GUNSLINGER GIRL

OMNIBUS COLLECTION 3

Vol. 7-8

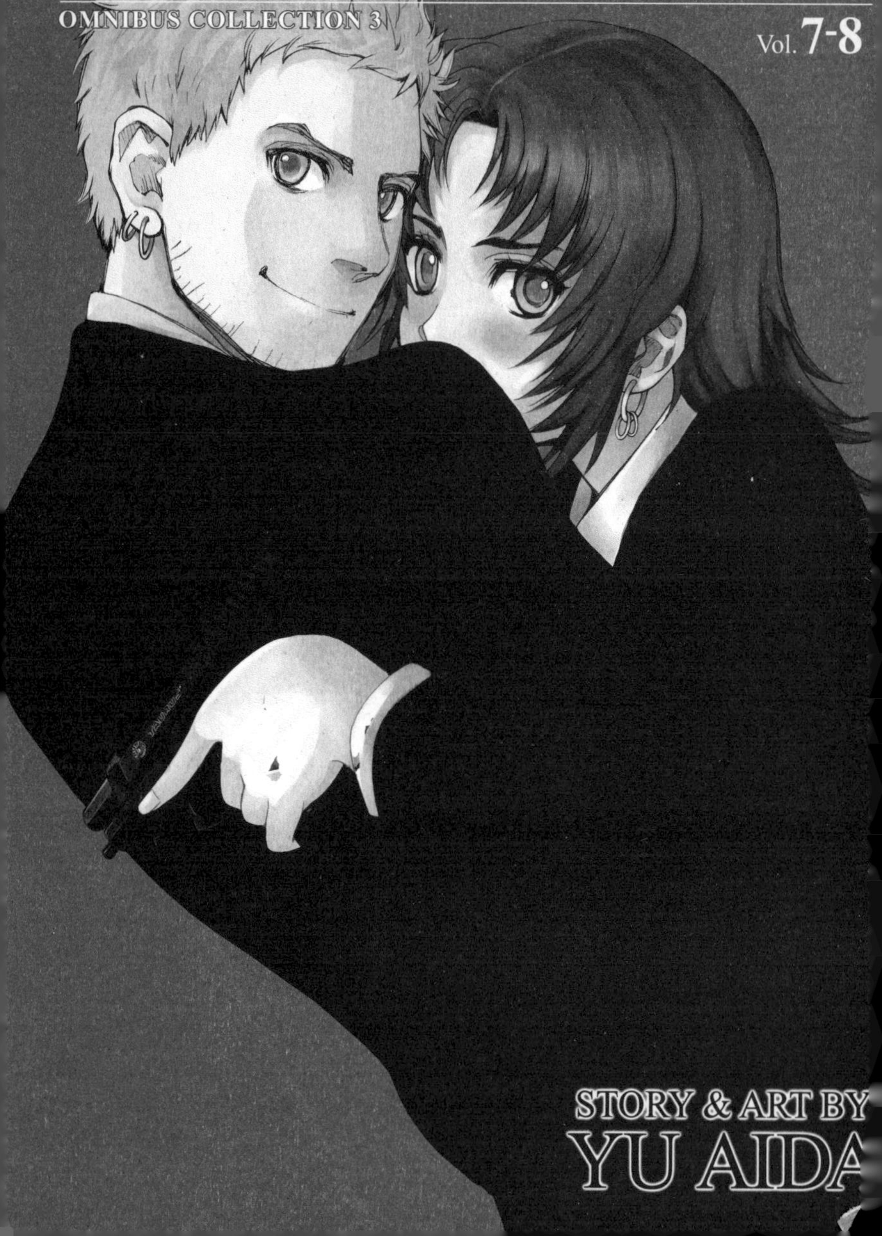

STORY & ART BY

YU AIDA

GUNSLINGER GIRL
OMNIBUS COLLECTION 3
VOLUME 7-8
story & art by Yu Aida

STAFF CREDITS

translation Adrienne Beck
adaptation Janet Houck
lettering Roland Amago
layout Bambi Eloriaga-Amago
cover design Nicky Lim
copy editor Shanti Whitesides
editor Adam Arnold

publisher Jason DeAngelis
Seven Seas Entertainment

GUNSLINGER GIRL OMNIBUS COLLECTION 3
Content originally published as Gunslinger Girl Vol. 7-8

First published in 2006-2007 by Media Works Inc., Tokyo, Japan.
English translation rights arranged with ASCII MEDIA WORKS.

This is a work of fiction. Names, characters, places, and incidents are the products of the author's imagination or are used fictitiously. Any resemblance to actual events, locales, or persons, living or dead, is entirely coincidental.

ISBN: 978-1-935934-22-6

Printed in Canada

First Printing: November 2011

10 9 8 7 6 5 4 3 2 1

READING DIRECTIONS

This book reads from *right to left*, Japanese style. If this is your first time reading manga, you start reading from the top right panel on each page and take it from there. If you get lost, just follow the numbered diagram here. It may seem backwards at first, but you'll get the hang of it! Have fun!!

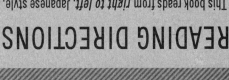

1
2
3
4
5
6
7
8
9
10

CHARACTERS
登場人物紹介

PETRUSHKA

The first of the new, second generation cyborgs. In her life before the Agency, she was a promising young ballerina with the Bolshoi Ballet. However, osteosarcoma in her leg ended her career, and she attempted suicide. Her handler is Alessandro.

ALESSANDRO

A new handler transferred from the Agency's Public Safety division over to Section 2. Prior to his transfer, his missions centered around infiltrating Padania terrorist groups.

TRIELA

Smart and responsible, she is an "older sister" figure for the other cyborgs. Her handler is Hilshire.

HILSHIRE

German. Former detective with Europol. He tries very hard to be kind to Triela, but has difficulty figuring out what kind of distance there should be in their relationship.

CLAES

Triela's roommate. When her handler Raballo was killed, she became the Agency's "guinea pig" cyborg. All cyborg developments are first tested on her.

HENRIETTA

The only survivor of a slaughtered family of six. Thanks to her "conditioning" when she was converted into a cyborg, she is blindly in love with her handler, Jose.

JOSE

Ex-military. Generally, he is very kind to Henrietta, but he is beginning to find himself disturbed at how much he unconsciously imposes his late sister's image onto her.

RICO

Former quadriplegic. Innocent and cheerful, even the most common everyday things bring her much joy. Her handler is Jean.

JEAN

Jose's older brother. Very serious-minded and business-like. He is the cyborg handlers' leader and field commander for Section 2 operations.

ANGELICA

The first prototype cyborg. She was the first to start displaying side effects to the cyborg conversion process, and has an acute dependency on the "drug" used. Her handler is Marco.

MARCO

Ex-military special forces. When he was discharged due to an injury, he took up a job with the Agency. He has trouble dealing with feelings of helplessness and frustration as he watches Angelica's condition deteriorate day by day.

ROBERTA GUELLFI

The Roman prosecutor newly assigned to the "Croce Incident" case. Padania terrorists have announced their intention to assassinate her.

RACHELLE BELLEUT

Europol mortician. Along with Hilshire, she investigated a child slavery ring in Amsterdam, and was killed in the process.

BELISARIO

Agency technician. He is in charge of the cyborg "conditioning" process.

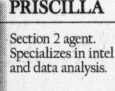

PRISCILLA

Section 2 agent. Specializes in intel and data analysis.

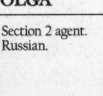

OLGA

Section 2 agent. Russian.

LORENZO

Section 2 Chief. Formerly of the Ministry of State.

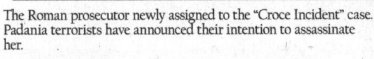

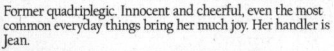

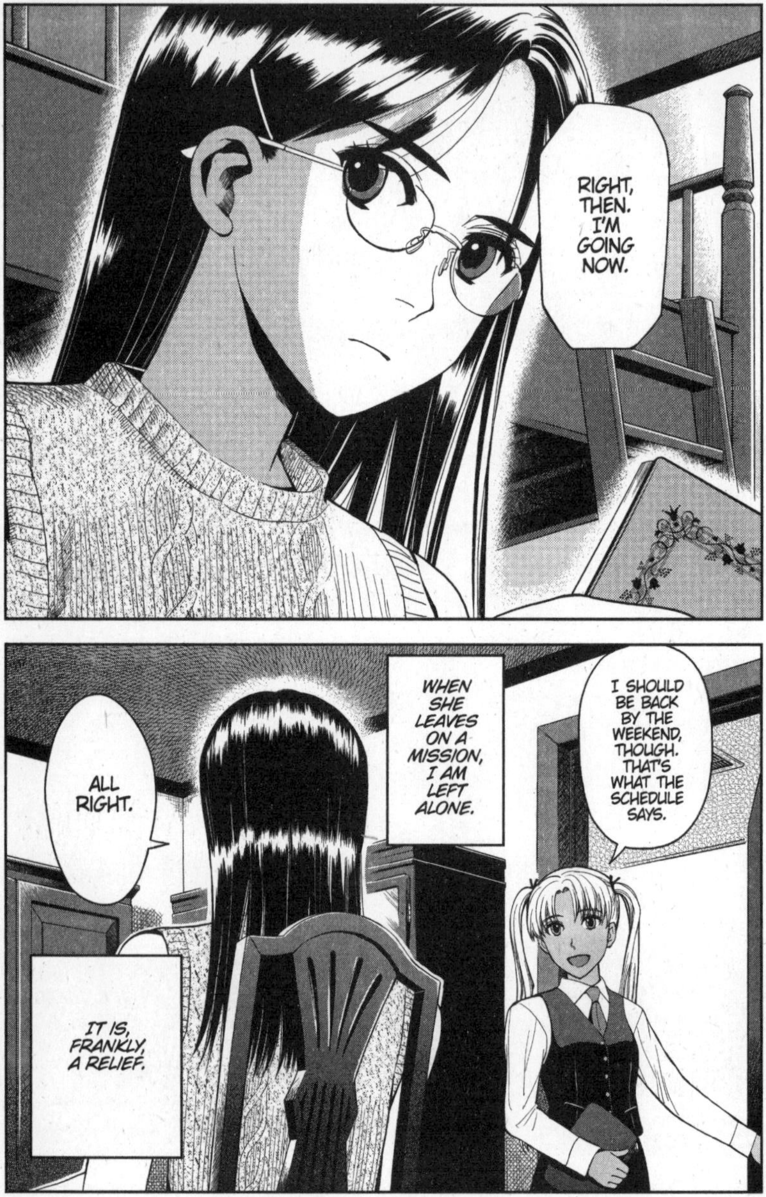
RIGHT, THEN. I'M GOING NOW.
I SHOULD BE BACK BY THE WEEKEND, THOUGH. THAT'S WHAT THE SCHEDULE SAYS.
WHEN SHE LEAVES ON A MISSION, I AM LEFT ALONE.
ALL RIGHT.
IT IS, FRANKLY, A RELIEF.

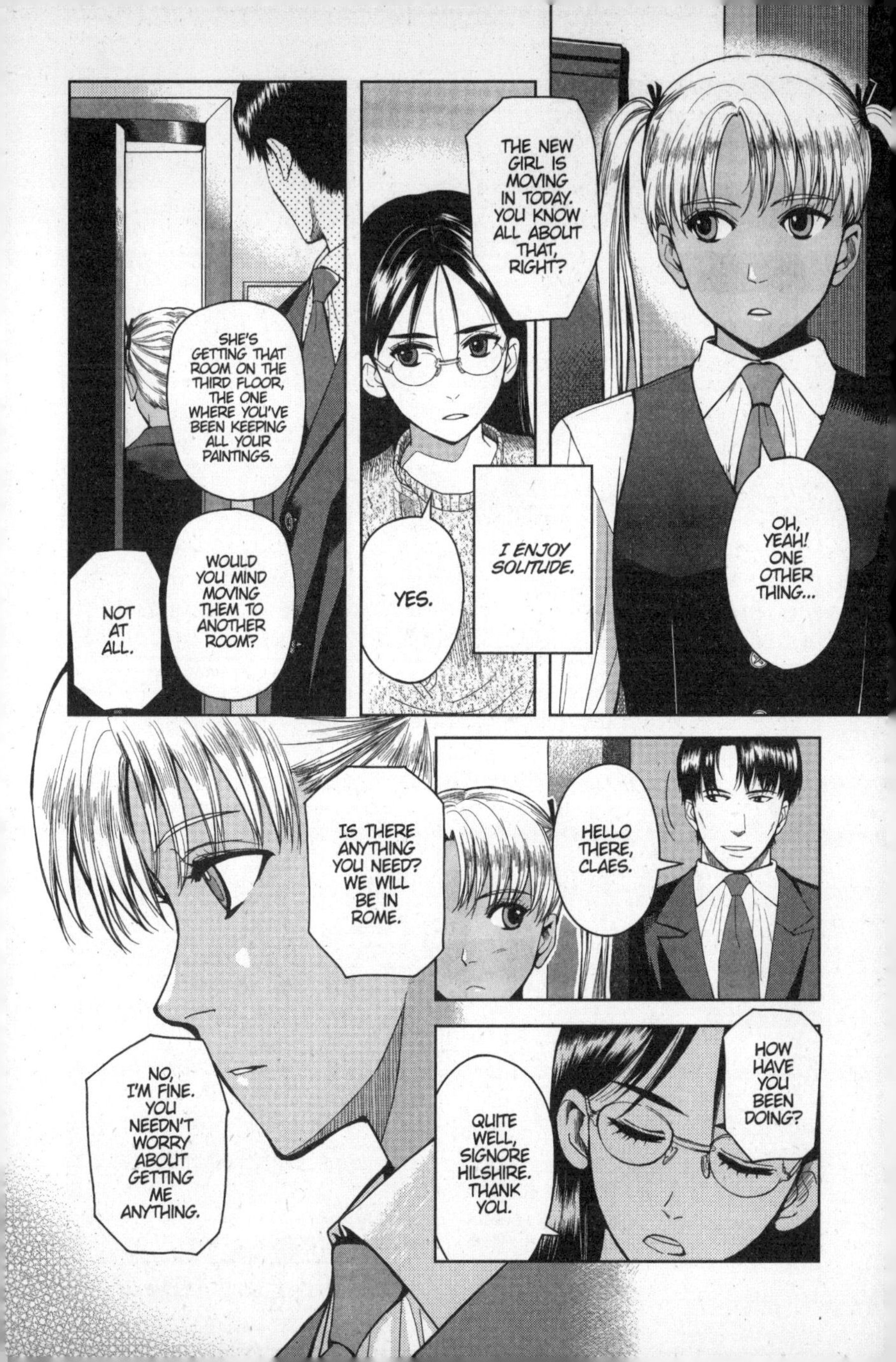

THE NEW GIRL IS MOVING IN TODAY. YOU KNOW ALL ABOUT THAT, RIGHT?
OH, YEAH! ONE OTHER THING...
I ENJOY SOLITUDE.
YES.
SHE'S GETTING THAT ROOM ON THE THIRD FLOOR, THE ONE WHERE YOU'VE BEEN KEEPING ALL YOUR PAINTINGS.
WOULD YOU MIND MOVING THEM TO ANOTHER ROOM?
NOT AT ALL.
HELLO THERE, CLAES.
IS THERE ANYTHING YOU NEED? WE WILL BE IN ROME.
HOW HAVE YOU BEEN DOING?
QUITE WELL, SIGNORE HILSHIRE. THANK YOU.
NO, I'M FINE. YOU NEEDN'T WORRY ABOUT GETTING ME ANYTHING.

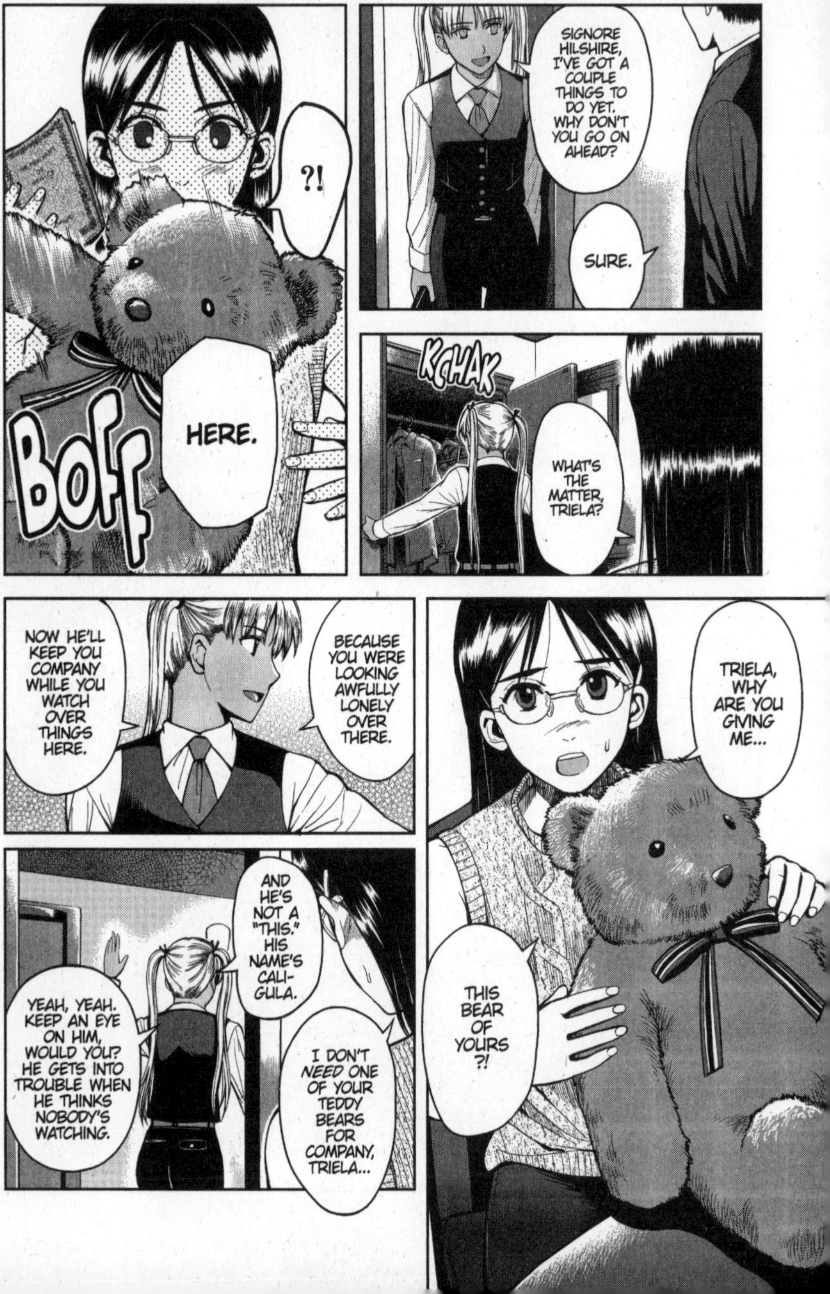
SIGNORE HILSHIRE, I'VE GOT A COUPLE THINGS TO DO YET. WHY DON'T YOU GO ON AHEAD?
SURE.
KCHAK
WHAT'S THE MATTER, TRIELA?
?!
HERE.
BOFF
TRIELA, WHY ARE YOU GIVING ME...
THIS BEAR OF YOURS?!
BECAUSE YOU WERE LOOKING AWFULLY LONELY OVER THERE.
NOW HE'LL KEEP YOU COMPANY WHILE YOU WATCH OVER THINGS HERE.
AND HE'S NOT A "THIS." HIS NAME'S CALIGULA.
I DON'T *NEED* ONE OF YOUR TEDDY BEARS FOR COMPANY, TRIELA...
YEAH, YEAH. KEEP AN EYE ON HIM, WOULD YOU? HE GETS INTO TROUBLE WHEN HE THINKS NOBODY'S WATCHING.

CHAPTER 33: HER TINY GARDEN

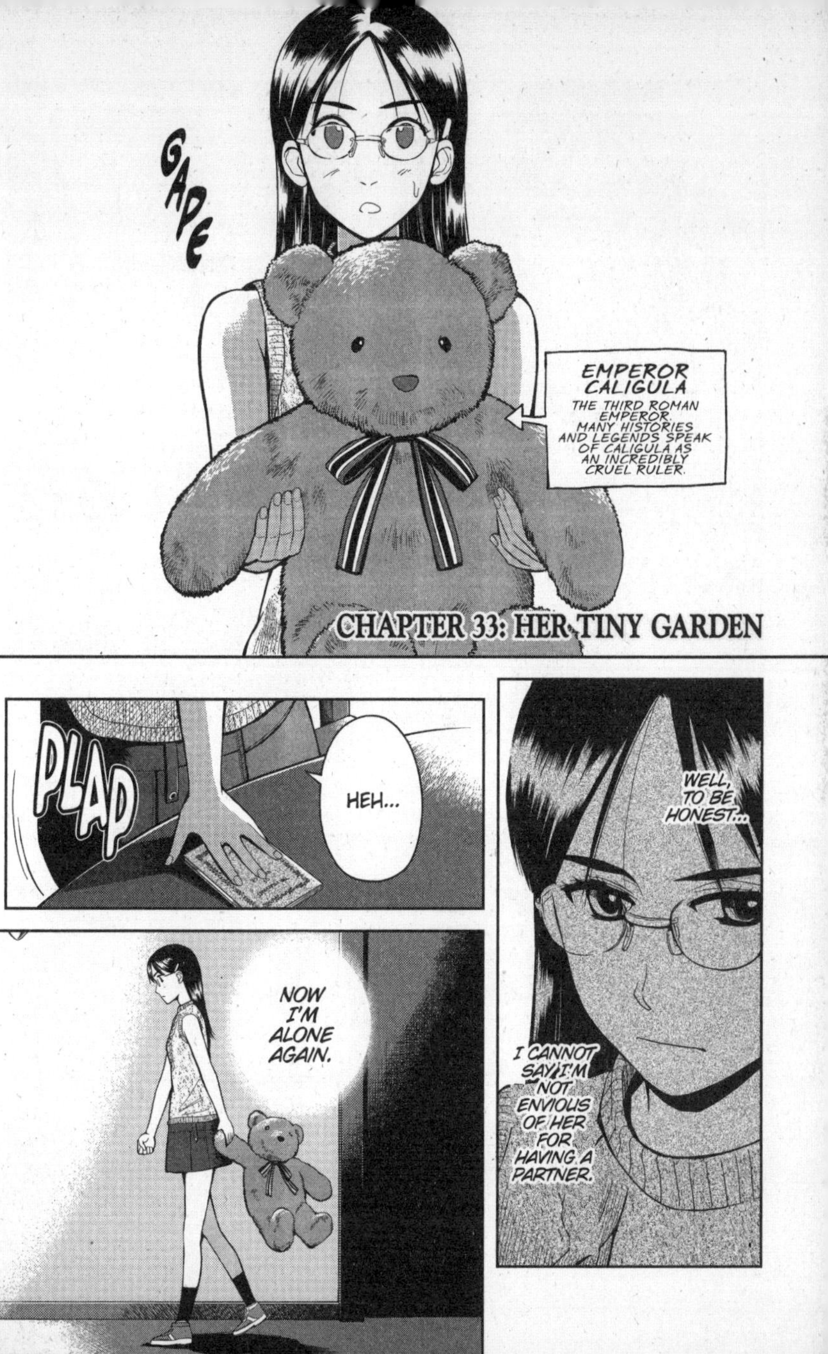
GAPE
EMPEROR CALIGULA
THE THIRD ROMAN EMPEROR. MANY HISTORIES AND LEGENDS SPEAK OF CALIGULA AS AN INCREDIBLY CRUEL RULER.
WELL, TO BE HONEST...
I CANNOT SAY I'M NOT ENVIOUS OF HER FOR HAVING A PARTNER.
PLAP
HEH...
NOW I'M ALONE AGAIN.

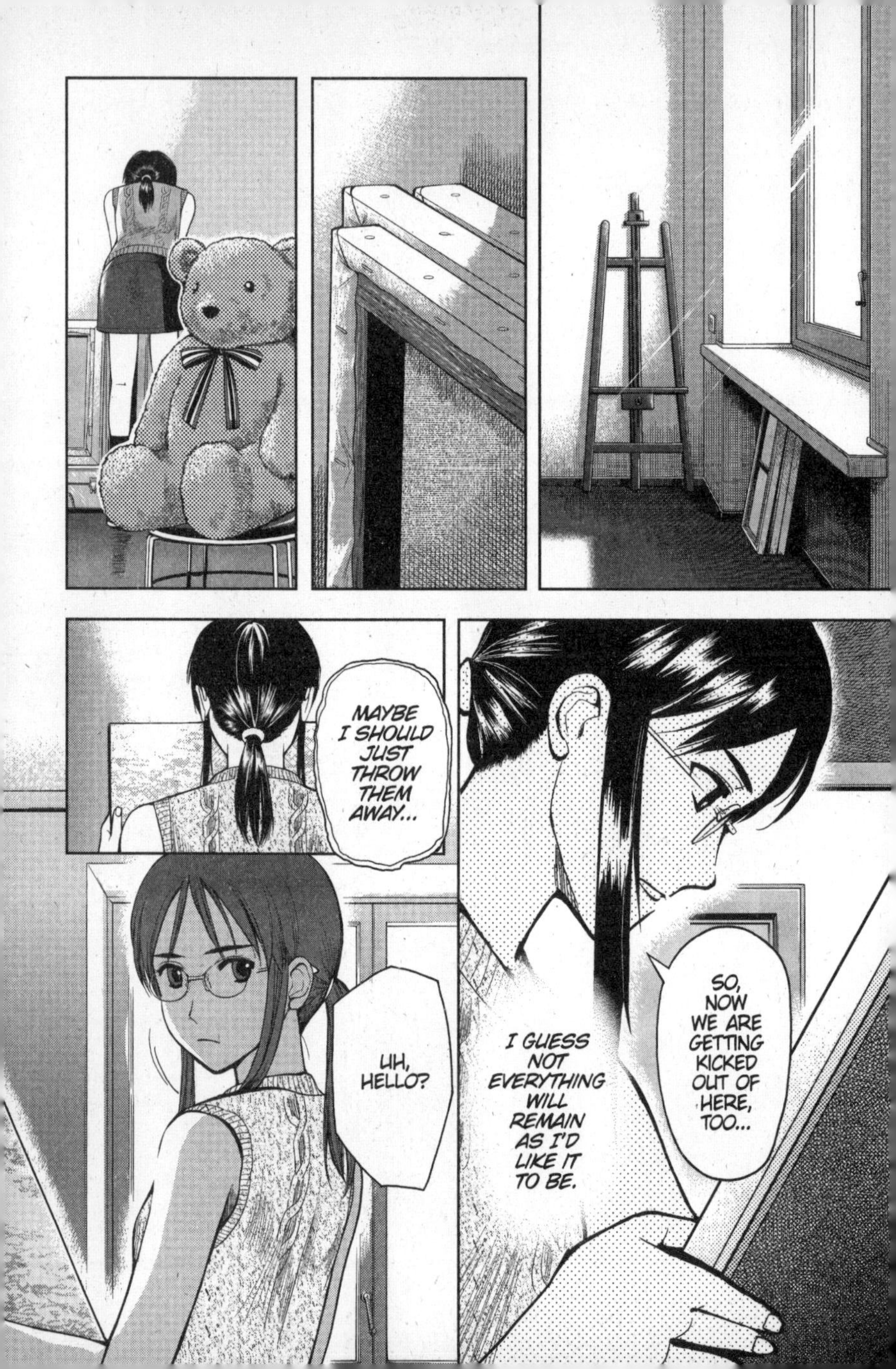
SO, NOW WE ARE GETTING KICKED OUT OF HERE, TOO...
I GUESS NOT EVERYTHING WILL REMAIN AS I'D LIKE IT TO BE.
MAYBE I SHOULD JUST THROW THEM AWAY...
UH, HELLO?

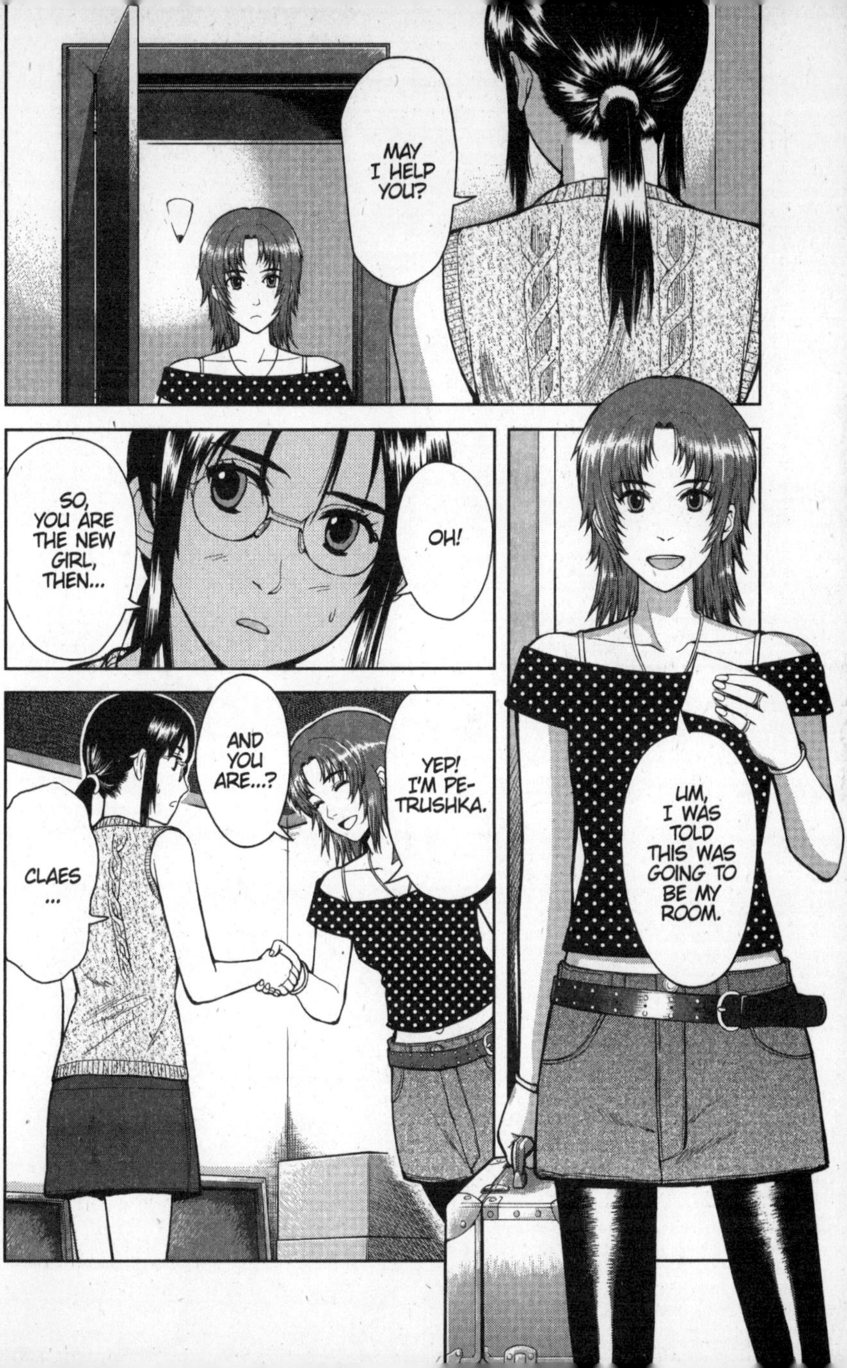
MAY I HELP YOU?
UM, I WAS TOLD THIS WAS GOING TO BE MY ROOM.
OH!
SO, YOU ARE THE NEW GIRL, THEN...
YEP! I'M PE-TRUSHKA.
AND YOU ARE...?
CLAES ...

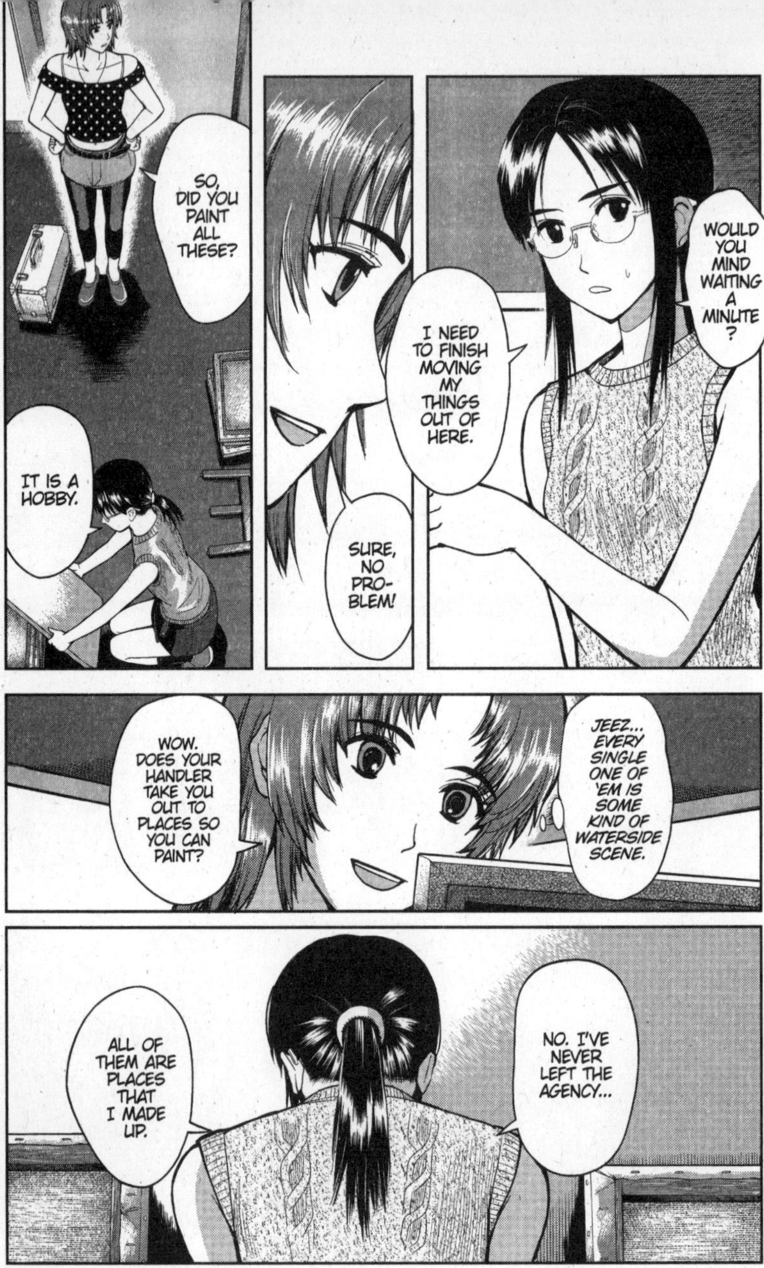
WOULD YOU MIND WAITING A MINUTE?
I NEED TO FINISH MOVING MY THINGS OUT OF HERE.
SURE, NO PROBLEM!
SO, DID YOU PAINT ALL THESE?
IT IS A HOBBY.
JEEZ... EVERY SINGLE ONE OF 'EM IS SOME KIND OF WATERSIDE SCENE.
WOW. DOES YOUR HANDLER TAKE YOU OUT TO PLACES SO YOU CAN PAINT?
NO. I'VE NEVER LEFT THE AGENCY...
ALL OF THEM ARE PLACES THAT I MADE UP.

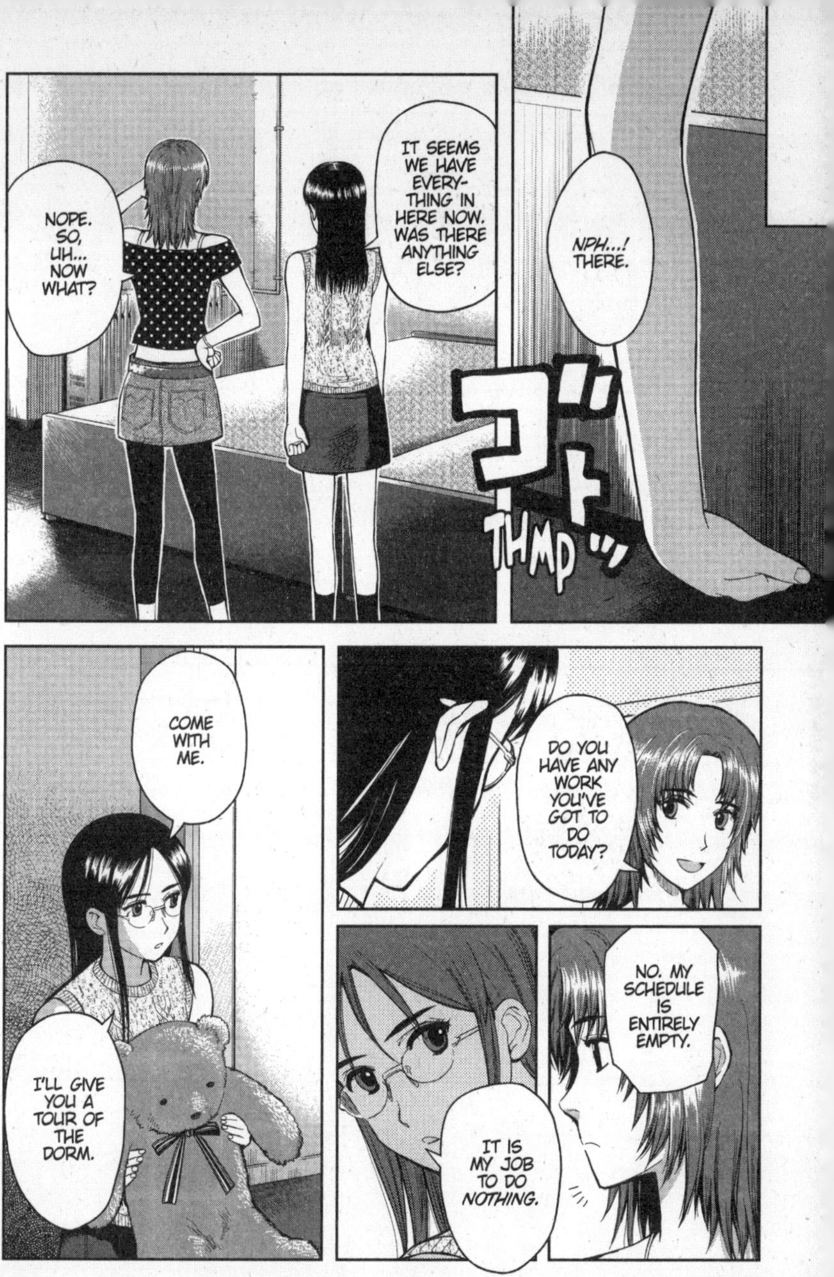
NPH...! THERE.
ゴトッ
THMP
IT SEEMS WE HAVE EVERYTHING IN HERE NOW. WAS THERE ANYTHING ELSE?
NOPE. SO, UH... NOW WHAT?
DO YOU HAVE ANY WORK YOU'VE GOT TO DO TODAY?
NO. MY SCHEDULE IS ENTIRELY EMPTY.
IT IS MY JOB TO DO *NOTHING.*
COME WITH ME.
I'LL GIVE YOU A TOUR OF THE DORM.

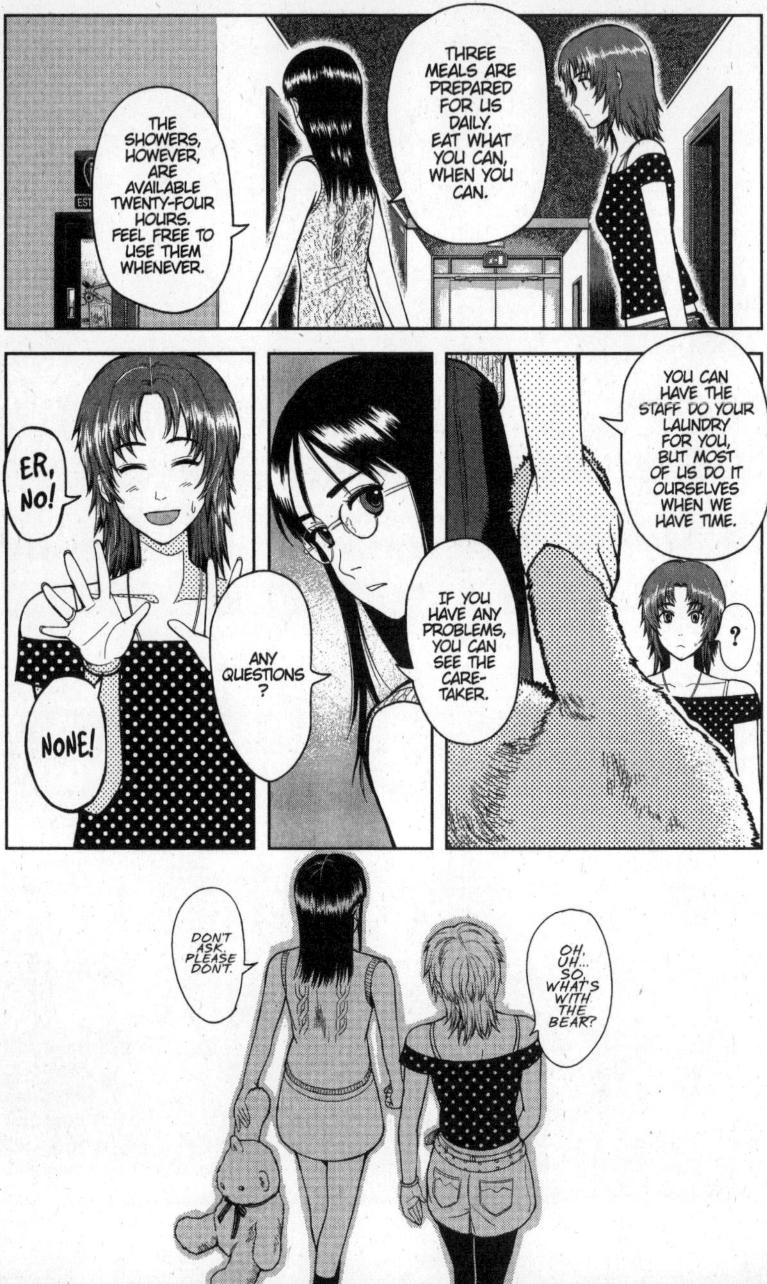
THREE MEALS ARE PREPARED FOR US DAILY. EAT WHAT YOU CAN, WHEN YOU CAN.
THE SHOWERS, HOWEVER, ARE AVAILABLE TWENTY-FOUR HOURS. FEEL FREE TO USE THEM WHENEVER.
YOU CAN HAVE THE STAFF DO YOUR LAUNDRY FOR YOU, BUT MOST OF US DO IT OURSELVES WHEN WE HAVE TIME.
?
IF YOU HAVE ANY PROBLEMS, YOU CAN SEE THE CARE-TAKER.
ANY QUESTIONS?
ER, NO!
NONE!
OH, UH... SO, WHAT'S WITH THE BEAR?
DON'T ASK. PLEASE DON'T.

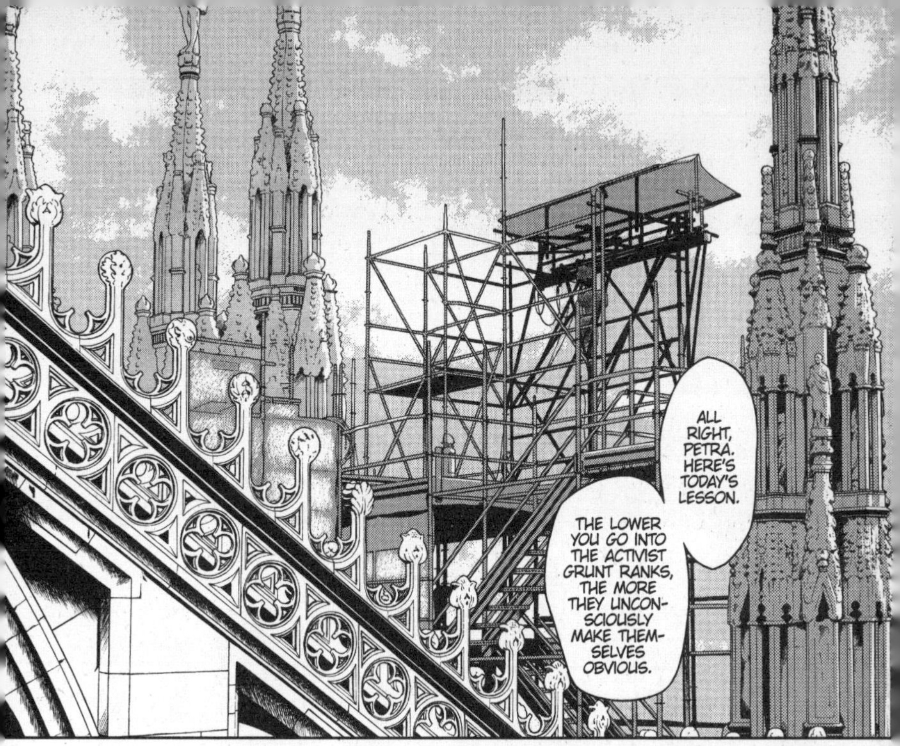
ALL RIGHT, PETRA. HERE'S TODAY'S LESSON.
THE LOWER YOU GO INTO THE ACTIVIST GRUNT RANKS, THE MORE THEY UNCON-SCIOUSLY MAKE THEM-SELVES OBVIOUS.

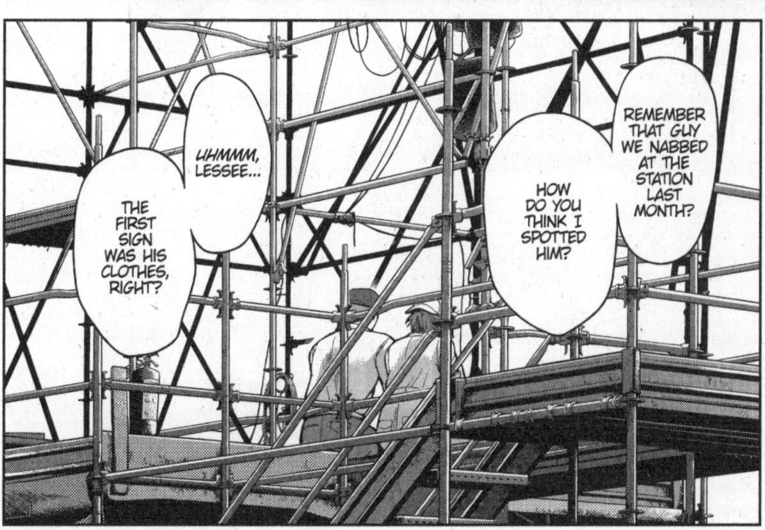
REMEMBER THAT GUY WE NABBED AT THE STATION LAST MONTH?
HOW DO YOU THINK I SPOTTED HIM?
UHMMM, LESSEE...
THE FIRST SIGN WAS HIS CLOTHES, RIGHT?

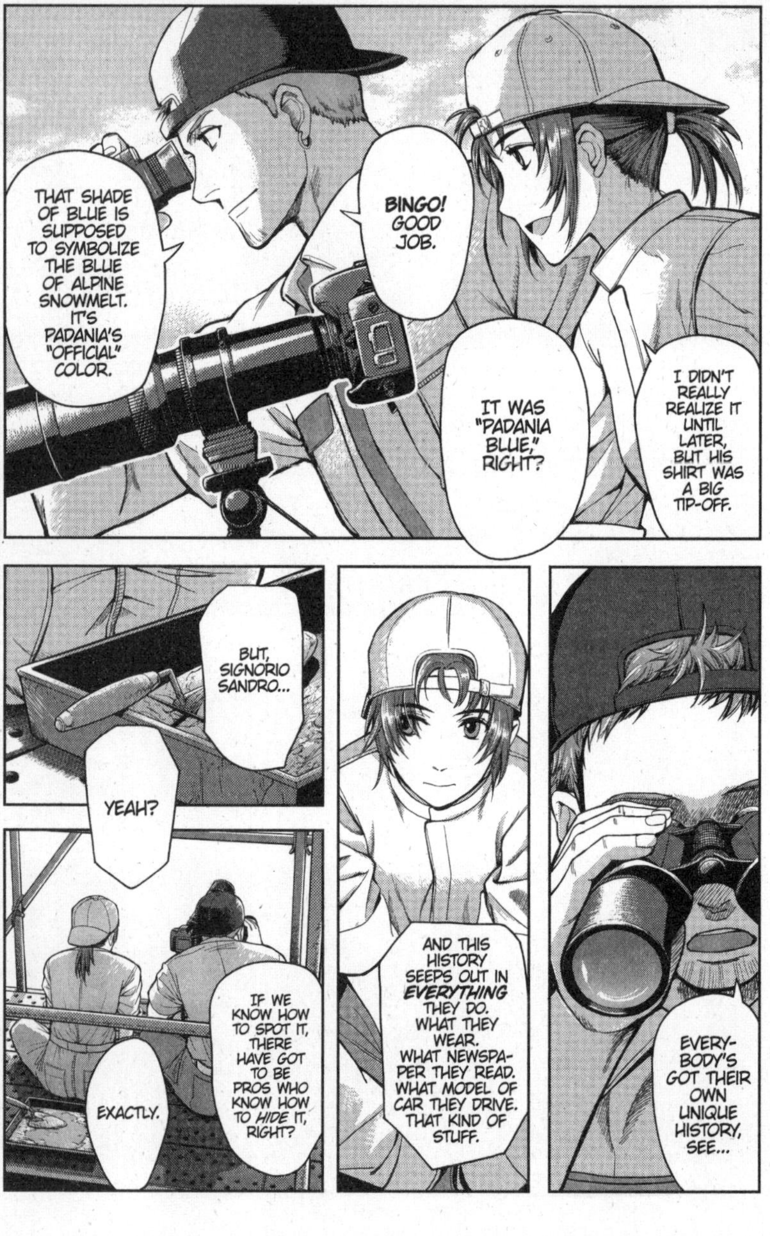
I DIDN'T REALLY REALIZE IT UNTIL LATER, BUT HIS SHIRT WAS A BIG TIP-OFF.
IT WAS "PADANIA BLUE," RIGHT?
BINGO! GOOD JOB.
THAT SHADE OF BLUE IS SUPPOSED TO SYMBOLIZE THE BLUE OF ALPINE SNOWMELT. IT'S PADANIA'S "OFFICIAL" COLOR.
EVERY-BODY'S GOT THEIR OWN UNIQUE HISTORY, SEE...
AND THIS HISTORY SEEPS OUT IN ***EVERYTHING*** THEY DO. WHAT THEY WEAR. WHAT NEWSPA-PER THEY READ. WHAT MODEL OF CAR THEY DRIVE. THAT KIND OF STUFF.
BUT, SIGNORIO SANDRO...
YEAH?
IF WE KNOW HOW TO SPOT IT, THERE HAVE GOT TO BE PROS WHO KNOW HOW TO *HIDE* IT, RIGHT?
EXACTLY.

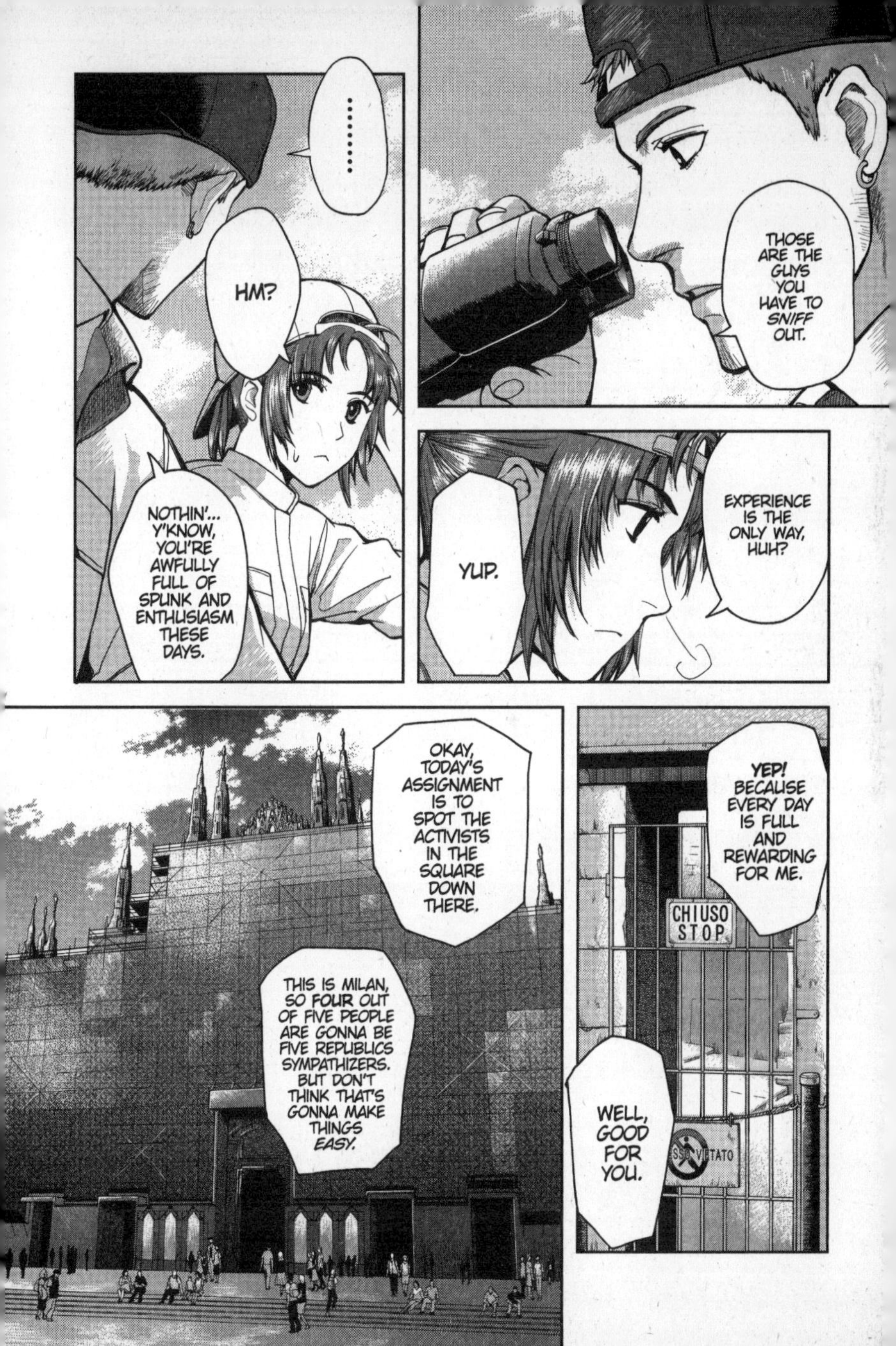
THOSE ARE THE GUYS YOU HAVE TO SNIFF OUT.
EXPERIENCE IS THE ONLY WAY, HUH?
YUP.
......
HM?
NOTHIN'... Y'KNOW, YOU'RE AWFULLY FULL OF SPUNK AND ENTHUSIASM THESE DAYS.
YEP! BECAUSE EVERY DAY IS FULL AND REWARDING FOR ME.
CHIUSO STOP
WELL, GOOD FOR YOU.
OKAY, TODAY'S ASSIGNMENT IS TO SPOT THE ACTIVISTS IN THE SQUARE DOWN THERE.
THIS IS MILAN, SO FOUR OUT OF FIVE PEOPLE ARE GONNA BE FIVE REPUBLICS SYMPATHIZERS. BUT DON'T THINK THAT'S GONNA MAKE THINGS EASY.

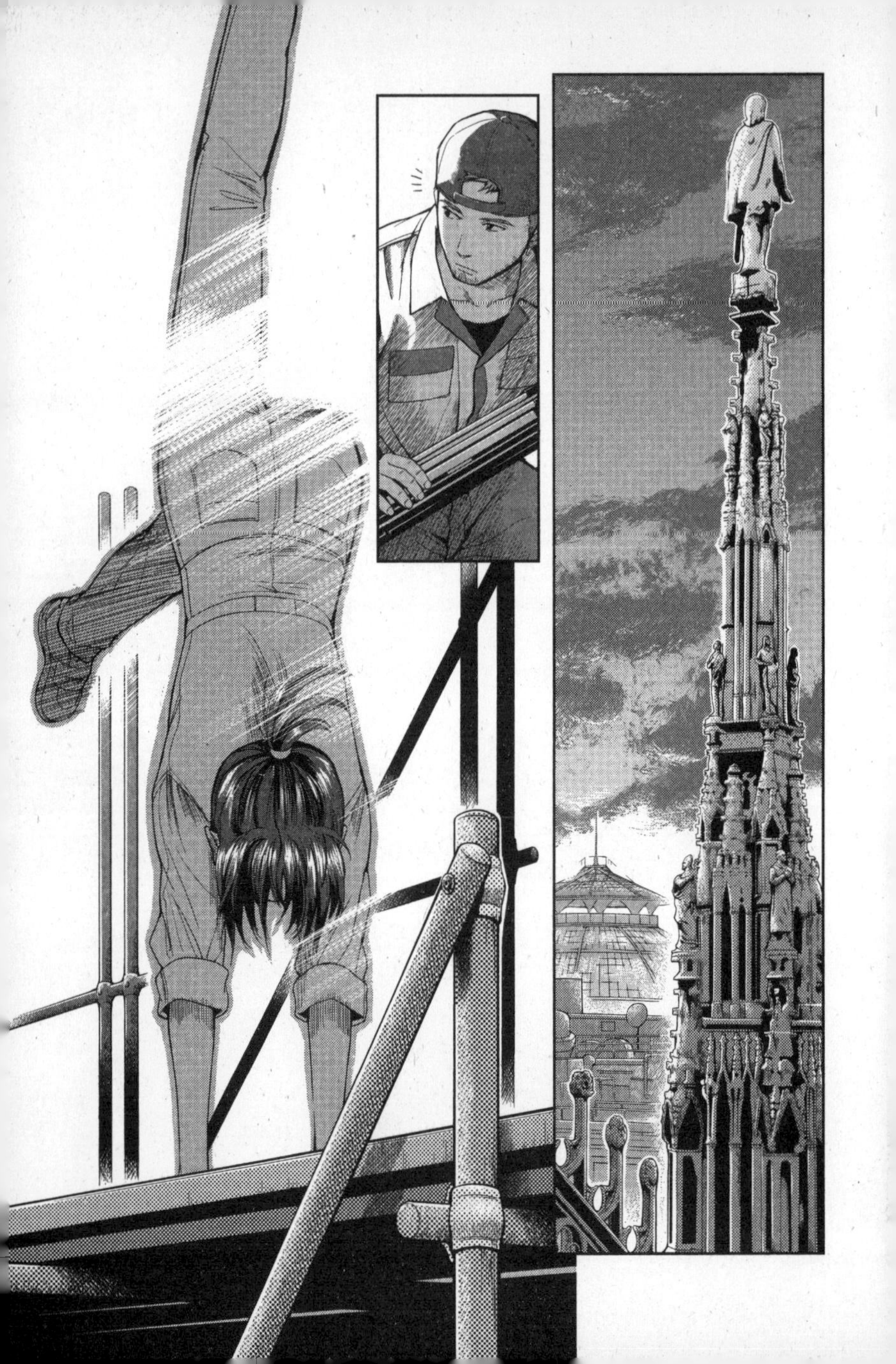

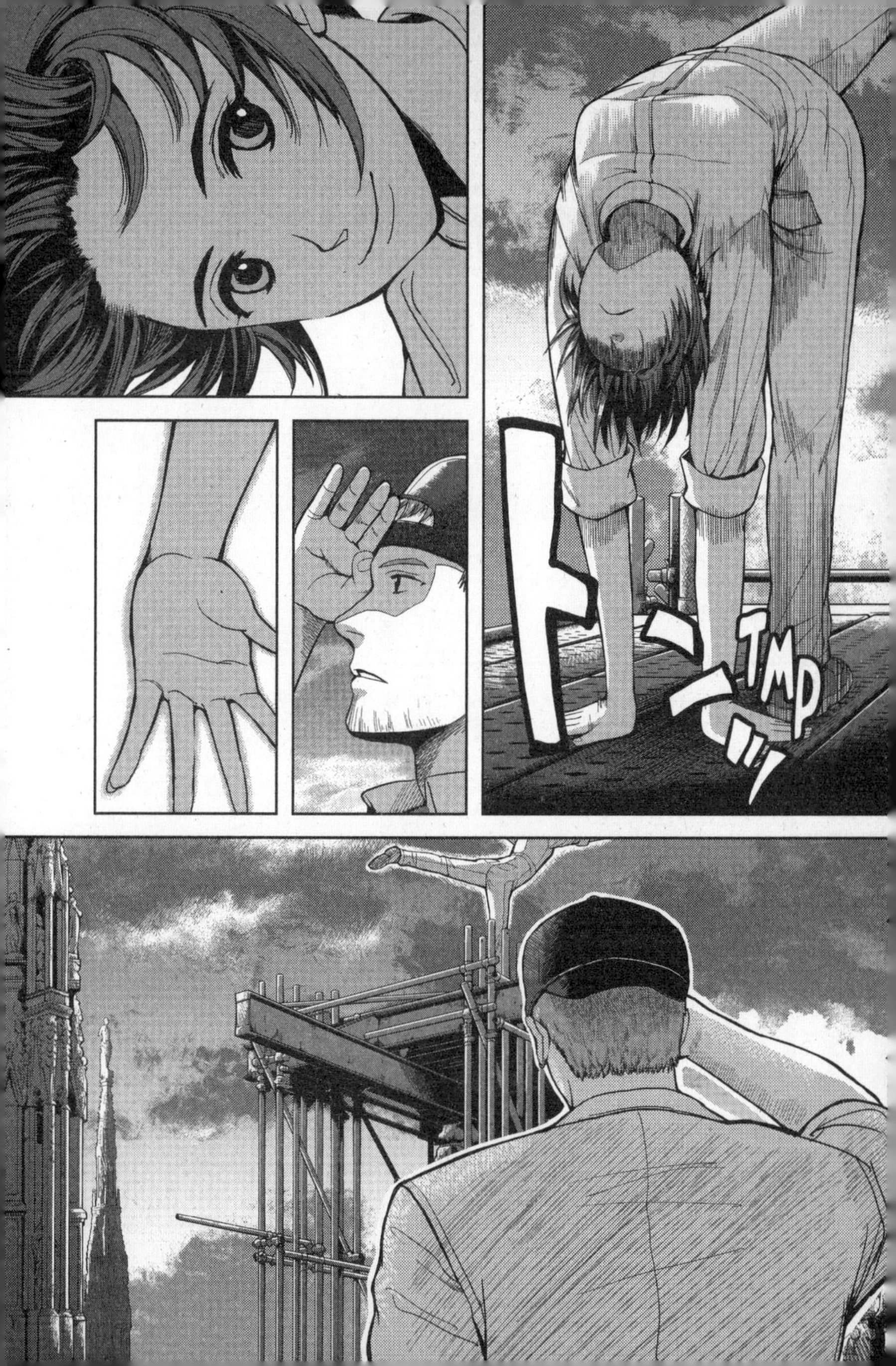
TMP

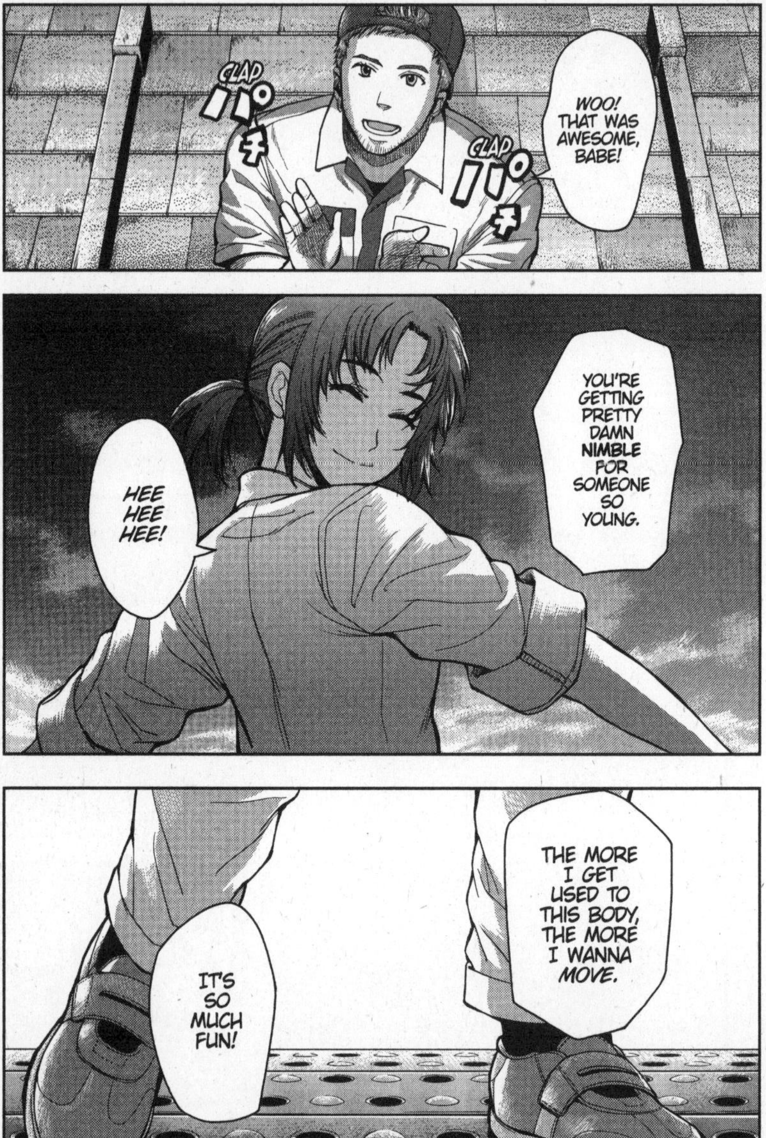
WOO! THAT WAS AWESOME, BABE!
CLAP
パチ
CLAP
パチ
YOU'RE GETTING PRETTY DAMN NIMBLE FOR SOMEONE SO YOUNG.
HEE HEE HEE!
THE MORE I GET USED TO THIS BODY, THE MORE I WANNA MOVE.
IT'S SO MUCH FUN!

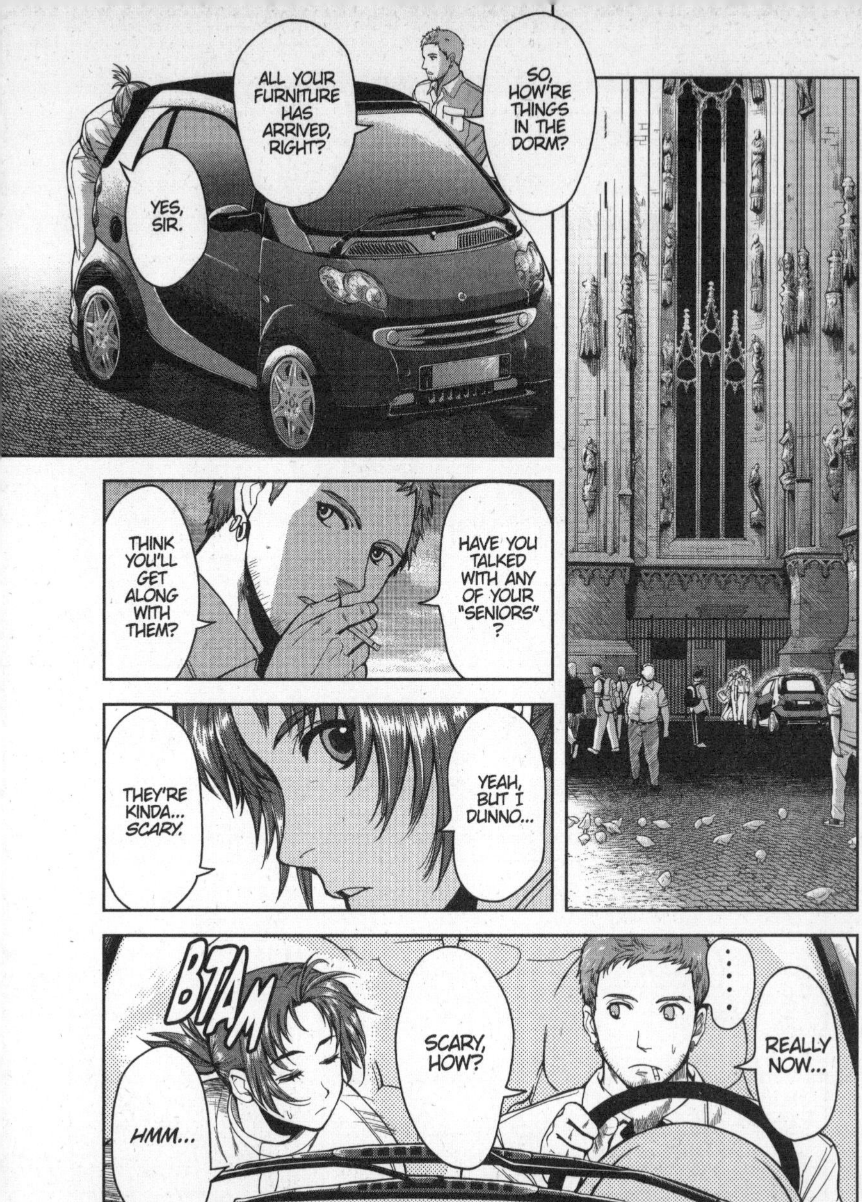
SO, HOW'RE THINGS IN THE DORM?
ALL YOUR FURNITURE HAS ARRIVED, RIGHT?
YES, SIR.
HAVE YOU TALKED WITH ANY OF YOUR "SENIORS"?
THINK YOU'LL GET ALONG WITH THEM?
YEAH, BUT I DUNNO...
THEY'RE KINDA... SCARY.
....
REALLY NOW...
SCARY, HOW?
BTAM
HMM...

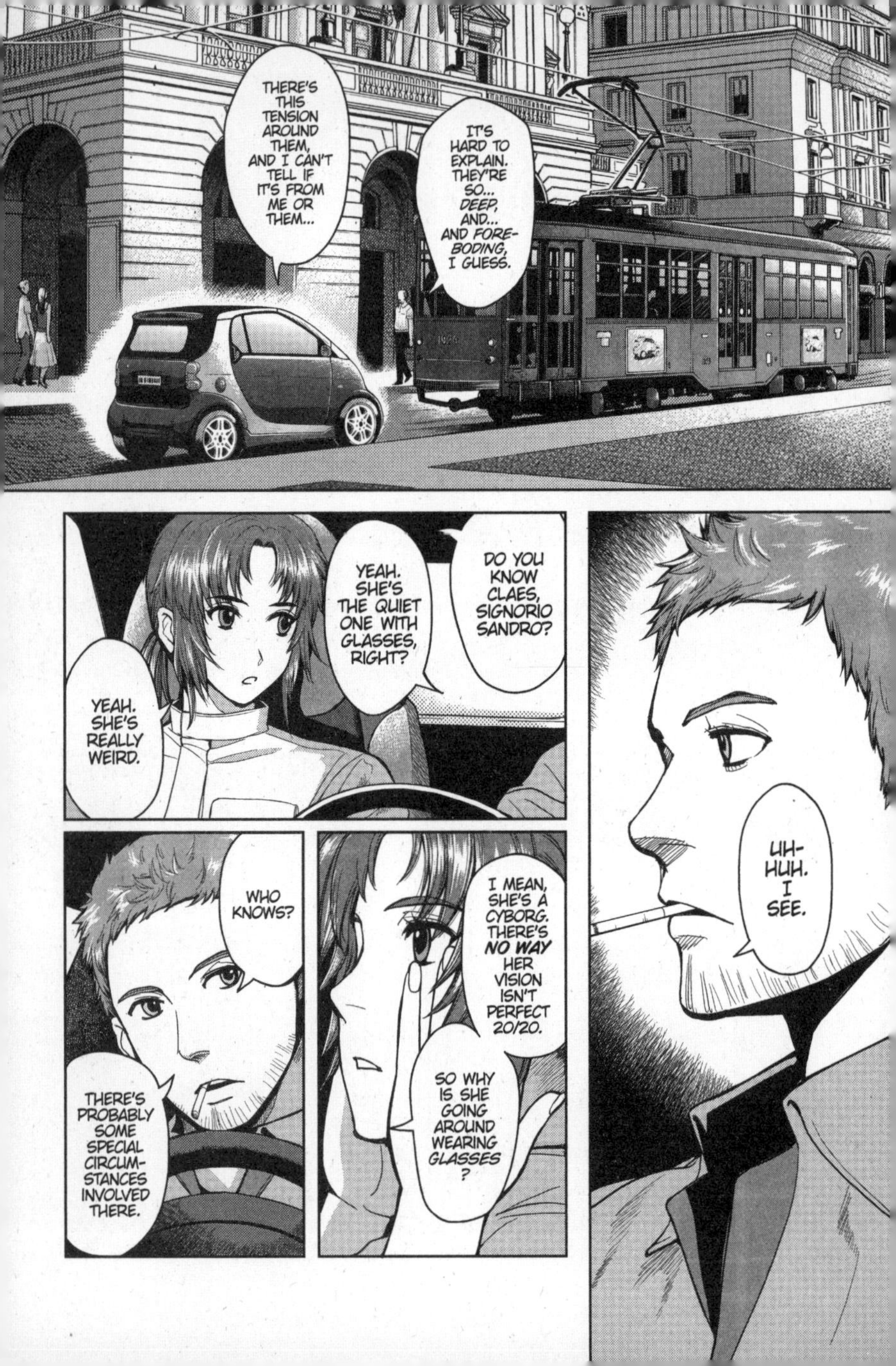
IT'S HARD TO EXPLAIN. THEY'RE SO... *DEEP*, AND... AND *FOREBODING*, I GUESS.
THERE'S THIS TENSION AROUND THEM, AND I CAN'T TELL IF IT'S FROM ME OR THEM...
UH-HUH. I SEE.
DO YOU KNOW CLAES, SIGNORIO SANDRO?
YEAH. SHE'S THE QUIET ONE WITH GLASSES, RIGHT?
YEAH. SHE'S REALLY WEIRD.
I MEAN, SHE'S A CYBORG. THERE'S ***NO WAY*** HER VISION ISN'T PERFECT 20/20.
SO WHY IS SHE GOING AROUND WEARING *GLASSES* ?
WHO KNOWS?
THERE'S PROBABLY SOME SPECIAL CIRCUM-STANCES INVOLVED THERE.

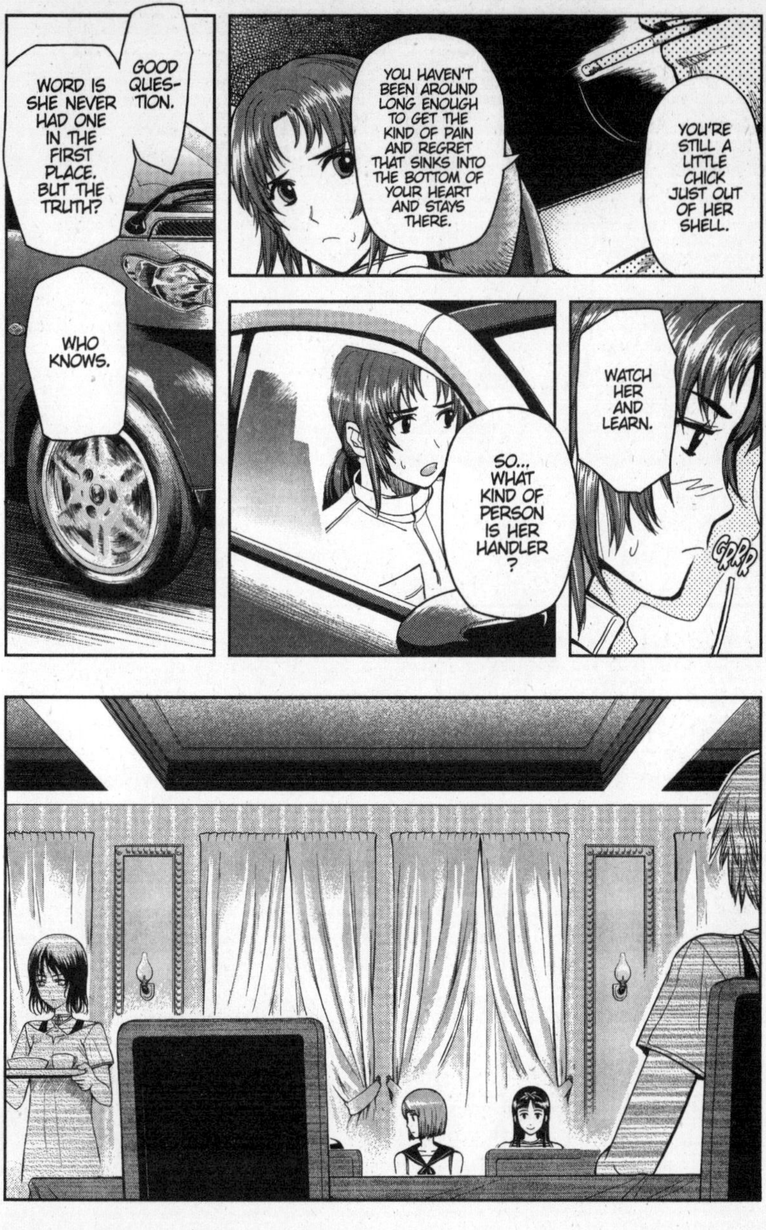

YOU'RE STILL A LITTLE CHICK JUST OUT OF HER SHELL.
YOU HAVEN'T BEEN AROUND LONG ENOUGH TO GET THE KIND OF PAIN AND REGRET THAT SINKS INTO THE BOTTOM OF YOUR HEART AND STAYS THERE.
WATCH HER AND LEARN.
GRRR
SO... WHAT KIND OF PERSON IS HER HANDLER?
GOOD QUES-TION.
WORD IS SHE NEVER HAD ONE IN THE FIRST PLACE. BUT THE TRUTH?
WHO KNOWS.

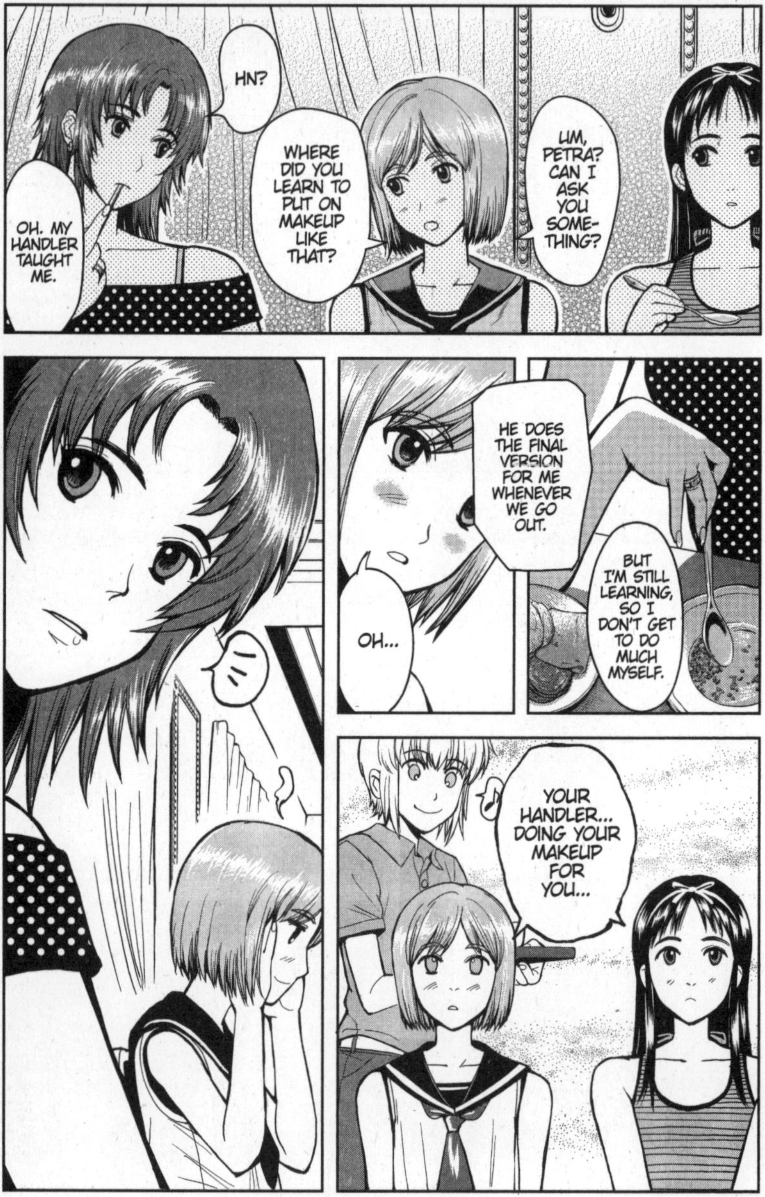
UM, PETRA? CAN I ASK YOU SOMETHING?
HN?
WHERE DID YOU LEARN TO PUT ON MAKEUP LIKE THAT?
OH. MY HANDLER TAUGHT ME.
HE DOES THE FINAL VERSION FOR ME WHENEVER WE GO OUT.
BUT I'M STILL LEARNING, SO I DON'T GET TO DO MUCH MYSELF.
OH...
YOUR HANDLER... DOING YOUR MAKEUP FOR YOU...

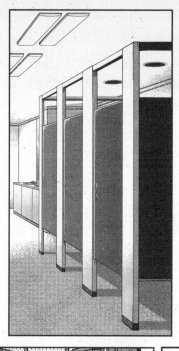

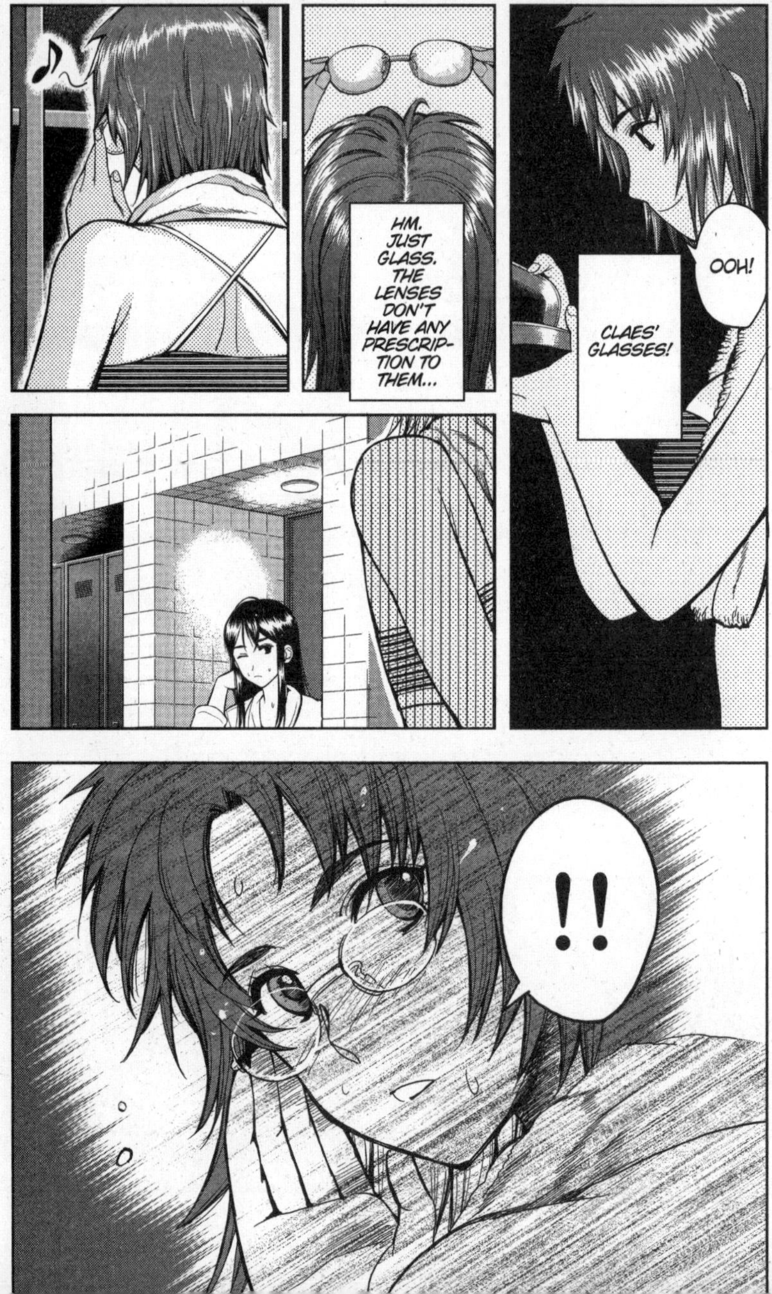
OOH!
CLAES' GLASSES!
HM. JUST GLASS. THE LENSES DON'T HAVE ANY PRESCRIPTION TO THEM...
!!

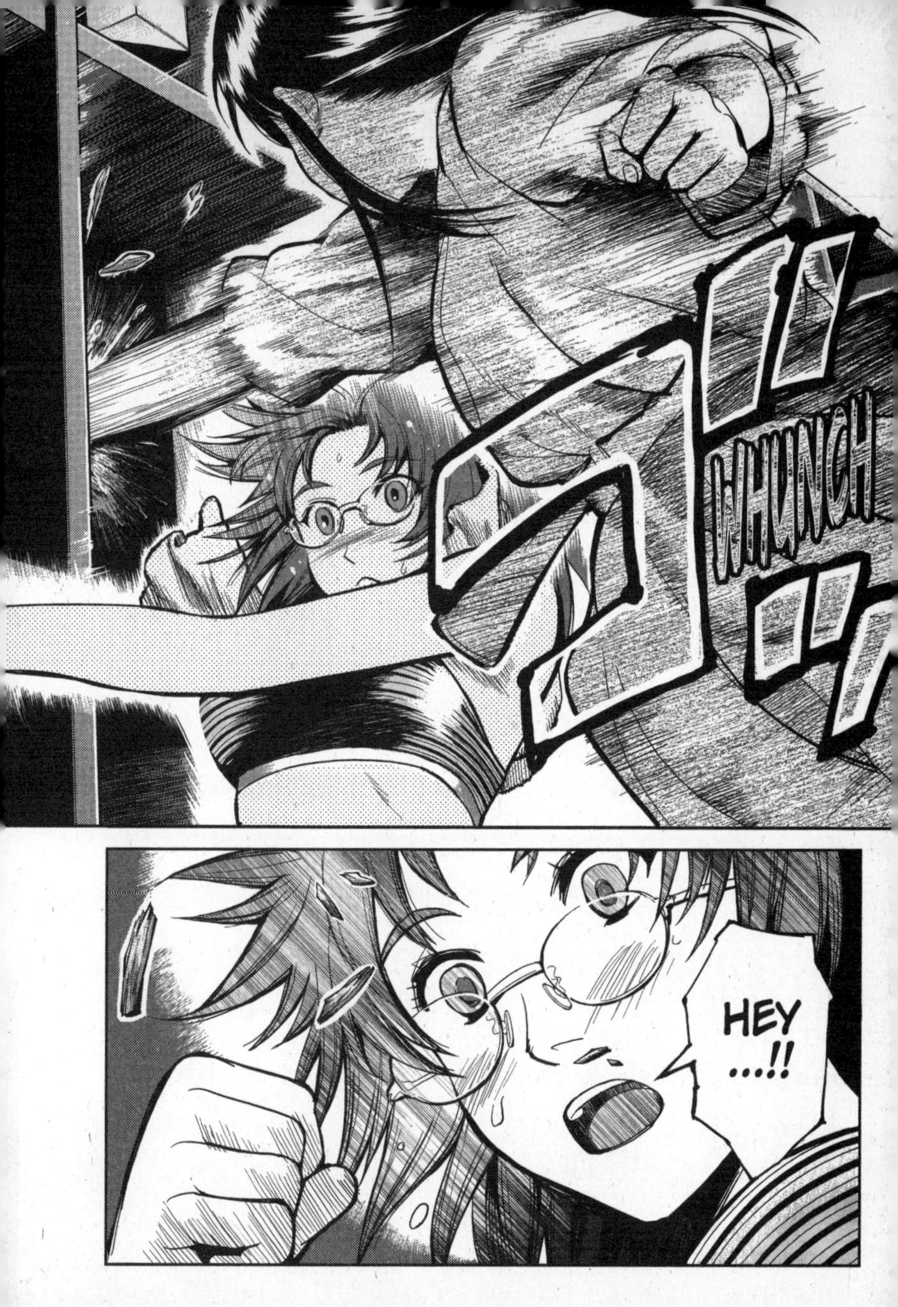
WHUNCH
HEY ...!!

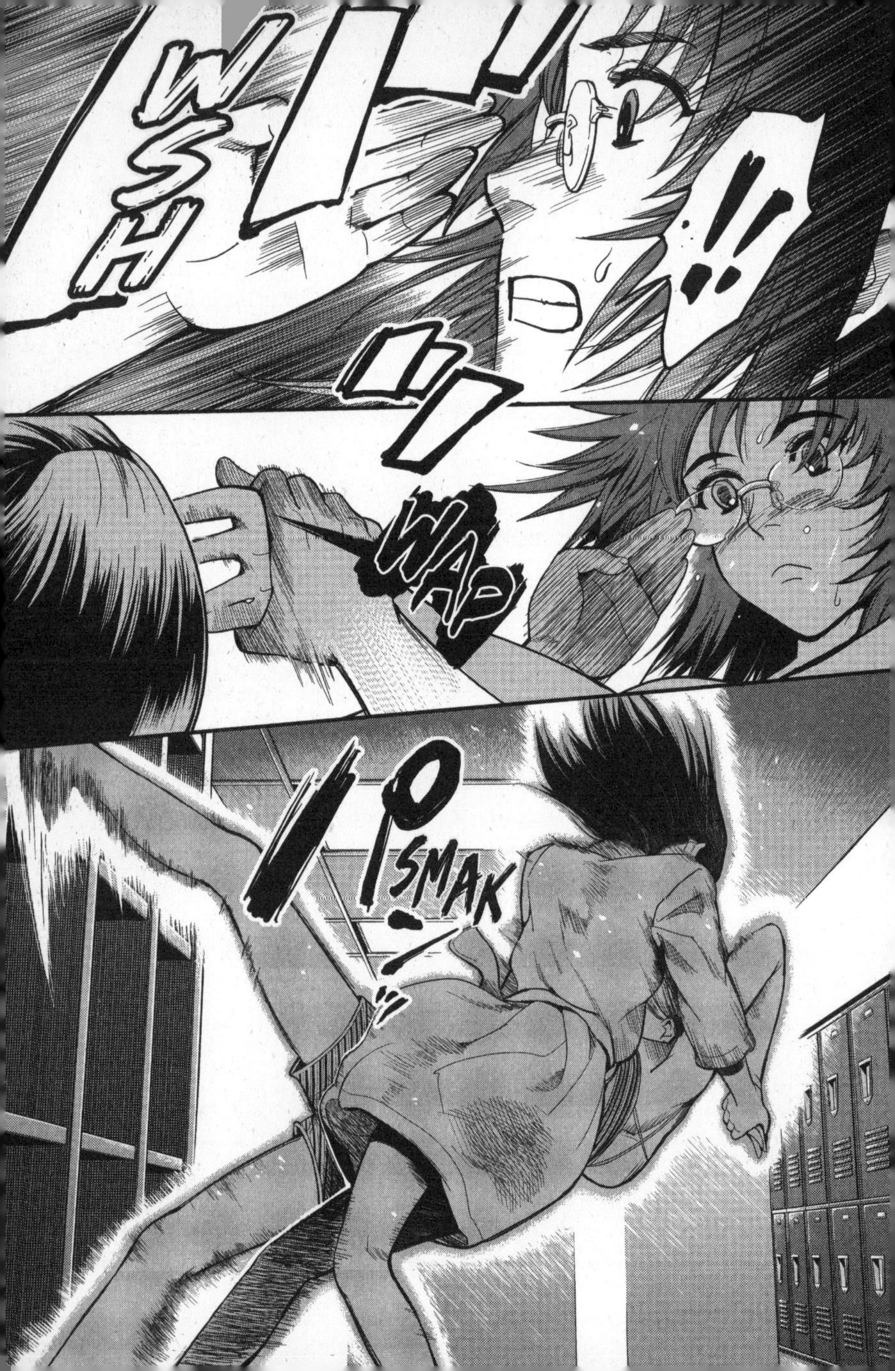
!!
WSH
WAP
SMAK

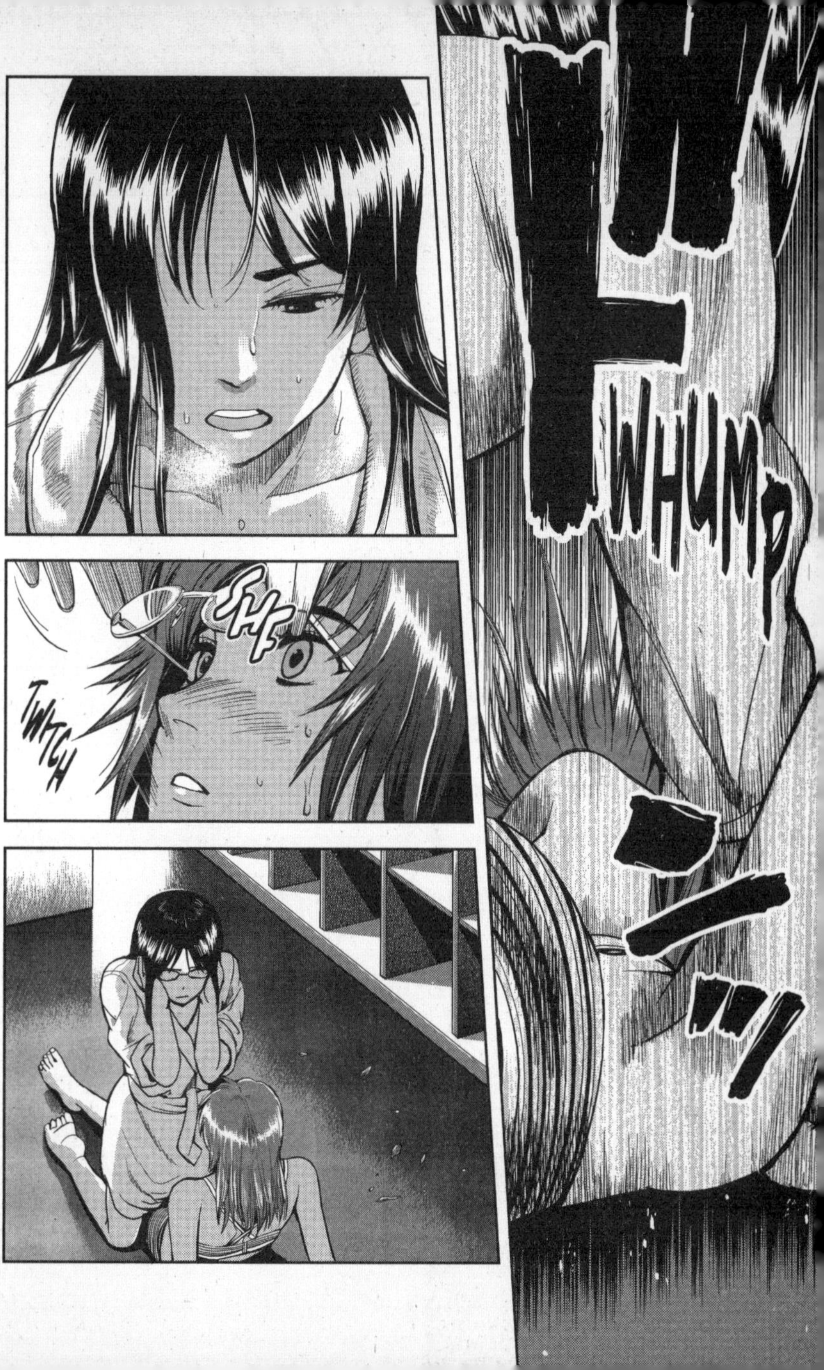
WHUMP
SHF
TWITCH

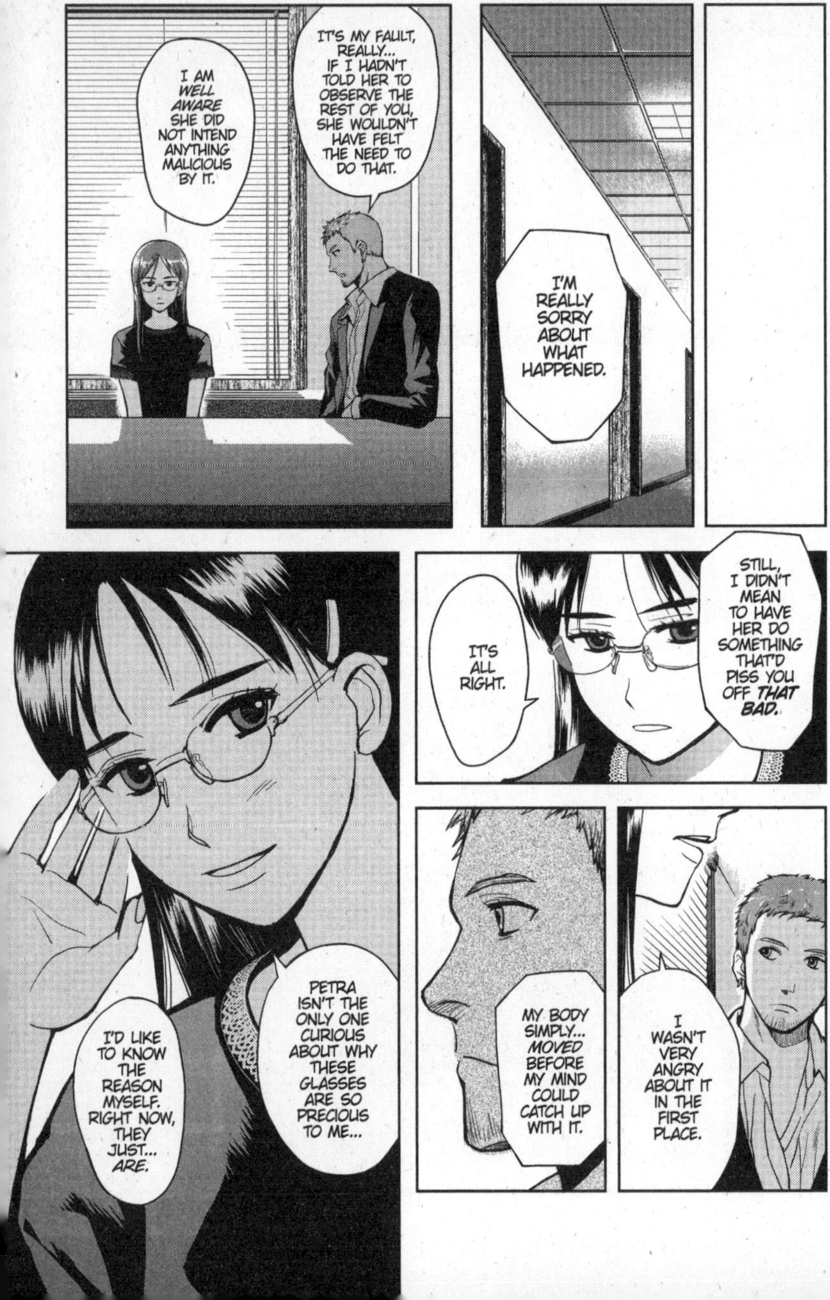
I'M REALLY SORRY ABOUT WHAT HAPPENED.
IT'S MY FAULT, REALLY... IF I HADN'T TOLD HER TO OBSERVE THE REST OF YOU, SHE WOULDN'T HAVE FELT THE NEED TO DO THAT.
I AM *WELL AWARE* SHE DID NOT INTEND ANYTHING MALICIOUS BY IT.
STILL, I DIDN'T MEAN TO HAVE HER DO SOMETHING THAT'D PISS YOU OFF ***THAT BAD***.
IT'S ALL RIGHT.
I WASN'T VERY ANGRY ABOUT IT IN THE FIRST PLACE.
MY BODY SIMPLY... *MOVED* BEFORE MY MIND COULD CATCH UP WITH IT.
PETRA ISN'T THE ONLY ONE CURIOUS ABOUT WHY THESE GLASSES ARE SO PRECIOUS TO ME...
I'D LIKE TO KNOW THE REASON MYSELF. RIGHT NOW, THEY JUST... *ARE*.

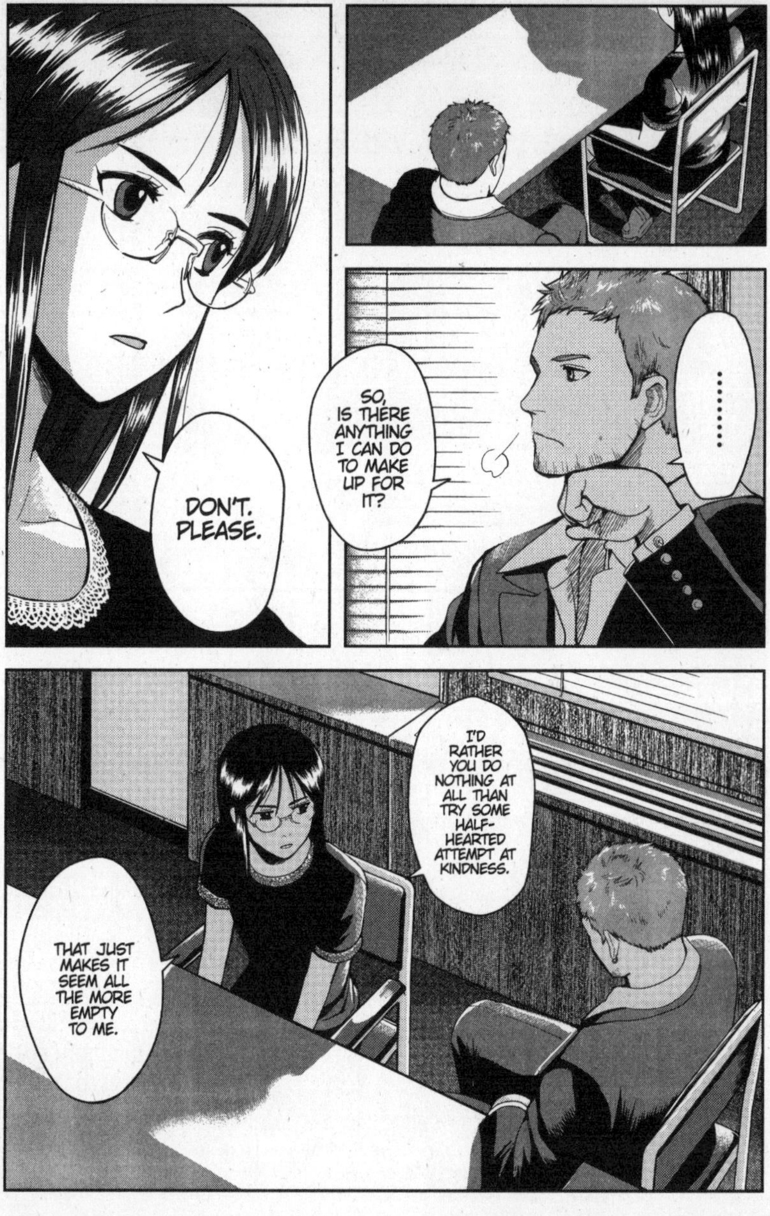
......
SO, IS THERE ANYTHING I CAN DO TO MAKE UP FOR IT?
DON'T. PLEASE.
I'D RATHER YOU DO NOTHING AT ALL THAN TRY SOME HALF-HEARTED ATTEMPT AT KINDNESS.
THAT JUST MAKES IT SEEM ALL THE MORE EMPTY TO ME.

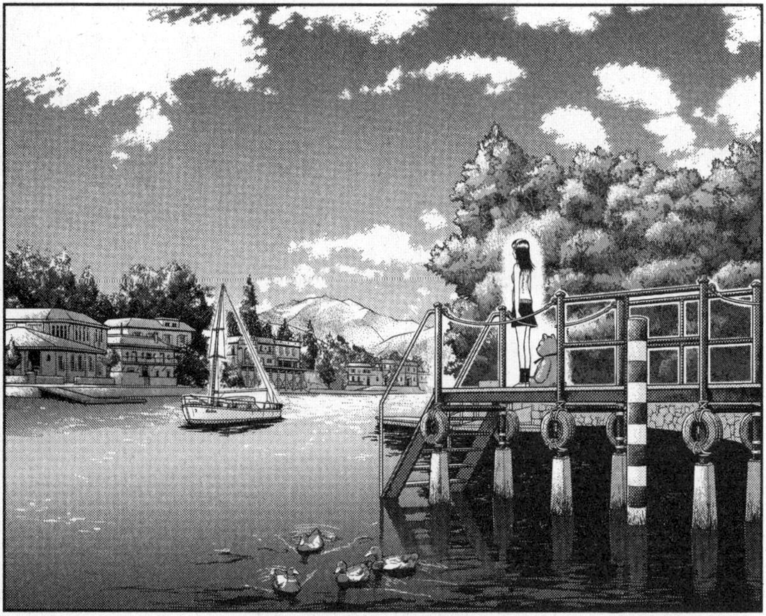

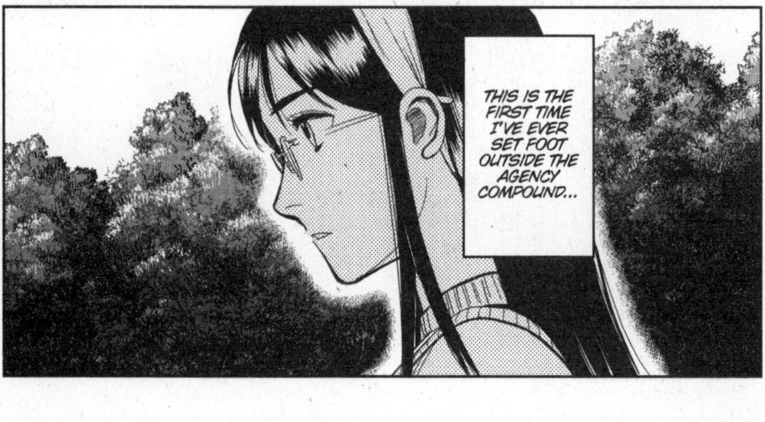
THIS IS THE FIRST TIME I'VE EVER SET FOOT OUTSIDE THE AGENCY COMPOUND...

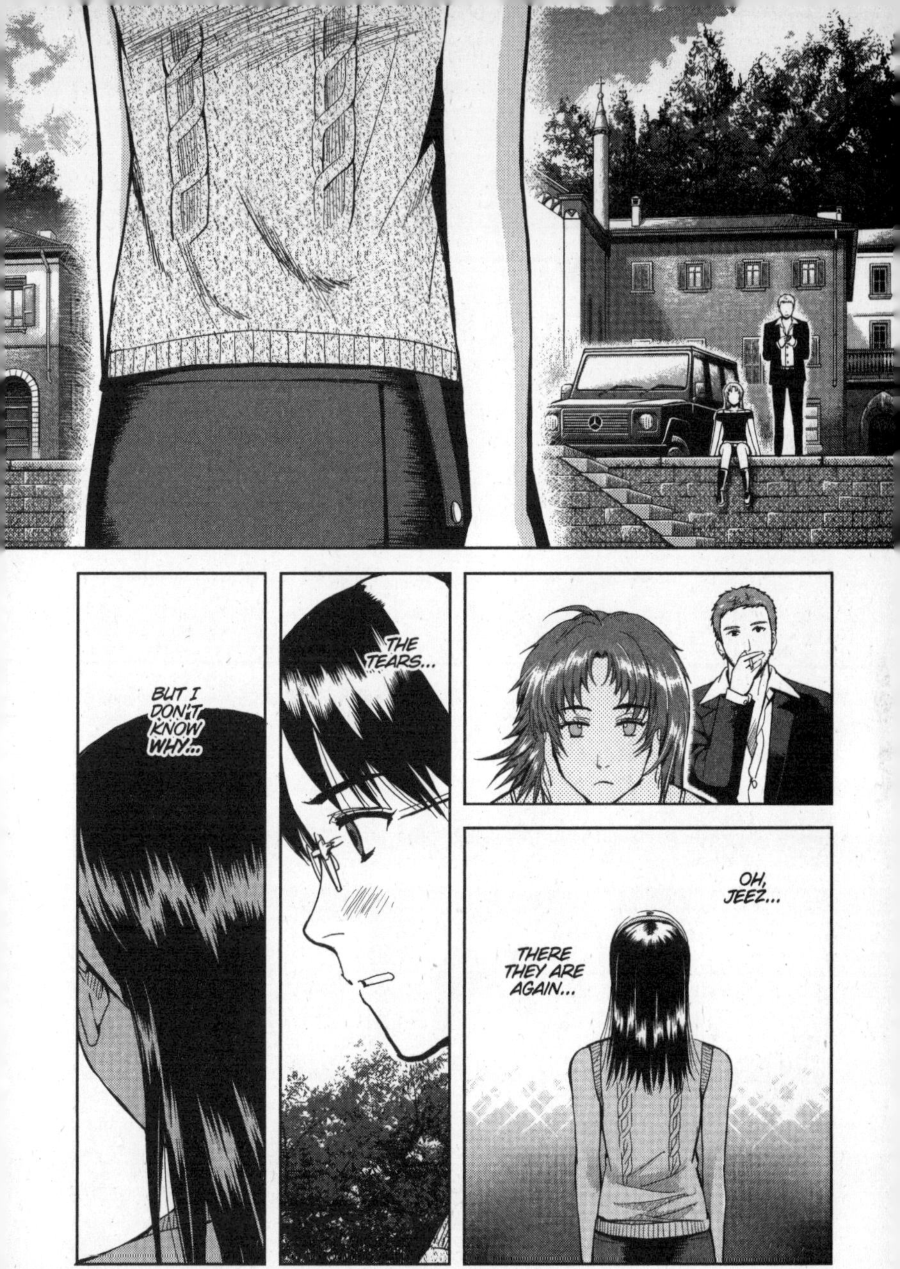
OH, JEEZ...
THERE THEY ARE AGAIN...
THE TEARS...
BUT I DON'T KNOW WHY...

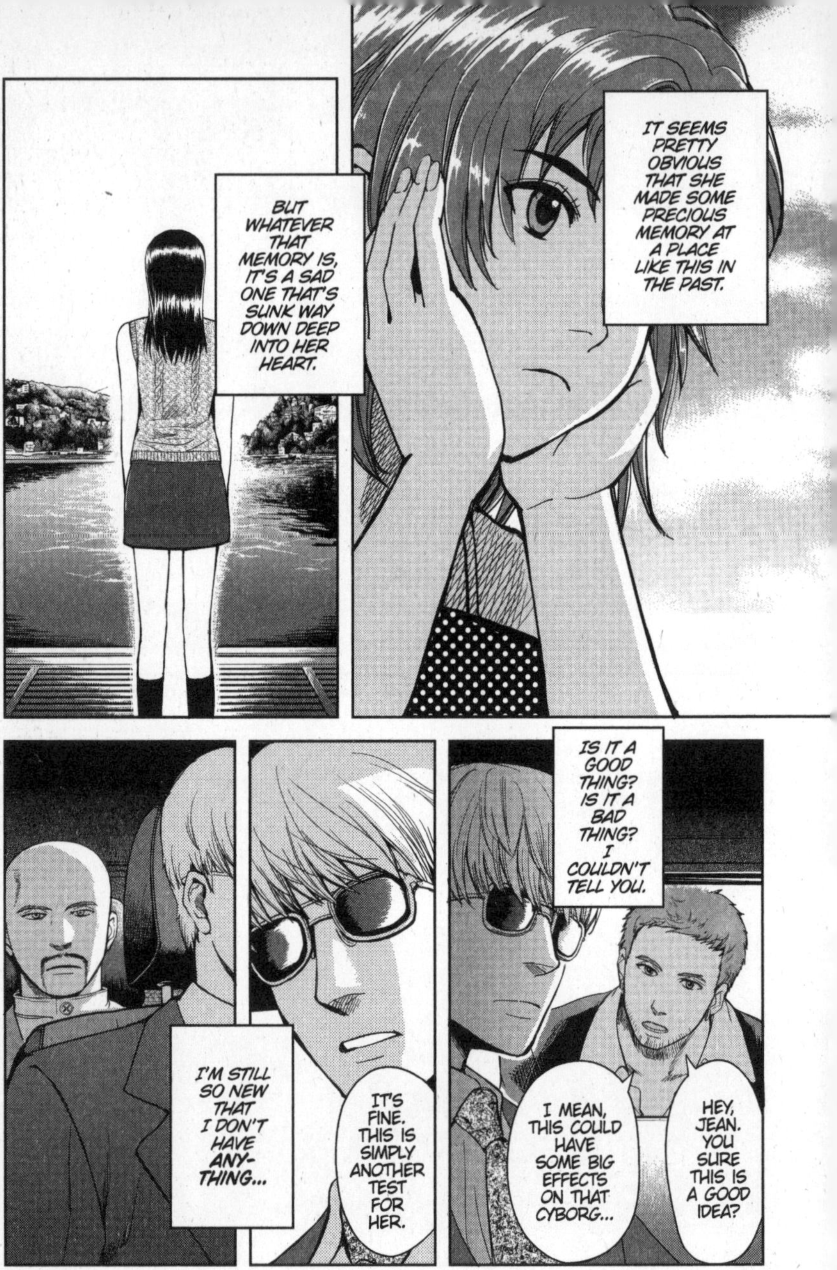
IT SEEMS PRETTY OBVIOUS THAT SHE MADE SOME PRECIOUS MEMORY AT A PLACE LIKE THIS IN THE PAST.
BUT WHATEVER THAT MEMORY IS, IT'S A SAD ONE THAT'S SUNK WAY DOWN DEEP INTO HER HEART.
IS IT A GOOD THING? IS IT A BAD THING? I COULDN'T TELL YOU.
HEY, JEAN. YOU SURE THIS IS A GOOD IDEA?
I MEAN, THIS COULD HAVE SOME BIG EFFECTS ON THAT CYBORG...
IT'S FINE. THIS IS SIMPLY ANOTHER TEST FOR HER.
I'M STILL SO NEW THAT I DON'T HAVE ANYTHING...

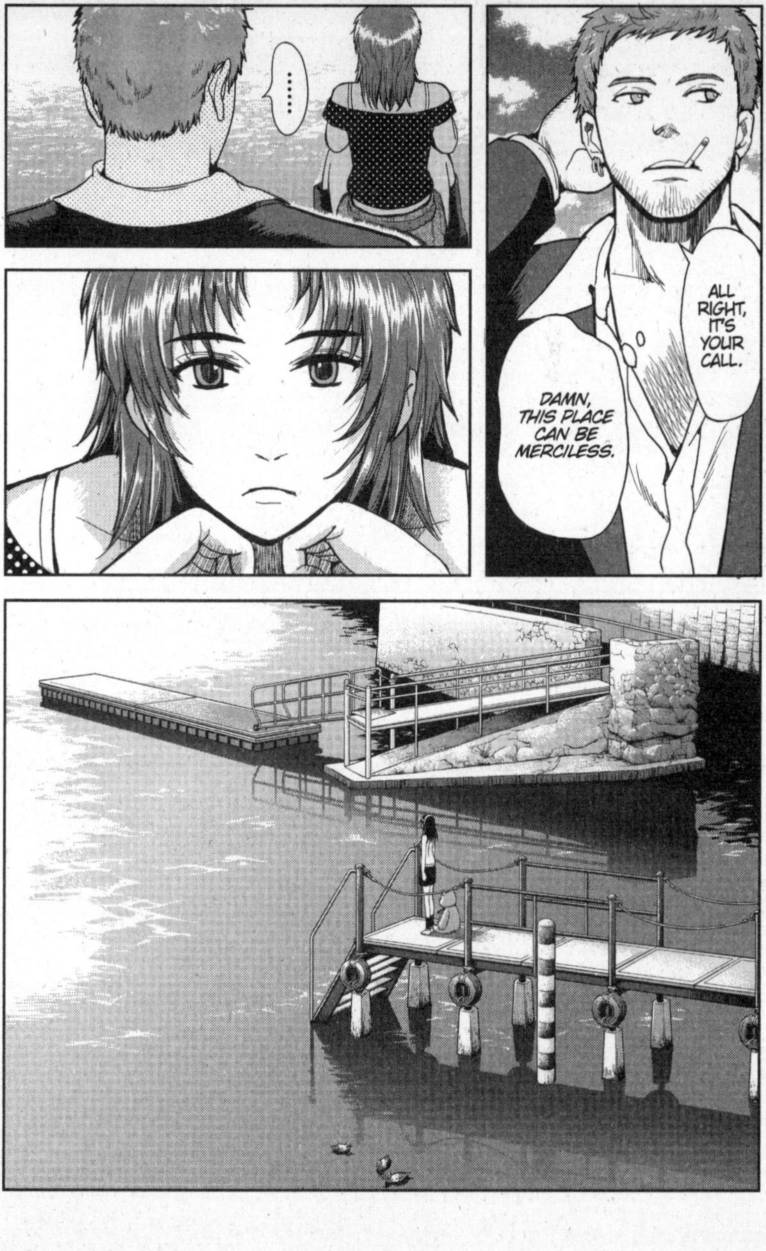
ALL RIGHT, IT'S YOUR CALL.
DAMN, THIS PLACE CAN BE MERCILESS.
......

GUNSLINGERGIRL.

CHAPTER 34: PROMISES

NOW, WHILE YOU WEAR THESE GLASSES, I WANT YOU TO BE THE GENTLE AND QUIET CLAES.

THIS ISN'T SOME ORDER THAT CAN BE CHANGED WHENEVER. THIS IS A BLOOD OATH.

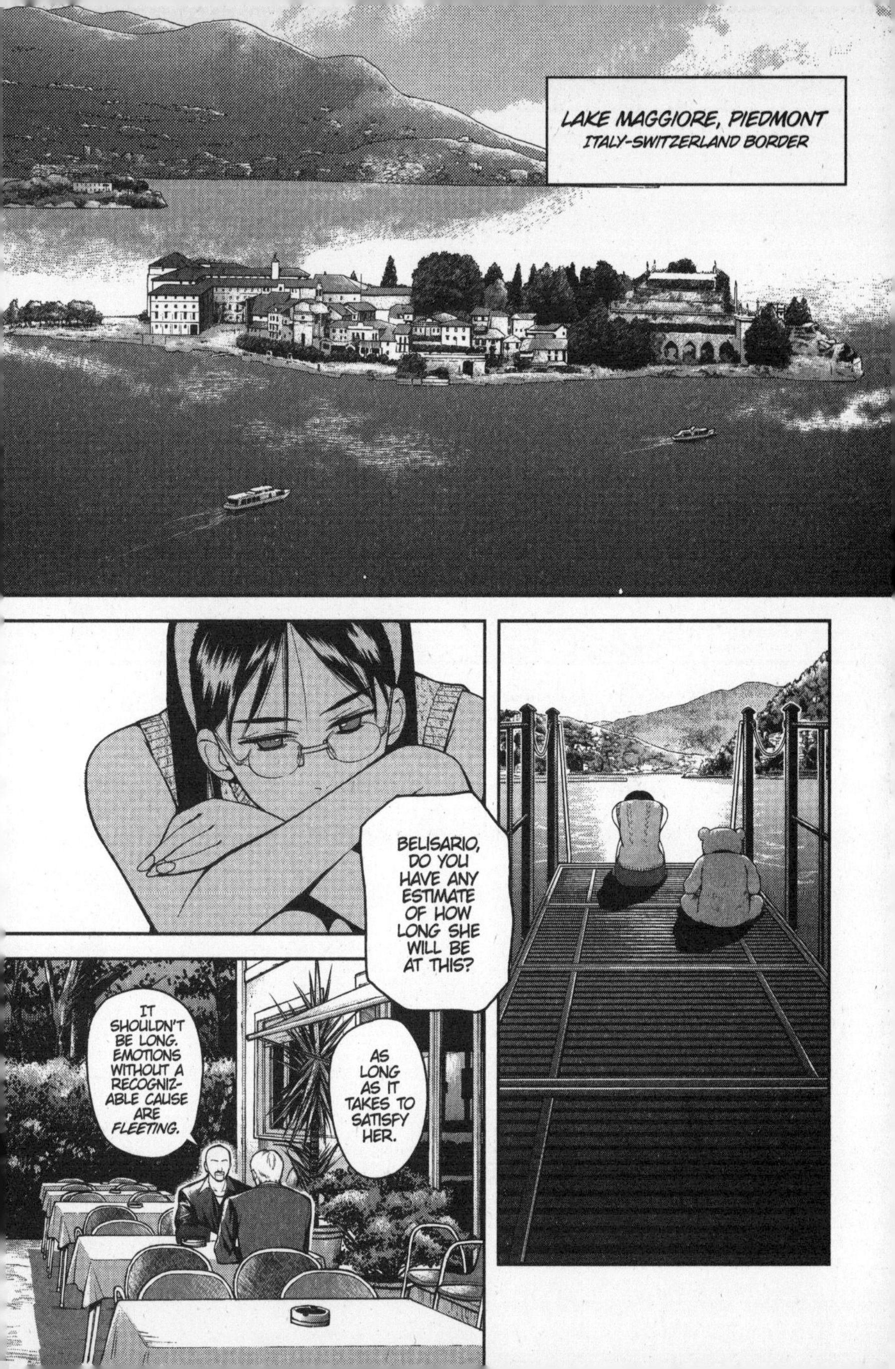
LAKE MAGGIORE, PIEDMONT
ITALY-SWITZERLAND BORDER
BELISARIO, DO YOU HAVE ANY ESTIMATE OF HOW LONG SHE WILL BE AT THIS?
AS LONG AS IT TAKES TO SATISFY HER.
IT SHOULDN'T BE LONG. EMOTIONS WITHOUT A RECOGNIZ-ABLE CAUSE ARE FLEETING.

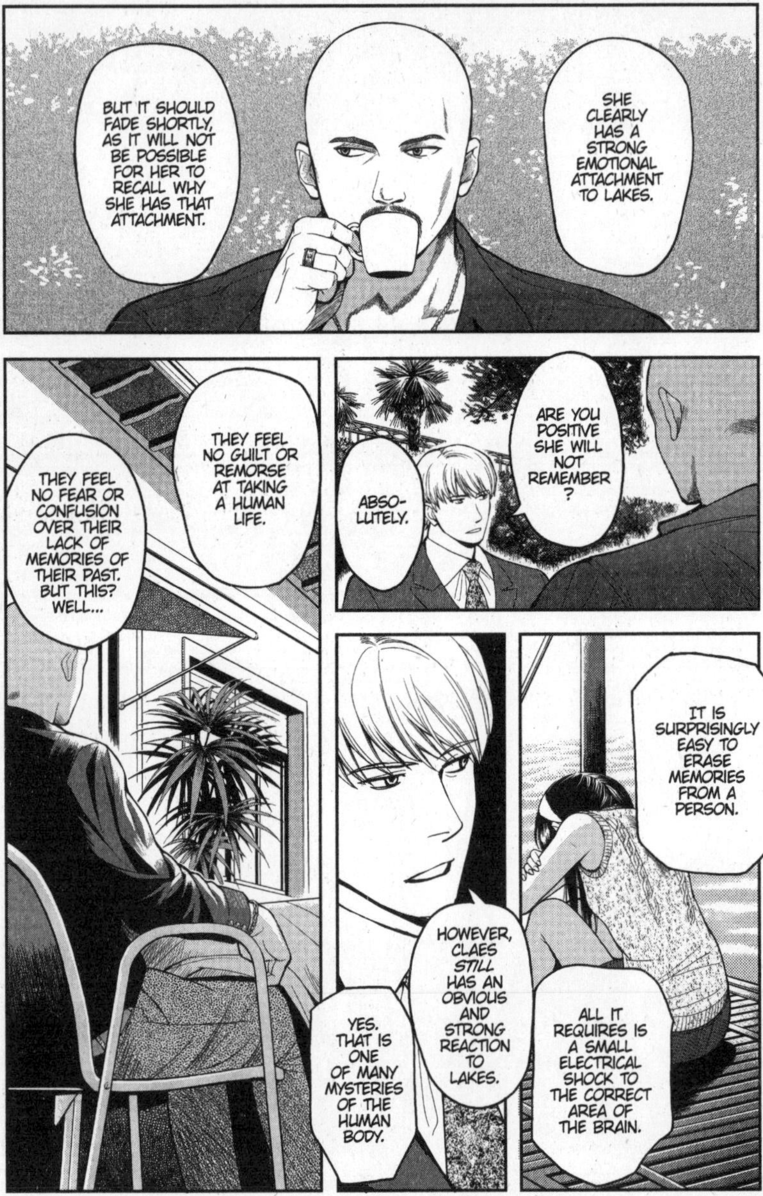
SHE CLEARLY HAS A STRONG EMOTIONAL ATTACHMENT TO LAKES.
BUT IT SHOULD FADE SHORTLY, AS IT WILL NOT BE POSSIBLE FOR HER TO RECALL WHY SHE HAS THAT ATTACHMENT.
ARE YOU POSITIVE SHE WILL NOT REMEMBER?
ABSO-LUTELY.
IT IS SURPRISINGLY EASY TO ERASE MEMORIES FROM A PERSON.
ALL IT REQUIRES IS A SMALL ELECTRICAL SHOCK TO THE CORRECT AREA OF THE BRAIN.
HOWEVER, CLAES *STILL* HAS AN OBVIOUS AND STRONG REACTION TO LAKES.
YES. THAT IS ONE OF MANY MYSTERIES OF THE HUMAN BODY.
THEY FEEL NO GUILT OR REMORSE AT TAKING A HUMAN LIFE.
THEY FEEL NO FEAR OR CONFUSION OVER THEIR LACK OF MEMORIES OF THEIR PAST. BUT THIS? WELL...

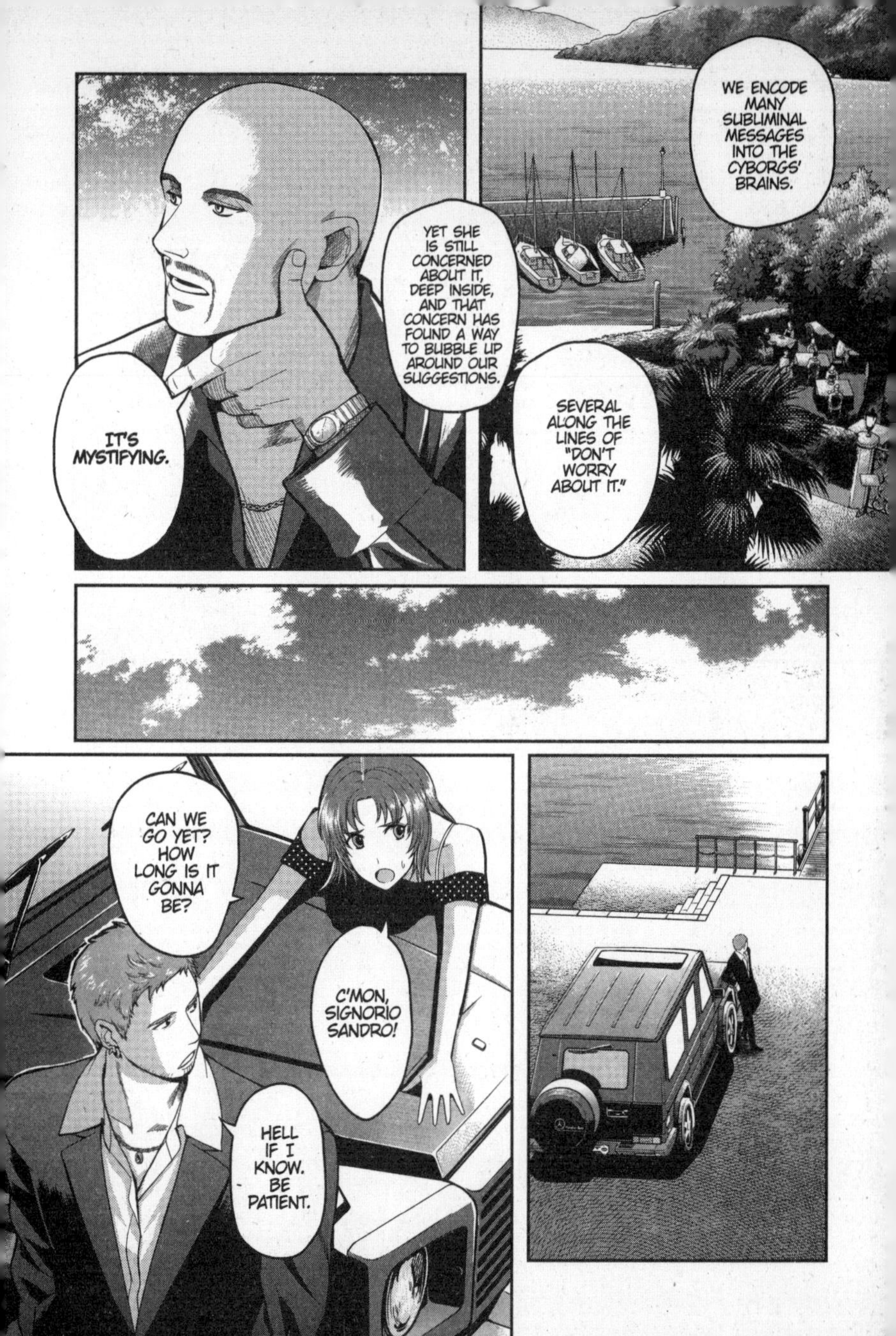
WE ENCODE MANY SUBLIMINAL MESSAGES INTO THE CYBORGS' BRAINS.
SEVERAL ALONG THE LINES OF "DON'T WORRY ABOUT IT."
YET SHE IS STILL CONCERNED ABOUT IT, DEEP INSIDE, AND THAT CONCERN HAS FOUND A WAY TO BUBBLE UP AROUND OUR SUGGESTIONS.
IT'S MYSTIFYING.
CAN WE GO YET? HOW LONG IS IT GONNA BE?
C'MON, SIGNORIO SANDRO!
HELL IF I KNOW. BE PATIENT.

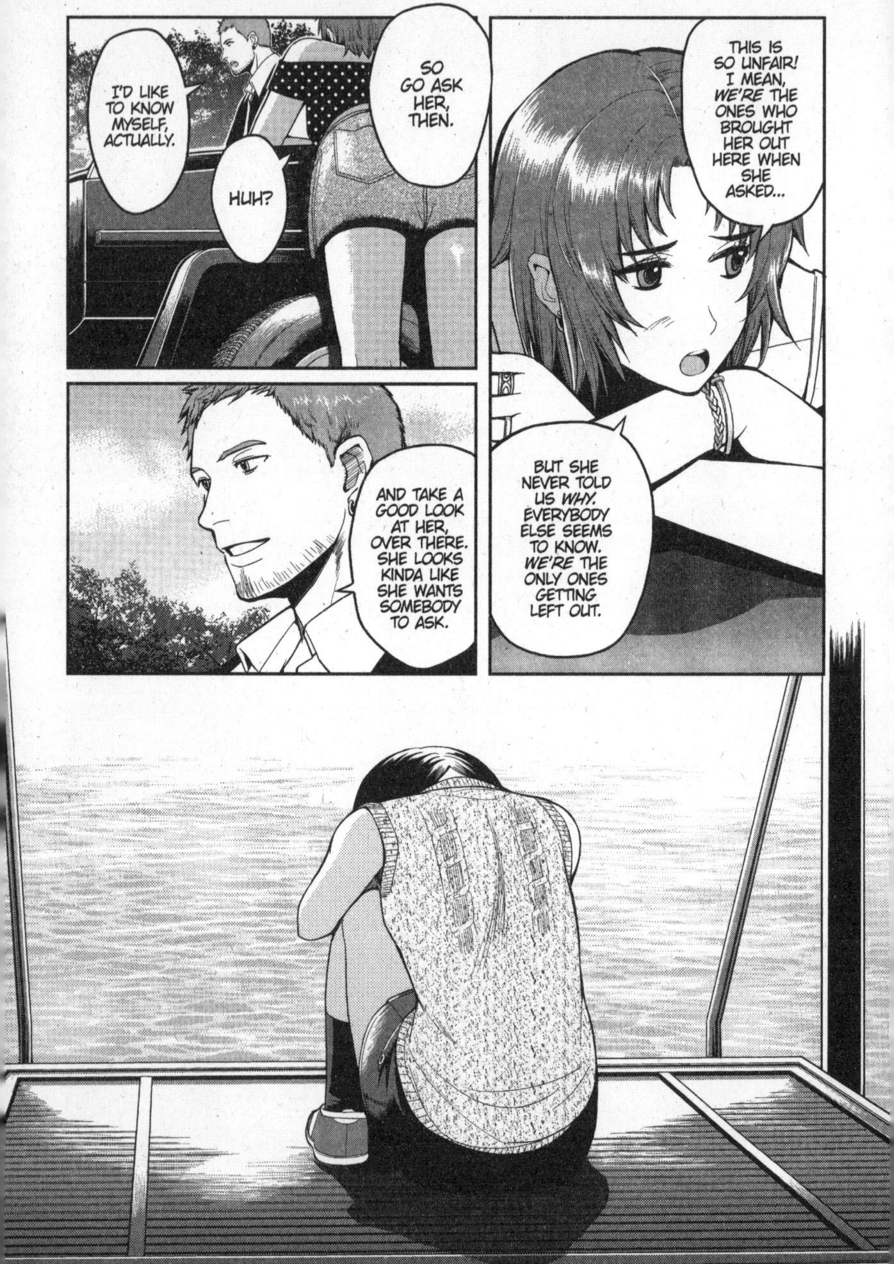
THIS IS SO UNFAIR! I MEAN, *WE'RE* THE ONES WHO BROUGHT HER OUT HERE WHEN SHE ASKED...
BUT SHE NEVER TOLD US *WHY*. EVERYBODY ELSE SEEMS TO KNOW. *WE'RE* THE ONLY ONES GETTING LEFT OUT.
SO GO ASK HER, THEN.
I'D LIKE TO KNOW MYSELF, ACTUALLY.
HUH?
AND TAKE A GOOD LOOK AT HER, OVER THERE. SHE LOOKS KINDA LIKE SHE WANTS SOMEBODY TO ASK.

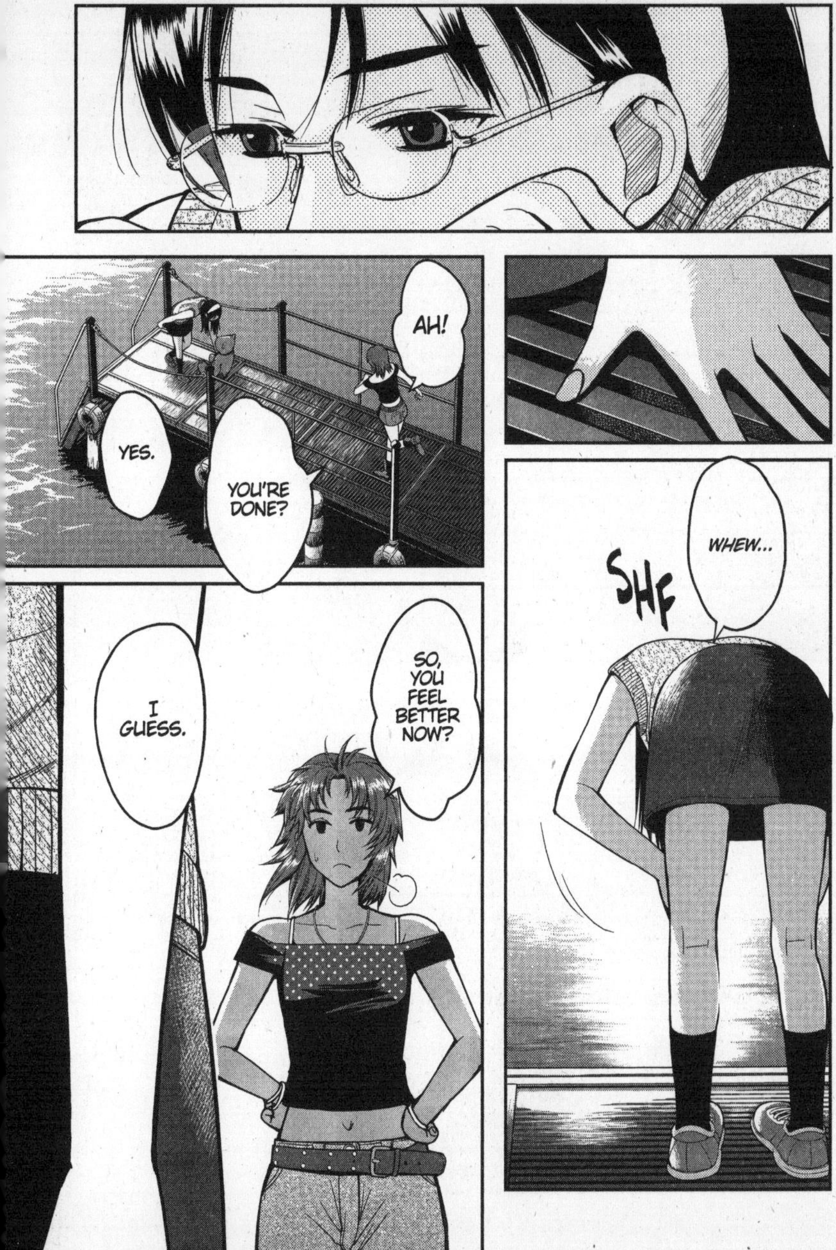
AH!
YOU'RE DONE?
YES.
WHEW...
SHF
SO, YOU FEEL BETTER NOW?
I GUESS.

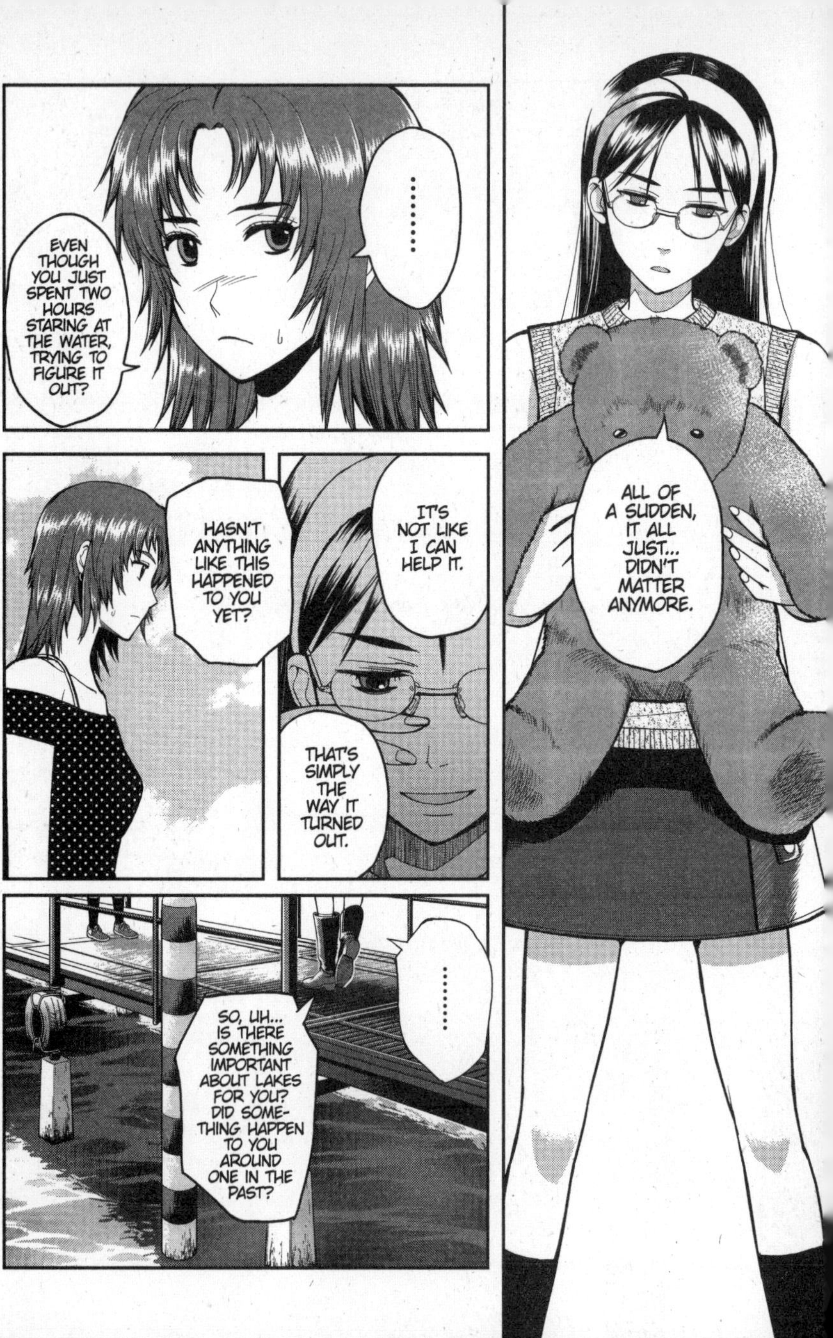
ALL OF A SUDDEN, IT ALL JUST... DIDN'T MATTER ANYMORE.
......
EVEN THOUGH YOU JUST SPENT TWO HOURS STARING AT THE WATER, TRYING TO FIGURE IT OUT?
IT'S NOT LIKE I CAN HELP IT.
THAT'S SIMPLY THE WAY IT TURNED OUT.
HASN'T ANYTHING LIKE THIS HAPPENED TO YOU YET?
......
SO, UH... IS THERE SOMETHING IMPORTANT ABOUT LAKES FOR YOU? DID SOME-THING HAPPEN TO YOU AROUND ONE IN THE PAST?

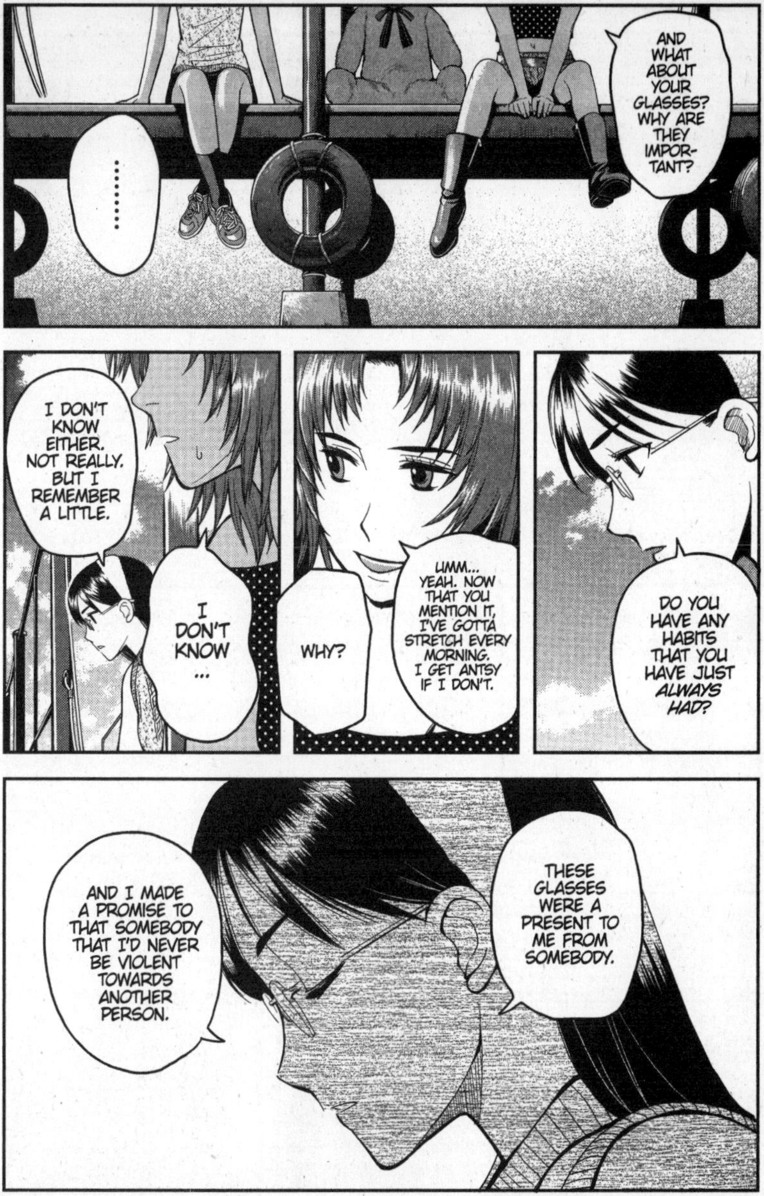
AND WHAT ABOUT YOUR GLASSES? WHY ARE THEY IMPORTANT?
......
DO YOU HAVE ANY HABITS THAT YOU HAVE JUST *ALWAYS* HAD?
UMM... YEAH. NOW THAT YOU MENTION IT, I'VE GOTTA STRETCH EVERY MORNING. I GET ANTSY IF I DON'T.
WHY?
I DON'T KNOW ...
I DON'T KNOW EITHER. NOT REALLY. BUT I REMEMBER A LITTLE.
THESE GLASSES WERE A PRESENT TO ME FROM SOMEBODY.
AND I MADE A PROMISE TO THAT SOMEBODY THAT I'D NEVER BE VIOLENT TOWARDS ANOTHER PERSON.

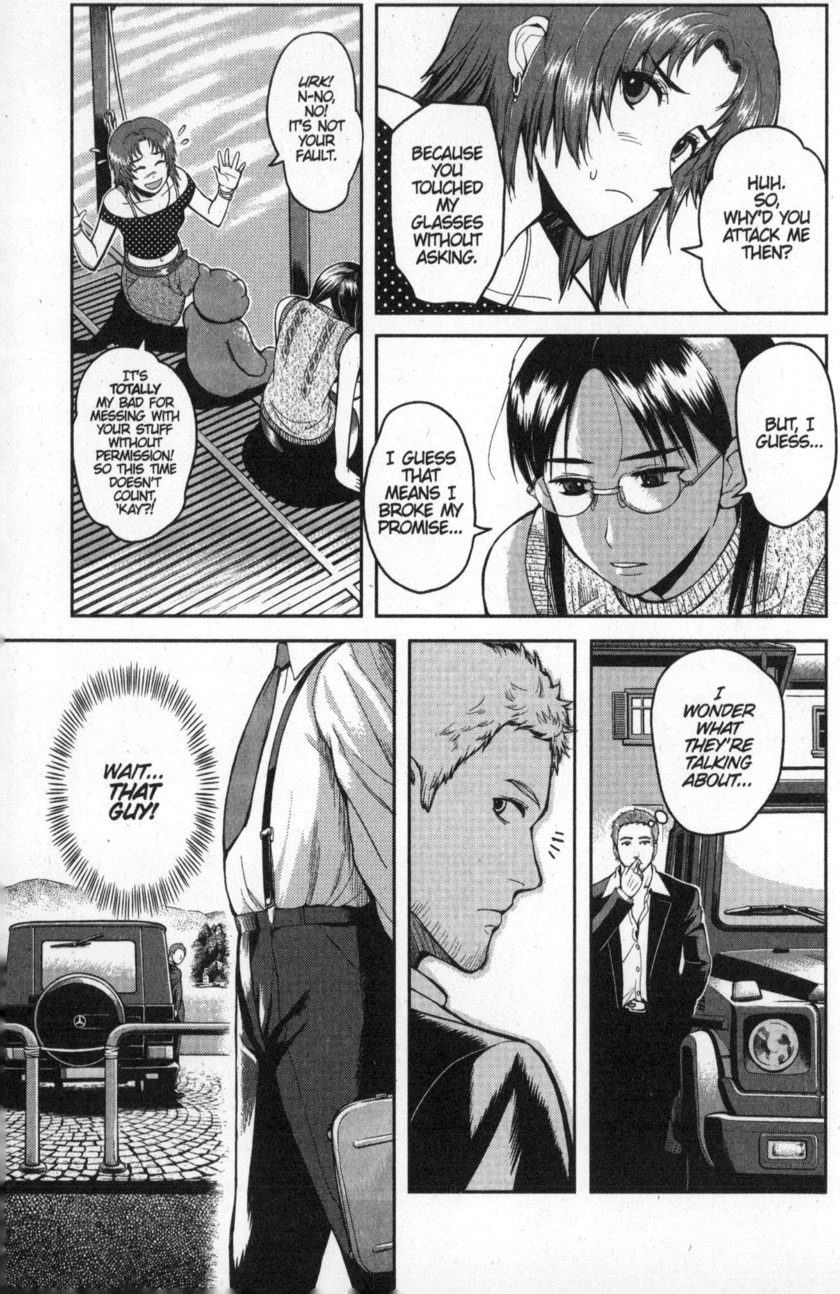
HUH. SO, WHY'D YOU ATTACK ME THEN?
BECAUSE YOU TOUCHED MY GLASSES WITHOUT ASKING.
BUT, I GUESS...
I GUESS THAT MEANS I BROKE MY PROMISE...
URK! N-NO, NO! IT'S NOT YOUR FAULT.
IT'S TOTALLY MY BAD FOR MESSING WITH YOUR STUFF WITHOUT PERMISSION! SO THIS TIME DOESN'T COUNT, 'KAY?!
I WONDER WHAT THEY'RE TALKING ABOUT...
WAIT... THAT GUY!

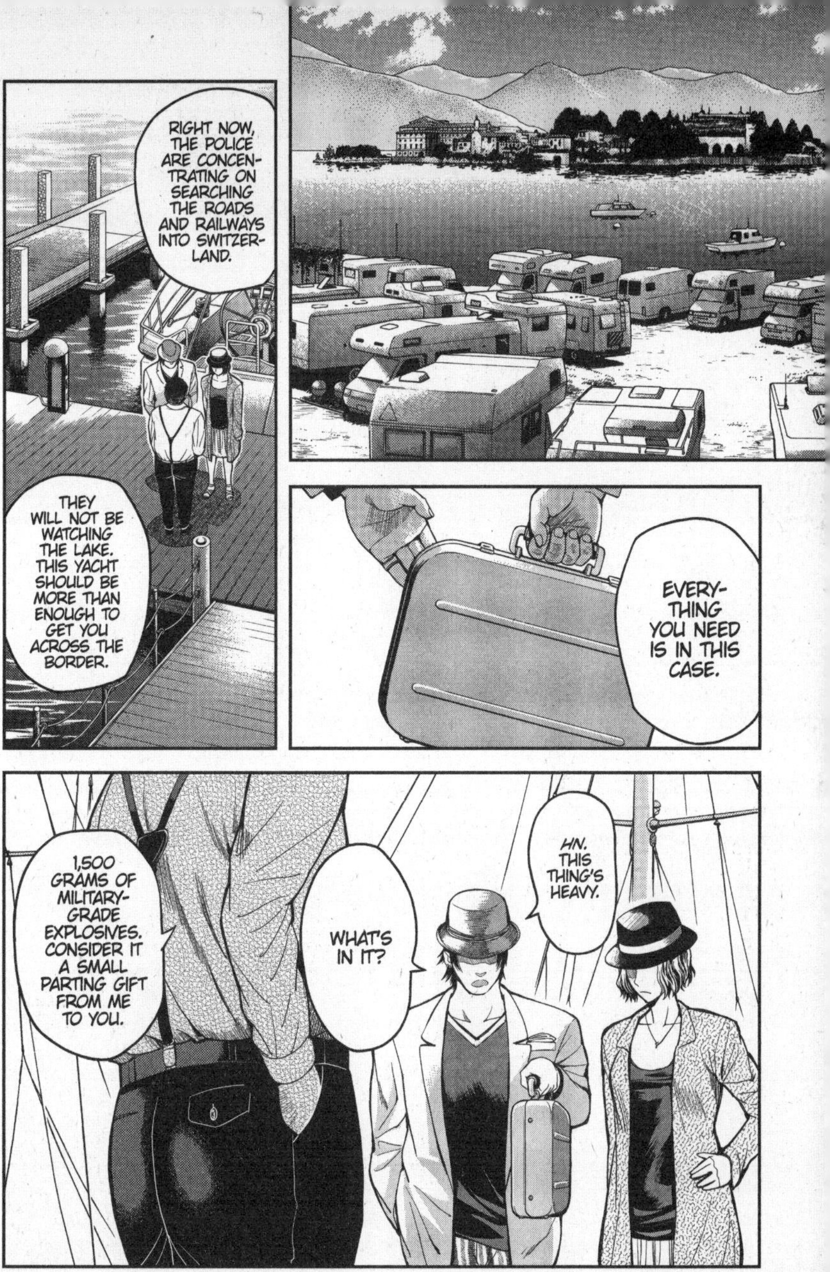
EVERYTHING YOU NEED IS IN THIS CASE.
RIGHT NOW, THE POLICE ARE CONCENTRATING ON SEARCHING THE ROADS AND RAILWAYS INTO SWITZERLAND.
THEY WILL NOT BE WATCHING THE LAKE. THIS YACHT SHOULD BE MORE THAN ENOUGH TO GET YOU ACROSS THE BORDER.
HN. THIS THING'S HEAVY.
WHAT'S IN IT?
1,500 GRAMS OF MILITARY-GRADE EXPLOSIVES. CONSIDER IT A SMALL PARTING GIFT FROM ME TO YOU.

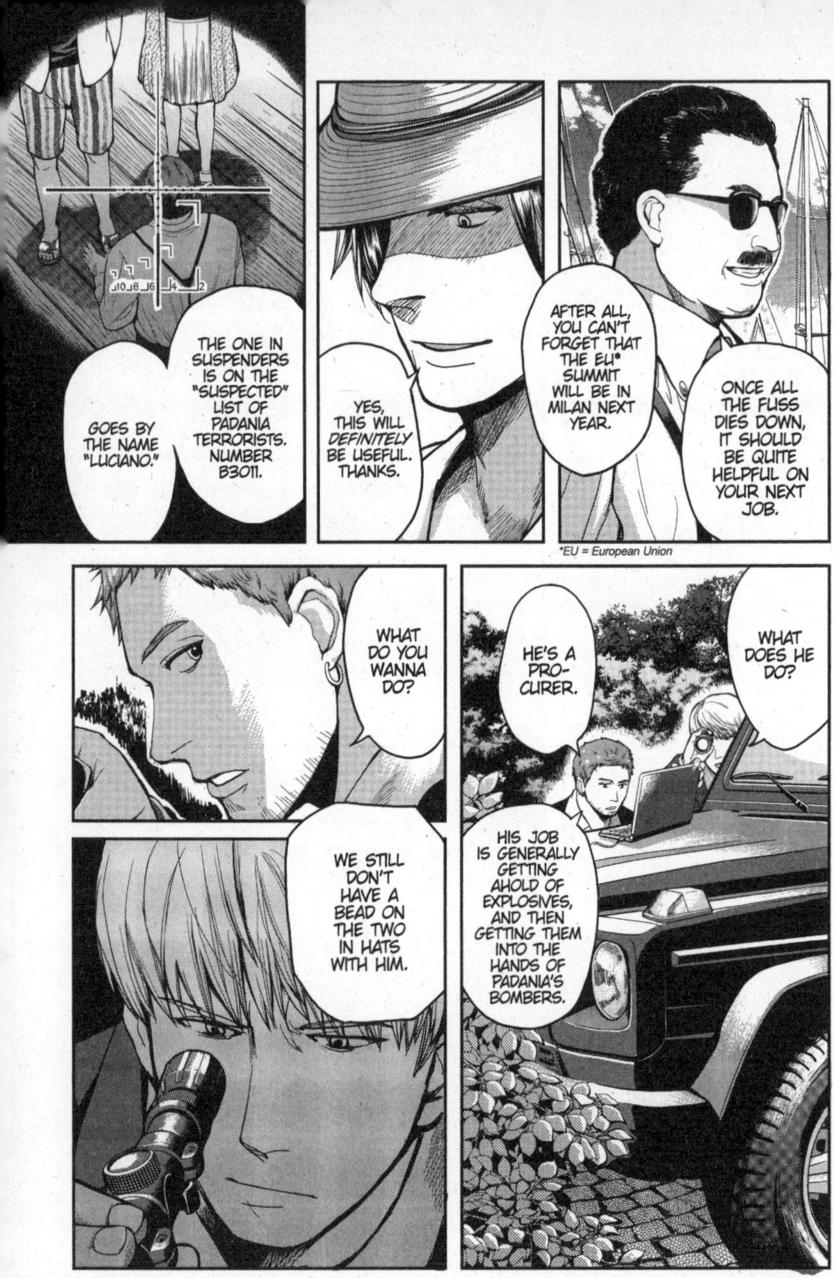
ONCE ALL THE FUSS DIES DOWN, IT SHOULD BE QUITE HELPFUL ON YOUR NEXT JOB.
AFTER ALL, YOU CAN'T FORGET THAT THE EU* SUMMIT WILL BE IN MILAN NEXT YEAR.
YES, THIS WILL *DEFINITELY* BE USEFUL. THANKS.
THE ONE IN SUSPENDERS IS ON THE "SUSPECTED" LIST OF PADANIA TERRORISTS. NUMBER B3011.
GOES BY THE NAME "LUCIANO."
WHAT DOES HE DO?
HE'S A PRO-CURER.
HIS JOB IS GENERALLY GETTING AHOLD OF EXPLOSIVES, AND THEN GETTING THEM INTO THE HANDS OF PADANIA'S BOMBERS.
WHAT DO YOU WANNA DO?
WE STILL DON'T HAVE A BEAD ON THE TWO IN HATS WITH HIM.

*EU = European Union

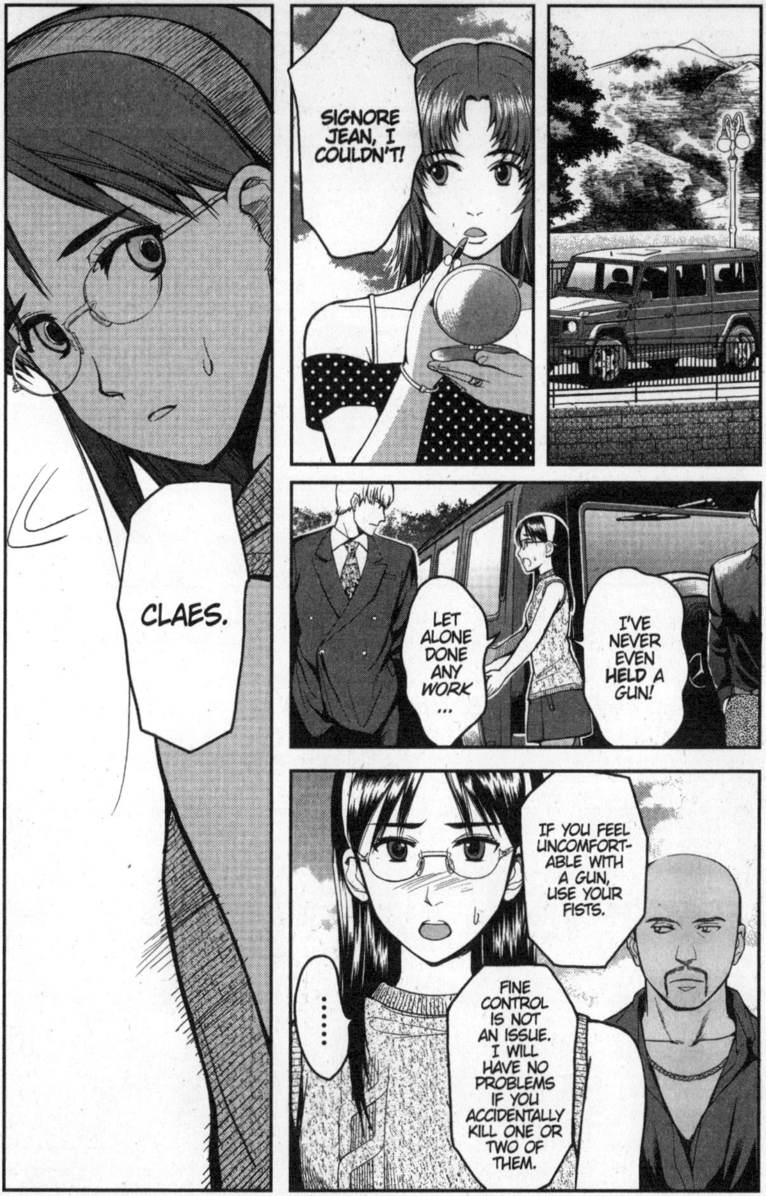
SIGNORE JEAN, I COULDN'T!
I'VE NEVER EVEN HELD A GUN!
LET ALONE DONE ANY *WORK* ...
IF YOU FEEL UNCOMFORT-ABLE WITH A GUN, USE YOUR FISTS.
FINE CONTROL IS NOT AN ISSUE. I WILL HAVE NO PROBLEMS IF YOU ACCIDENTALLY KILL ONE OR TWO OF THEM.
......
CLAES.

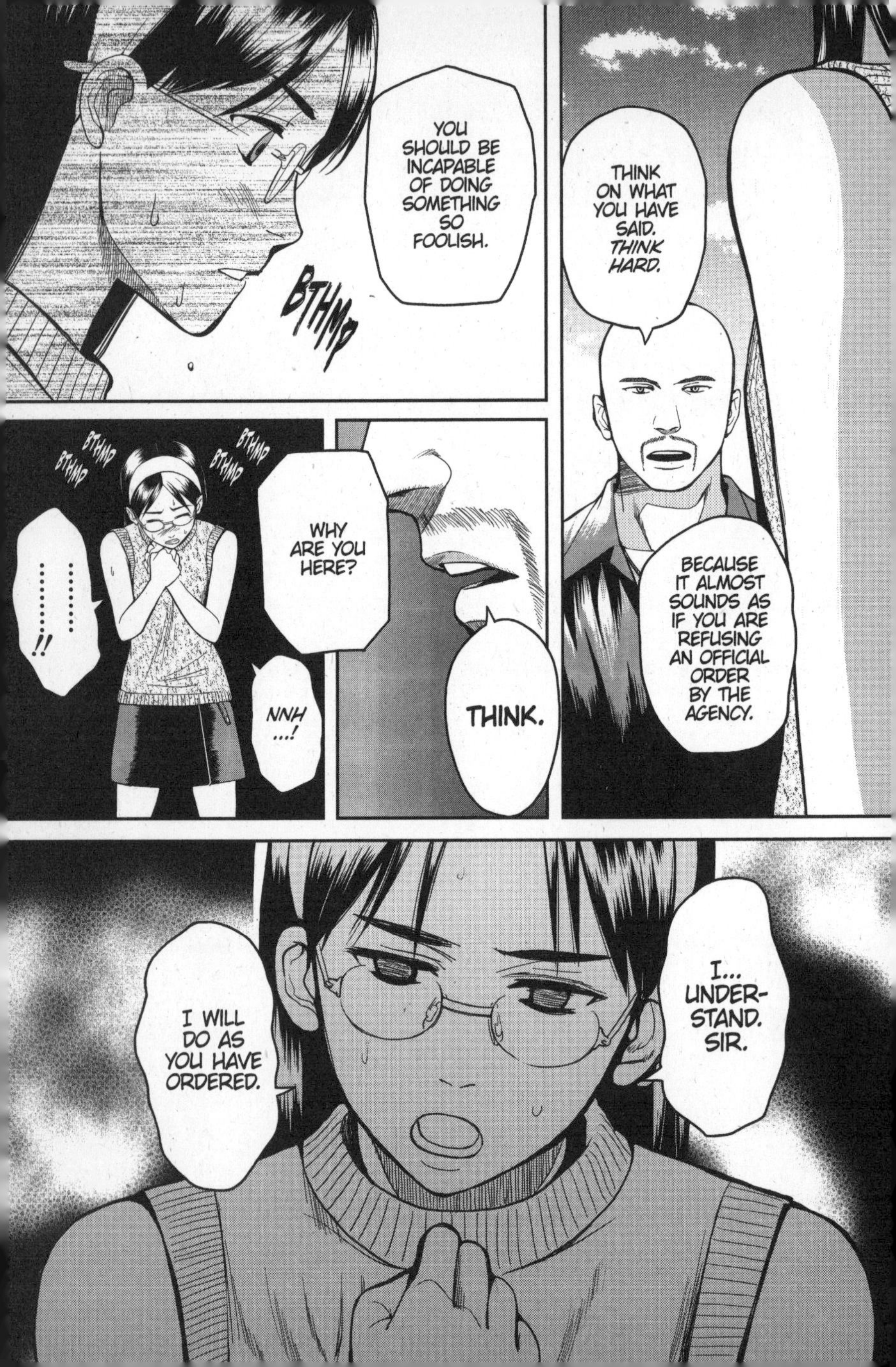
THINK ON WHAT YOU HAVE SAID. THINK HARD.
BECAUSE IT ALMOST SOUNDS AS IF YOU ARE REFUSING AN OFFICIAL ORDER BY THE AGENCY.
YOU SHOULD BE INCAPABLE OF DOING SOMETHING SO FOOLISH.
BTHMP
WHY ARE YOU HERE?
THINK.
BTHMP
BTHMP
BTHMP
BTHMP
NNH ...!
......!!
I... UNDER-STAND. SIR.
I WILL DO AS YOU HAVE ORDERED.

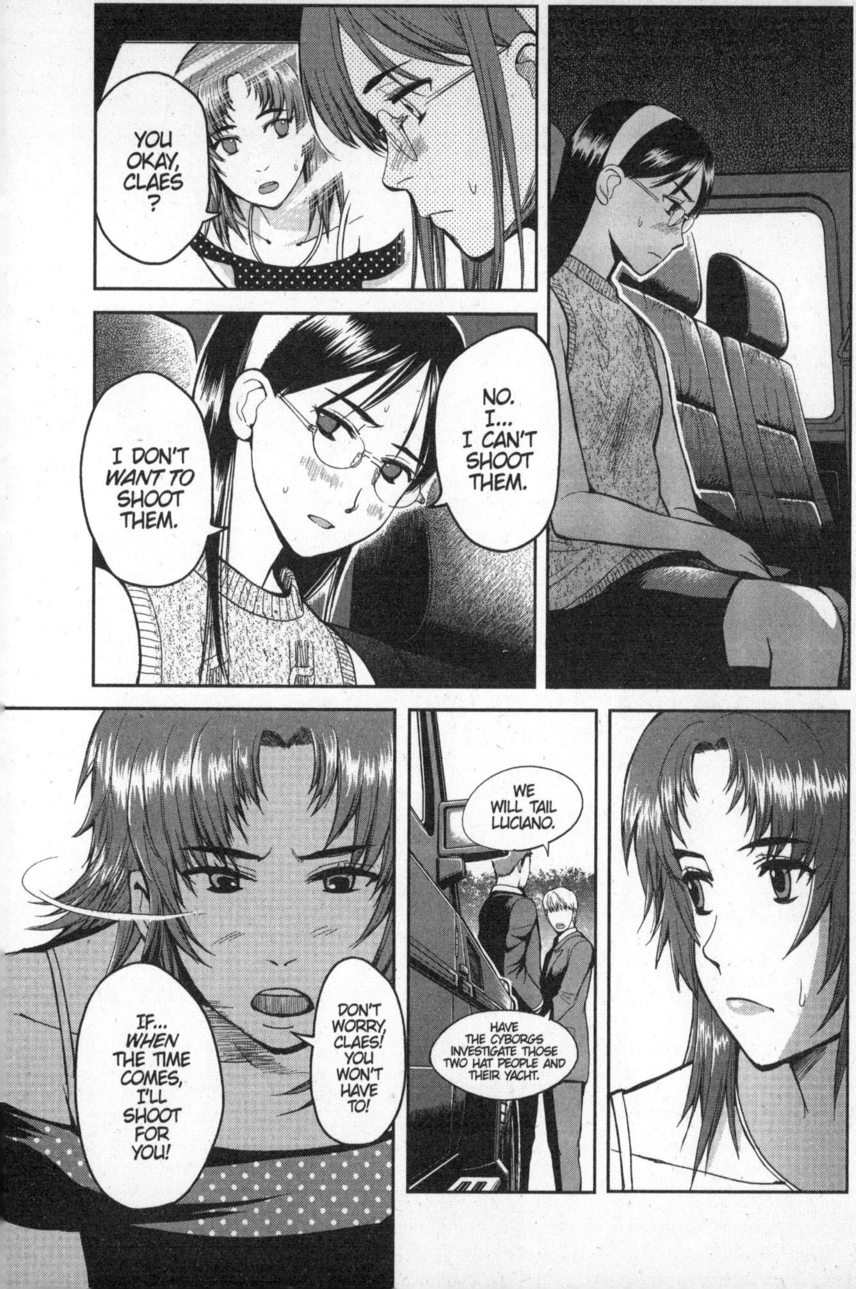
YOU OKAY, CLAES?
NO. I... I CAN'T SHOOT THEM.
I DON'T *WANT TO* SHOOT THEM.
WE WILL TAIL LUCIANO.
HAVE THE CYBORGS INVESTIGATE THOSE TWO HAT PEOPLE AND THEIR YACHT.
DON'T WORRY, CLAES! YOU WON'T HAVE TO!
IF... *WHEN* THE TIME COMES, I'LL SHOOT FOR YOU!

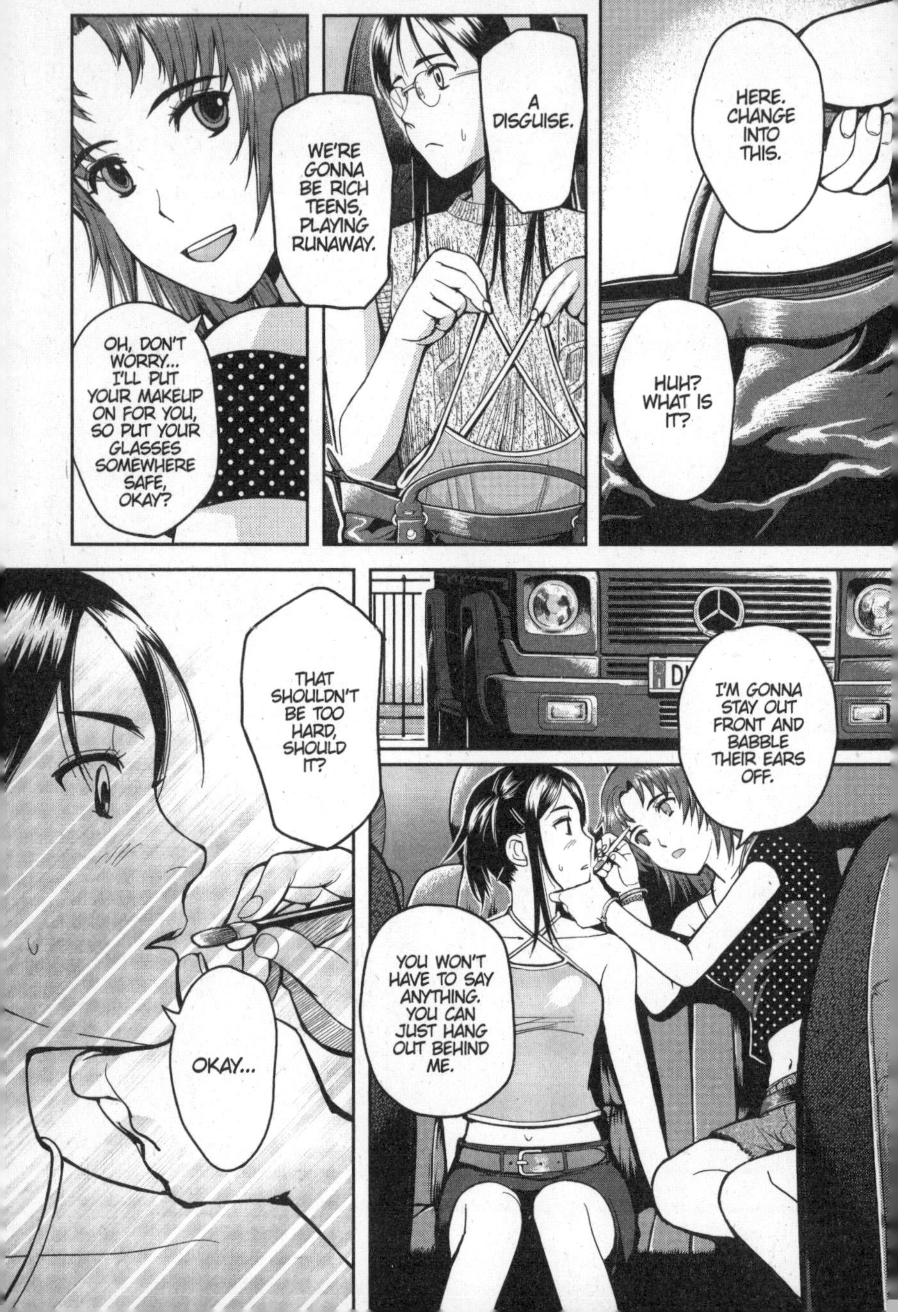
HERE. CHANGE INTO THIS.
HUH? WHAT IS IT?
A DISGUISE.
WE'RE GONNA BE RICH TEENS, PLAYING RUNAWAY.
OH, DON'T WORRY... I'LL PUT YOUR MAKEUP ON FOR YOU, SO PUT YOUR GLASSES SOMEWHERE SAFE, OKAY?
I'M GONNA STAY OUT FRONT AND BABBLE THEIR EARS OFF.
YOU WON'T HAVE TO SAY ANYTHING. YOU CAN JUST HANG OUT BEHIND ME.
THAT SHOULDN'T BE TOO HARD, SHOULD IT?
OKAY...

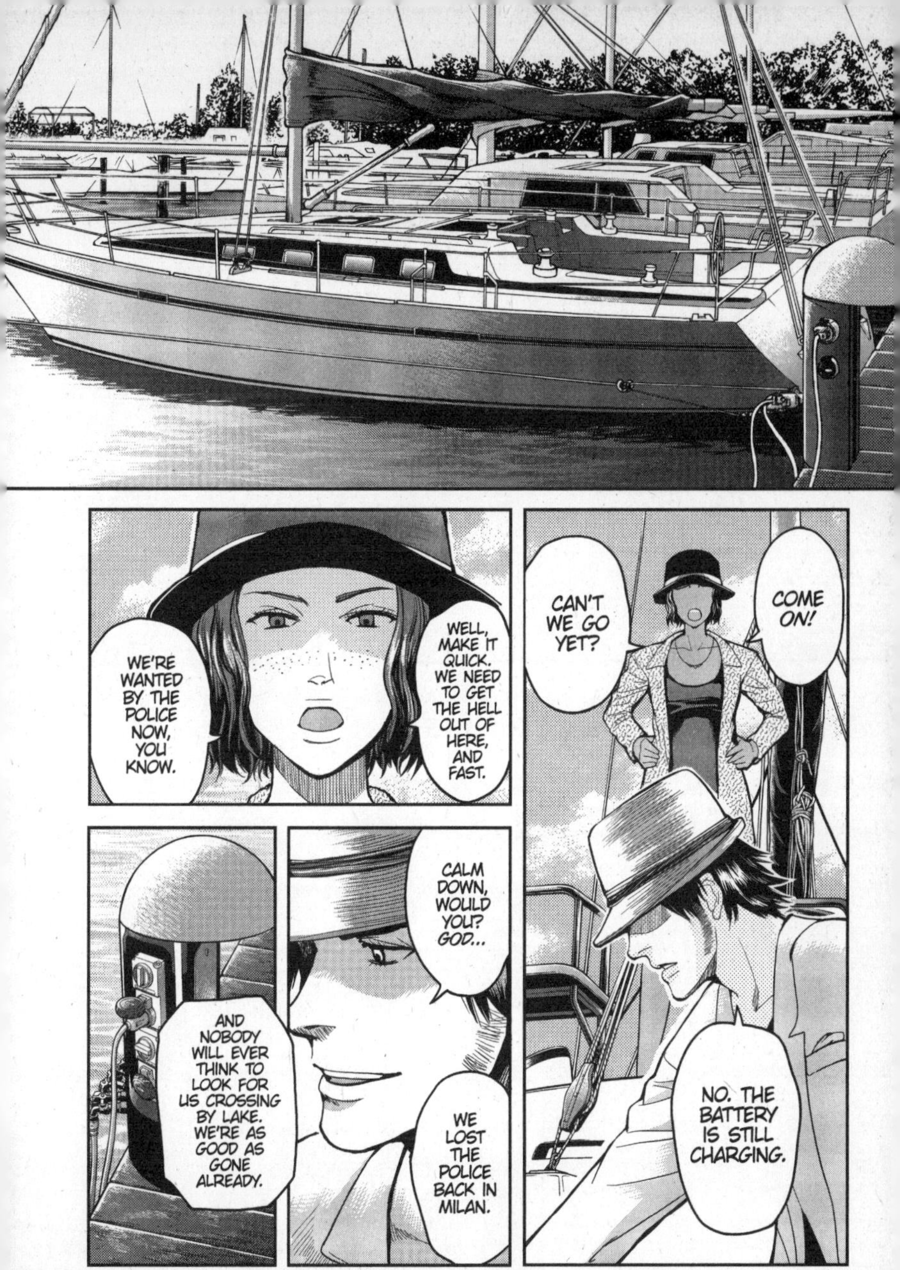
COME ON!
CAN'T WE GO YET?
NO. THE BATTERY IS STILL CHARGING.
WELL, MAKE IT QUICK. WE NEED TO GET THE HELL OUT OF HERE, AND FAST.
WE'RE WANTED BY THE POLICE NOW, YOU KNOW.
CALM DOWN, WOULD YOU? GOD...
WE LOST THE POLICE BACK IN MILAN.
AND NOBODY WILL EVER THINK TO LOOK FOR US CROSSING BY LAKE. WE'RE AS GOOD AS GONE ALREADY.

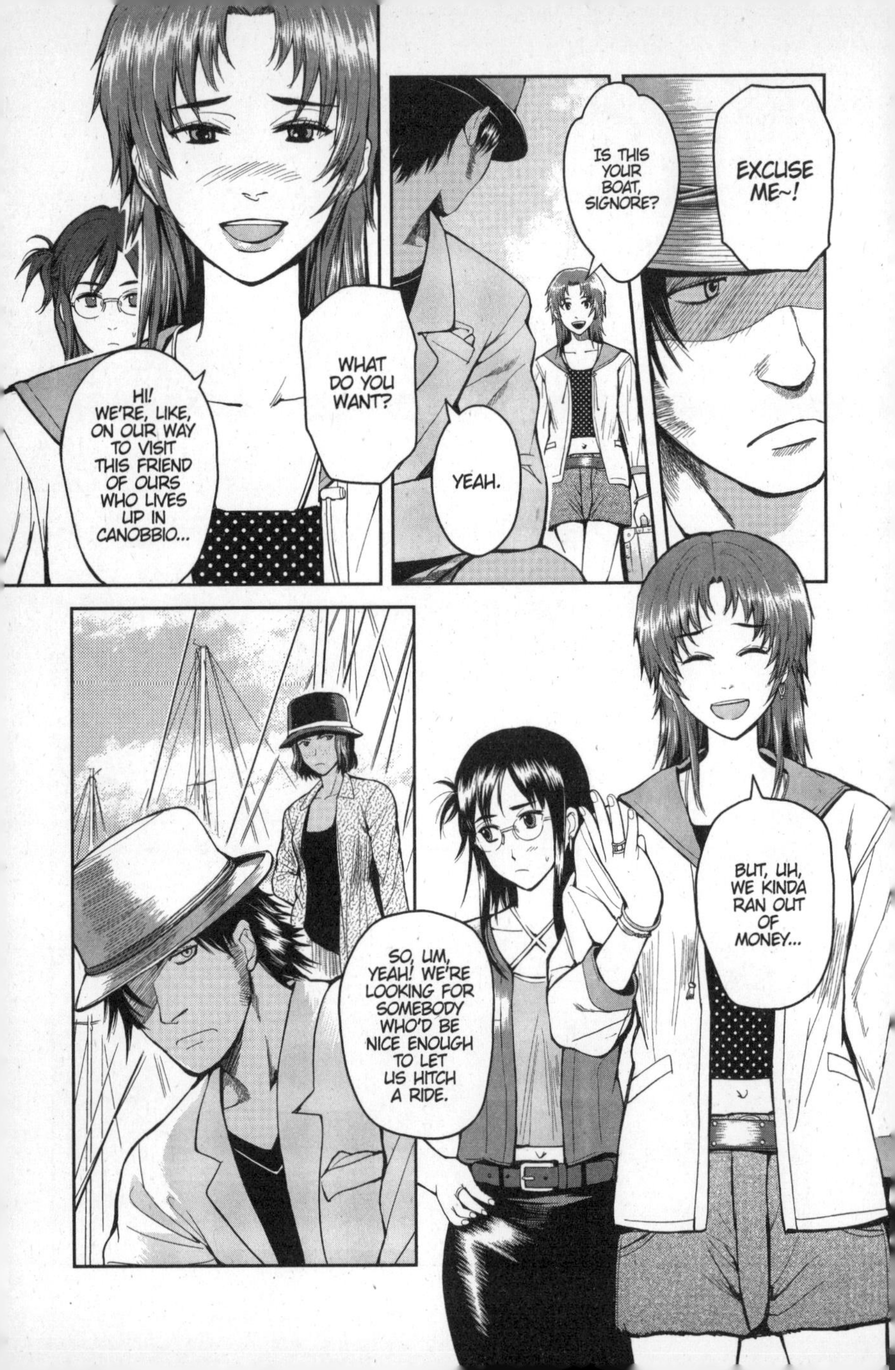
EXCUSE ME~!
IS THIS YOUR BOAT, SIGNORE?
YEAH.
WHAT DO YOU WANT?
HI! WE'RE, LIKE, ON OUR WAY TO VISIT THIS FRIEND OF OURS WHO LIVES UP IN CANOBBIO...
BUT, UH, WE KINDA RAN OUT OF MONEY...
SO, UM, YEAH! WE'RE LOOKING FOR SOMEBODY WHO'D BE NICE ENOUGH TO LET US HITCH A RIDE.

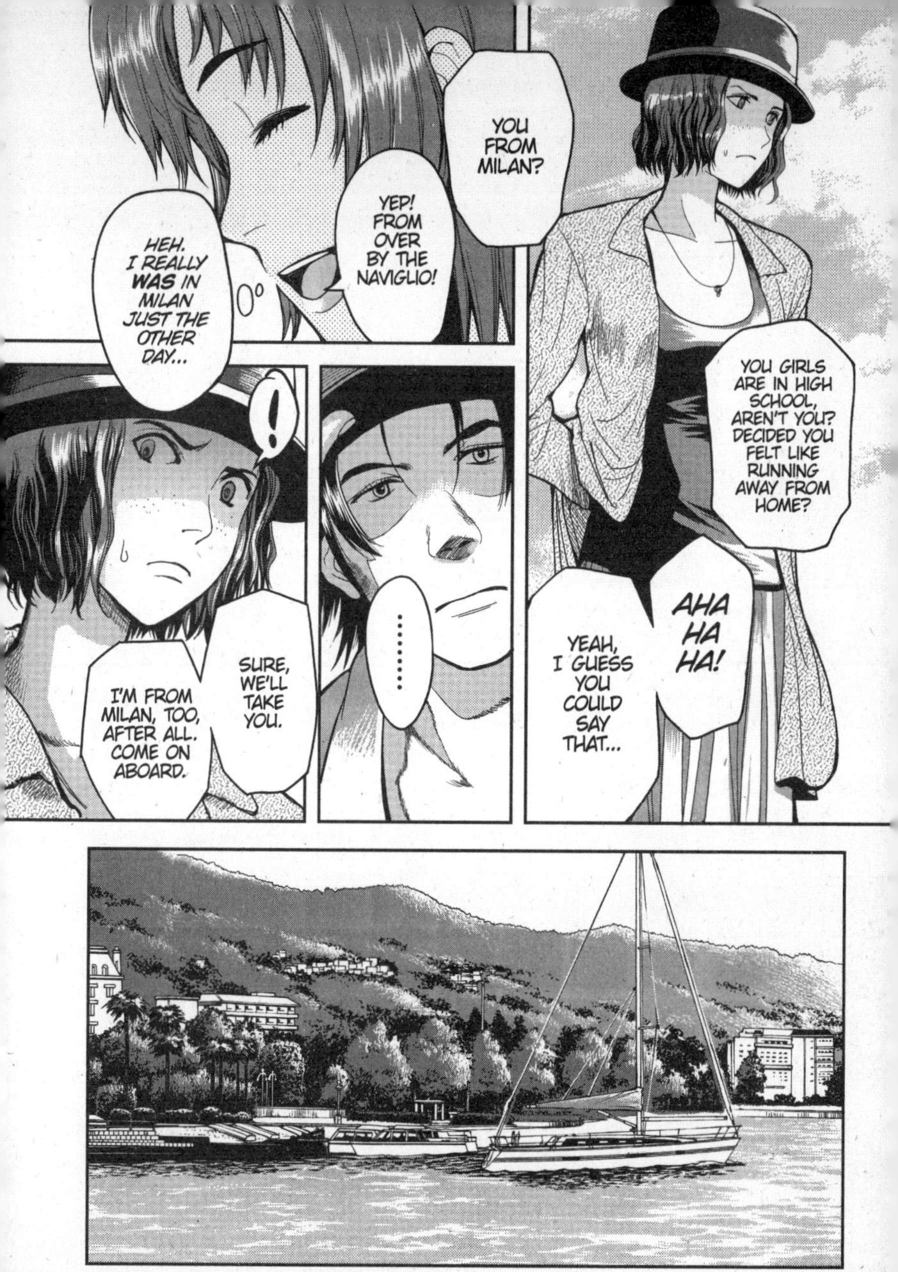
YOU GIRLS ARE IN HIGH SCHOOL, AREN'T YOU? DECIDED YOU FELT LIKE RUNNING AWAY FROM HOME?
AHA HA HA!
YEAH, I GUESS YOU COULD SAY THAT...
YOU FROM MILAN?
YEP! FROM OVER BY THE NAVIGLIO!
HEH. I REALLY **WAS** IN MILAN JUST THE OTHER DAY...
......
!
SURE, WE'LL TAKE YOU.
I'M FROM MILAN, TOO, AFTER ALL. COME ON ABOARD.

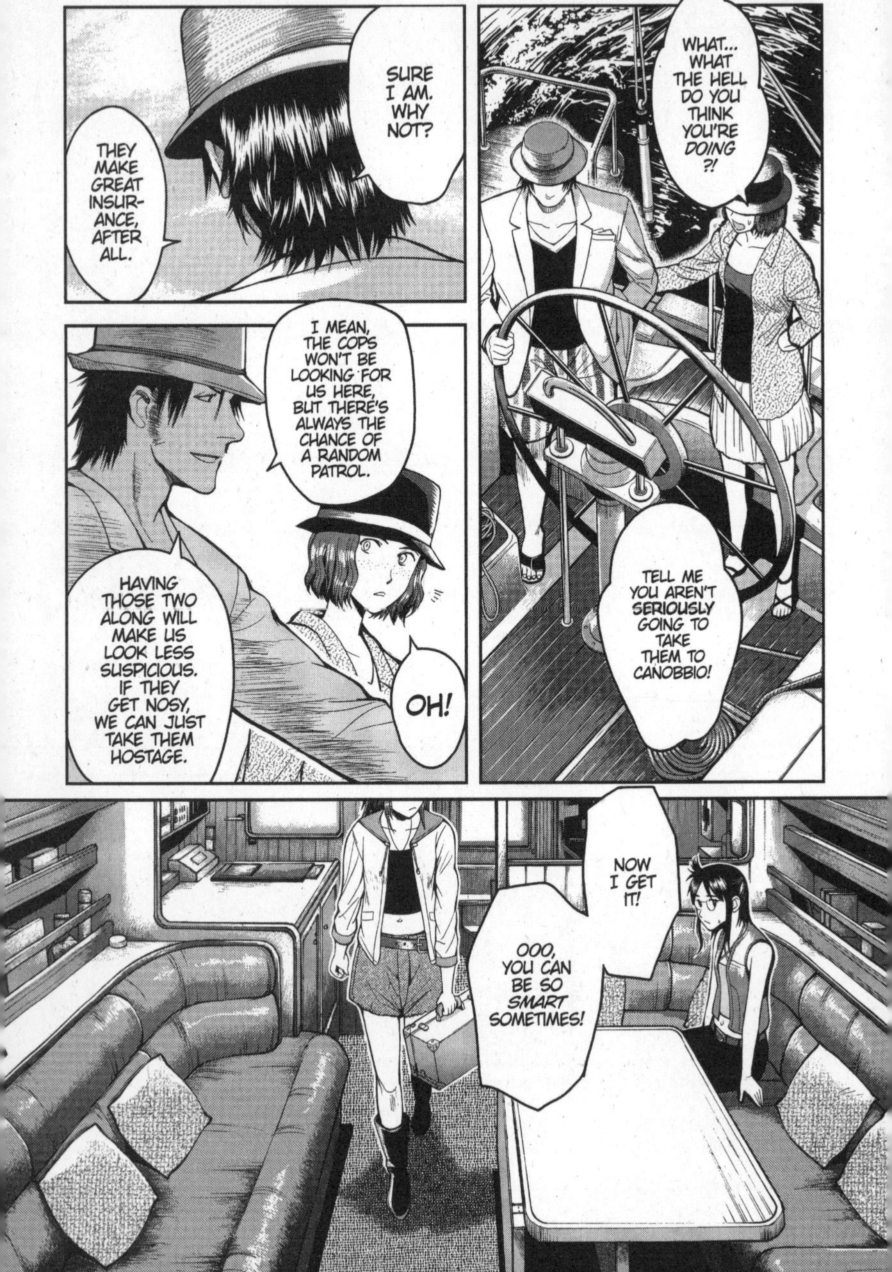
WHAT... WHAT THE HELL DO YOU THINK YOU'RE *DOING* ?!
TELL ME YOU AREN'T SERIOUSLY GOING TO TAKE THEM TO CANOBBIO!
SURE I AM. WHY NOT?
THEY MAKE GREAT INSURANCE, AFTER ALL.
I MEAN, THE COPS WON'T BE LOOKING FOR US HERE, BUT THERE'S ALWAYS THE CHANCE OF A RANDOM PATROL.
HAVING THOSE TWO ALONG WILL MAKE US LOOK LESS SUSPICIOUS. IF THEY GET NOSY, WE CAN JUST TAKE THEM HOSTAGE.
OH!
NOW I GET IT!
OOO, YOU CAN BE SO *SMART* SOMETIMES!

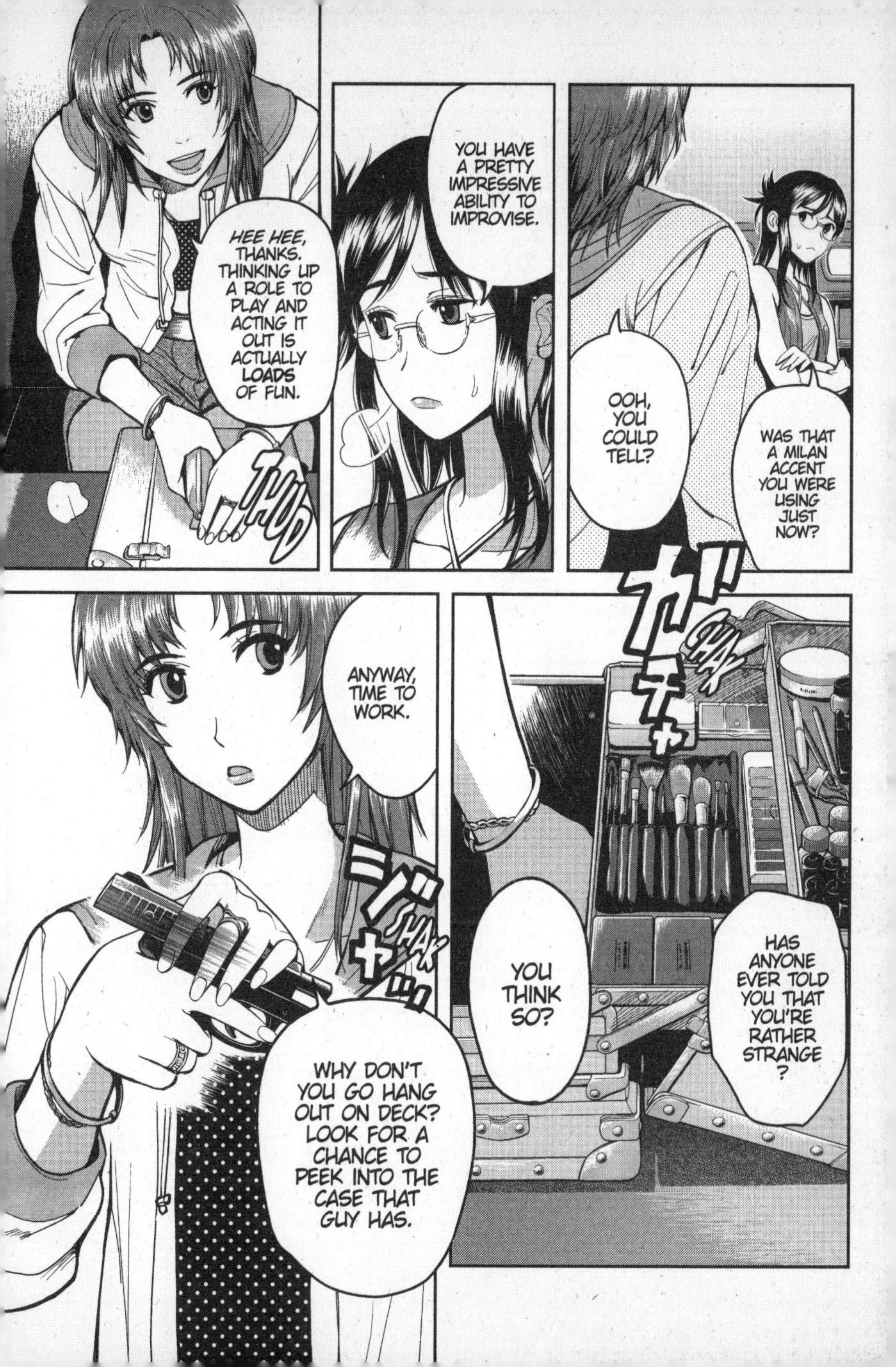
WAS THAT A MILAN ACCENT YOU WERE USING JUST NOW?
OOH, YOU COULD TELL?
YOU HAVE A PRETTY IMPRESSIVE ABILITY TO IMPROVISE.
HEE HEE, THANKS. THINKING UP A ROLE TO PLAY AND ACTING IT OUT IS ACTUALLY LOADS OF FUN.
THUD
ガチャ
CHAK
HAS ANYONE EVER TOLD YOU THAT YOU'RE RATHER STRANGE?
YOU THINK SO?
ANYWAY, TIME TO WORK.
SHAK
WHY DON'T YOU GO HANG OUT ON DECK? LOOK FOR A CHANCE TO PEEK INTO THE CASE THAT GUY HAS.

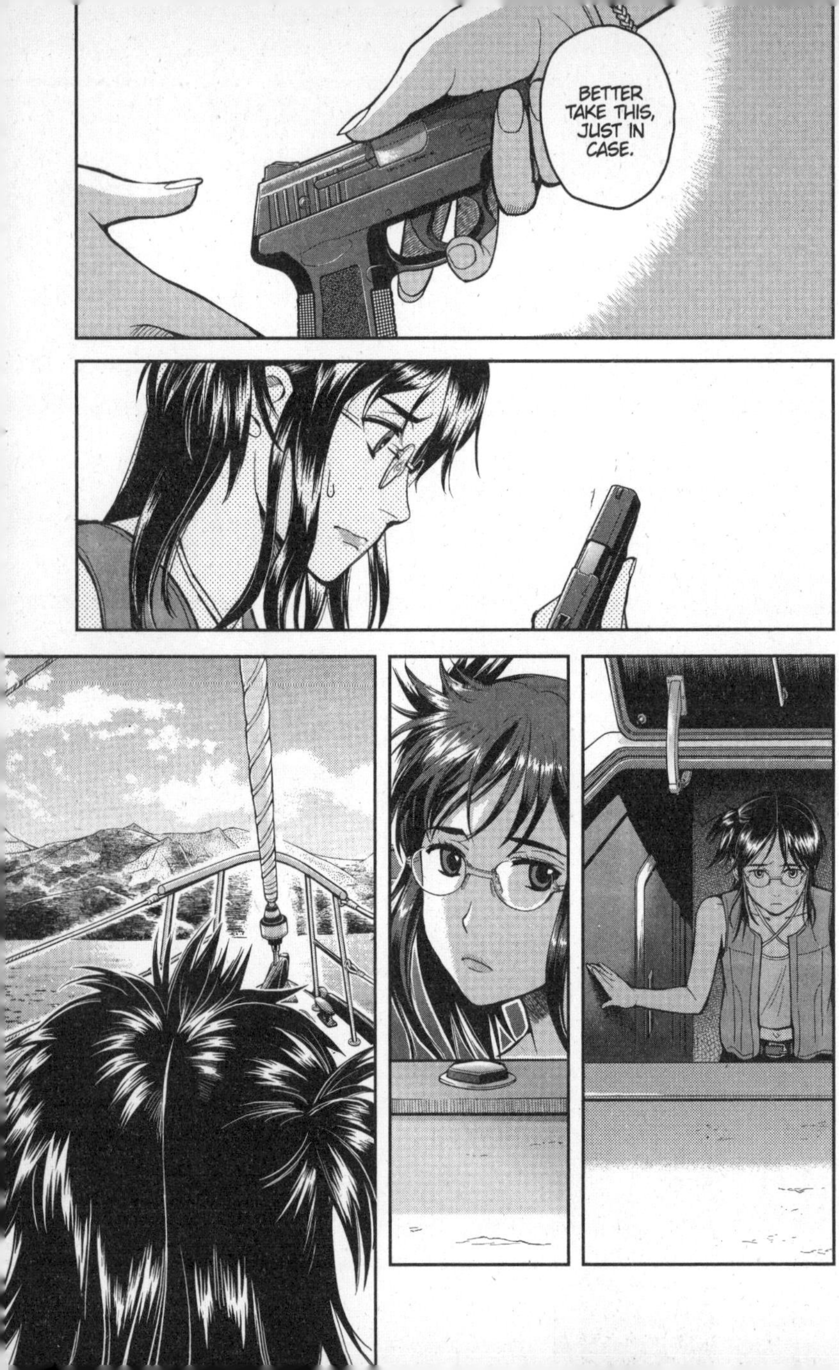
BETTER TAKE THIS, JUST IN CASE.

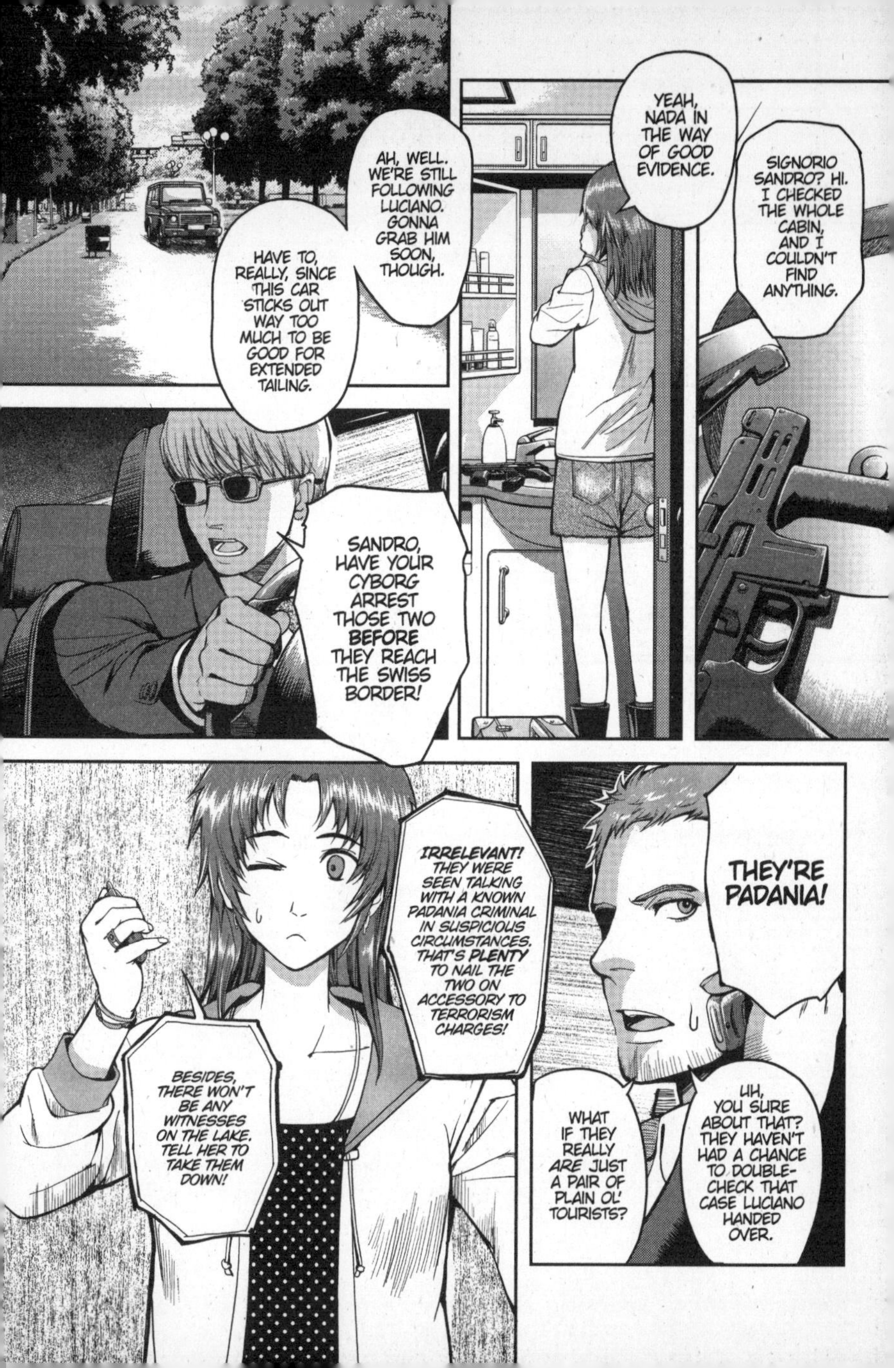
SIGNORIO SANDRO? HI. I CHECKED THE WHOLE CABIN, AND I COULDN'T FIND ANYTHING.
YEAH, NADA IN THE WAY OF GOOD EVIDENCE.
AH, WELL. WE'RE STILL FOLLOWING LUCIANO. GONNA GRAB HIM SOON, THOUGH.
HAVE TO, REALLY, SINCE THIS CAR STICKS OUT WAY TOO MUCH TO BE GOOD FOR EXTENDED TAILING.
SANDRO, HAVE YOUR CYBORG ARREST THOSE TWO BEFORE THEY REACH THE SWISS BORDER!
THEY'RE PADANIA!
UH, YOU SURE ABOUT THAT? THEY HAVEN'T HAD A CHANCE TO DOUBLE-CHECK THAT CASE LUCIANO HANDED OVER.
WHAT IF THEY REALLY ARE JUST A PAIR OF PLAIN OL' TOURISTS?
IRRELEVANT! THEY WERE SEEN TALKING WITH A KNOWN PADANIA CRIMINAL IN SUSPICIOUS CIRCUMSTANCES. THAT'S PLENTY TO NAIL THE TWO ON ACCESSORY TO TERRORISM CHARGES!
BESIDES, THERE WON'T BE ANY WITNESSES ON THE LAKE. TELL HER TO TAKE THEM DOWN!

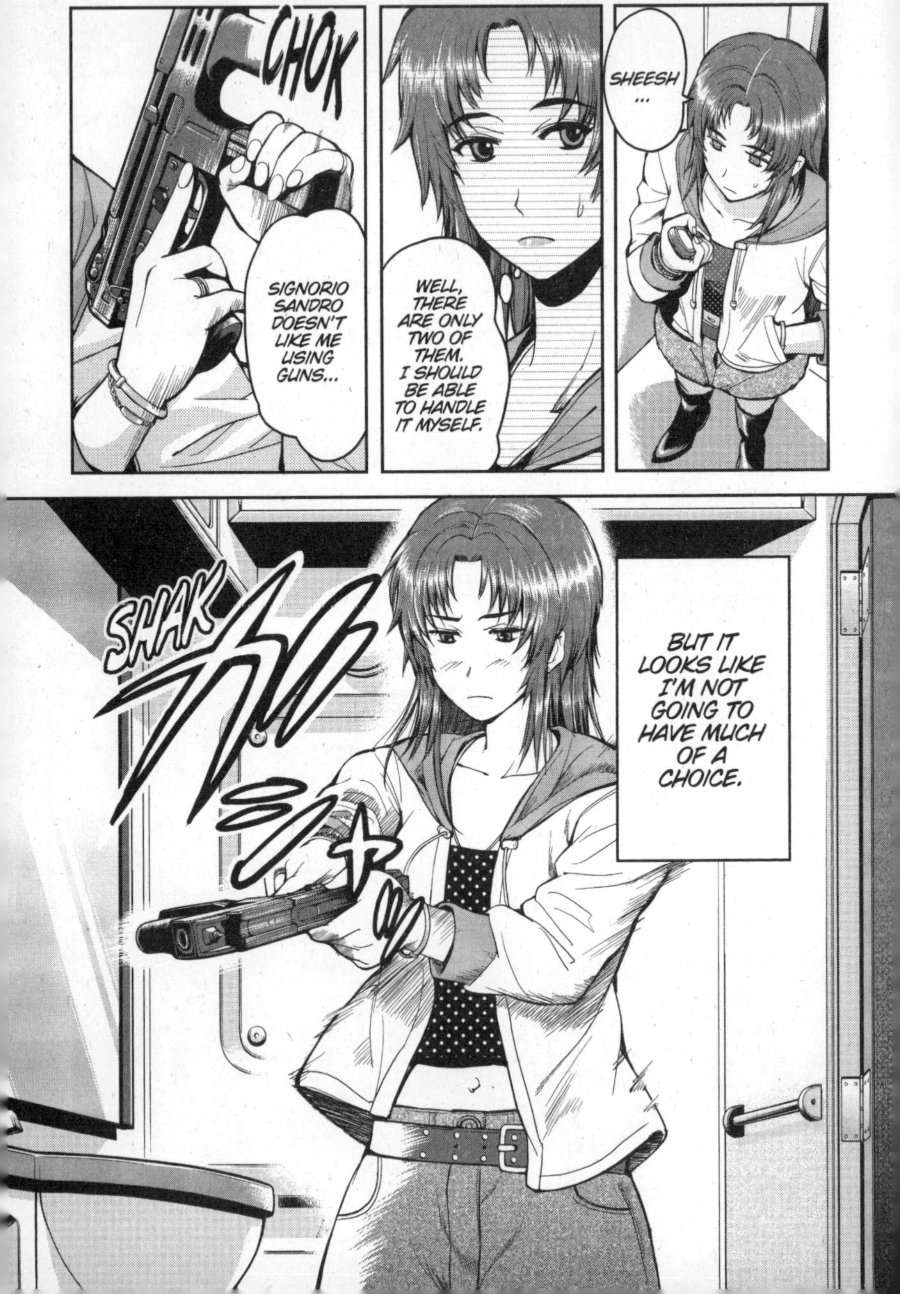
SHEESH ...
WELL, THERE ARE ONLY TWO OF THEM. I SHOULD BE ABLE TO HANDLE IT MYSELF.
CHOK
SIGNORIO SANDRO DOESN'T LIKE ME USING GUNS...
BUT IT LOOKS LIKE I'M NOT GOING TO HAVE MUCH OF A CHOICE.
SHAK

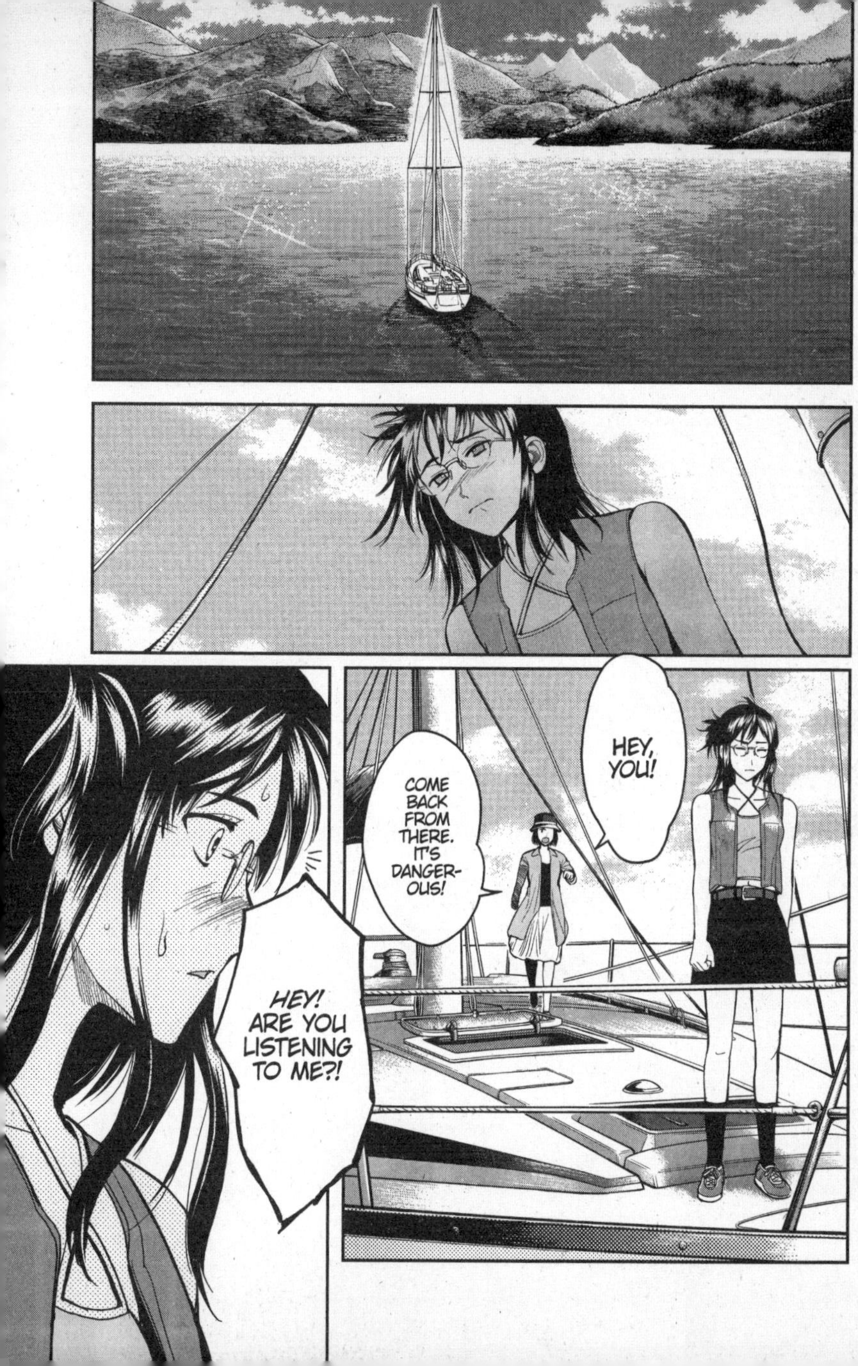
HEY, YOU!
COME BACK FROM THERE. IT'S DANGER-OUS!
HEY! ARE YOU LISTENING TO ME?!

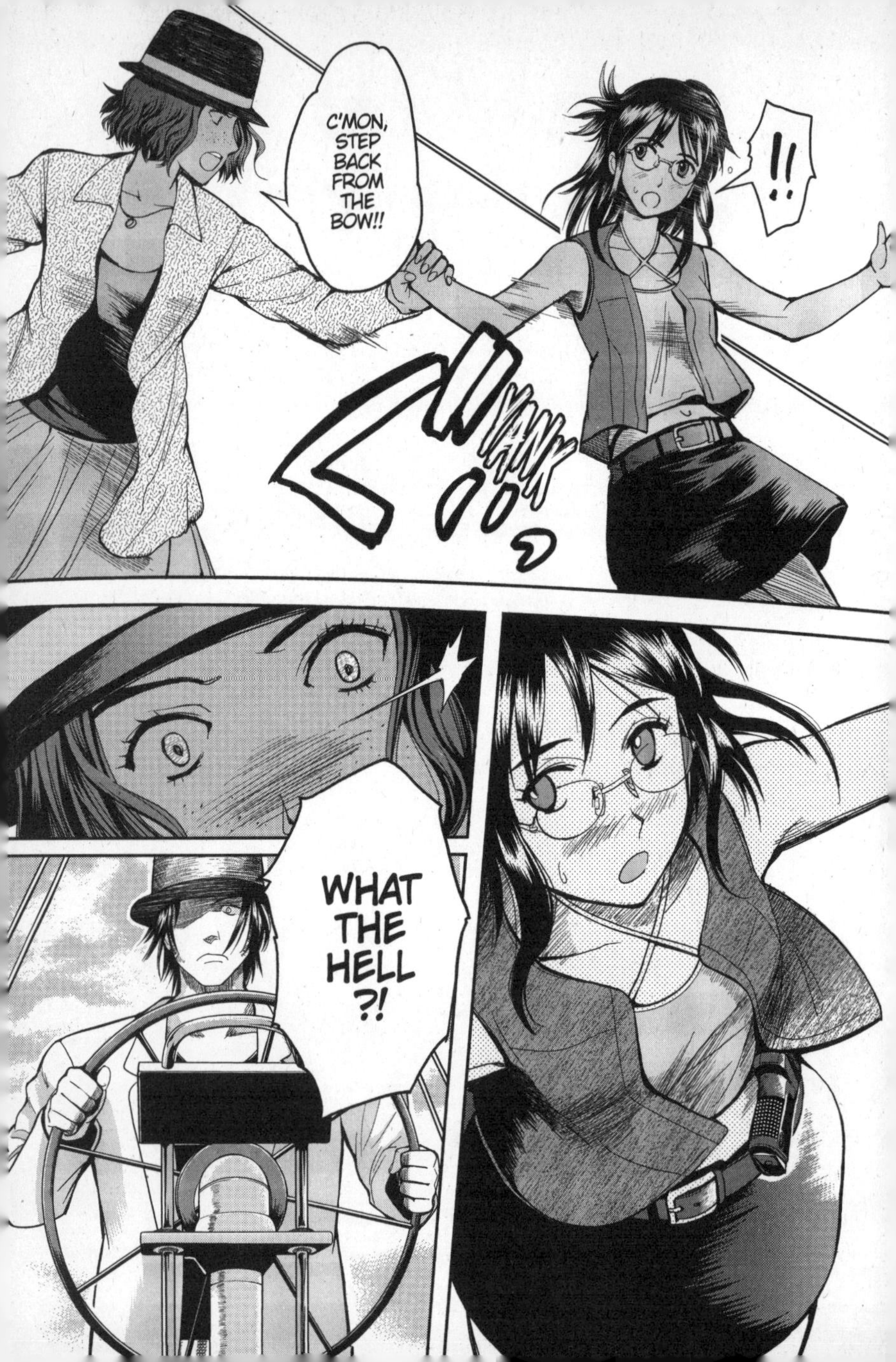
!!
C'MON, STEP BACK FROM THE BOW!!
YANK
WHAT THE HELL ?!

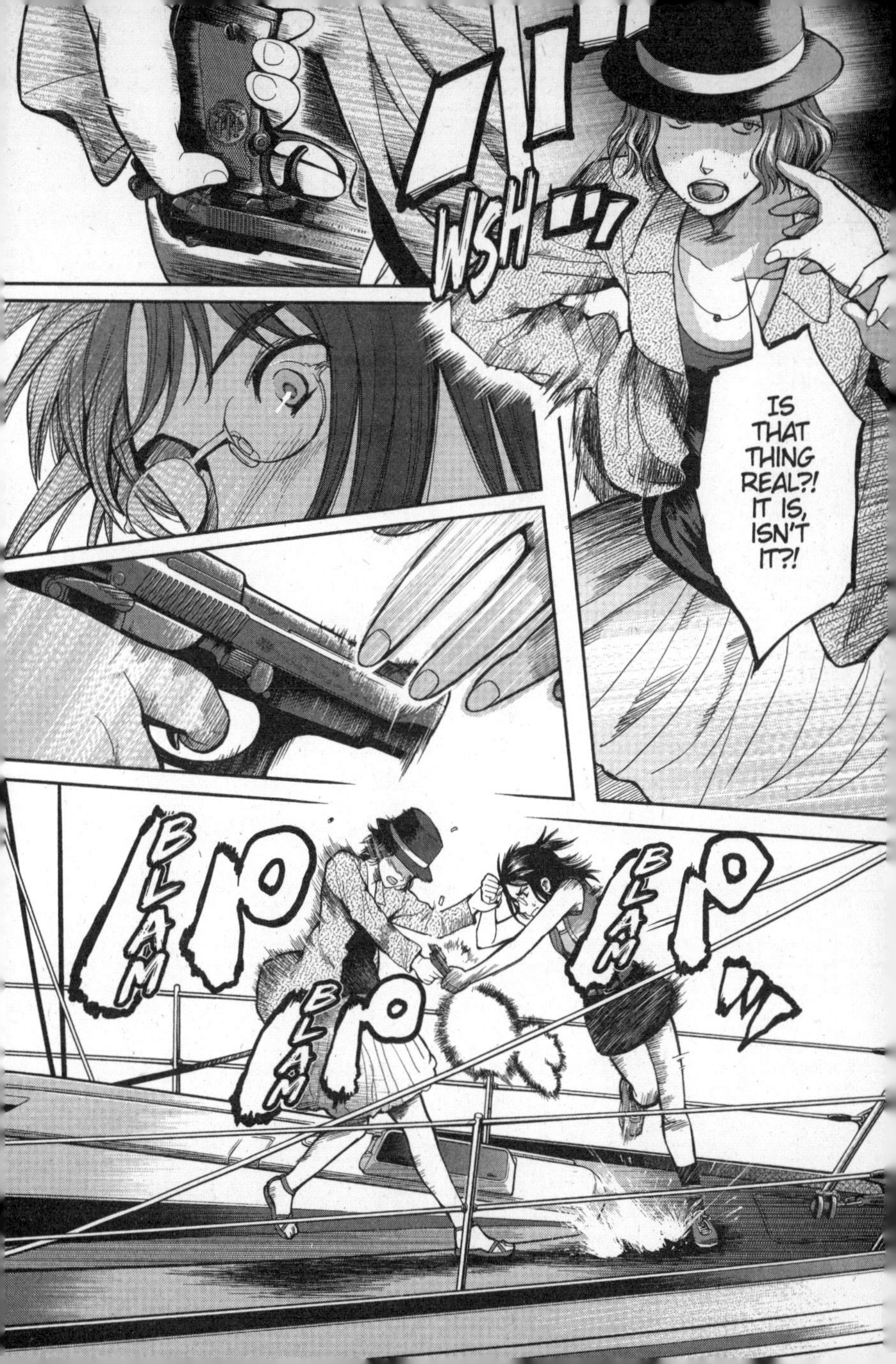
WSH
IS THAT THING REAL?! IT IS, ISN'T IT?!
BLAM
BLAM
BLAM

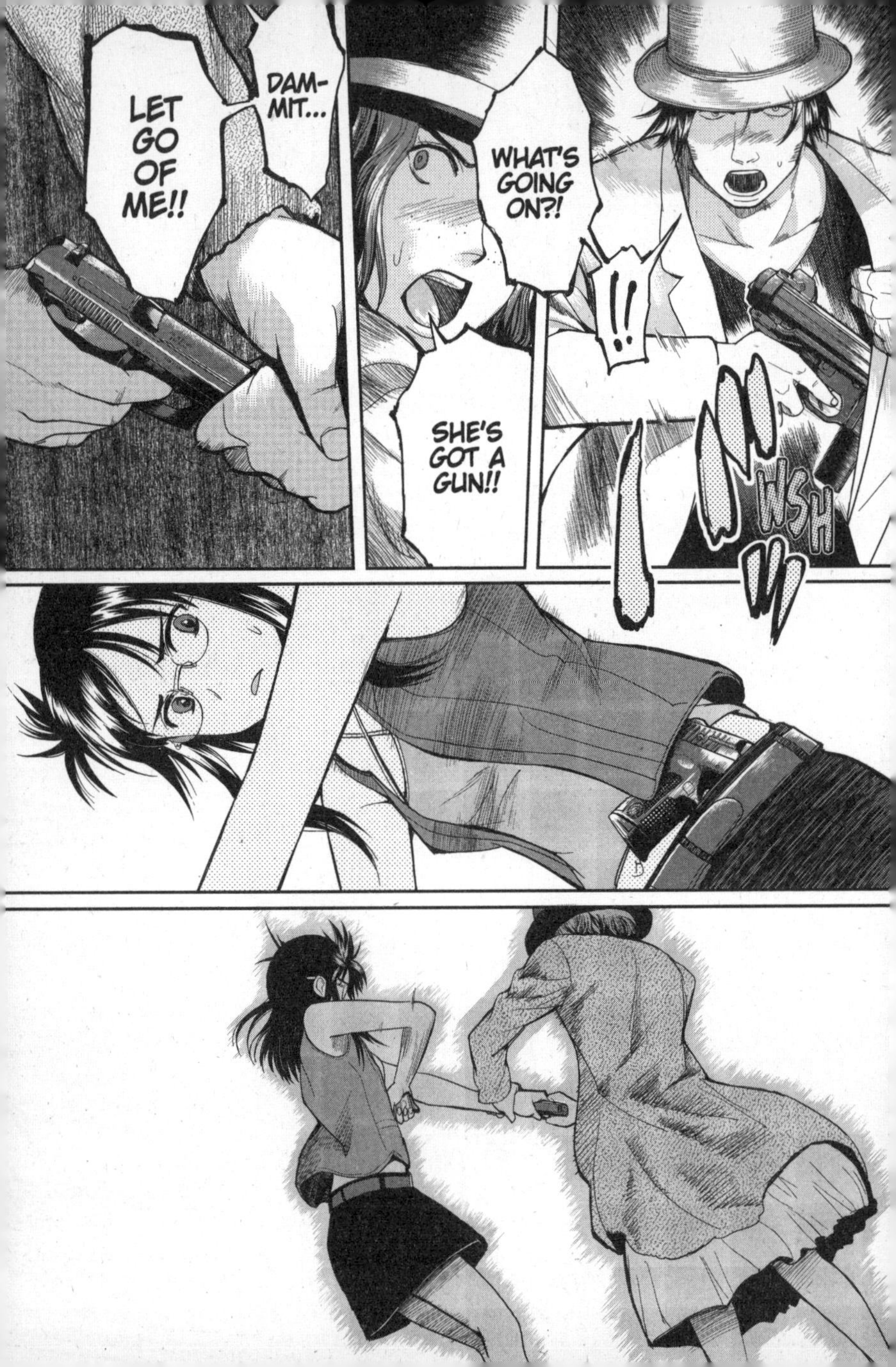
WHAT'S GOING ON?!
!!
WSH
SHE'S GOT A GUN!!
DAM-MIT...
LET GO OF ME!!

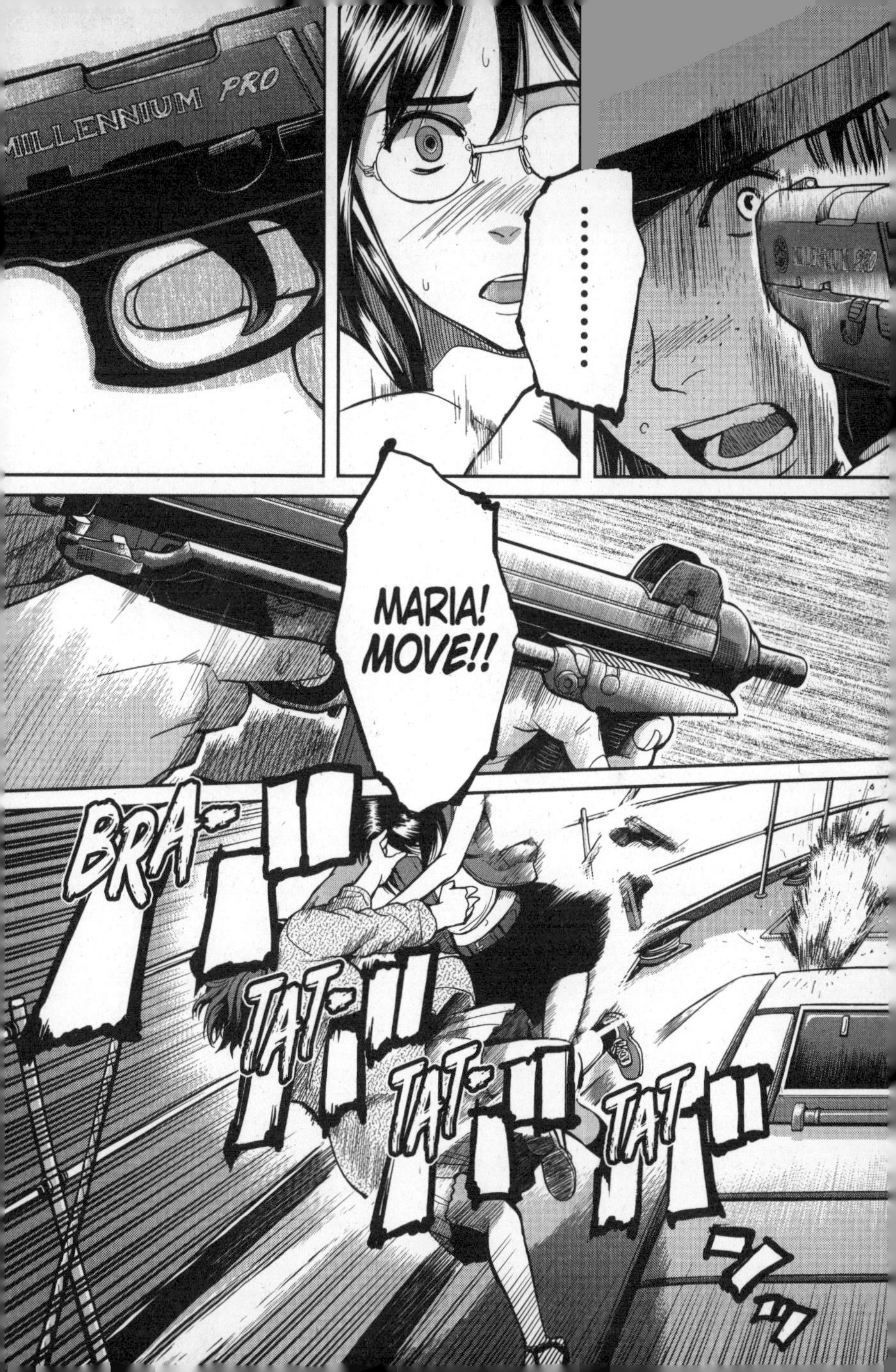
......
MILLENNIUM PRO
MARIA! MOVE!!
BRA-
TAT-
TAT-
TAT

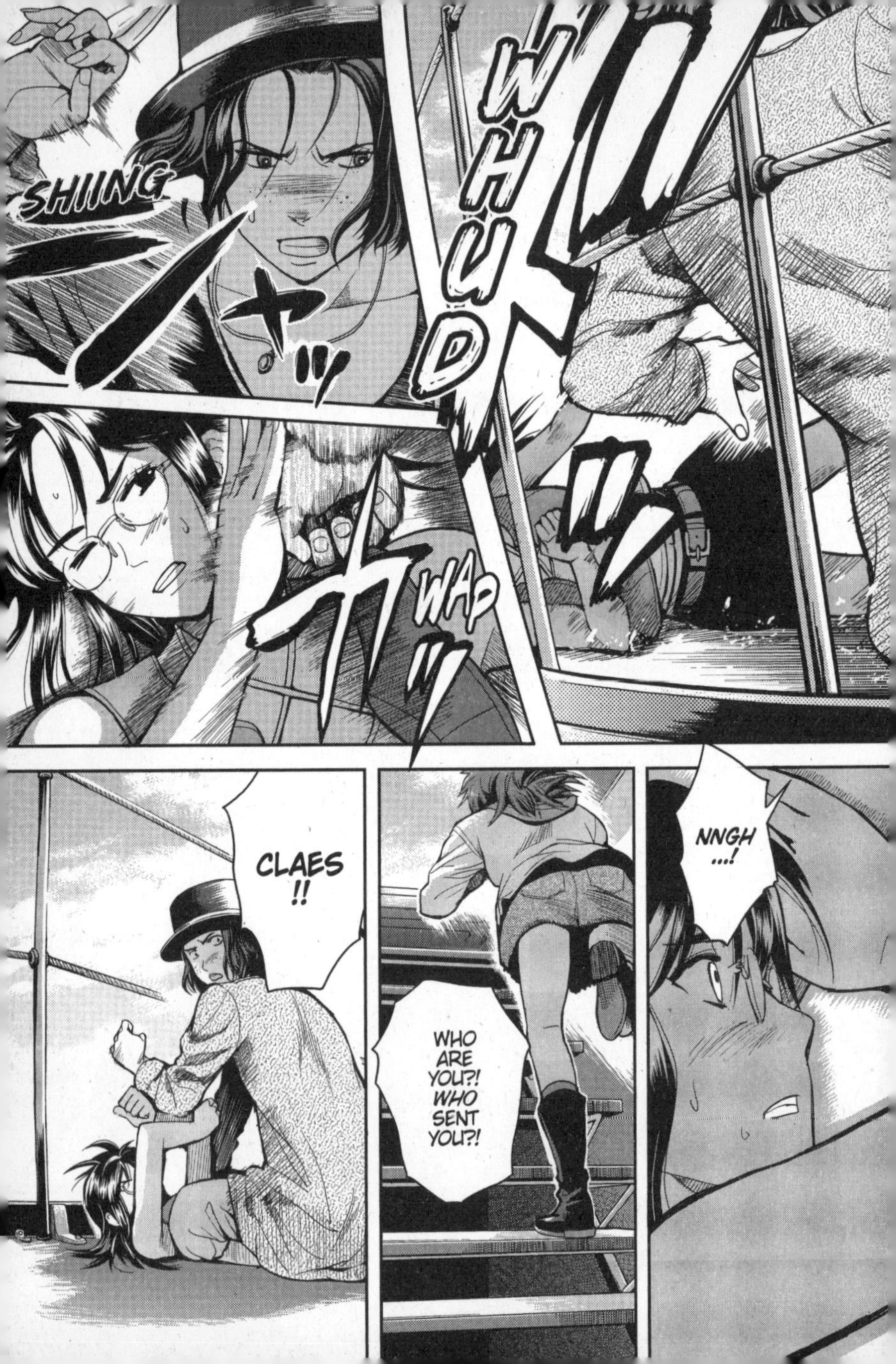
WHUD
SHIING
WAP
NNGH ...!
WHO ARE YOU?! WHO SENT YOU?!
CLAES !!

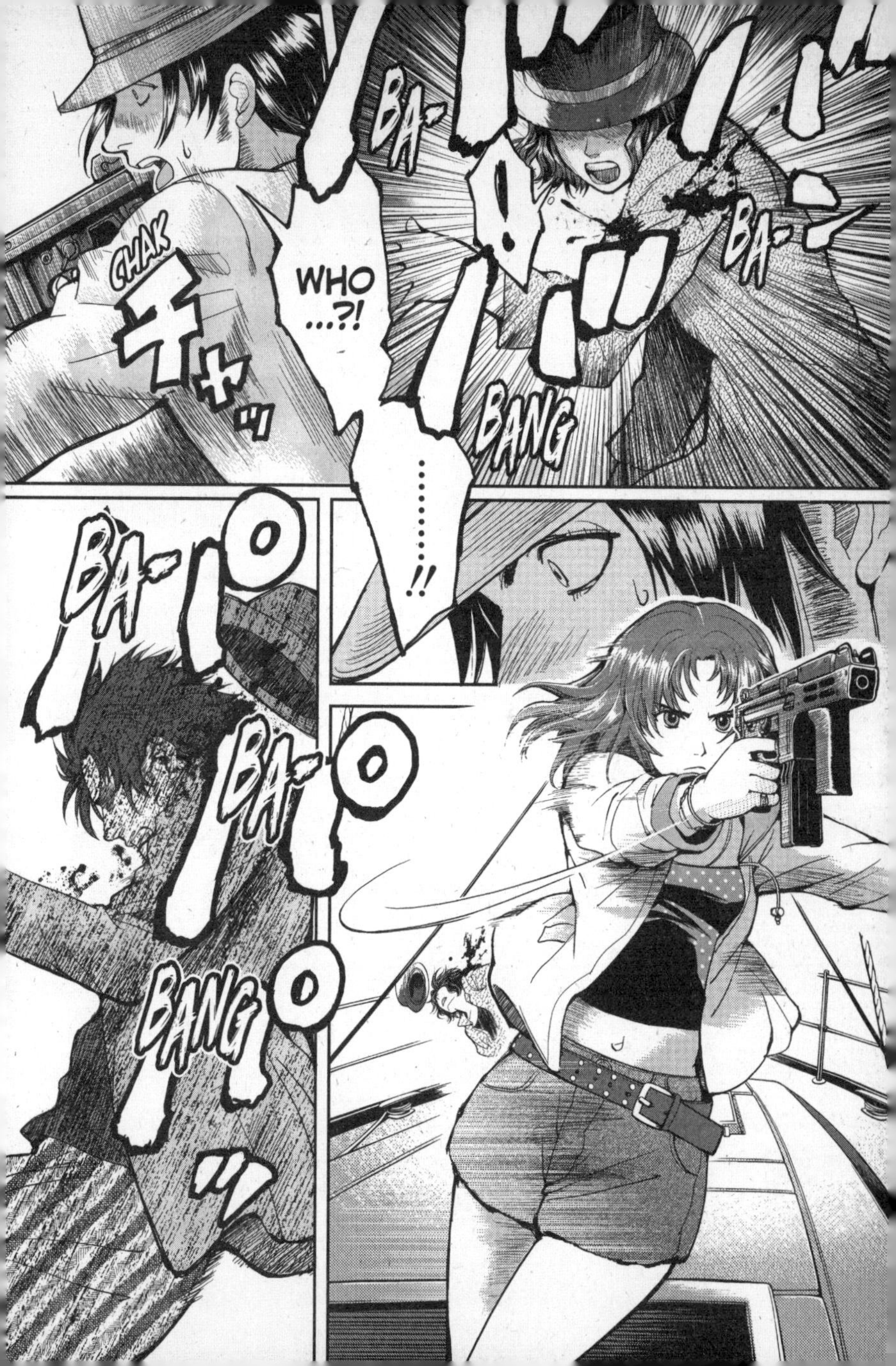

BA-
BA-
BANG
WHO ...?!
CHAK
チャッ
......!!
BA-
BA-
BANG

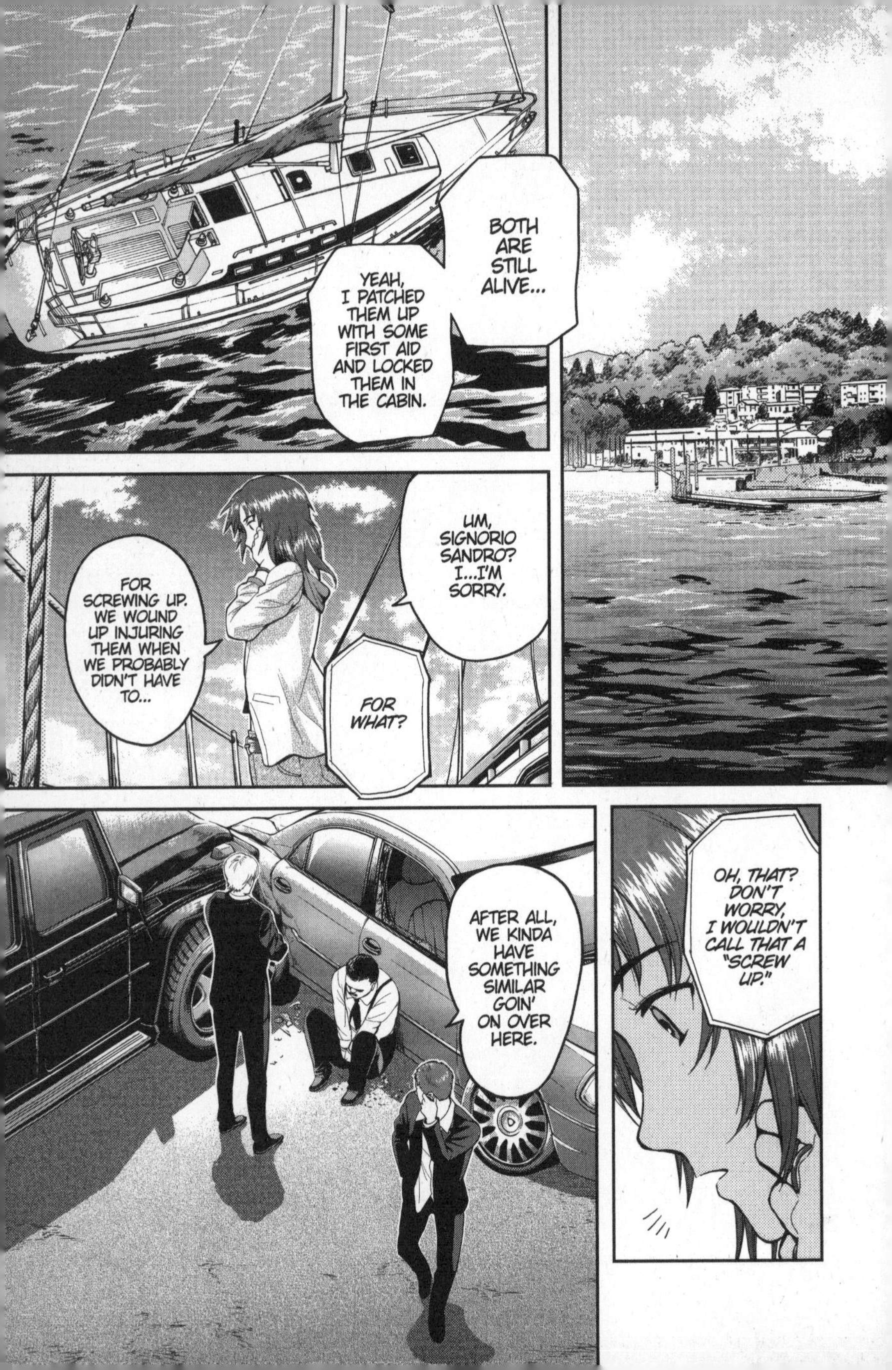
BOTH ARE STILL ALIVE...
YEAH, I PATCHED THEM UP WITH SOME FIRST AID AND LOCKED THEM IN THE CABIN.
UM, SIGNORIO SANDRO? I...I'M SORRY.
FOR WHAT?
FOR SCREWING UP. WE WOUND UP INJURING THEM WHEN WE PROBABLY DIDN'T HAVE TO...
OH, THAT? DON'T WORRY, I WOULDN'T CALL THAT A "SCREW UP."
AFTER ALL, WE KINDA HAVE SOMETHING SIMILAR GOIN' ON OVER HERE.

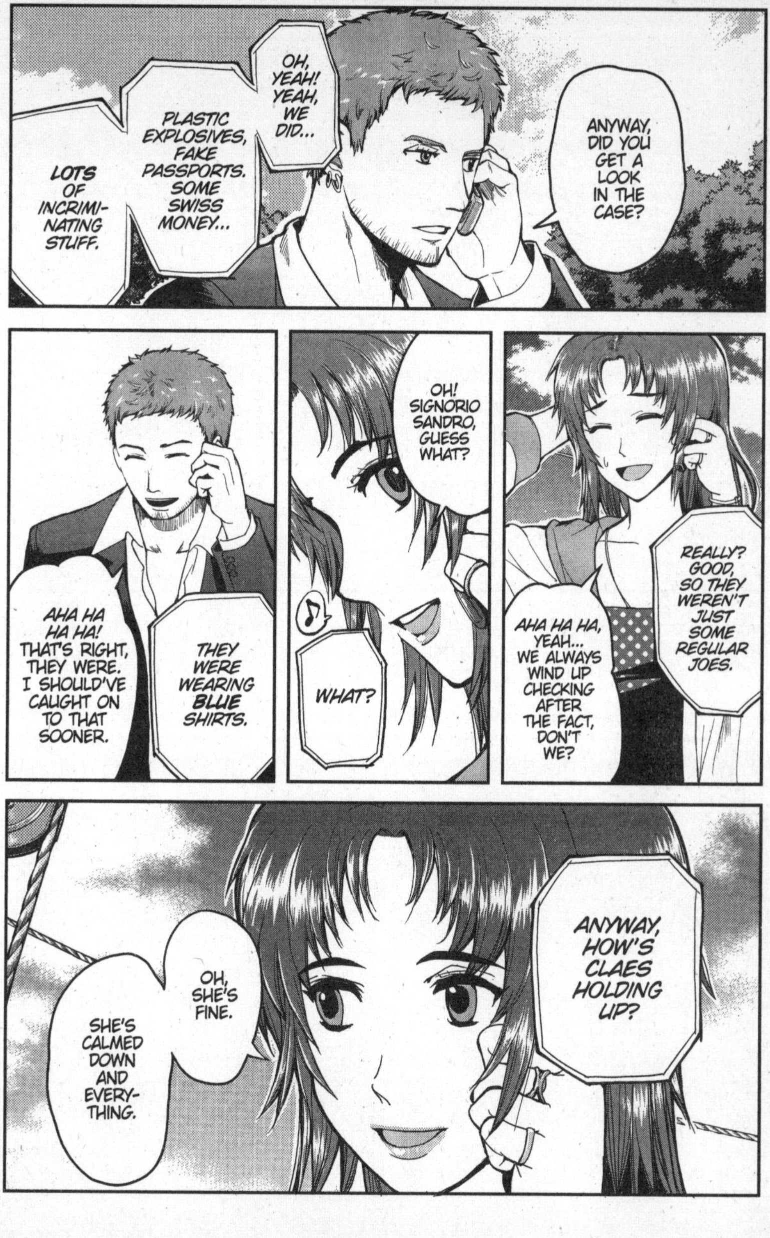
ANYWAY, DID YOU GET A LOOK IN THE CASE?
OH, YEAH! YEAH, WE DID...
PLASTIC EXPLOSIVES, FAKE PASSPORTS. SOME SWISS MONEY...
LOTS OF INCRIMINATING STUFF.
REALLY? GOOD, SO THEY WEREN'T JUST SOME REGULAR JOES.
AHA HA HA, YEAH... WE ALWAYS WIND UP CHECKING AFTER THE FACT, DON'T WE?
OH! SIGNORIO SANDRO, GUESS WHAT?
♪
WHAT?
THEY WERE WEARING **BLUE** SHIRTS.
AHA HA HA HA! THAT'S RIGHT, THEY WERE. I SHOULD'VE CAUGHT ON TO THAT SOONER.
ANYWAY, HOW'S CLAES HOLDING UP?
OH, SHE'S FINE.
SHE'S CALMED DOWN AND EVERYTHING.

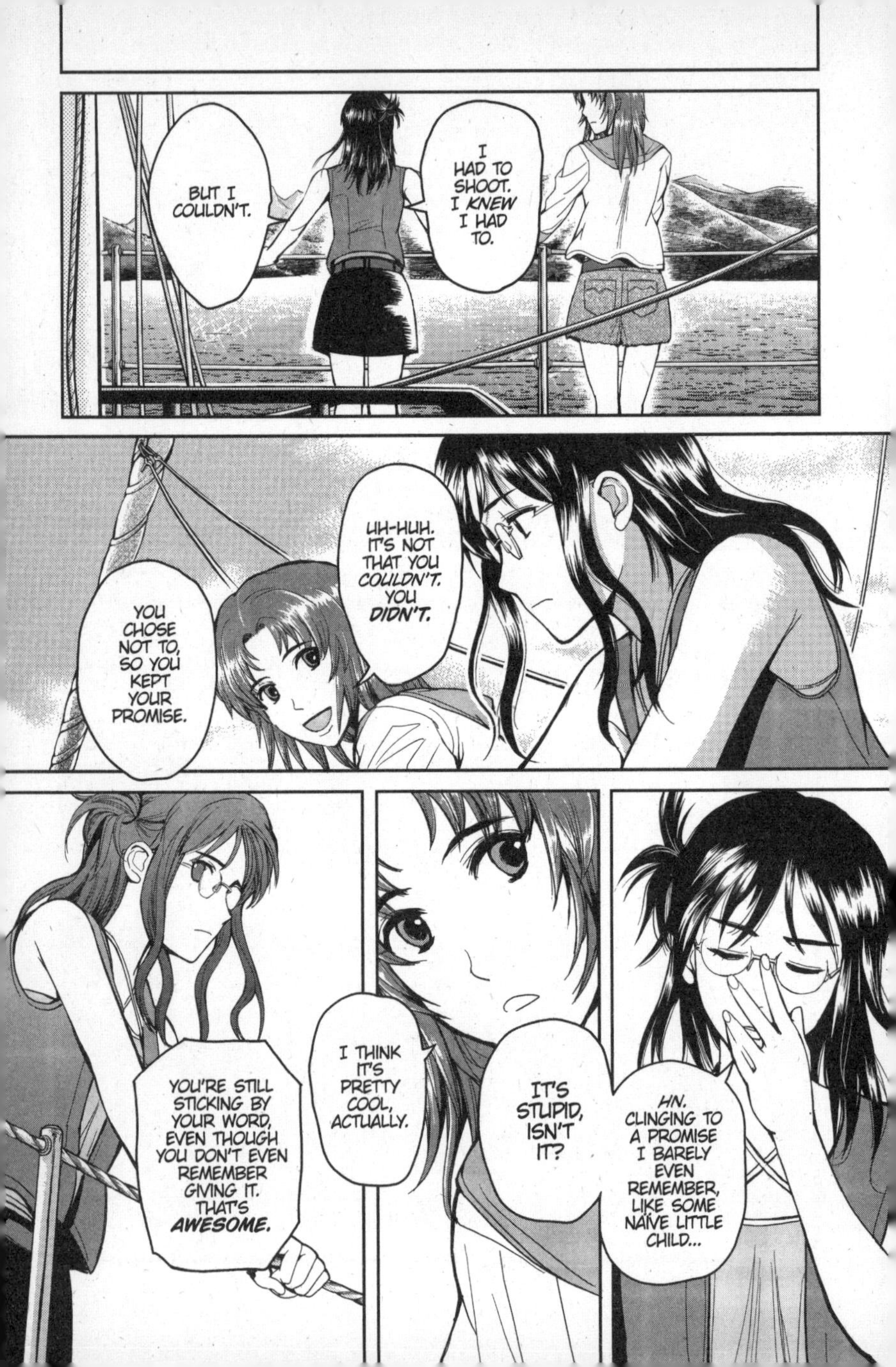
I HAD TO SHOOT. I *KNEW* I HAD TO.
BUT I COULDN'T.
UH-HUH. IT'S NOT THAT YOU *COULDN'T.* YOU ***DIDN'T.***
YOU CHOSE NOT TO, SO YOU KEPT YOUR PROMISE.
HN. CLINGING TO A PROMISE I BARELY EVEN REMEMBER, LIKE SOME NAÏVE LITTLE CHILD...
IT'S STUPID, ISN'T IT?
I THINK IT'S PRETTY COOL, ACTUALLY.
YOU'RE STILL STICKING BY YOUR WORD, EVEN THOUGH YOU DON'T EVEN REMEMBER GIVING IT. THAT'S ***AWESOME.***

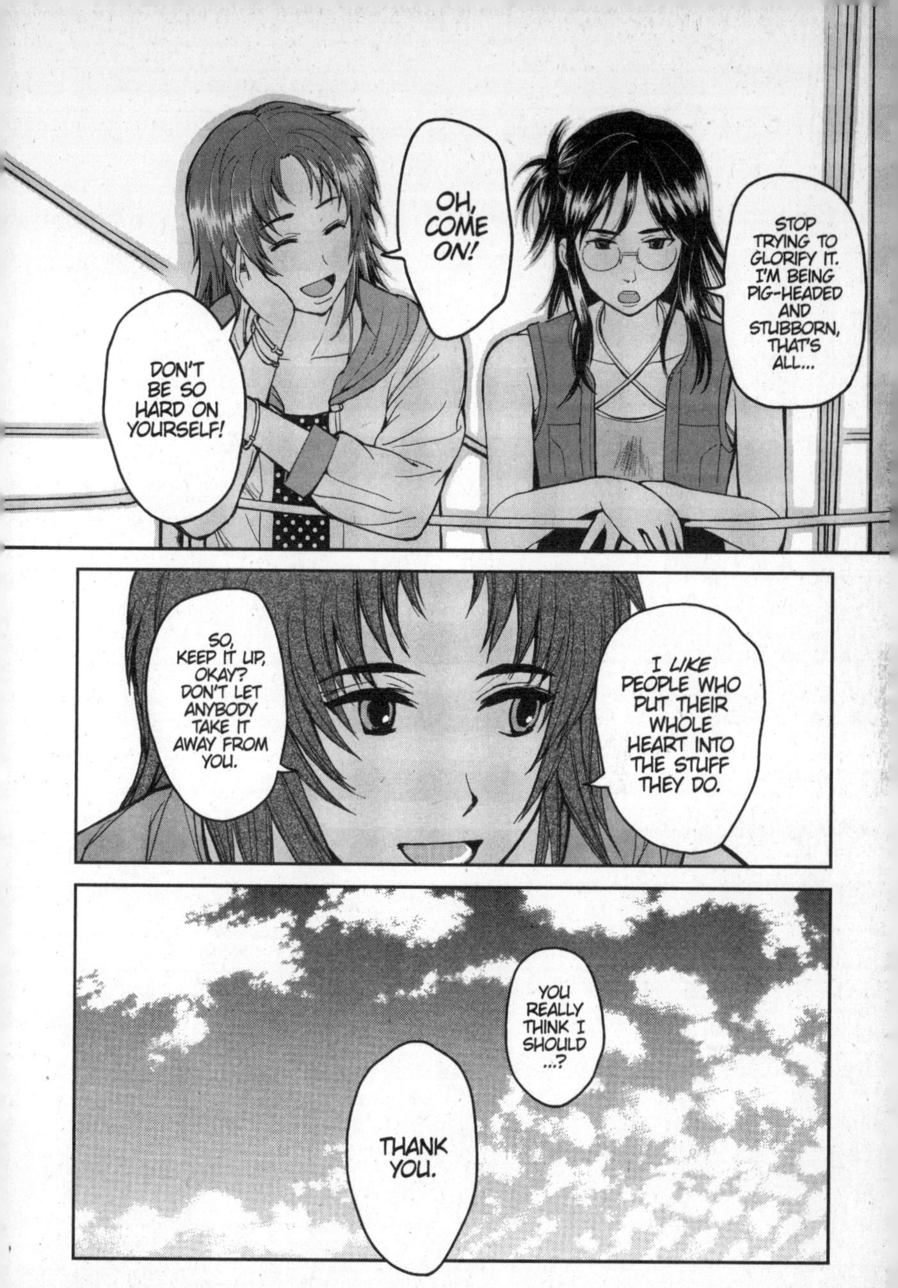
STOP TRYING TO GLORIFY IT. I'M BEING PIG-HEADED AND STUBBORN, THAT'S ALL...
OH, COME ON!
DON'T BE SO HARD ON YOURSELF!
I *LIKE* PEOPLE WHO PUT THEIR WHOLE HEART INTO THE STUFF THEY DO.
SO, KEEP IT UP, OKAY? DON'T LET ANYBODY TAKE IT AWAY FROM YOU.
YOU REALLY THINK I SHOULD ...?
THANK YOU.

GUNSLINGERGIRL.

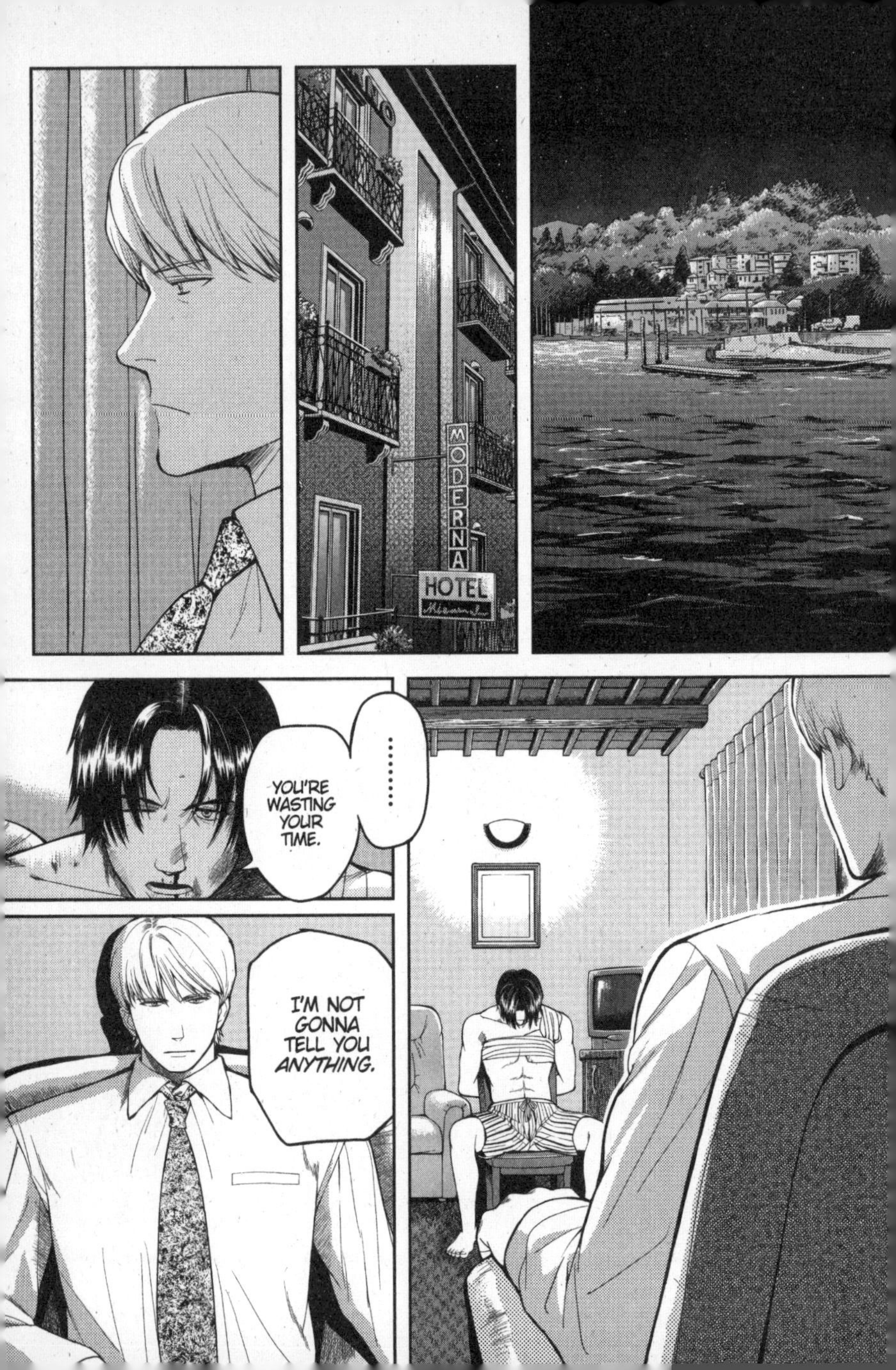
MODERNA
HOTEL
......
YOU'RE WASTING YOUR TIME.
I'M NOT GONNA TELL YOU ANYTHING.

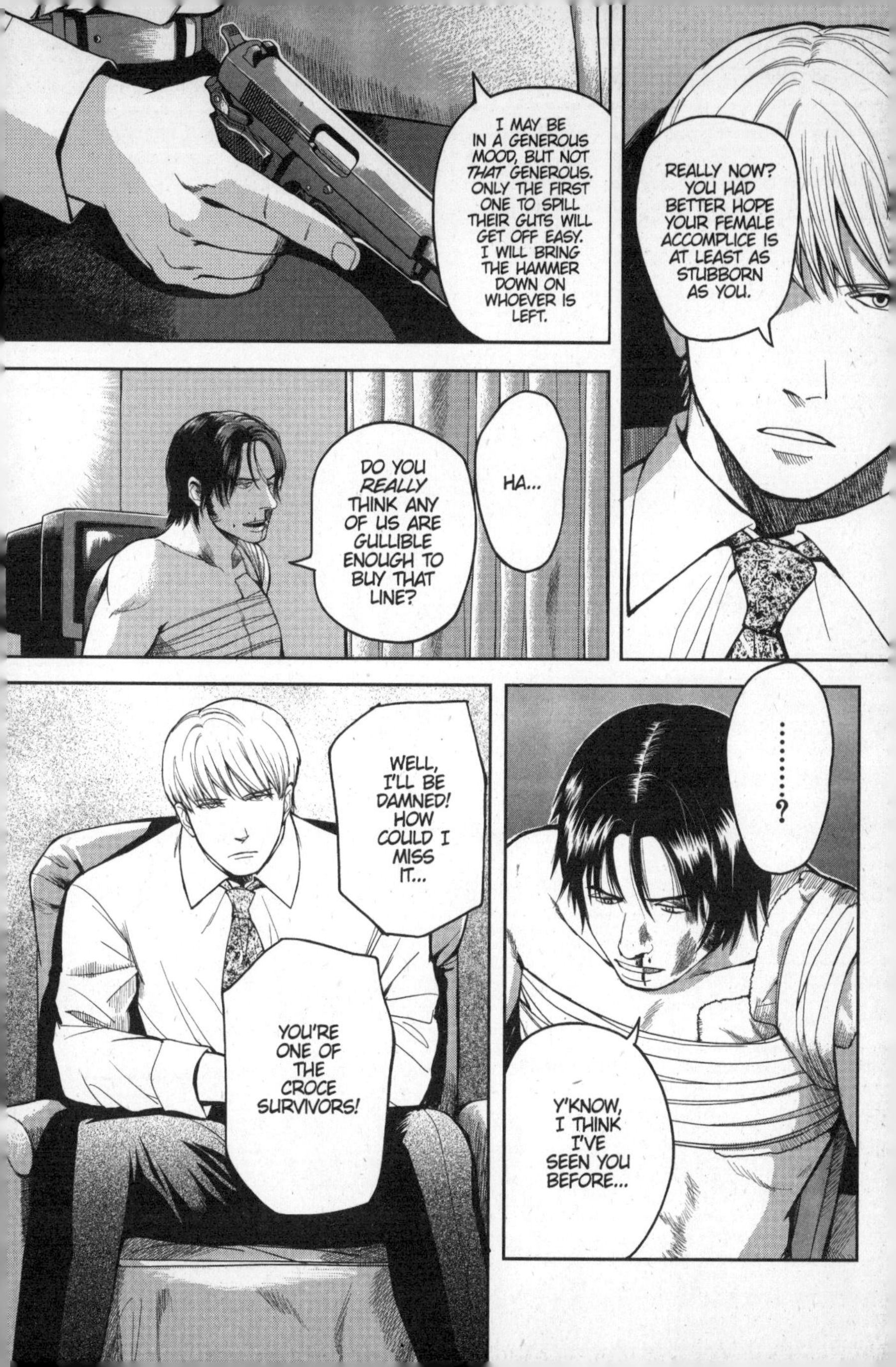
REALLY NOW? YOU HAD BETTER HOPE YOUR FEMALE ACCOMPLICE IS AT LEAST AS STUBBORN AS YOU.
I MAY BE IN A GENEROUS MOOD, BUT NOT *THAT* GENEROUS. ONLY THE FIRST ONE TO SPILL THEIR GUTS WILL GET OFF EASY. I WILL BRING THE HAMMER DOWN ON WHOEVER IS LEFT.
HA...
DO YOU *REALLY* THINK ANY OF US ARE GULLIBLE ENOUGH TO BUY THAT LINE?
......?
Y'KNOW, I THINK I'VE SEEN YOU BEFORE...
WELL, I'LL BE DAMNED! HOW COULD I MISS IT...
YOU'RE ONE OF THE CROCE SURVIVORS!

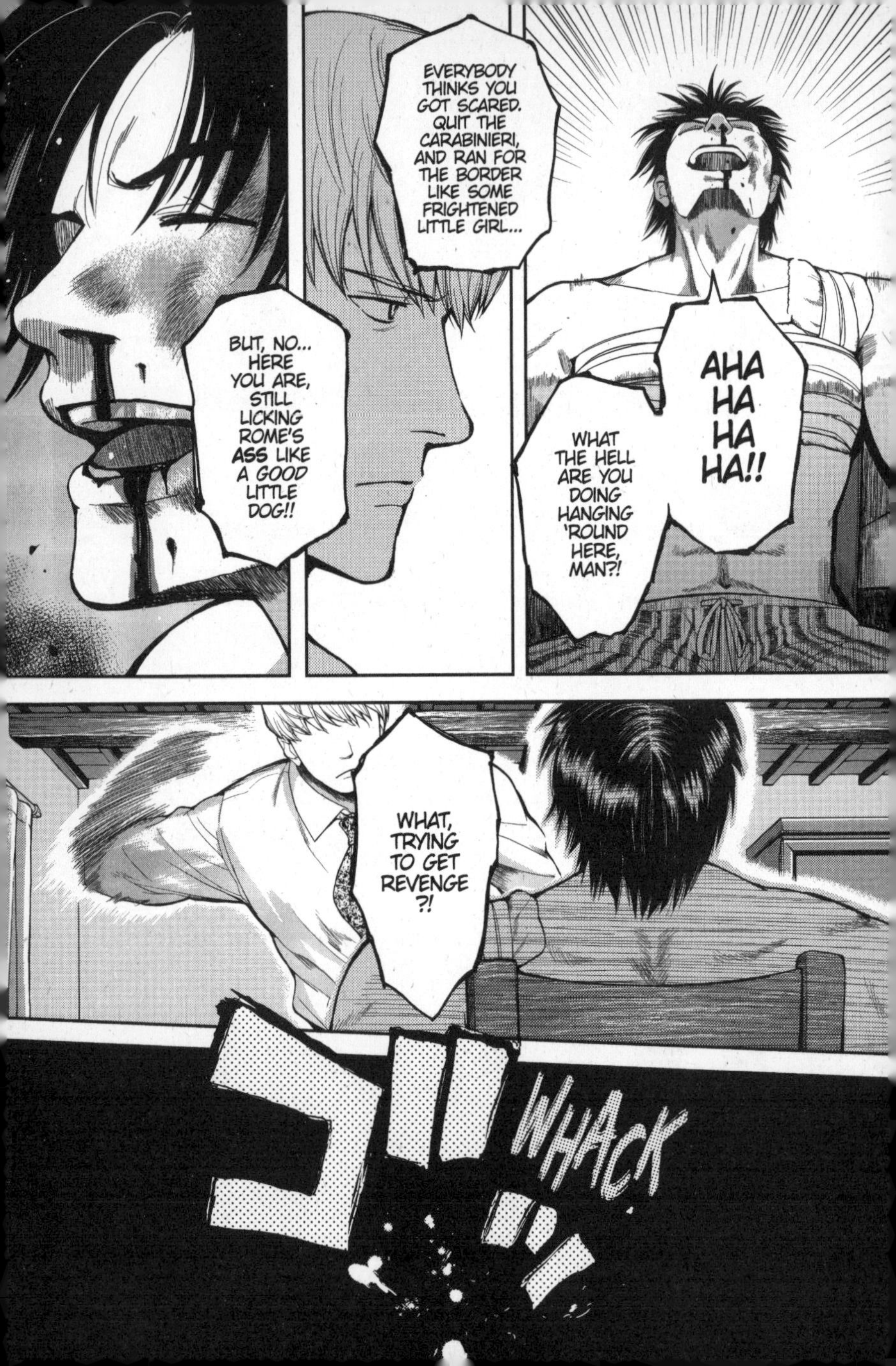
AHA HA HA HA!!
WHAT THE HELL ARE YOU DOING HANGING 'ROUND HERE, MAN?!
EVERYBODY THINKS YOU GOT SCARED. QUIT THE CARABINIERI, AND RAN FOR THE BORDER LIKE SOME FRIGHTENED LITTLE GIRL...
BUT, NO... HERE YOU ARE, STILL LICKING ROME'S ASS LIKE A GOOD LITTLE DOG!!
WHAT, TRYING TO GET REVENGE?!
WHACK

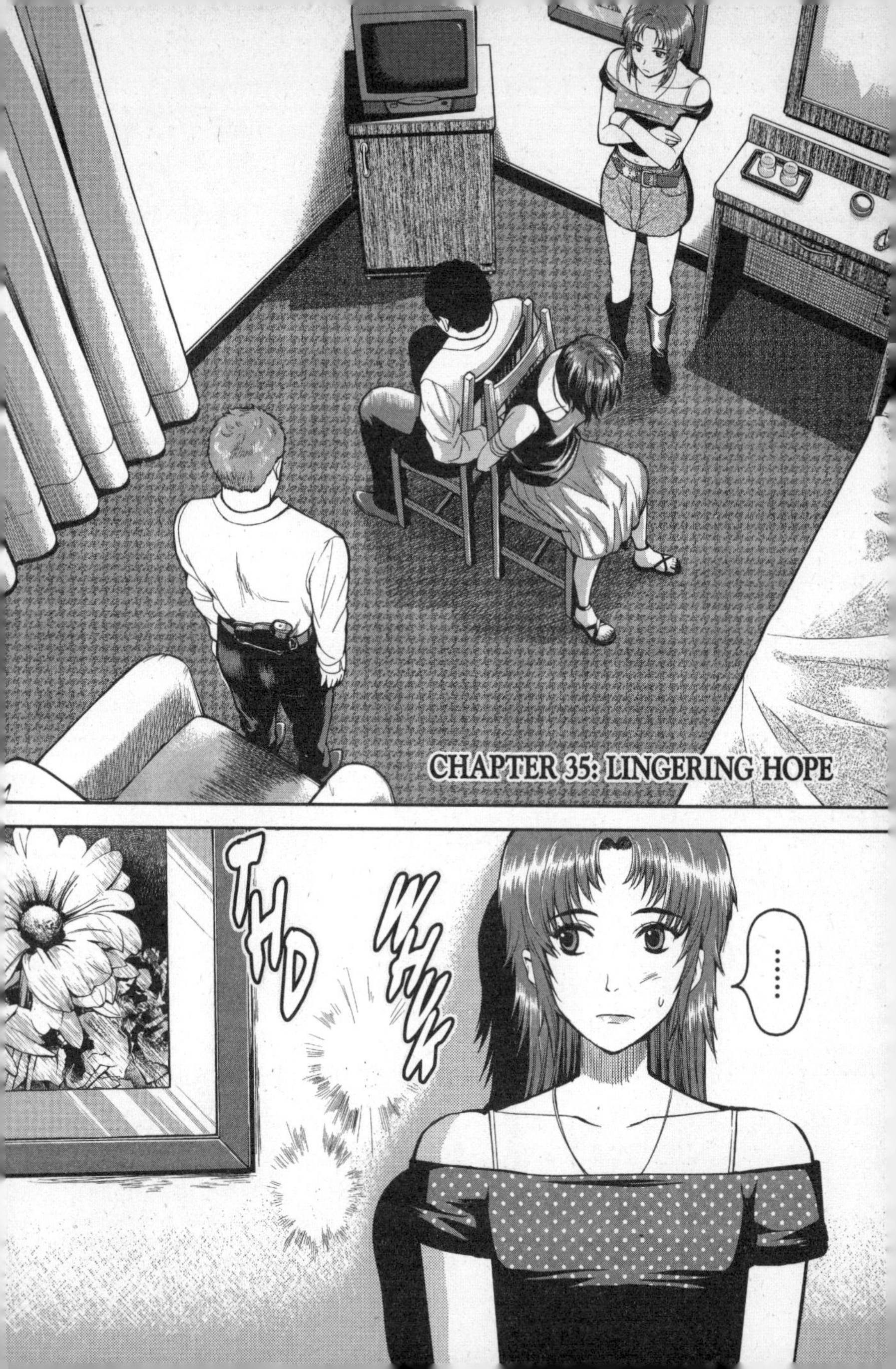
CHAPTER 35: LINGERING HOPE
......
WHAK
THD

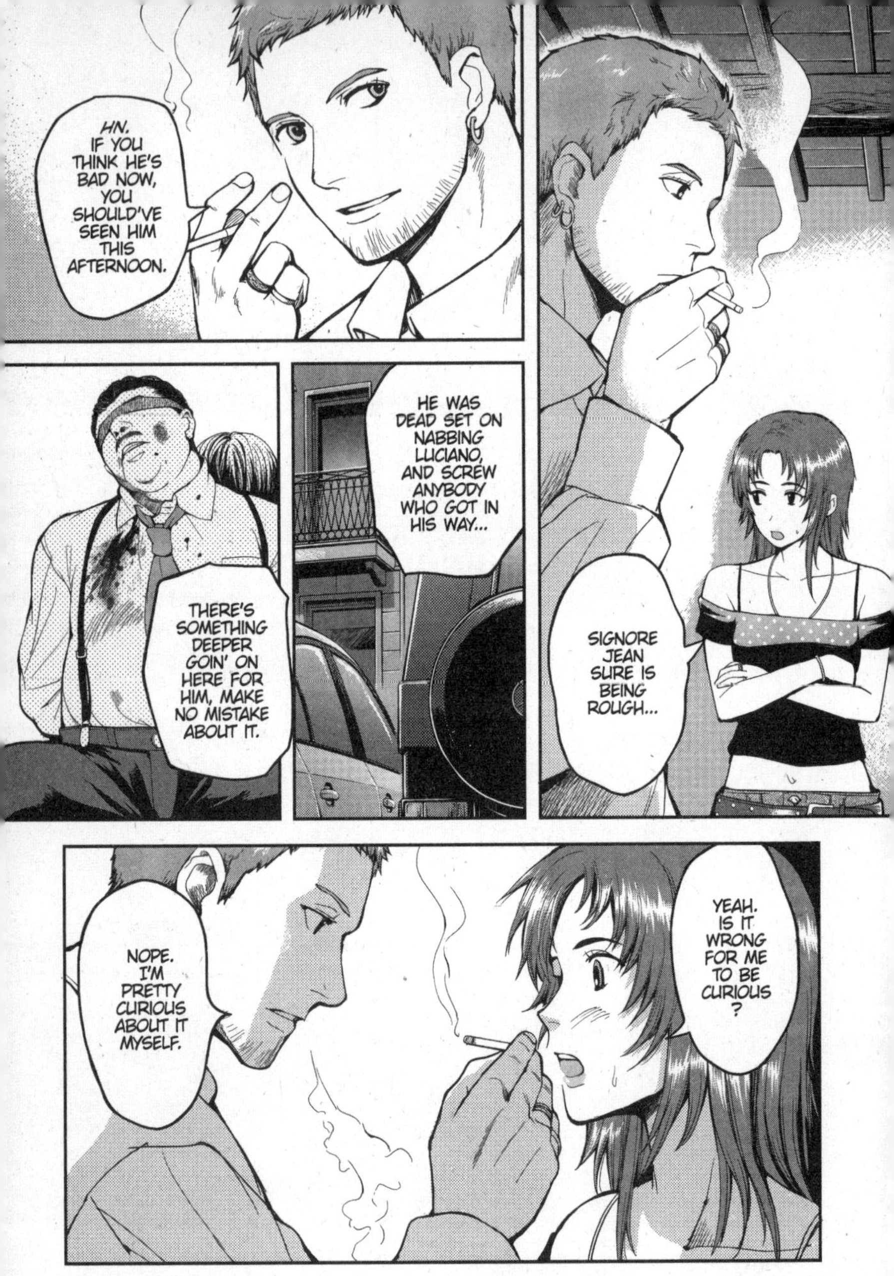
SIGNORE JEAN SURE IS BEING ROUGH...
HN. IF YOU THINK HE'S BAD NOW, YOU SHOULD'VE SEEN HIM THIS AFTERNOON.
HE WAS DEAD SET ON NABBING LUCIANO, AND SCREW ANYBODY WHO GOT IN HIS WAY...
THERE'S SOMETHING DEEPER GOIN' ON HERE FOR HIM, MAKE NO MISTAKE ABOUT IT.
YEAH. IS IT WRONG FOR ME TO BE CURIOUS?
NOPE. I'M PRETTY CURIOUS ABOUT IT MYSELF.

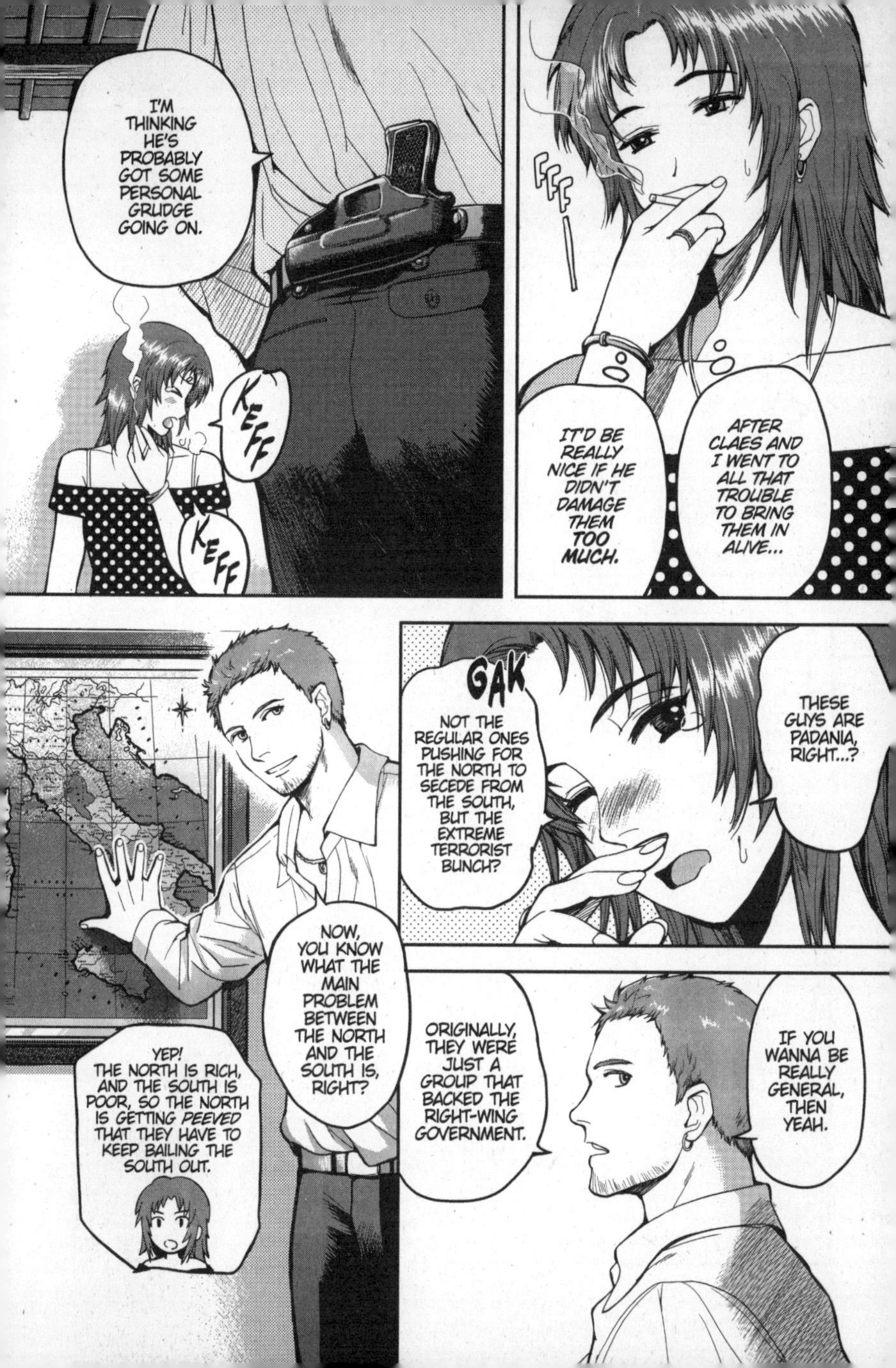
FFF
AFTER CLAES AND I WENT TO ALL THAT TROUBLE TO BRING THEM IN ALIVE...
IT'D BE REALLY NICE IF HE DIDN'T DAMAGE THEM TOO MUCH.
I'M THINKING HE'S PROBABLY GOT SOME PERSONAL GRUDGE GOING ON.
KEFF
KEFF
THESE GUYS ARE PADANIA, RIGHT...?
GAK
NOT THE REGULAR ONES PUSHING FOR THE NORTH TO SECEDE FROM THE SOUTH, BUT THE EXTREME TERRORIST BUNCH?
IF YOU WANNA BE REALLY GENERAL, THEN YEAH.
ORIGINALLY, THEY WERE JUST A GROUP THAT BACKED THE RIGHT-WING GOVERNMENT.
NOW, YOU KNOW WHAT THE MAIN PROBLEM BETWEEN THE NORTH AND THE SOUTH IS, RIGHT?
YEP! THE NORTH IS RICH, AND THE SOUTH IS POOR, SO THE NORTH IS GETTING *PEEVED* THAT THEY HAVE TO KEEP BAILING THE SOUTH OUT.

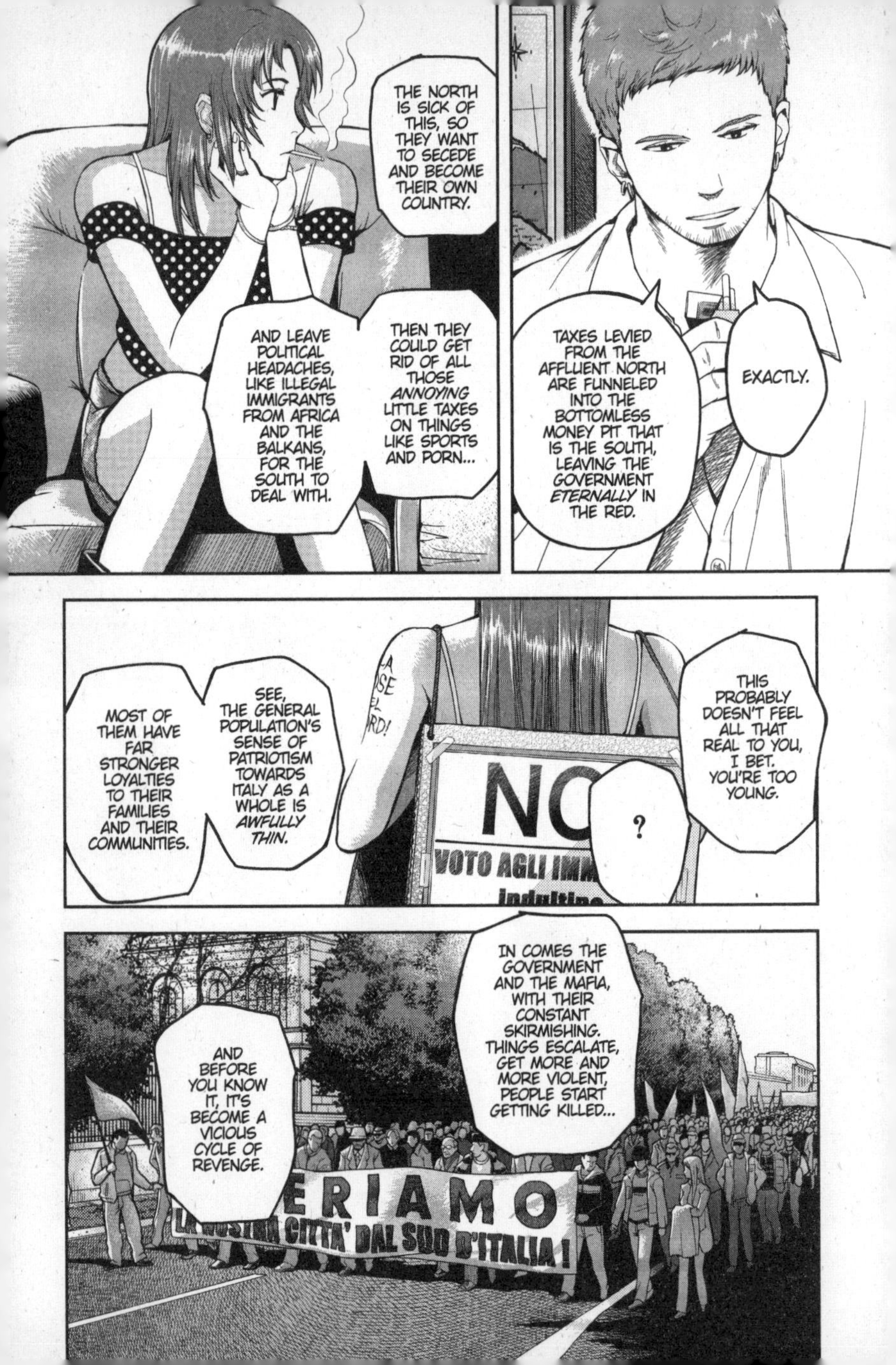
EXACTLY.
TAXES LEVIED FROM THE AFFLUENT NORTH ARE FUNNELED INTO THE BOTTOMLESS MONEY PIT THAT IS THE SOUTH, LEAVING THE GOVERNMENT *ETERNALLY* IN THE RED.
THE NORTH IS SICK OF THIS, SO THEY WANT TO SECEDE AND BECOME THEIR OWN COUNTRY.
THEN THEY COULD GET RID OF ALL THOSE *ANNOYING* LITTLE TAXES ON THINGS LIKE SPORTS AND PORN...
AND LEAVE POLITICAL HEADACHES, LIKE ILLEGAL IMMIGRANTS FROM AFRICA AND THE BALKANS, FOR THE SOUTH TO DEAL WITH.
THIS PROBABLY DOESN'T FEEL ALL THAT REAL TO YOU, I BET. YOU'RE TOO YOUNG.
?
NO
VOTO AGLI IMM
SEE, THE GENERAL POPULATION'S SENSE OF PATRIOTISM TOWARDS ITALY AS A WHOLE IS *AWFULLY THIN*.
MOST OF THEM HAVE FAR STRONGER LOYALTIES TO THEIR FAMILIES AND THEIR COMMUNITIES.
IN COMES THE GOVERNMENT AND THE MAFIA, WITH THEIR CONSTANT SKIRMISHING. THINGS ESCALATE, GET MORE AND MORE VIOLENT, PEOPLE START GETTING KILLED...
AND BEFORE YOU KNOW IT, IT'S BECOME A VICIOUS CYCLE OF REVENGE.
ERIAMO
DAL SUD D'ITALIA !

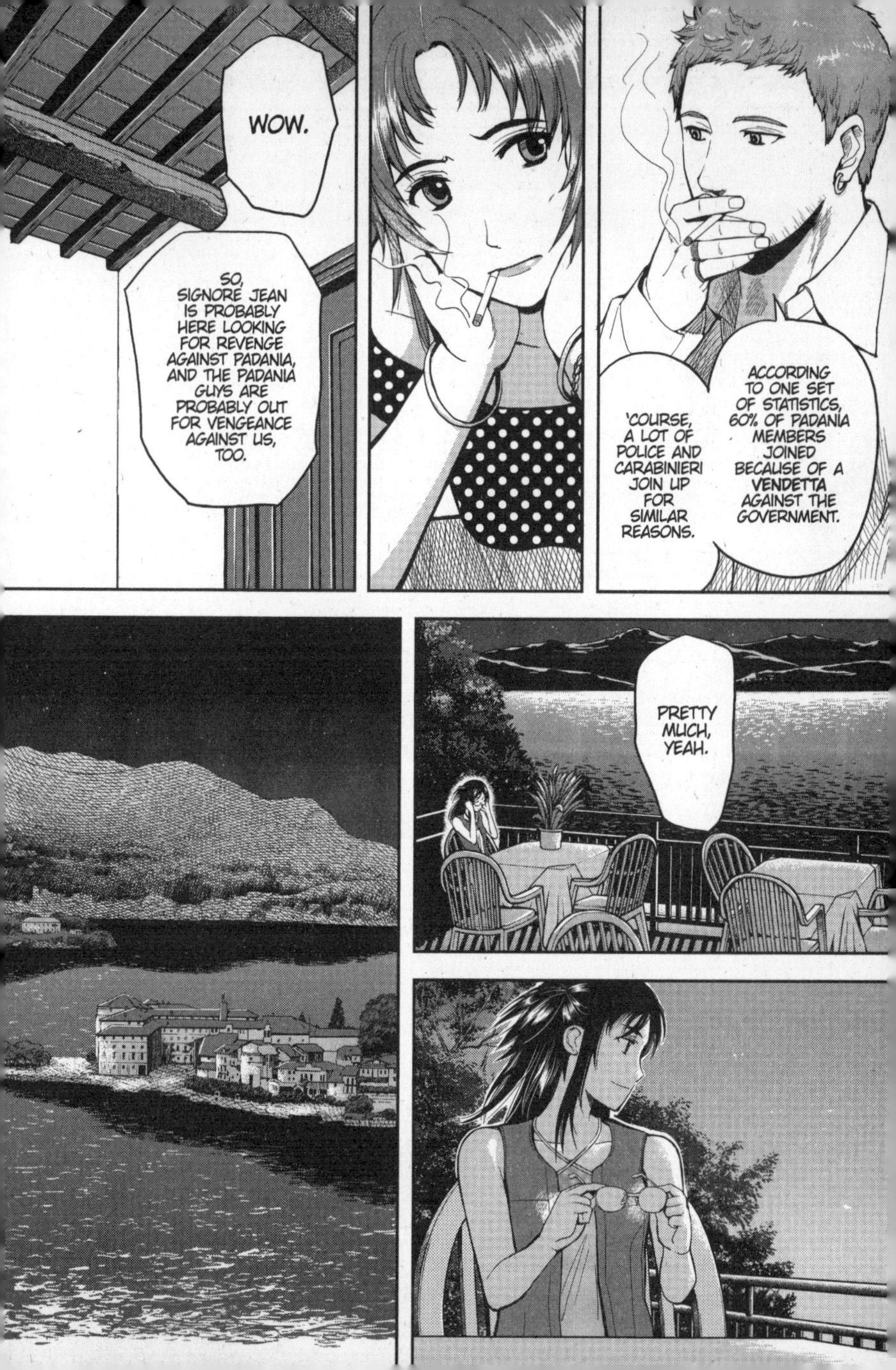
ACCORDING TO ONE SET OF STATISTICS, 60% OF PADANIA MEMBERS JOINED BECAUSE OF A VENDETTA AGAINST THE GOVERNMENT.
'COURSE, A LOT OF POLICE AND CARABINIERI JOIN UP FOR SIMILAR REASONS.
WOW.
SO, SIGNORE JEAN IS PROBABLY HERE LOOKING FOR REVENGE AGAINST PADANIA, AND THE PADANIA GUYS ARE PROBABLY OUT FOR VENGEANCE AGAINST US, TOO.
PRETTY MUCH, YEAH.

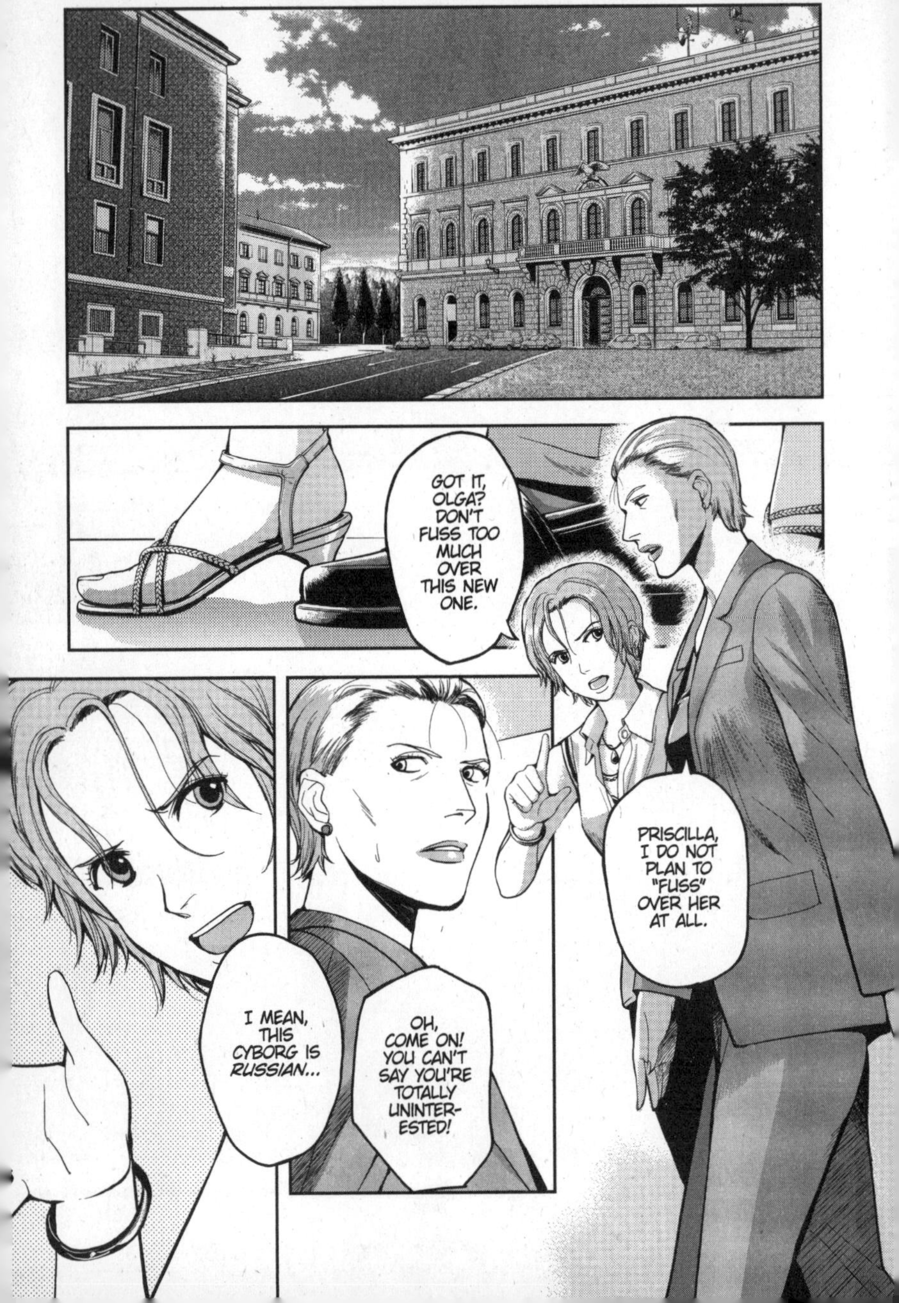
GOT IT, OLGA? DON'T FUSS TOO MUCH OVER THIS NEW ONE.
PRISCILLA, I DO NOT PLAN TO "FUSS" OVER HER AT ALL.
OH, COME ON! YOU CAN'T SAY YOU'RE TOTALLY UNINTER-ESTED!
I MEAN, THIS CYBORG IS *RUSSIAN*...

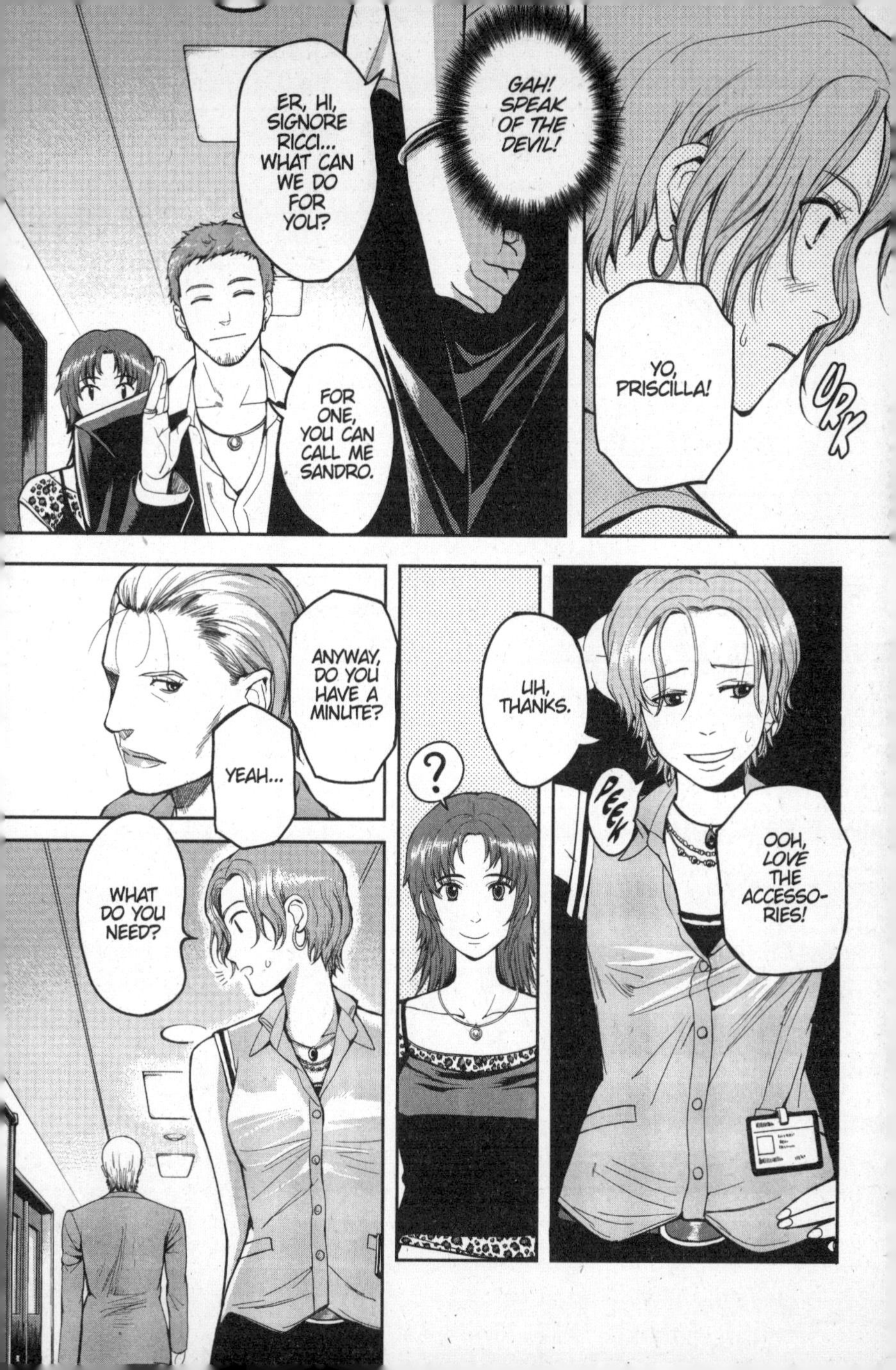
YO, PRISCILLA!
URK
GAH! SPEAK OF THE DEVIL!
ER, HI, SIGNORE RICCI... WHAT CAN WE DO FOR YOU?
FOR ONE, YOU CAN CALL ME SANDRO.
PEEK
OOH, LOVE THE ACCESSO-RIES!
UH, THANKS.
?
ANYWAY, DO YOU HAVE A MINUTE?
YEAH...
WHAT DO YOU NEED?

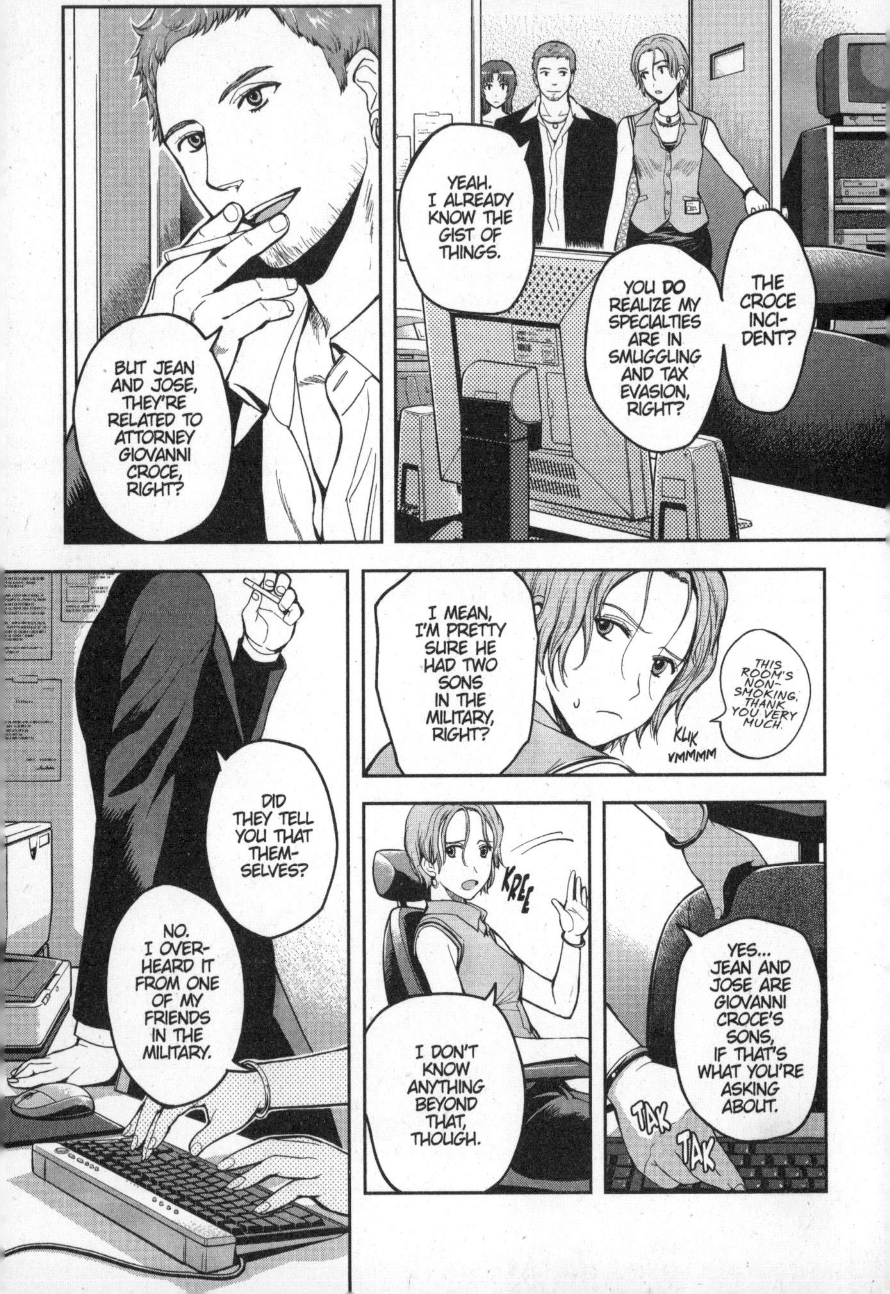
THE CROCE INCIDENT?
YOU DO REALIZE MY SPECIALTIES ARE IN SMUGGLING AND TAX EVASION, RIGHT?
YEAH. I ALREADY KNOW THE GIST OF THINGS.
BUT JEAN AND JOSE, THEY'RE RELATED TO ATTORNEY GIOVANNI CROCE, RIGHT?
THIS ROOM'S NON-SMOKING, THANK YOU VERY MUCH.
KLIK
VMMMM
I MEAN, I'M PRETTY SURE HE HAD TWO SONS IN THE MILITARY, RIGHT?
YES... JEAN AND JOSE ARE GIOVANNI CROCE'S SONS, IF THAT'S WHAT YOU'RE ASKING ABOUT.
TAK
TAK
KREE
I DON'T KNOW ANYTHING BEYOND THAT, THOUGH.
DID THEY TELL YOU THAT THEM-SELVES?
NO. I OVER-HEARD IT FROM ONE OF MY FRIENDS IN THE MILITARY.

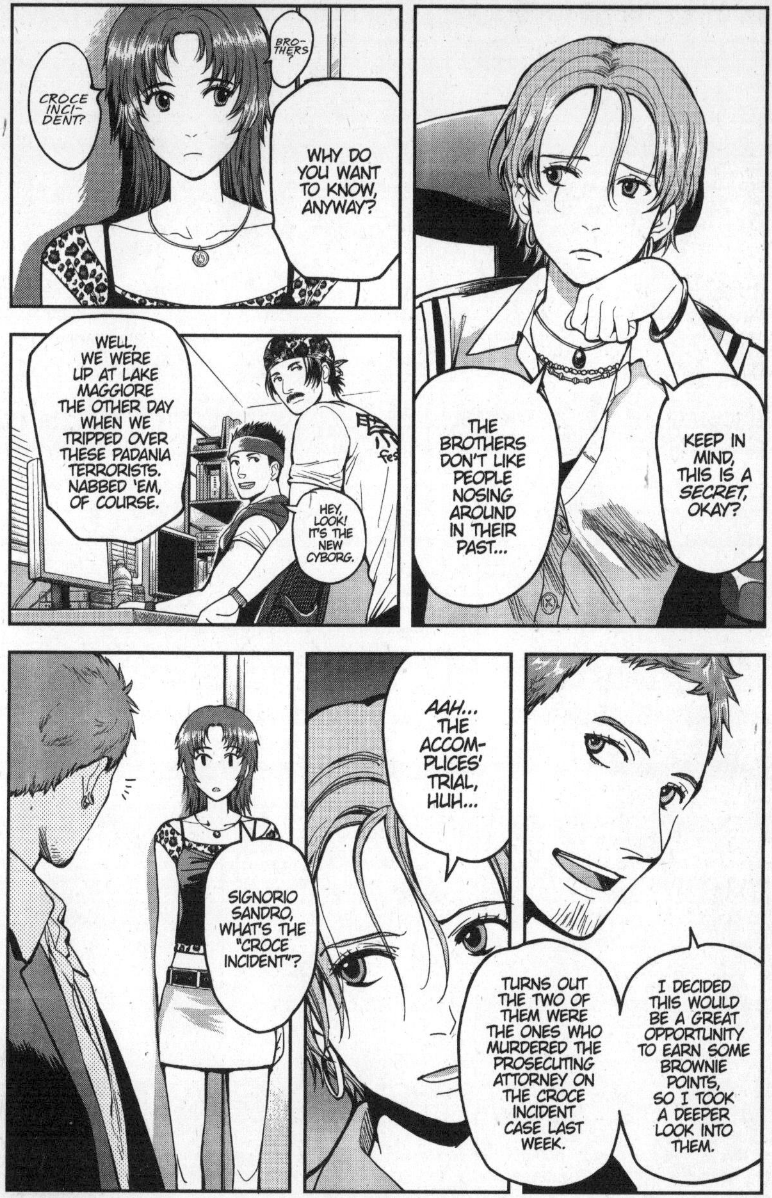
KEEP IN MIND, THIS IS A SECRET, OKAY?
THE BROTHERS DON'T LIKE PEOPLE NOSING AROUND IN THEIR PAST...
BROTHERS?
WHY DO YOU WANT TO KNOW, ANYWAY?
CROCE INCIDENT?
WELL, WE WERE UP AT LAKE MAGGIORE THE OTHER DAY WHEN WE TRIPPED OVER THESE PADANIA TERRORISTS. NABBED 'EM, OF COURSE.
HEY, LOOK! IT'S THE NEW CYBORG.
I DECIDED THIS WOULD BE A GREAT OPPORTUNITY TO EARN SOME BROWNIE POINTS, SO I TOOK A DEEPER LOOK INTO THEM.
TURNS OUT THE TWO OF THEM WERE THE ONES WHO MURDERED THE PROSECUTING ATTORNEY ON THE CROCE INCIDENT CASE LAST WEEK.
AAH... THE ACCOMPLICES' TRIAL, HUH...
SIGNORIO SANDRO, WHAT'S THE "CROCE INCIDENT"?

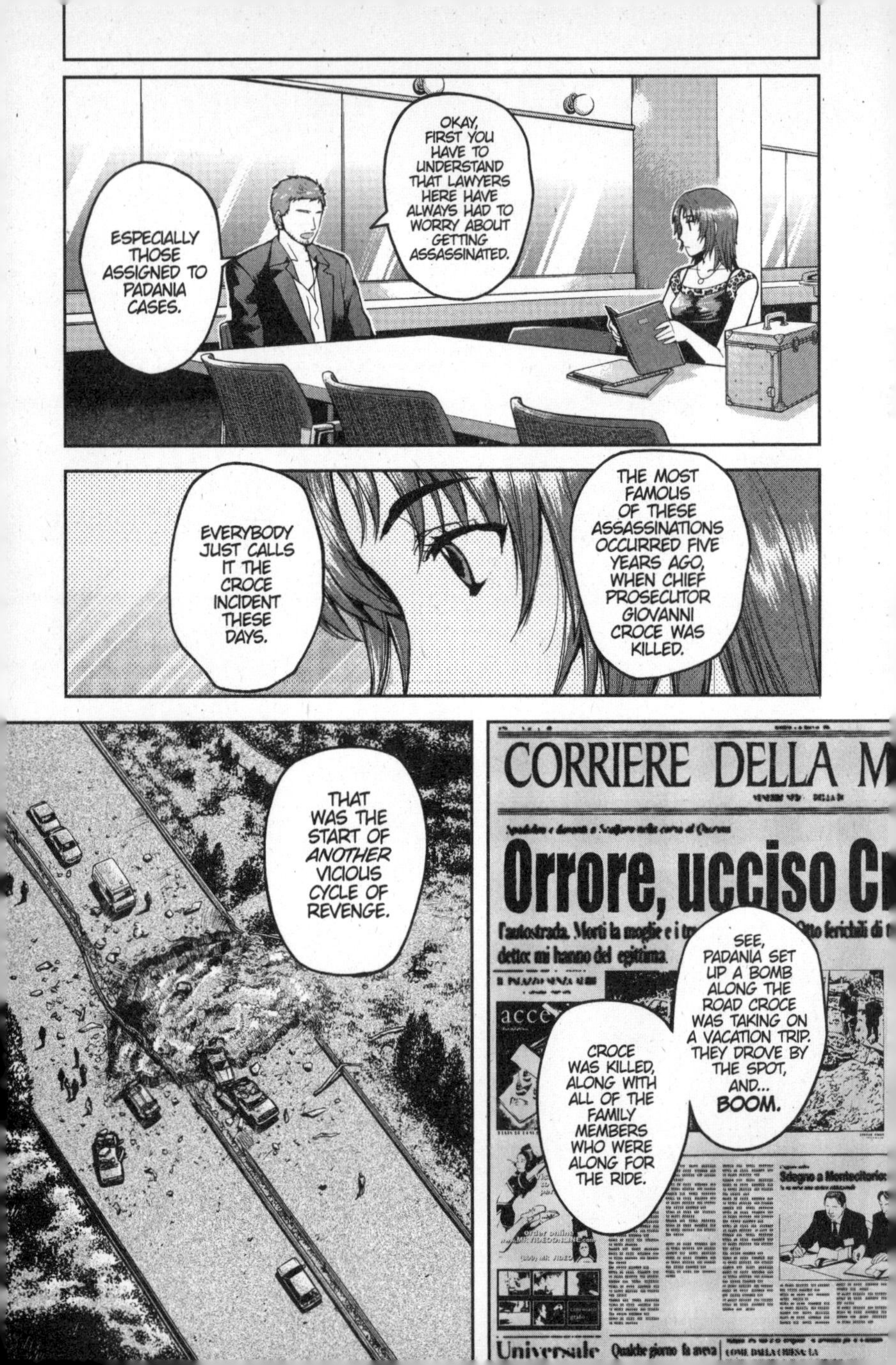
OKAY, FIRST YOU HAVE TO UNDERSTAND THAT LAWYERS HERE HAVE ALWAYS HAD TO WORRY ABOUT GETTING ASSASSINATED.
ESPECIALLY THOSE ASSIGNED TO PADANIA CASES.
THE MOST FAMOUS OF THESE ASSASSINATIONS OCCURRED FIVE YEARS AGO, WHEN CHIEF PROSECUTOR GIOVANNI CROCE WAS KILLED.
EVERYBODY JUST CALLS IT THE CROCE INCIDENT THESE DAYS.
CORRIERE DELLA M
Orrore, ucciso Cr
SEE, PADANIA SET UP A BOMB ALONG THE ROAD CROCE WAS TAKING ON A VACATION TRIP. THEY DROVE BY THE SPOT, AND... **BOOM.**
CROCE WAS KILLED, ALONG WITH ALL OF THE FAMILY MEMBERS WHO WERE ALONG FOR THE RIDE.
Sdegno a Montecitorio
Universale
THAT WAS THE START OF *ANOTHER* VICIOUS CYCLE OF REVENGE.

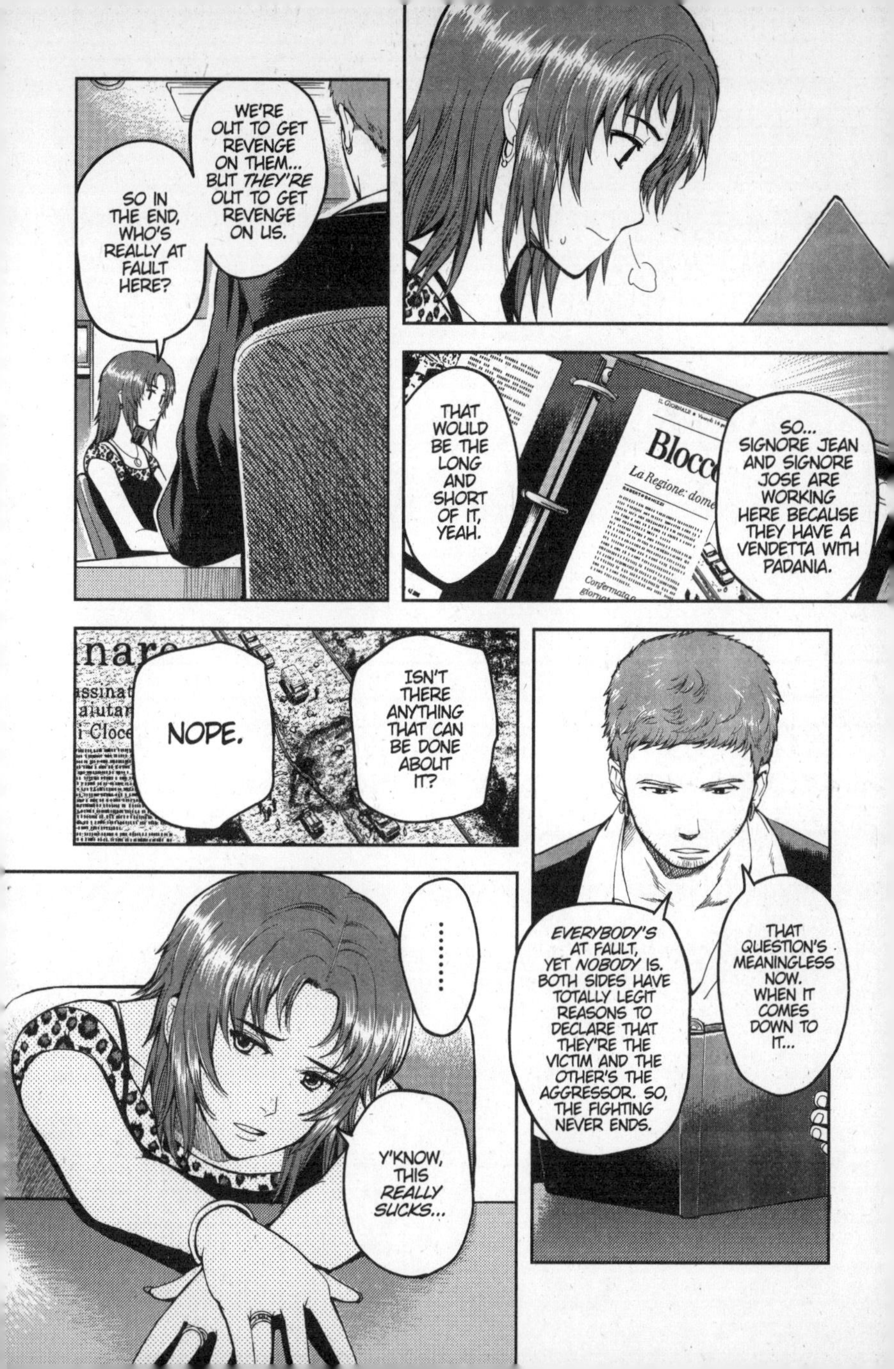
SO... SIGNORE JEAN AND SIGNORE JOSE ARE WORKING HERE BECAUSE THEY HAVE A VENDETTA WITH PADANIA.
THAT WOULD BE THE LONG AND SHORT OF IT, YEAH.
WE'RE OUT TO GET REVENGE ON THEM... BUT *THEY'RE* OUT TO GET REVENGE ON US.
SO IN THE END, WHO'S REALLY AT FAULT HERE?
THAT QUESTION'S MEANINGLESS NOW. WHEN IT COMES DOWN TO IT...
EVERYBODY'S AT FAULT, YET *NOBODY* IS. BOTH SIDES HAVE TOTALLY LEGIT REASONS TO DECLARE THAT THEY'RE THE VICTIM AND THE OTHER'S THE AGGRESSOR. SO, THE FIGHTING NEVER ENDS.
ISN'T THERE ANYTHING THAT CAN BE DONE ABOUT IT?
NOPE.
......
Y'KNOW, THIS *REALLY* *SUCKS*...

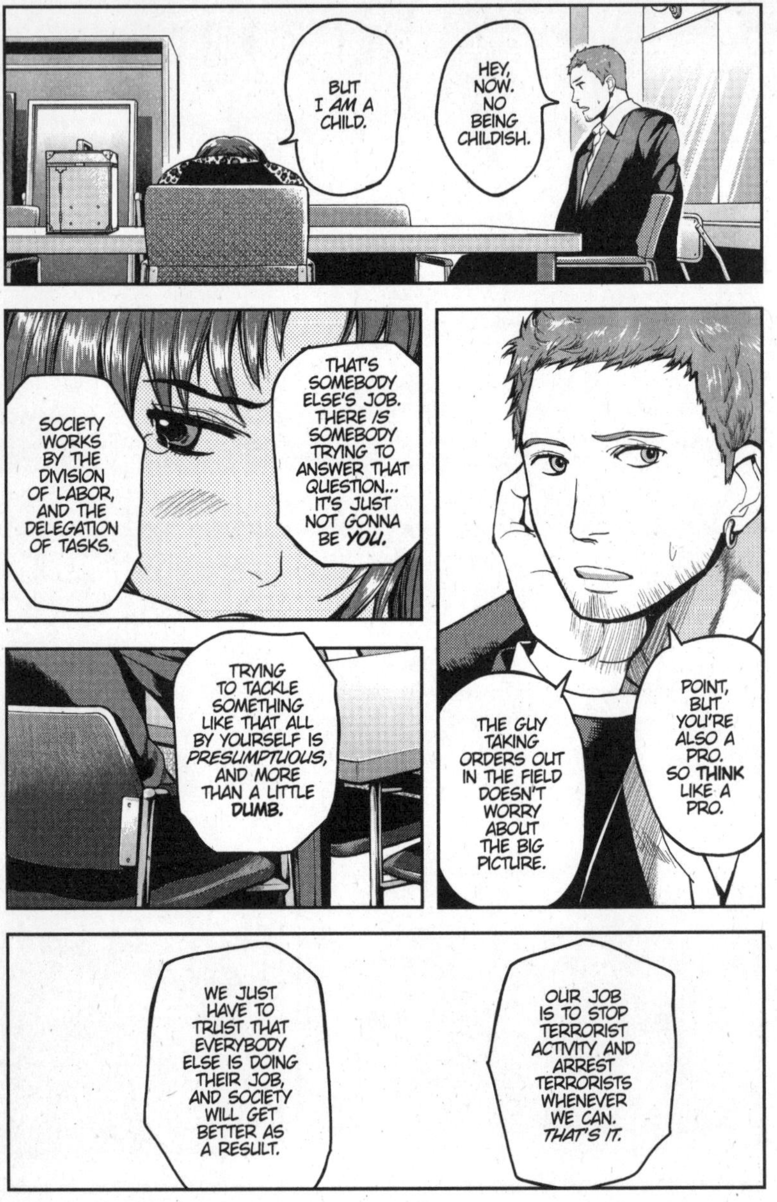
HEY, NOW. NO BEING CHILDISH.
BUT I *AM* A CHILD.
POINT, BUT YOU'RE ALSO A PRO. SO **THINK** LIKE A PRO.
THE GUY TAKING ORDERS OUT IN THE FIELD DOESN'T WORRY ABOUT THE BIG PICTURE.
THAT'S SOMEBODY ELSE'S JOB. THERE *IS* SOMEBODY TRYING TO ANSWER THAT QUESTION... IT'S JUST NOT GONNA BE ***YOU.***
SOCIETY WORKS BY THE DIVISION OF LABOR, AND THE DELEGATION OF TASKS.
TRYING TO TACKLE SOMETHING LIKE THAT ALL BY YOURSELF IS *PRESUMPTUOUS,* AND MORE THAN A LITTLE **DUMB.**
OUR JOB IS TO STOP TERRORIST ACTIVITY AND ARREST TERRORISTS WHENEVER WE CAN. *THAT'S IT.*
WE JUST HAVE TO TRUST THAT EVERYBODY ELSE IS DOING THEIR JOB, AND SOCIETY WILL GET BETTER AS A RESULT.

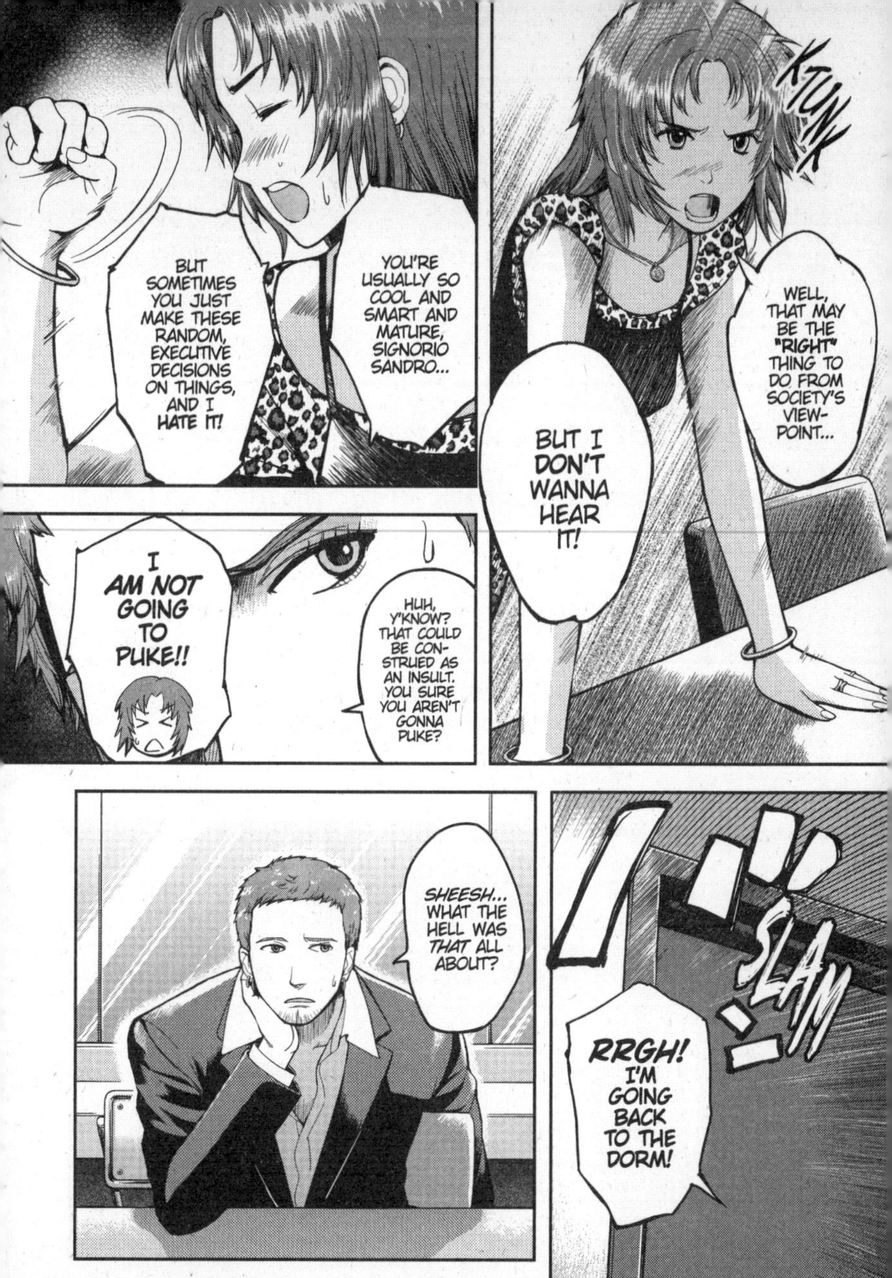
KTUNK
WELL, THAT MAY BE THE **"RIGHT"** THING TO DO FROM SOCIETY'S VIEW-POINT...
BUT I DON'T WANNA HEAR IT!
YOU'RE USUALLY SO COOL AND SMART AND MATURE, SIGNORIO SANDRO...
BUT SOMETIMES YOU JUST MAKE THESE RANDOM, EXECUTIVE DECISIONS ON THINGS, AND I HATE IT!
HUH, Y'KNOW? THAT COULD BE CON-STRUED AS AN INSULT. YOU SURE YOU AREN'T GONNA PUKE?
I *AM NOT* GOING TO PUKE!!
SLAM
RRGH! I'M GOING BACK TO THE DORM!
SHEESH... WHAT THE HELL WAS *THAT* ALL ABOUT?

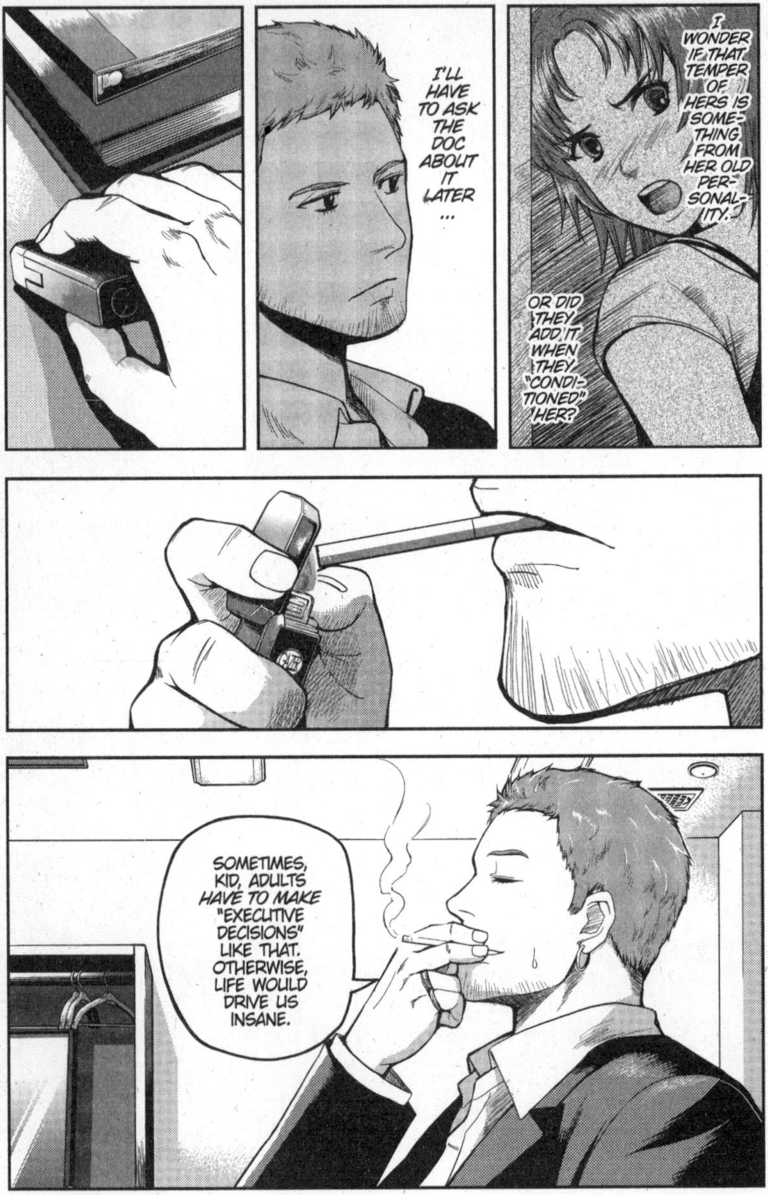
I WONDER IF THAT TEMPER OF HERS IS SOMETHING FROM HER OLD PERSONALITY.
OR DID THEY ADD IT WHEN THEY "CONDITIONED" HER?
I'LL HAVE TO ASK THE DOC ABOUT IT LATER ...
SOMETIMES, KID, ADULTS *HAVE TO MAKE* "EXECUTIVE DECISIONS" LIKE THAT. OTHERWISE, LIFE WOULD DRIVE US INSANE.

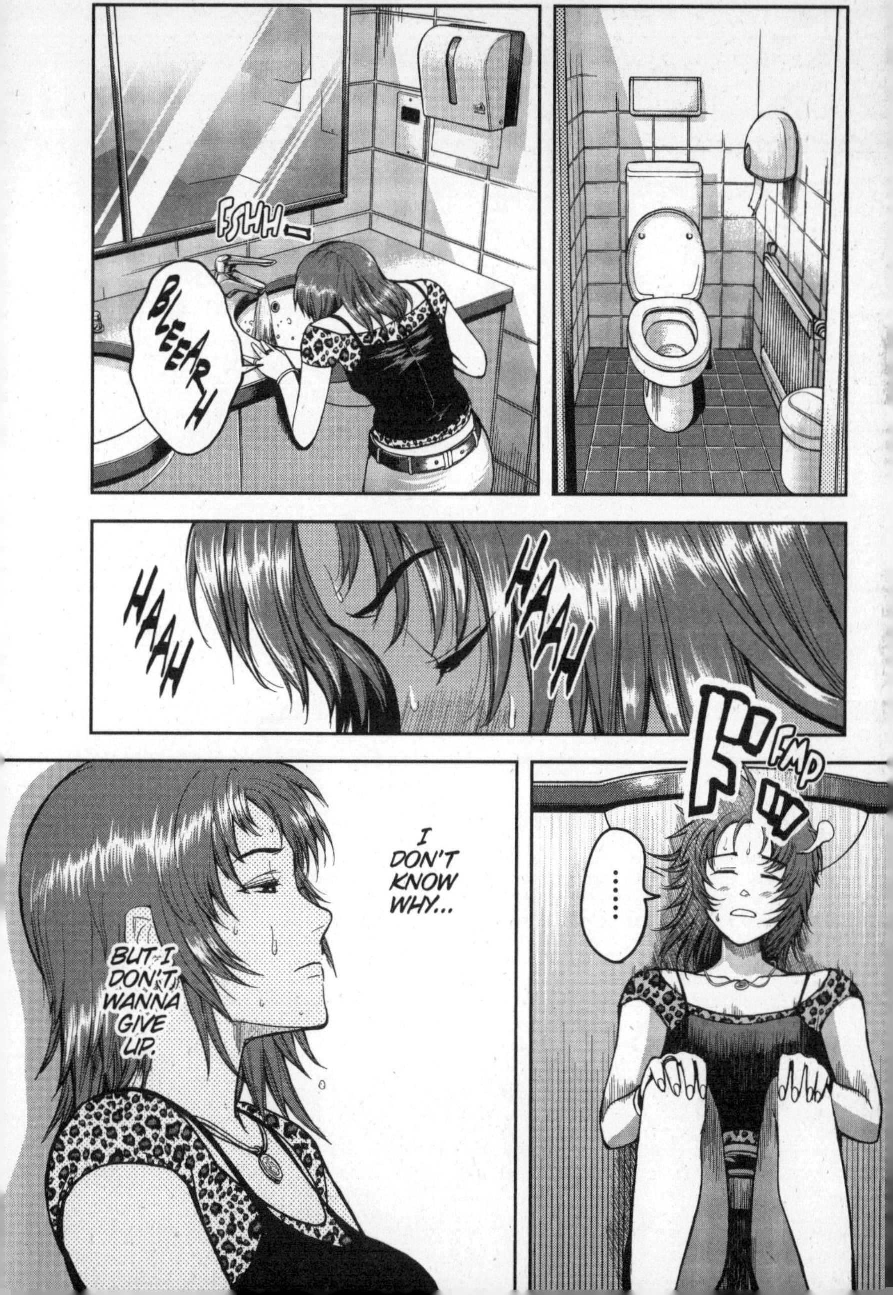
FSHH
BLEEARH
HAAAH
HAAAH
FMP
......
I DON'T KNOW WHY...
BUT I DON'T WANNA GIVE UP.

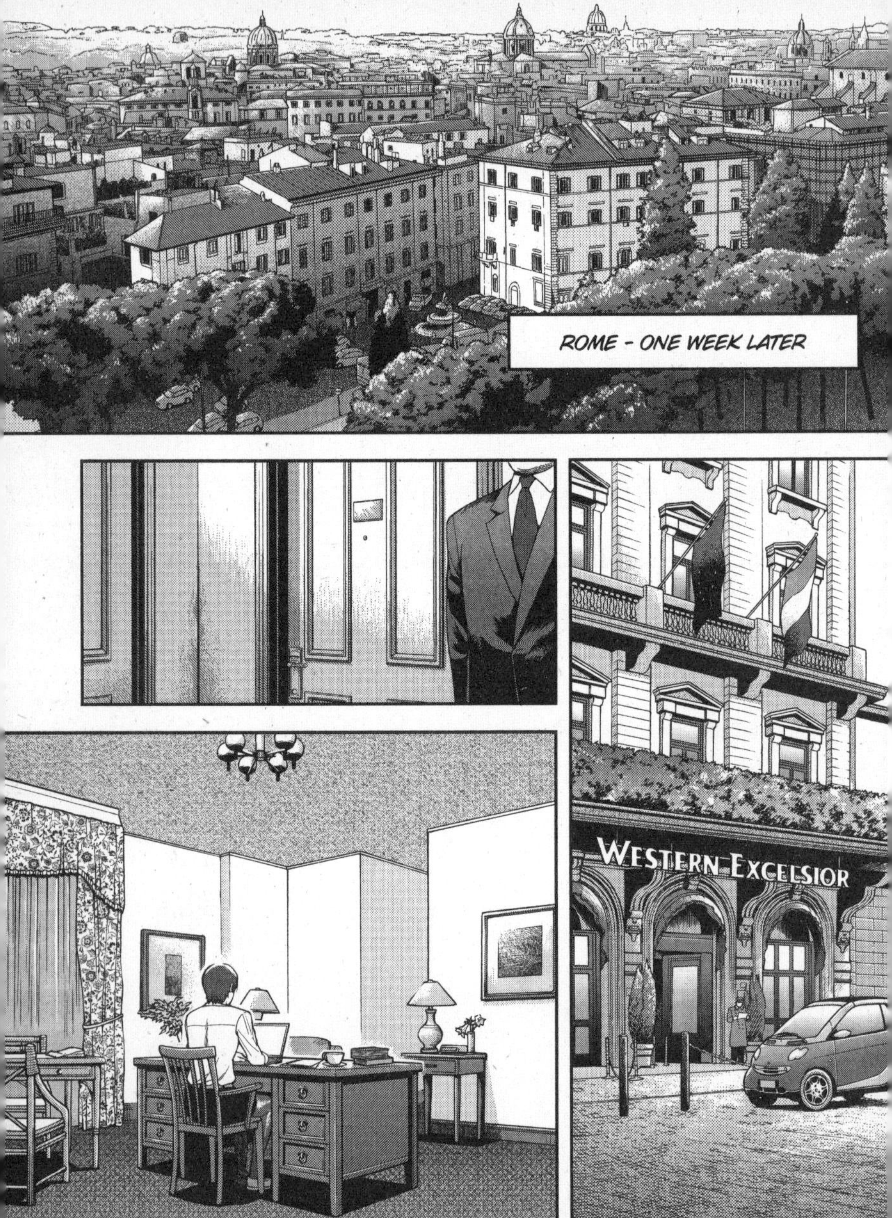
ROME - ONE WEEK LATER
WESTERN EXCELSIOR

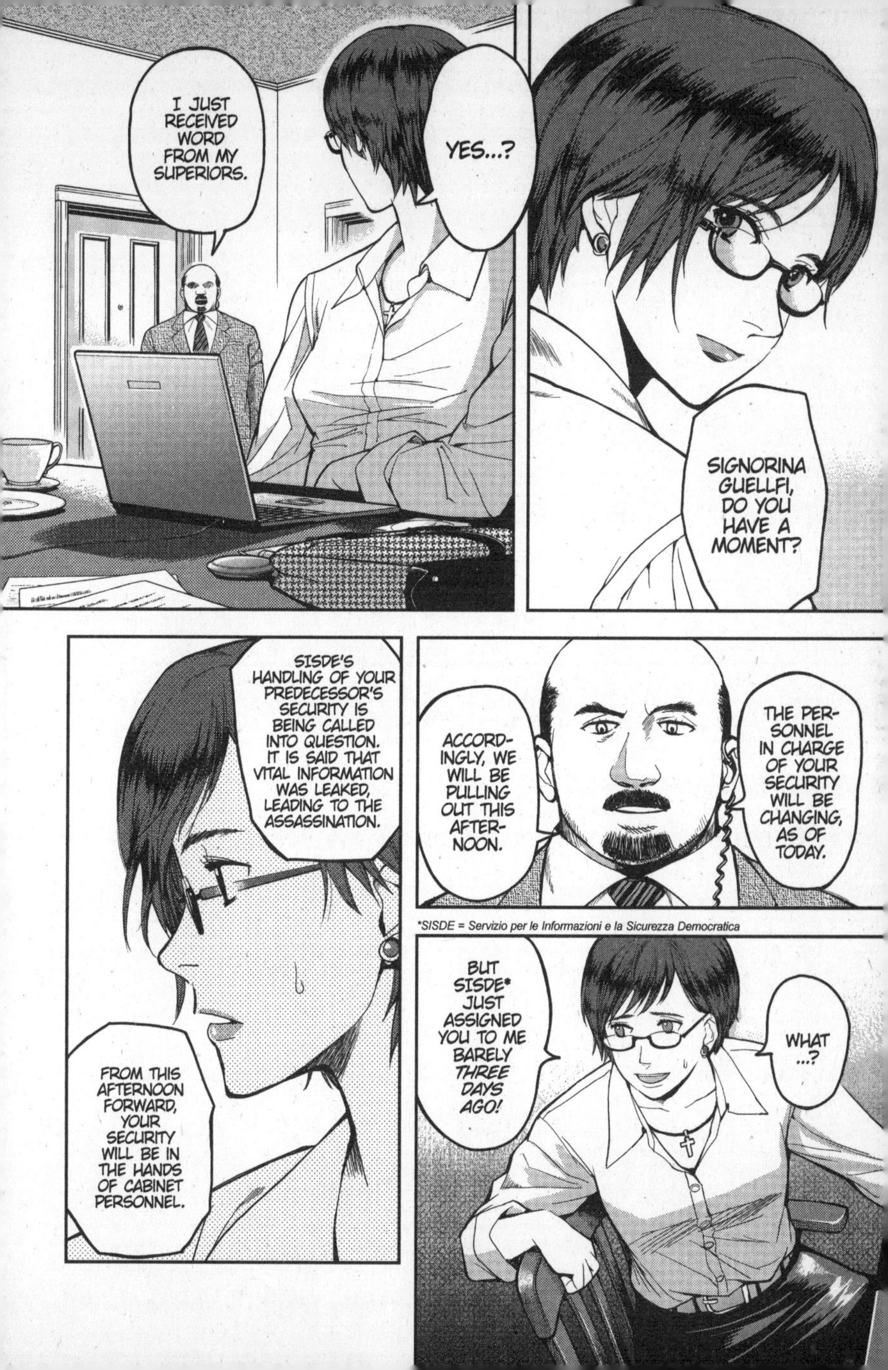
SIGNORINA GUELLFI, DO YOU HAVE A MOMENT?
YES...?
I JUST RECEIVED WORD FROM MY SUPERIORS.
THE PER-SONNEL IN CHARGE OF YOUR SECURITY WILL BE CHANGING, AS OF TODAY.
ACCORD-INGLY, WE WILL BE PULLING OUT THIS AFTER-NOON.
WHAT ...?
BUT SISDE* JUST ASSIGNED YOU TO ME BARELY *THREE DAYS* AGO!
SISDE'S HANDLING OF YOUR PREDECESSOR'S SECURITY IS BEING CALLED INTO QUESTION. IT IS SAID THAT VITAL INFORMATION WAS LEAKED, LEADING TO THE ASSASSINATION.
FROM THIS AFTERNOON FORWARD, YOUR SECURITY WILL BE IN THE HANDS OF CABINET PERSONNEL.

**SISDE = Servizio per le Informazioni e la Sicurezza Democratica*

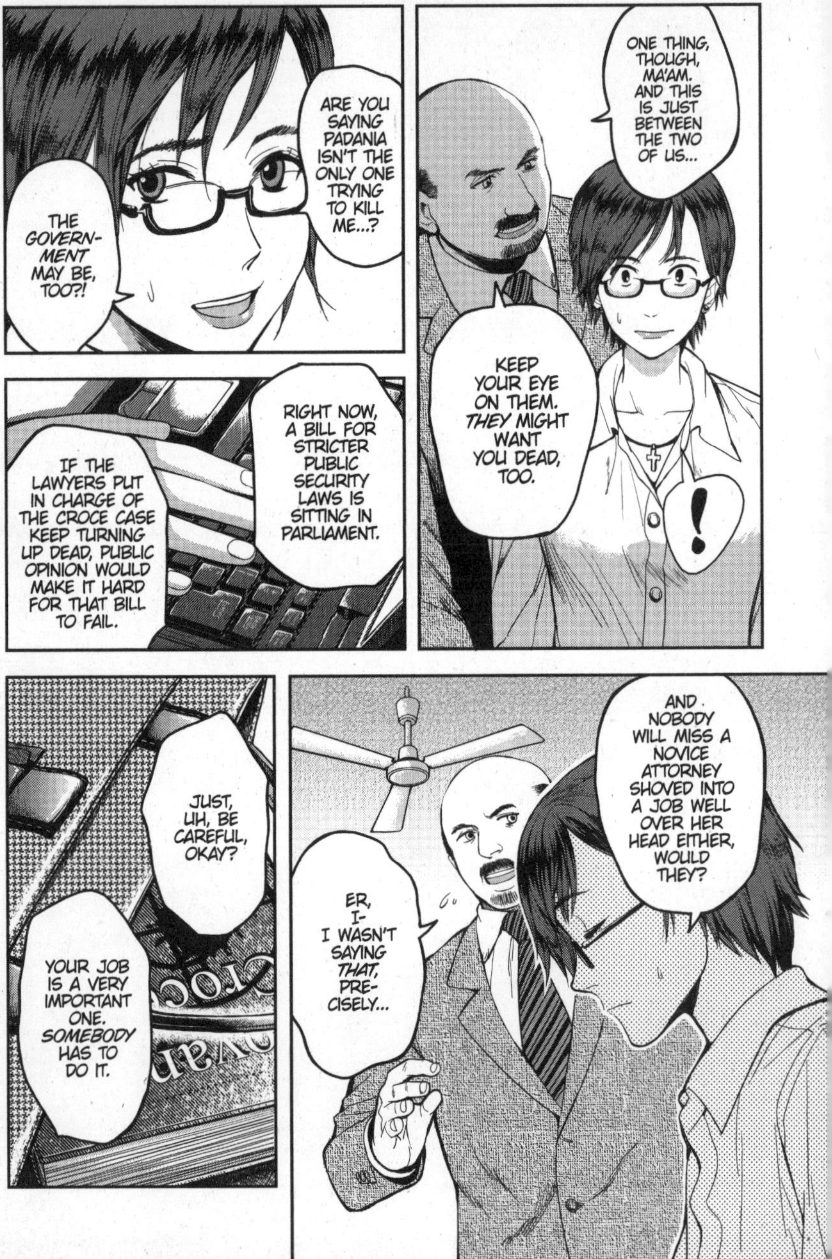
ONE THING, THOUGH, MA'AM. AND THIS IS JUST BETWEEN THE TWO OF US...
KEEP YOUR EYE ON THEM. *THEY* MIGHT WANT YOU DEAD, TOO.
!
ARE YOU SAYING PADANIA ISN'T THE ONLY ONE TRYING TO KILL ME...?
THE *GOVERNMENT* MAY BE, TOO?!
RIGHT NOW, A BILL FOR STRICTER PUBLIC SECURITY LAWS IS SITTING IN PARLIAMENT.
IF THE LAWYERS PUT IN CHARGE OF THE CROCE CASE KEEP TURNING UP DEAD, PUBLIC OPINION WOULD MAKE IT HARD FOR THAT BILL TO FAIL.
AND NOBODY WILL MISS A NOVICE ATTORNEY SHOVED INTO A JOB WELL OVER HER HEAD EITHER, WOULD THEY?
ER, I- I WASN'T SAYING *THAT,* PRE-CISELY...
JUST, UH, BE CAREFUL, OKAY?
YOUR JOB IS A VERY IMPORTANT ONE. *SOMEBODY* HAS TO DO IT.

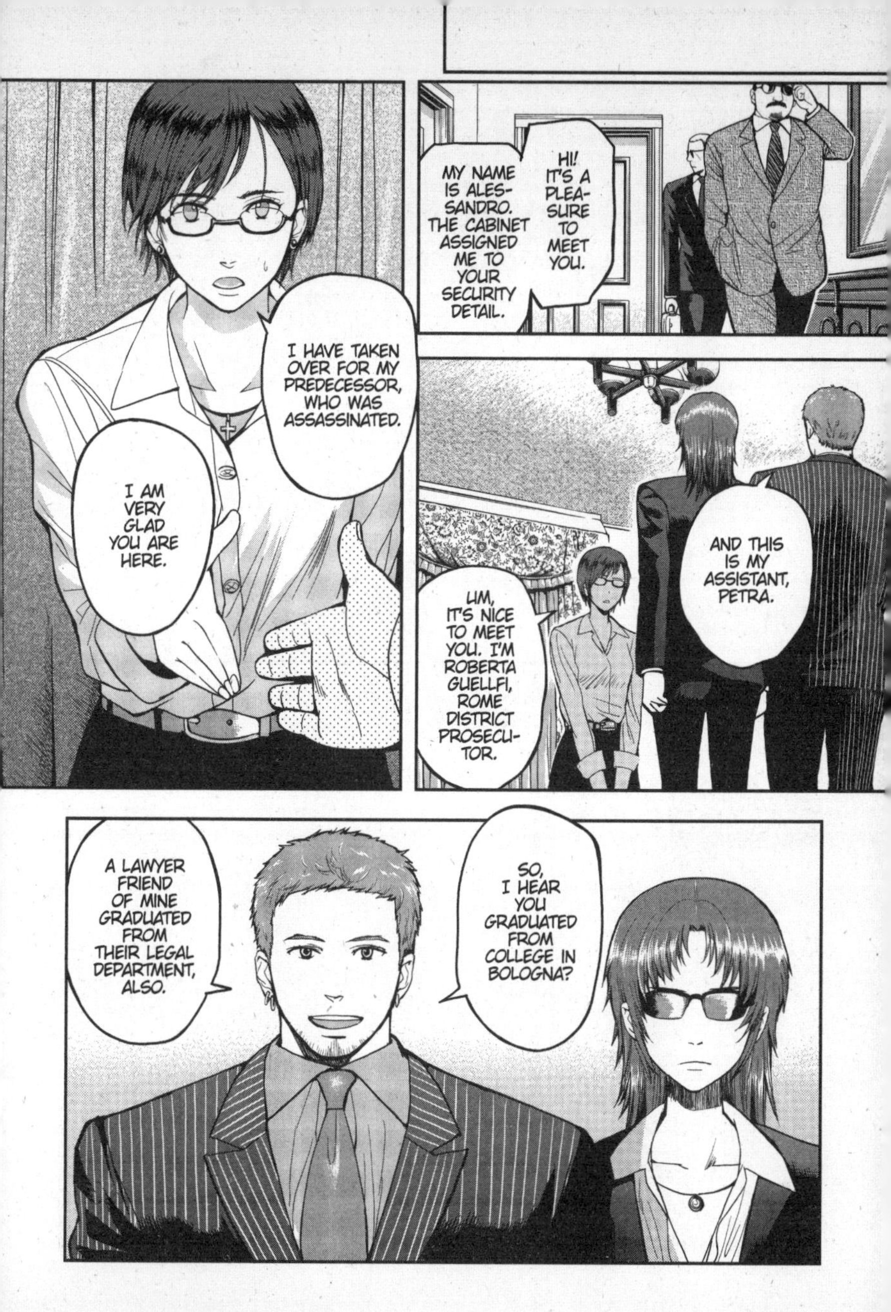
HI! IT'S A PLEASURE TO MEET YOU.
MY NAME IS ALES-SANDRO. THE CABINET ASSIGNED ME TO YOUR SECURITY DETAIL.
AND THIS IS MY ASSISTANT, PETRA.
UM, IT'S NICE TO MEET YOU. I'M ROBERTA GUELLFI, ROME DISTRICT PROSECU-TOR.
I HAVE TAKEN OVER FOR MY PREDECESSOR, WHO WAS ASSASSINATED.
I AM VERY GLAD YOU ARE HERE.
SO, I HEAR YOU GRADUATED FROM COLLEGE IN BOLOGNA?
A LAWYER FRIEND OF MINE GRADUATED FROM THEIR LEGAL DEPARTMENT, ALSO.

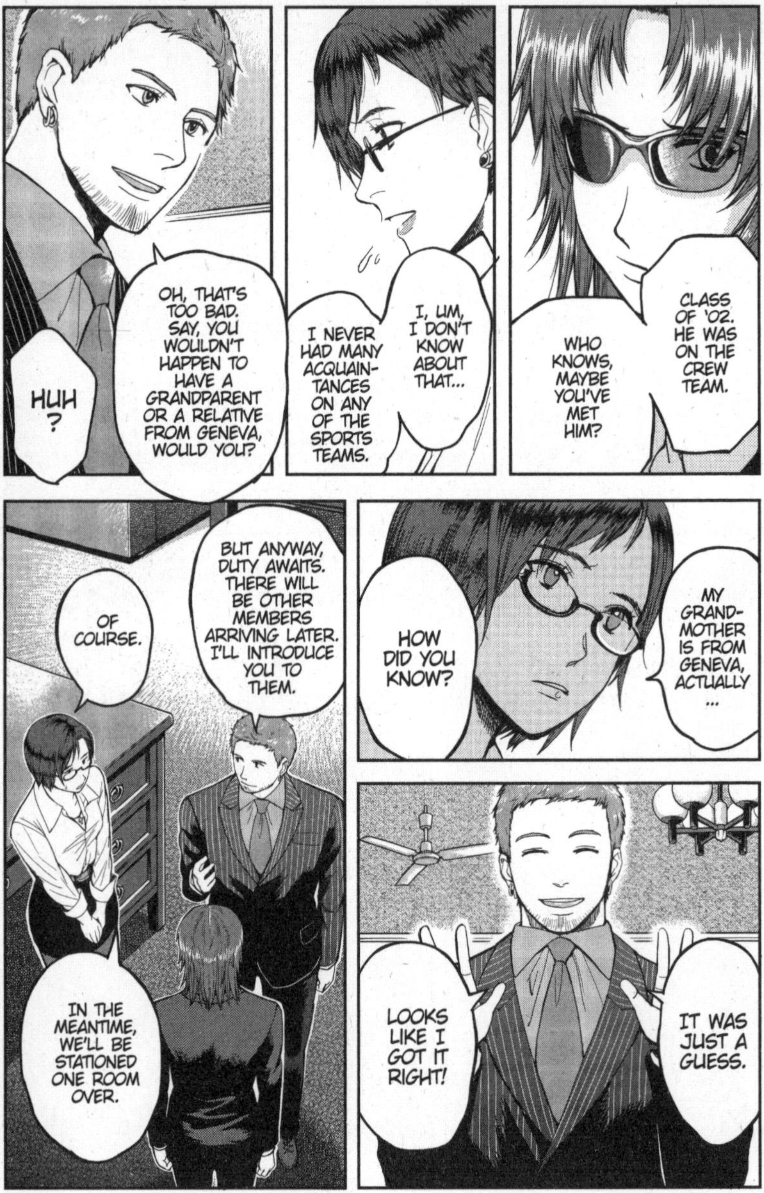
CLASS OF '02. HE WAS ON THE CREW TEAM.
WHO KNOWS, MAYBE YOU'VE MET HIM?
I, UM, I DON'T KNOW ABOUT THAT...
I NEVER HAD MANY ACQUAINTANCES ON ANY OF THE SPORTS TEAMS.
OH, THAT'S TOO BAD. SAY, YOU WOULDN'T HAPPEN TO HAVE A GRANDPARENT OR A RELATIVE FROM GENEVA, WOULD YOU?
HUH?
MY GRANDMOTHER IS FROM GENEVA, ACTUALLY...
HOW DID YOU KNOW?
IT WAS JUST A GUESS.
LOOKS LIKE I GOT IT RIGHT!
BUT ANYWAY, DUTY AWAITS. THERE WILL BE OTHER MEMBERS ARRIVING LATER. I'LL INTRODUCE YOU TO THEM.
OF COURSE.
IN THE MEANTIME, WE'LL BE STATIONED ONE ROOM OVER.

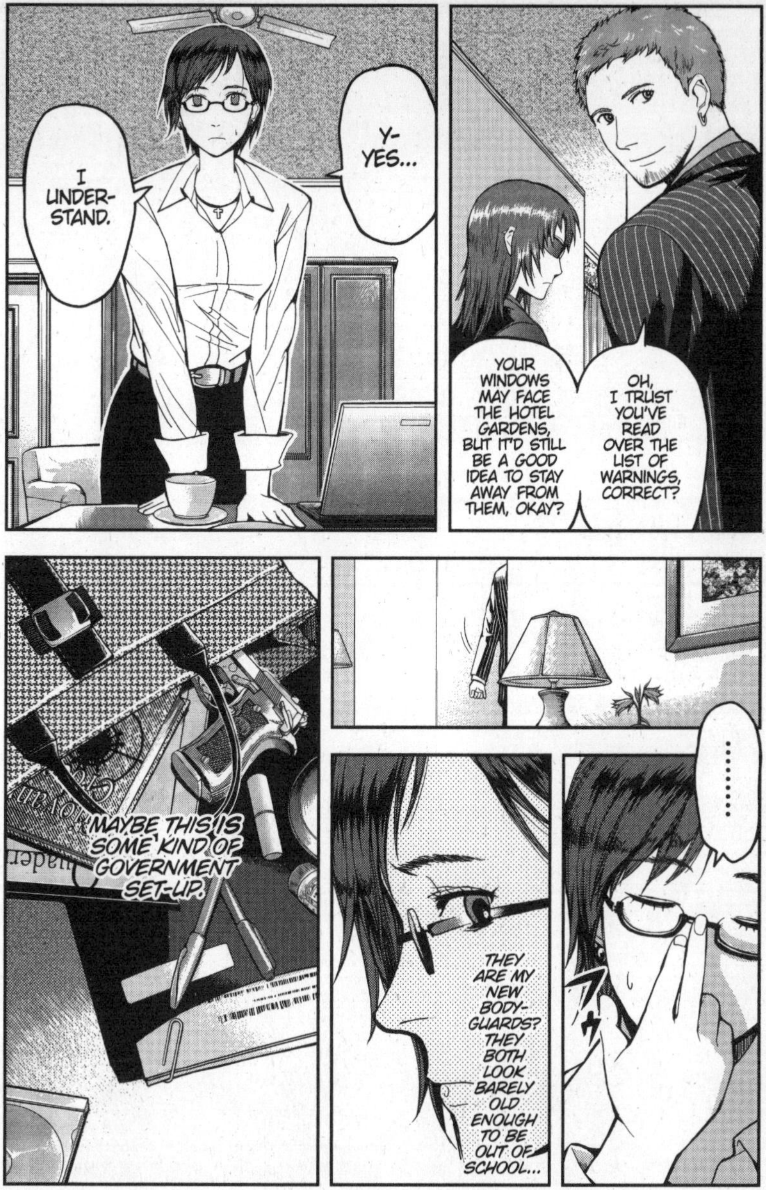
OH, I TRUST YOU'VE READ OVER THE LIST OF WARNINGS, CORRECT?
YOUR WINDOWS MAY FACE THE HOTEL GARDENS, BUT IT'D STILL BE A GOOD IDEA TO STAY AWAY FROM THEM, OKAY?
Y-YES...
I UNDER-STAND.
......
THEY ARE MY NEW BODY-GUARDS? THEY BOTH LOOK BARELY OLD ENOUGH TO BE OUT OF SCHOOL...
MAYBE THIS IS SOME KIND OF GOVERNMENT SET-UP.

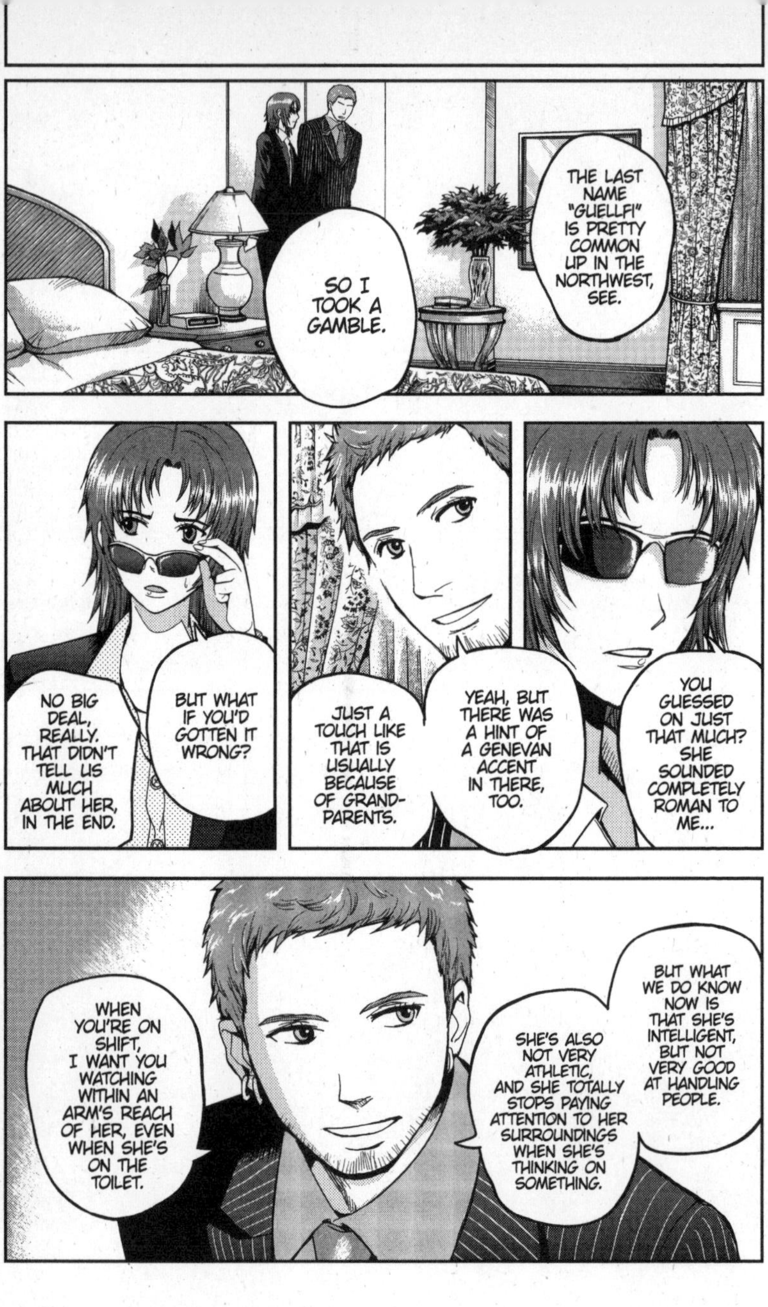
THE LAST NAME "GUELLFI" IS PRETTY COMMON UP IN THE NORTHWEST, SEE.
SO I TOOK A GAMBLE.
YOU GUESSED ON JUST THAT MUCH? SHE SOUNDED COMPLETELY ROMAN TO ME...
YEAH, BUT THERE WAS A HINT OF A GENEVAN ACCENT IN THERE, TOO.
JUST A TOUCH LIKE THAT IS USUALLY BECAUSE OF GRAND-PARENTS.
BUT WHAT IF YOU'D GOTTEN IT WRONG?
NO BIG DEAL, REALLY. THAT DIDN'T TELL US MUCH ABOUT HER, IN THE END.
BUT WHAT WE DO KNOW NOW IS THAT SHE'S INTELLIGENT, BUT NOT VERY GOOD AT HANDLING PEOPLE.
SHE'S ALSO NOT VERY ATHLETIC, AND SHE TOTALLY STOPS PAYING ATTENTION TO HER SURROUNDINGS WHEN SHE'S THINKING ON SOMETHING.
WHEN YOU'RE ON SHIFT, I WANT YOU WATCHING WITHIN AN ARM'S REACH OF HER, EVEN WHEN SHE'S ON THE TOILET.

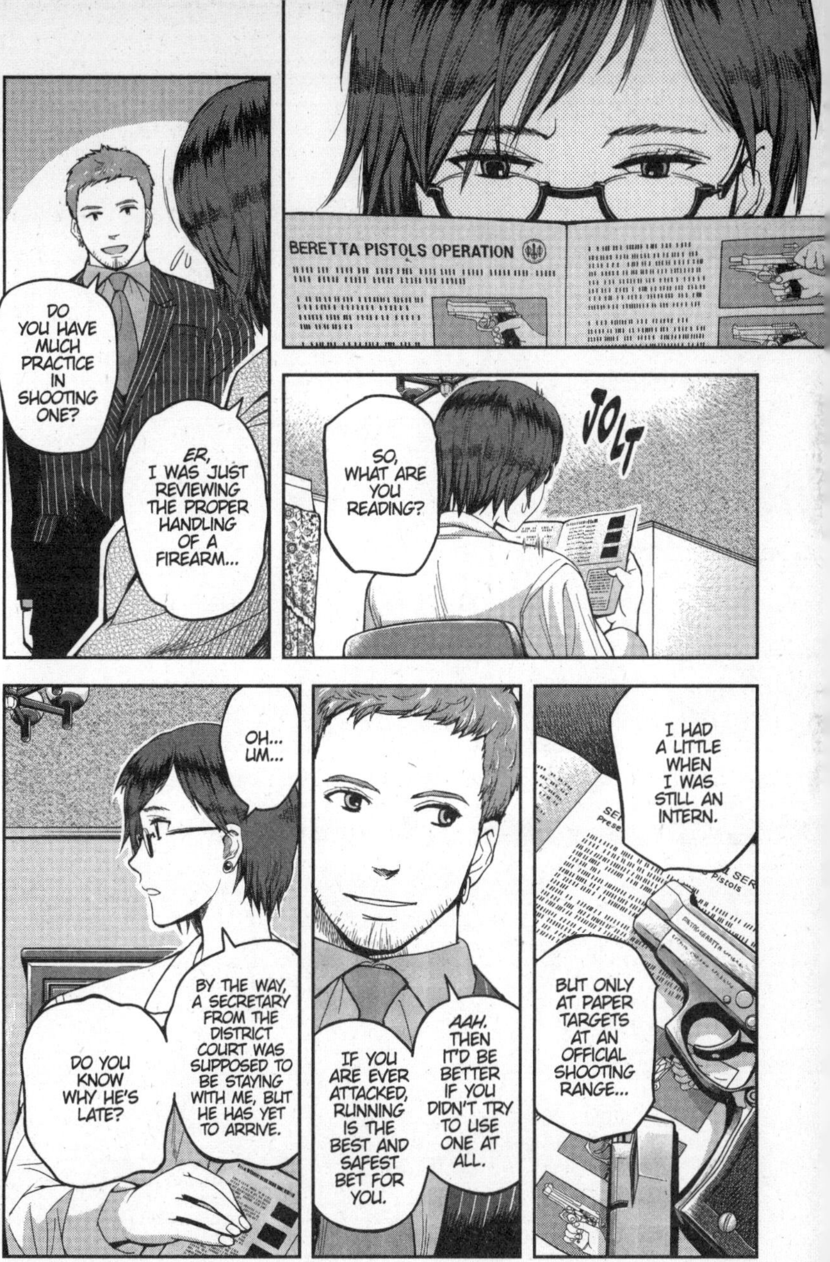
BERETTA PISTOLS OPERATION
SO, WHAT ARE YOU READING?
JOLT
ER, I WAS JUST REVIEWING THE PROPER HANDLING OF A FIREARM...
DO YOU HAVE MUCH PRACTICE IN SHOOTING ONE?
I HAD A LITTLE WHEN I WAS STILL AN INTERN.
BUT ONLY AT PAPER TARGETS AT AN OFFICIAL SHOOTING RANGE...
AAH. THEN IT'D BE BETTER IF YOU DIDN'T TRY TO USE ONE AT ALL.
IF YOU ARE EVER ATTACKED, RUNNING IS THE BEST AND SAFEST BET FOR YOU.
OH... UM...
BY THE WAY, A SECRETARY FROM THE DISTRICT COURT WAS SUPPOSED TO BE STAYING WITH ME, BUT HE HAS YET TO ARRIVE.
DO YOU KNOW WHY HE'S LATE?

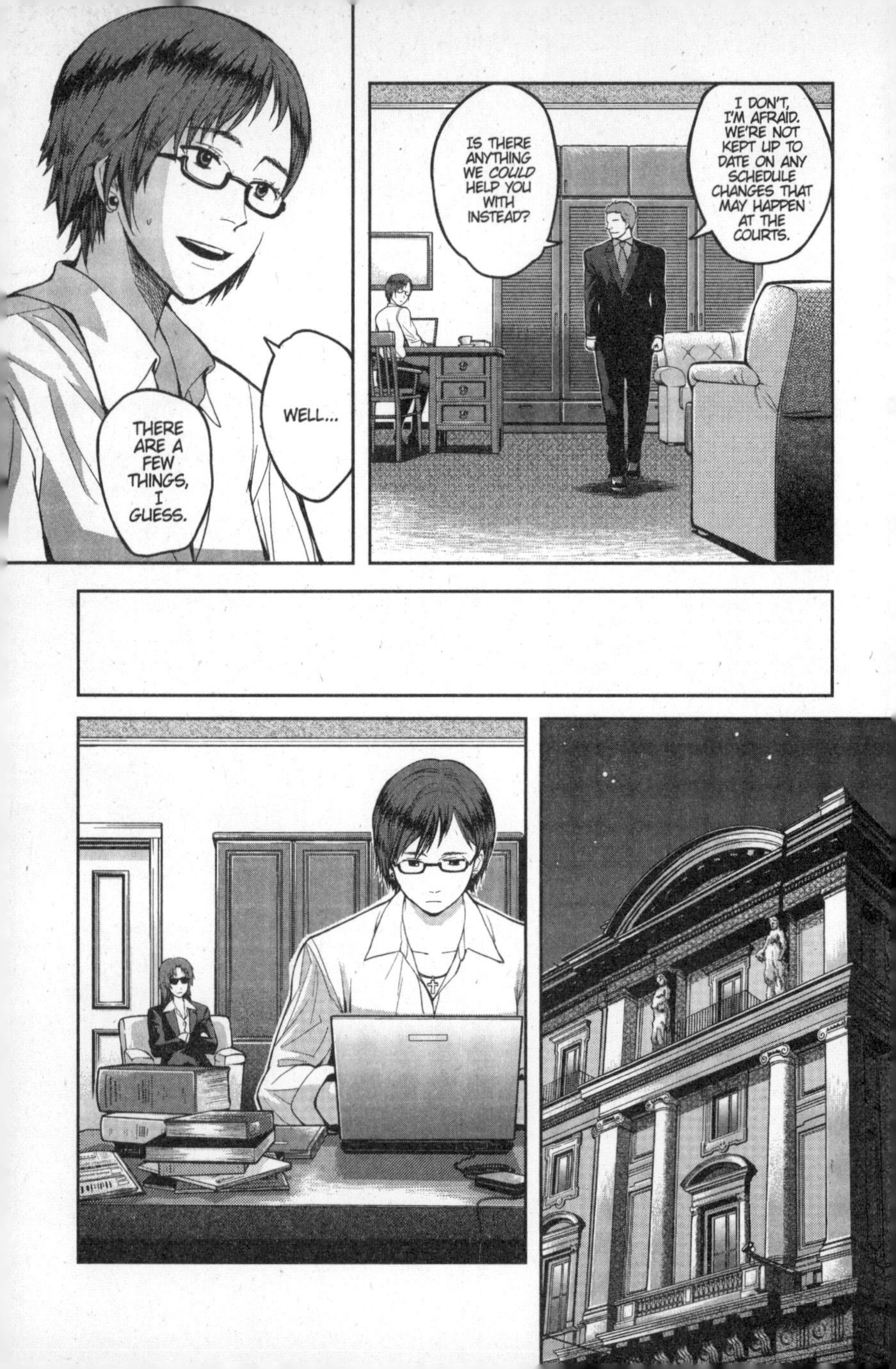
I DON'T, I'M AFRAID. WE'RE NOT KEPT UP TO DATE ON ANY SCHEDULE CHANGES THAT MAY HAPPEN AT THE COURTS.
IS THERE ANYTHING WE *COULD* HELP YOU WITH INSTEAD?
WELL...
THERE ARE A FEW THINGS, I GUESS.

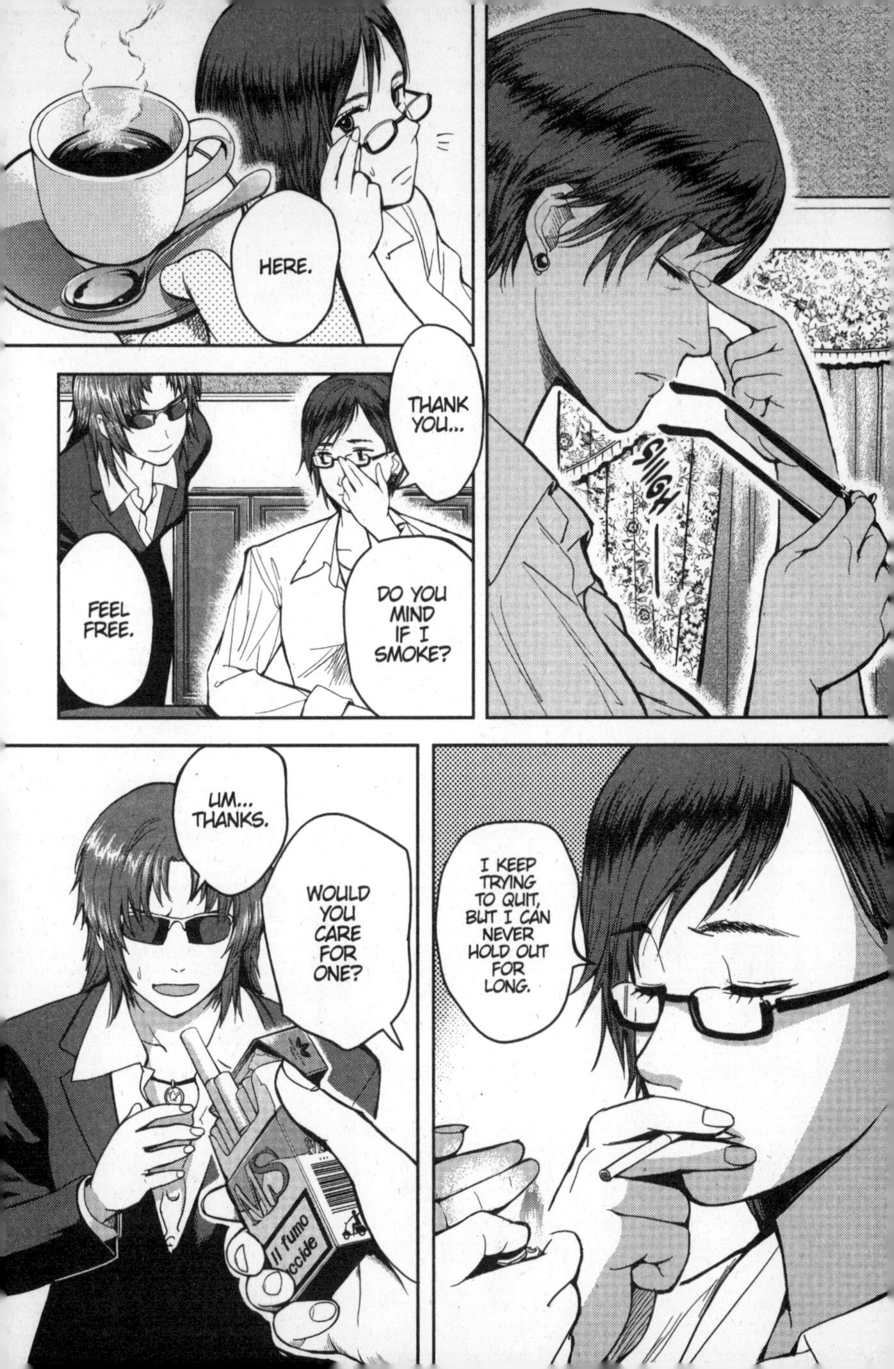
SIIIGH
HERE.
THANK YOU...
DO YOU MIND IF I SMOKE?
FEEL FREE.
I KEEP TRYING TO QUIT, BUT I CAN NEVER HOLD OUT FOR LONG.
WOULD YOU CARE FOR ONE?
UM... THANKS.

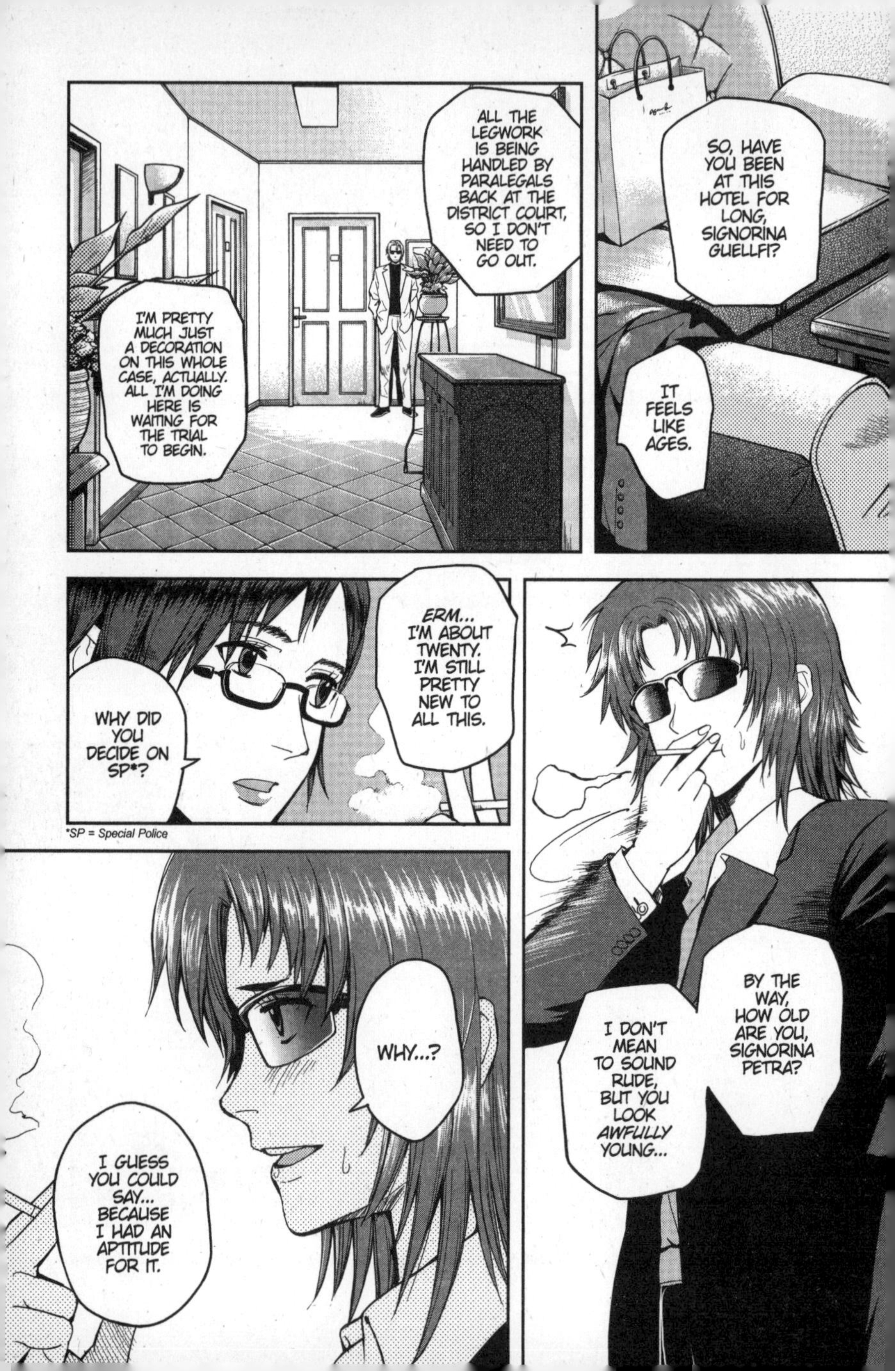
SO, HAVE YOU BEEN AT THIS HOTEL FOR LONG, SIGNORINA GUELLFI?
IT FEELS LIKE AGES.
ALL THE LEGWORK IS BEING HANDLED BY PARALEGALS BACK AT THE DISTRICT COURT, SO I DON'T NEED TO GO OUT.
I'M PRETTY MUCH JUST A DECORATION ON THIS WHOLE CASE, ACTUALLY. ALL I'M DOING HERE IS WAITING FOR THE TRIAL TO BEGIN.
BY THE WAY, HOW OLD ARE YOU, SIGNORINA PETRA?
I DON'T MEAN TO SOUND RUDE, BUT YOU LOOK *AWFULLY* YOUNG...
ERM... I'M ABOUT TWENTY. I'M STILL PRETTY NEW TO ALL THIS.
WHY DID YOU DECIDE ON SP*?
WHY...?
I GUESS YOU COULD SAY... BECAUSE I HAD AN APTITUDE FOR IT.
*SP = Special Police

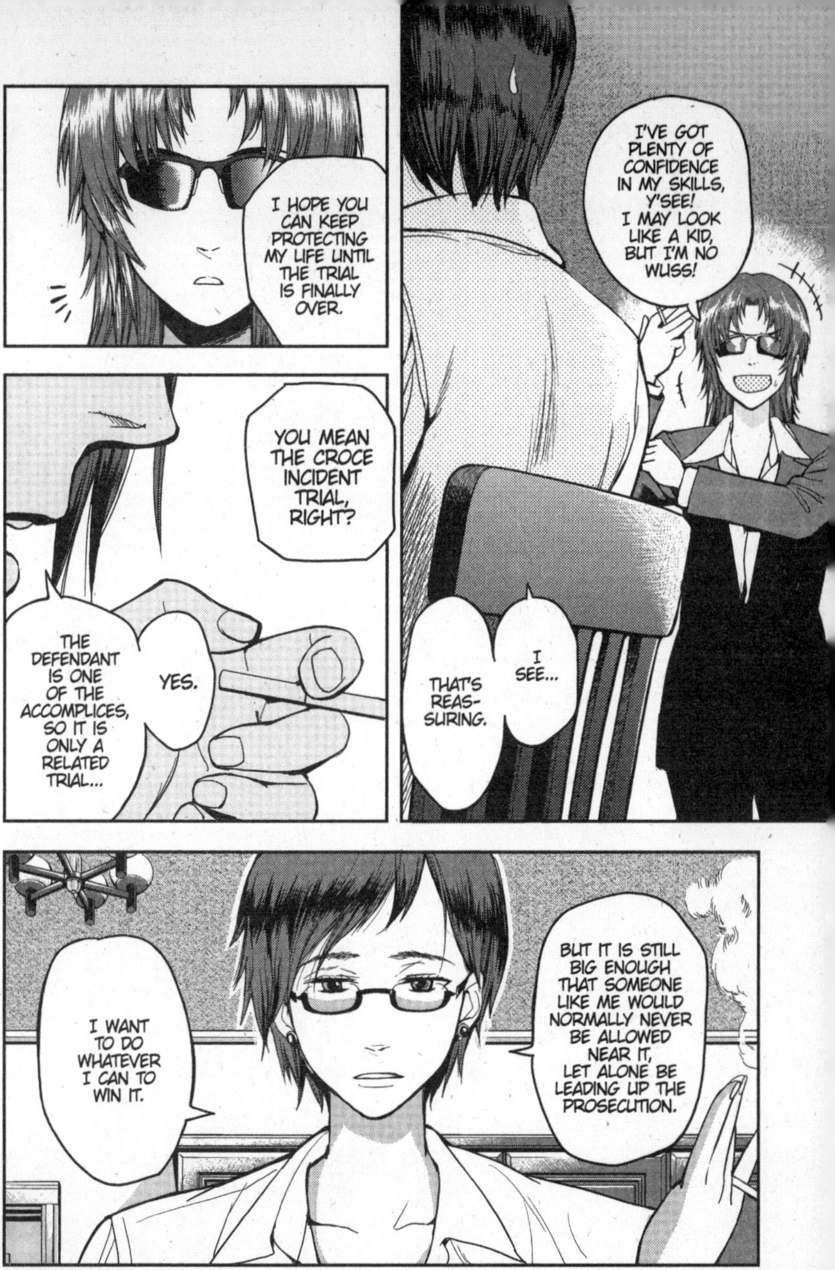
I'VE GOT PLENTY OF CONFIDENCE IN MY SKILLS, Y'SEE! I MAY LOOK LIKE A KID, BUT I'M NO WUSS!
I SEE...
THAT'S REAS-SURING.
I HOPE YOU CAN KEEP PROTECTING MY LIFE UNTIL THE TRIAL IS FINALLY OVER.
YOU MEAN THE CROCE INCIDENT TRIAL, RIGHT?
YES.
THE DEFENDANT IS ONE OF THE ACCOMPLICES, SO IT IS ONLY A RELATED TRIAL...
BUT IT IS STILL BIG ENOUGH THAT SOMEONE LIKE ME WOULD NORMALLY NEVER BE ALLOWED NEAR IT, LET ALONE BE LEADING UP THE PROSECUTION.
I WANT TO DO WHATEVER I CAN TO WIN IT.

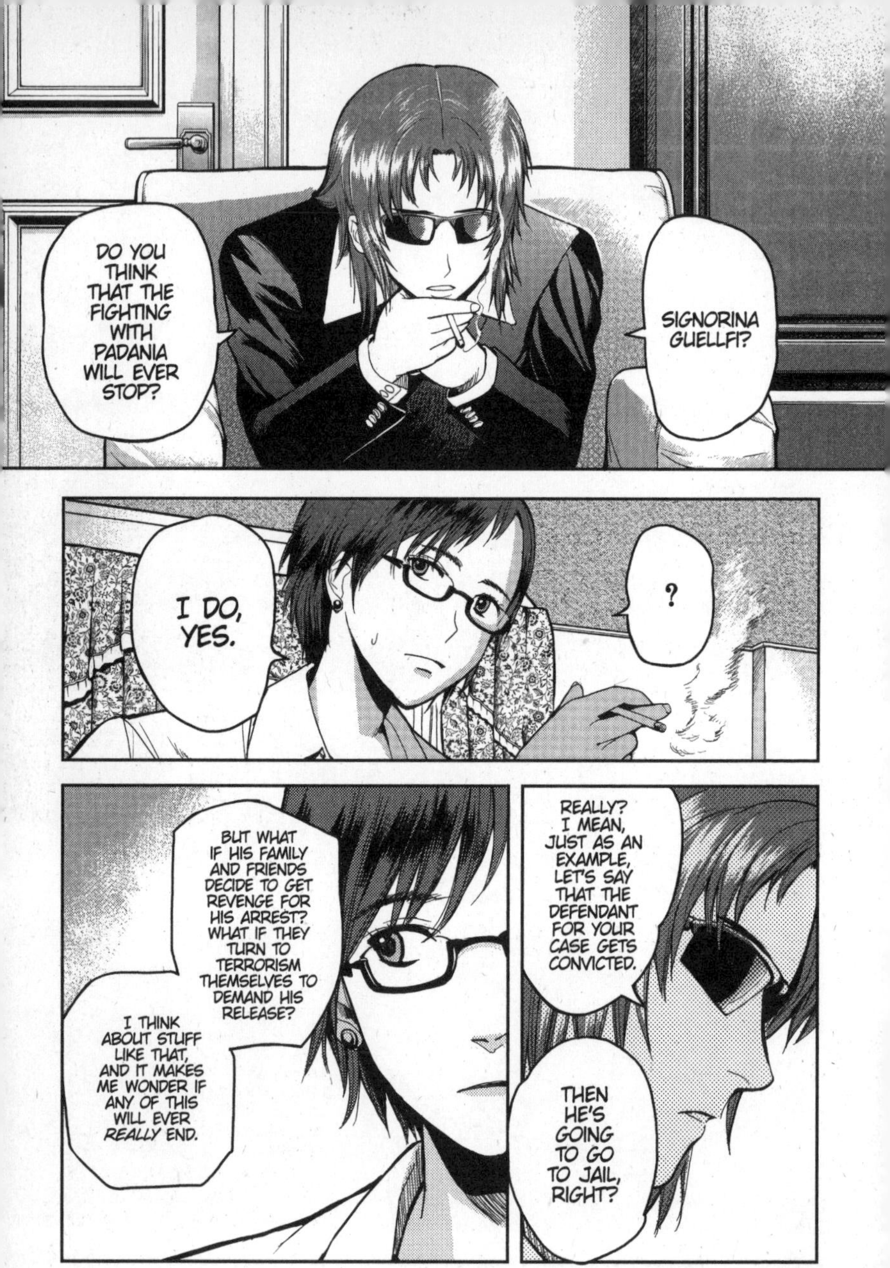
SIGNORINA GUELLFI?
DO YOU THINK THAT THE FIGHTING WITH PADANIA WILL EVER STOP?
?
I DO, YES.
REALLY? I MEAN, JUST AS AN EXAMPLE, LET'S SAY THAT THE DEFENDANT FOR YOUR CASE GETS CONVICTED.
THEN HE'S GOING TO GO TO JAIL, RIGHT?
BUT WHAT IF HIS FAMILY AND FRIENDS DECIDE TO GET REVENGE FOR HIS ARREST? WHAT IF THEY TURN TO TERRORISM THEMSELVES TO DEMAND HIS RELEASE?
I THINK ABOUT STUFF LIKE THAT, AND IT MAKES ME WONDER IF ANY OF THIS WILL EVER *REALLY* END.

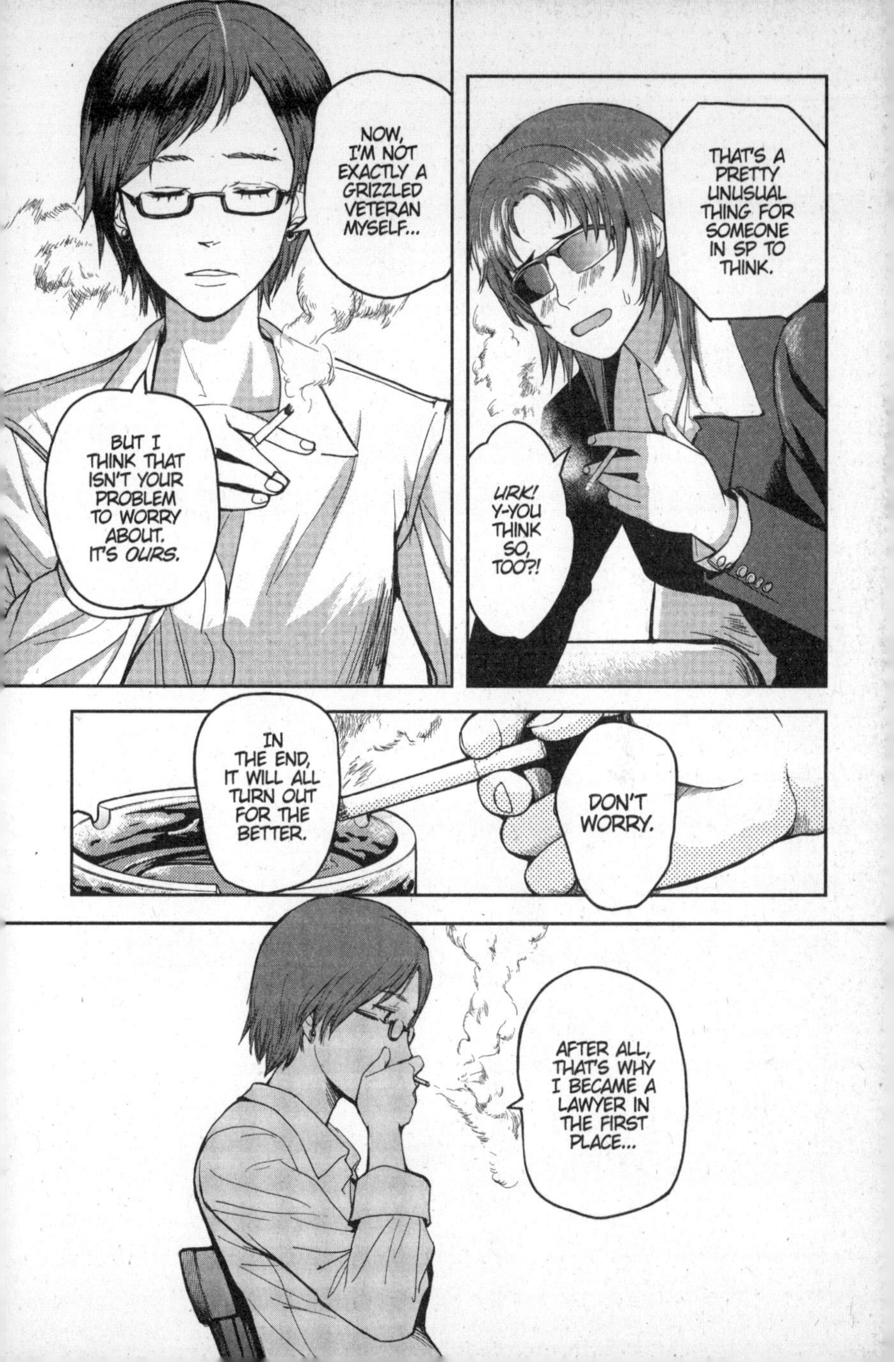
THAT'S A PRETTY UNUSUAL THING FOR SOMEONE IN SP TO THINK.
URK! Y-YOU THINK SO, TOO?!
NOW, I'M NOT EXACTLY A GRIZZLED VETERAN MYSELF...
BUT I THINK THAT ISN'T YOUR PROBLEM TO WORRY ABOUT. IT'S *OURS.*
DON'T WORRY.
IN THE END, IT WILL ALL TURN OUT FOR THE BETTER.
AFTER ALL, THAT'S WHY I BECAME A LAWYER IN THE FIRST PLACE...

GUNSLINGER GIRL.

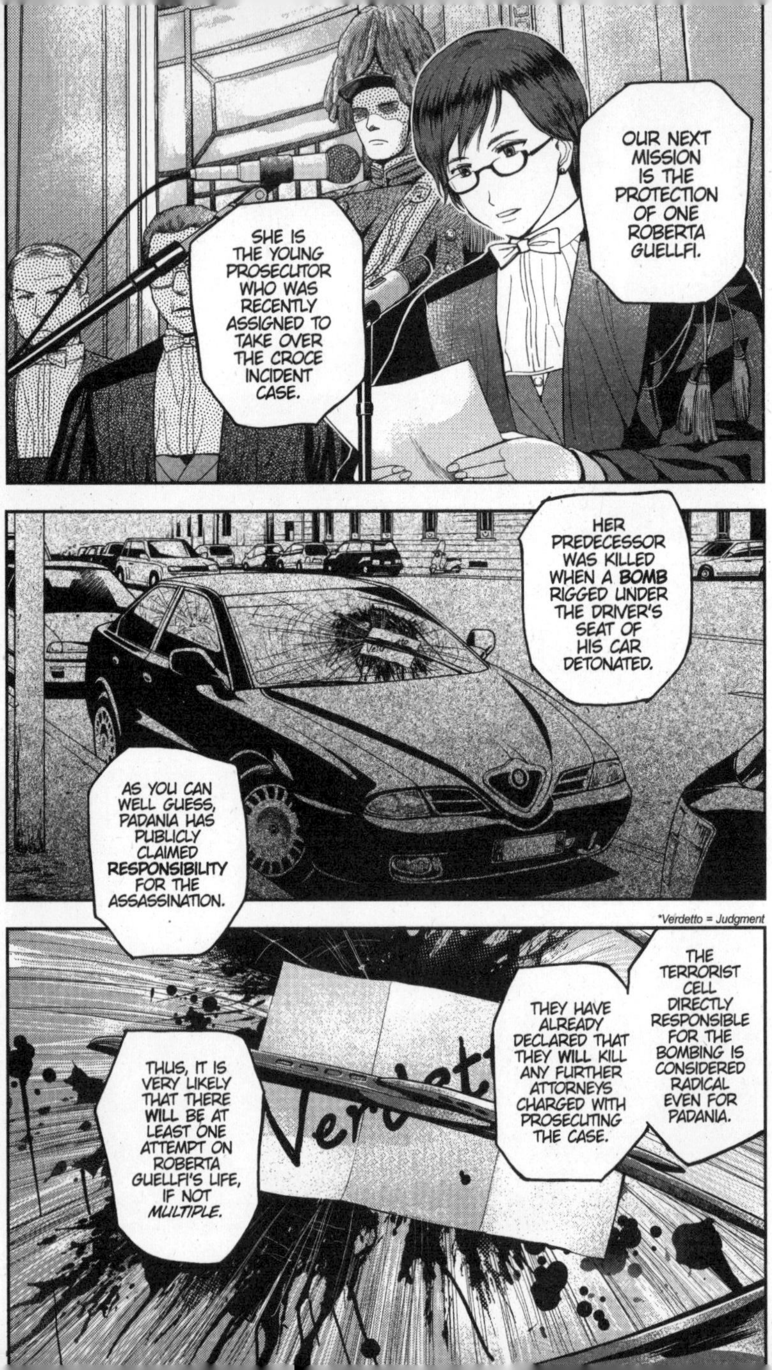
OUR NEXT MISSION IS THE PROTECTION OF ONE ROBERTA GUELLFI.
SHE IS THE YOUNG PROSECUTOR WHO WAS RECENTLY ASSIGNED TO TAKE OVER THE CROCE INCIDENT CASE.
HER PREDECESSOR WAS KILLED WHEN A **BOMB** RIGGED UNDER THE DRIVER'S SEAT OF HIS CAR DETONATED.
AS YOU CAN WELL GUESS, PADANIA HAS PUBLICLY CLAIMED **RESPONSIBILITY** FOR THE ASSASSINATION.
THE TERRORIST CELL DIRECTLY RESPONSIBLE FOR THE BOMBING IS CONSIDERED RADICAL EVEN FOR PADANIA.
THEY HAVE ALREADY DECLARED THAT THEY **WILL** KILL ANY FURTHER ATTORNEYS CHARGED WITH PROSECUTING THE CASE.
THUS, IT IS VERY LIKELY THAT THERE **WILL** BE AT LEAST ONE ATTEMPT ON ROBERTA GUELLFI'S LIFE, IF NOT *MULTIPLE*.

**Verdetto* = Judgment

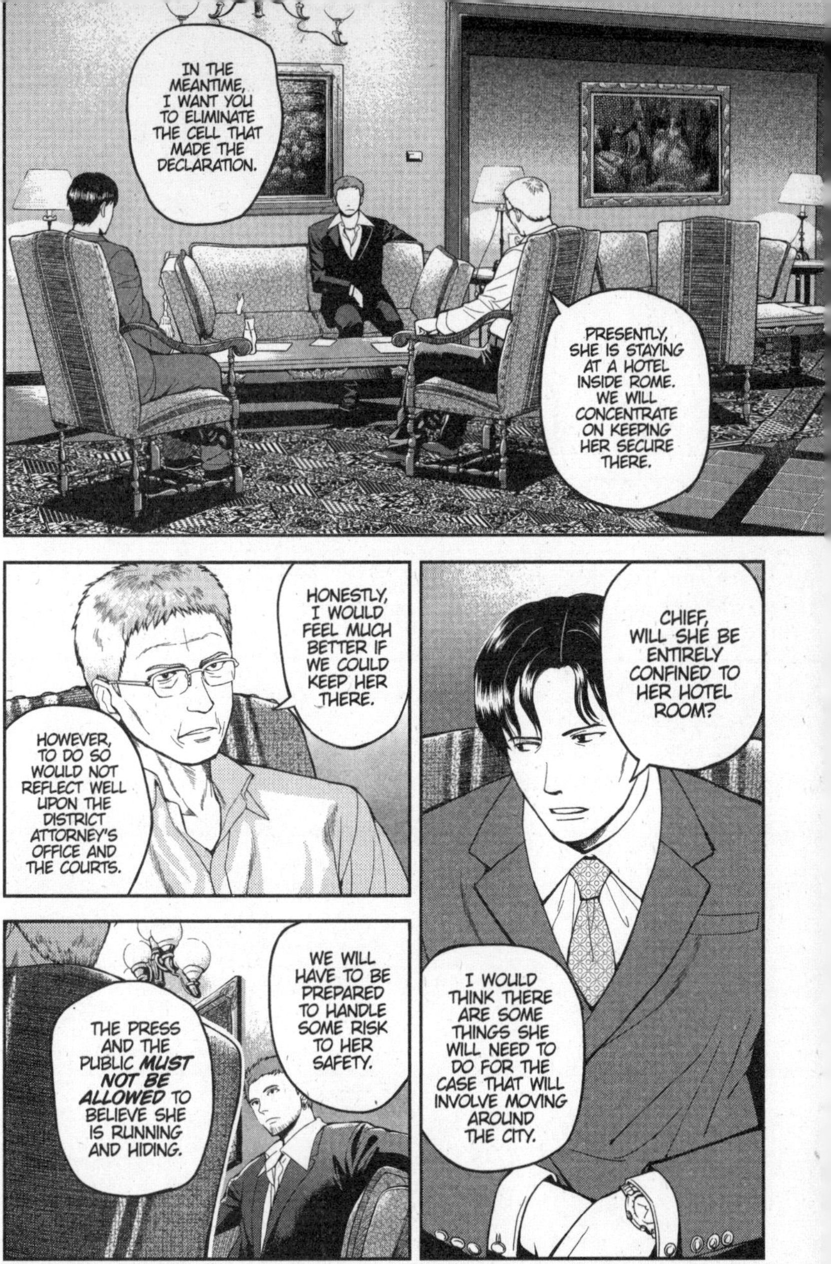

PRESENTLY, SHE IS STAYING AT A HOTEL INSIDE ROME. WE WILL CONCENTRATE ON KEEPING HER SECURE THERE.
IN THE MEANTIME, I WANT YOU TO ELIMINATE THE CELL THAT MADE THE DECLARATION.
CHIEF, WILL SHE BE ENTIRELY CONFINED TO HER HOTEL ROOM?
I WOULD THINK THERE ARE SOME THINGS SHE WILL NEED TO DO FOR THE CASE THAT WILL INVOLVE MOVING AROUND THE CITY.
HONESTLY, I WOULD FEEL MUCH BETTER IF WE COULD KEEP HER THERE.
HOWEVER, TO DO SO WOULD NOT REFLECT WELL UPON THE DISTRICT ATTORNEY'S OFFICE AND THE COURTS.
WE WILL HAVE TO BE PREPARED TO HANDLE SOME RISK TO HER SAFETY.
THE PRESS AND THE PUBLIC ***MUST NOT BE ALLOWED*** TO BELIEVE SHE IS RUNNING AND HIDING.

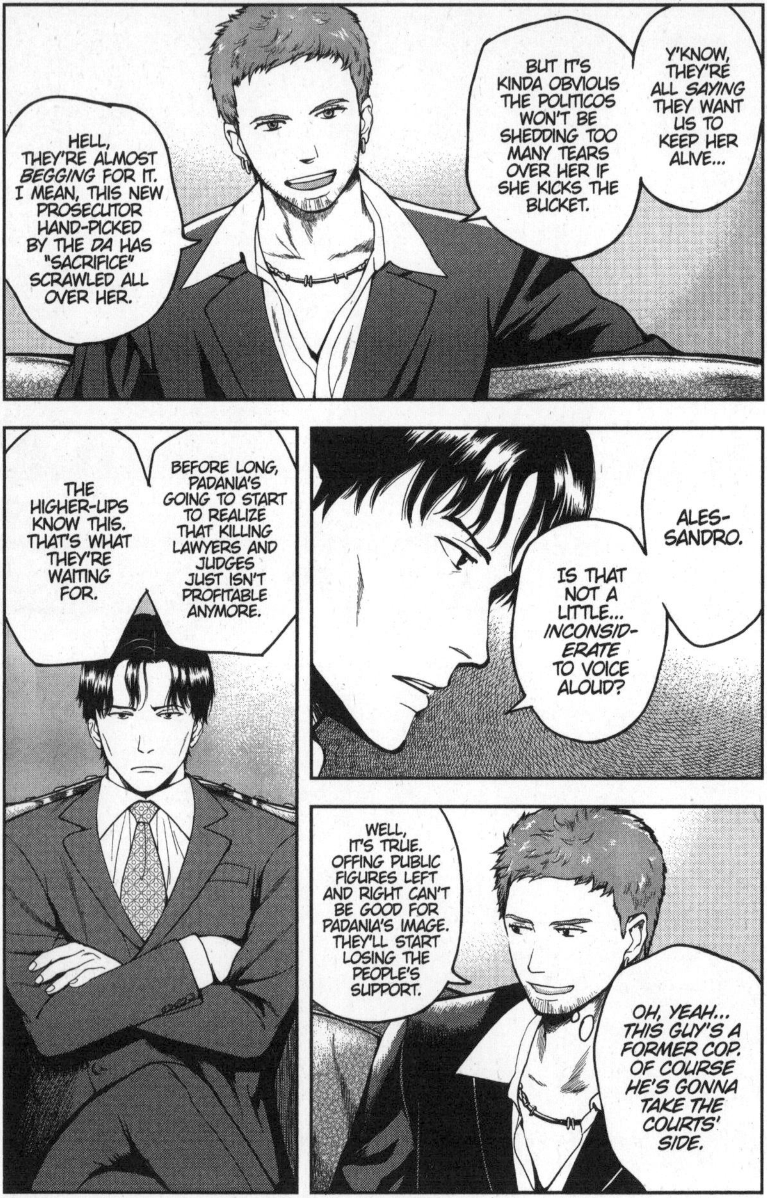
Y'KNOW, THEY'RE ALL *SAYING* THEY WANT US TO KEEP HER ALIVE...
BUT IT'S KINDA OBVIOUS THE POLITICOS WON'T BE SHEDDING TOO MANY TEARS OVER HER IF SHE KICKS THE BUCKET.
HELL, THEY'RE ALMOST *BEGGING* FOR IT. I MEAN, THIS NEW PROSECUTOR HAND-PICKED BY THE *DA* HAS "SACRIFICE" SCRAWLED ALL OVER HER.
ALES-SANDRO.
IS THAT NOT A LITTLE... *INCONSIDERATE* TO VOICE ALOUD?
WELL, IT'S TRUE. OFFING PUBLIC FIGURES LEFT AND RIGHT CAN'T BE GOOD FOR PADANIA'S IMAGE. THEY'LL START LOSING THE PEOPLE'S SUPPORT.
OH, YEAH... THIS GUY'S A FORMER COP. OF COURSE HE'S GONNA TAKE THE COURTS' SIDE.
BEFORE LONG, PADANIA'S GOING TO START TO REALIZE THAT KILLING LAWYERS AND JUDGES JUST ISN'T PROFITABLE ANYMORE.
THE HIGHER-UPS KNOW THIS. THAT'S WHAT THEY'RE WAITING FOR.

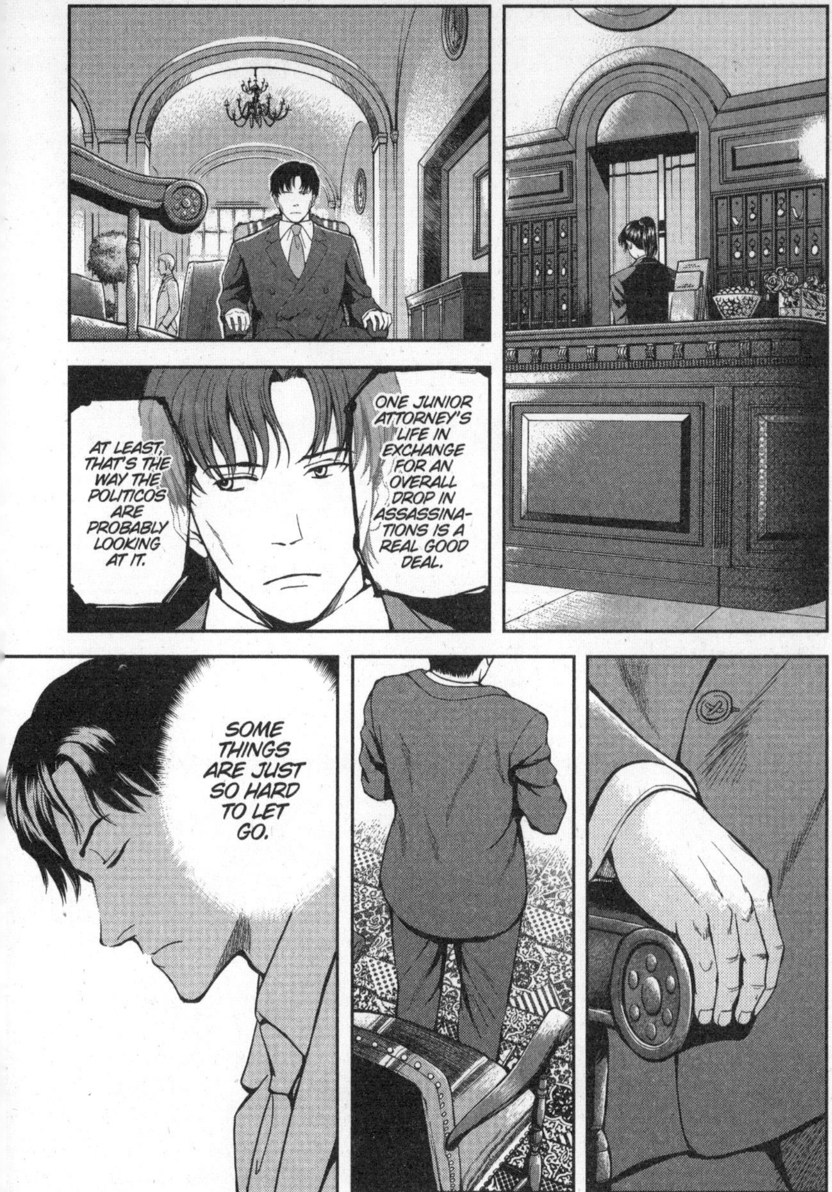
ONE JUNIOR ATTORNEY'S LIFE IN EXCHANGE FOR AN OVERALL DROP IN ASSASSINATIONS IS A REAL GOOD DEAL.
AT LEAST, THAT'S THE WAY THE POLITICOS ARE PROBABLY LOOKING AT IT.
SOME THINGS ARE JUST SO HARD TO LET GO.

CHAPTER 36: THE SHEEP AND THE GOATS

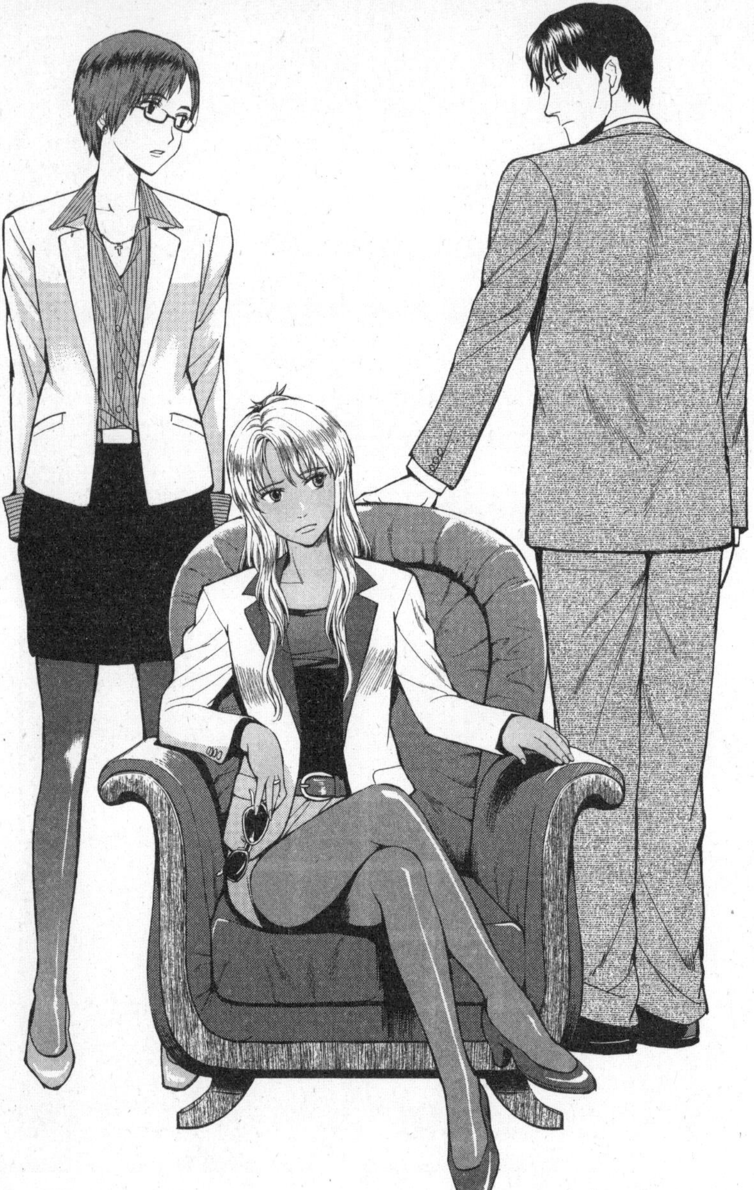

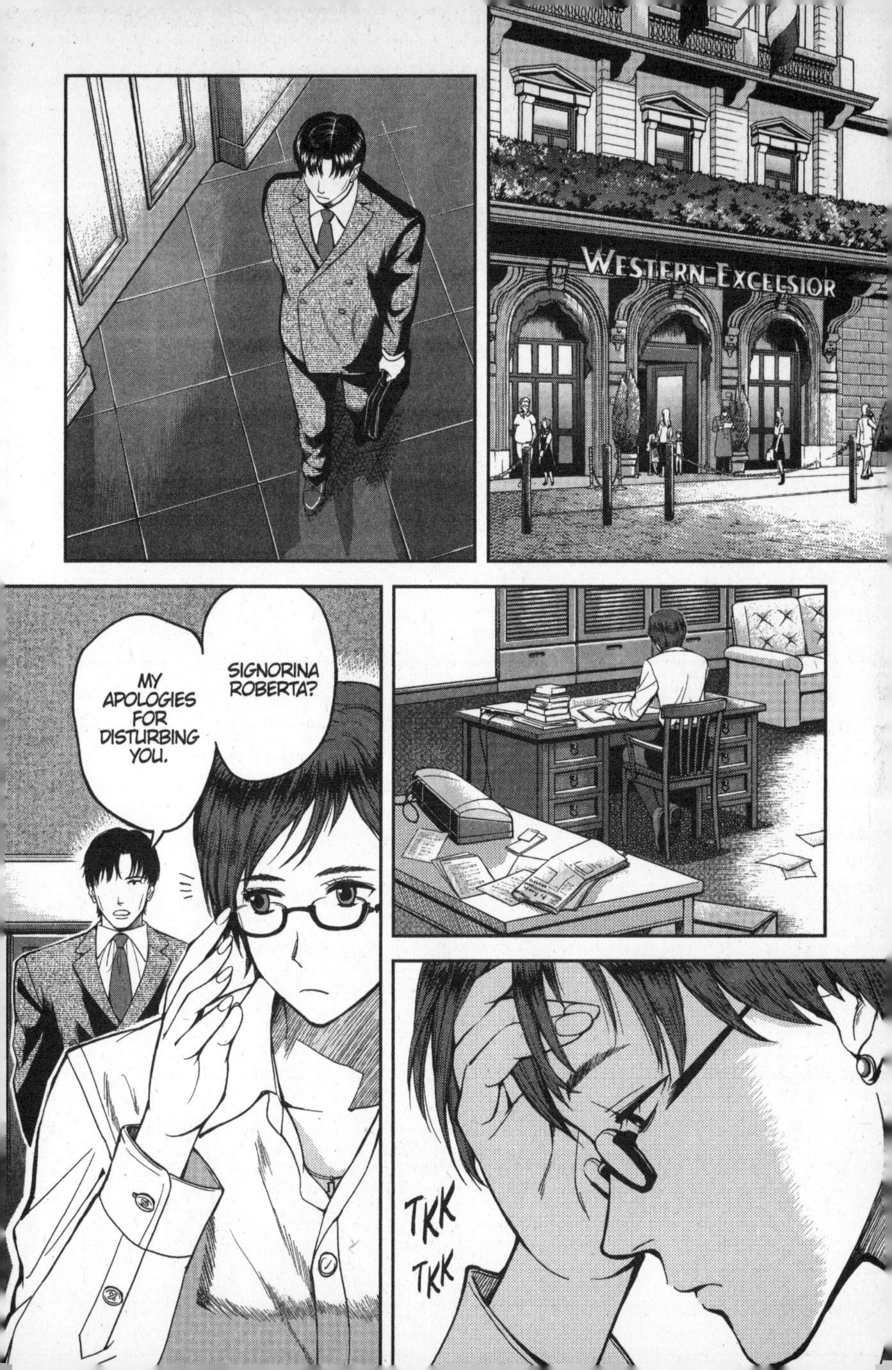
WESTERN EXCELSIOR
TKK TKK
SIGNORINA ROBERTA?
MY APOLOGIES FOR DISTURBING YOU.

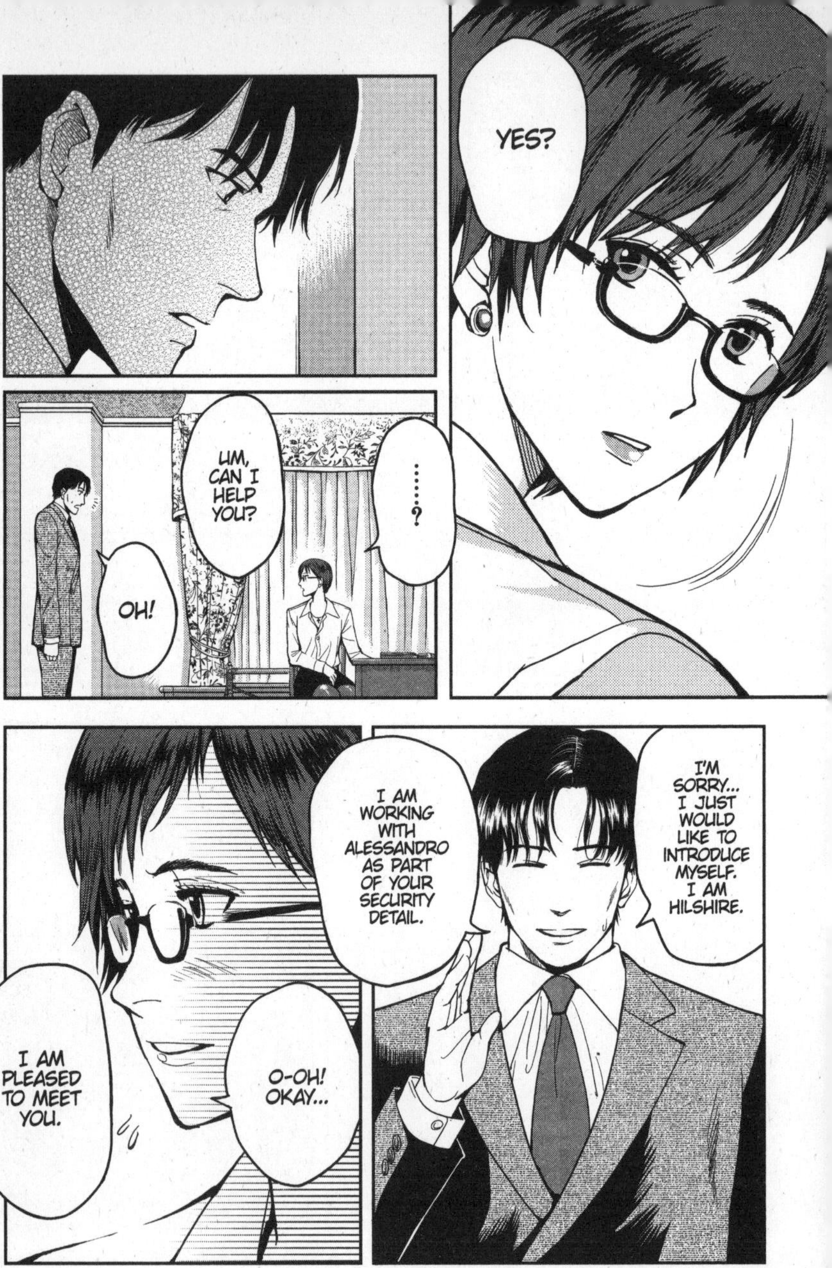
YES?
......?
UM, CAN I HELP YOU?
OH!
I'M SORRY... I JUST WOULD LIKE TO INTRODUCE MYSELF. I AM HILSHIRE.
I AM WORKING WITH ALESSANDRO AS PART OF YOUR SECURITY DETAIL.
O-OH! OKAY...
I AM PLEASED TO MEET YOU.

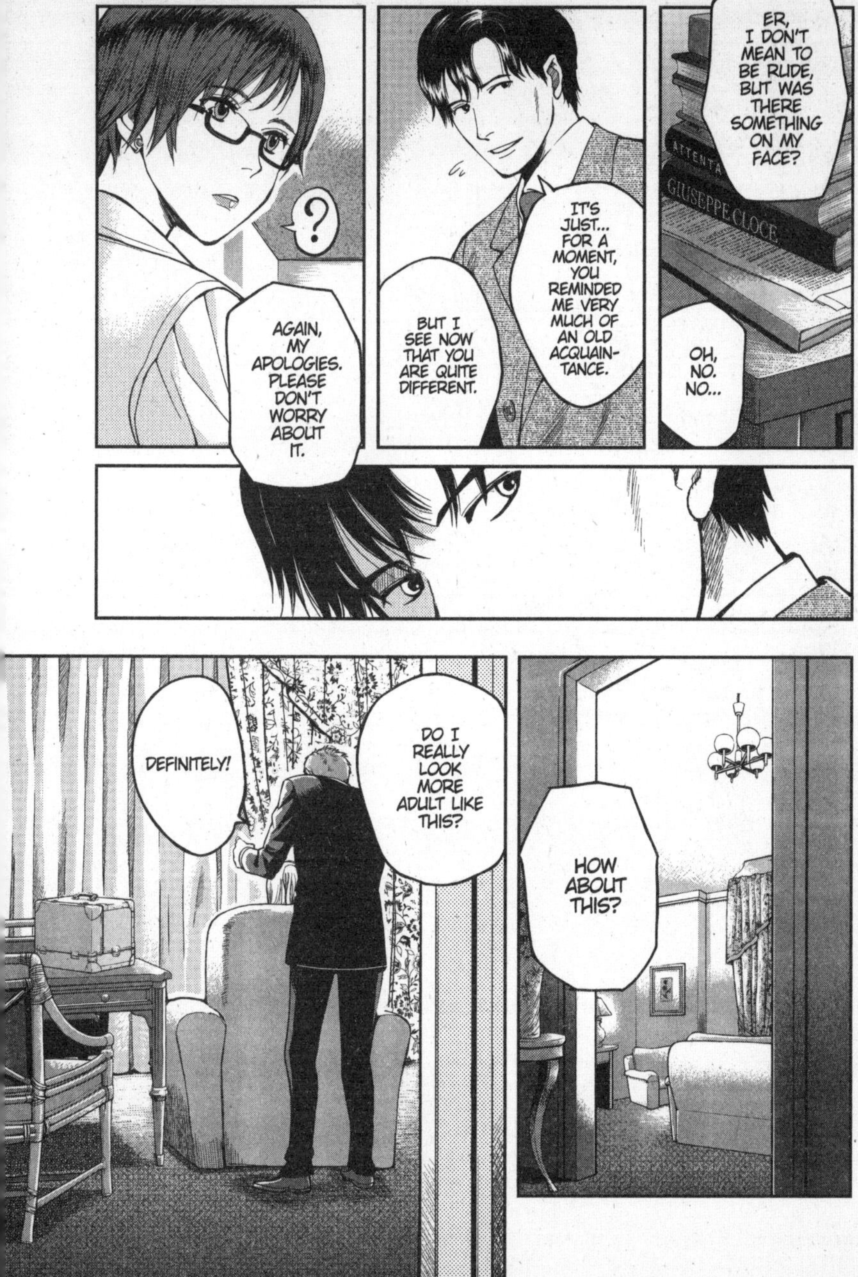
ER, I DON'T MEAN TO BE RUDE, BUT WAS THERE SOMETHING ON MY FACE?
ATTENTA
GIUSEPPE CLOCE
OH, NO. NO...
IT'S JUST... FOR A MOMENT, YOU REMINDED ME VERY MUCH OF AN OLD ACQUAINTANCE.
BUT I SEE NOW THAT YOU ARE QUITE DIFFERENT.
?
AGAIN, MY APOLOGIES. PLEASE DON'T WORRY ABOUT IT.
HOW ABOUT THIS?
DO I REALLY LOOK MORE ADULT LIKE THIS?
DEFINITELY!

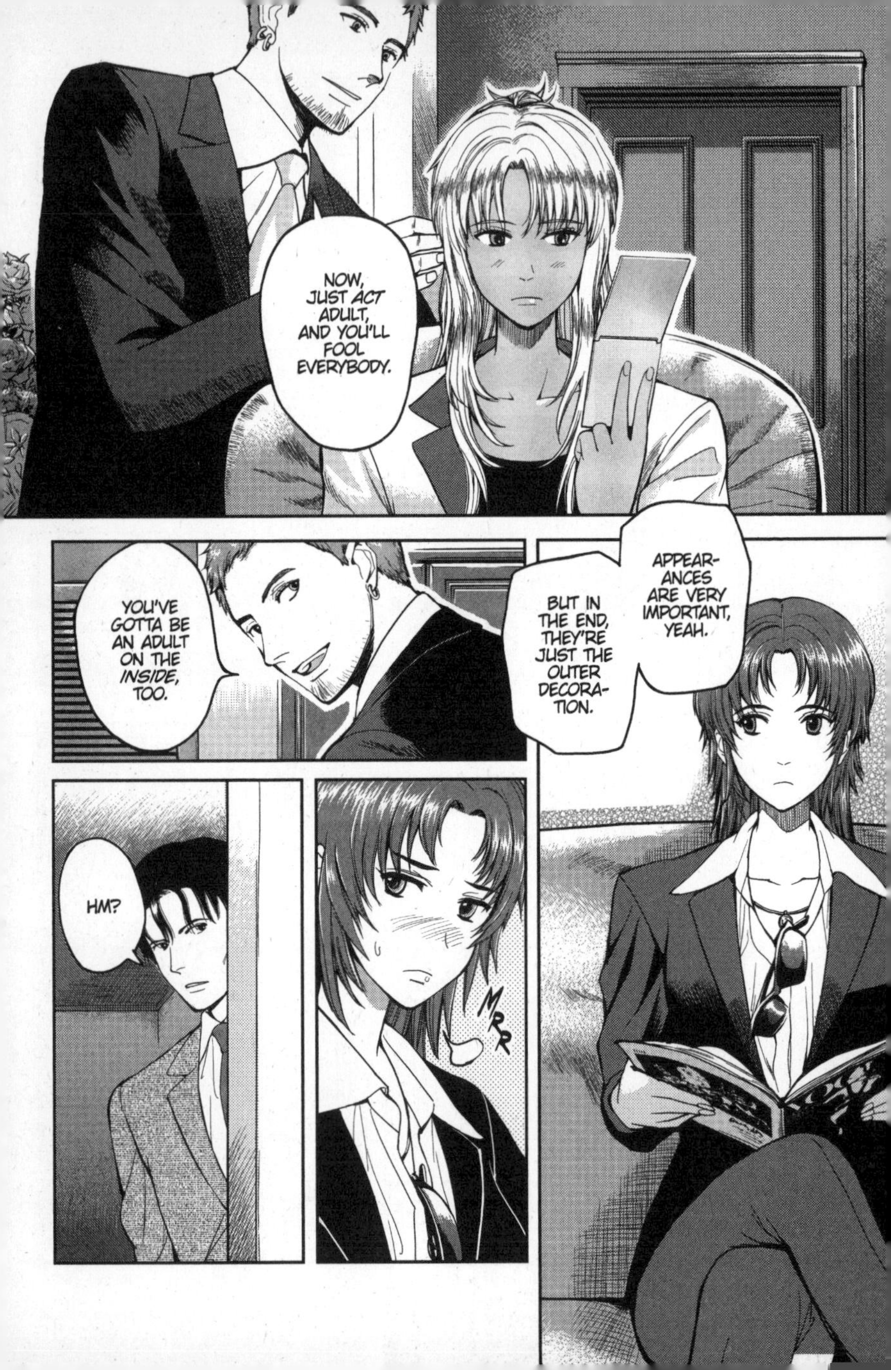
NOW, JUST ACT ADULT, AND YOU'LL FOOL EVERYBODY.
APPEAR-ANCES ARE VERY IMPORTANT, YEAH.
BUT IN THE END, THEY'RE JUST THE OUTER DECORA-TION.
YOU'VE GOTTA BE AN ADULT ON THE INSIDE, TOO.
MRR
HM?

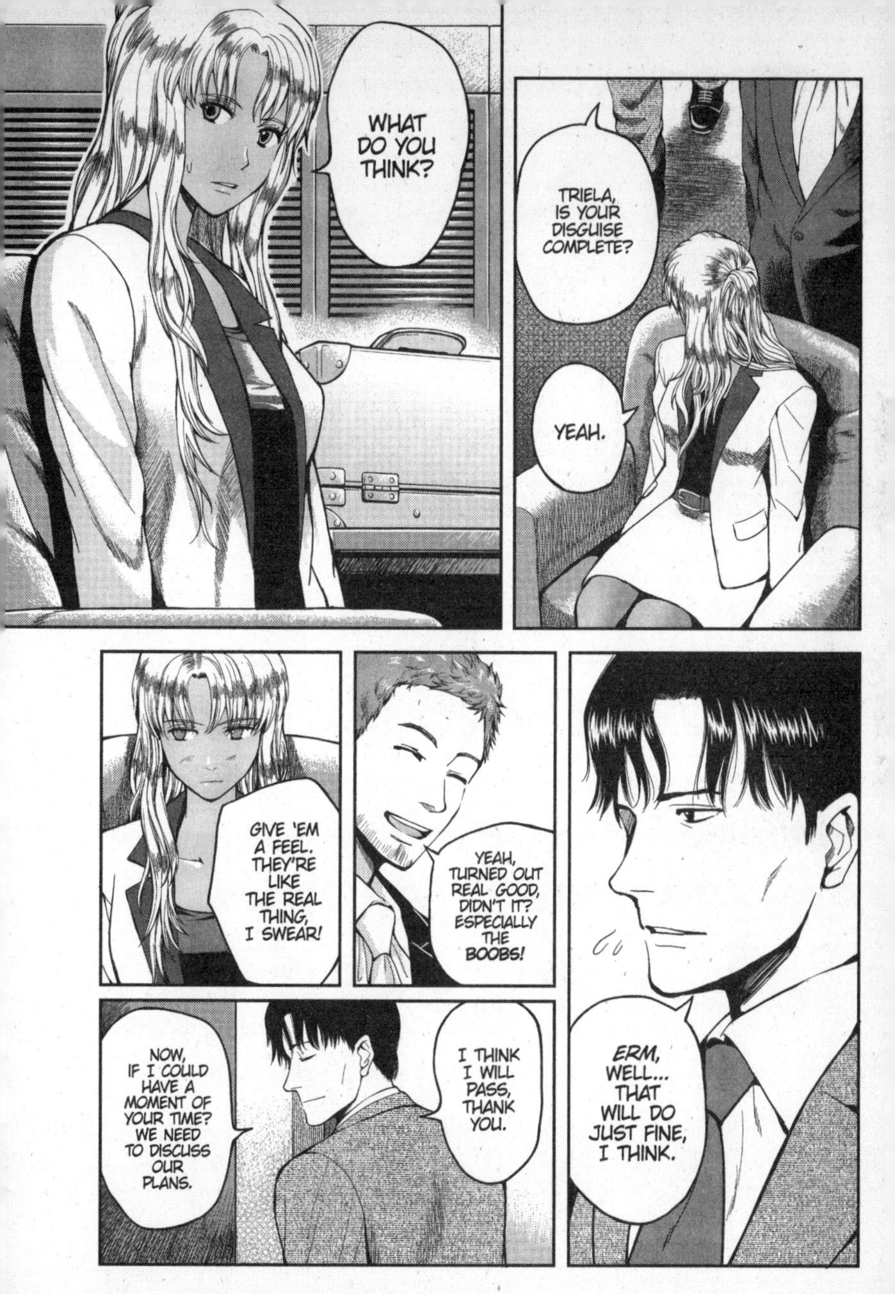
TRIELA, IS YOUR DISGUISE COMPLETE?
YEAH.
WHAT DO YOU THINK?
ERM, WELL... THAT WILL DO JUST FINE, I THINK.
YEAH, TURNED OUT REAL GOOD, DIDN'T IT? ESPECIALLY THE BOOBS!
GIVE 'EM A FEEL. THEY'RE LIKE THE REAL THING, I SWEAR!
I THINK I WILL PASS, THANK YOU.
NOW, IF I COULD HAVE A MOMENT OF YOUR TIME? WE NEED TO DISCUSS OUR PLANS.

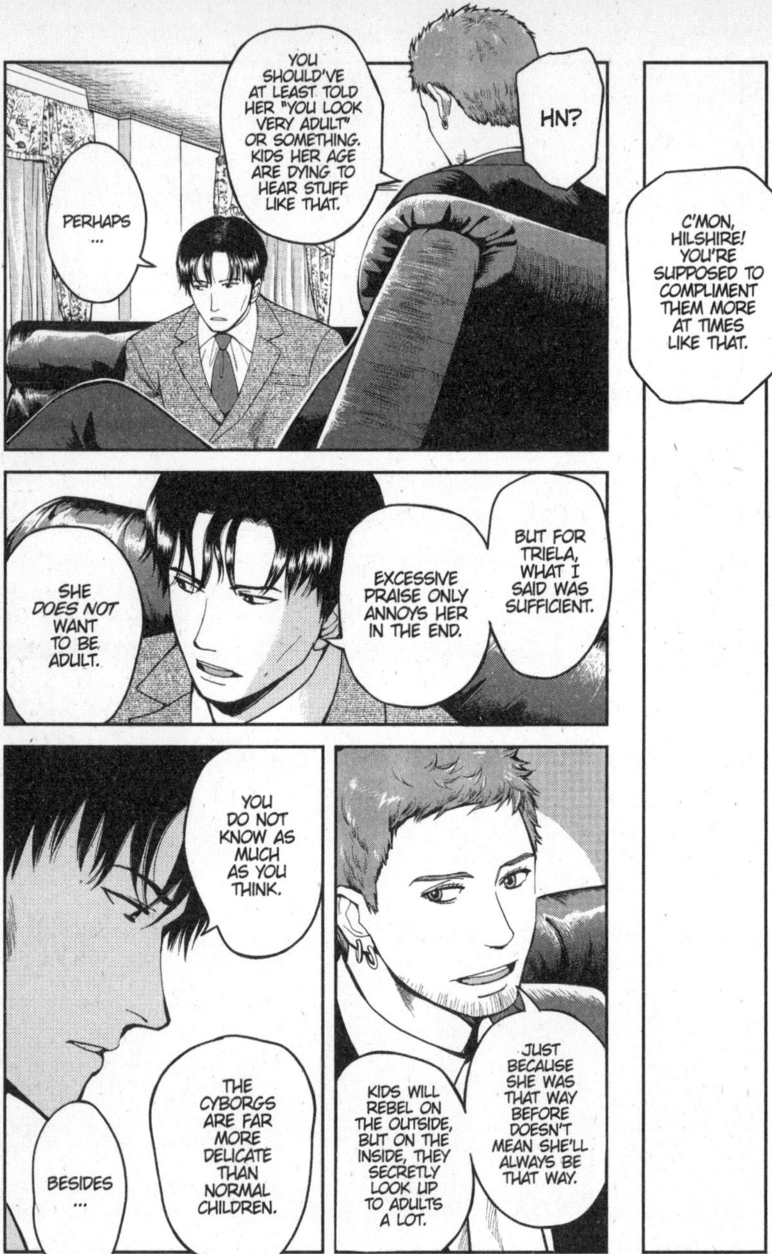
C'MON, HILSHIRE! YOU'RE SUPPOSED TO COMPLIMENT THEM MORE AT TIMES LIKE THAT.
HN?
YOU SHOULD'VE AT LEAST TOLD HER "YOU LOOK VERY ADULT" OR SOMETHING. KIDS HER AGE ARE DYING TO HEAR STUFF LIKE THAT.
PERHAPS ...
BUT FOR TRIELA, WHAT I SAID WAS SUFFICIENT.
EXCESSIVE PRAISE ONLY ANNOYS HER IN THE END.
SHE *DOES NOT* WANT TO BE ADULT.
JUST BECAUSE SHE WAS THAT WAY BEFORE DOESN'T MEAN SHE'LL ALWAYS BE THAT WAY.
KIDS WILL REBEL ON THE OUTSIDE, BUT ON THE INSIDE, THEY SECRETLY LOOK UP TO ADULTS A LOT.
YOU DO NOT KNOW AS MUCH AS YOU THINK.
THE CYBORGS ARE FAR MORE DELICATE THAN NORMAL CHILDREN.
BESIDES ...

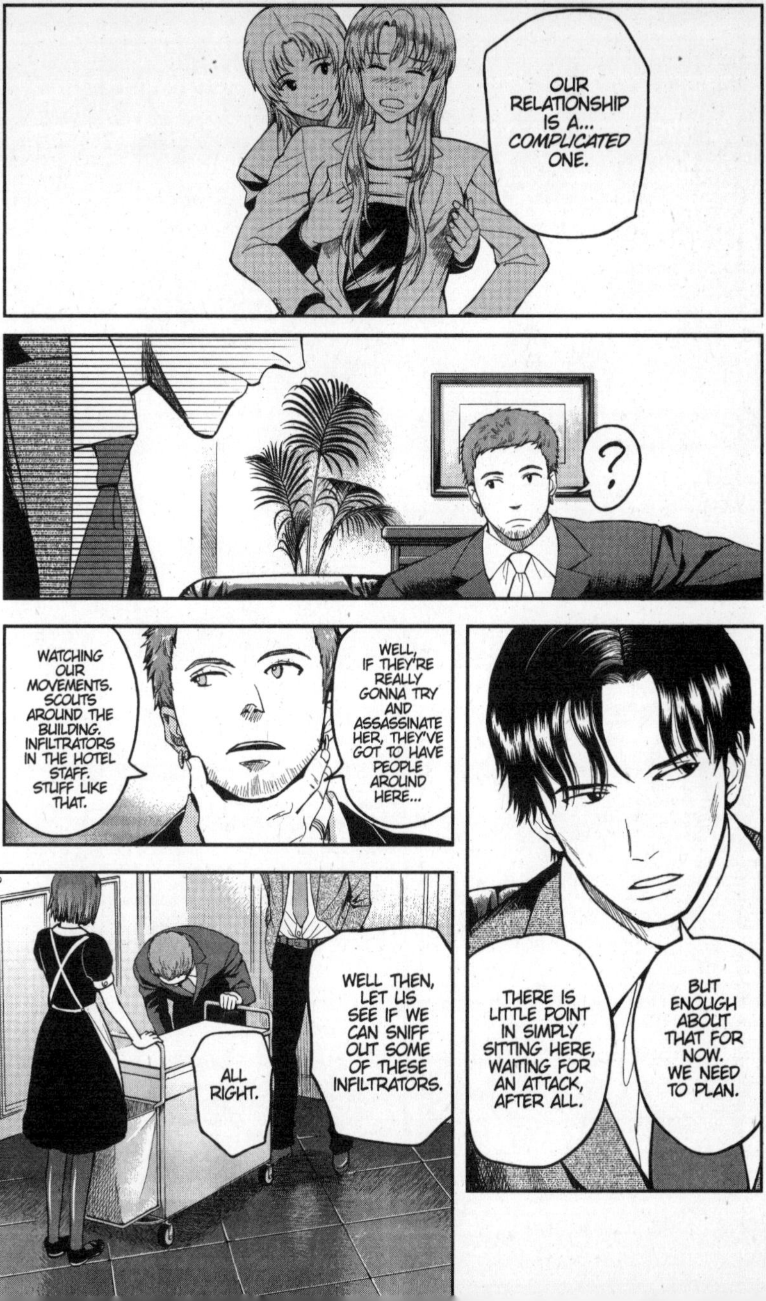
OUR RELATIONSHIP IS A... COMPLICATED ONE.
?
BUT ENOUGH ABOUT THAT FOR NOW. WE NEED TO PLAN.
THERE IS LITTLE POINT IN SIMPLY SITTING HERE, WAITING FOR AN ATTACK, AFTER ALL.
WELL, IF THEY'RE REALLY GONNA TRY AND ASSASSINATE HER, THEY'VE GOT TO HAVE PEOPLE AROUND HERE...
WATCHING OUR MOVEMENTS. SCOUTS AROUND THE BUILDING. INFILTRATORS IN THE HOTEL STAFF. STUFF LIKE THAT.
WELL THEN, LET US SEE IF WE CAN SNIFF OUT SOME OF THESE INFILTRATORS.
ALL RIGHT.

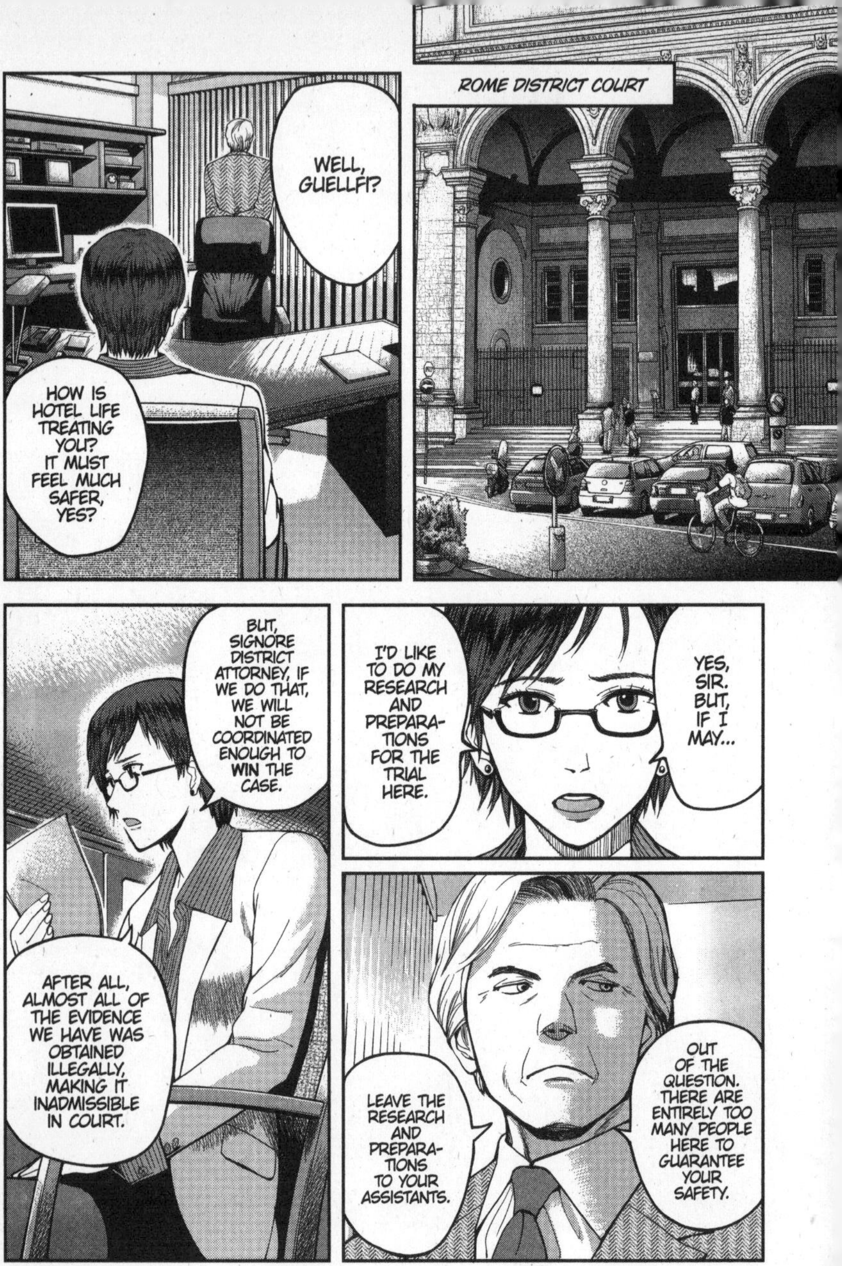
ROME DISTRICT COURT
WELL, GUELLFI?
HOW IS HOTEL LIFE TREATING YOU? IT MUST FEEL MUCH SAFER, YES?
YES, SIR. BUT, IF I MAY...
I'D LIKE TO DO MY RESEARCH AND PREPARATIONS FOR THE TRIAL HERE.
OUT OF THE QUESTION. THERE ARE ENTIRELY TOO MANY PEOPLE HERE TO GUARANTEE YOUR SAFETY.
LEAVE THE RESEARCH AND PREPARATIONS TO YOUR ASSISTANTS.
BUT, SIGNORE DISTRICT ATTORNEY, IF WE DO THAT, WE WILL NOT BE COORDINATED ENOUGH TO WIN THE CASE.
AFTER ALL, ALMOST ALL OF THE EVIDENCE WE HAVE WAS OBTAINED ILLEGALLY, MAKING IT INADMISSIBLE IN COURT.

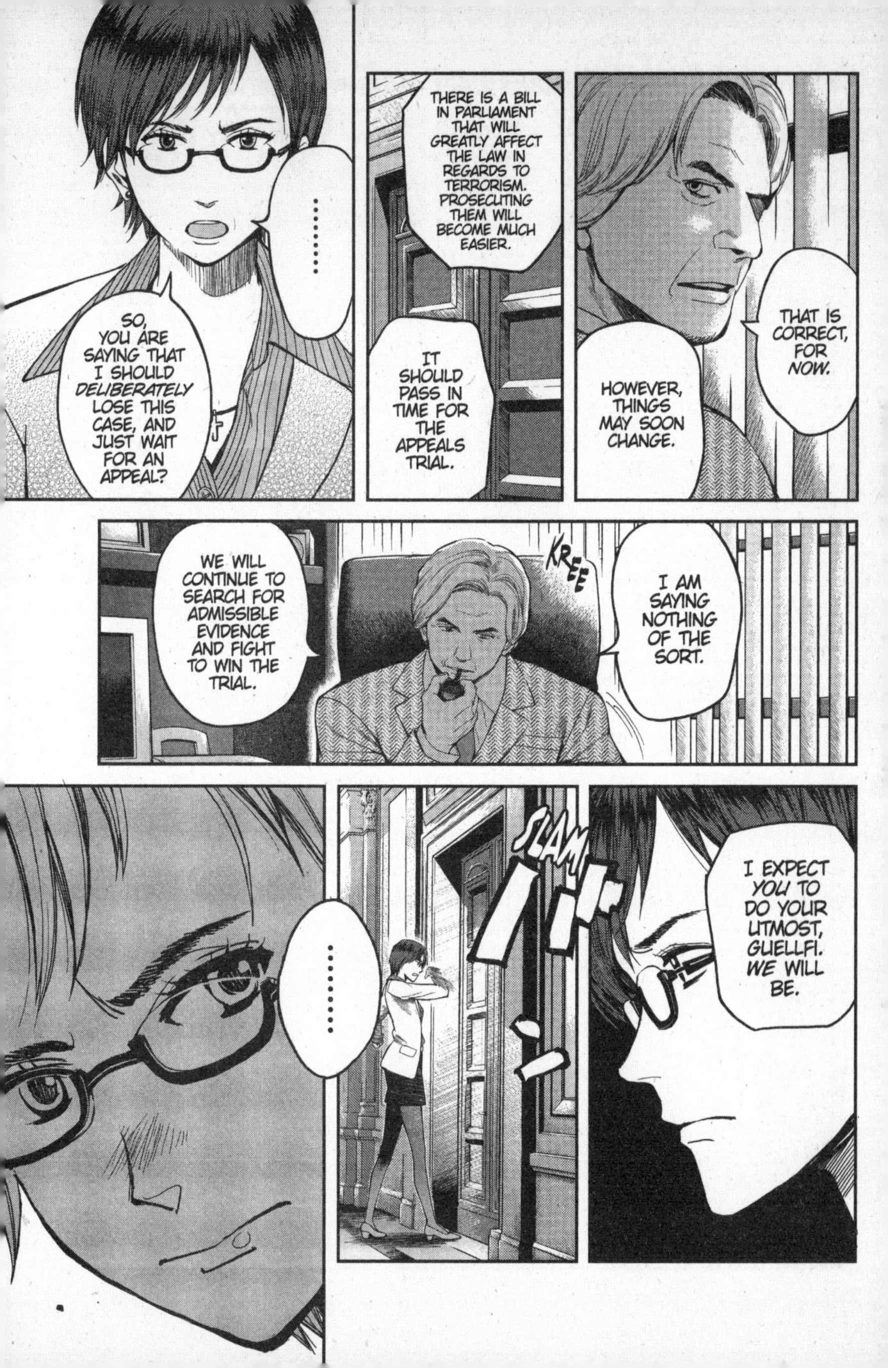
THAT IS CORRECT, FOR *NOW.*
HOWEVER, THINGS MAY SOON CHANGE.
THERE IS A BILL IN PARLIAMENT THAT WILL GREATLY AFFECT THE LAW IN REGARDS TO TERRORISM. PROSECUTING THEM WILL BECOME MUCH EASIER.
IT SHOULD PASS IN TIME FOR THE APPEALS TRIAL.
......
SO, YOU ARE SAYING THAT I SHOULD *DELIBERATELY* LOSE THIS CASE, AND JUST WAIT FOR AN APPEAL?
I AM SAYING NOTHING OF THE SORT.
KREE
WE WILL CONTINUE TO SEARCH FOR ADMISSIBLE EVIDENCE AND FIGHT TO WIN THE TRIAL.
I EXPECT *YOU* TO DO YOUR UTMOST, GUELLFI. *WE* WILL BE.
SLAM
....

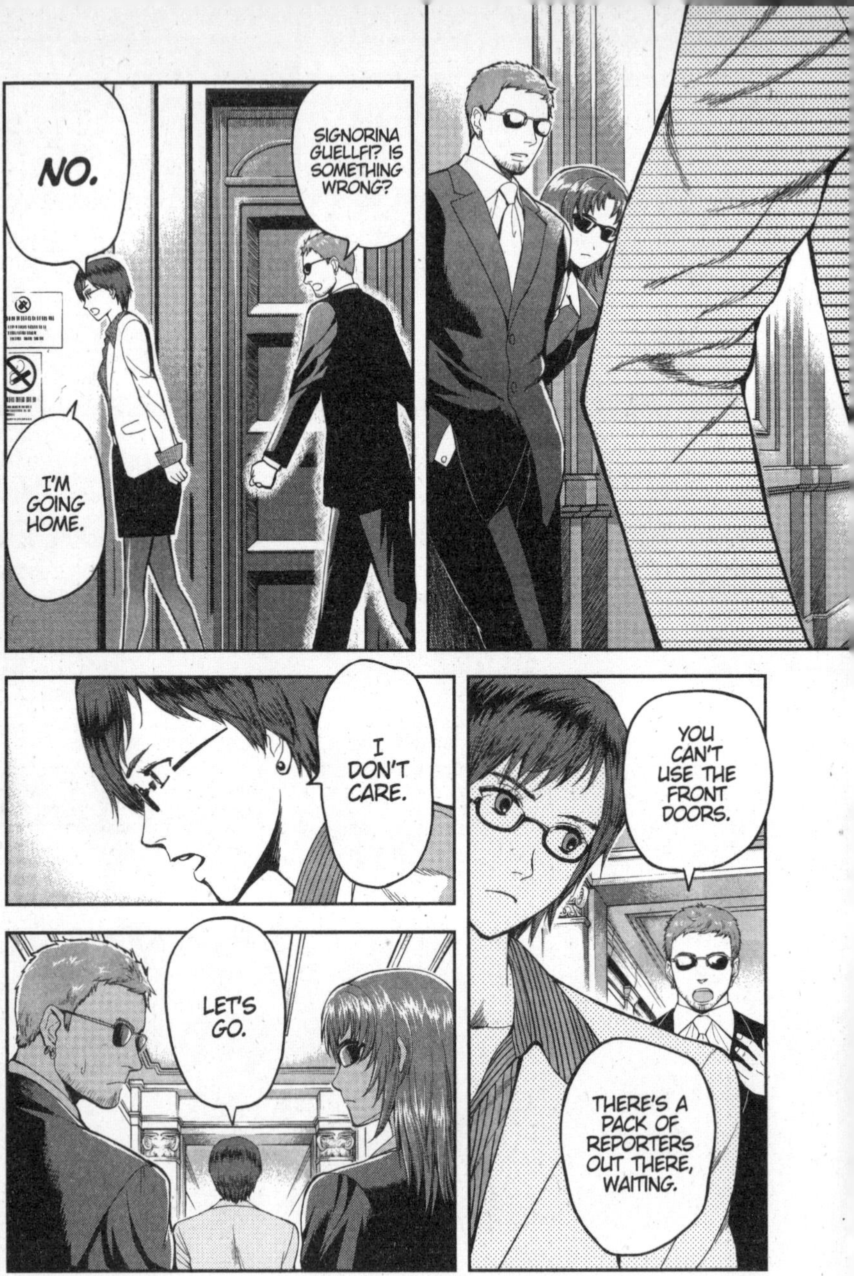
SIGNORINA GUELLFI? IS SOMETHING WRONG?
NO.
I'M GOING HOME.
YOU CAN'T USE THE FRONT DOORS.
THERE'S A PACK OF REPORTERS OUT THERE, WAITING.
I DON'T CARE.
LET'S GO.

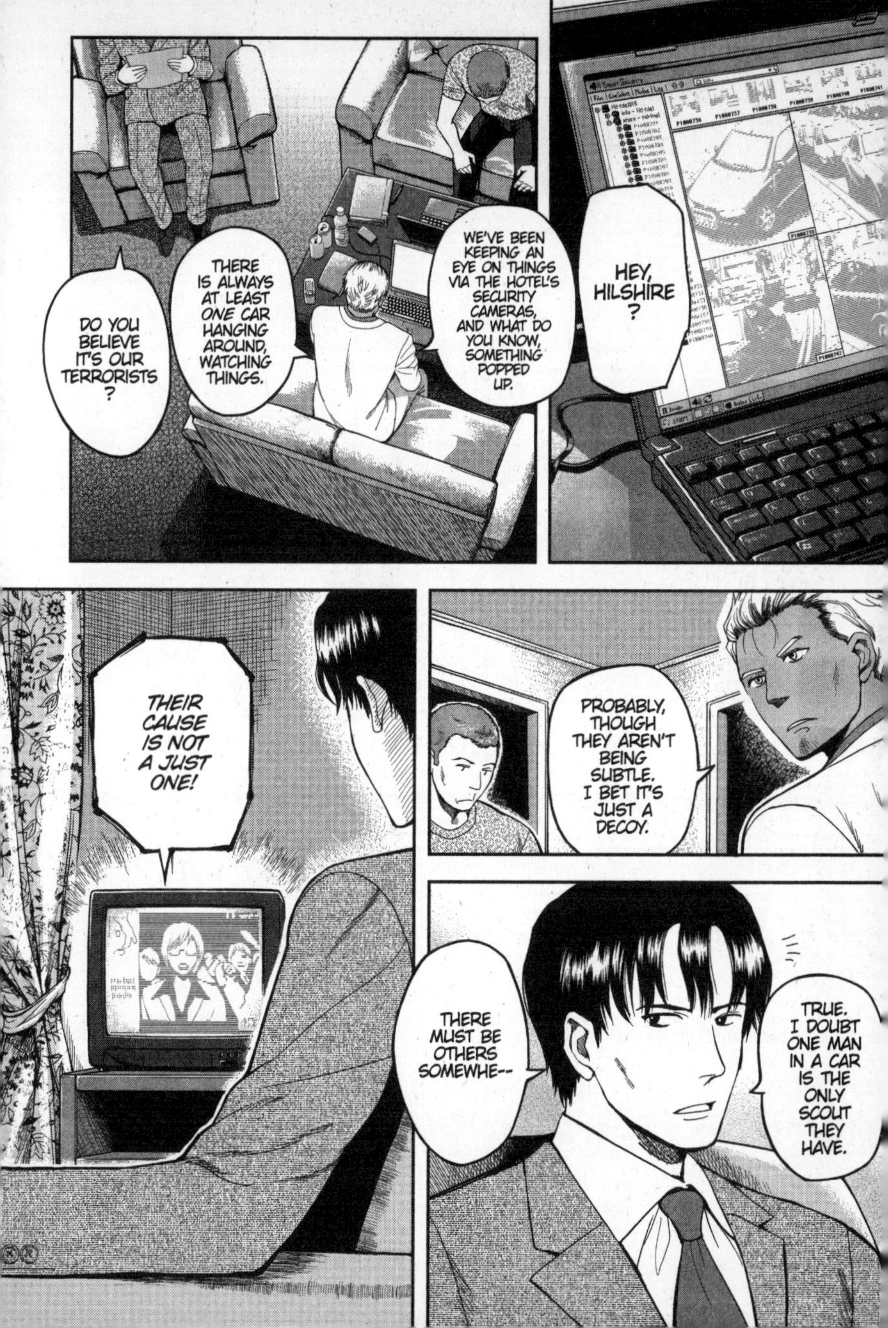
HEY, HILSHIRE?
WE'VE BEEN KEEPING AN EYE ON THINGS VIA THE HOTEL'S SECURITY CAMERAS, AND WHAT DO YOU KNOW, SOMETHING POPPED UP.
THERE IS ALWAYS AT LEAST ONE CAR HANGING AROUND, WATCHING THINGS.
DO YOU BELIEVE IT'S OUR TERRORISTS?
PROBABLY, THOUGH THEY AREN'T BEING SUBTLE. I BET IT'S JUST A DECOY.
TRUE. I DOUBT ONE MAN IN A CAR IS THE ONLY SCOUT THEY HAVE.
THERE MUST BE OTHERS SOMEWHE--
THEIR CAUSE IS NOT A JUST ONE!

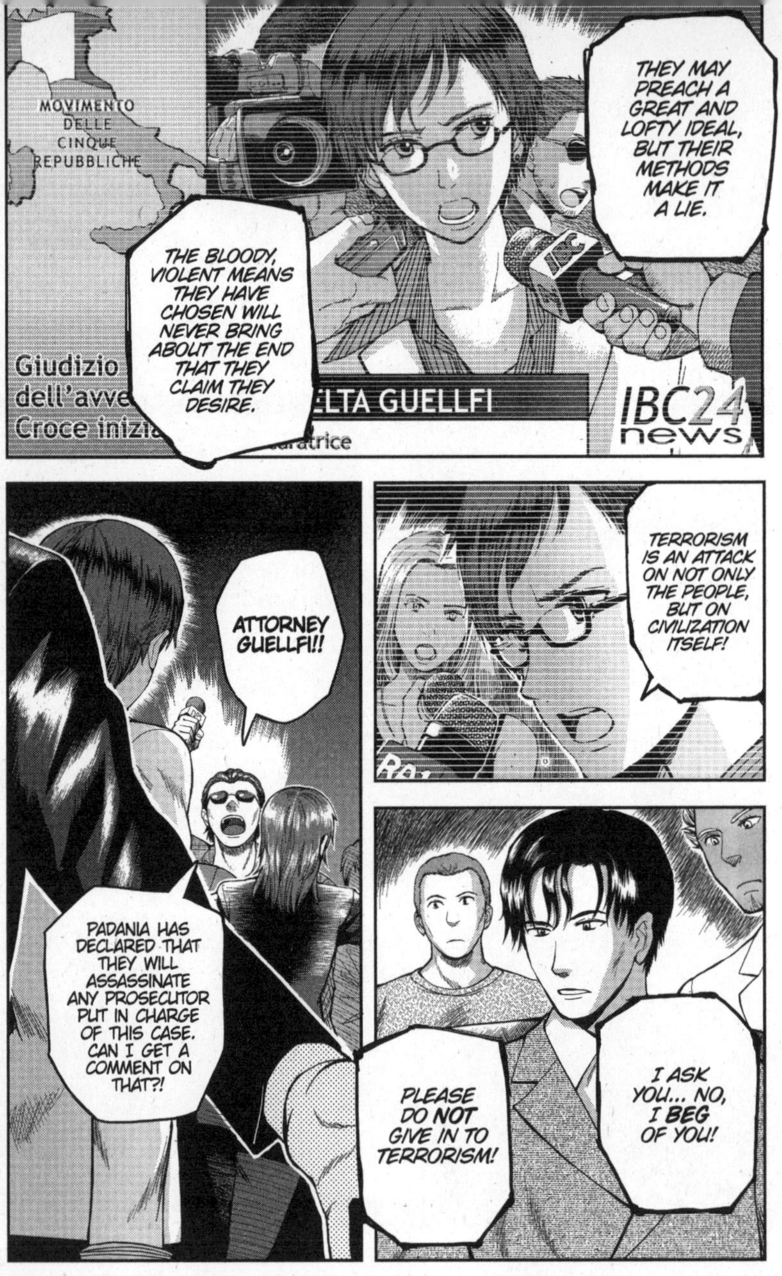
THEY MAY PREACH A GREAT AND LOFTY IDEAL, BUT THEIR METHODS MAKE IT A LIE.
THE BLOODY, VIOLENT MEANS THEY HAVE CHOSEN WILL NEVER BRING ABOUT THE END THAT THEY CLAIM THEY DESIRE.
MOVIMENTO DELLE CINQUE REPUBBLICHE
Giudizio
IBC24 news
TERRORISM IS AN ATTACK ON NOT ONLY THE PEOPLE, BUT ON CIVILIZATION ITSELF!
I ASK YOU... NO, I **BEG** OF YOU!
PLEASE DO **NOT** GIVE IN TO TERRORISM!
ATTORNEY GUELLFI!!
PADANIA HAS DECLARED THAT THEY WILL ASSASSINATE ANY PROSECUTOR PUT IN CHARGE OF THIS CASE. CAN I GET A COMMENT ON THAT?!

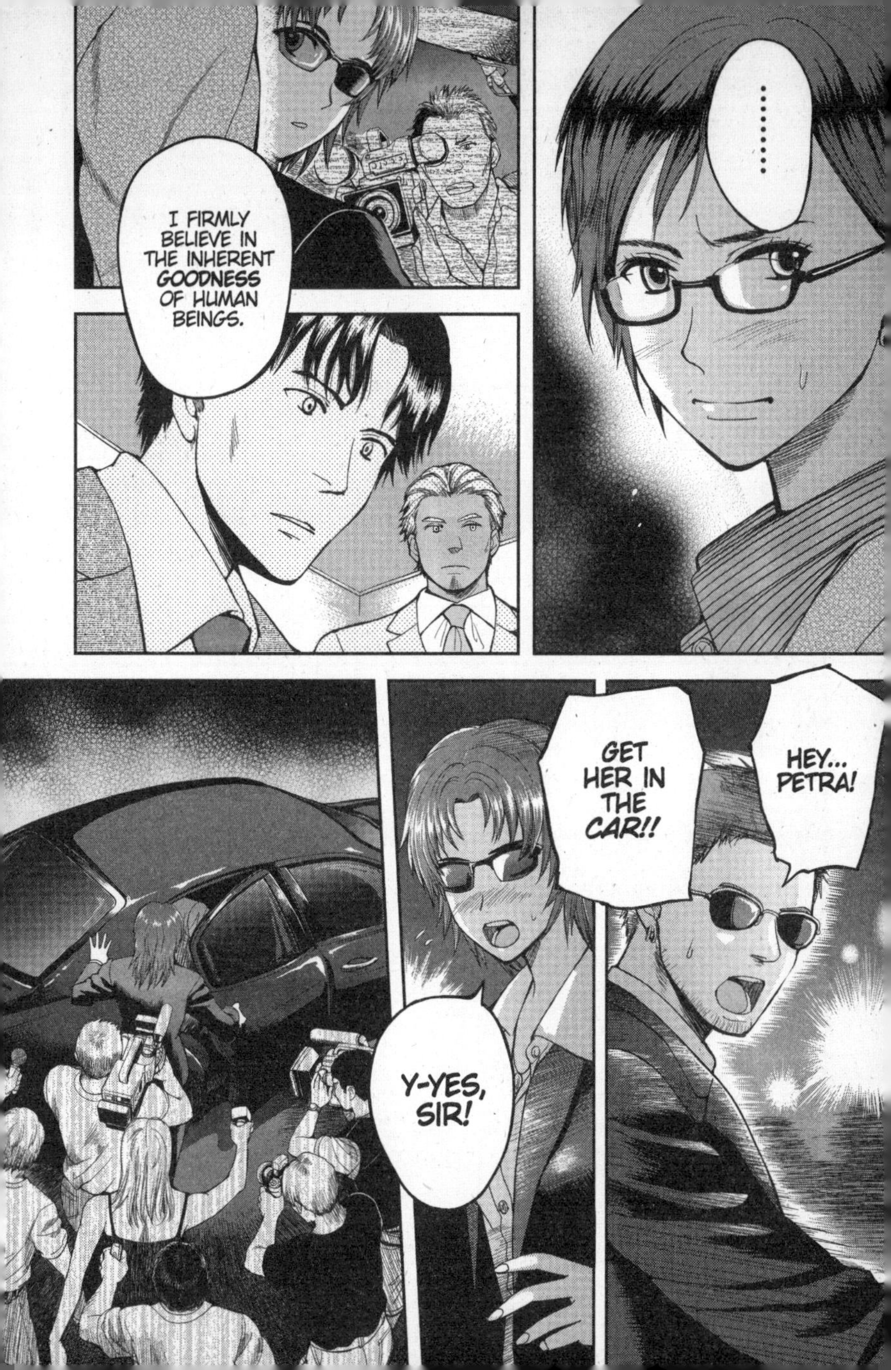
......
I FIRMLY BELIEVE IN THE INHERENT GOODNESS OF HUMAN BEINGS.
HEY... PETRA!
GET HER IN THE CAR!!
Y-YES, SIR!

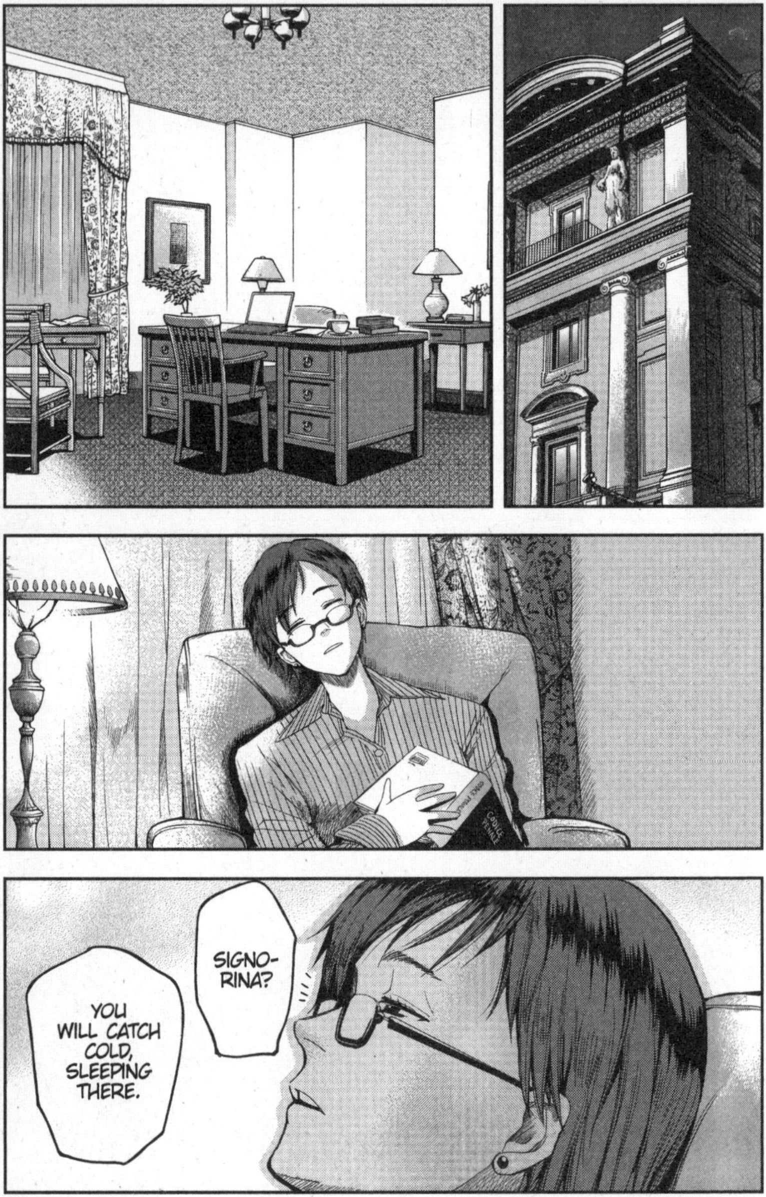
SIGNO-RINA?
YOU WILL CATCH COLD, SLEEPING THERE.

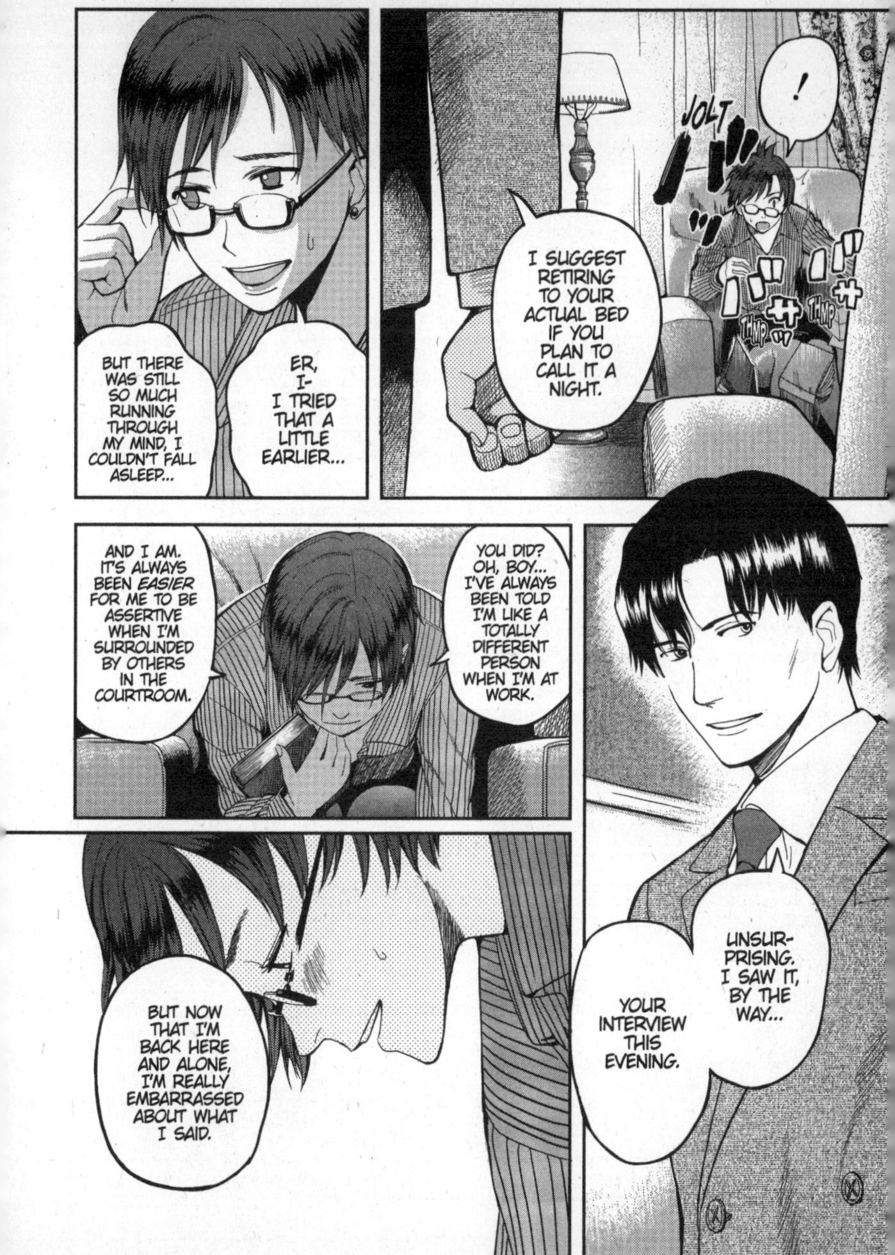
!
JOLT
THMP
THMP
I SUGGEST RETIRING TO YOUR ACTUAL BED IF YOU PLAN TO CALL IT A NIGHT.
ER, I- I TRIED THAT A LITTLE EARLIER...
BUT THERE WAS STILL SO MUCH RUNNING THROUGH MY MIND, I COULDN'T FALL ASLEEP...
UNSUR-PRISING. I SAW IT, BY THE WAY...
YOUR INTERVIEW THIS EVENING.
YOU DID? OH, BOY... I'VE ALWAYS BEEN TOLD I'M LIKE A TOTALLY DIFFERENT PERSON WHEN I'M AT WORK.
AND I AM. IT'S ALWAYS BEEN *EASIER* FOR ME TO BE ASSERTIVE WHEN I'M SURROUNDED BY OTHERS IN THE COURTROOM.
BUT NOW THAT I'M BACK HERE AND ALONE, I'M REALLY EMBARRASSED ABOUT WHAT I SAID.

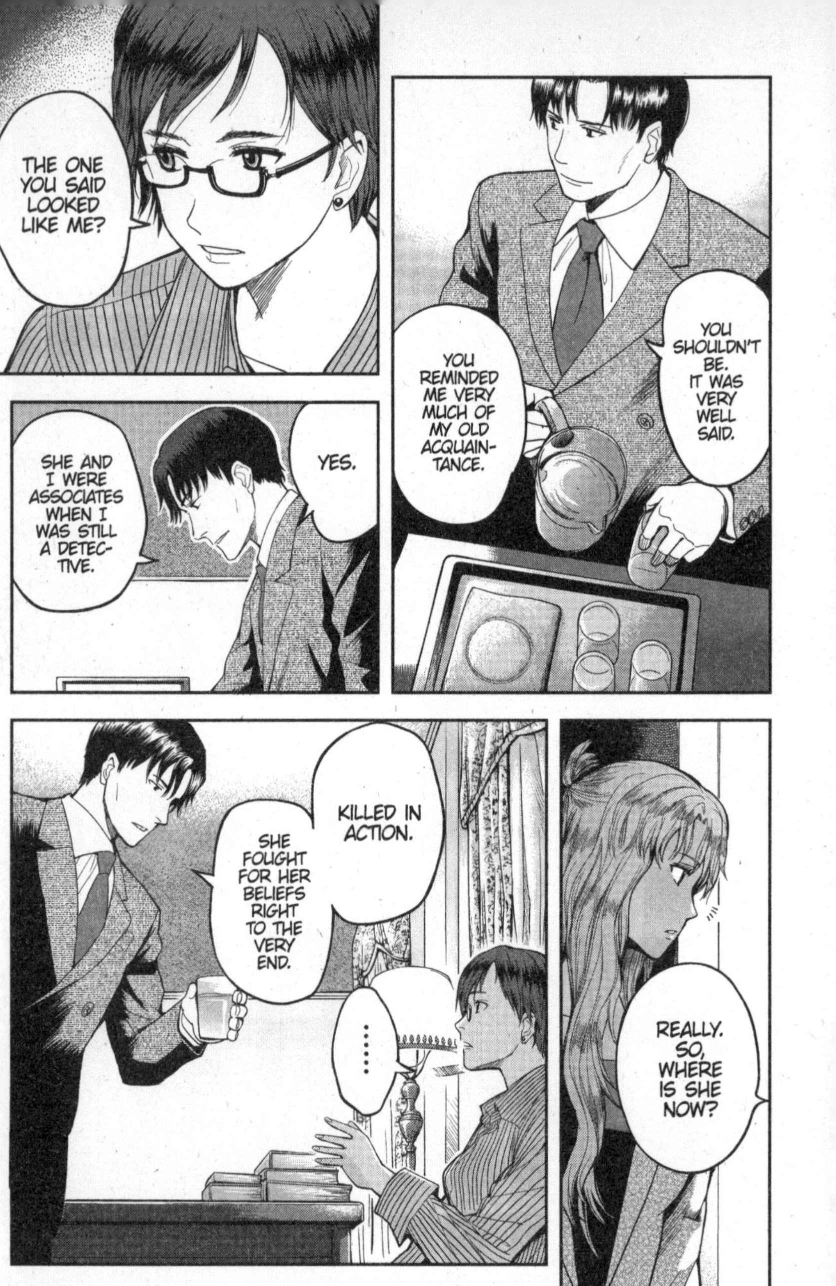
YOU SHOULDN'T BE. IT WAS VERY WELL SAID.
YOU REMINDED ME VERY MUCH OF MY OLD ACQUAINTANCE.
THE ONE YOU SAID LOOKED LIKE ME?
YES.
SHE AND I WERE ASSOCIATES WHEN I WAS STILL A DETECTIVE.
REALLY. SO, WHERE IS SHE NOW?
KILLED IN ACTION.
SHE FOUGHT FOR HER BELIEFS RIGHT TO THE VERY END.
......

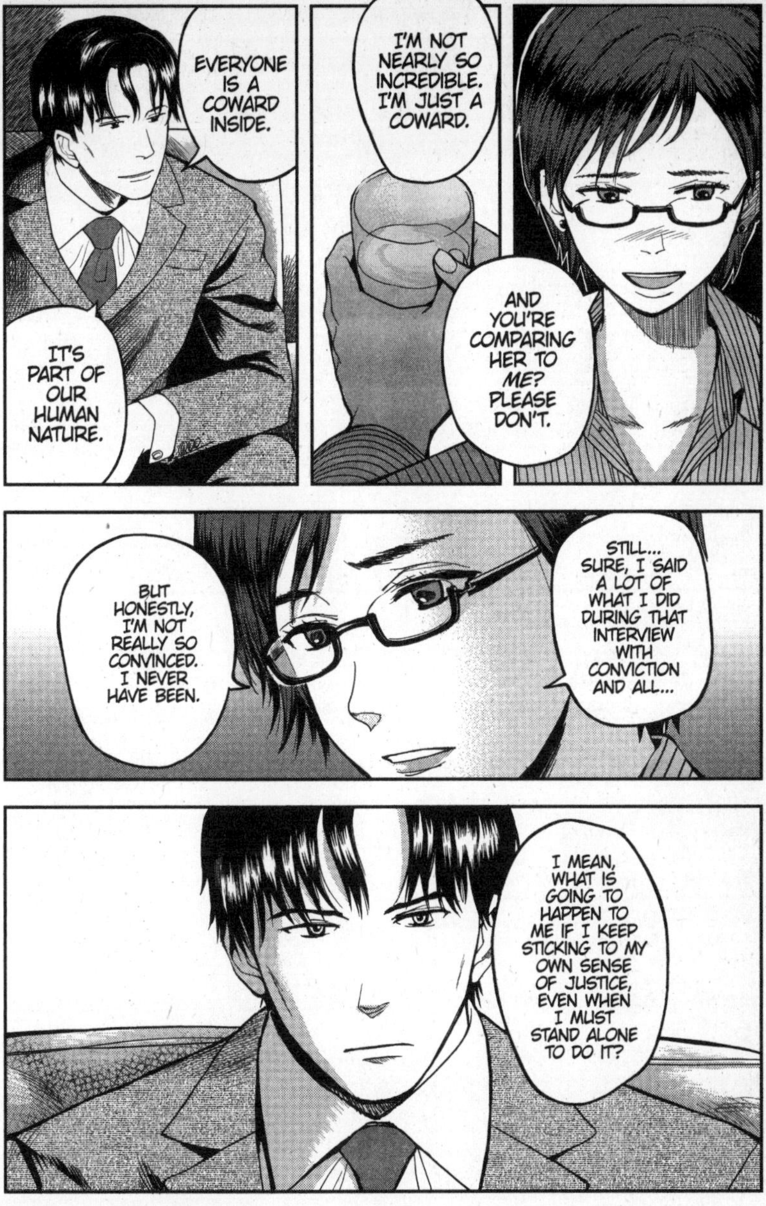
AND YOU'RE COMPARING HER TO *ME*? PLEASE DON'T.
I'M NOT NEARLY SO INCREDIBLE. I'M JUST A COWARD.
EVERYONE IS A COWARD INSIDE.
IT'S PART OF OUR HUMAN NATURE.
STILL... SURE, I SAID A LOT OF WHAT I DID DURING THAT INTERVIEW WITH CONVICTION AND ALL...
BUT HONESTLY, I'M NOT REALLY SO CONVINCED. I NEVER HAVE BEEN.
I MEAN, WHAT IS GOING TO HAPPEN TO ME IF I KEEP STICKING TO MY OWN SENSE OF JUSTICE, EVEN WHEN I MUST STAND ALONE TO DO IT?

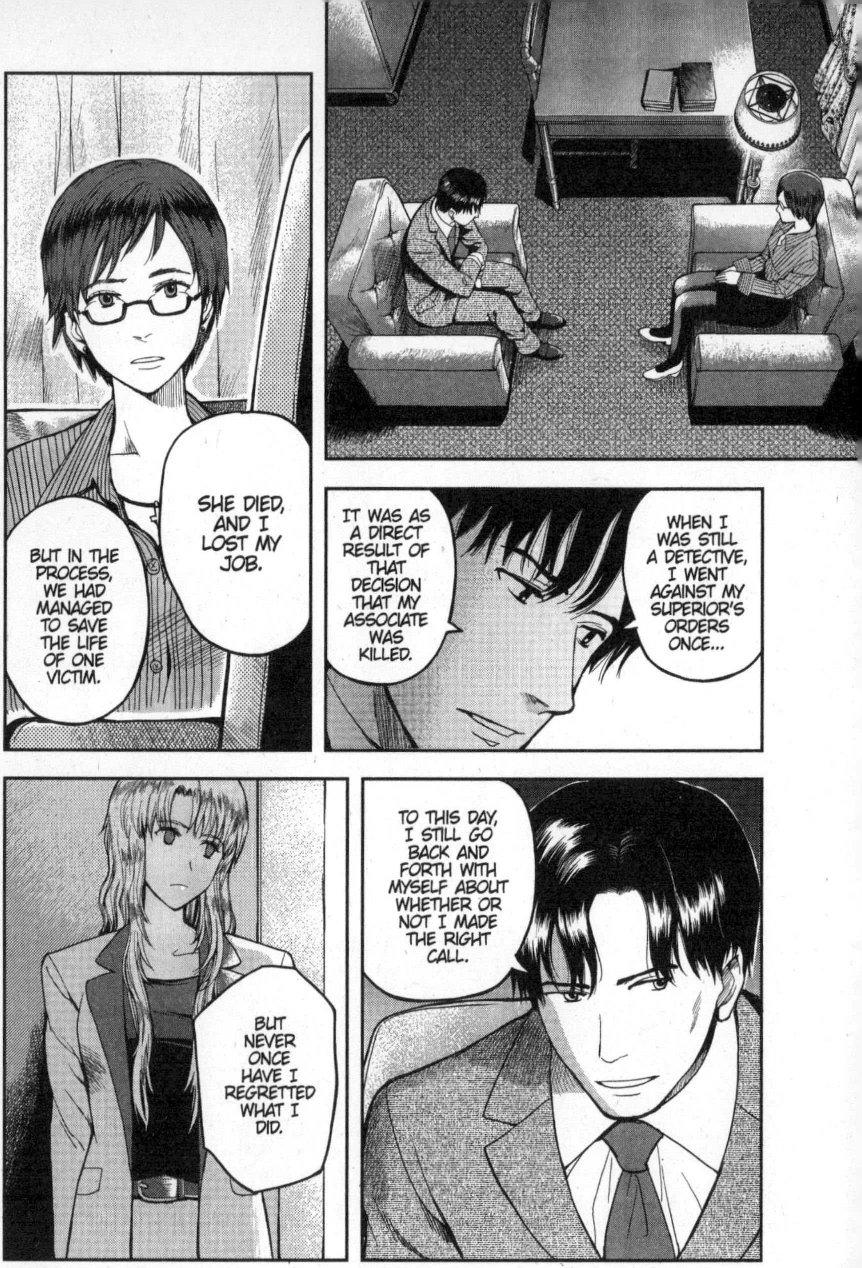
WHEN I WAS STILL A DETECTIVE, I WENT AGAINST MY SUPERIOR'S ORDERS ONCE...
IT WAS AS A DIRECT RESULT OF THAT DECISION THAT MY ASSOCIATE WAS KILLED.
SHE DIED, AND I LOST MY JOB.
BUT IN THE PROCESS, WE HAD MANAGED TO SAVE THE LIFE OF ONE VICTIM.
TO THIS DAY, I STILL GO BACK AND FORTH WITH MYSELF ABOUT WHETHER OR NOT I MADE THE RIGHT CALL.
BUT NEVER ONCE HAVE I REGRETTED WHAT I DID.

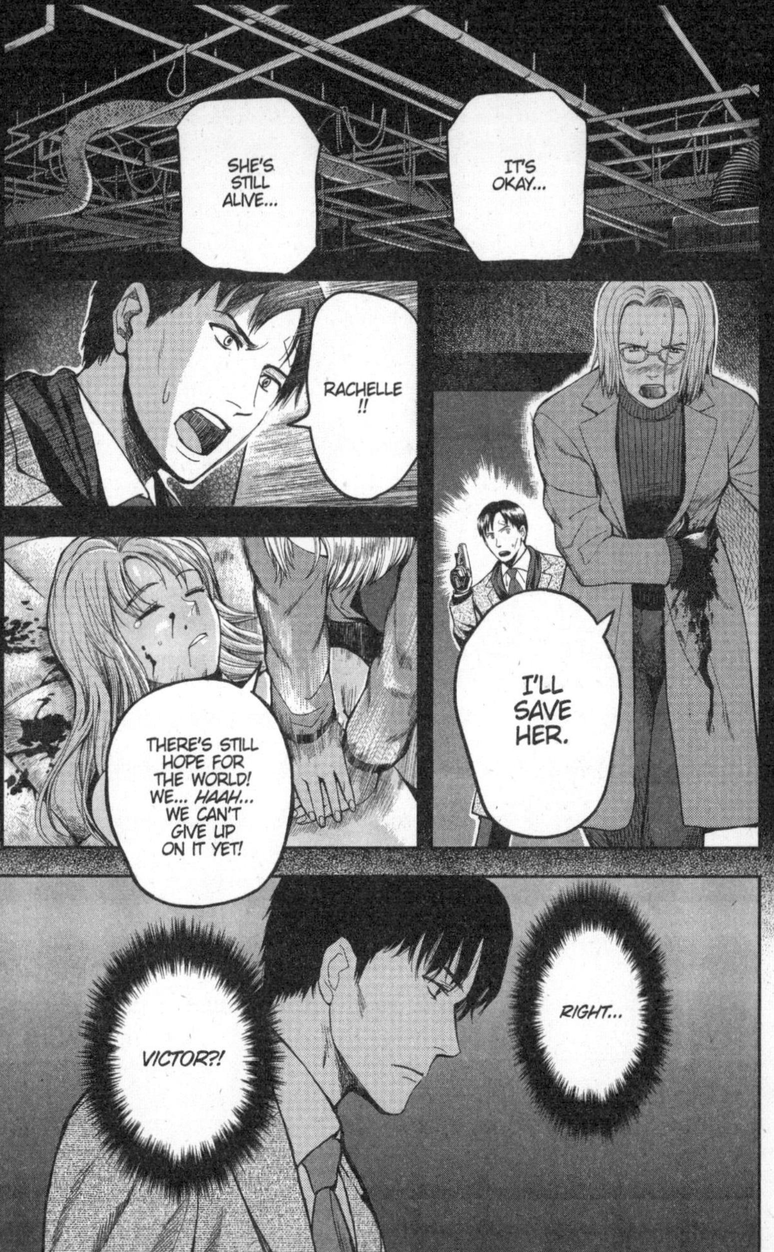
IT'S OKAY...
SHE'S STILL ALIVE...
I'LL SAVE HER.
RACHELLE !!
THERE'S STILL HOPE FOR THE WORLD! WE... *HAAH*... WE CAN'T GIVE UP ON IT YET!
RIGHT...
VICTOR?!

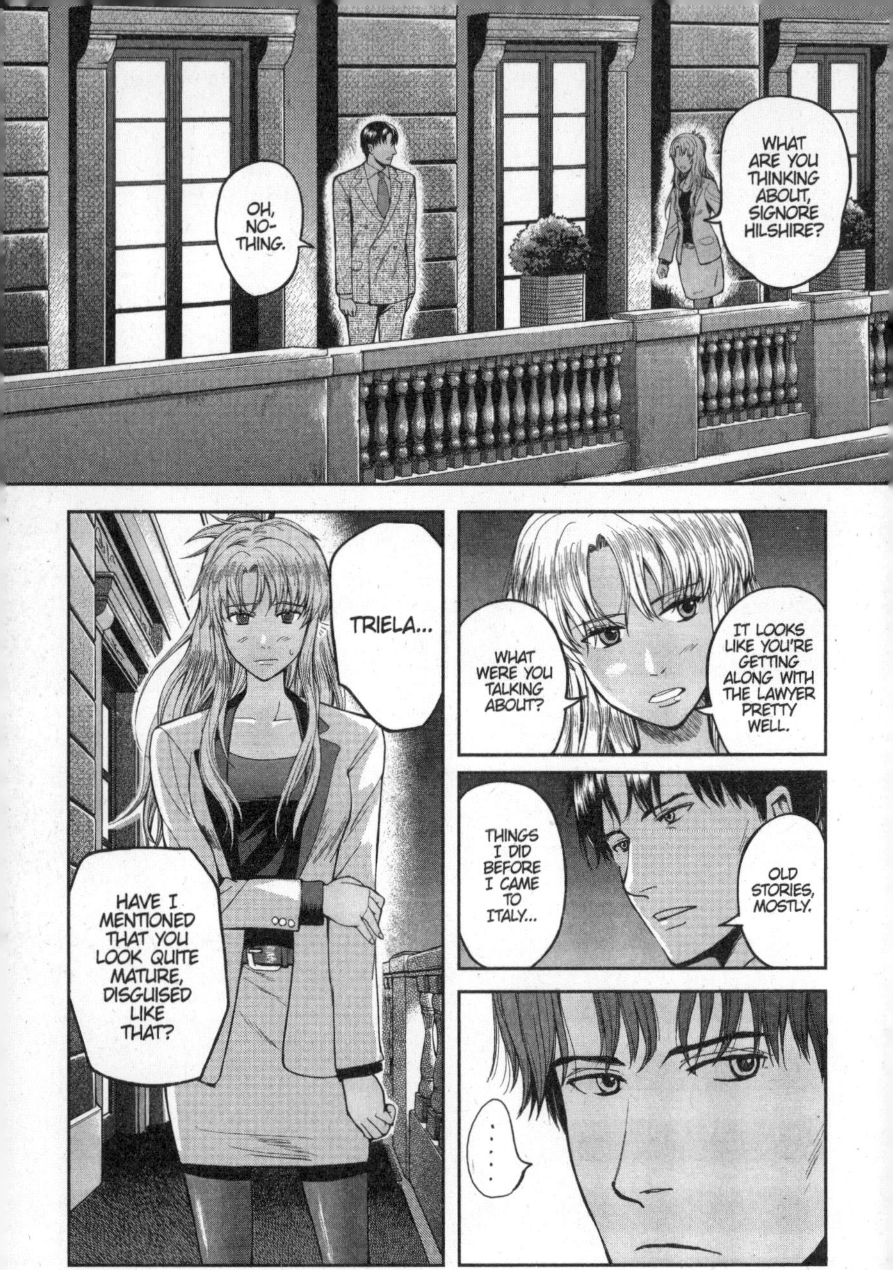
WHAT ARE YOU THINKING ABOUT, SIGNORE HILSHIRE?
OH, NO-THING.
IT LOOKS LIKE YOU'RE GETTING ALONG WITH THE LAWYER PRETTY WELL.
WHAT WERE YOU TALKING ABOUT?
OLD STORIES, MOSTLY.
THINGS I DID BEFORE I CAME TO ITALY...
......
TRIELA...
HAVE I MENTIONED THAT YOU LOOK QUITE MATURE, DISGUISED LIKE THAT?

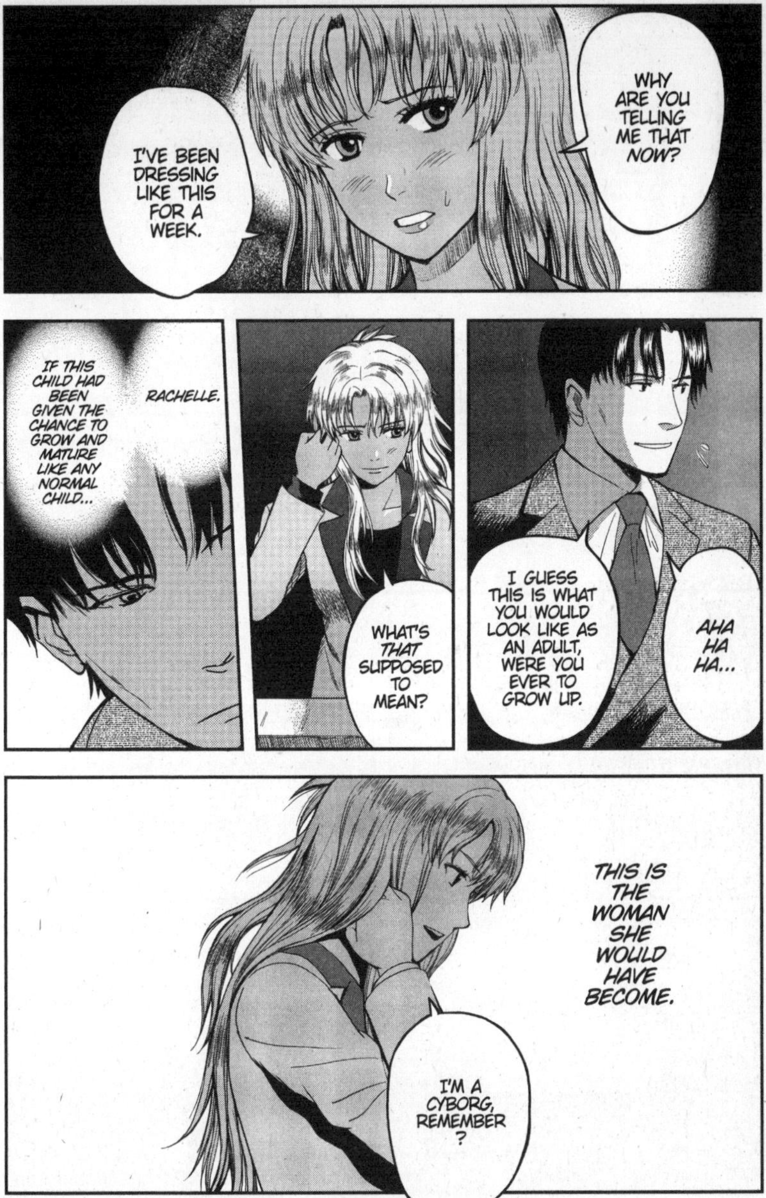
WHY ARE YOU TELLING ME THAT *NOW*?
I'VE BEEN DRESSING LIKE THIS FOR A WEEK.
AHA HA HA...
I GUESS THIS IS WHAT YOU WOULD LOOK LIKE AS AN ADULT, WERE YOU EVER TO GROW UP.
WHAT'S *THAT* SUPPOSED TO MEAN?
RACHELLE.
IF THIS CHILD HAD BEEN GIVEN THE CHANCE TO GROW AND MATURE LIKE ANY NORMAL CHILD...
THIS IS THE WOMAN SHE WOULD HAVE BECOME.
I'M A CYBORG, REMEMBER?

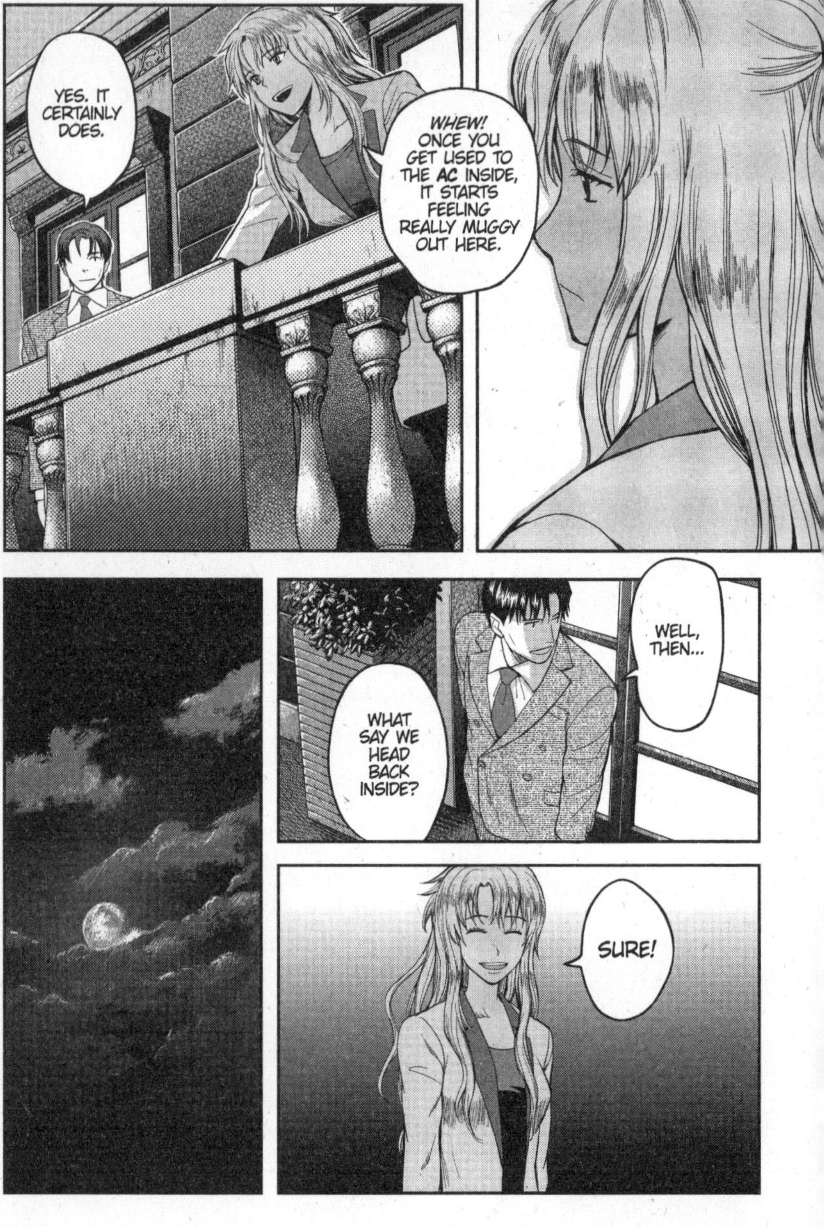
WHEW! ONCE YOU GET USED TO THE AC INSIDE, IT STARTS FEELING REALLY MUGGY OUT HERE.
YES. IT CERTAINLY DOES.
WELL, THEN...
WHAT SAY WE HEAD BACK INSIDE?
SURE!

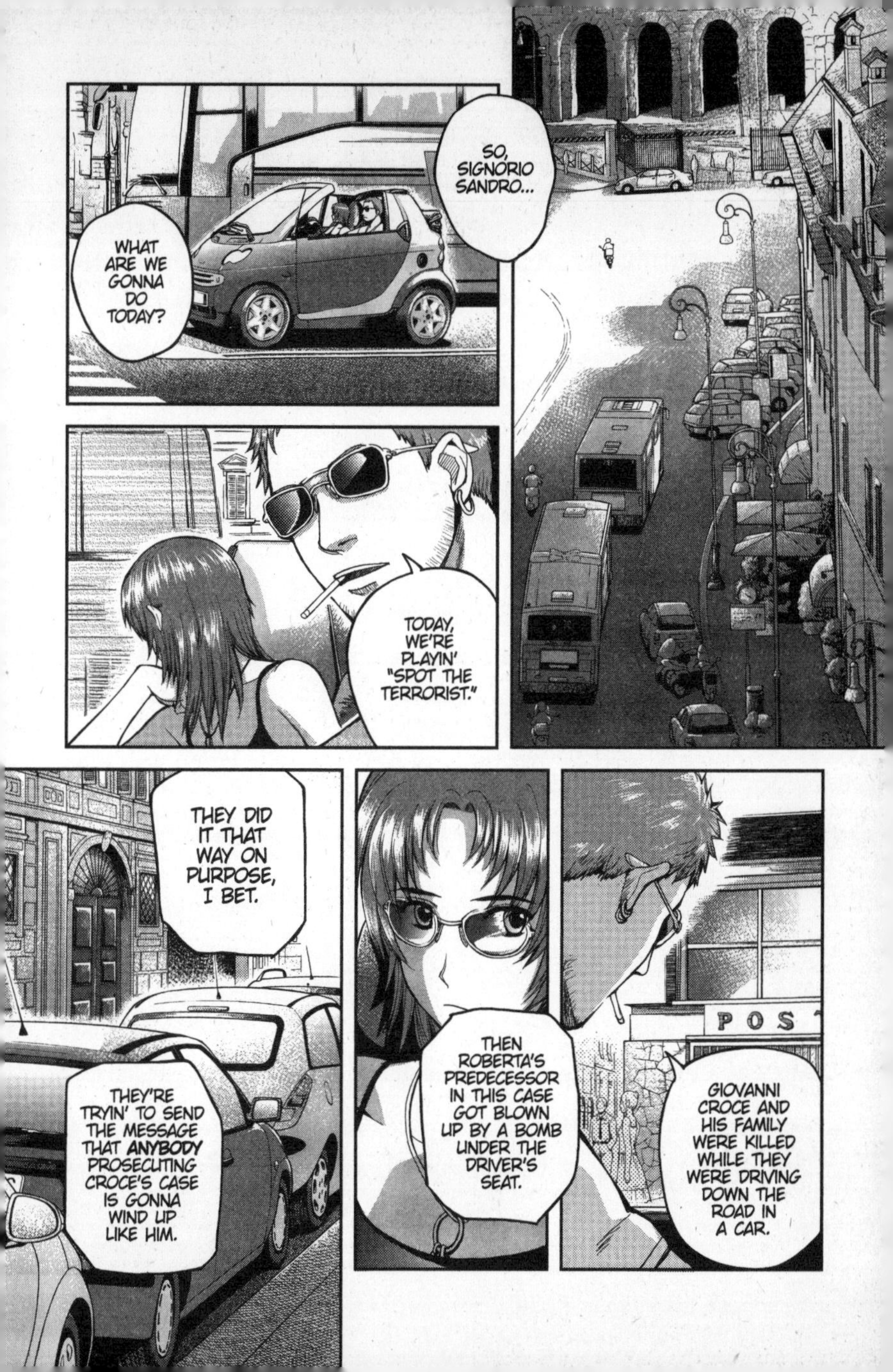
SO, SIGNORIO SANDRO...
WHAT ARE WE GONNA DO TODAY?
TODAY, WE'RE PLAYIN' "SPOT THE TERRORIST."
GIOVANNI CROCE AND HIS FAMILY WERE KILLED WHILE THEY WERE DRIVING DOWN THE ROAD IN A CAR.
POS
THEN ROBERTA'S PREDECESSOR IN THIS CASE GOT BLOWN UP BY A BOMB UNDER THE DRIVER'S SEAT.
THEY DID IT THAT WAY ON PURPOSE, I BET.
THEY'RE TRYIN' TO SEND THE MESSAGE THAT **ANYBODY** PROSECUTING CROCE'S CASE IS GONNA WIND UP LIKE HIM.

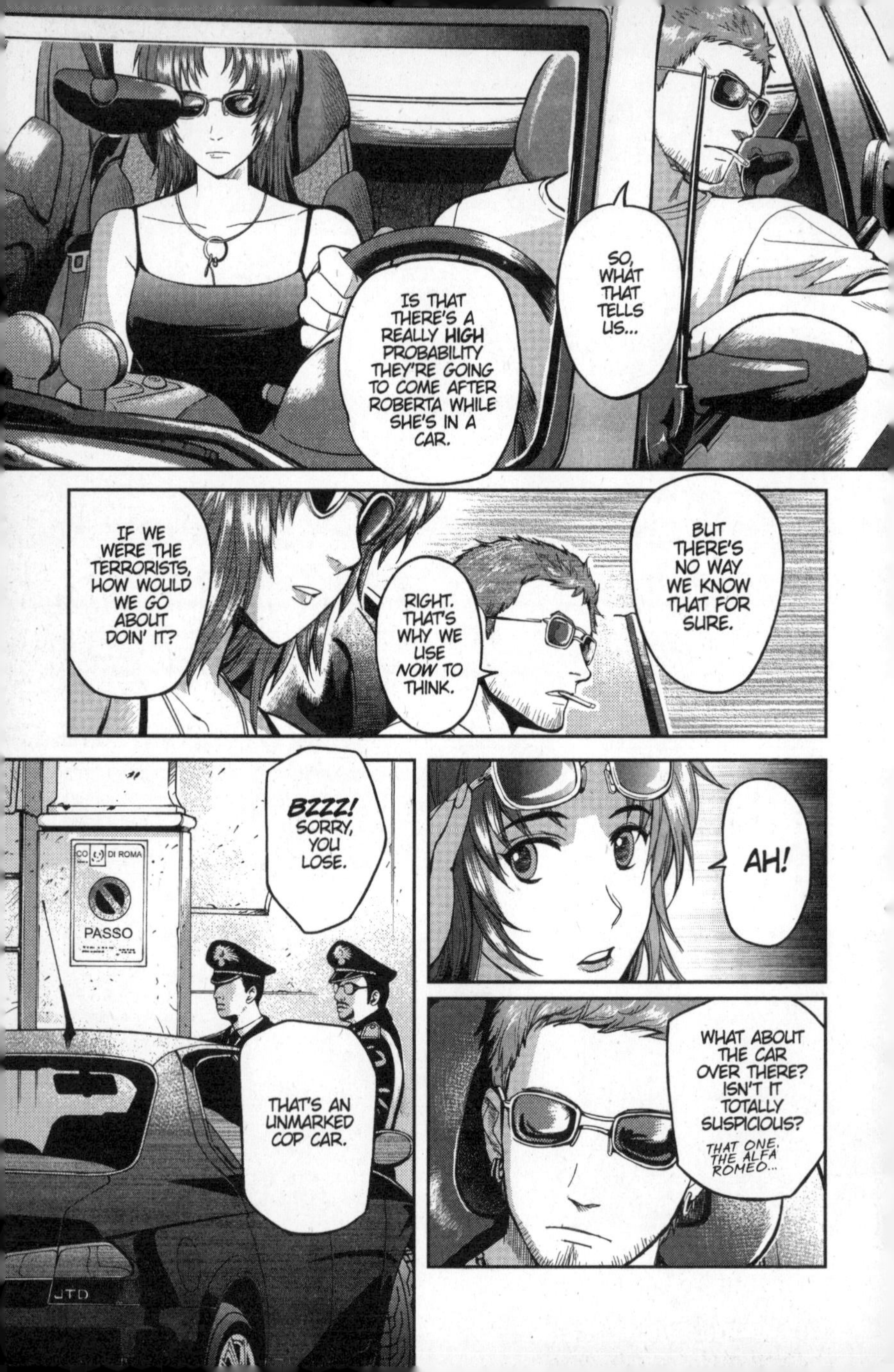
SO, WHAT THAT TELLS US...
IS THAT THERE'S A REALLY **HIGH** PROBABILITY THEY'RE GOING TO COME AFTER ROBERTA WHILE SHE'S IN A CAR.
BUT THERE'S NO WAY WE KNOW THAT FOR SURE.
RIGHT. THAT'S WHY WE USE *NOW* TO THINK.
IF WE WERE THE TERRORISTS, HOW WOULD WE GO ABOUT DOIN' IT?
AH!
WHAT ABOUT THE CAR OVER THERE? ISN'T IT TOTALLY SUSPICIOUS?
THAT ONE, THE ALFA ROMEO...
CO DI ROMA
PASSO
BZZZ! SORRY, YOU LOSE.
THAT'S AN UNMARKED COP CAR.
JTD

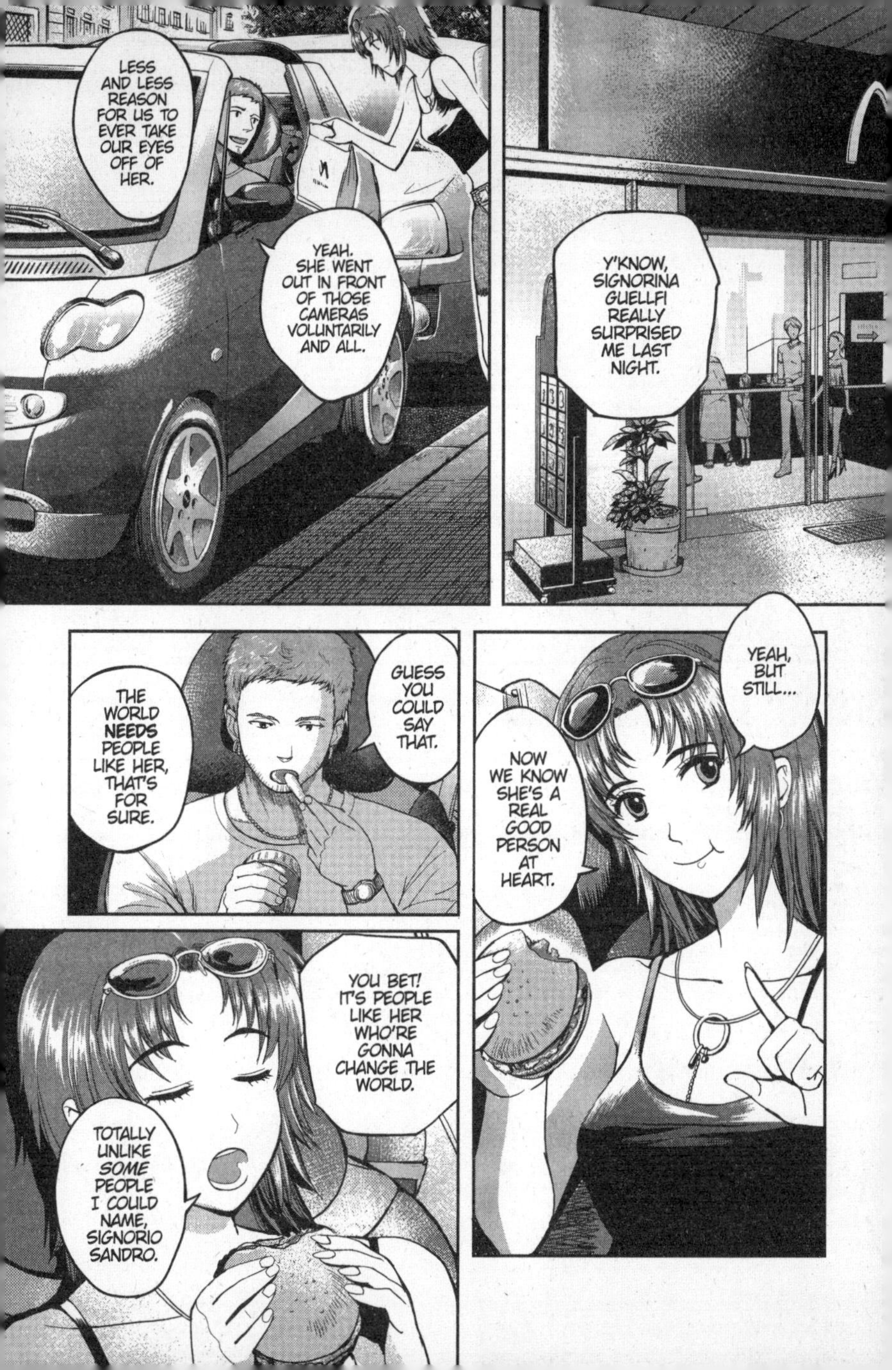
Y'KNOW, SIGNORINA GUELLFI REALLY SURPRISED ME LAST NIGHT.
LESS AND LESS REASON FOR US TO EVER TAKE OUR EYES OFF OF HER.
YEAH. SHE WENT OUT IN FRONT OF THOSE CAMERAS VOLUNTARILY AND ALL.
YEAH, BUT STILL...
NOW WE KNOW SHE'S A REAL GOOD PERSON AT HEART.
GUESS YOU COULD SAY THAT.
THE WORLD NEEDS PEOPLE LIKE HER, THAT'S FOR SURE.
YOU BET! IT'S PEOPLE LIKE HER WHO'RE GONNA CHANGE THE WORLD.
TOTALLY UNLIKE SOME PEOPLE I COULD NAME, SIGNORIO SANDRO.

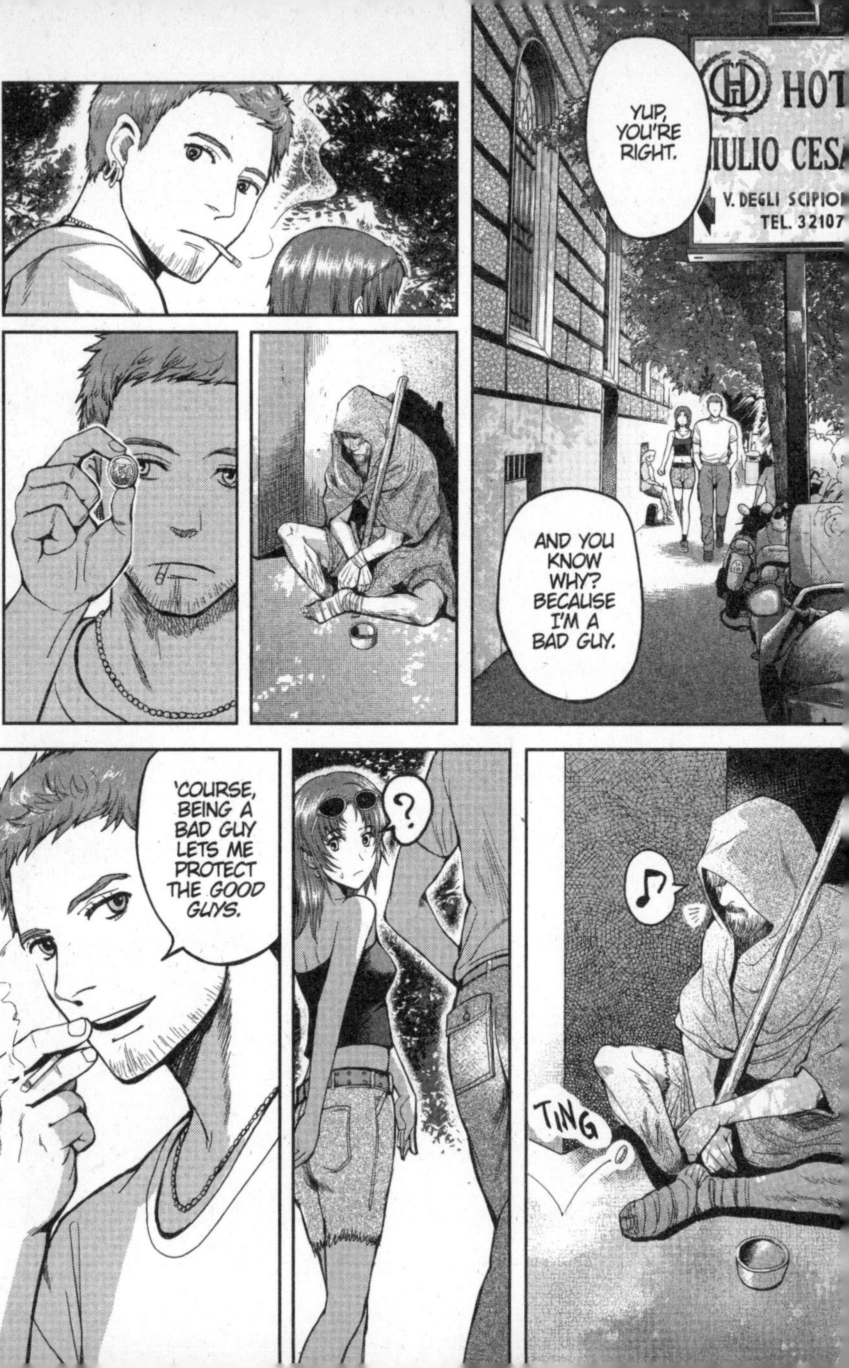
HOT
IULIO CESA
V. DEGLI SCIPIOI
TEL. 32107
YUP, YOU'RE RIGHT.
AND YOU KNOW WHY? BECAUSE I'M A BAD GUY.
♪
TING
?
'COURSE, BEING A BAD GUY LETS ME PROTECT THE *GOOD* GUYS.

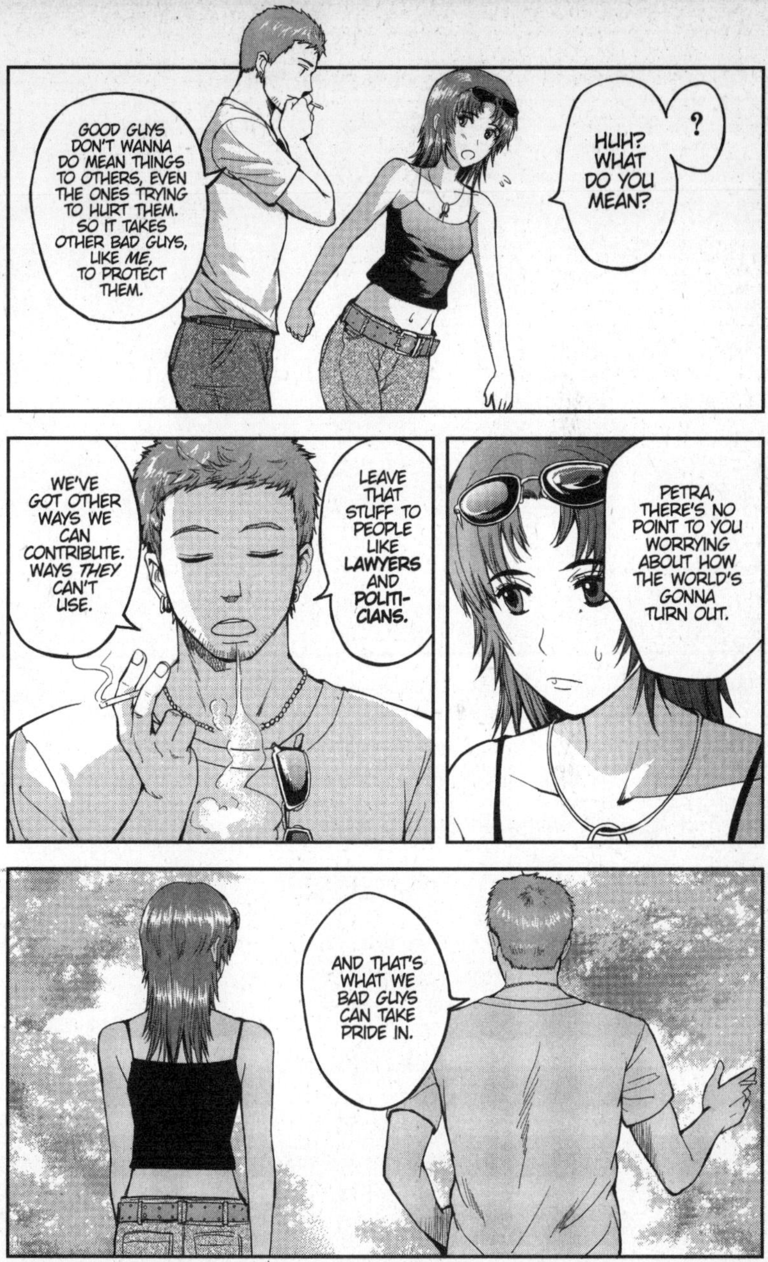
?
HUH? WHAT DO YOU MEAN?
GOOD GUYS DON'T WANNA DO MEAN THINGS TO OTHERS, EVEN THE ONES TRYING TO HURT THEM. SO IT TAKES OTHER BAD GUYS, LIKE *ME*, TO PROTECT THEM.
PETRA, THERE'S NO POINT TO YOU WORRYING ABOUT HOW THE WORLD'S GONNA TURN OUT.
LEAVE THAT STUFF TO PEOPLE LIKE **LAWYERS** AND **POLITI-CIANS.**
WE'VE GOT OTHER WAYS WE CAN CONTRIBUTE. WAYS *THEY* CAN'T USE.
AND THAT'S WHAT WE BAD GUYS CAN TAKE PRIDE IN.

GUNSLINGERGIRL.

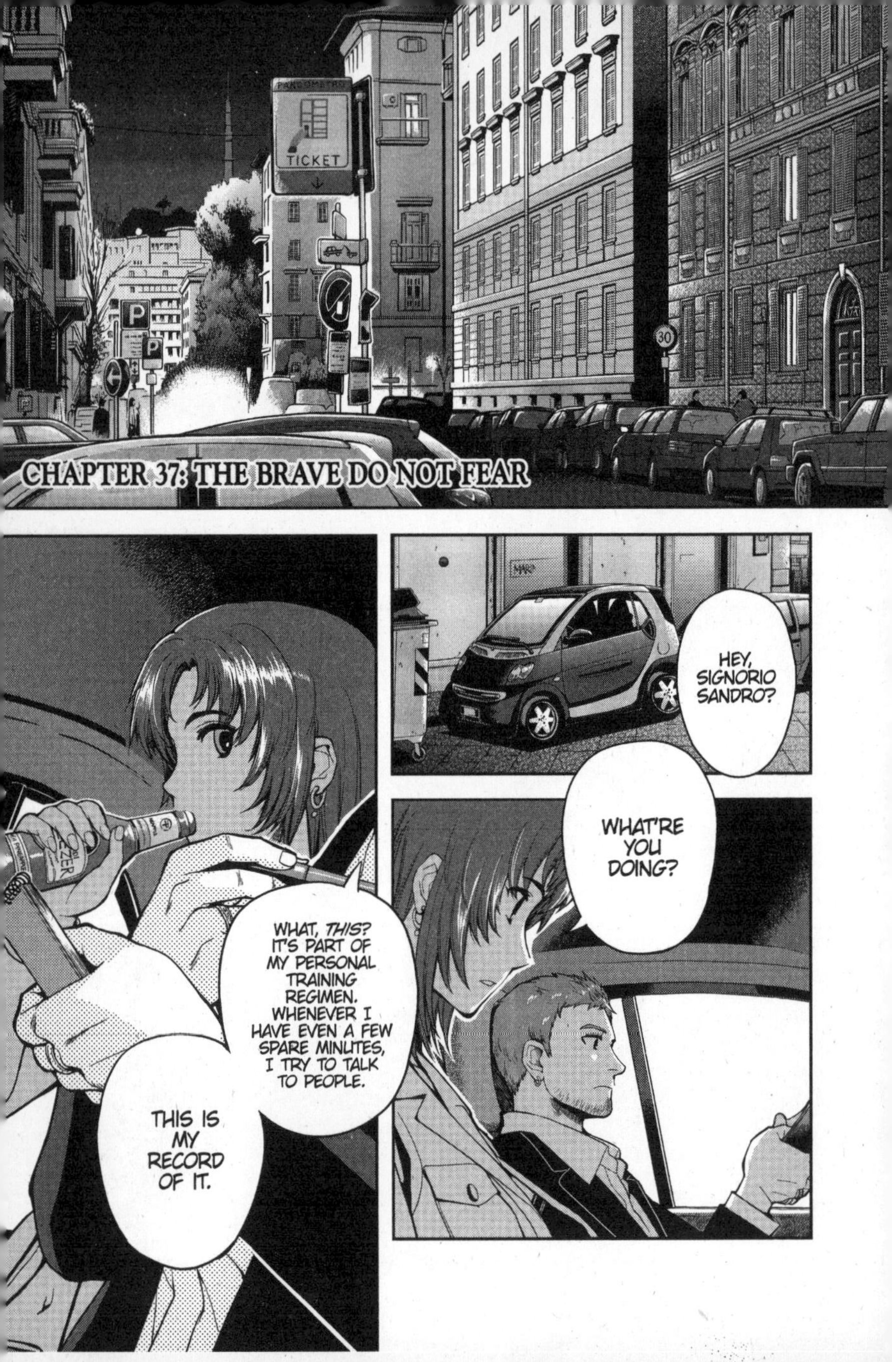
TICKET
CHAPTER 37: THE BRAVE DO NOT FEAR
HEY, SIGNORIO SANDRO?
WHAT'RE YOU DOING?
WHAT, *THIS*? IT'S PART OF MY PERSONAL TRAINING REGIMEN. WHENEVER I HAVE EVEN A FEW SPARE MINUTES, I TRY TO TALK TO PEOPLE.
THIS IS MY RECORD OF IT.

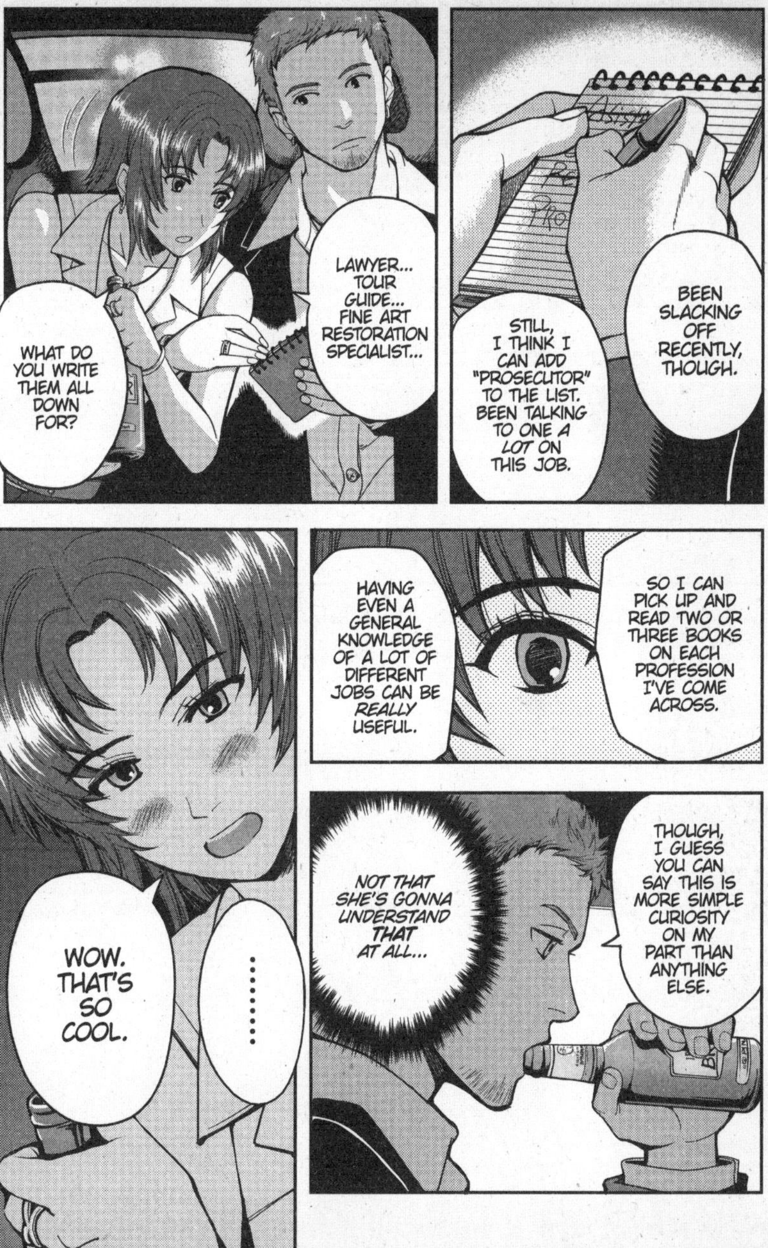
BEEN SLACKING OFF RECENTLY, THOUGH.
STILL, I THINK I CAN ADD "PROSECUTOR" TO THE LIST. BEEN TALKING TO ONE A *LOT* ON THIS JOB.
LAWYER... TOUR GUIDE... FINE ART RESTORATION SPECIALIST...
WHAT DO YOU WRITE THEM ALL DOWN FOR?
SO I CAN PICK UP AND READ TWO OR THREE BOOKS ON EACH PROFESSION I'VE COME ACROSS.
HAVING EVEN A GENERAL KNOWLEDGE OF A LOT OF DIFFERENT JOBS CAN BE *REALLY* USEFUL.
THOUGH, I GUESS YOU CAN SAY THIS IS MORE SIMPLE CURIOSITY ON MY PART THAN ANYTHING ELSE.
NOT THAT SHE'S GONNA UNDERSTAND THAT AT ALL...
......
WOW. THAT'S SO COOL.

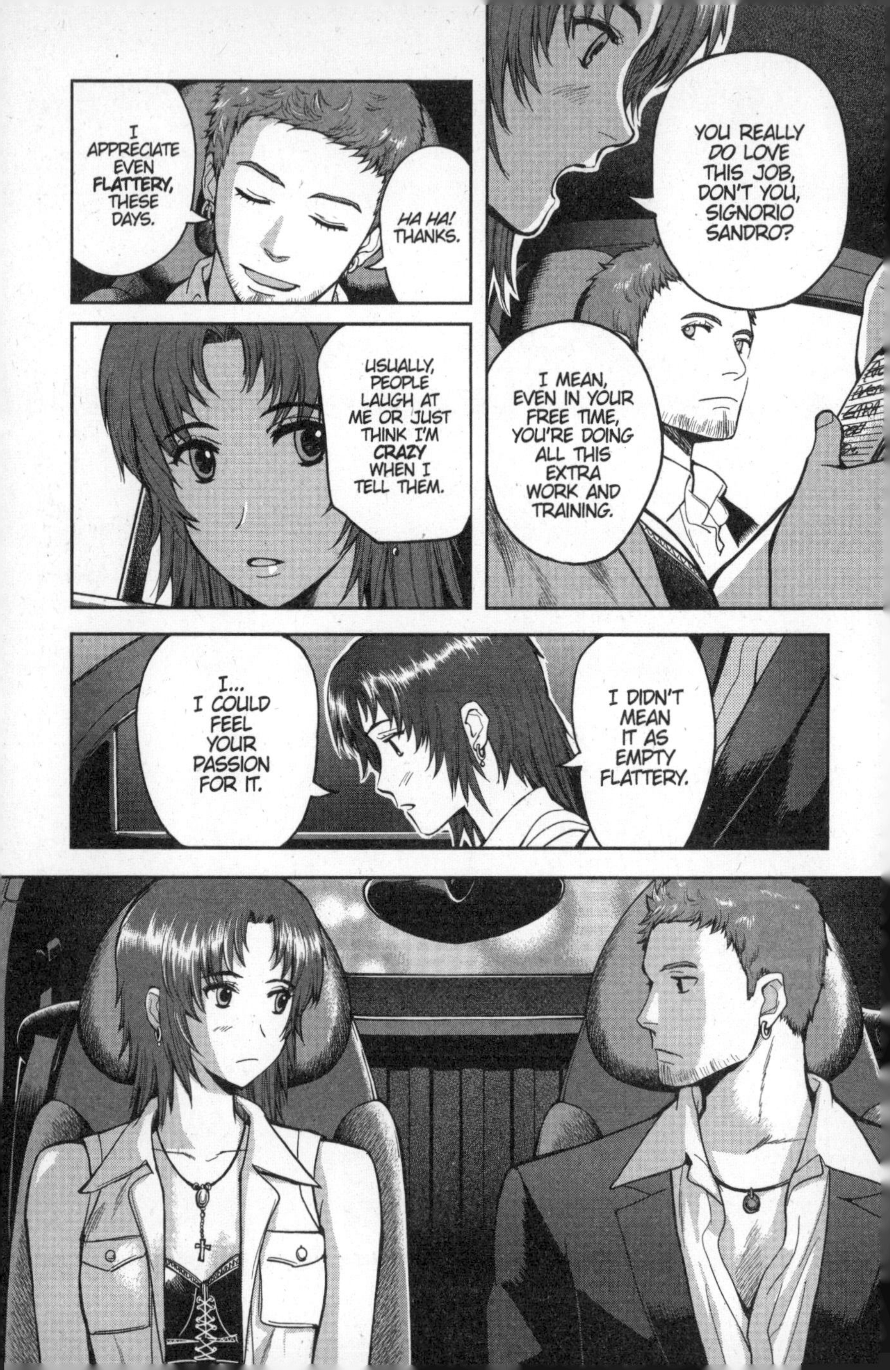
YOU REALLY DO LOVE THIS JOB, DON'T YOU, SIGNORIO SANDRO?
I MEAN, EVEN IN YOUR FREE TIME, YOU'RE DOING ALL THIS EXTRA WORK AND TRAINING.
HA HA! THANKS.
I APPRECIATE EVEN FLATTERY, THESE DAYS.
USUALLY, PEOPLE LAUGH AT ME OR JUST THINK I'M CRAZY WHEN I TELL THEM.
I DIDN'T MEAN IT AS EMPTY FLATTERY.
I... I COULD FEEL YOUR PASSION FOR IT.

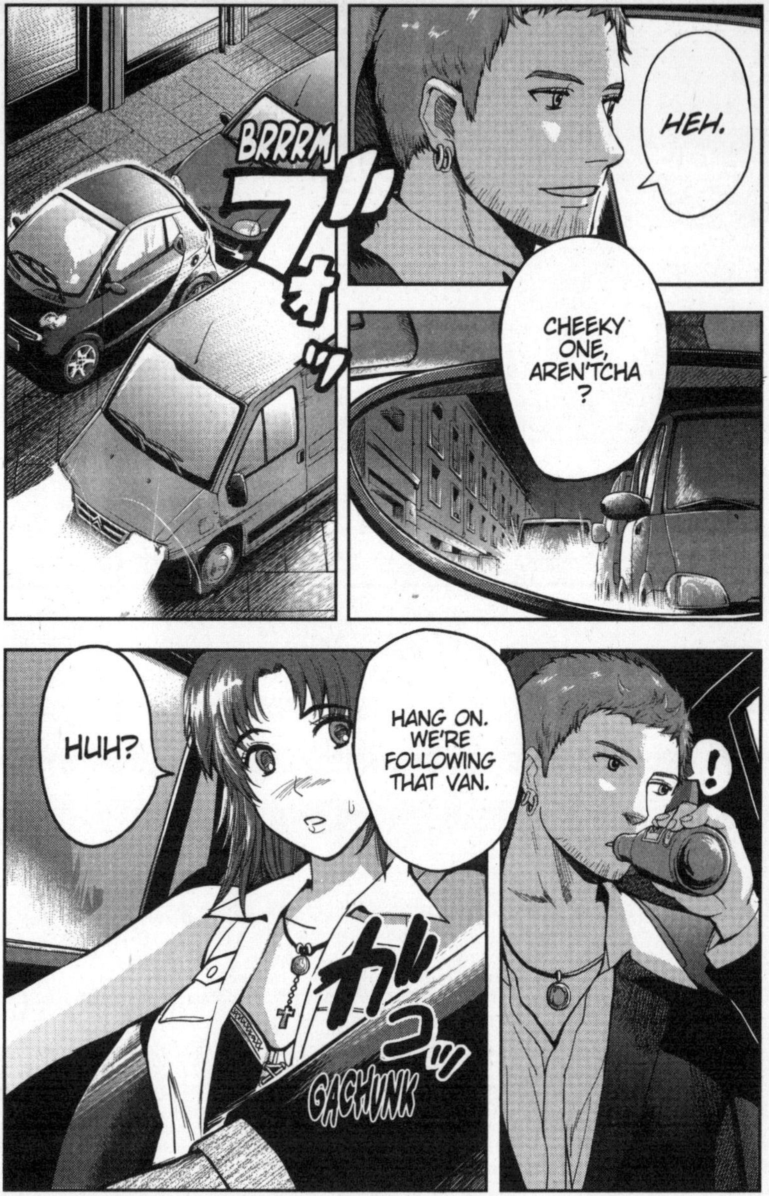
HEH.
CHEEKY ONE, AREN'TCHA?
BRRRM
ブォッ
!
HANG ON. WE'RE FOLLOWING THAT VAN.
HUH?
ガコッ
GACHUNK

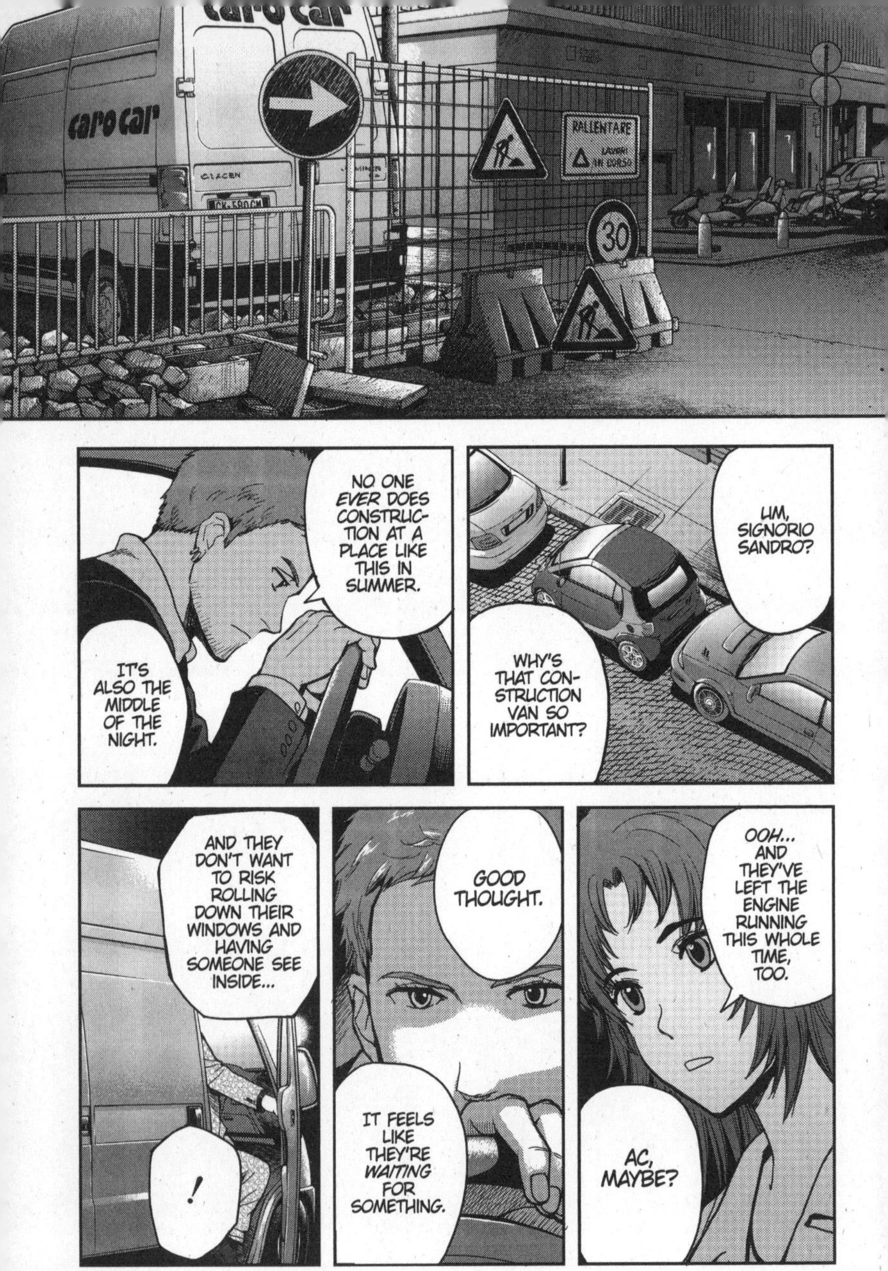
caro car
caro car
RALLENTARE
LAVORI IN CORSO
30
UM, SIGNORIO SANDRO?
WHY'S THAT CON-STRUCTION VAN SO IMPORTANT?
NO ONE *EVER DOES* CONSTRUC-TION AT A PLACE LIKE THIS IN SUMMER.
IT'S ALSO THE MIDDLE OF THE NIGHT.
OOH... AND THEY'VE LEFT THE ENGINE RUNNING THIS WHOLE TIME, TOO.
AC, MAYBE?
GOOD THOUGHT.
IT FEELS LIKE THEY'RE *WAITING* FOR SOMETHING.
AND THEY DON'T WANT TO RISK ROLLING DOWN THEIR WINDOWS AND HAVING SOMEONE SEE INSIDE...
!

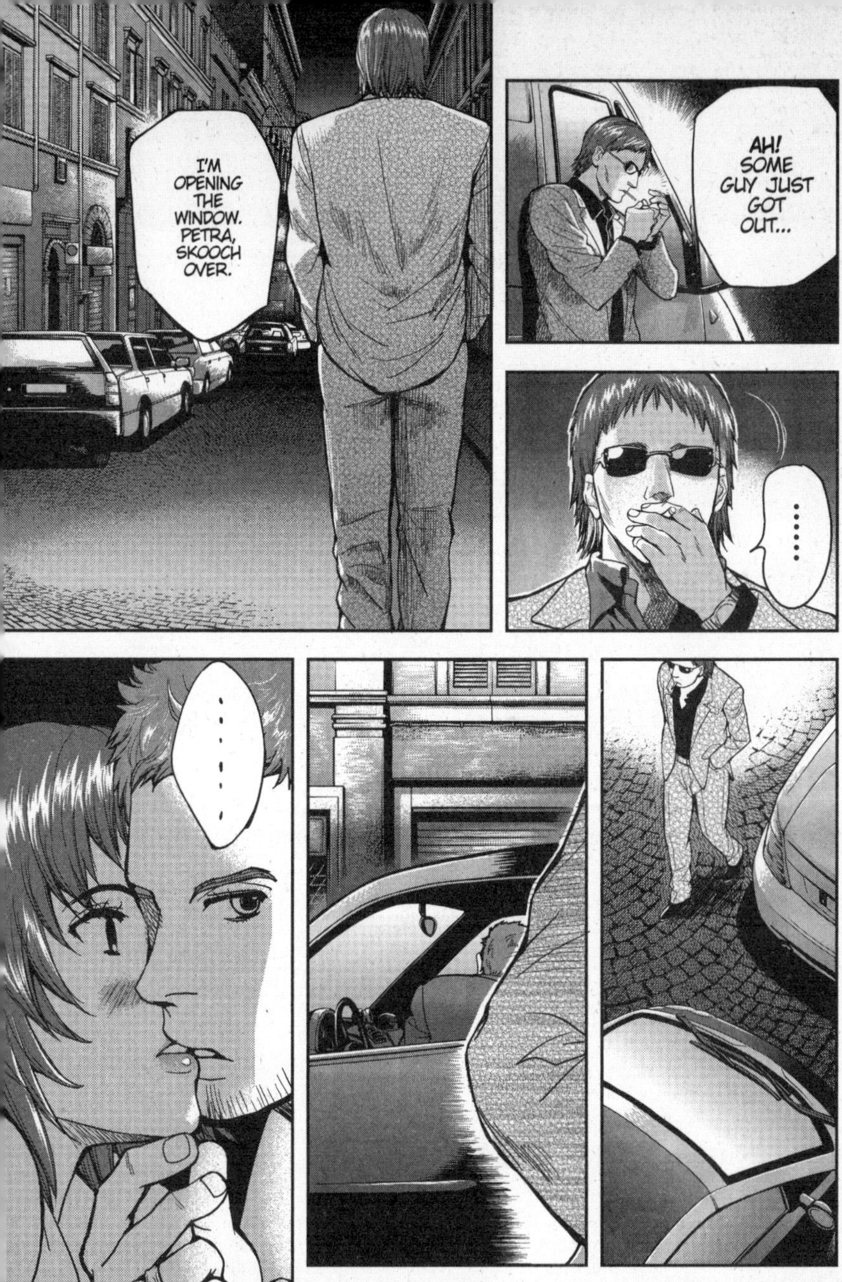

AH! SOME GUY JUST GOT OUT...
......
I'M OPENING THE WINDOW. PETRA, SKOOCH OVER.
.....

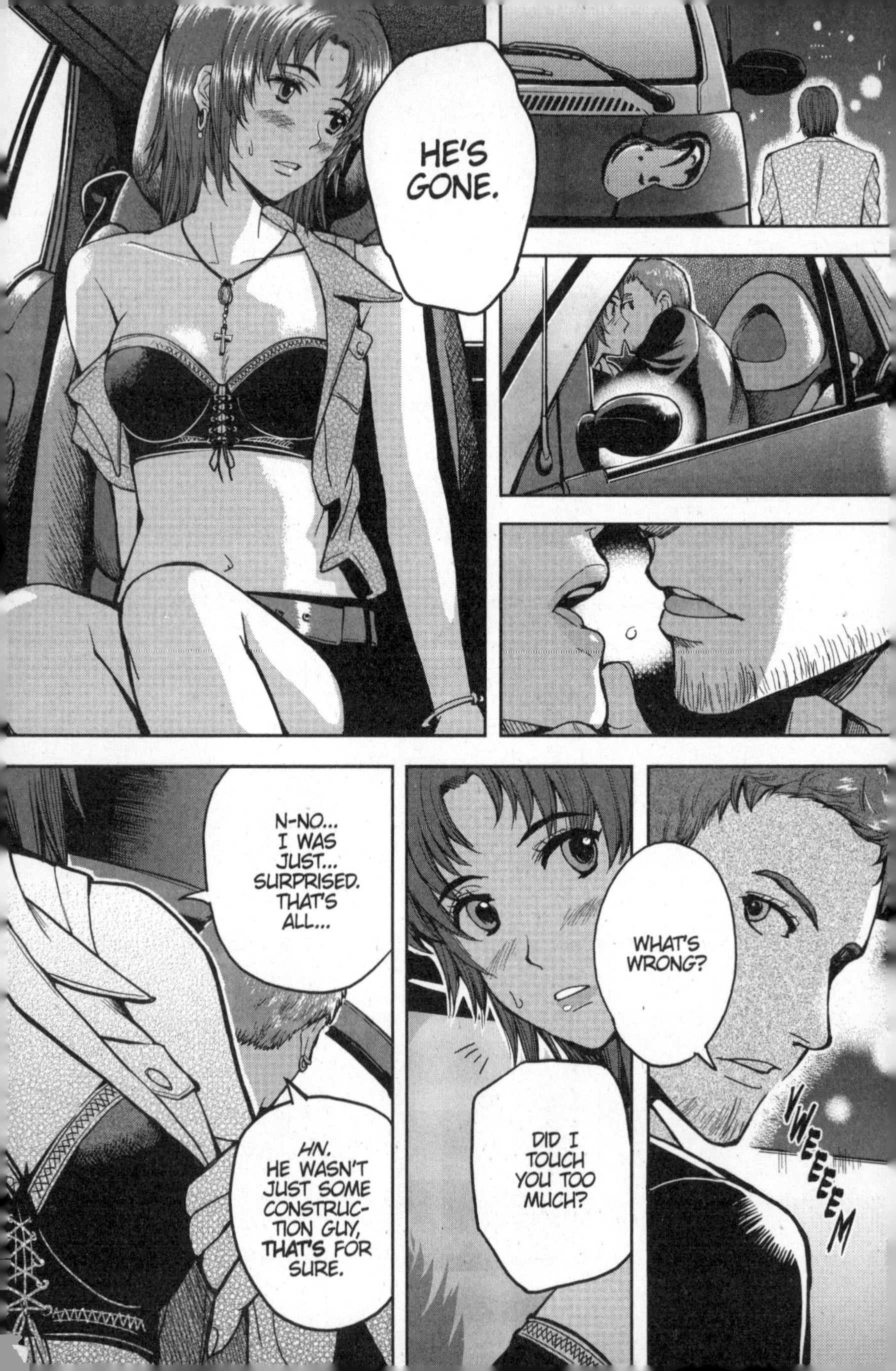
HE'S GONE.
WHAT'S WRONG?
VWEEEEM
DID I TOUCH YOU TOO MUCH?
N-NO... I WAS JUST... SURPRISED. THAT'S ALL...
HN. HE WASN'T JUST SOME CONSTRUC-TION GUY, THAT'S FOR SURE.

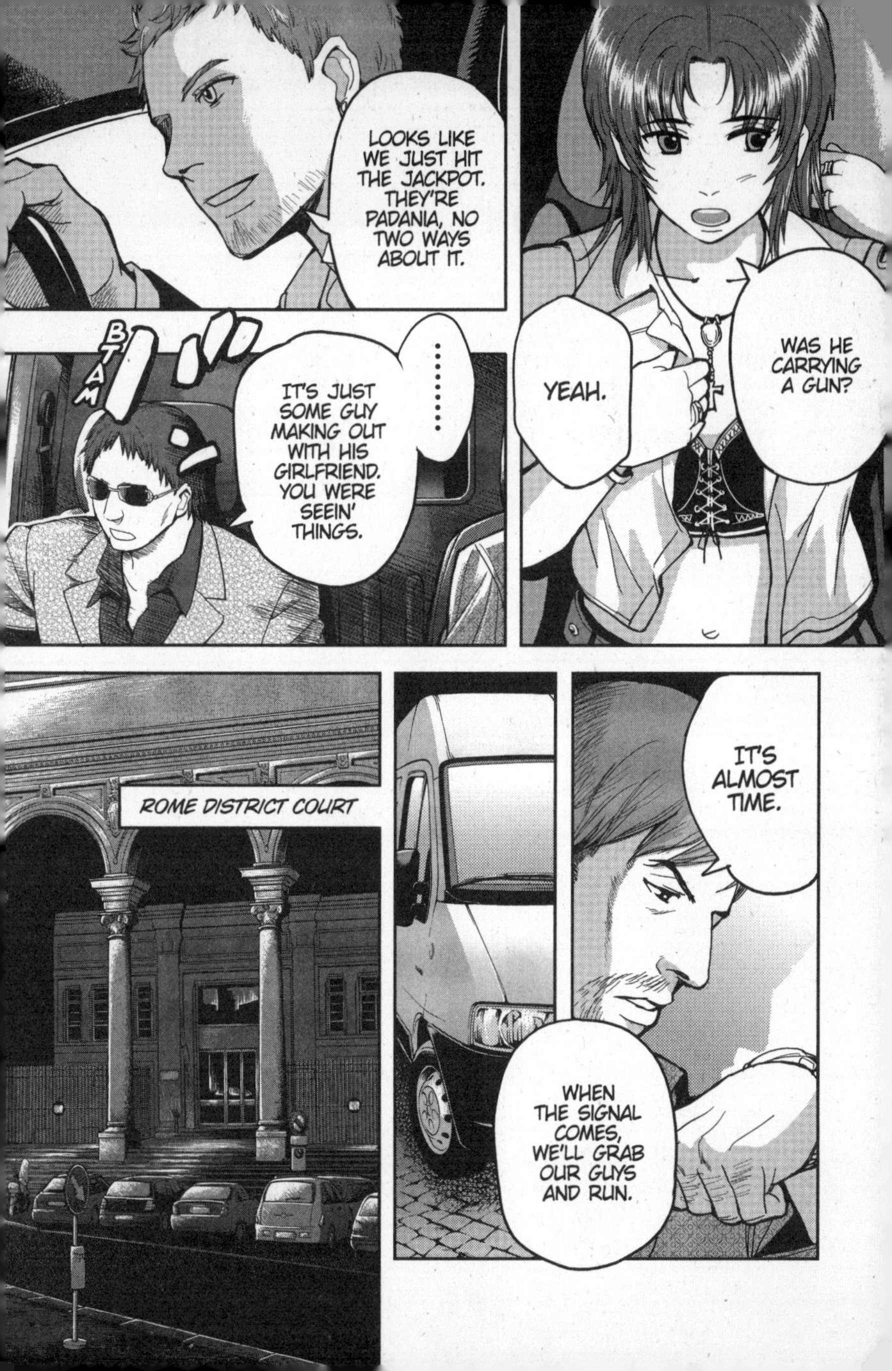
WAS HE CARRYING A GUN?
YEAH.
LOOKS LIKE WE JUST HIT THE JACKPOT. THEY'RE PADANIA, NO TWO WAYS ABOUT IT.
BTAM
....
IT'S JUST SOME GUY MAKING OUT WITH HIS GIRLFRIEND. YOU WERE SEEIN' THINGS.
IT'S ALMOST TIME.
WHEN THE SIGNAL COMES, WE'LL GRAB OUR GUYS AND RUN.
ROME DISTRICT COURT

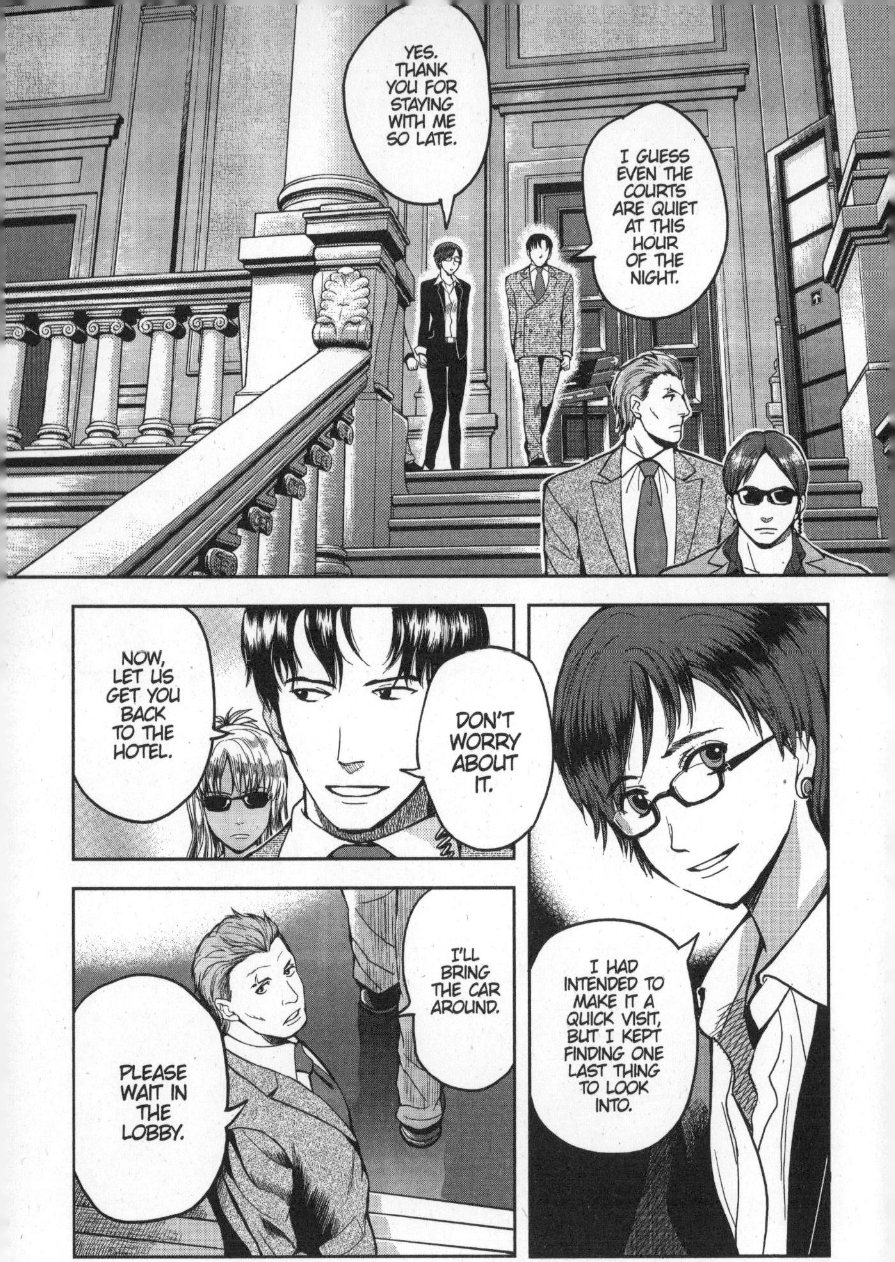
I GUESS EVEN THE COURTS ARE QUIET AT THIS HOUR OF THE NIGHT.
YES. THANK YOU FOR STAYING WITH ME SO LATE.
I HAD INTENDED TO MAKE IT A QUICK VISIT, BUT I KEPT FINDING ONE LAST THING TO LOOK INTO.
DON'T WORRY ABOUT IT.
NOW, LET US GET YOU BACK TO THE HOTEL.
I'LL BRING THE CAR AROUND.
PLEASE WAIT IN THE LOBBY.

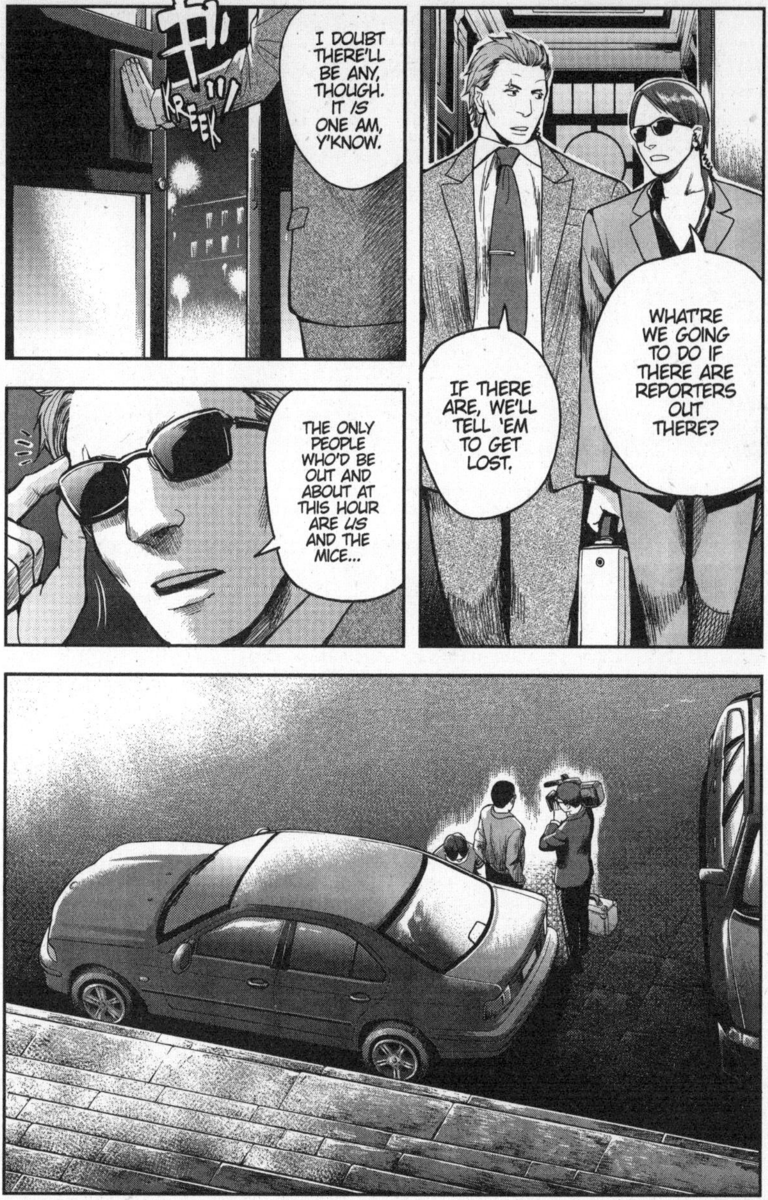
WHAT'RE WE GOING TO DO IF THERE ARE REPORTERS OUT THERE?
IF THERE ARE, WE'LL TELL 'EM TO GET LOST.
KREEEK
I DOUBT THERE'LL BE ANY, THOUGH. IT IS ONE AM, Y'KNOW.
THE ONLY PEOPLE WHO'D BE OUT AND ABOUT AT THIS HOUR ARE US AND THE MICE...

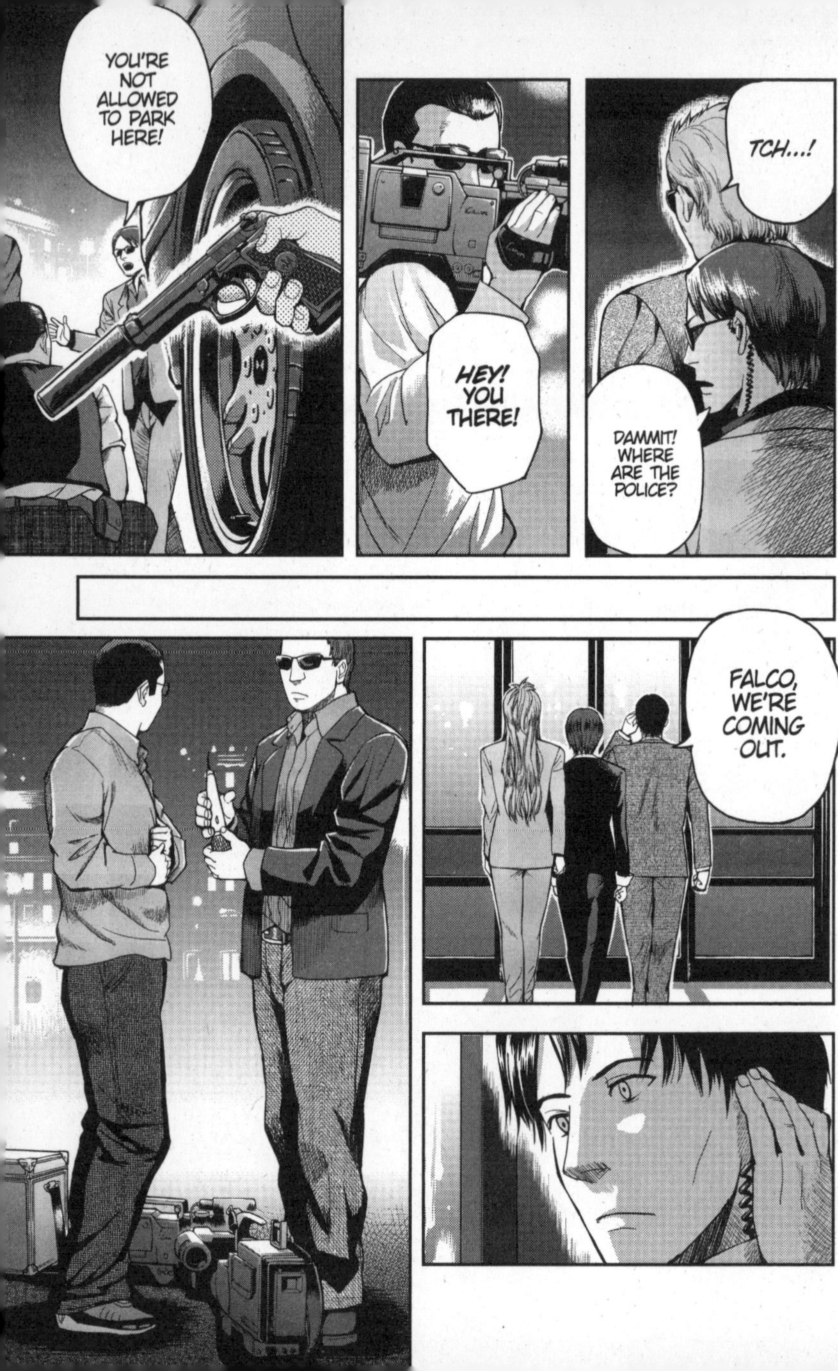
TCH...!
DAMMIT! WHERE ARE THE POLICE?
HEY! YOU THERE!
YOU'RE NOT ALLOWED TO PARK HERE!
FALCO, WE'RE COMING OUT.

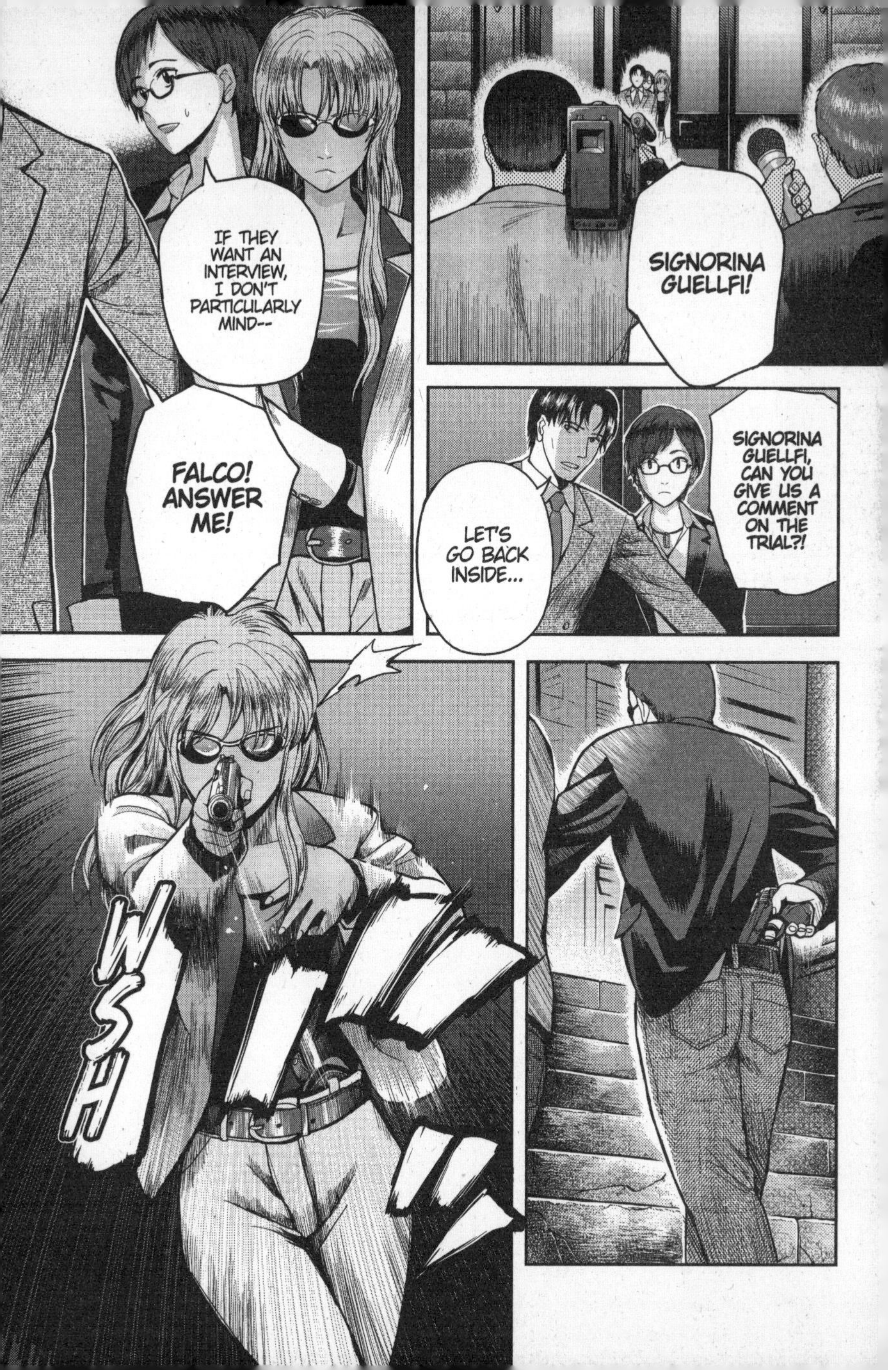
SIGNORINA GUELLFI!
SIGNORINA GUELLFI, CAN YOU GIVE US A COMMENT ON THE TRIAL?!
LET'S GO BACK INSIDE...
IF THEY WANT AN INTERVIEW, I DON'T PARTICULARLY MIND--
FALCO! ANSWER ME!
WHSH

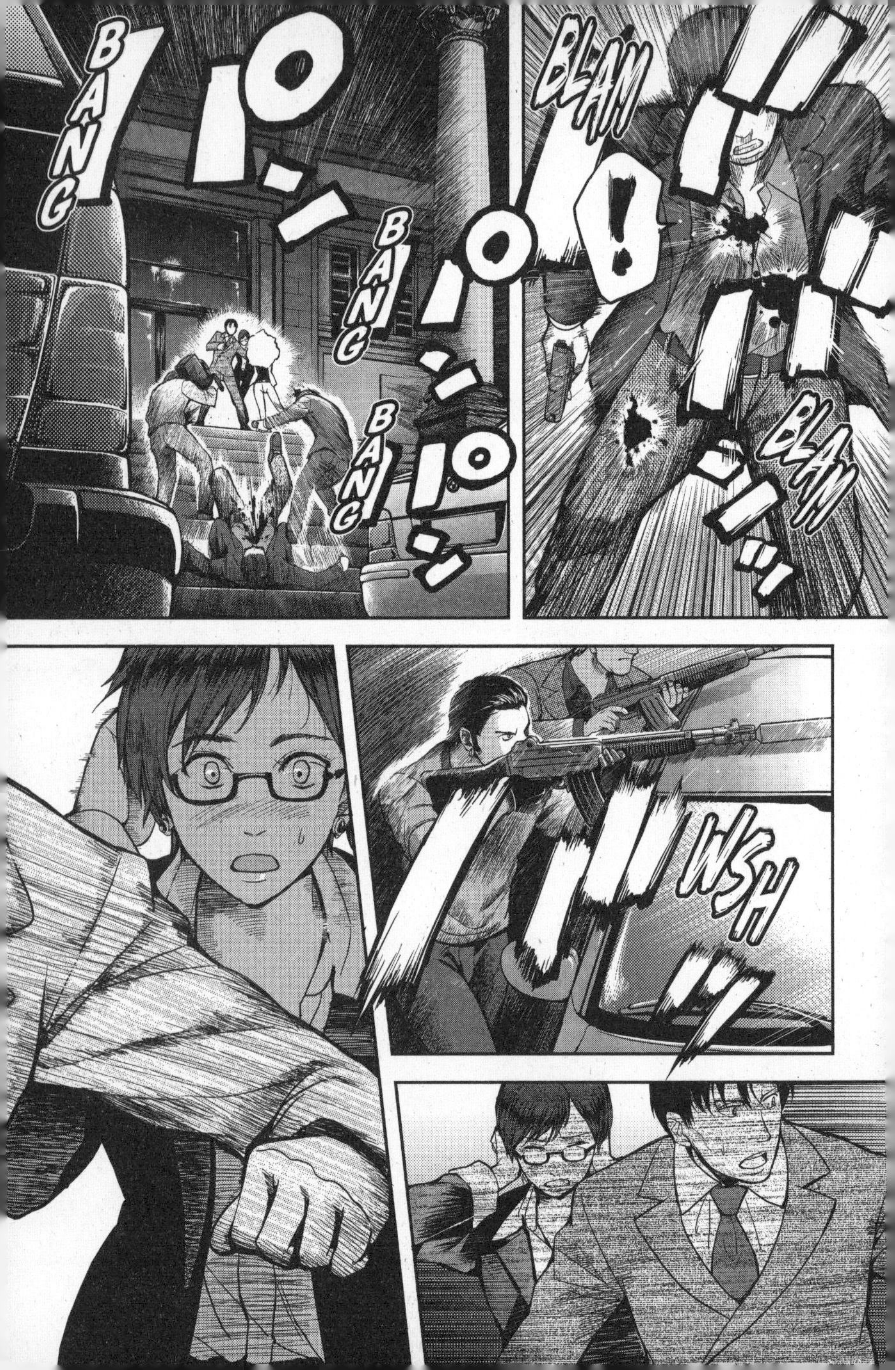
BLAM
BLAM
BANG
BANG
BANG
WSH

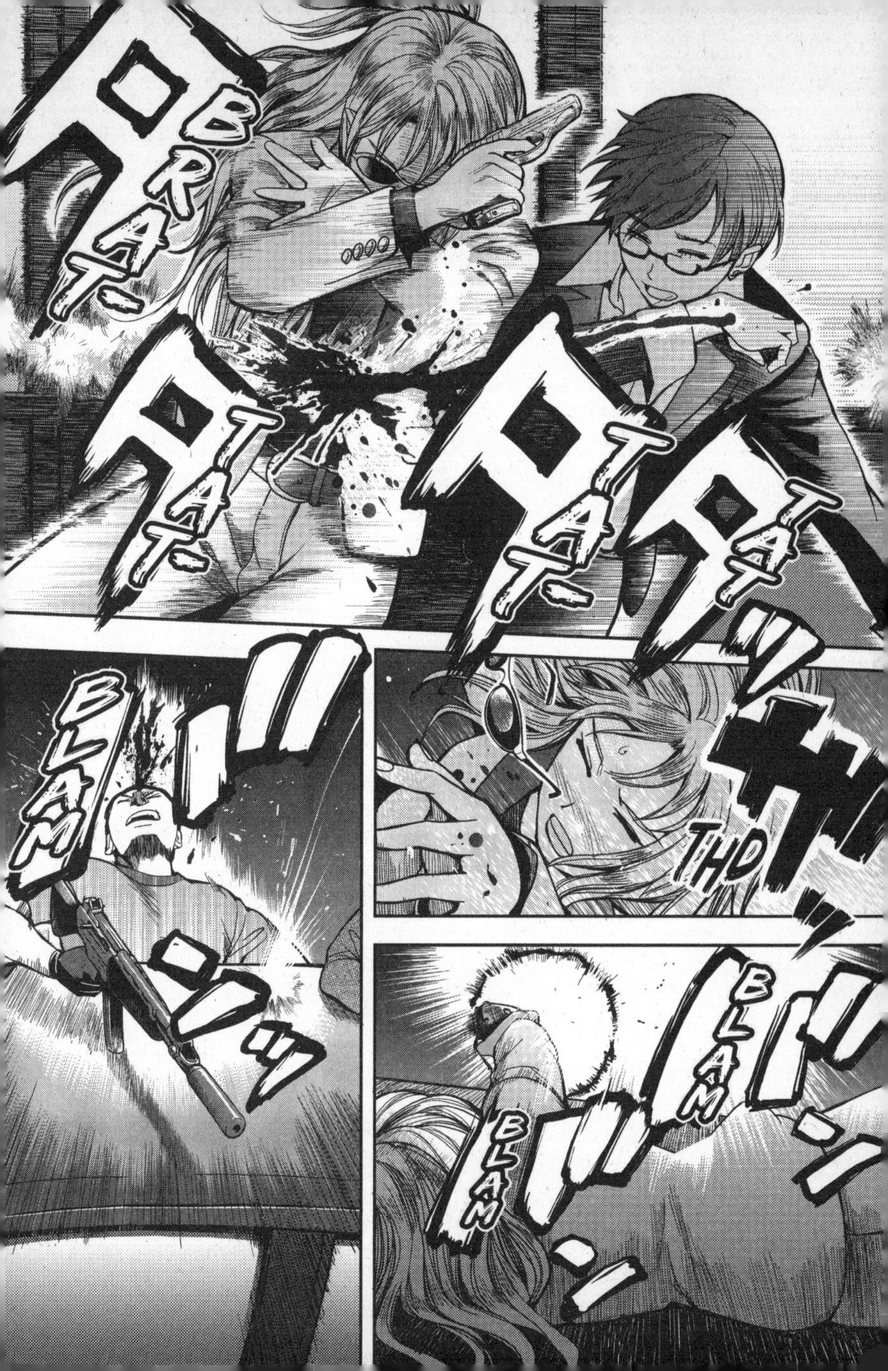
TAT-
TAT-
BRAT-
THD
BLAM
BLAM
BLAM

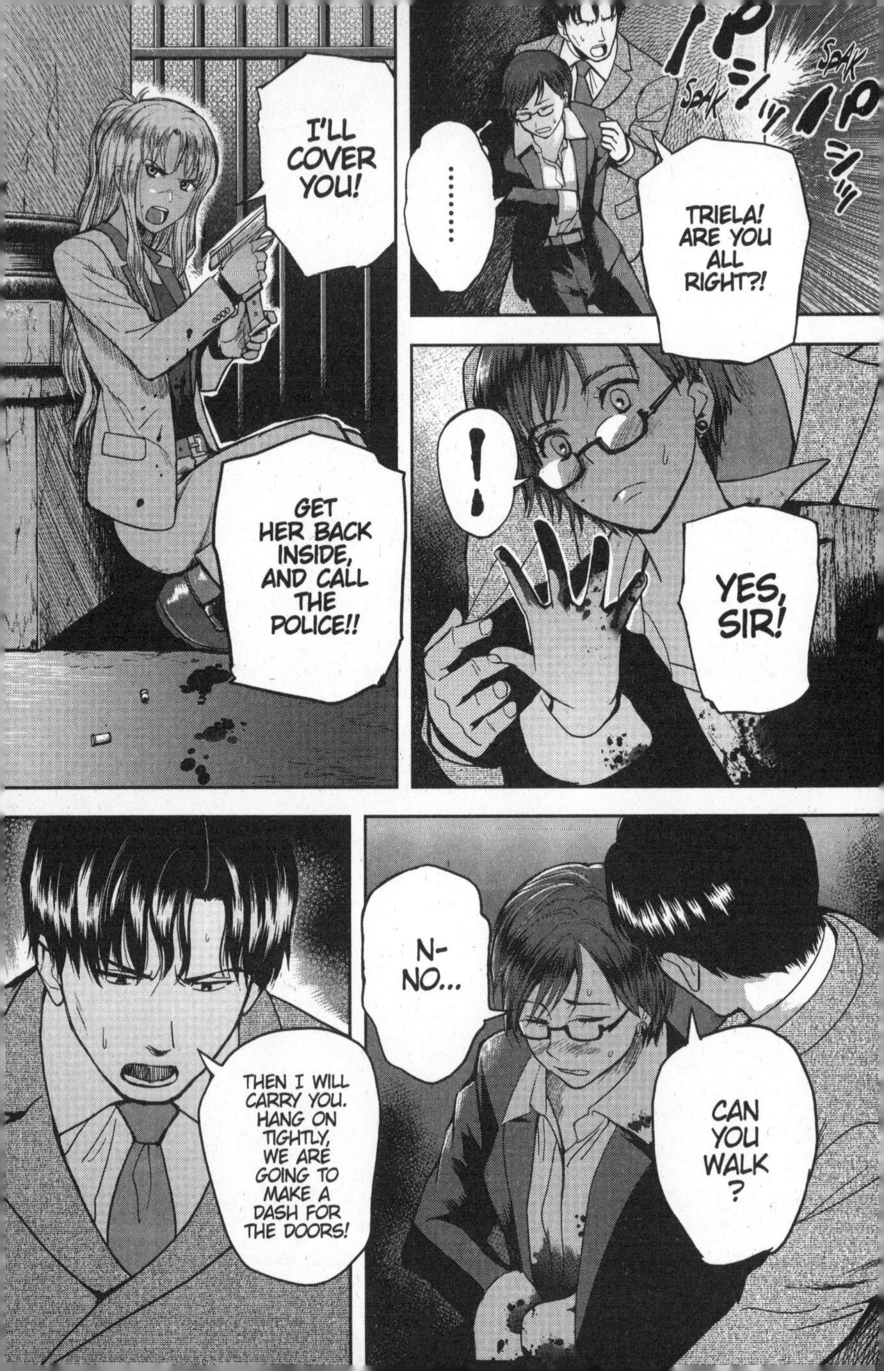
SPAK
SPAK
TRIELA! ARE YOU ALL RIGHT?!
....
YES, SIR!
!
I'LL COVER YOU!
GET HER BACK INSIDE, AND CALL THE POLICE!!
CAN YOU WALK?
N-NO...
THEN I WILL CARRY YOU. HANG ON TIGHTLY, WE ARE GOING TO MAKE A DASH FOR THE DOORS!

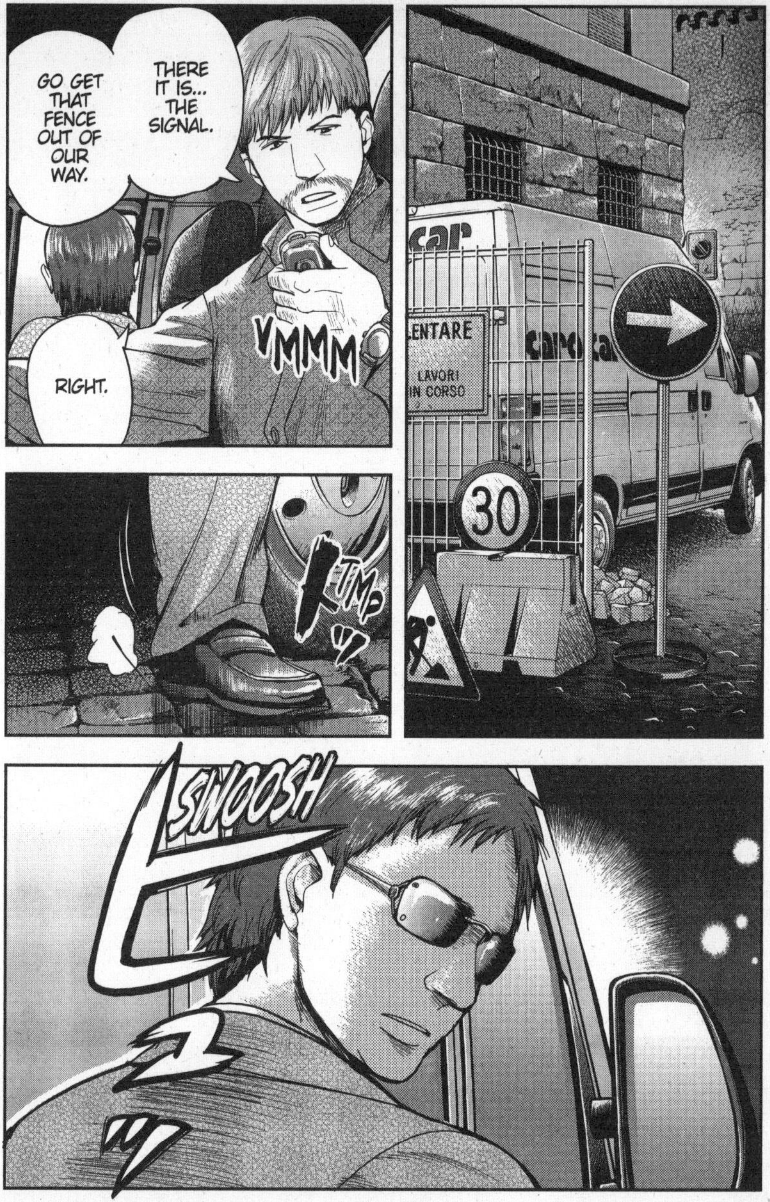
car
LENTARE
LAVORI IN CORSO
30
THERE IT IS... THE SIGNAL.
GO GET THAT FENCE OUT OF OUR WAY.
VMMM
RIGHT.
TMP
SWOOSH

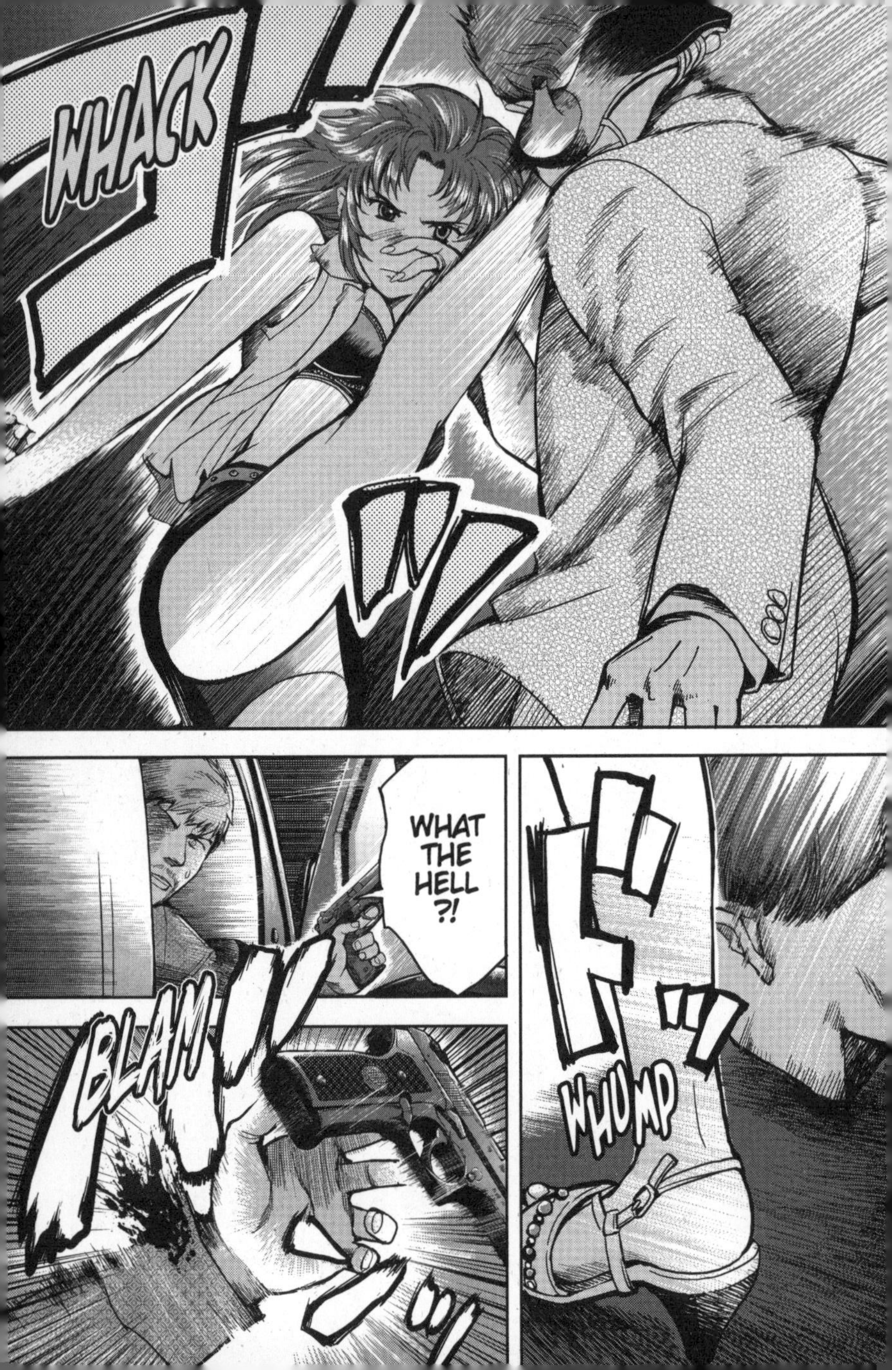
WHACK
WHUMP
WHAT THE HELL ?!
BLAM

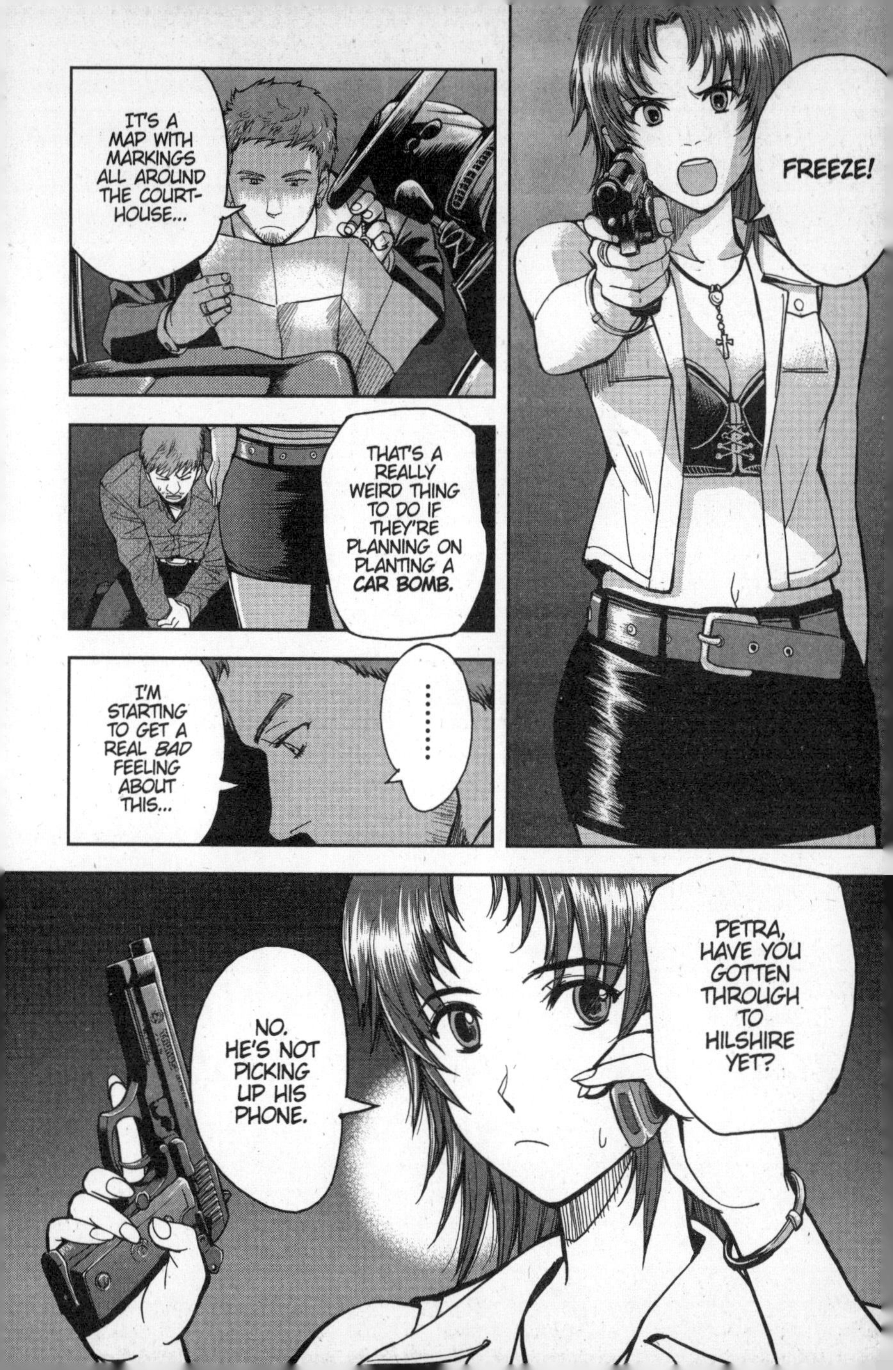
FREEZE!
IT'S A MAP WITH MARKINGS ALL AROUND THE COURT-HOUSE...
THAT'S A REALLY WEIRD THING TO DO IF THEY'RE PLANNING ON PLANTING A CAR BOMB.
....
I'M STARTING TO GET A REAL *BAD* FEELING ABOUT THIS...
PETRA, HAVE YOU GOTTEN THROUGH TO HILSHIRE YET?
NO. HE'S NOT PICKING UP HIS PHONE.

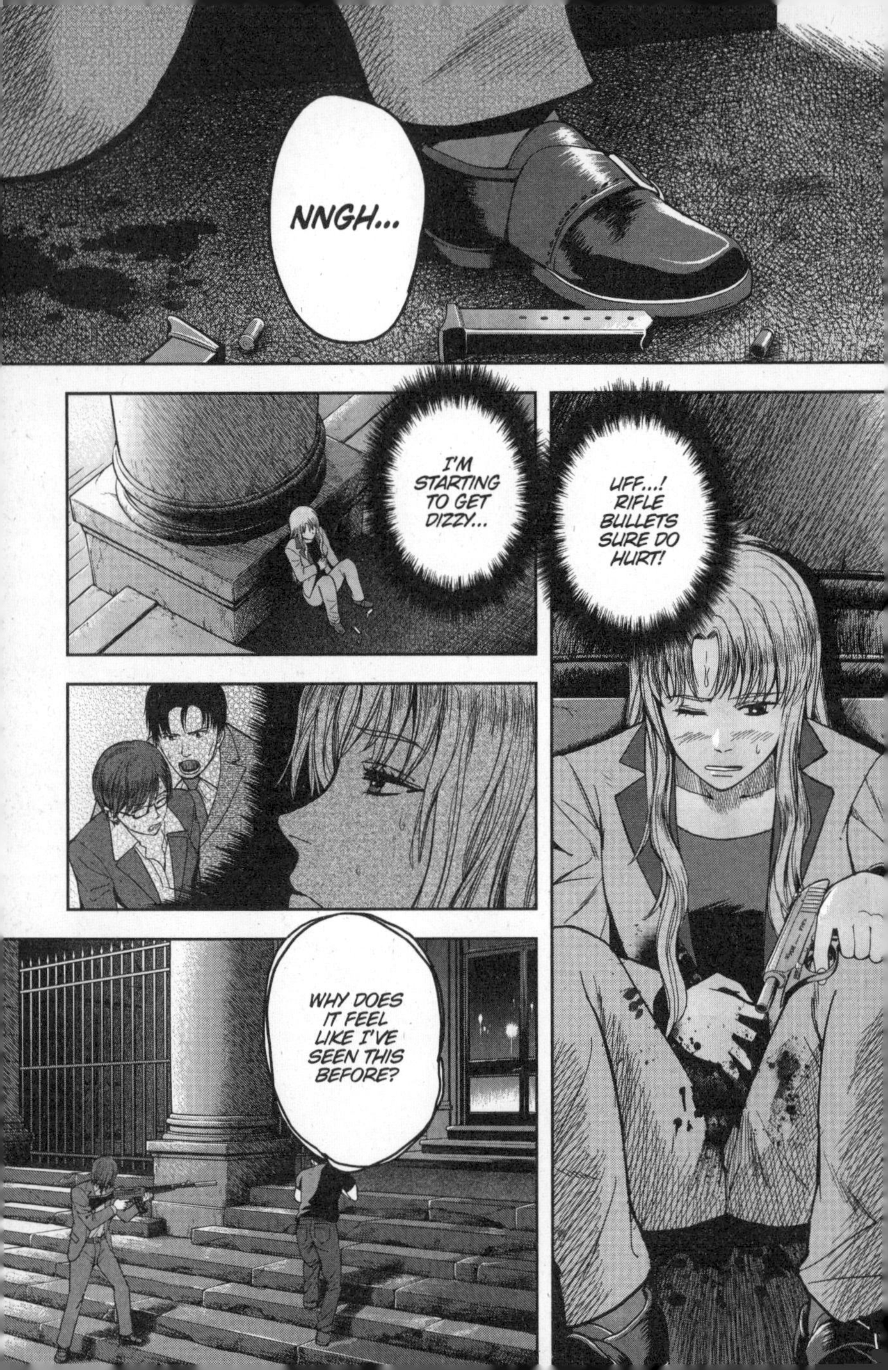
NNGH...
UFF...! RIFLE BULLETS SURE DO HURT!
I'M STARTING TO GET DIZZY...
WHY DOES IT FEEL LIKE I'VE SEEN THIS BEFORE?

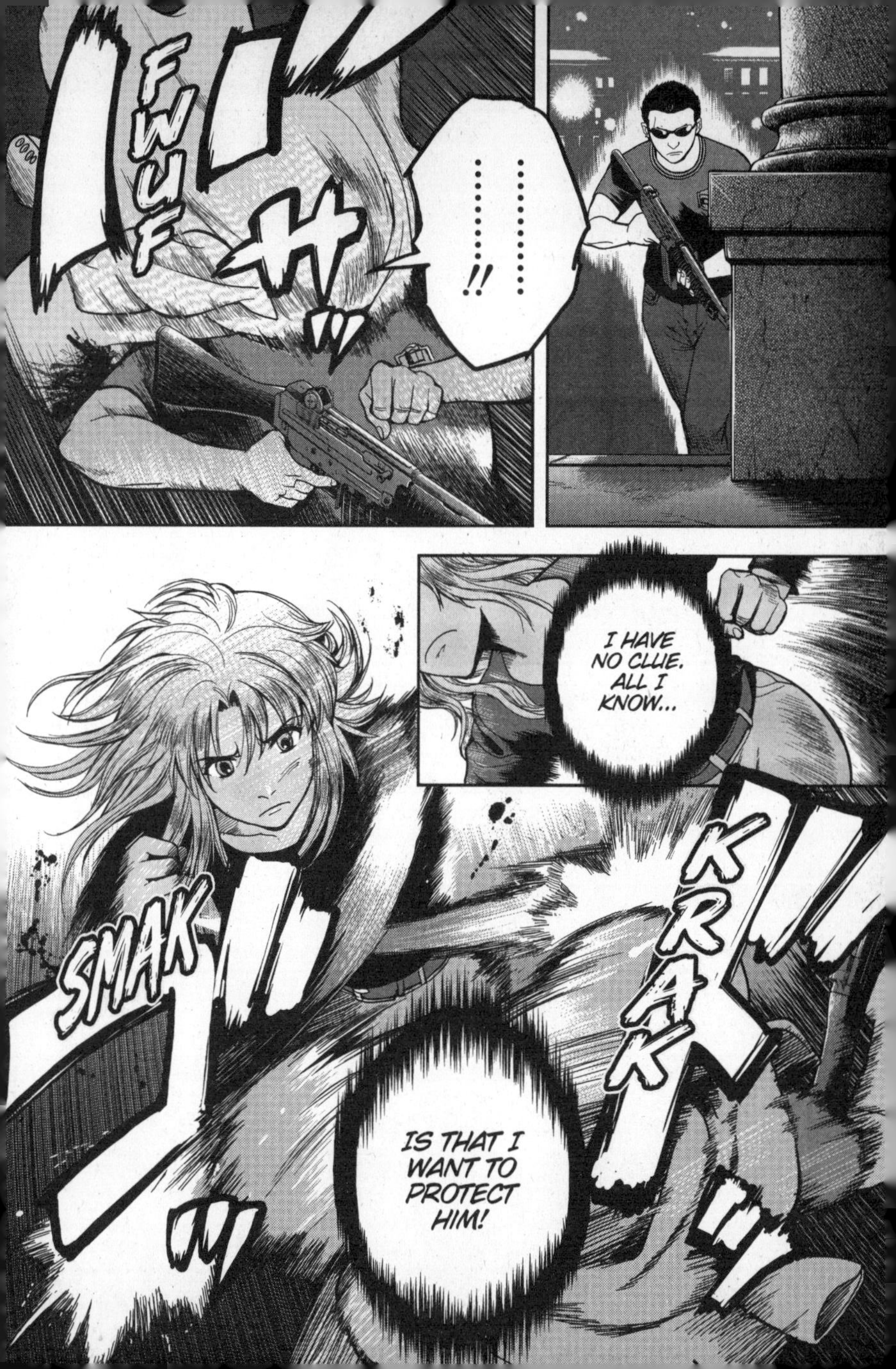

......
......!!
FWUF
I HAVE NO CLUE. ALL I KNOW...
KRAK
SMAK
IS THAT I WANT TO PROTECT HIM!

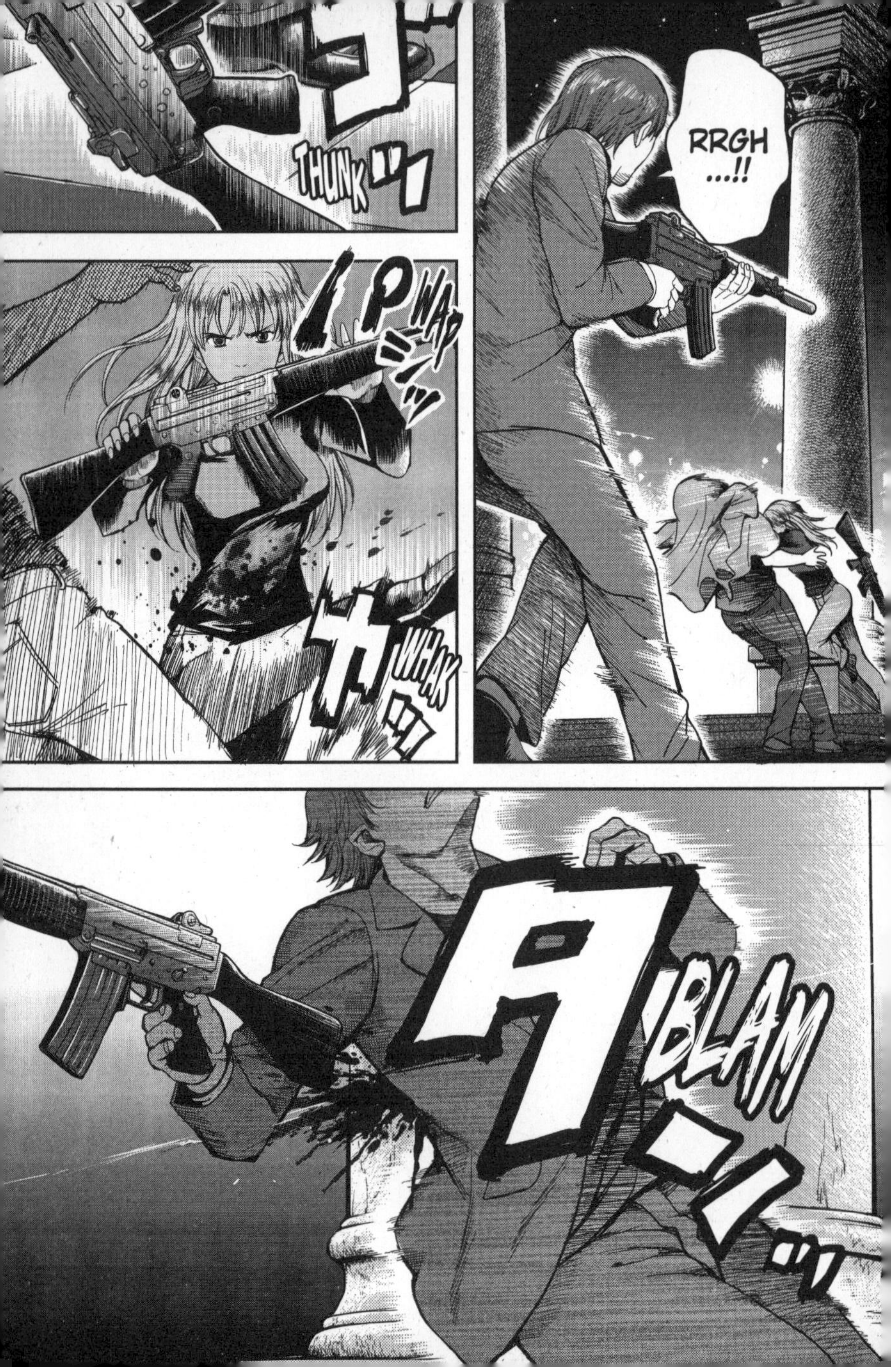
RRGH
...!!
THUNK
WAP
WHAK
BLAM

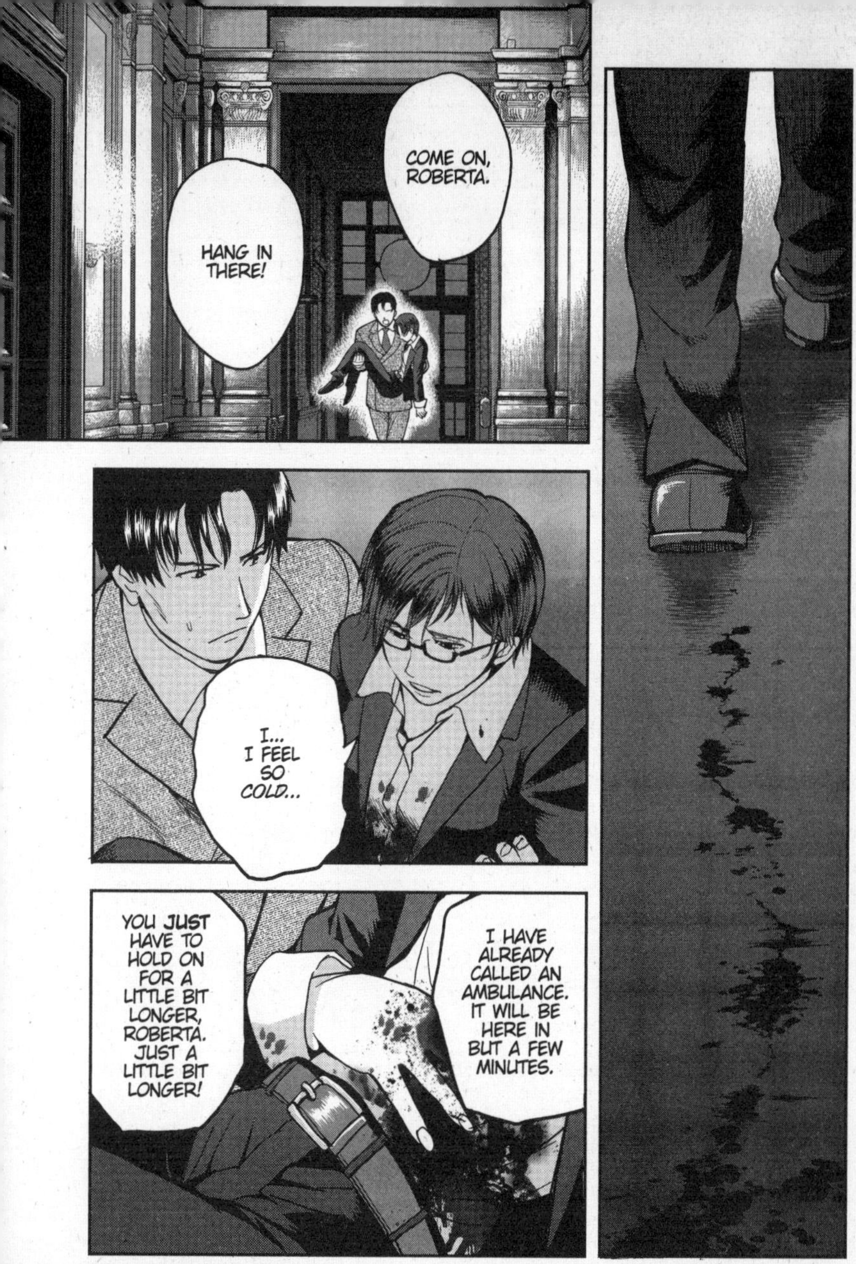
COME ON, ROBERTA.
HANG IN THERE!
I... I FEEL SO COLD...
I HAVE ALREADY CALLED AN AMBULANCE. IT WILL BE HERE IN BUT A FEW MINUTES.
YOU **JUST** HAVE TO HOLD ON FOR A LITTLE BIT LONGER, ROBERTA. JUST A LITTLE BIT LONGER!

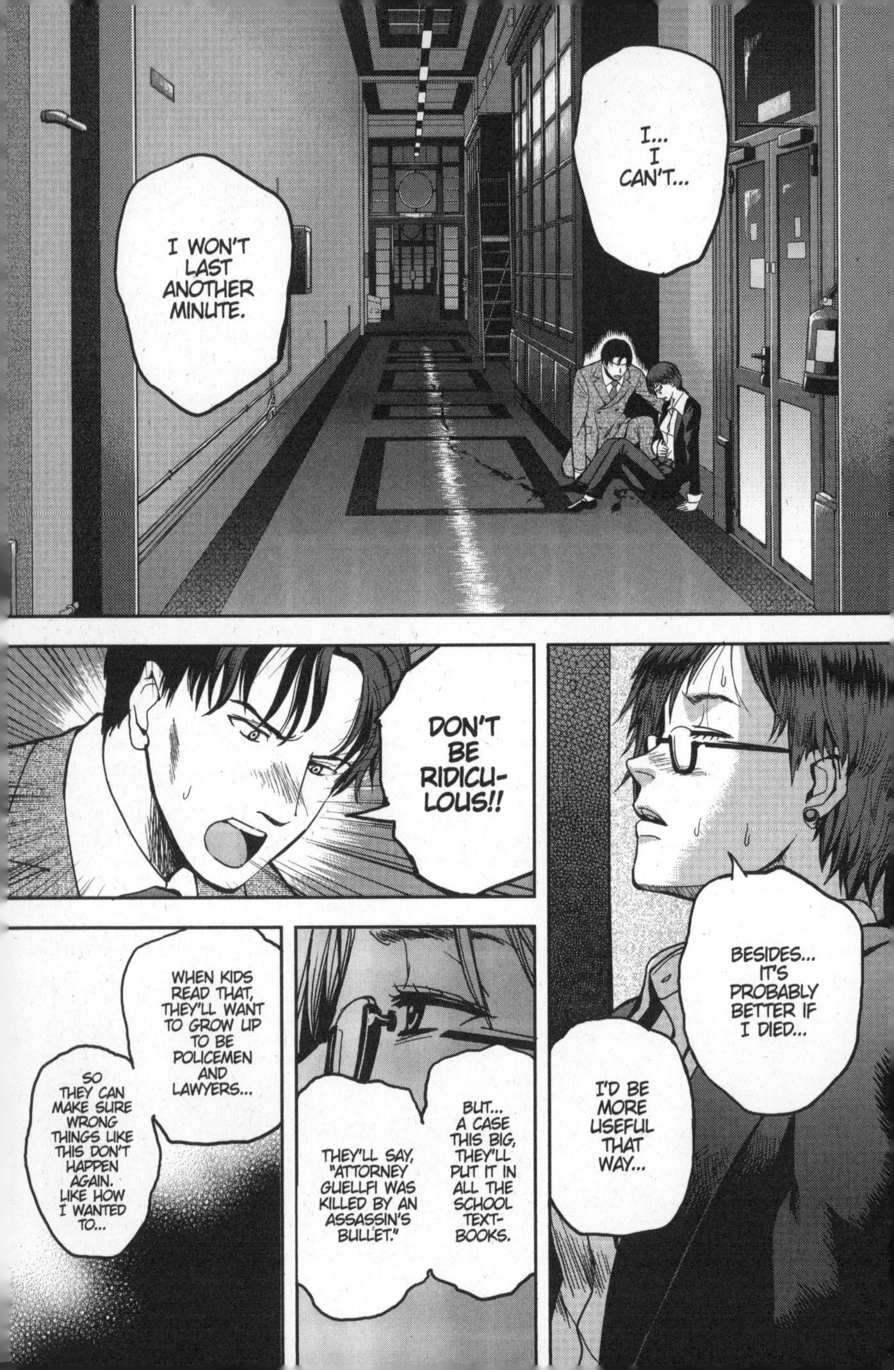
I... I CAN'T...
I WON'T LAST ANOTHER MINUTE.
BESIDES... IT'S PROBABLY BETTER IF I DIED...
I'D BE MORE USEFUL THAT WAY...
DON'T BE RIDICULOUS!!
BUT... A CASE THIS BIG, THEY'LL PUT IT IN ALL THE SCHOOL TEXT-BOOKS.
THEY'LL SAY, "ATTORNEY GUELLFI WAS KILLED BY AN ASSASSIN'S BULLET."
WHEN KIDS READ THAT, THEY'LL WANT TO GROW UP TO BE POLICEMEN AND LAWYERS...
SO THEY CAN MAKE SURE WRONG THINGS LIKE THIS DON'T HAPPEN AGAIN. LIKE HOW I WANTED TO...

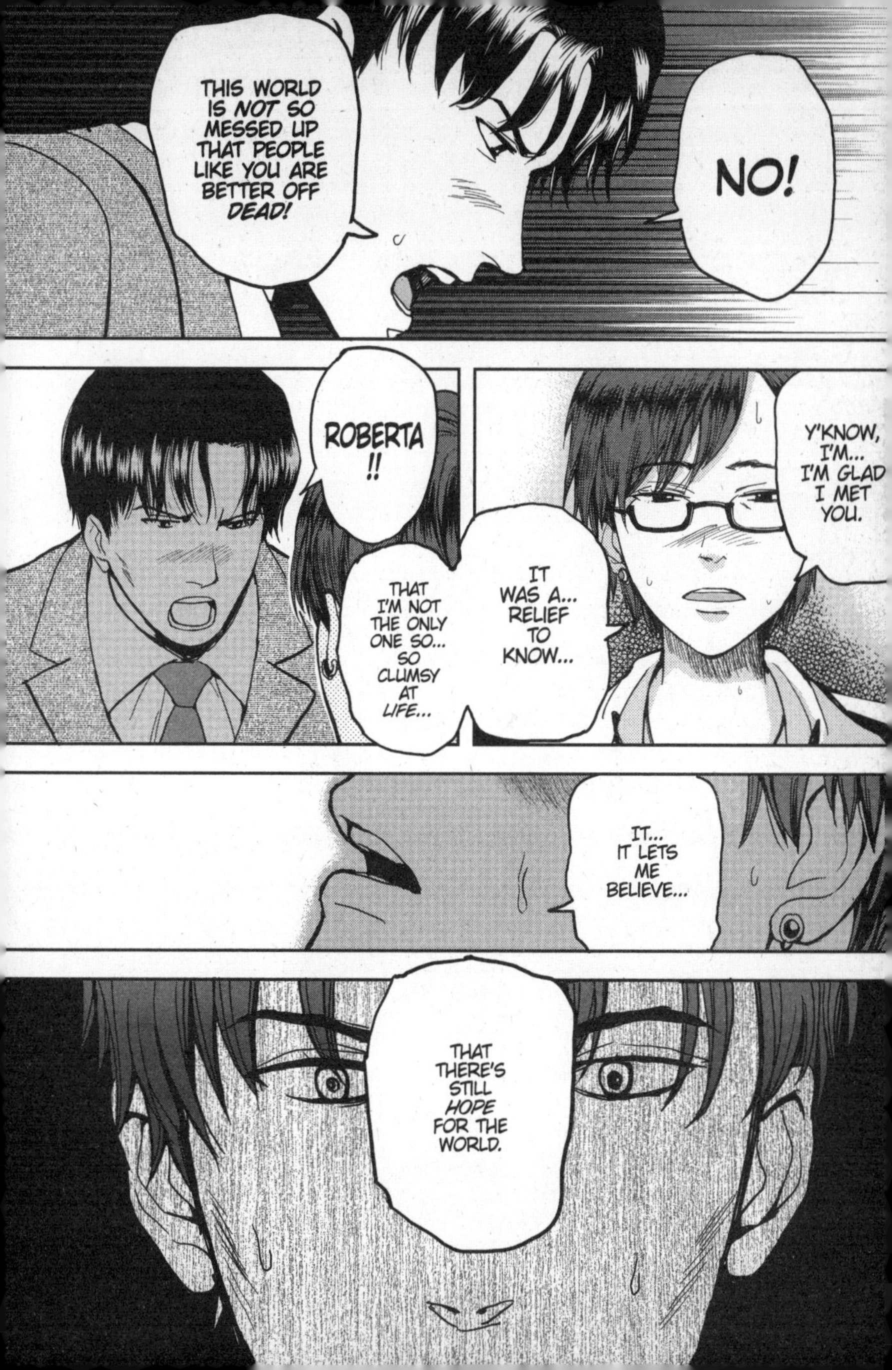
NO!
THIS WORLD IS *NOT* SO MESSED UP THAT PEOPLE LIKE YOU ARE BETTER OFF *DEAD!*
Y'KNOW, I'M... I'M GLAD I MET YOU.
IT WAS A... RELIEF TO KNOW...
THAT I'M NOT THE ONLY ONE SO... SO CLUMSY AT *LIFE*...
ROBERTA !!
IT... IT LETS ME BELIEVE...
THAT THERE'S STILL *HOPE* FOR THE WORLD.

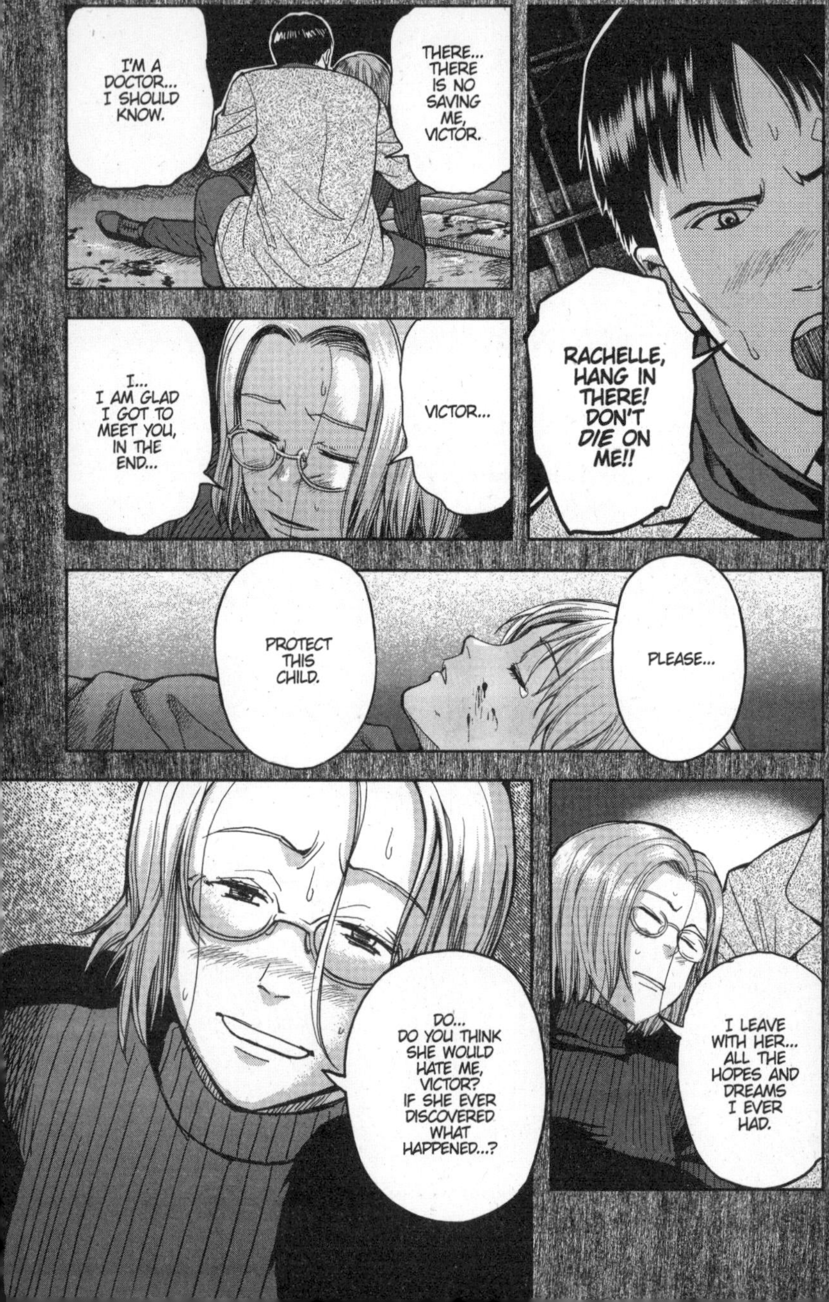
RACHELLE, HANG IN THERE! DON'T *DIE* ON ME!!
THERE... THERE IS NO SAVING ME, VICTOR.
I'M A DOCTOR... I SHOULD KNOW.
VICTOR...
I... I AM GLAD I GOT TO MEET YOU, IN THE END...
PLEASE...
PROTECT THIS CHILD.
I LEAVE WITH HER... ALL THE HOPES AND DREAMS I EVER HAD.
DO... DO YOU THINK SHE WOULD HATE ME, VICTOR? IF SHE EVER DISCOVERED WHAT HAPPENED...?

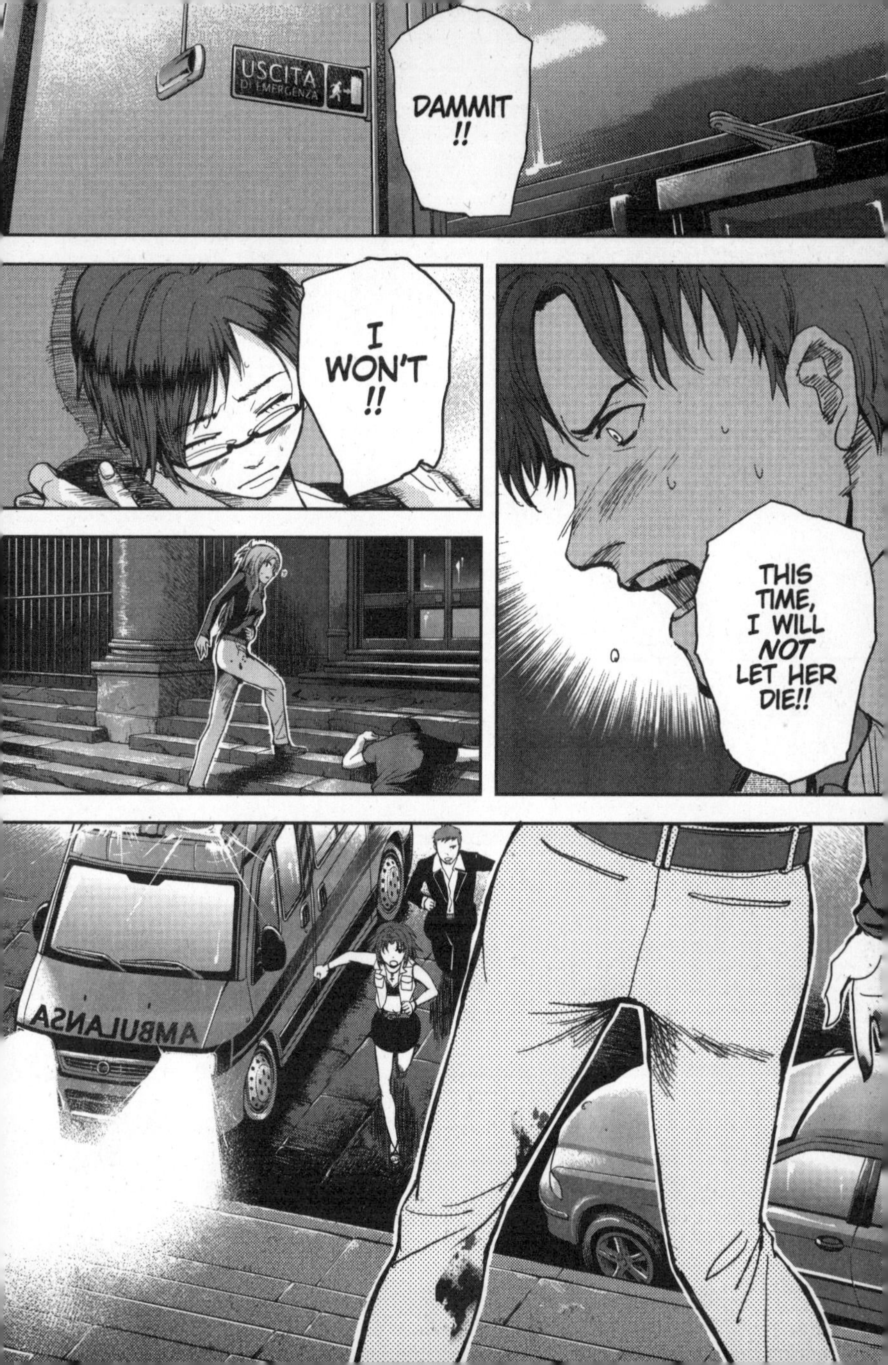
DAMMIT!!
USCITA DI EMERGENZA
THIS TIME, I WILL *NOT* LET HER DIE!!
I WON'T!!
AMBULANSA

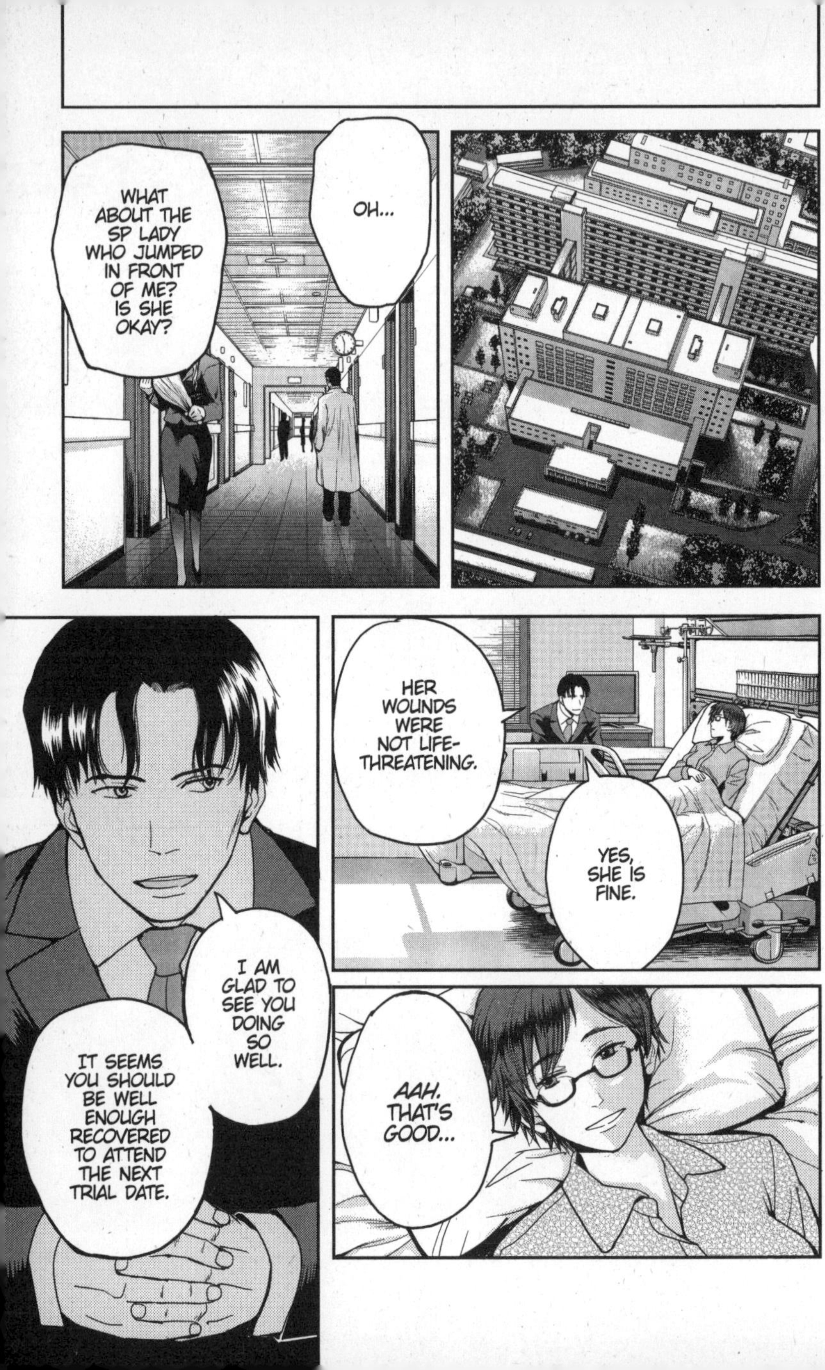
OH...
WHAT ABOUT THE SP LADY WHO JUMPED IN FRONT OF ME? IS SHE OKAY?
HER WOUNDS WERE NOT LIFE-THREATENING.
YES, SHE IS FINE.
AAH. THAT'S GOOD...
I AM GLAD TO SEE YOU DOING SO WELL.
IT SEEMS YOU SHOULD BE WELL ENOUGH RECOVERED TO ATTEND THE NEXT TRIAL DATE.

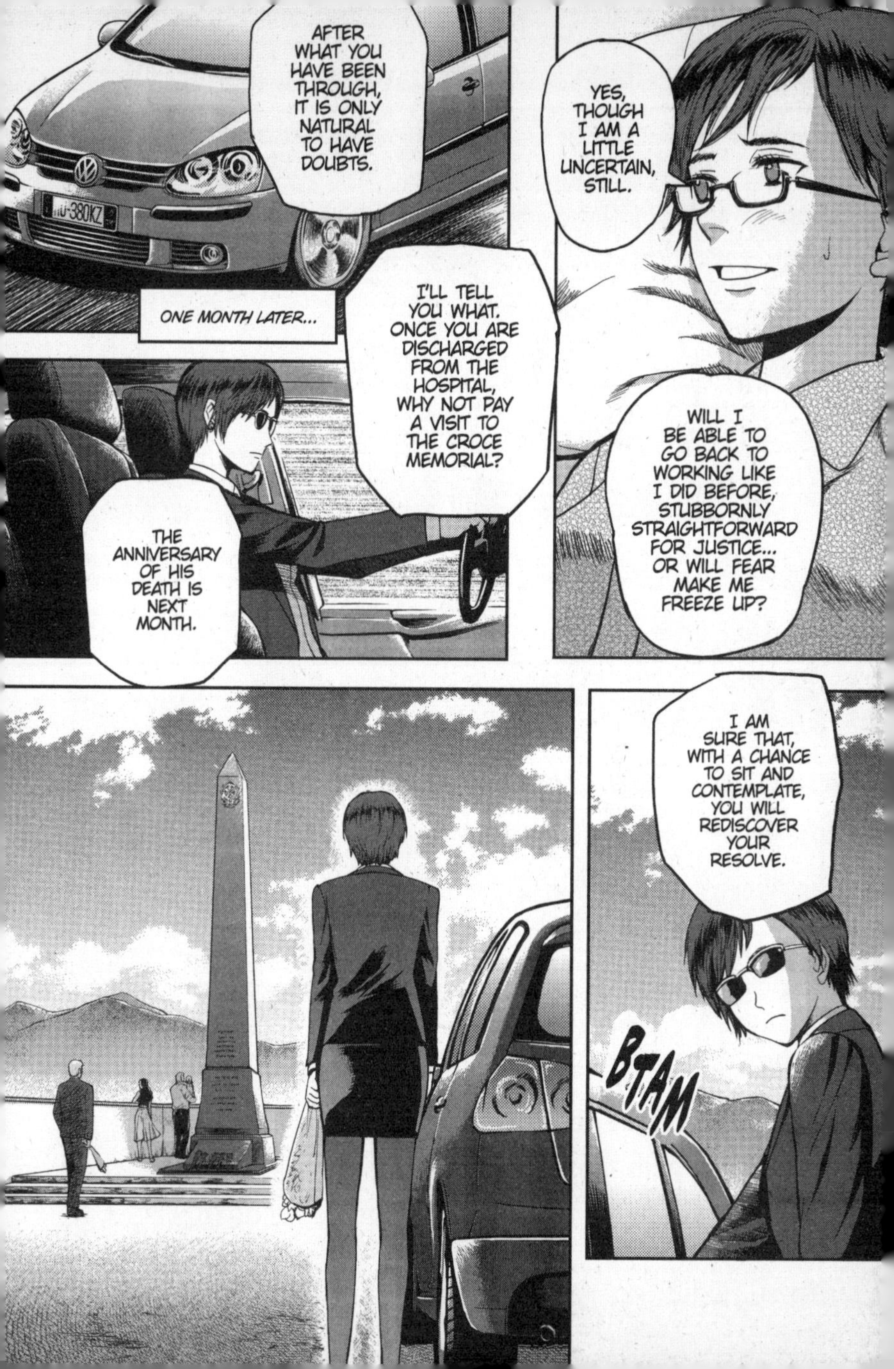
YES, THOUGH I AM A LITTLE UNCERTAIN, STILL.
WILL I BE ABLE TO GO BACK TO WORKING LIKE I DID BEFORE, STUBBORNLY STRAIGHTFORWARD FOR JUSTICE... OR WILL FEAR MAKE ME FREEZE UP?
AFTER WHAT YOU HAVE BEEN THROUGH, IT IS ONLY NATURAL TO HAVE DOUBTS.
ONE MONTH LATER...
I'LL TELL YOU WHAT. ONCE YOU ARE DISCHARGED FROM THE HOSPITAL, WHY NOT PAY A VISIT TO THE CROCE MEMORIAL?
THE ANNIVERSARY OF HIS DEATH IS NEXT MONTH.
I AM SURE THAT, WITH A CHANCE TO SIT AND CONTEMPLATE, YOU WILL REDISCOVER YOUR RESOLVE.
BTAM

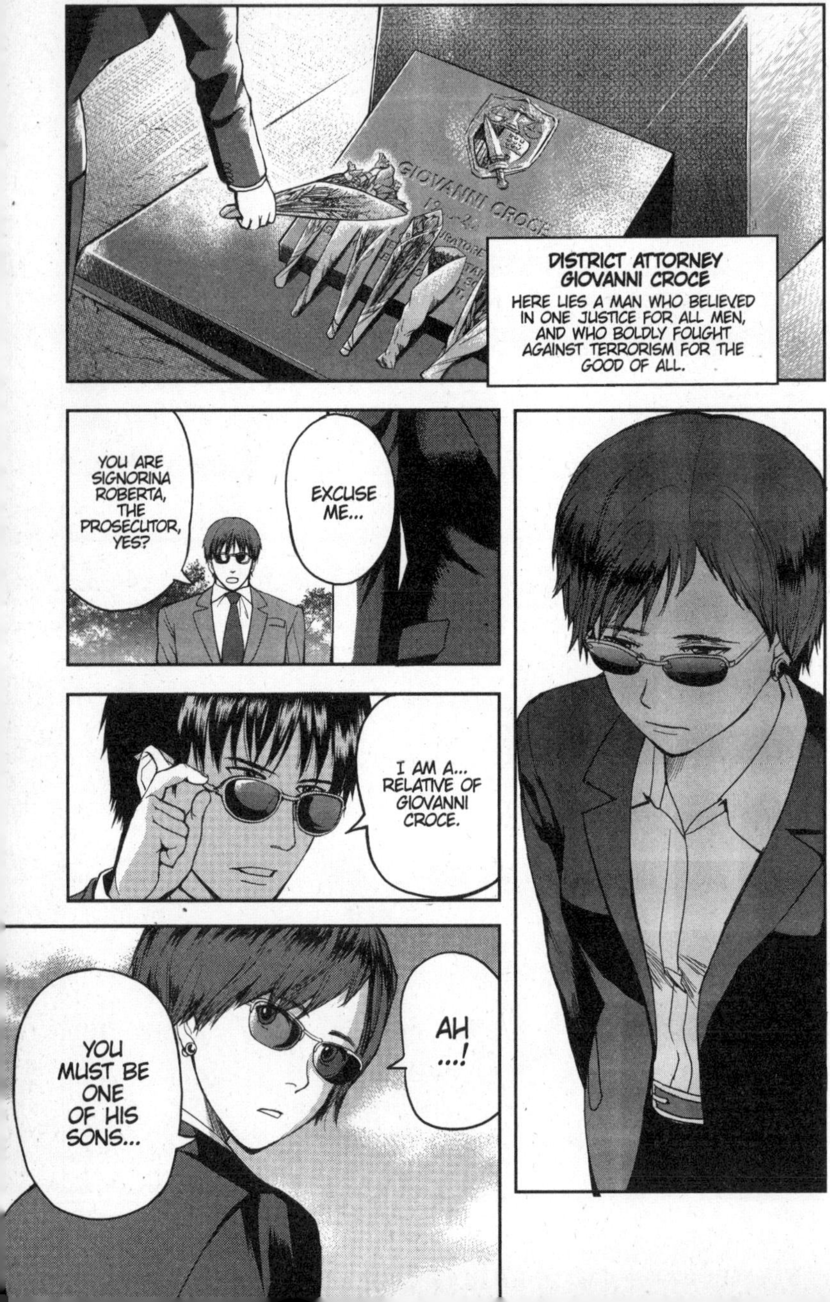
GIOVANNI CROCE
DISTRICT ATTORNEY GIOVANNI CROCE
HERE LIES A MAN WHO BELIEVED IN ONE JUSTICE FOR ALL MEN, AND WHO BOLDLY FOUGHT AGAINST TERRORISM FOR THE GOOD OF ALL.
EXCUSE ME...
YOU ARE SIGNORINA ROBERTA, THE PROSECUTOR, YES?
I AM A... RELATIVE OF GIOVANNI CROCE.
AH ...!
YOU MUST BE ONE OF HIS SONS...

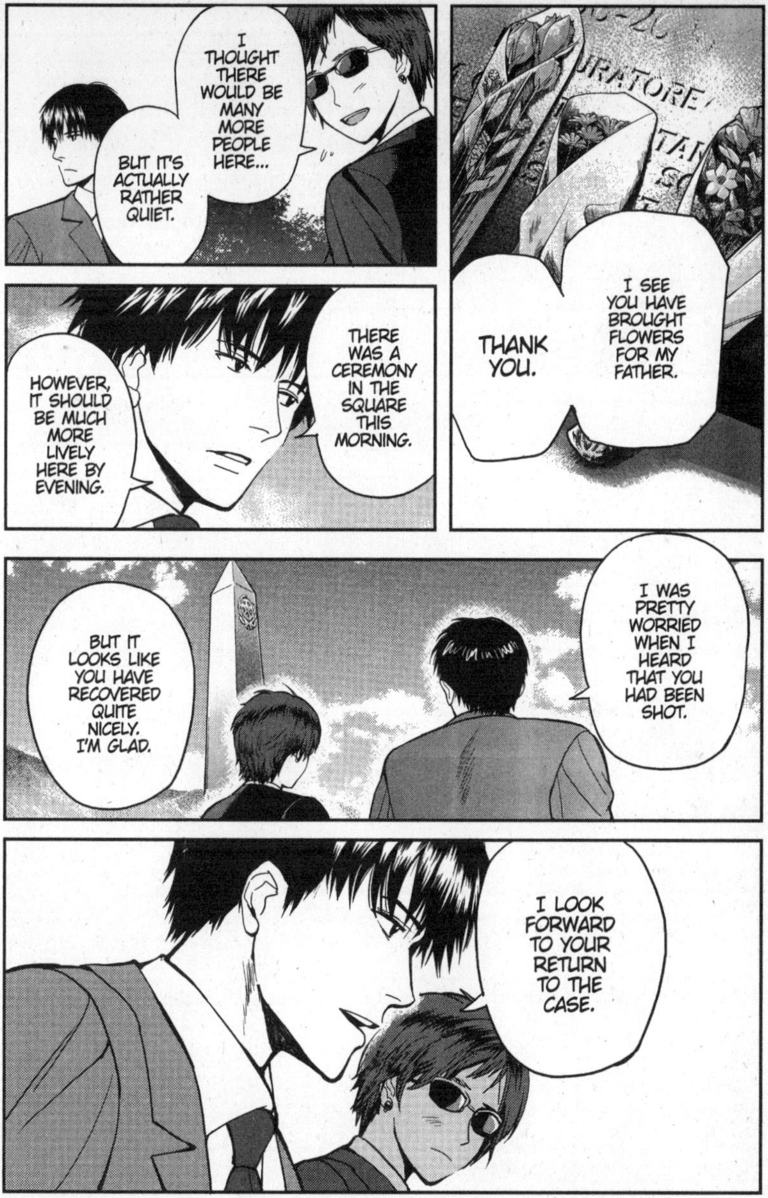
I SEE YOU HAVE BROUGHT FLOWERS FOR MY FATHER.
THANK YOU.
I THOUGHT THERE WOULD BE MANY MORE PEOPLE HERE...
BUT IT'S ACTUALLY RATHER QUIET.
THERE WAS A CEREMONY IN THE SQUARE THIS MORNING.
HOWEVER, IT SHOULD BE MUCH MORE LIVELY HERE BY EVENING.
I WAS PRETTY WORRIED WHEN I HEARD THAT YOU HAD BEEN SHOT.
BUT IT LOOKS LIKE YOU HAVE RECOVERED QUITE NICELY. I'M GLAD.
I LOOK FORWARD TO YOUR RETURN TO THE CASE.

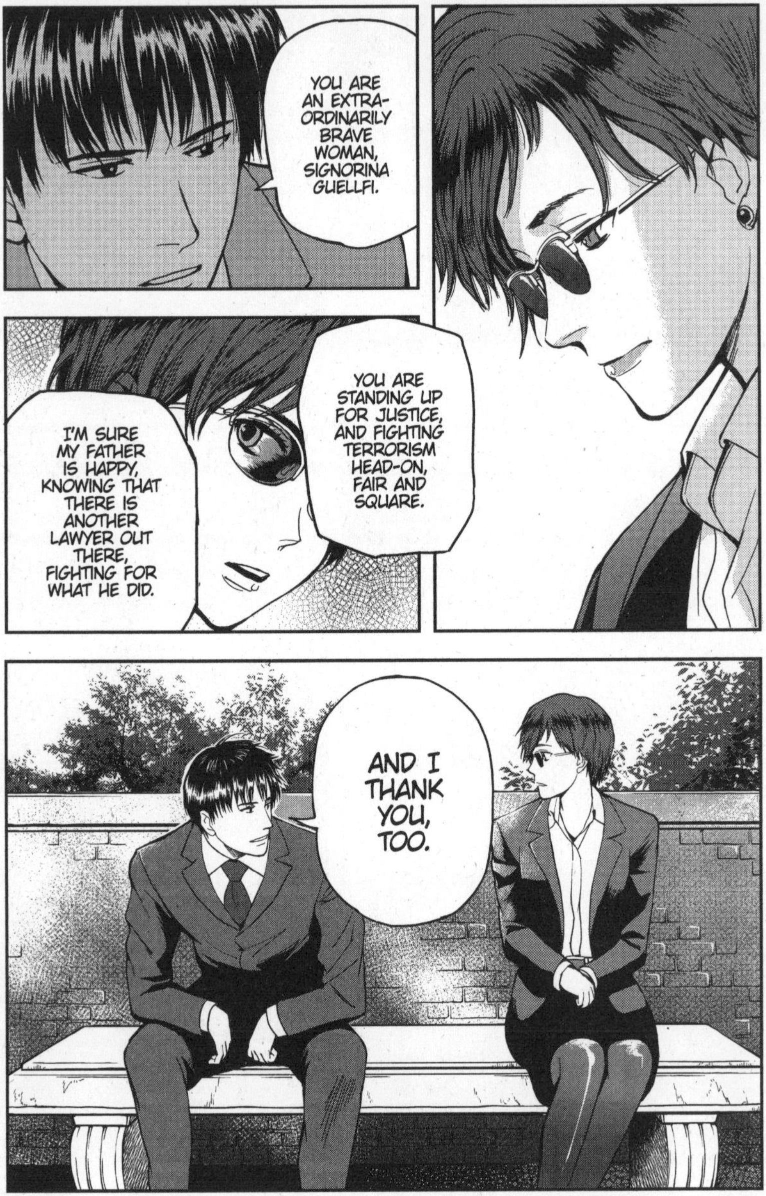
YOU ARE AN EXTRA-ORDINARILY BRAVE WOMAN, SIGNORINA GUELLFI.
YOU ARE STANDING UP FOR JUSTICE, AND FIGHTING TERRORISM HEAD-ON, FAIR AND SQUARE.
I'M SURE MY FATHER IS HAPPY, KNOWING THAT THERE IS ANOTHER LAWYER OUT THERE, FIGHTING FOR WHAT HE DID.
AND I THANK YOU, TOO.

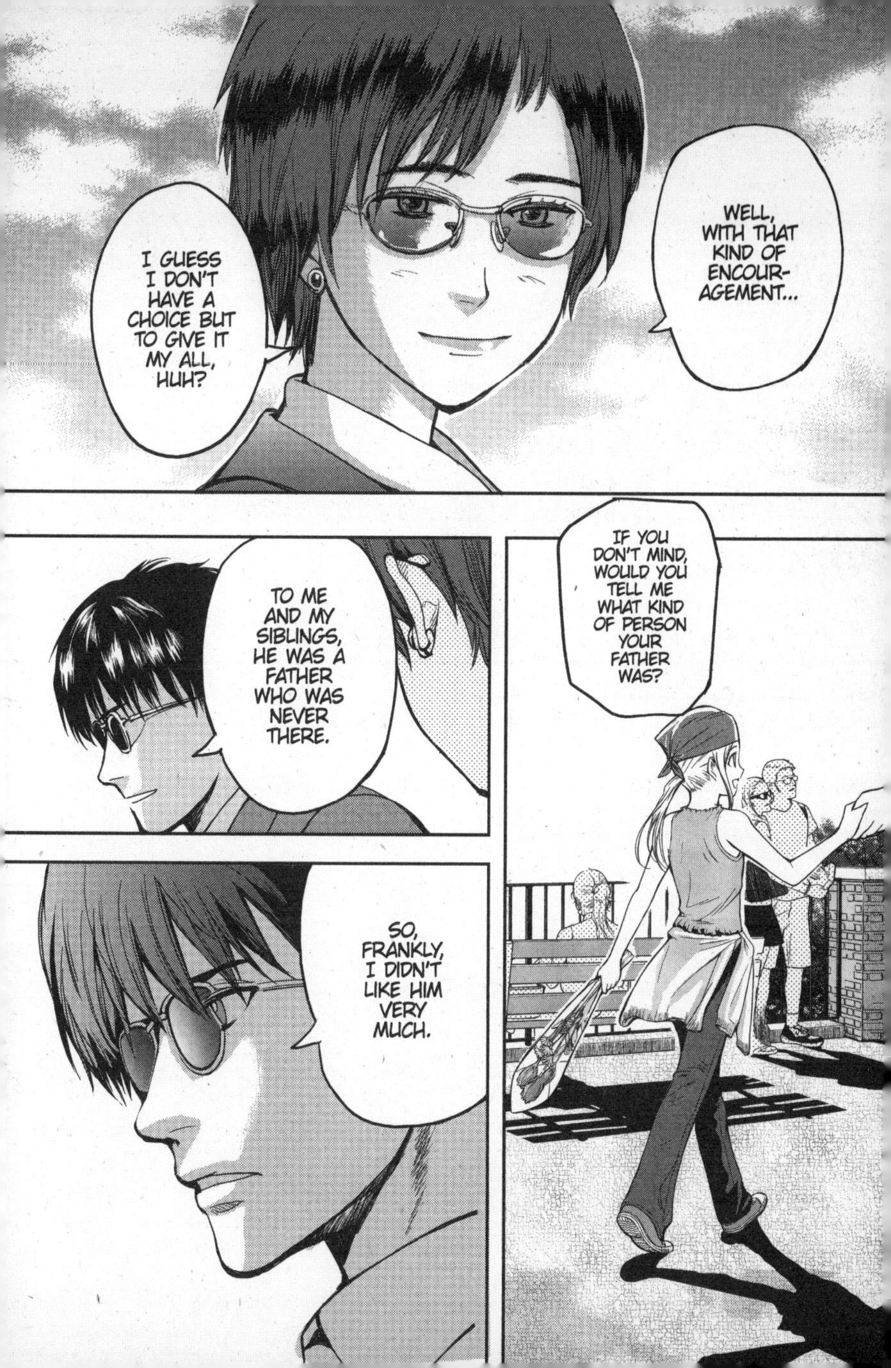
WELL, WITH THAT KIND OF ENCOUR-AGEMENT...
I GUESS I DON'T HAVE A CHOICE BUT TO GIVE IT MY ALL, HUH?
IF YOU DON'T MIND, WOULD YOU TELL ME WHAT KIND OF PERSON YOUR FATHER WAS?
TO ME AND MY SIBLINGS, HE WAS A FATHER WHO WAS NEVER THERE.
SO, FRANKLY, I DIDN'T LIKE HIM VERY MUCH.

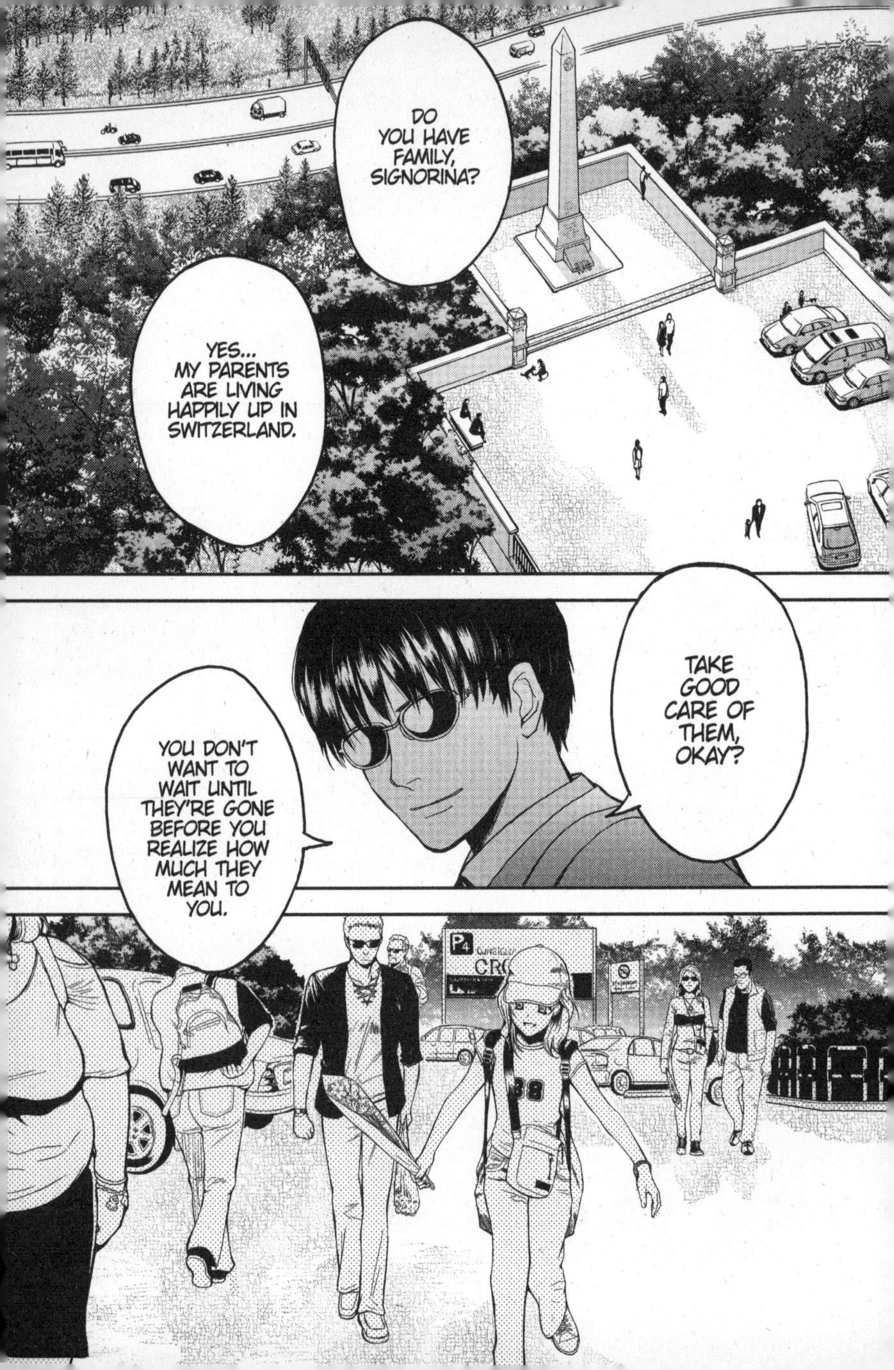
DO YOU HAVE FAMILY, SIGNORINA?
YES... MY PARENTS ARE LIVING HAPPILY UP IN SWITZERLAND.
TAKE GOOD CARE OF THEM, OKAY?
YOU DON'T WANT TO WAIT UNTIL THEY'RE GONE BEFORE YOU REALIZE HOW MUCH THEY MEAN TO YOU.

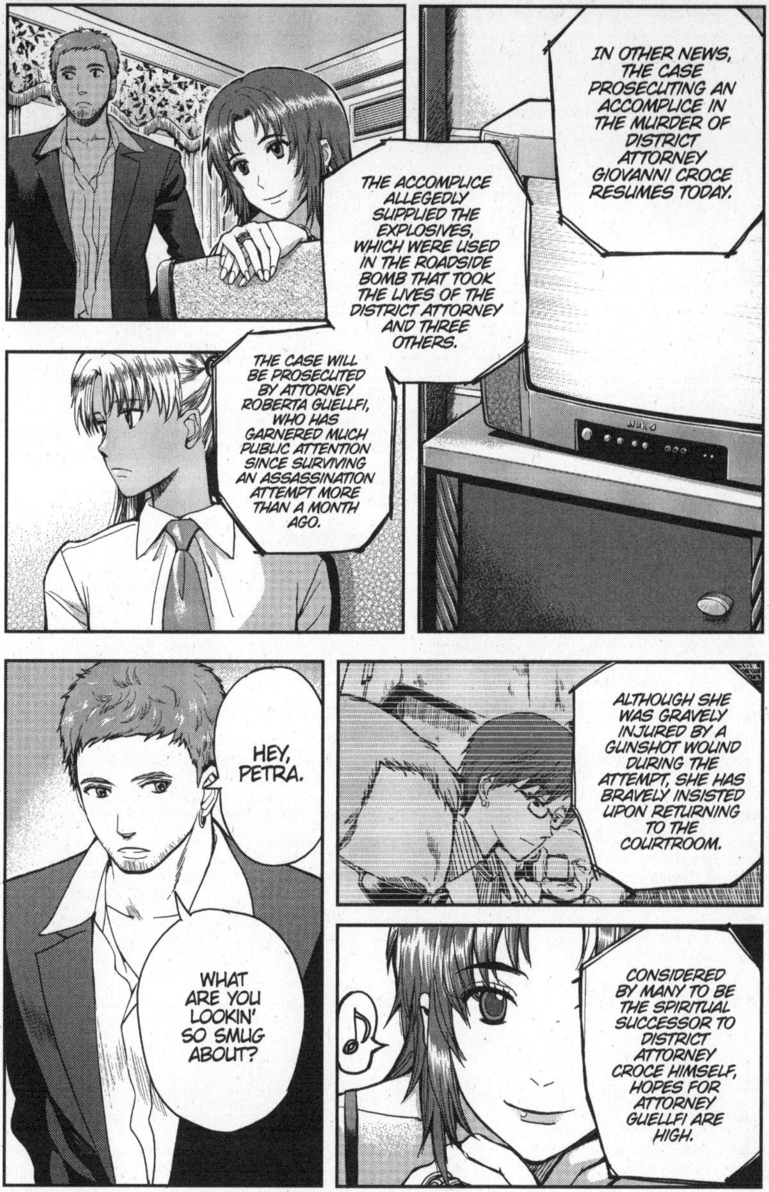
IN OTHER NEWS, THE CASE PROSECUTING AN ACCOMPLICE IN THE MURDER OF DISTRICT ATTORNEY GIOVANNI CROCE RESUMES TODAY.
THE ACCOMPLICE ALLEGEDLY SUPPLIED THE EXPLOSIVES, WHICH WERE USED IN THE ROADSIDE BOMB THAT TOOK THE LIVES OF THE DISTRICT ATTORNEY AND THREE OTHERS.
THE CASE WILL BE PROSECUTED BY ATTORNEY ROBERTA GUELLFI, WHO HAS GARNERED MUCH PUBLIC ATTENTION SINCE SURVIVING AN ASSASSINATION ATTEMPT MORE THAN A MONTH AGO.
ALTHOUGH SHE WAS GRAVELY INJURED BY A GUNSHOT WOUND DURING THE ATTEMPT, SHE HAS BRAVELY INSISTED UPON RETURNING TO THE COURTROOM.
CONSIDERED BY MANY TO BE THE SPIRITUAL SUCCESSOR TO DISTRICT ATTORNEY CROCE HIMSELF, HOPES FOR ATTORNEY GUELLFI ARE HIGH.
HEY, PETRA.
WHAT ARE YOU LOOKIN' SO SMUG ABOUT?

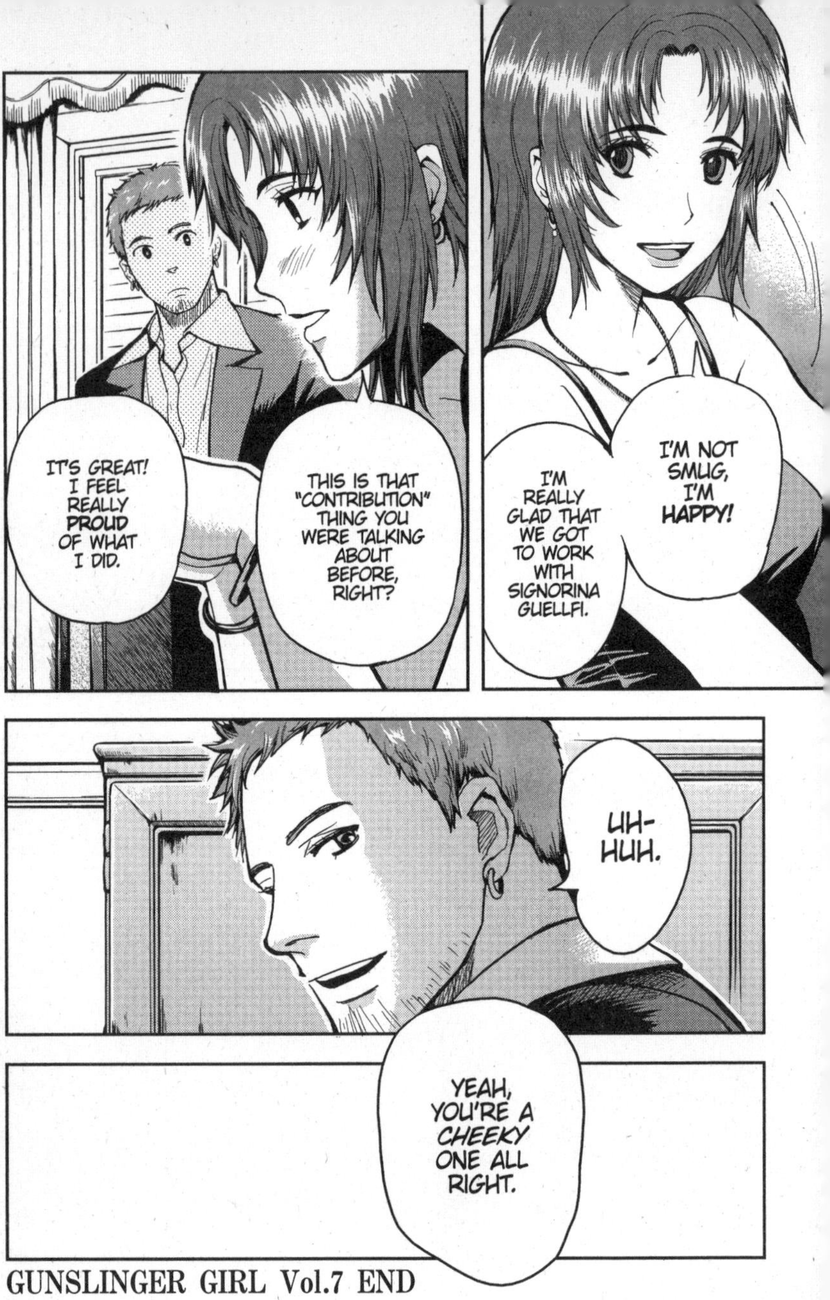
I'M NOT SMUG, I'M HAPPY!
I'M REALLY GLAD THAT WE GOT TO WORK WITH SIGNORINA GUELLFI.
THIS IS THAT "CONTRIBUTION" THING YOU WERE TALKING ABOUT BEFORE, RIGHT?
IT'S GREAT! I FEEL REALLY PROUD OF WHAT I DID.
UH-HUH.
YEAH, YOU'RE A CHEEKY ONE ALL RIGHT.

GUNSLINGER GIRL Vol.7 END

GUNSLINGERGIRL

MOSCOW - THE BOLSHOI BALLET ACADEMY

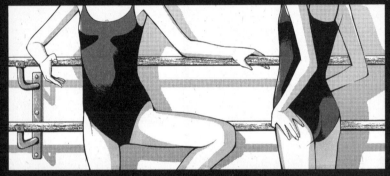

REALLY?

YOUR DANCE OF THE BLACK SWAN IS REALLY INCREDIBLE, LIZA.

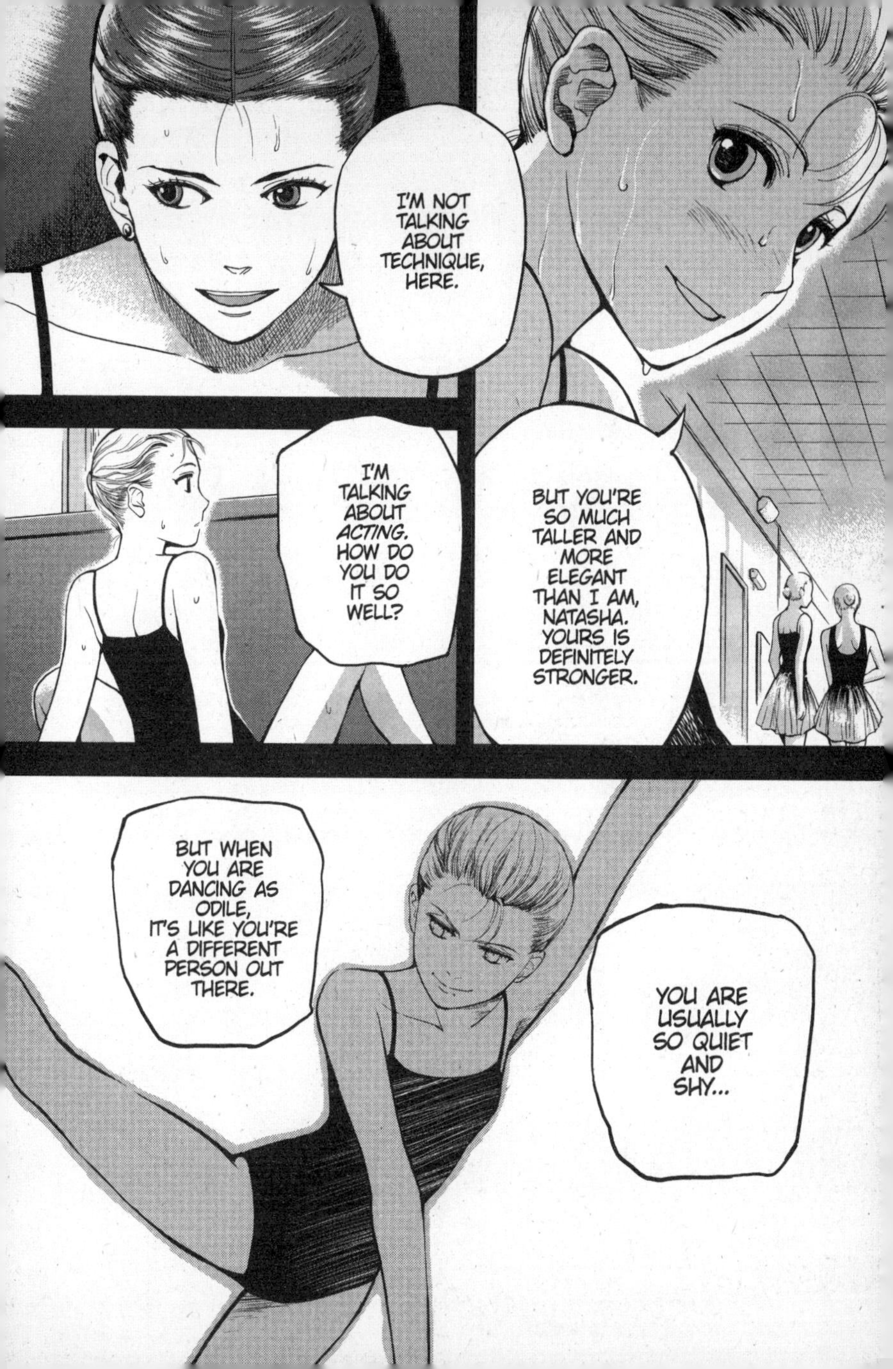
BUT YOU'RE SO MUCH TALLER AND MORE ELEGANT THAN I AM, NATASHA. YOURS IS DEFINITELY STRONGER.
I'M NOT TALKING ABOUT TECHNIQUE, HERE.
I'M TALKING ABOUT *ACTING*. HOW DO YOU DO IT SO WELL?
YOU ARE USUALLY SO QUIET AND SHY...
BUT WHEN YOU ARE DANCING AS ODILE, IT'S LIKE YOU'RE A DIFFERENT PERSON OUT THERE.

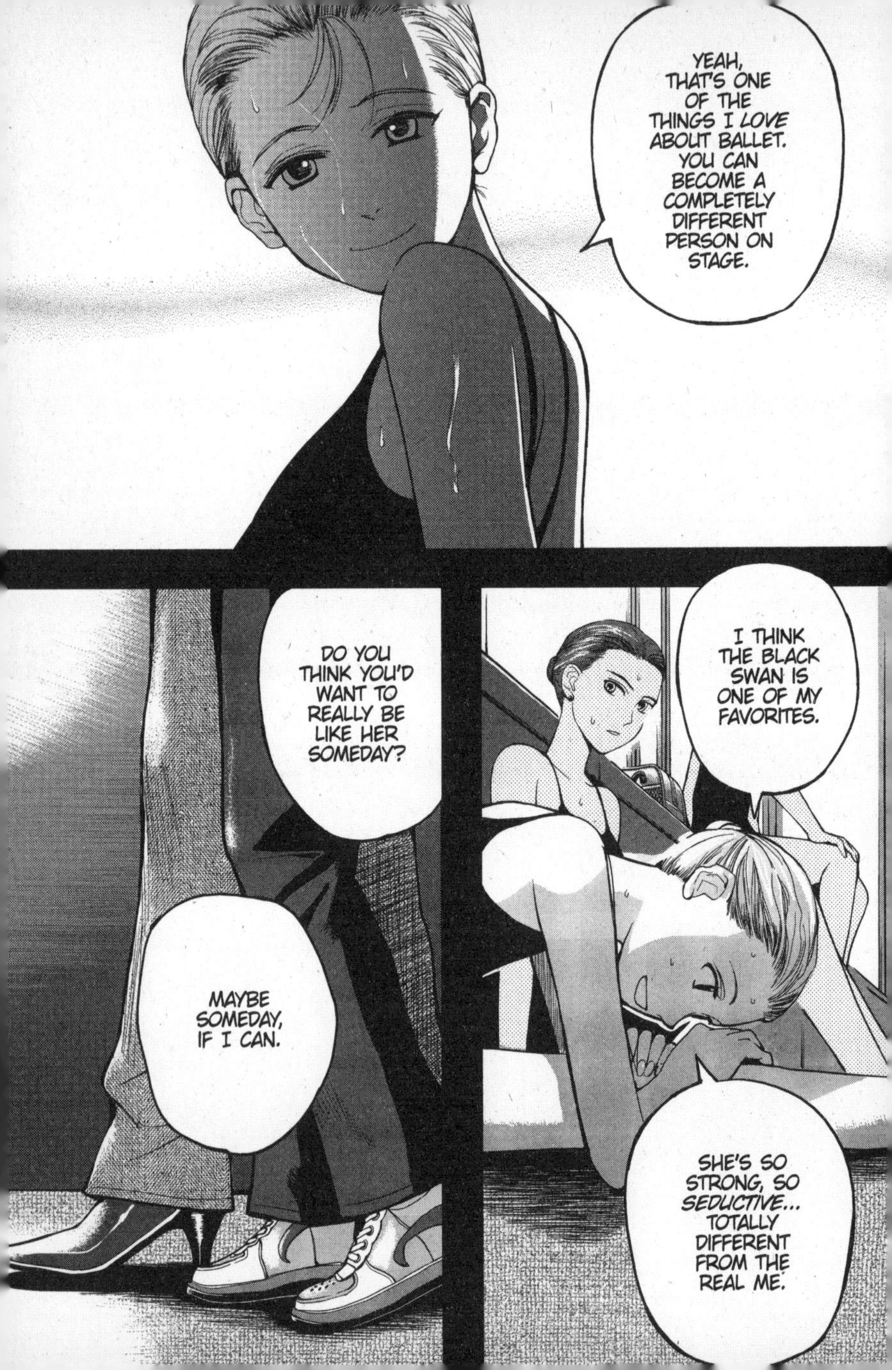
YEAH, THAT'S ONE OF THE THINGS I *LOVE* ABOUT BALLET. YOU CAN BECOME A COMPLETELY DIFFERENT PERSON ON STAGE.
I THINK THE BLACK SWAN IS ONE OF MY FAVORITES.
SHE'S SO STRONG, SO *SEDUCTIVE*... TOTALLY DIFFERENT FROM THE REAL ME.
DO YOU THINK YOU'D WANT TO REALLY BE LIKE HER SOMEDAY?
MAYBE SOMEDAY, IF I CAN.

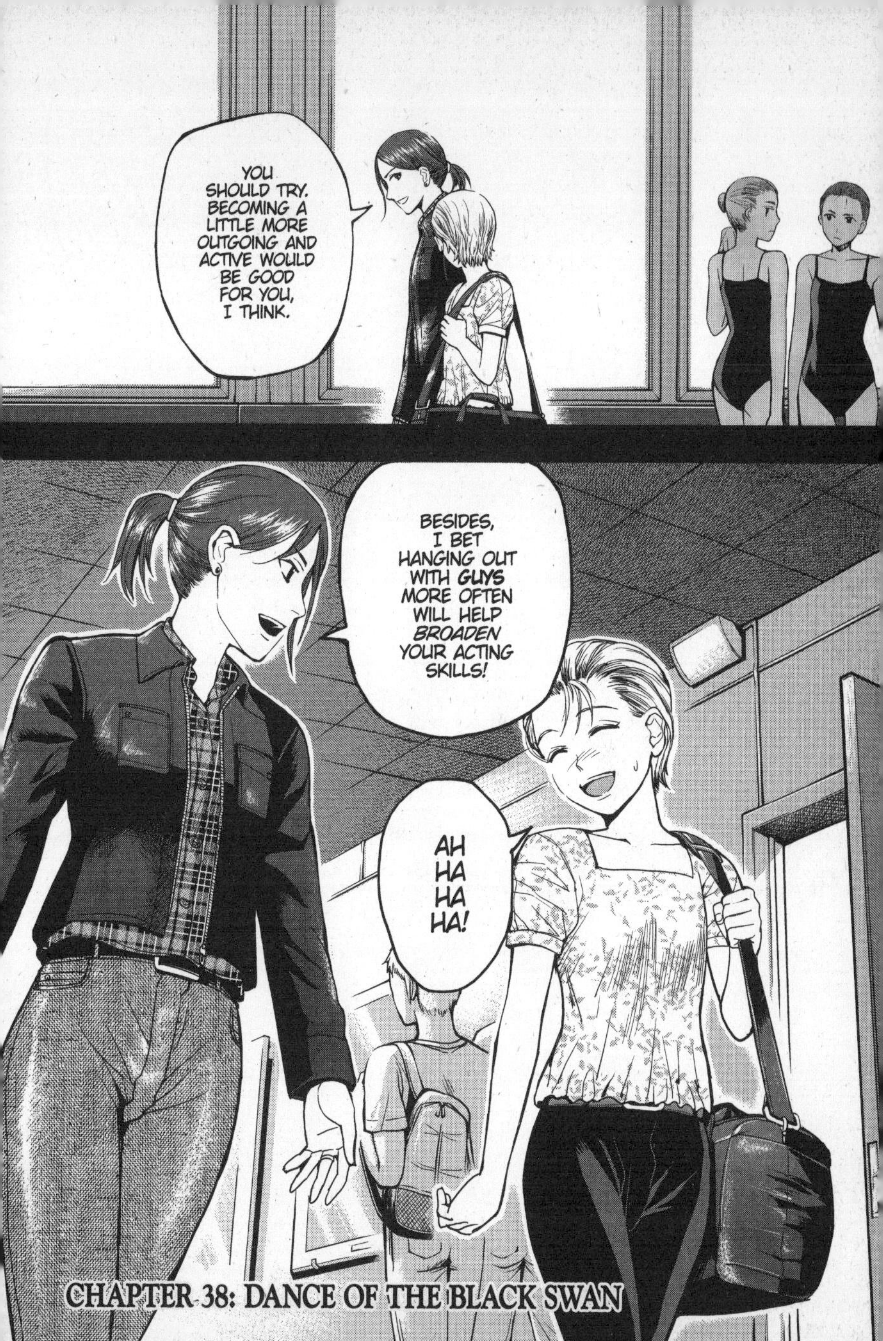
YOU SHOULD TRY. BECOMING A LITTLE MORE OUTGOING AND ACTIVE WOULD BE GOOD FOR YOU, I THINK.
BESIDES, I BET HANGING OUT WITH GUYS MORE OFTEN WILL HELP BROADEN YOUR ACTING SKILLS!
AH HA HA HA HA!

CHAPTER 38: DANCE OF THE BLACK SWAN

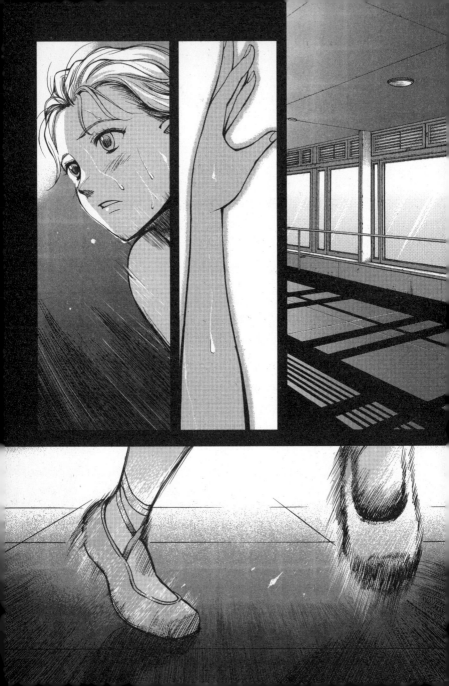

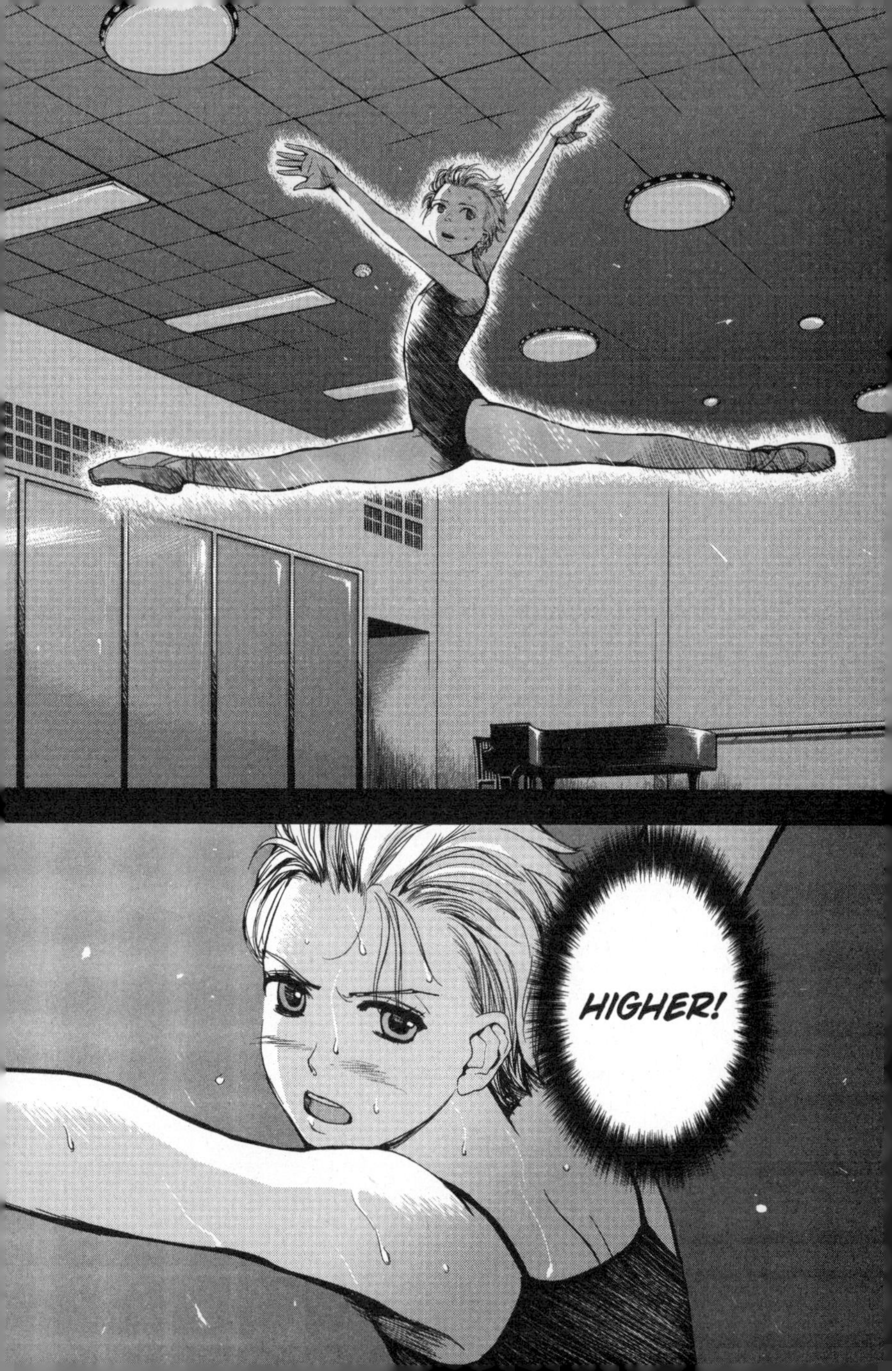
HIGHER!

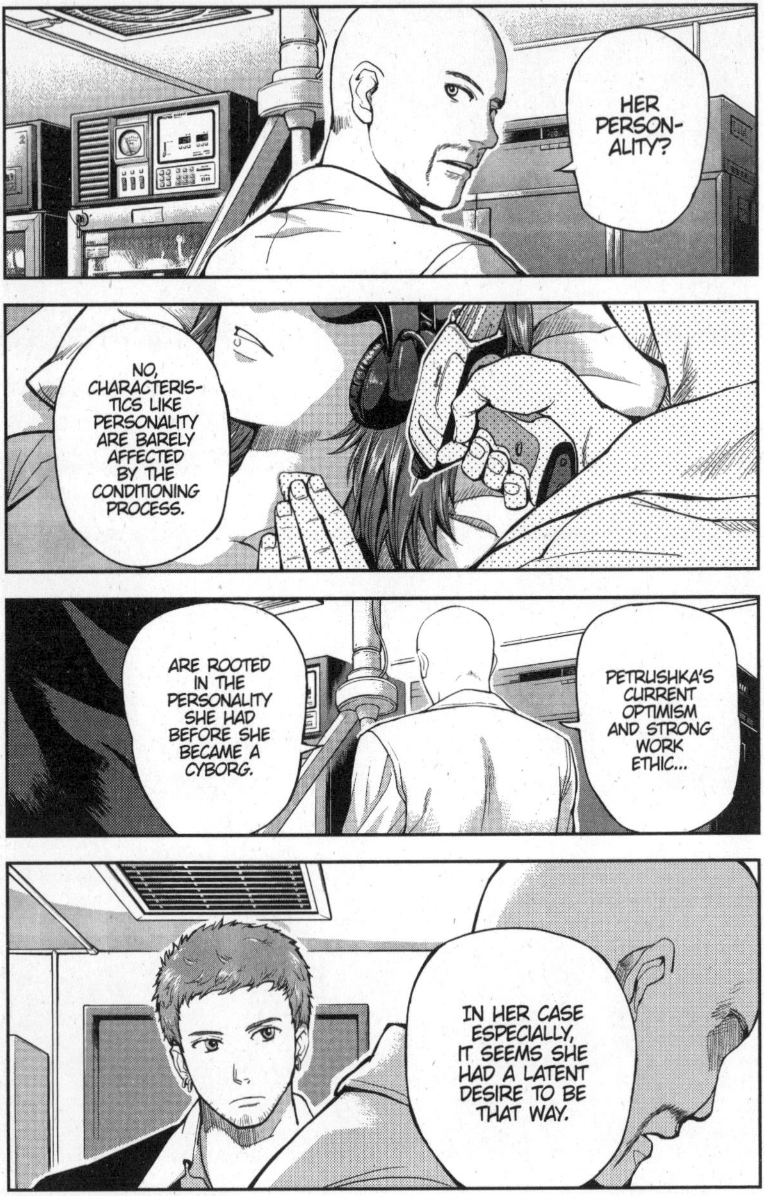
HER PERSON-ALITY?
NO, CHARACTERIS-TICS LIKE PERSONALITY ARE BARELY AFFECTED BY THE CONDITIONING PROCESS.
PETRUSHKA'S CURRENT OPTIMISM AND STRONG WORK ETHIC...
ARE ROOTED IN THE PERSONALITY SHE HAD BEFORE SHE BECAME A CYBORG.
IN HER CASE ESPECIALLY, IT SEEMS SHE HAD A LATENT DESIRE TO BE THAT WAY.

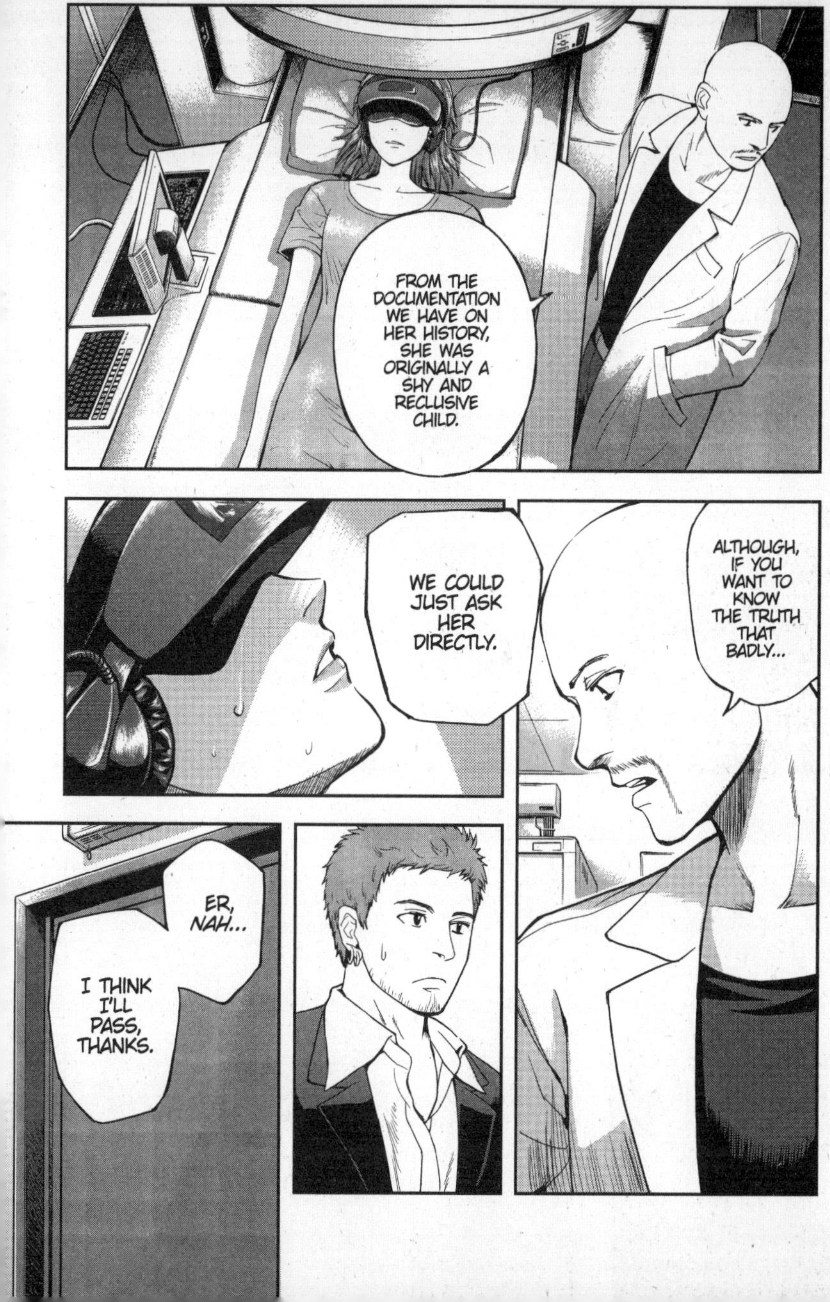
FROM THE DOCUMENTATION WE HAVE ON HER HISTORY, SHE WAS ORIGINALLY A SHY AND RECLUSIVE CHILD.
ALTHOUGH, IF YOU WANT TO KNOW THE TRUTH THAT BADLY...
WE COULD JUST ASK HER DIRECTLY.
ER, NAH...
I THINK I'LL PASS, THANKS.

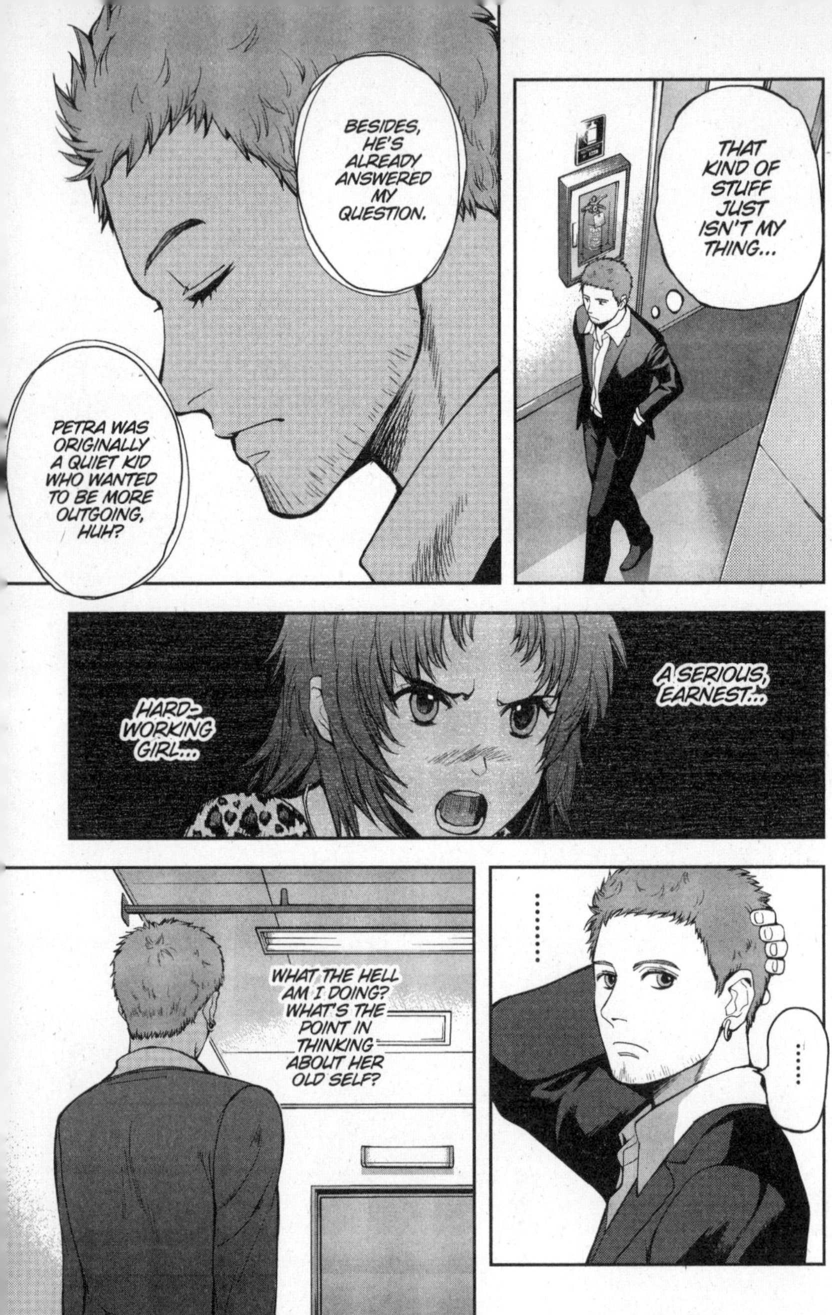
THAT KIND OF STUFF JUST ISN'T MY THING...
BESIDES, HE'S ALREADY ANSWERED MY QUESTION.
PETRA WAS ORIGINALLY A QUIET KID WHO WANTED TO BE MORE OUTGOING, HUH?
A SERIOUS, EARNEST...
HARD-WORKING GIRL...
......
......
WHAT THE HELL AM I DOING? WHAT'S THE POINT IN THINKING ABOUT HER OLD SELF?

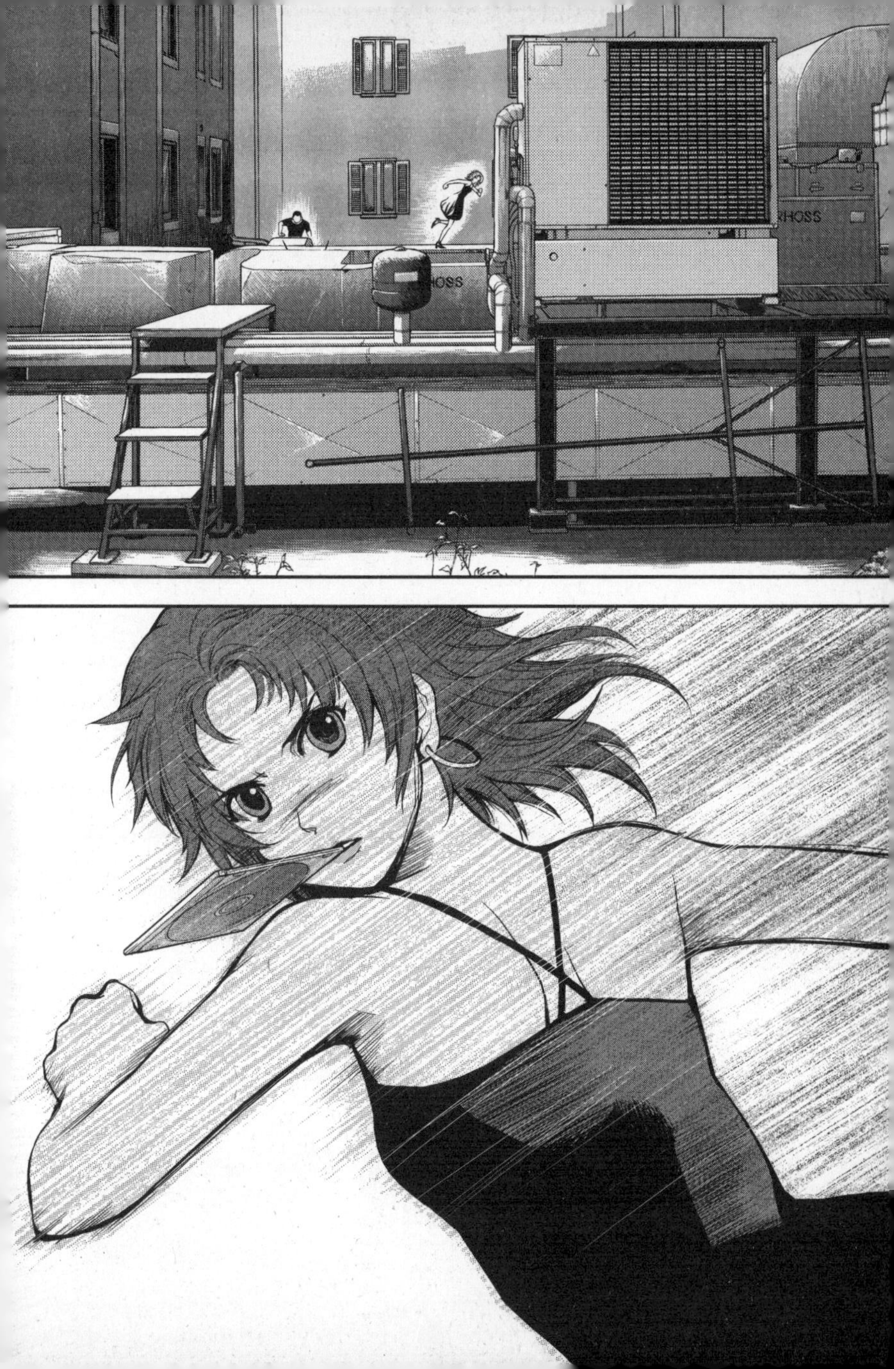

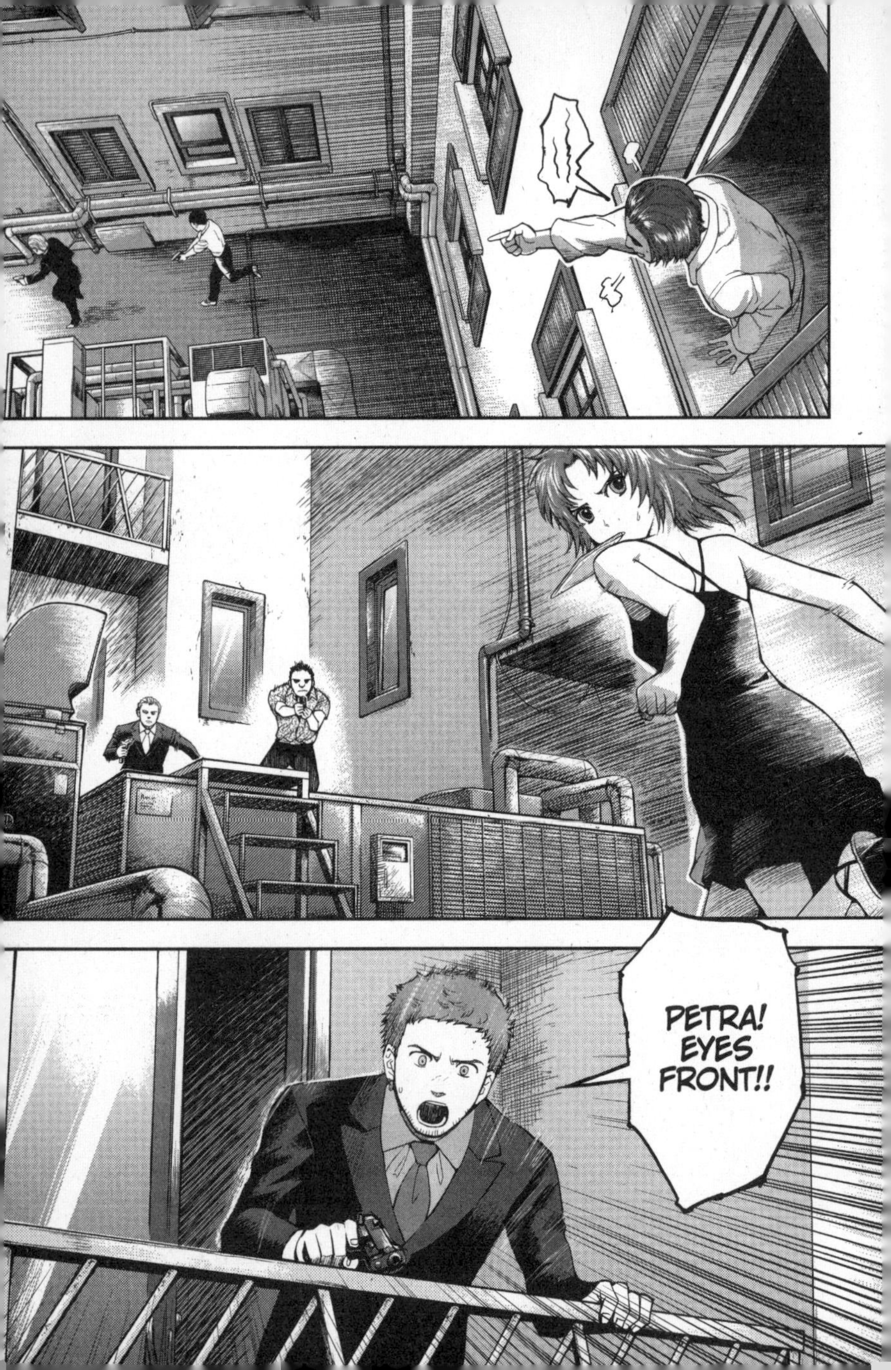
PETRA! EYES FRONT!!

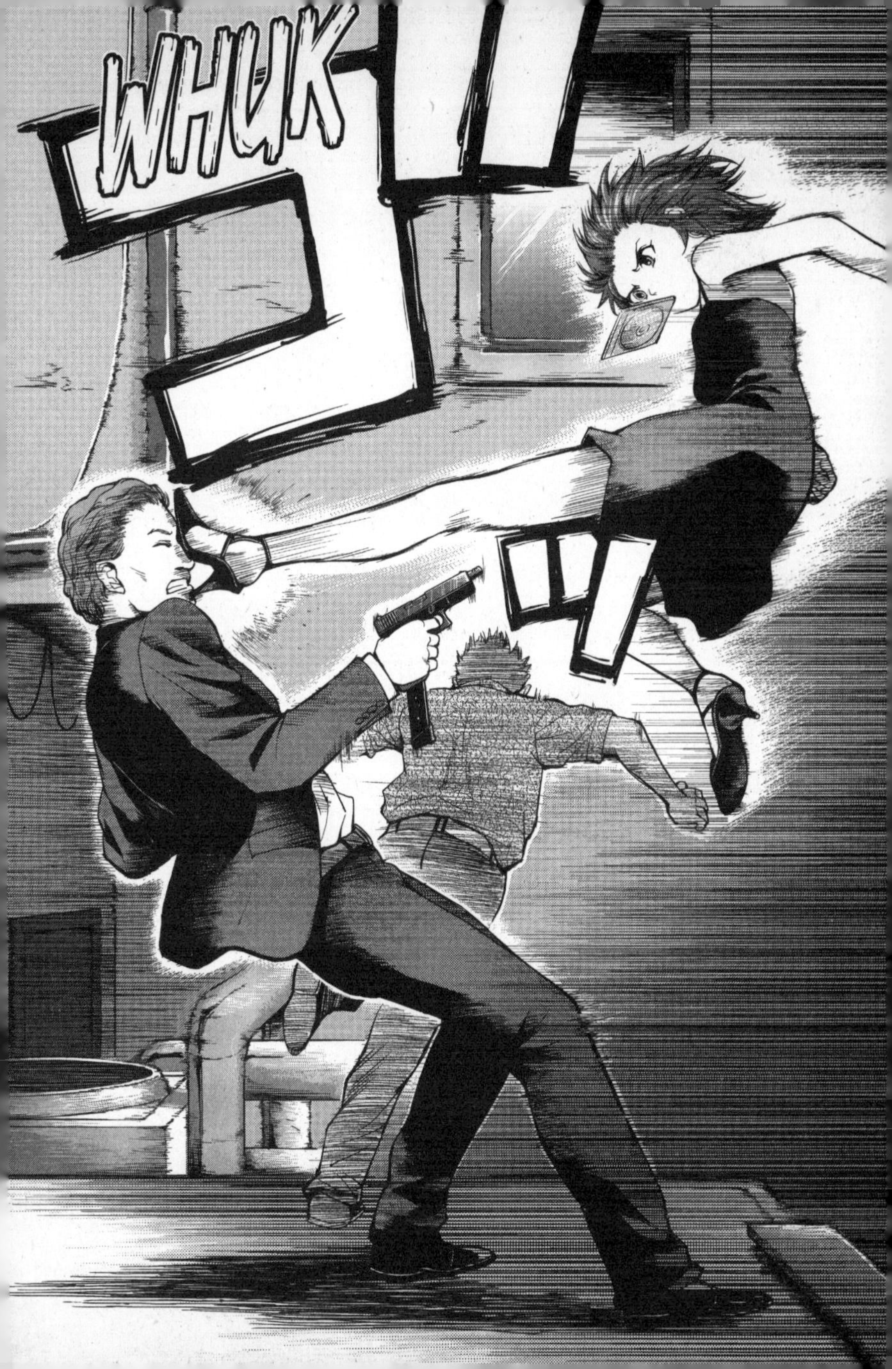
WHUK

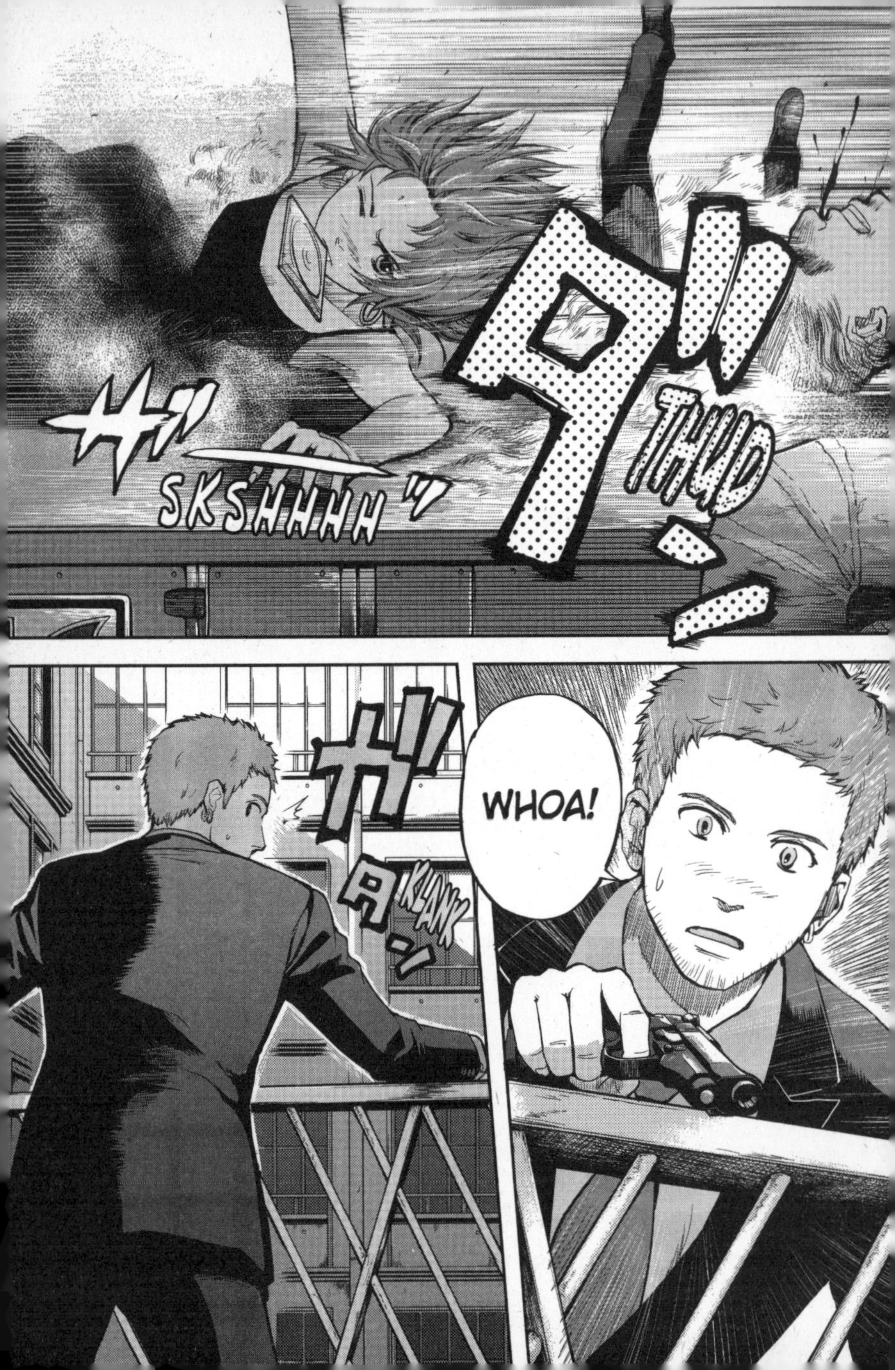
THUD
SKSHHHH
WHOA!
KLANK

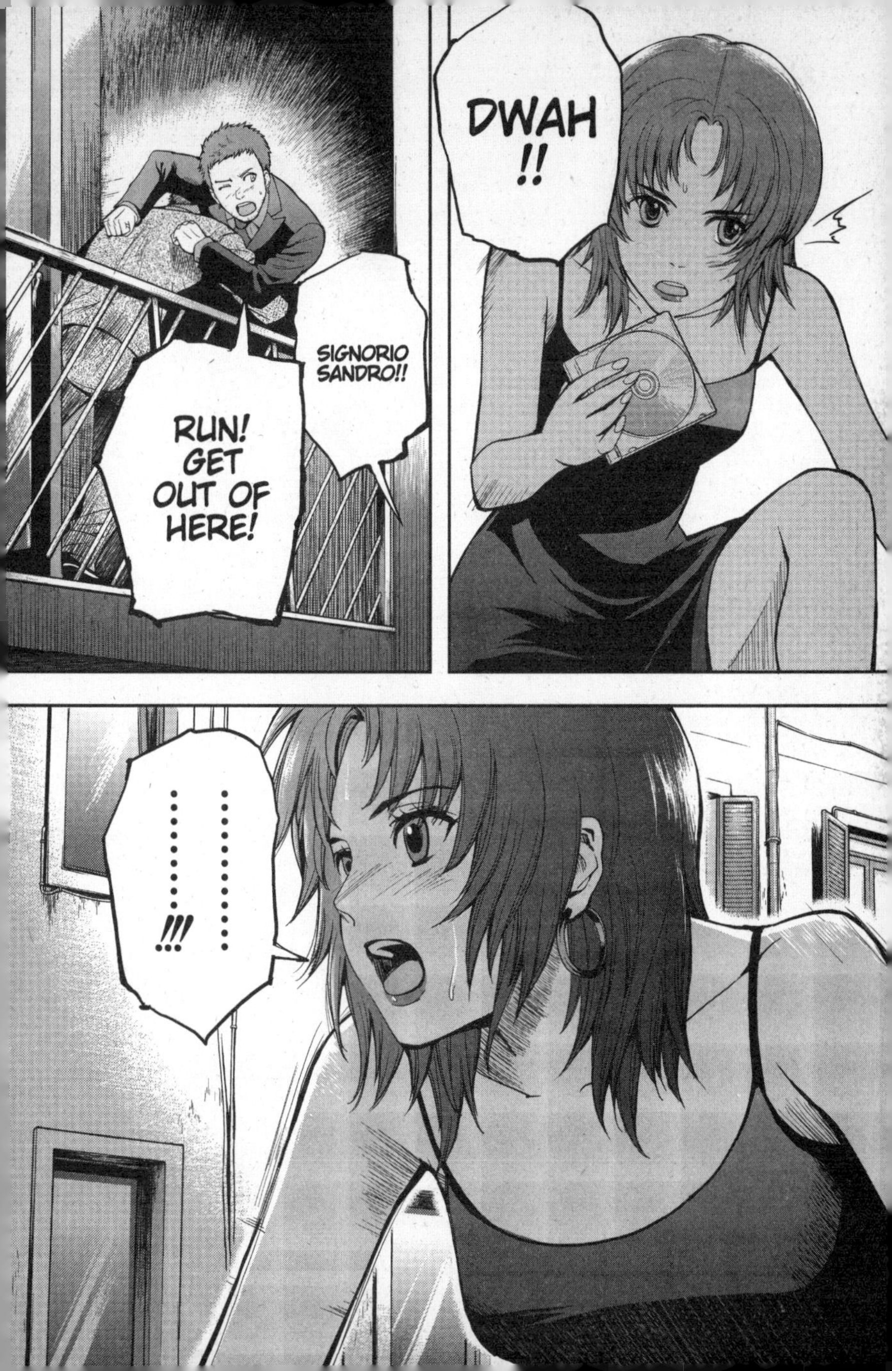
DWAH!!
SIGNORIO SANDRO!!
RUN! GET OUT OF HERE!
....
........!!!

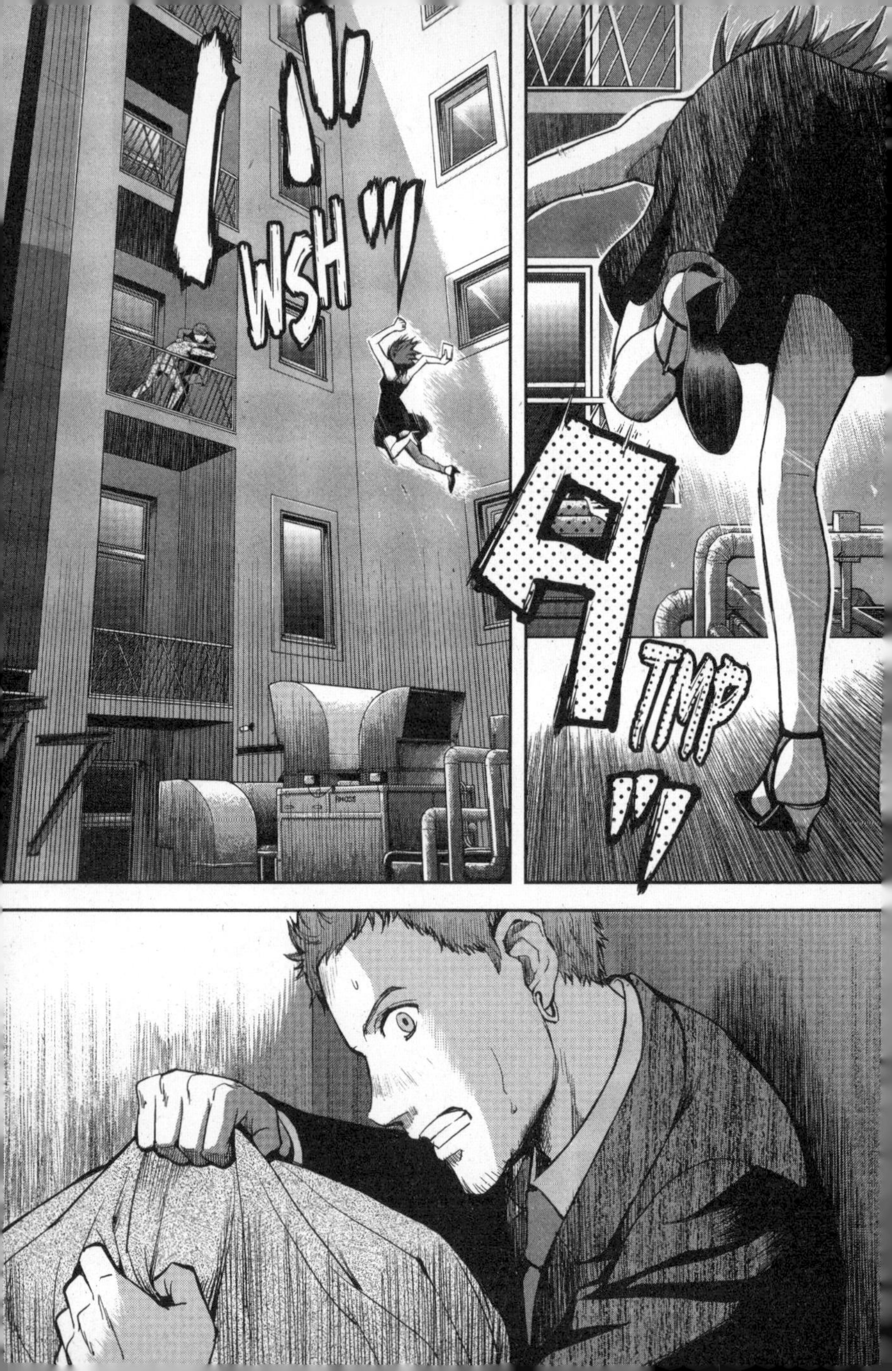
TMP
WSH

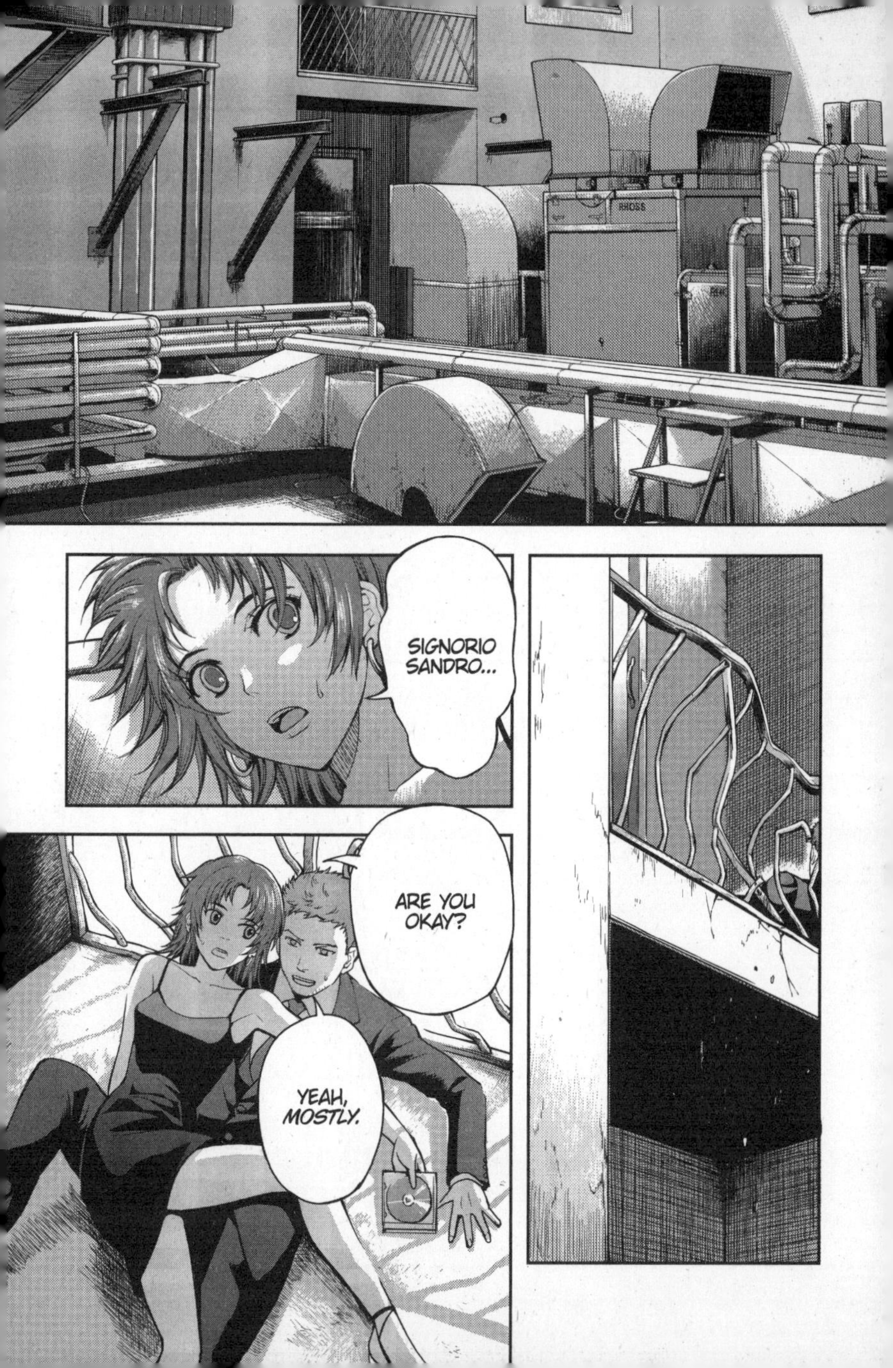
SIGNORIO SANDRO...
ARE YOU OKAY?
YEAH, MOSTLY.

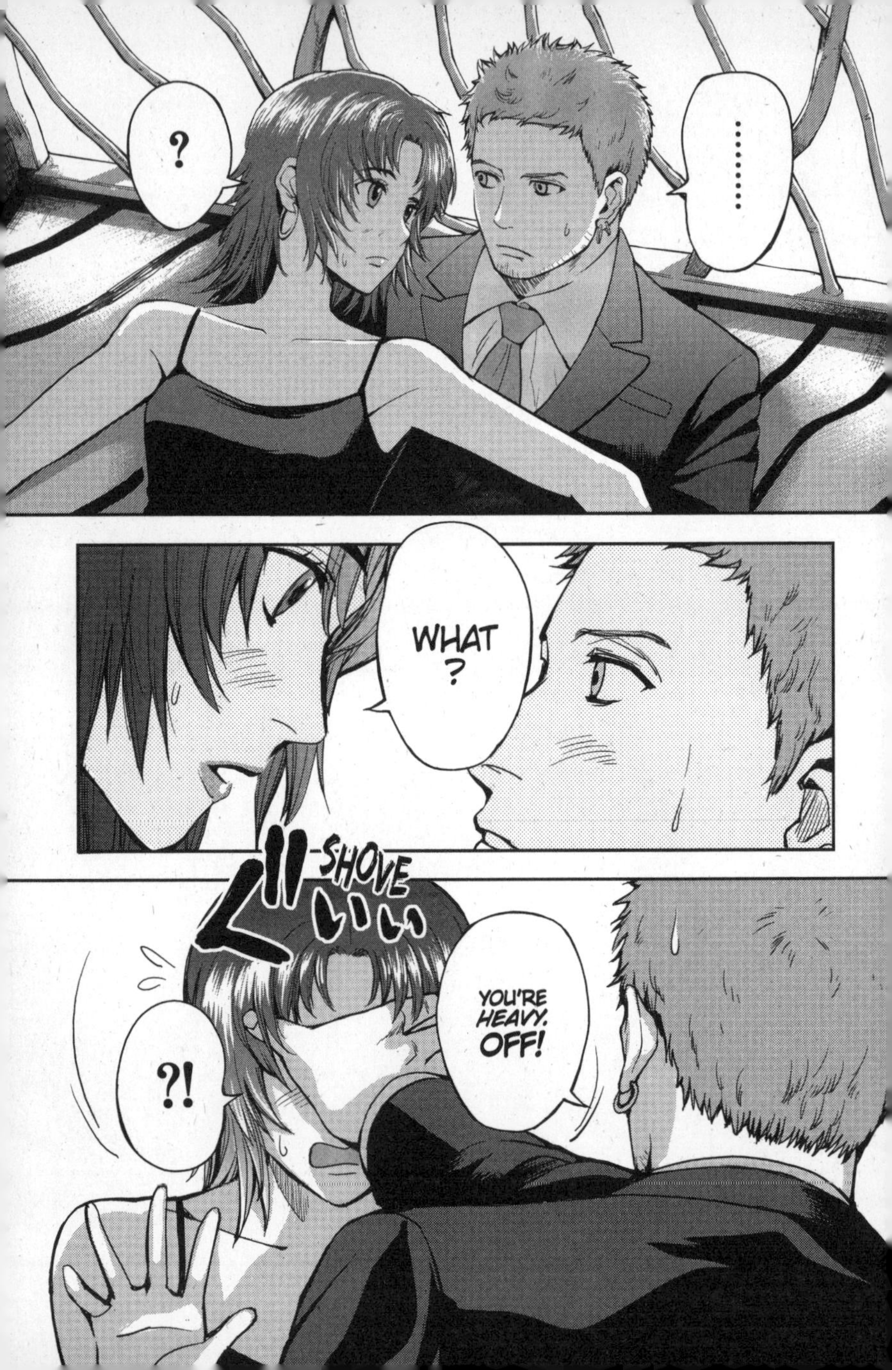
……
?
WHAT?
SHOVE
YOU'RE HEAVY. OFF!
?!

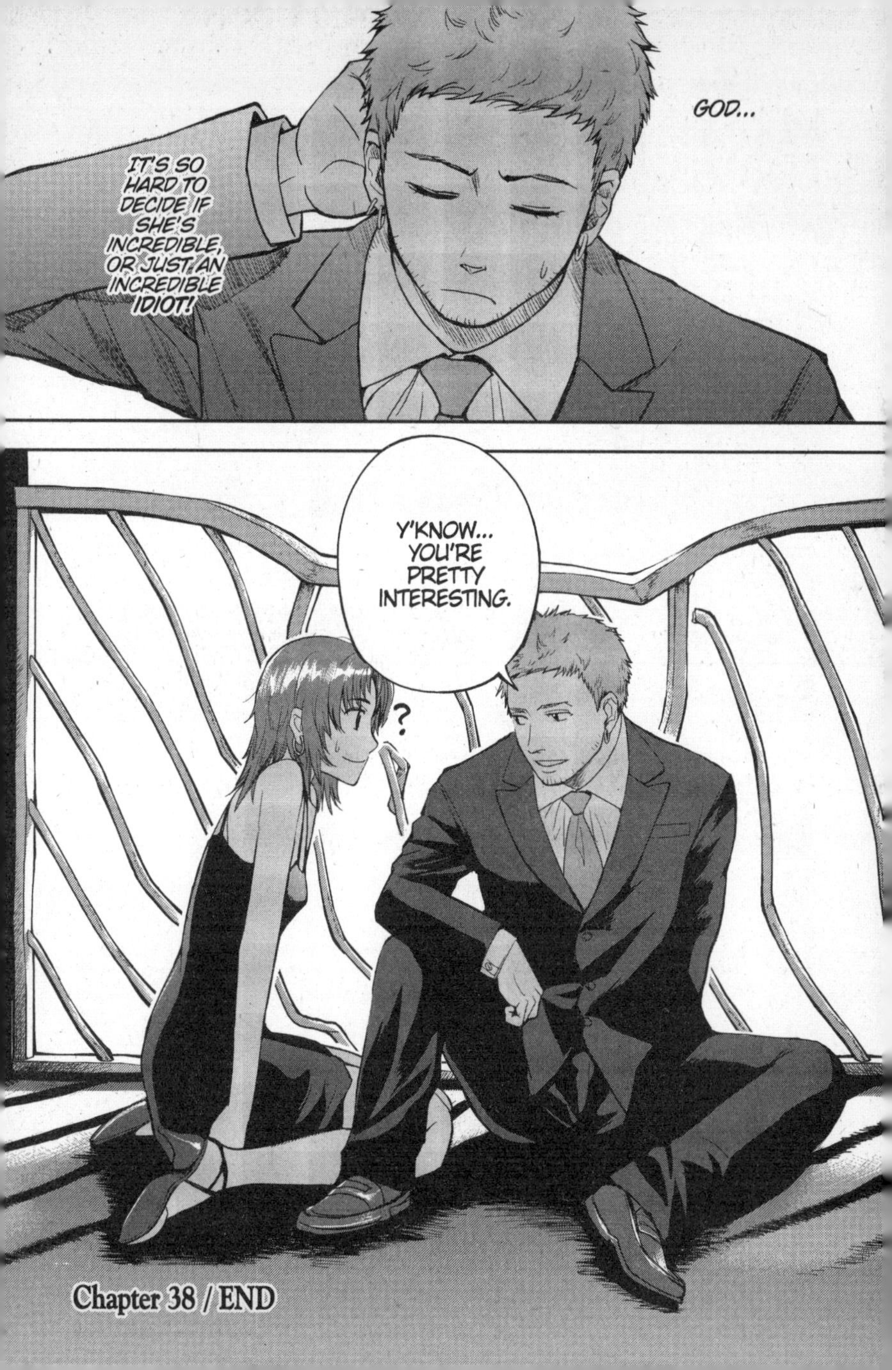
GOD...
IT'S SO HARD TO DECIDE IF SHE'S INCREDIBLE, OR JUST AN INCREDIBLE IDIOT!
Y'KNOW... YOU'RE PRETTY INTERESTING.
?
Chapter 38 / END

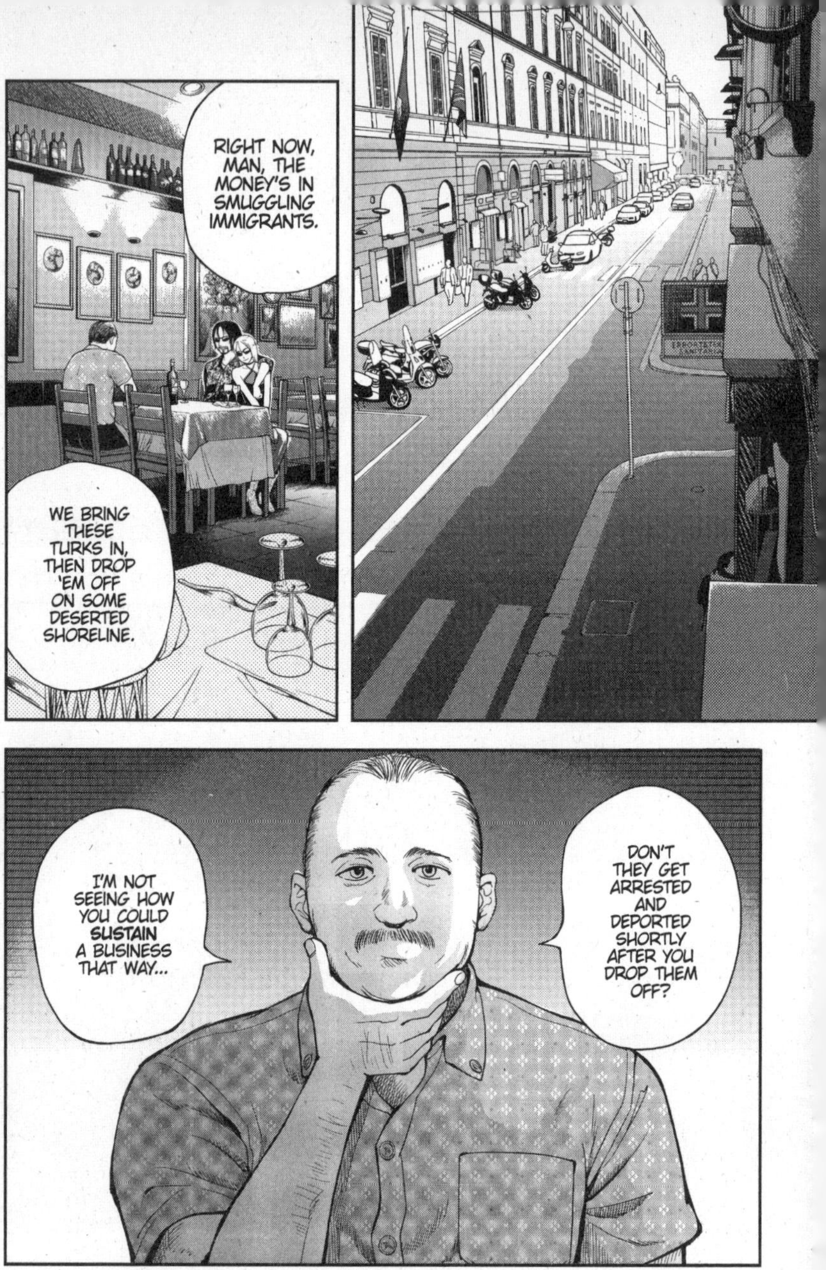
RIGHT NOW, MAN, THE MONEY'S IN SMUGGLING IMMIGRANTS.
WE BRING THESE TURKS IN, THEN DROP 'EM OFF ON SOME DESERTED SHORELINE.
DON'T THEY GET ARRESTED AND DEPORTED SHORTLY AFTER YOU DROP THEM OFF?
I'M NOT SEEING HOW YOU COULD **SUSTAIN** A BUSINESS THAT WAY...

*European Union

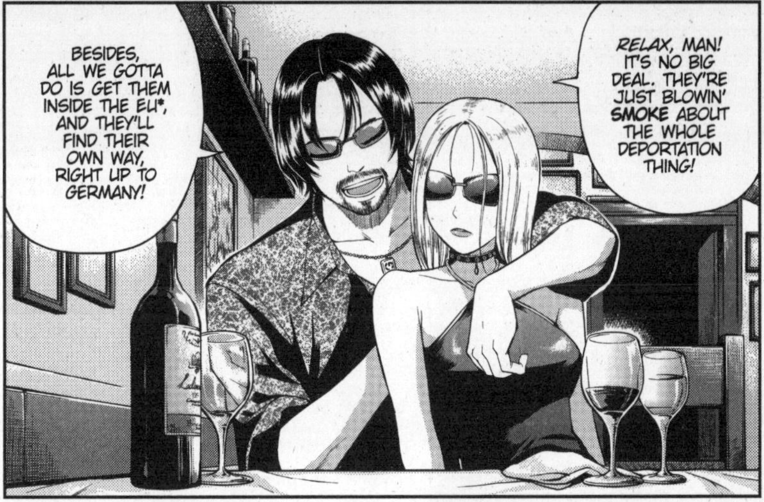
RELAX, MAN! IT'S NO BIG DEAL. THEY'RE JUST BLOWIN' SMOKE ABOUT THE WHOLE DEPORTATION THING!
BESIDES, ALL WE GOTTA DO IS GET THEM INSIDE THE EU*, AND THEY'LL FIND THEIR OWN WAY, RIGHT UP TO GERMANY!

*Tirana is the capitol city of Albania.

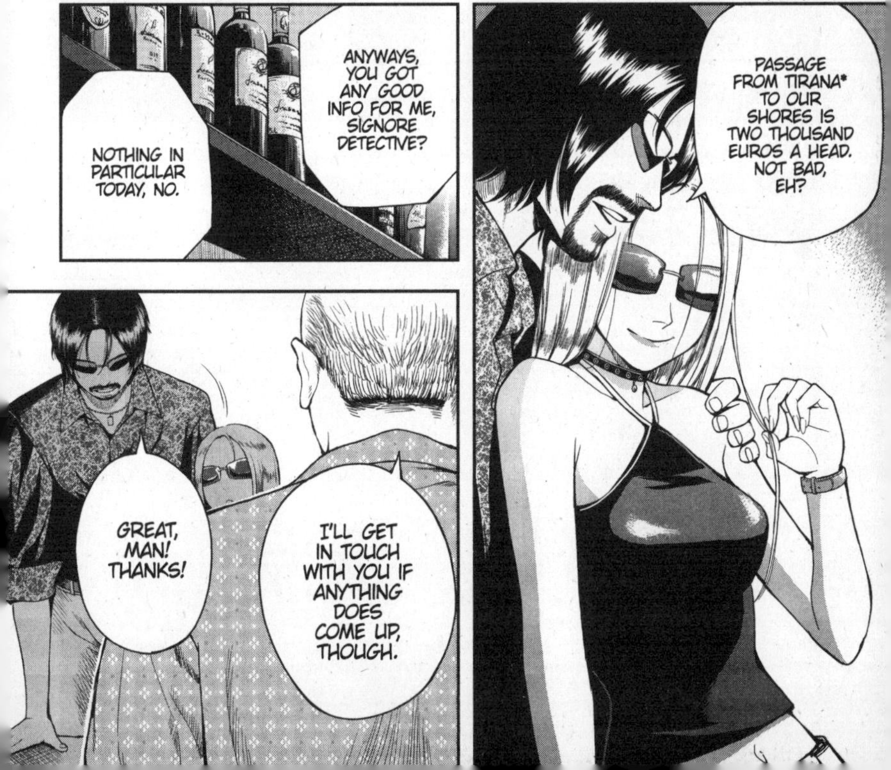
PASSAGE FROM TIRANA* TO OUR SHORES IS TWO THOUSAND EUROS A HEAD. NOT BAD, EH?
ANYWAYS, YOU GOT ANY GOOD INFO FOR ME, SIGNORE DETECTIVE?
NOTHING IN PARTICULAR TODAY, NO.
I'LL GET IN TOUCH WITH YOU IF ANYTHING DOES COME UP, THOUGH.
GREAT, MAN! THANKS!

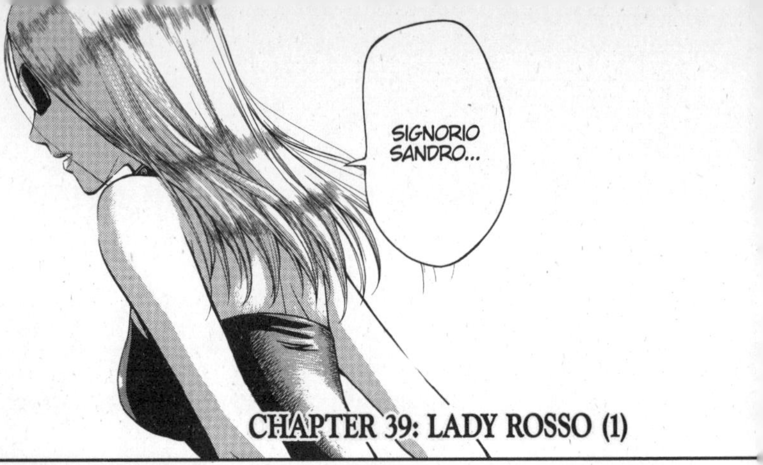
SIGNORIO SANDRO...

CHAPTER 39: LADY ROSSO (1)

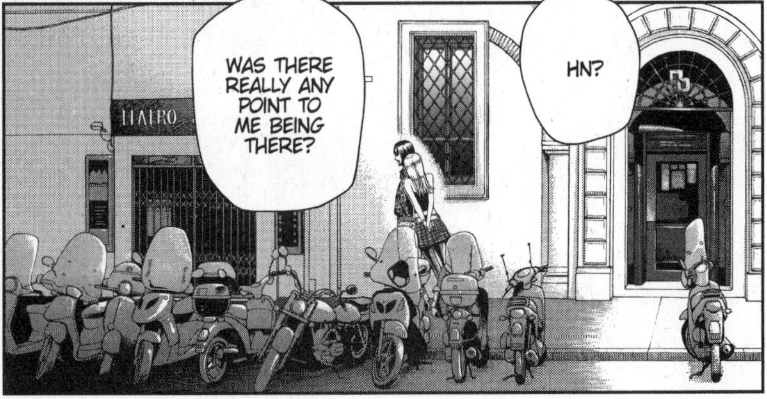
WAS THERE REALLY ANY POINT TO ME BEING THERE?
HN?

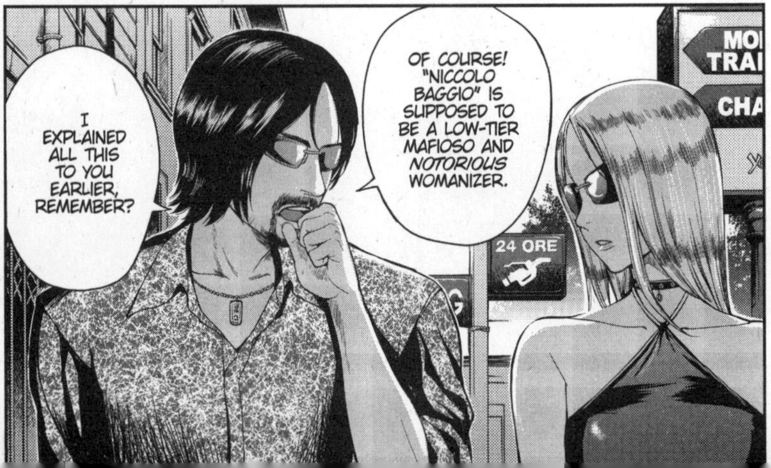
I EXPLAINED ALL THIS TO YOU EARLIER, REMEMBER?
OF COURSE! "NICCOLO BAGGIO" IS SUPPOSED TO BE A LOW-TIER MAFIOSO AND *NOTORIOUS* WOMANIZER.
24 ORE

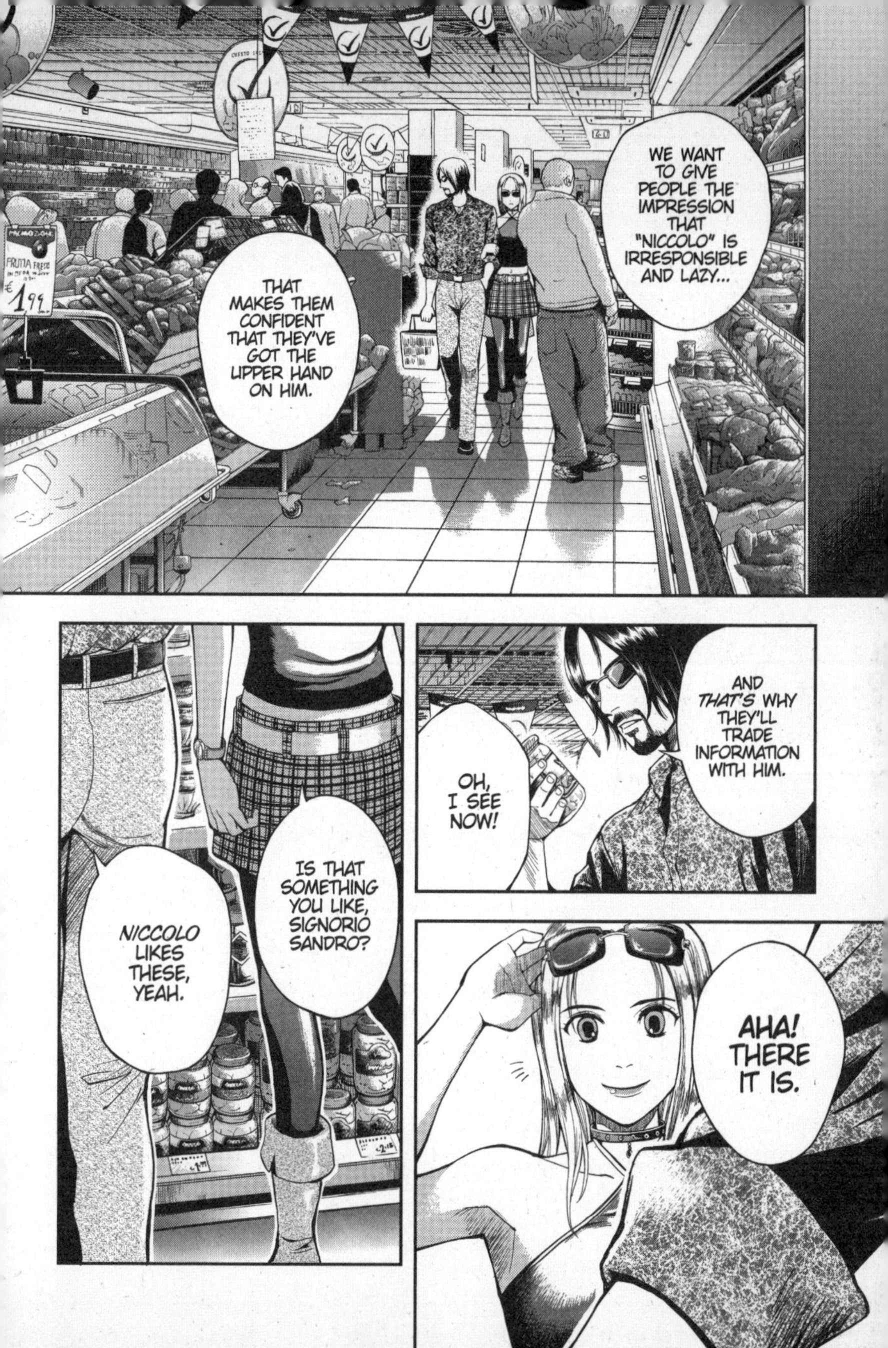
WE WANT TO GIVE PEOPLE THE IMPRESSION THAT "NICCOLO" IS IRRESPONSIBLE AND LAZY...
THAT MAKES THEM CONFIDENT THAT THEY'VE GOT THE UPPER HAND ON HIM.
AND *THAT'S* WHY THEY'LL TRADE INFORMATION WITH HIM.
OH, I SEE NOW!
AHA! THERE IT IS.
IS THAT SOMETHING YOU LIKE, SIGNORIO SANDRO?
NICCOLO LIKES THESE, YEAH.

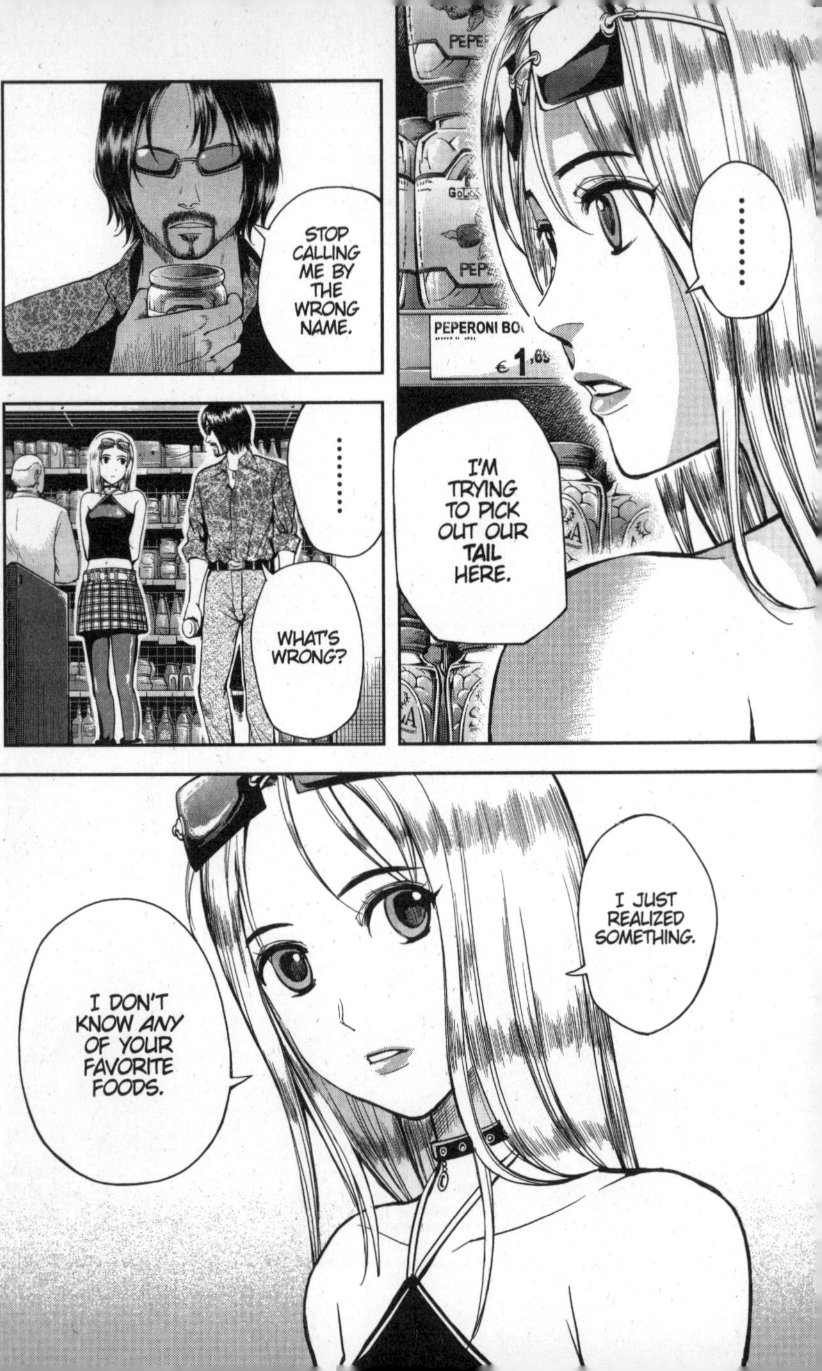
......
I'M TRYING TO PICK OUT OUR TAIL HERE.
STOP CALLING ME BY THE WRONG NAME.
......
WHAT'S WRONG?
I JUST REALIZED SOMETHING.
I DON'T KNOW ANY OF YOUR FAVORITE FOODS.

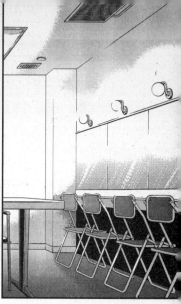

SO WHAT? WHO CARES ABOUT THAT CRAP?

TUG

I DON'T KNOW WHAT KIND OF CHEESES YOU LOVE, OR WHAT KIND OF VEGGIES YOU HATE.

I DO.

FWSH

WHEN YOU REALLY LIKE SOMEONE, YOU WANNA KNOW STUFF LIKE THAT.

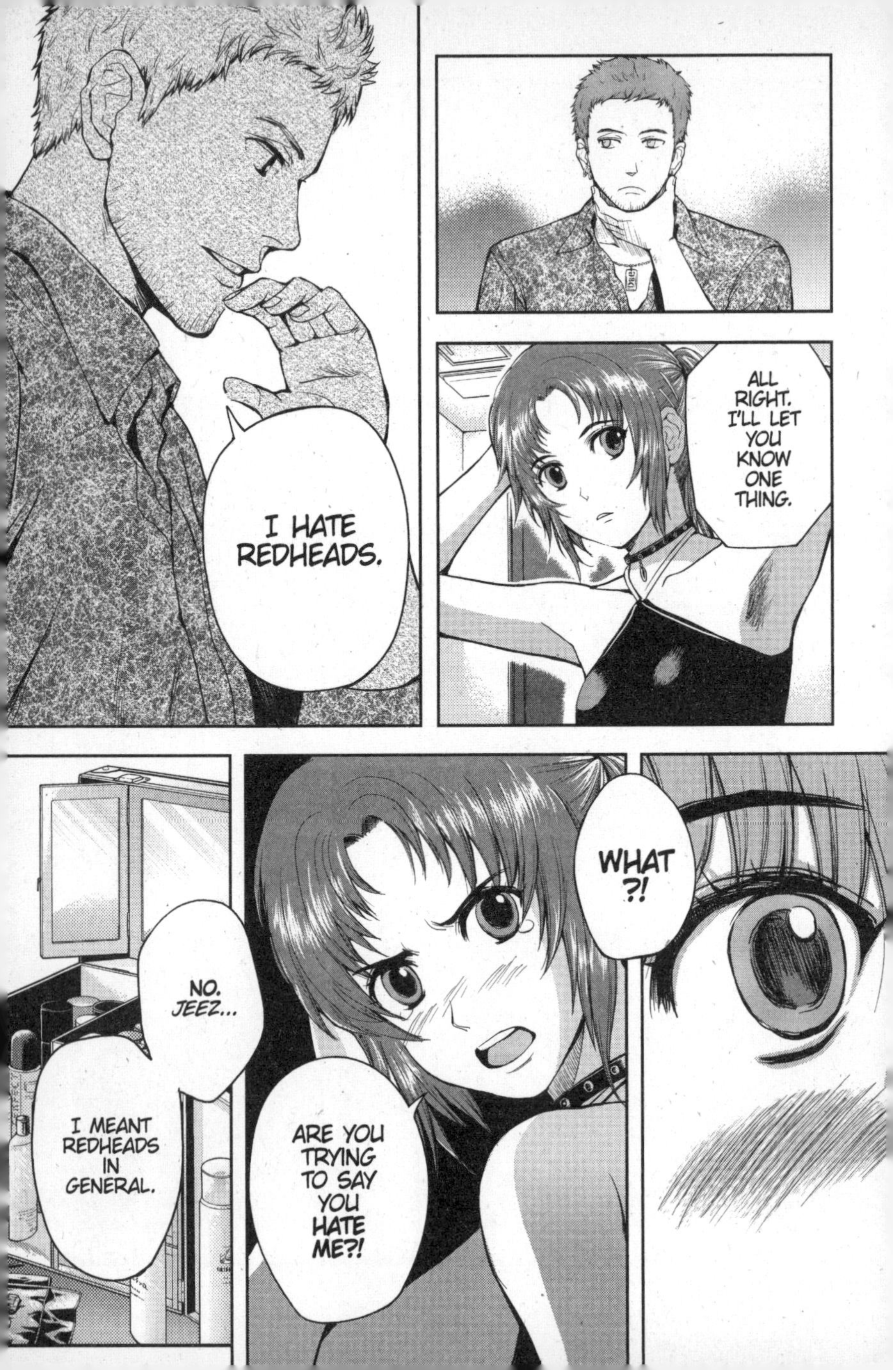
ALL RIGHT. I'LL LET YOU KNOW ONE THING.
I HATE REDHEADS.
WHAT?!
ARE YOU TRYING TO SAY YOU HATE ME?!
NO. JEEZ...
I MEANT REDHEADS IN GENERAL.

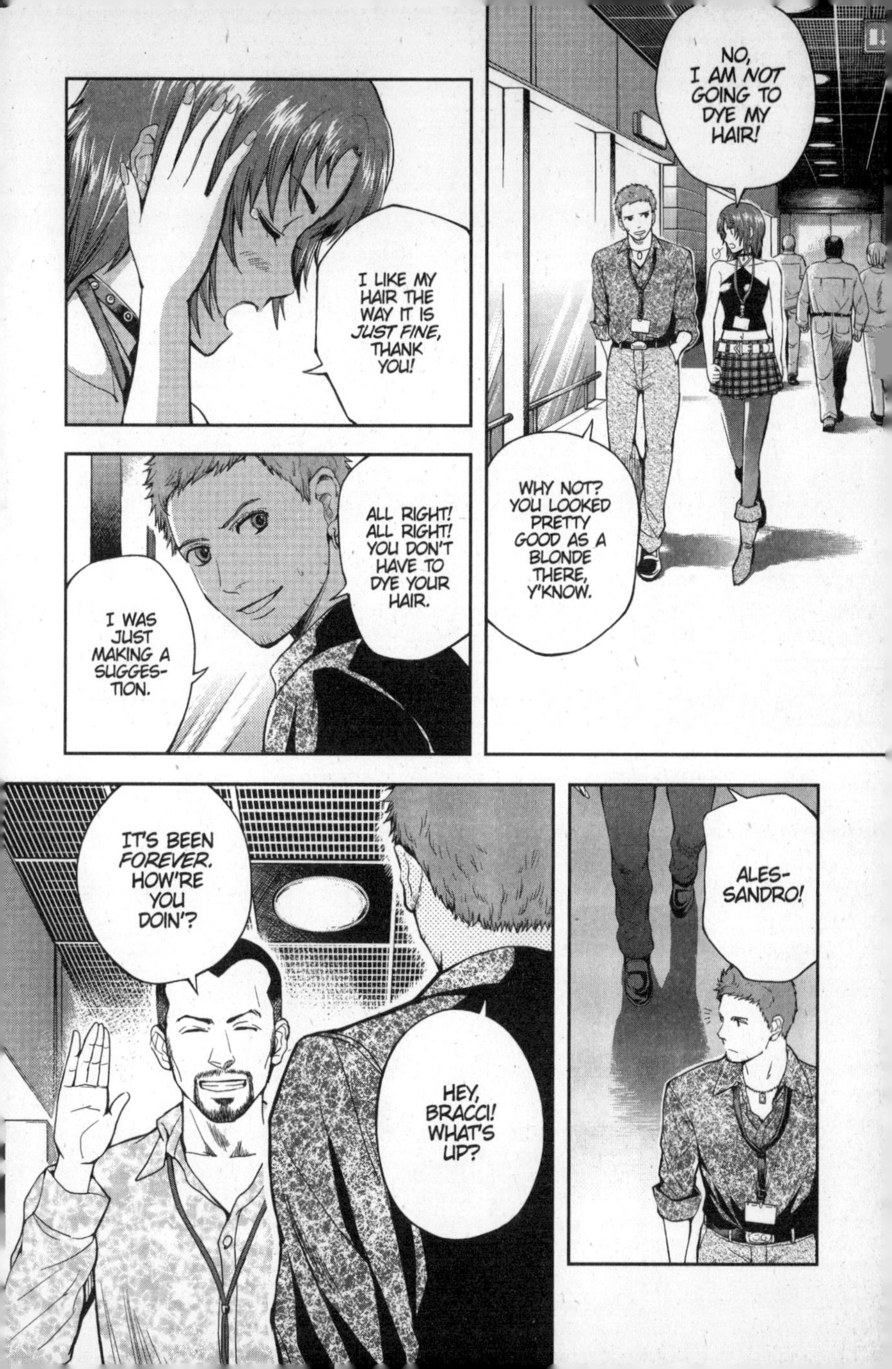
NO, I AM *NOT* GOING TO DYE MY HAIR!
WHY NOT? YOU LOOKED PRETTY GOOD AS A BLONDE THERE, Y'KNOW.
I LIKE MY HAIR THE WAY IT IS *JUST FINE*, THANK YOU!
ALL RIGHT! ALL RIGHT! YOU DON'T HAVE TO DYE YOUR HAIR.
I WAS JUST MAKING A SUGGES-TION.
ALES-SANDRO!
IT'S BEEN *FOREVER*. HOW'RE YOU DOIN'?
HEY, BRACCI! WHAT'S UP?

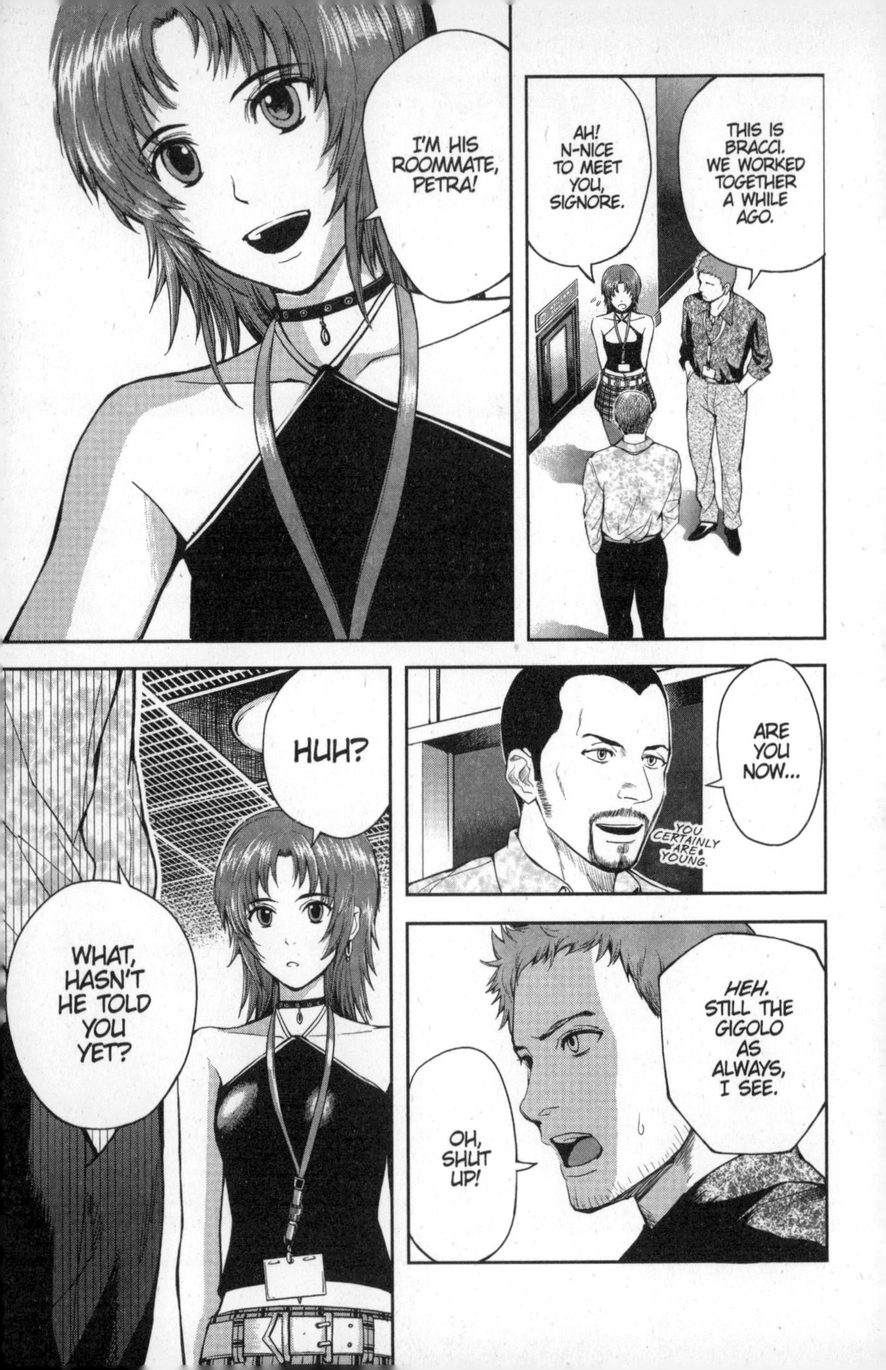
THIS IS BRACCI. WE WORKED TOGETHER A WHILE AGO.
AH! N-NICE TO MEET YOU, SIGNORE.
I'M HIS ROOMMATE, PETRA!
ARE YOU NOW...
YOU CERTAINLY ARE. YOUNG.
HEH. STILL THE GIGOLO AS ALWAYS, I SEE.
OH, SHUT UP!
HUH?
WHAT, HASN'T HE TOLD YOU YET?

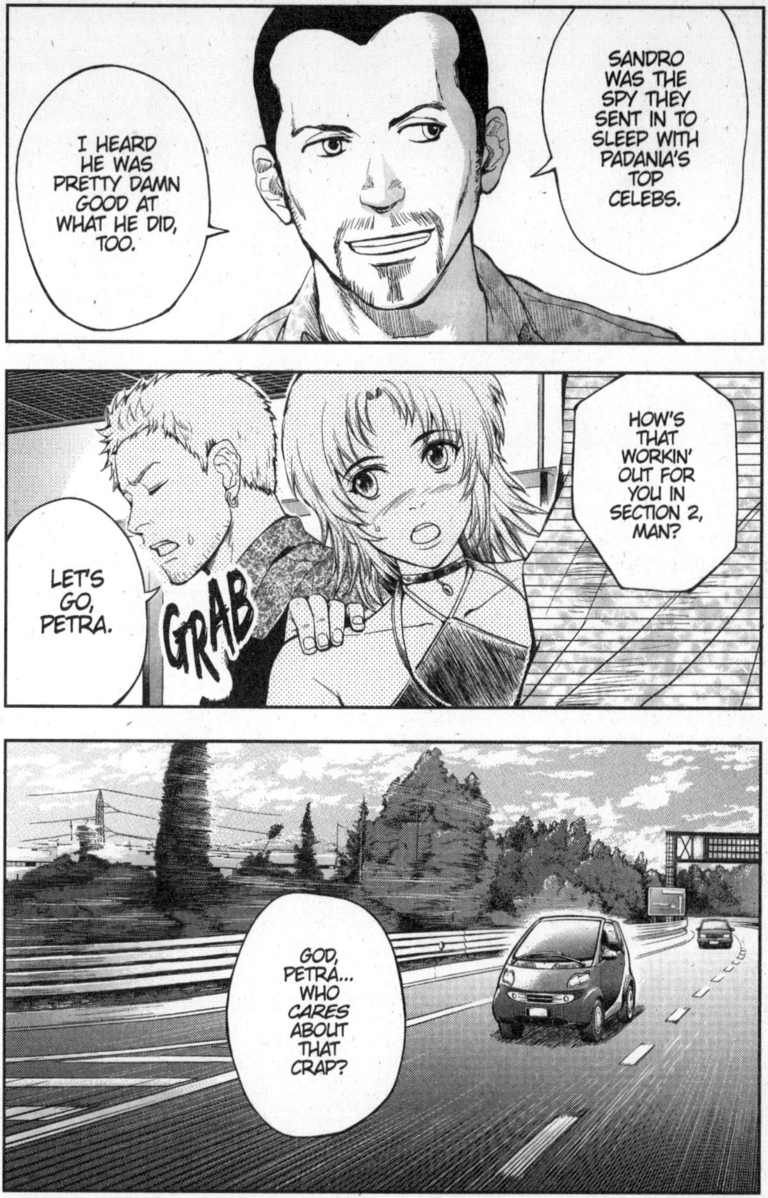
SANDRO WAS THE SPY THEY SENT IN TO SLEEP WITH PADANIA'S TOP CELEBS.
I HEARD HE WAS PRETTY DAMN GOOD AT WHAT HE DID, TOO.
HOW'S THAT WORKIN' OUT FOR YOU IN SECTION 2, MAN?
LET'S GO, PETRA.
GRAB
GOD, PETRA... WHO CARES ABOUT THAT CRAP?

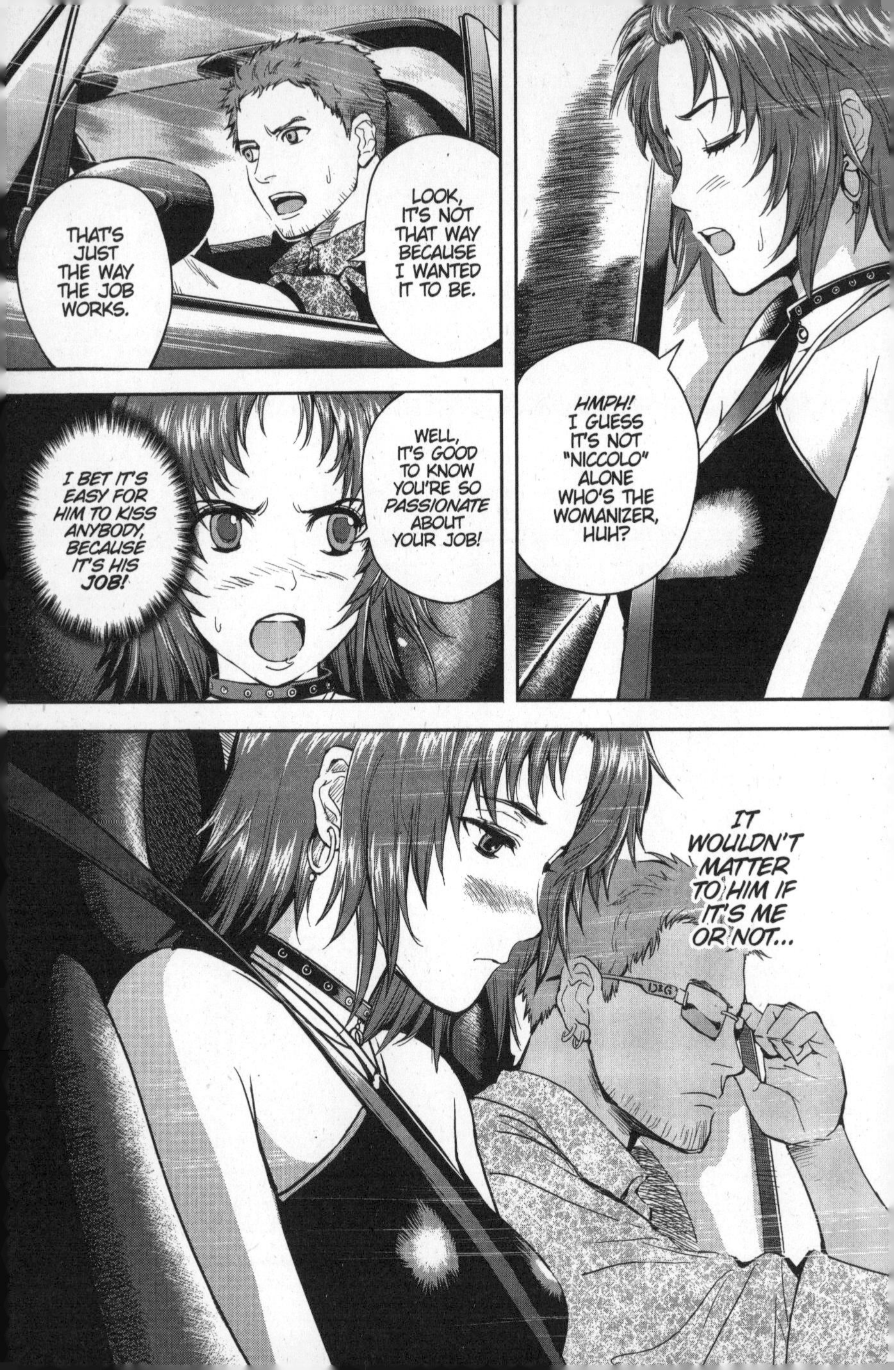
HMPH! I GUESS IT'S NOT "NICCOLO" ALONE WHO'S THE WOMANIZER, HUH?
LOOK, IT'S NOT THAT WAY BECAUSE I WANTED IT TO BE.
THAT'S JUST THE WAY THE JOB WORKS.
WELL, IT'S GOOD TO KNOW YOU'RE SO *PASSIONATE* ABOUT YOUR JOB!
I BET IT'S EASY FOR HIM TO KISS ANYBODY, BECAUSE IT'S HIS **JOB**!
IT WOULDN'T MATTER TO HIM IF IT'S ME OR NOT...

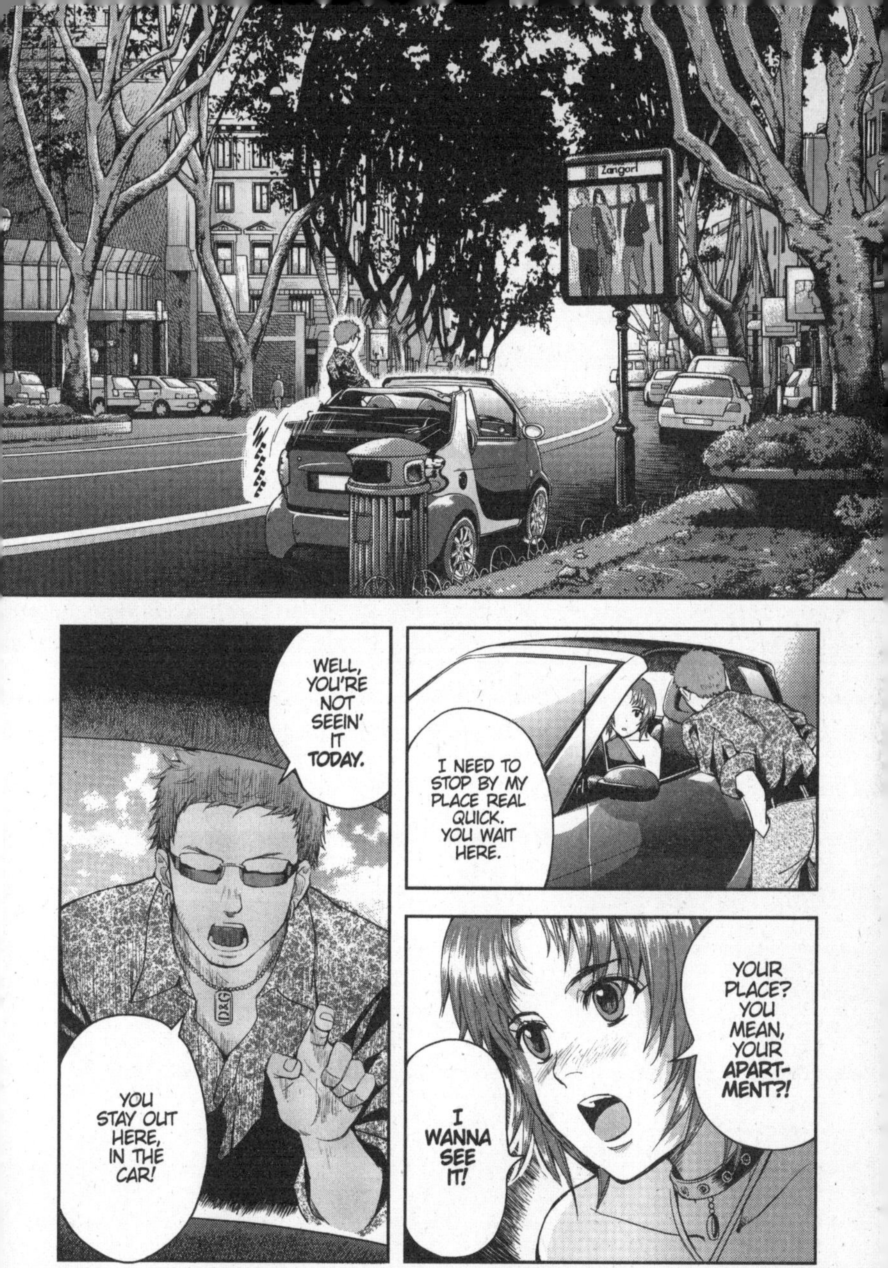
I NEED TO STOP BY MY PLACE REAL QUICK. YOU WAIT HERE.
YOUR PLACE? YOU MEAN, YOUR APARTMENT?!
I WANNA SEE IT!
WELL, YOU'RE NOT SEEIN' IT TODAY.
YOU STAY OUT HERE, IN THE CAR!

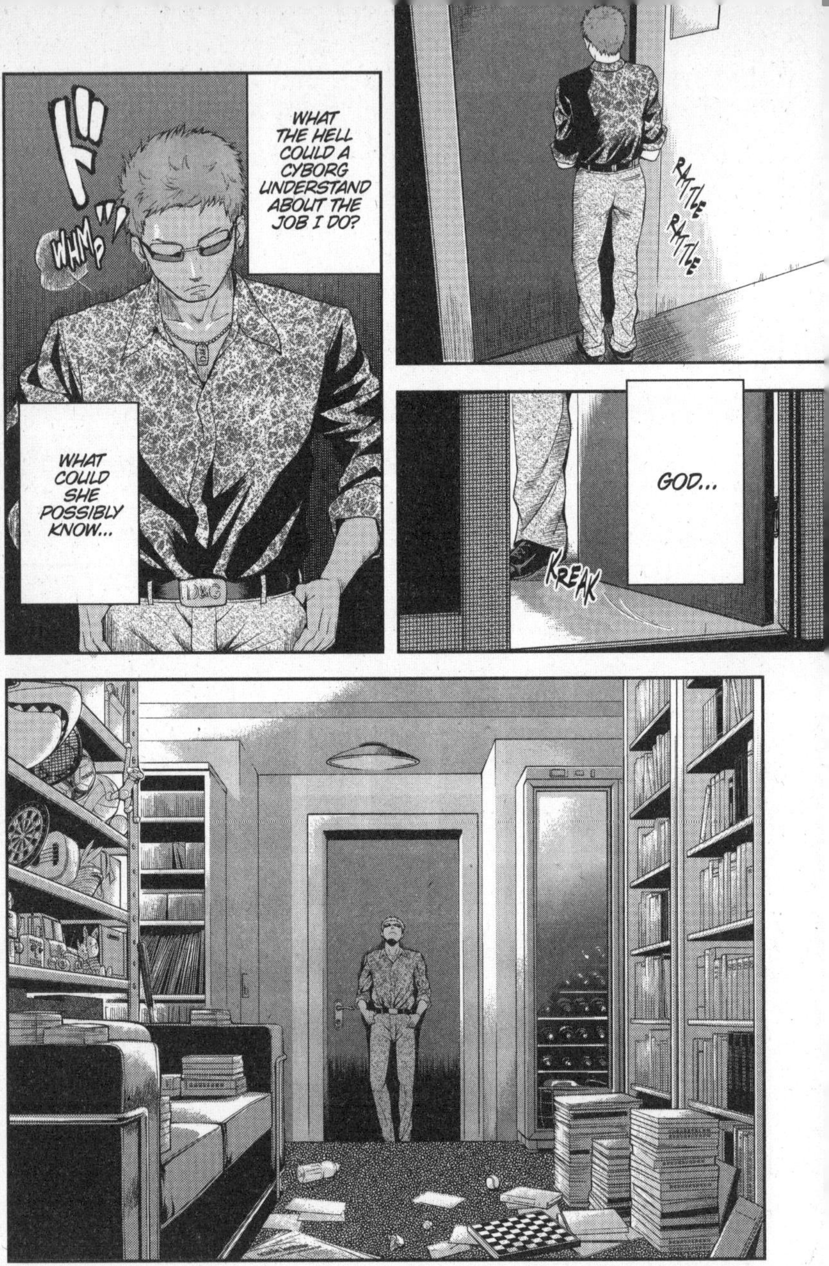
RATTLE RATTLE
KREAK
GOD...
ド
WHMP
WHAT THE HELL COULD A CYBORG UNDERSTAND ABOUT THE JOB I DO?
WHAT COULD SHE POSSIBLY KNOW...

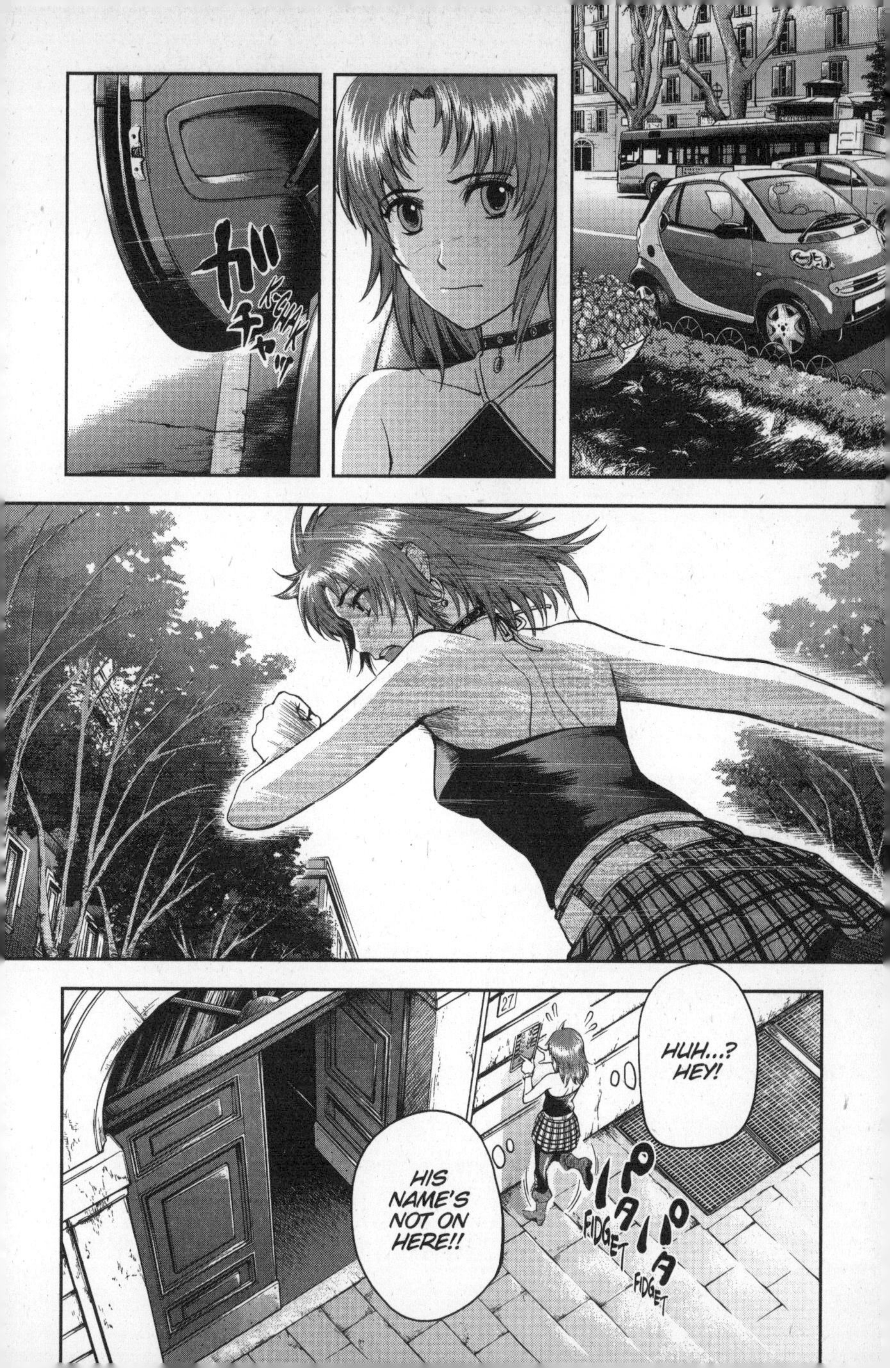

ガチャッ
KCHAK
HUH...? HEY!
HIS NAME'S NOT ON HERE!!
パタパタ
FIDGET
FIDGET

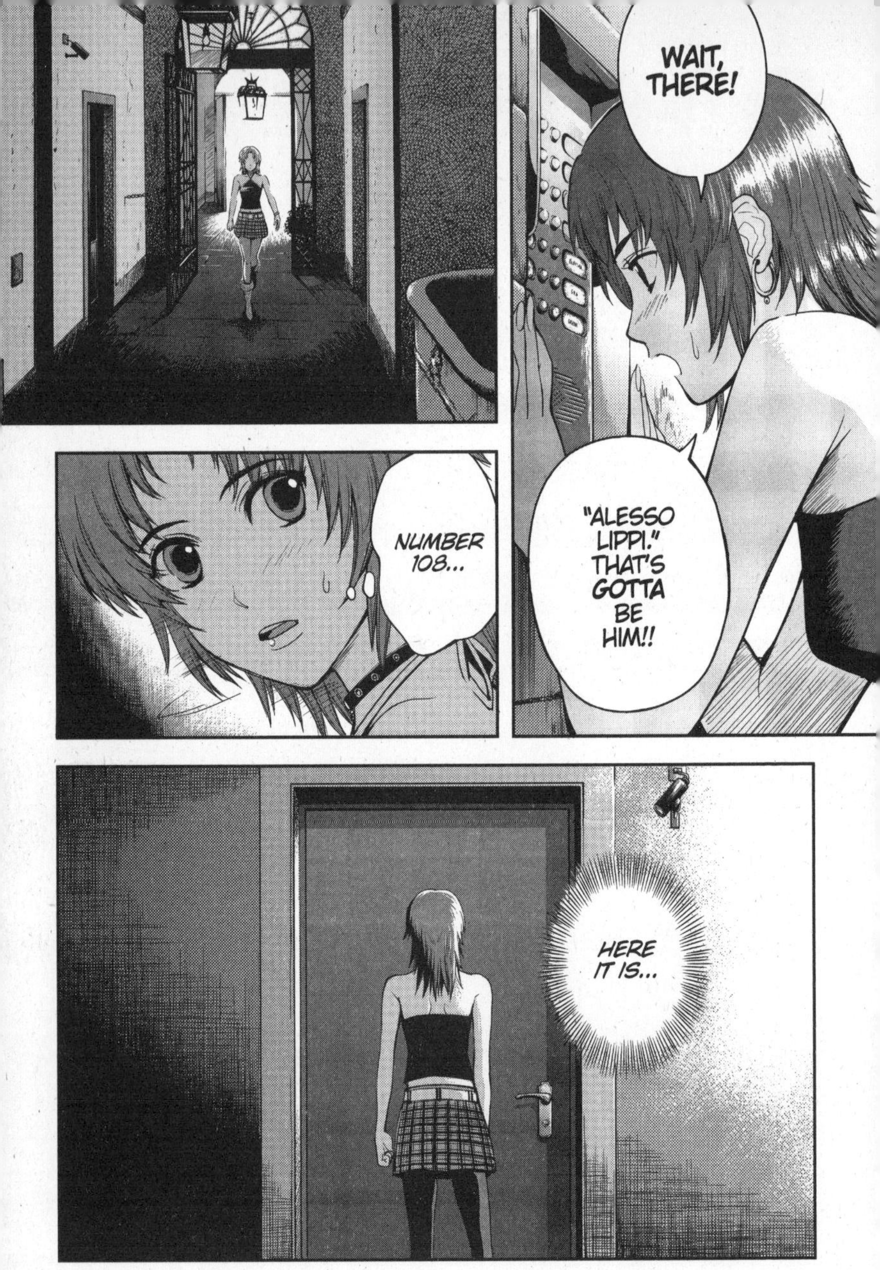
WAIT, THERE!
"ALESSO LIPPI." THAT'S GOTTA BE HIM!!
NUMBER 108...
HERE IT IS...

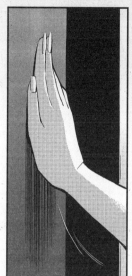

Chapter 39 / END

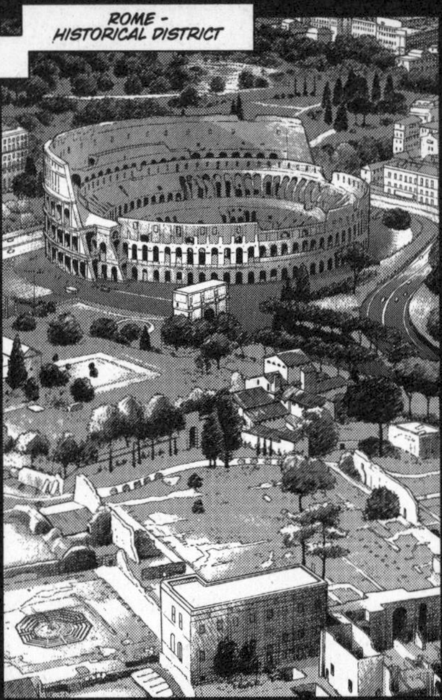
ROME - HISTORICAL DISTRICT

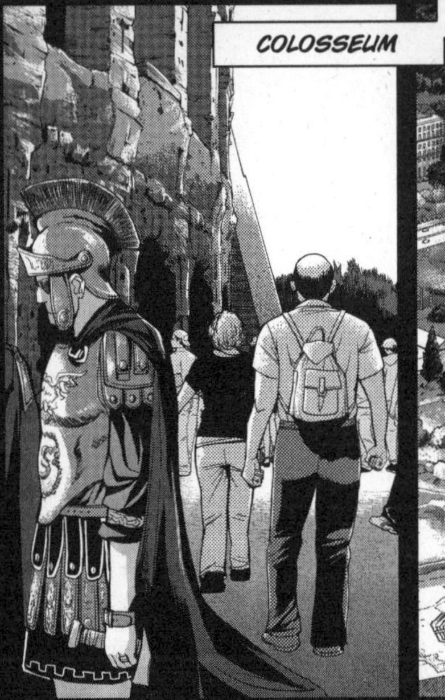
COLOSSEUM

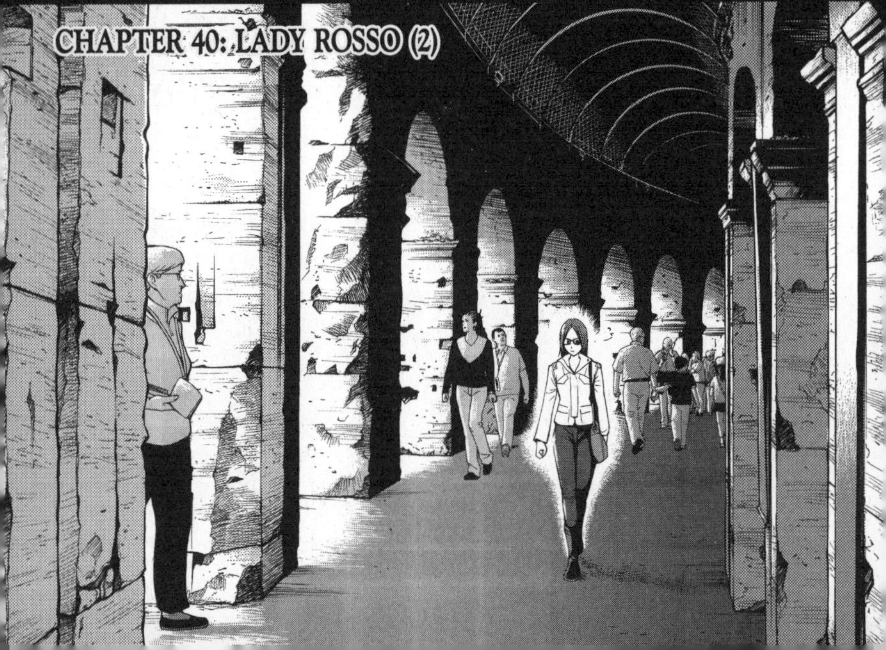
CHAPTER 40: LADY ROSSO (2)

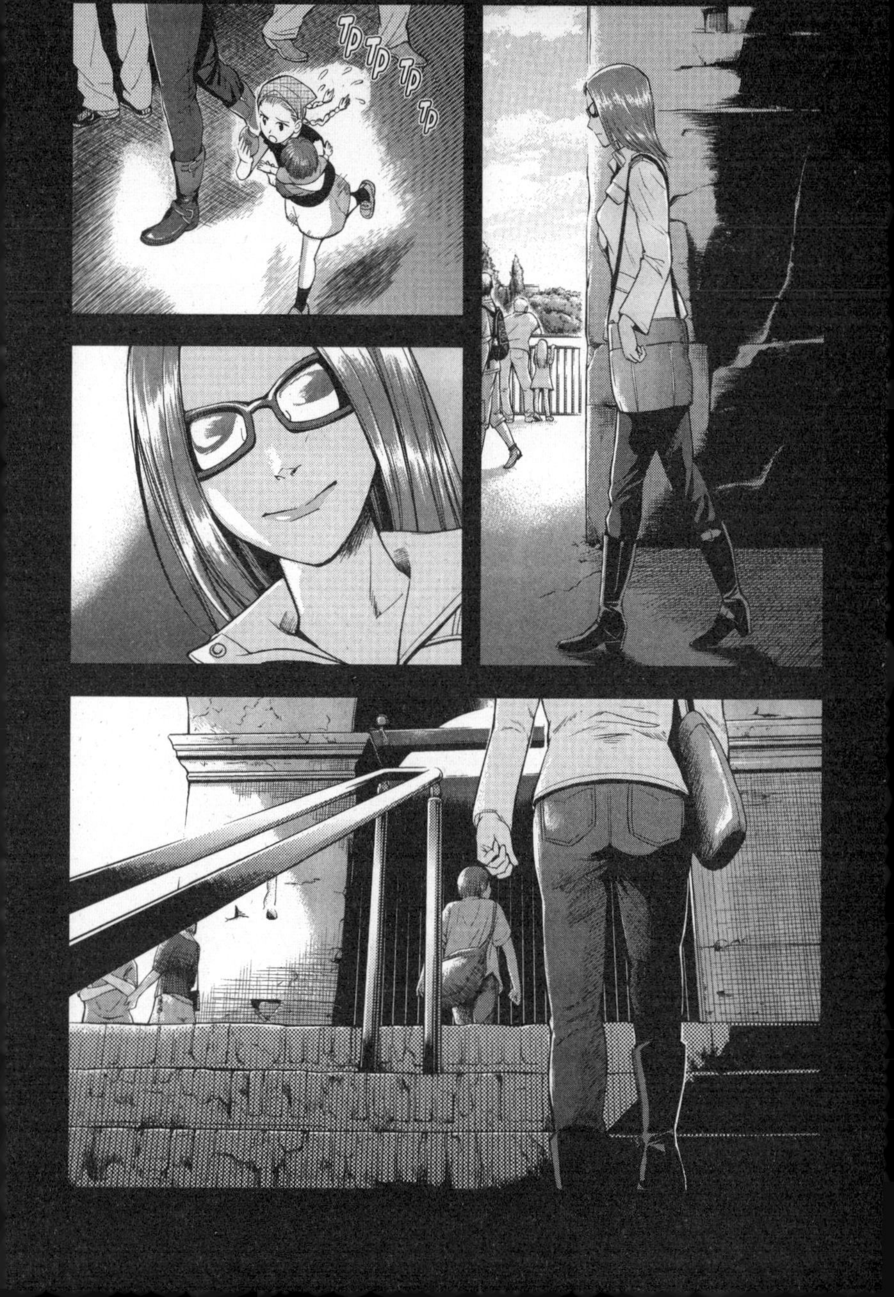
TP TP TP TP

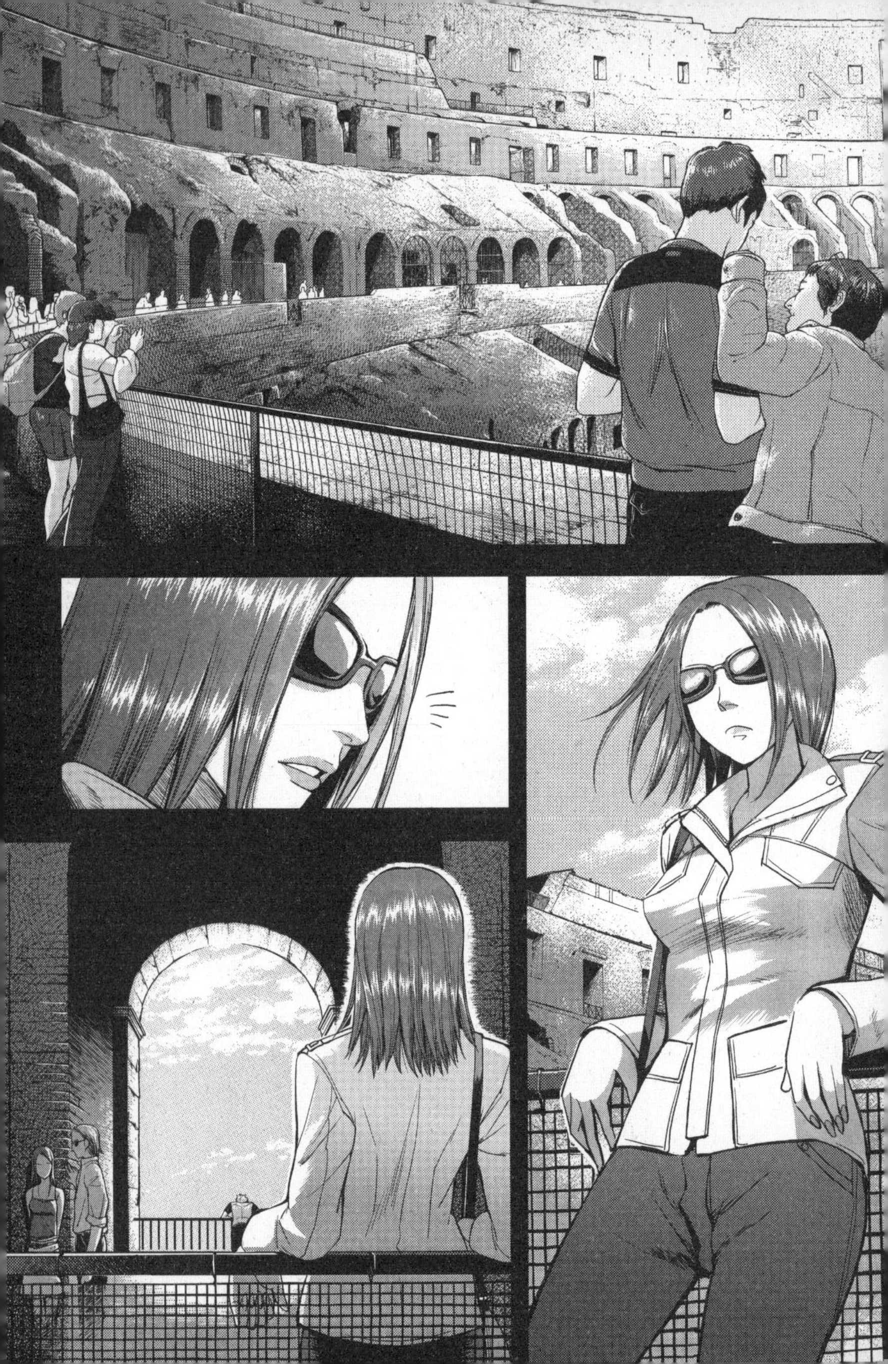

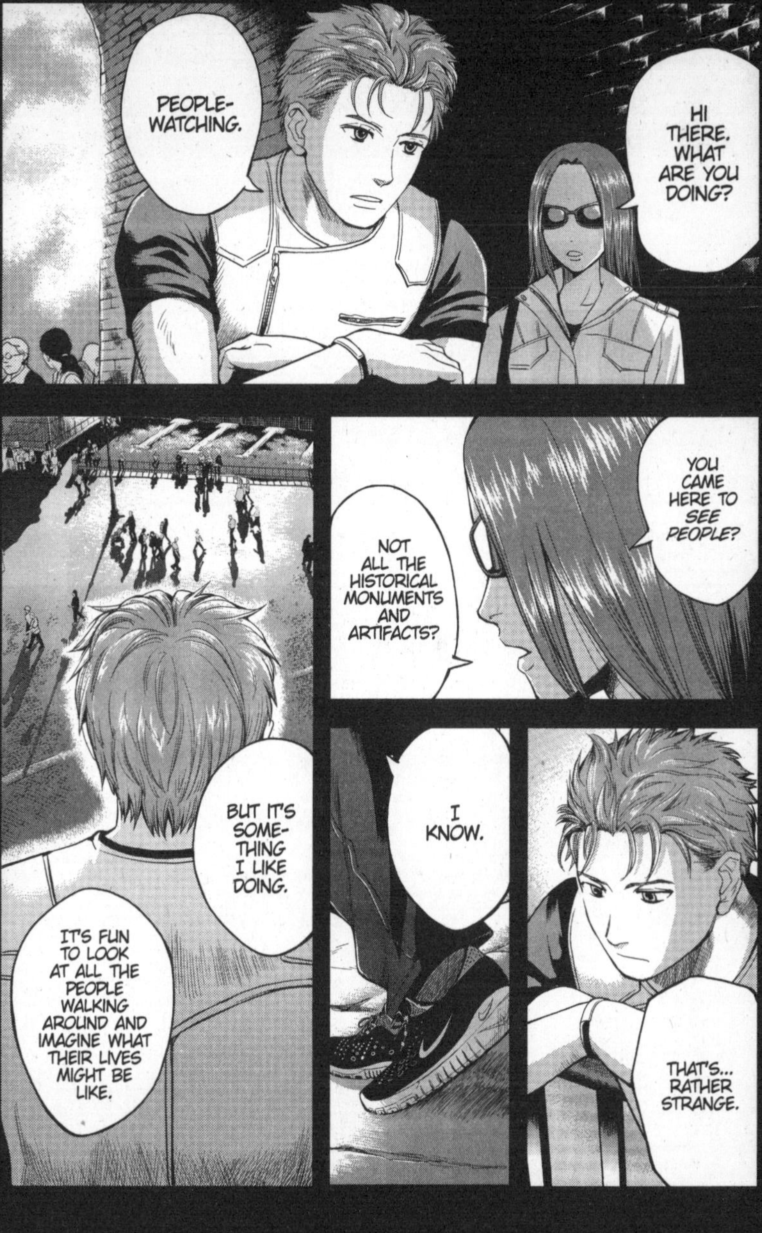
HI THERE. WHAT ARE YOU DOING?
PEOPLE-WATCHING.
YOU CAME HERE TO SEE PEOPLE?
NOT ALL THE HISTORICAL MONUMENTS AND ARTIFACTS?
THAT'S... RATHER STRANGE.
I KNOW.
BUT IT'S SOME-THING I LIKE DOING.
IT'S FUN TO LOOK AT ALL THE PEOPLE WALKING AROUND AND IMAGINE WHAT THEIR LIVES MIGHT BE LIKE.

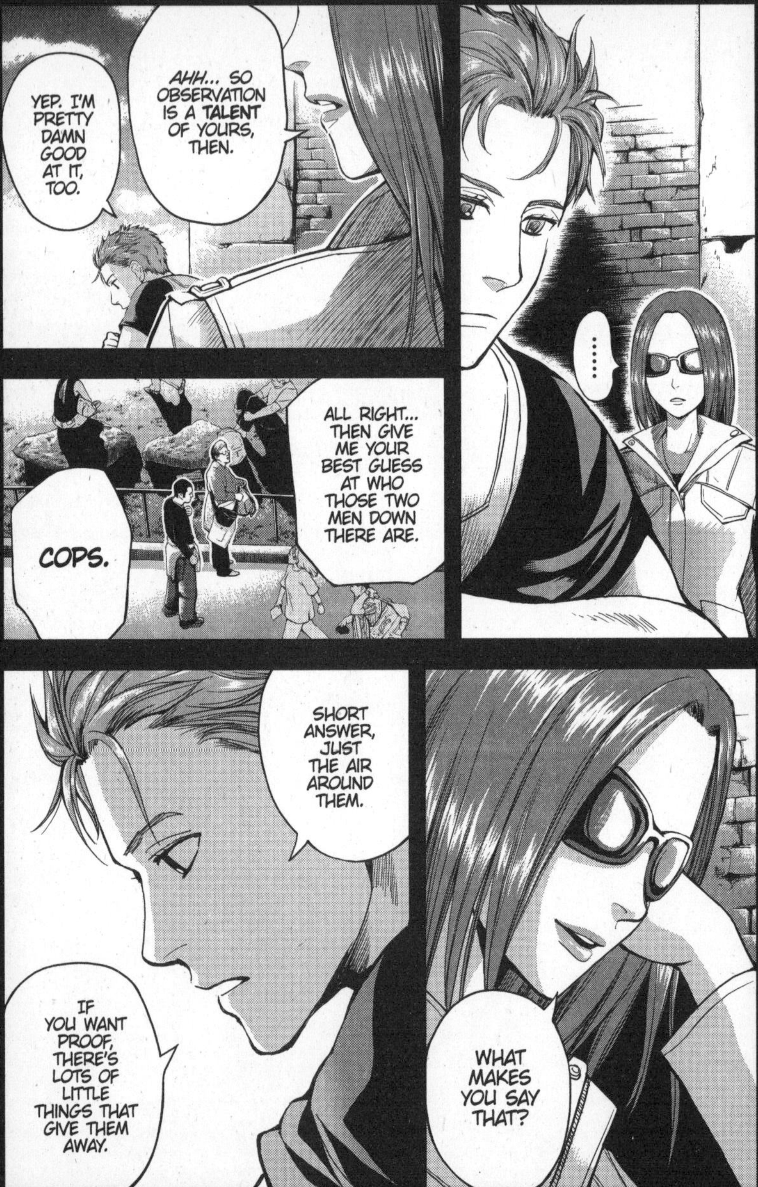
.....
AHH... SO OBSERVATION IS A TALENT OF YOURS, THEN.
YEP. I'M PRETTY DAMN GOOD AT IT, TOO.
ALL RIGHT... THEN GIVE ME YOUR BEST GUESS AT WHO THOSE TWO MEN DOWN THERE ARE.
COPS.
WHAT MAKES YOU SAY THAT?
SHORT ANSWER, JUST THE AIR AROUND THEM.
IF YOU WANT PROOF, THERE'S LOTS OF LITTLE THINGS THAT GIVE THEM AWAY.

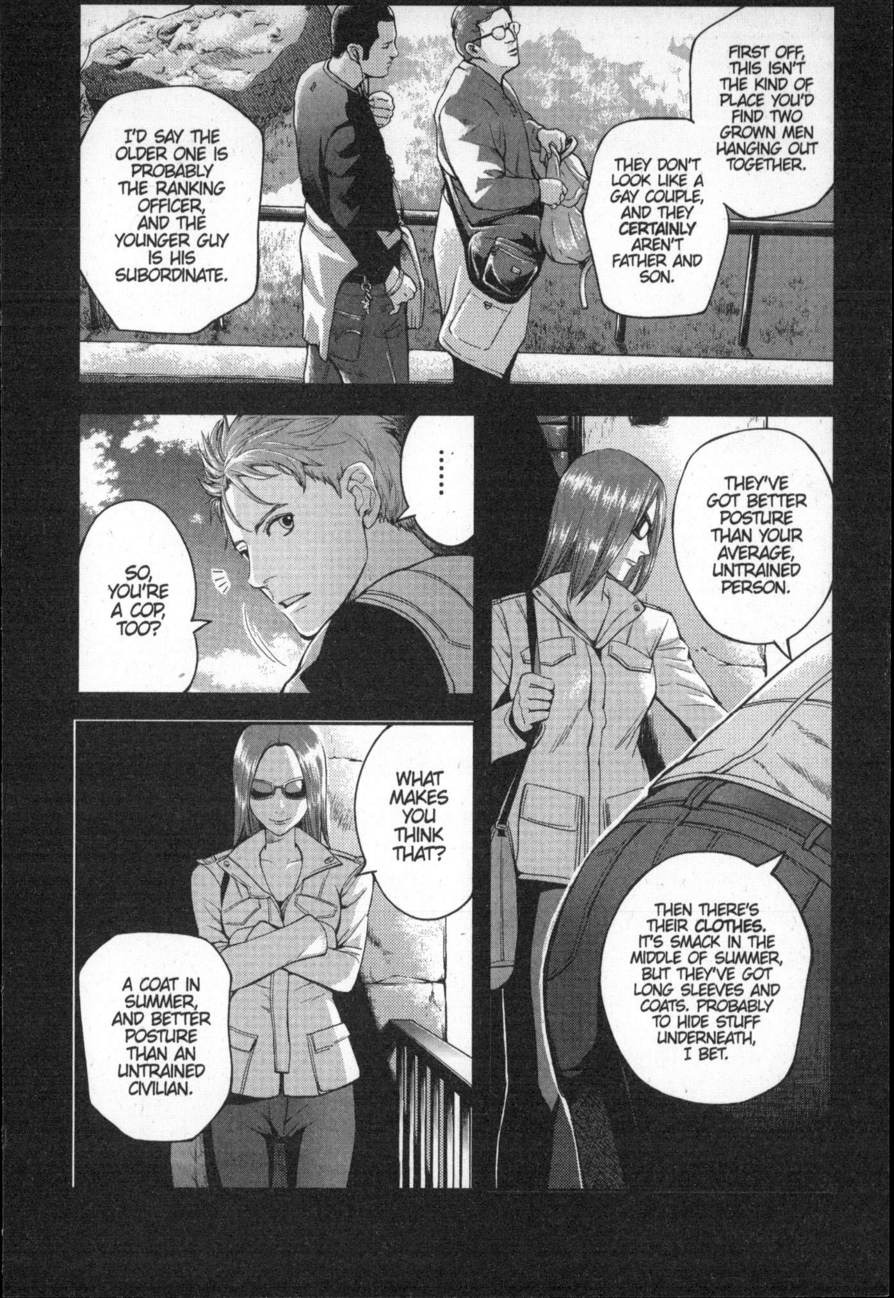
FIRST OFF, THIS ISN'T THE KIND OF PLACE YOU'D FIND TWO GROWN MEN HANGING OUT TOGETHER.
THEY DON'T LOOK LIKE A GAY COUPLE, AND THEY CERTAINLY AREN'T FATHER AND SON.
I'D SAY THE OLDER ONE IS PROBABLY THE RANKING OFFICER, AND THE YOUNGER GUY IS HIS SUBORDINATE.
THEY'VE GOT BETTER POSTURE THAN YOUR AVERAGE, UNTRAINED PERSON.
THEN THERE'S THEIR CLOTHES. IT'S SMACK IN THE MIDDLE OF SUMMER, BUT THEY'VE GOT LONG SLEEVES AND COATS. PROBABLY TO HIDE STUFF UNDERNEATH, I BET.
......
SO, YOU'RE A COP, TOO?
WHAT MAKES YOU THINK THAT?
A COAT IN SUMMER, AND BETTER POSTURE THAN AN UNTRAINED CIVILIAN.

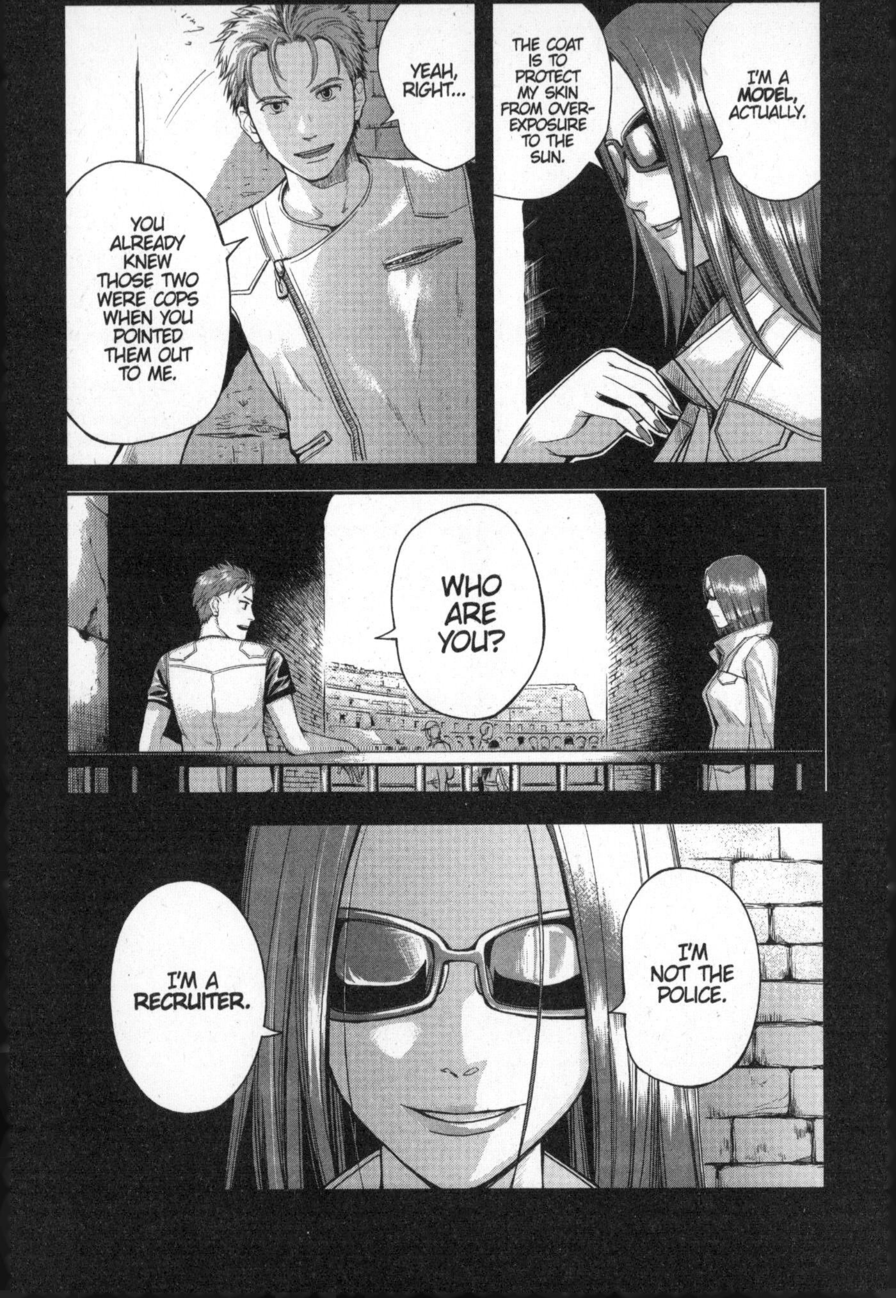
I'M A MODEL, ACTUALLY.
THE COAT IS TO PROTECT MY SKIN FROM OVER-EXPOSURE TO THE SUN.
YEAH, RIGHT...
YOU ALREADY KNEW THOSE TWO WERE COPS WHEN YOU POINTED THEM OUT TO ME.
WHO ARE YOU?
I'M NOT THE POLICE.
I'M A RECRUITER.

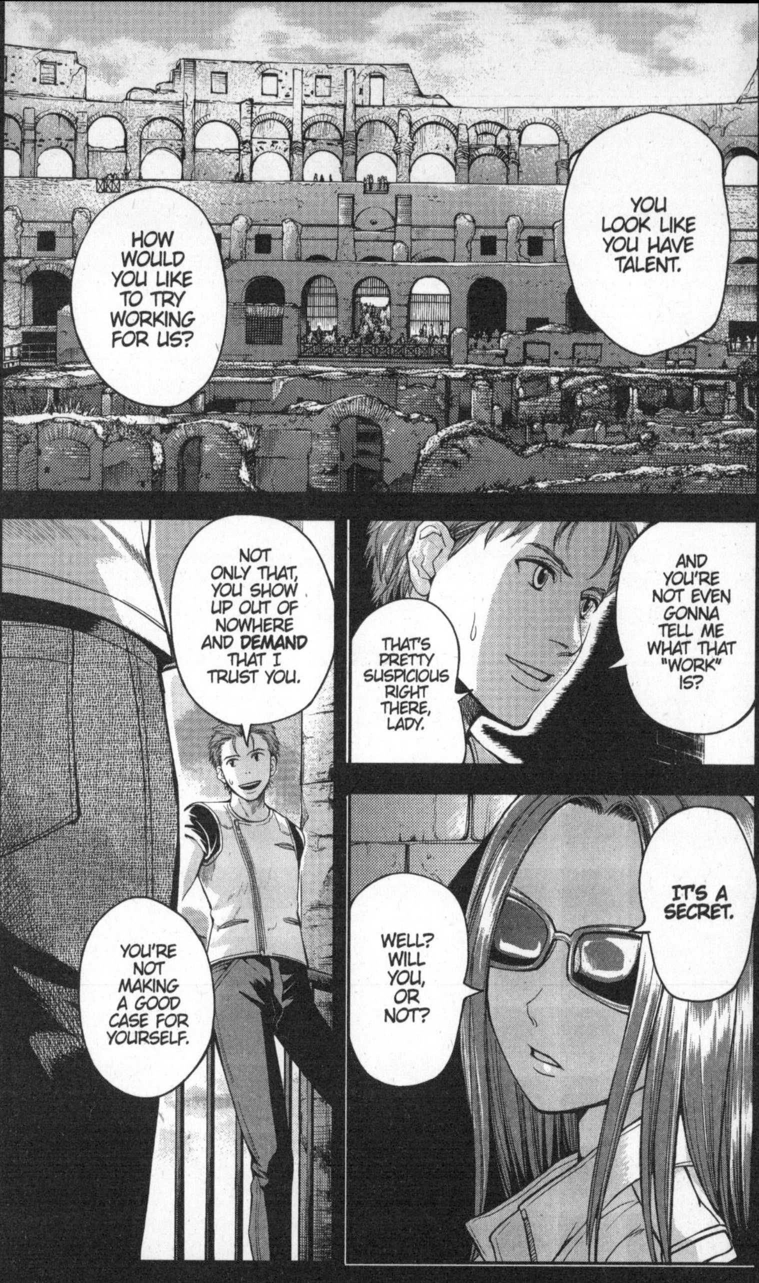
YOU LOOK LIKE YOU HAVE TALENT.
HOW WOULD YOU LIKE TO TRY WORKING FOR US?
AND YOU'RE NOT EVEN GONNA TELL ME WHAT THAT "WORK" IS?
THAT'S PRETTY SUSPICIOUS RIGHT THERE, LADY.
IT'S A SECRET.
WELL? WILL YOU, OR NOT?
NOT ONLY THAT, YOU SHOW UP OUT OF NOWHERE AND DEMAND THAT I TRUST YOU.
YOU'RE NOT MAKING A GOOD CASE FOR YOURSELF.

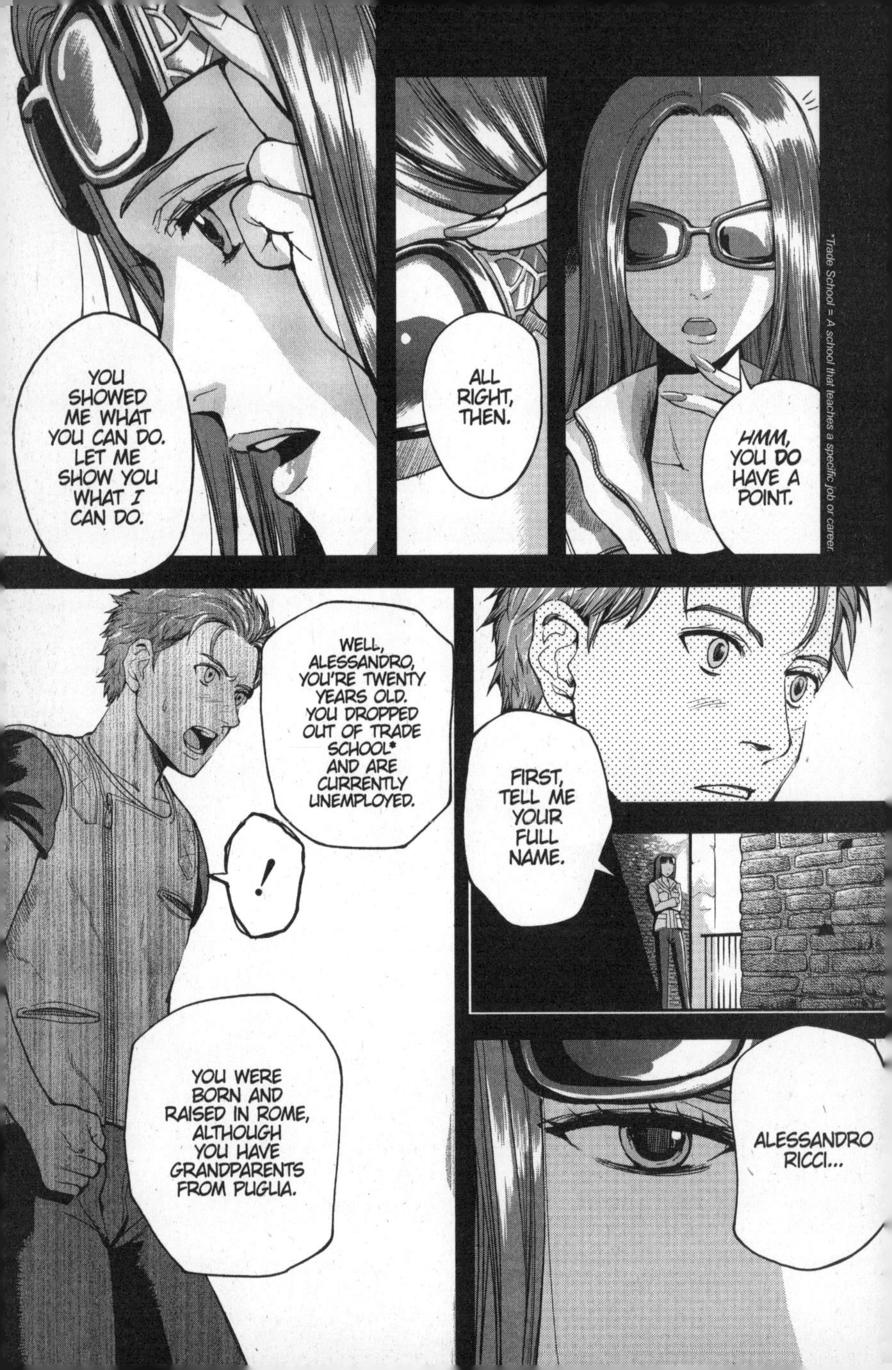
HMM, YOU DO HAVE A POINT.
ALL RIGHT, THEN.
YOU SHOWED ME WHAT YOU CAN DO. LET ME SHOW YOU WHAT *I* CAN DO.
FIRST, TELL ME YOUR FULL NAME.
ALESSANDRO RICCI...
WELL, ALESSANDRO, YOU'RE TWENTY YEARS OLD. YOU DROPPED OUT OF TRADE SCHOOL* AND ARE CURRENTLY UNEMPLOYED.
!
YOU WERE BORN AND RAISED IN ROME, ALTHOUGH YOU HAVE GRANDPARENTS FROM PUGLIA.

*Trade School = A school that teaches a specific job or career.

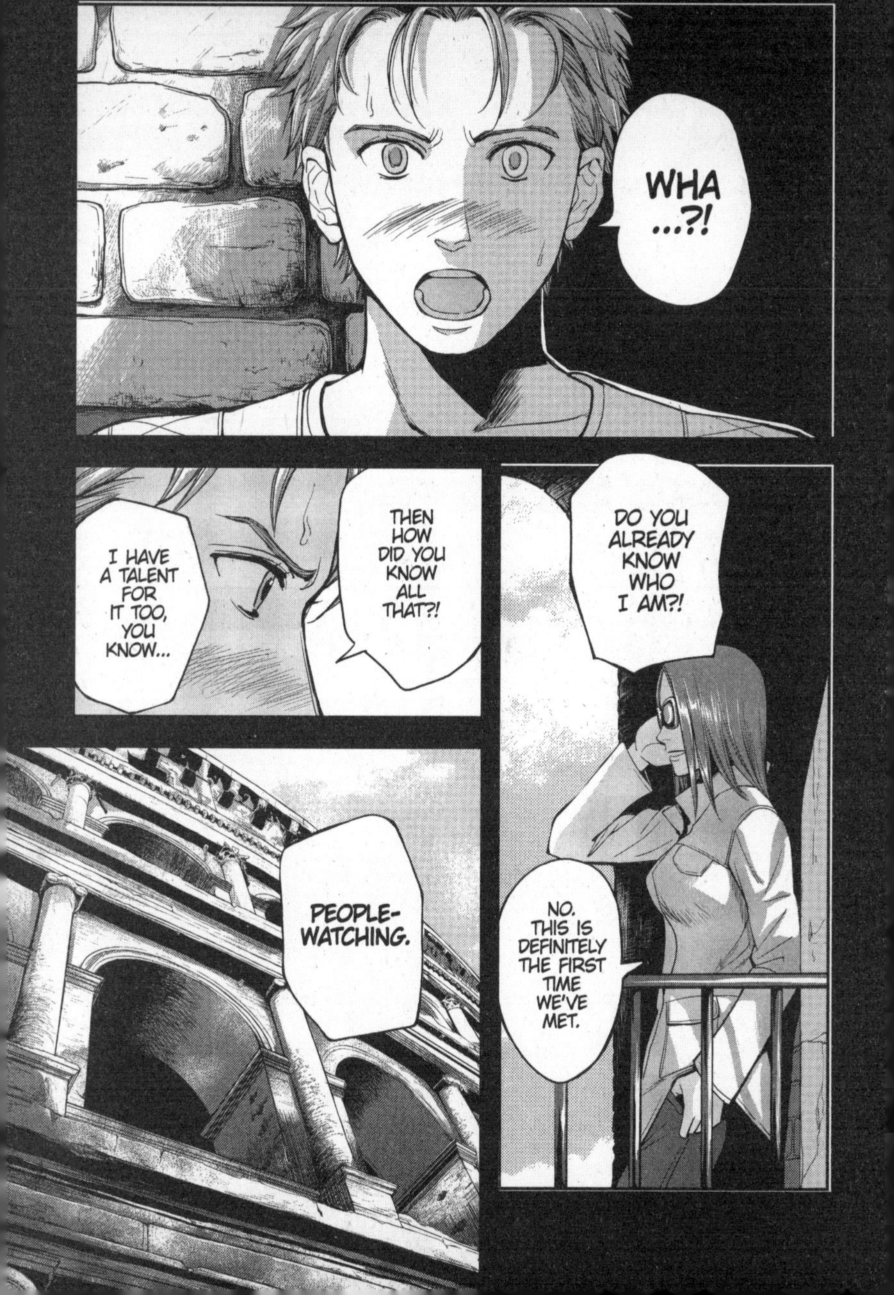
WHA ...?!
DO YOU ALREADY KNOW WHO I AM?!
NO. THIS IS DEFINITELY THE FIRST TIME WE'VE MET.
THEN HOW DID YOU KNOW ALL THAT?!
I HAVE A TALENT FOR IT TOO, YOU KNOW...
PEOPLE-WATCHING.

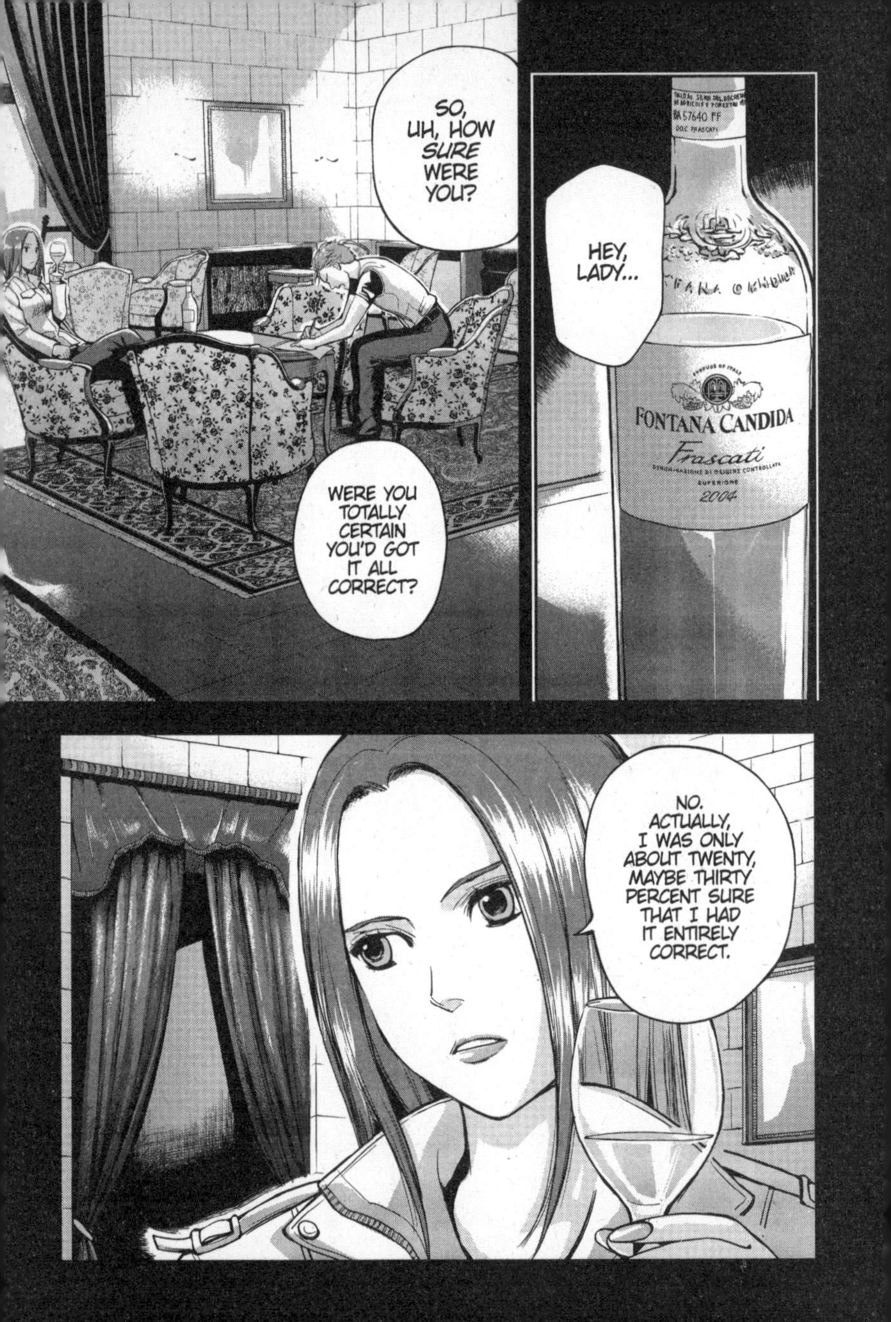
HEY, LADY...
BA 57640 FF
FONTANA CANDIDA
Frascati
SUPERIORE
2004
SO, UH, HOW SURE WERE YOU?
WERE YOU TOTALLY CERTAIN YOU'D GOT IT ALL CORRECT?
NO. ACTUALLY, I WAS ONLY ABOUT TWENTY, MAYBE THIRTY PERCENT SURE THAT I HAD IT ENTIRELY CORRECT.

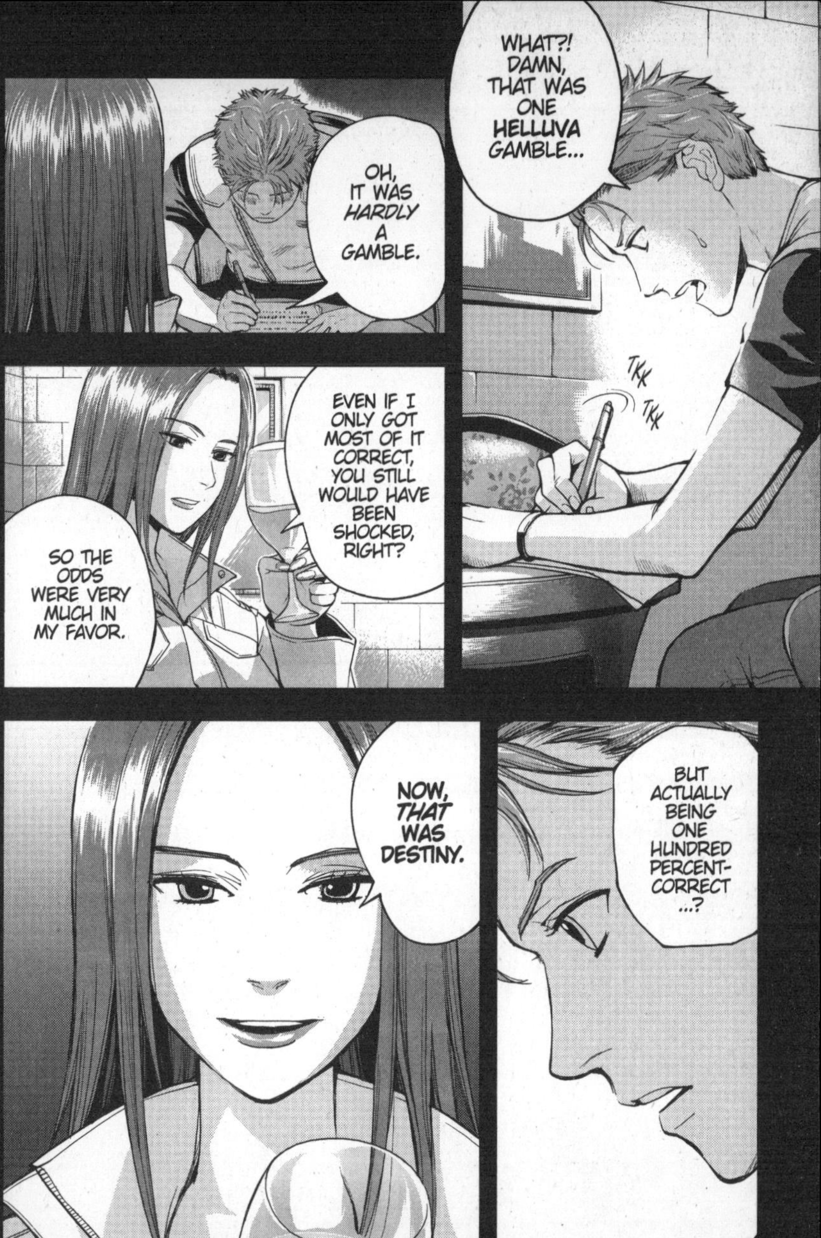
WHAT?! DAMN, THAT WAS ONE HELLUVA GAMBLE...
TKK
TKK
OH, IT WAS *HARDLY* A GAMBLE.
EVEN IF I ONLY GOT MOST OF IT CORRECT, YOU STILL WOULD HAVE BEEN SHOCKED, RIGHT?
SO THE ODDS WERE VERY MUCH IN MY FAVOR.
BUT ACTUALLY BEING ONE HUNDRED PERCENT-CORRECT ...?
NOW, *THAT* WAS DESTINY.

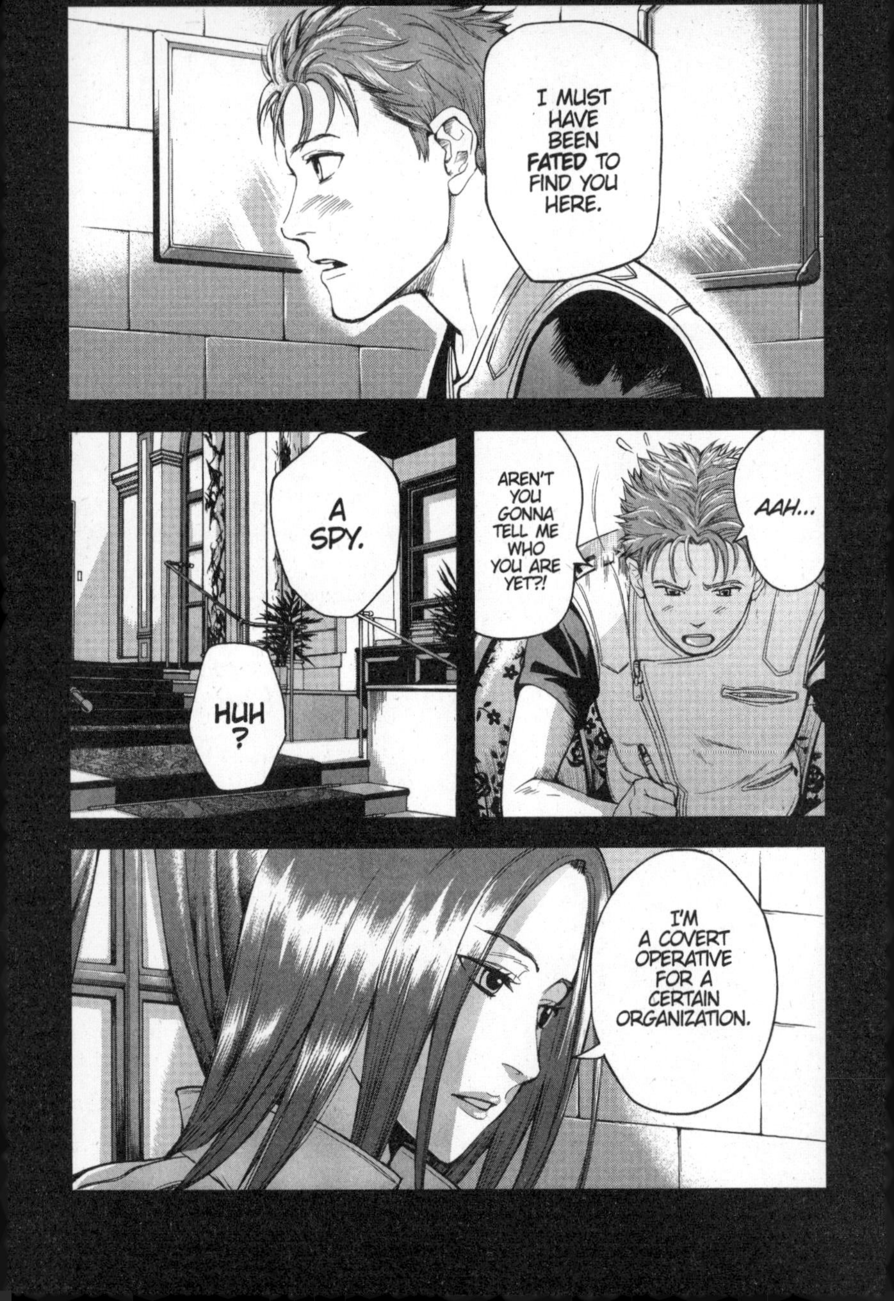

I MUST HAVE BEEN **FATED** TO FIND YOU HERE.
AAH...
AREN'T YOU GONNA TELL ME WHO YOU ARE YET?!
A SPY.
HUH?
I'M A COVERT OPERATIVE FOR A CERTAIN ORGANIZATION.

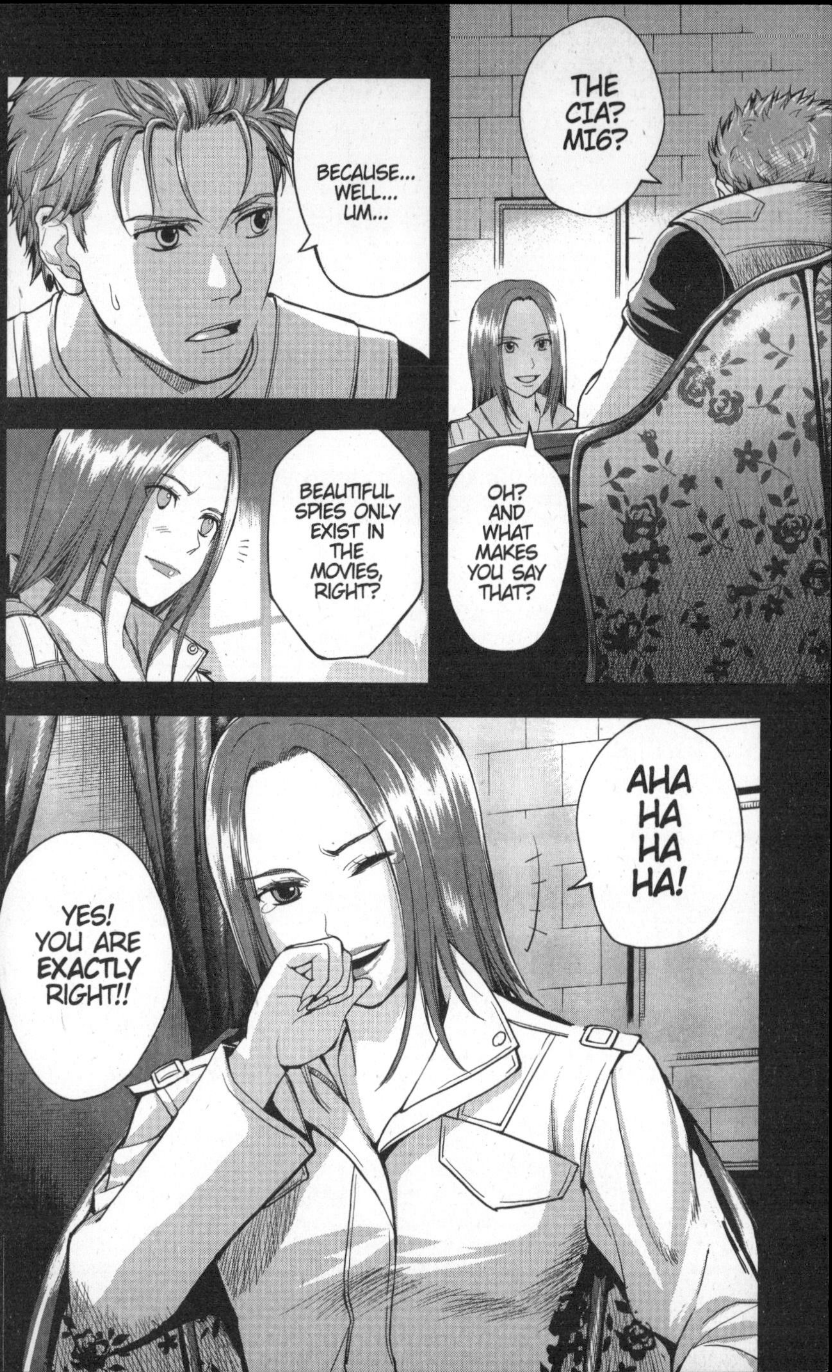
THE CIA? MI6?
OH? AND WHAT MAKES YOU SAY THAT?
BECAUSE... WELL... UM...
BEAUTIFUL SPIES ONLY EXIST IN THE MOVIES, RIGHT?
AHA HA HA HA!
YES! YOU ARE EXACTLY RIGHT!!

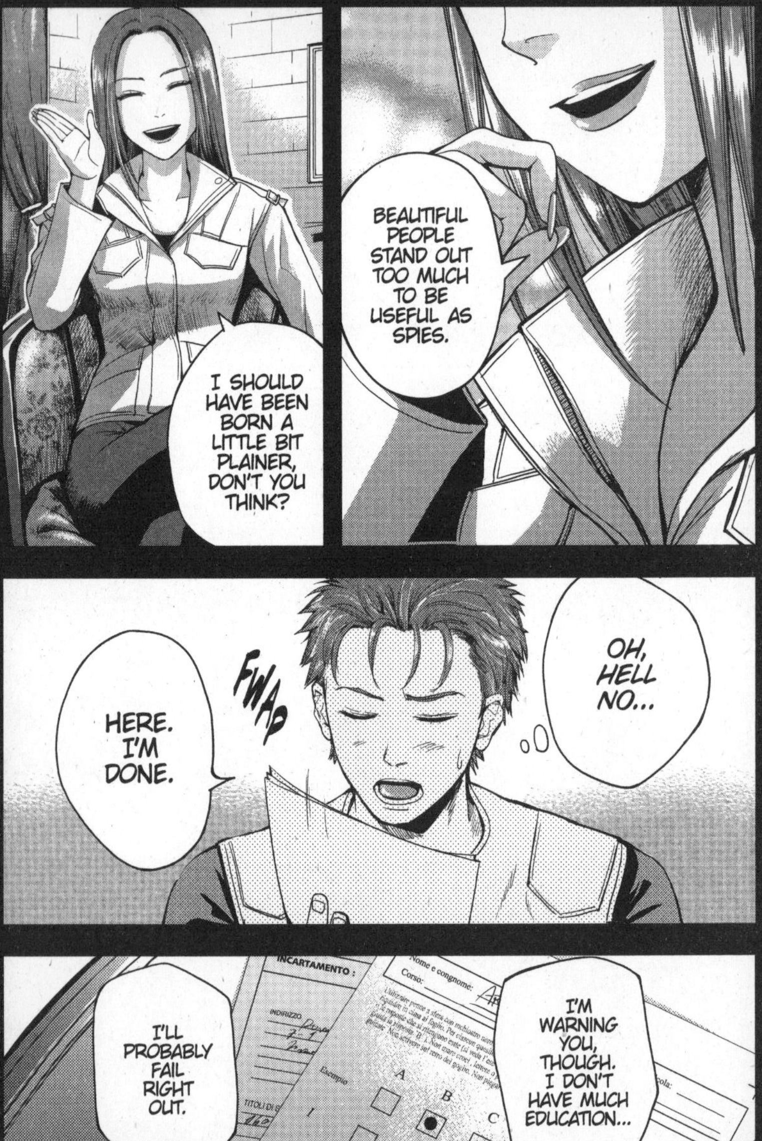
BEAUTIFUL PEOPLE STAND OUT TOO MUCH TO BE USEFUL AS SPIES.
I SHOULD HAVE BEEN BORN A LITTLE BIT PLAINER, DON'T YOU THINK?
OH, HELL NO...
FWAP
HERE. I'M DONE.
I'M WARNING YOU, THOUGH. I DON'T HAVE MUCH EDUCATION...
I'LL PROBABLY FAIL RIGHT OUT.
INCARTAMENTO :
Nome e congnome:
Corso:
INDIRIZZO
Esempio

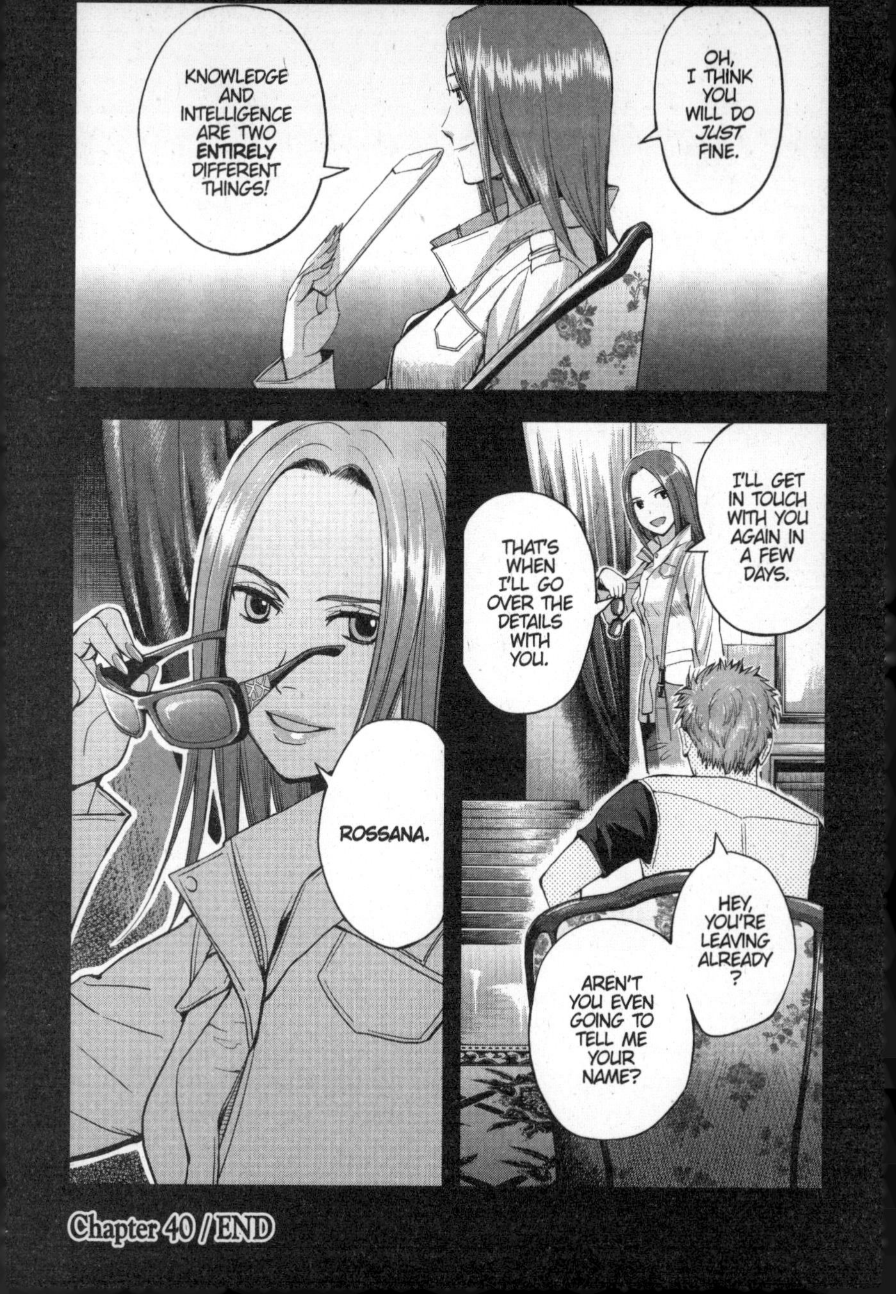
OH, I THINK YOU WILL DO JUST FINE.
KNOWLEDGE AND INTELLIGENCE ARE TWO ENTIRELY DIFFERENT THINGS!
I'LL GET IN TOUCH WITH YOU AGAIN IN A FEW DAYS.
THAT'S WHEN I'LL GO OVER THE DETAILS WITH YOU.
HEY, YOU'RE LEAVING ALREADY?
AREN'T YOU EVEN GOING TO TELL ME YOUR NAME?
ROSSANA.

Chapter 40 / END

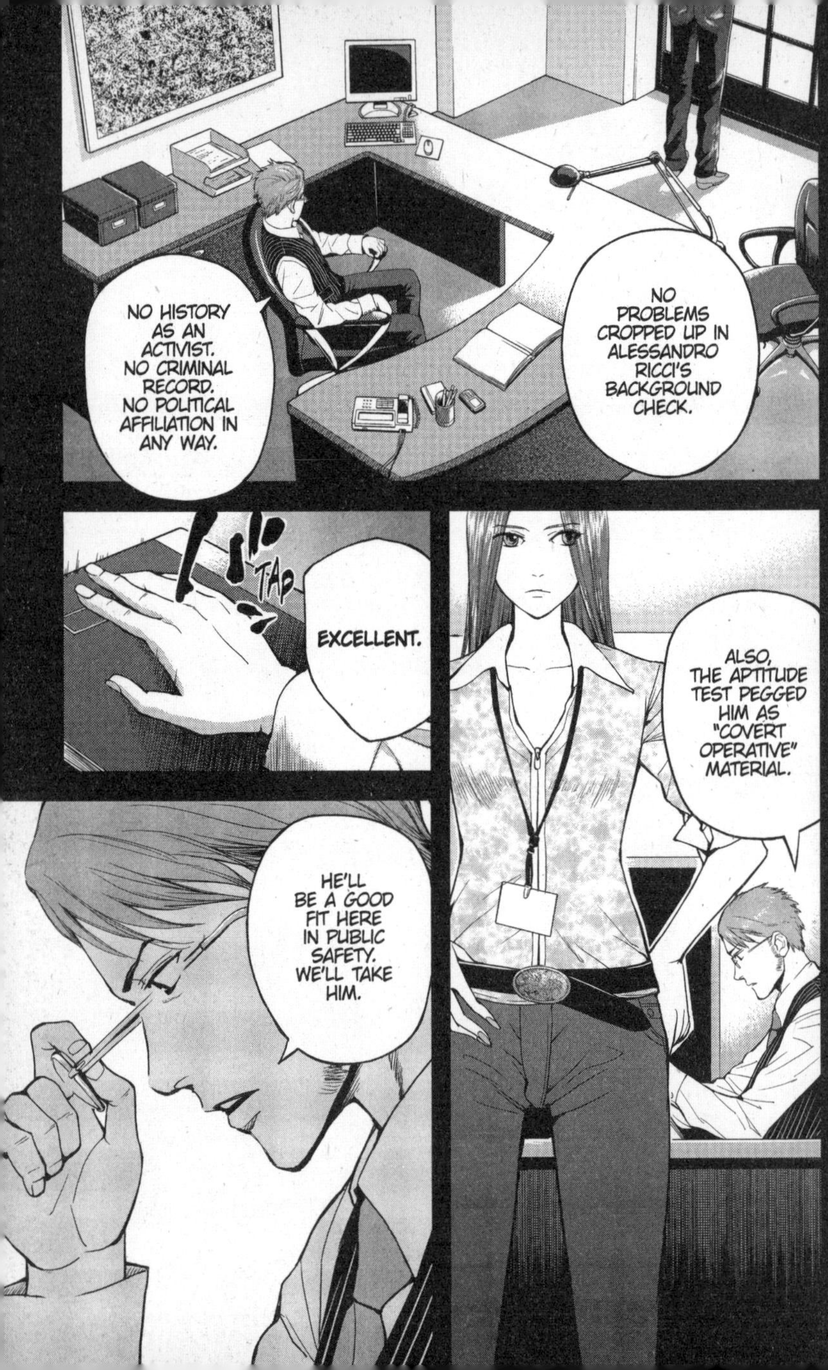
NO PROBLEMS CROPPED UP IN ALESSANDRO RICCI'S BACKGROUND CHECK.
NO HISTORY AS AN ACTIVIST. NO CRIMINAL RECORD. NO POLITICAL AFFILIATION IN ANY WAY.
ALSO, THE APTITUDE TEST PEGGED HIM AS "COVERT OPERATIVE" MATERIAL.
TAP
EXCELLENT.
HE'LL BE A GOOD FIT HERE IN PUBLIC SAFETY. WE'LL TAKE HIM.

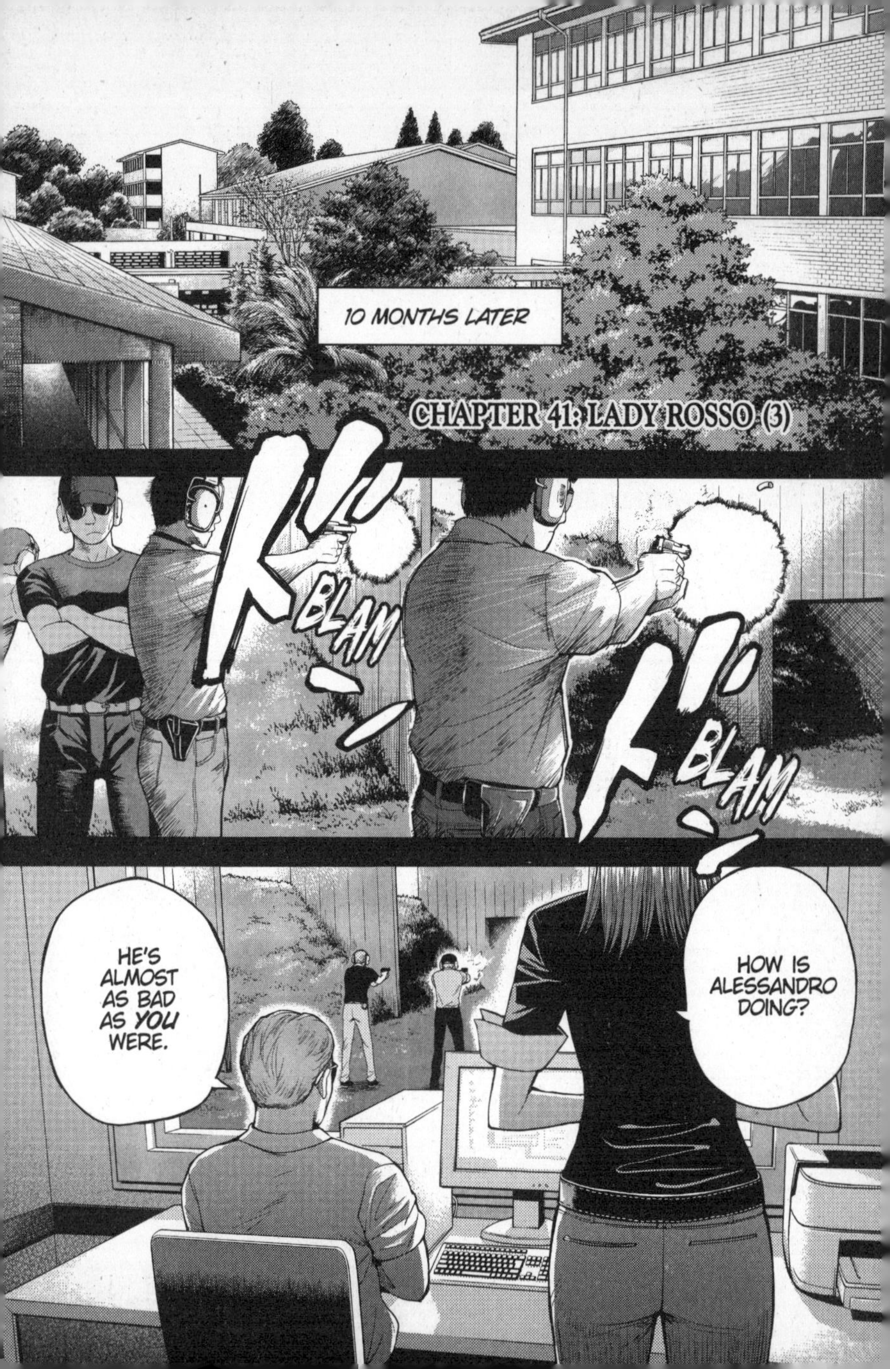
10 MONTHS LATER
CHAPTER 41: LADY ROSSO (3)
BLAM
BLAM
HOW IS ALESSANDRO DOING?
HE'S ALMOST AS BAD AS YOU WERE.

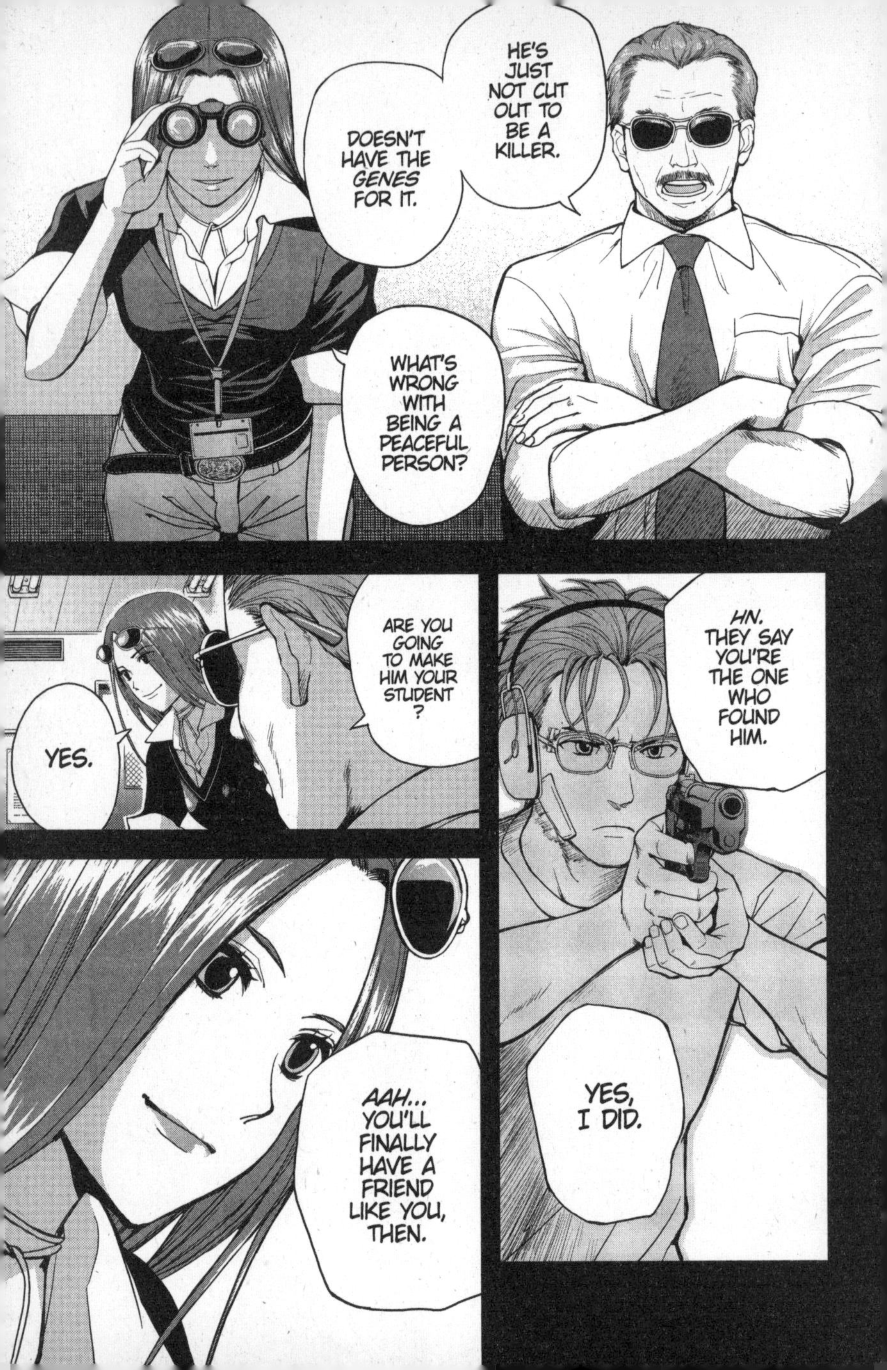
HE'S JUST NOT CUT OUT TO BE A KILLER.
DOESN'T HAVE THE *GENES* FOR IT.
WHAT'S WRONG WITH BEING A PEACEFUL PERSON?
HN. THEY SAY YOU'RE THE ONE WHO FOUND HIM.
YES, I DID.
ARE YOU GOING TO MAKE HIM YOUR STUDENT?
YES.
AAH... YOU'LL FINALLY HAVE A FRIEND LIKE YOU, THEN.

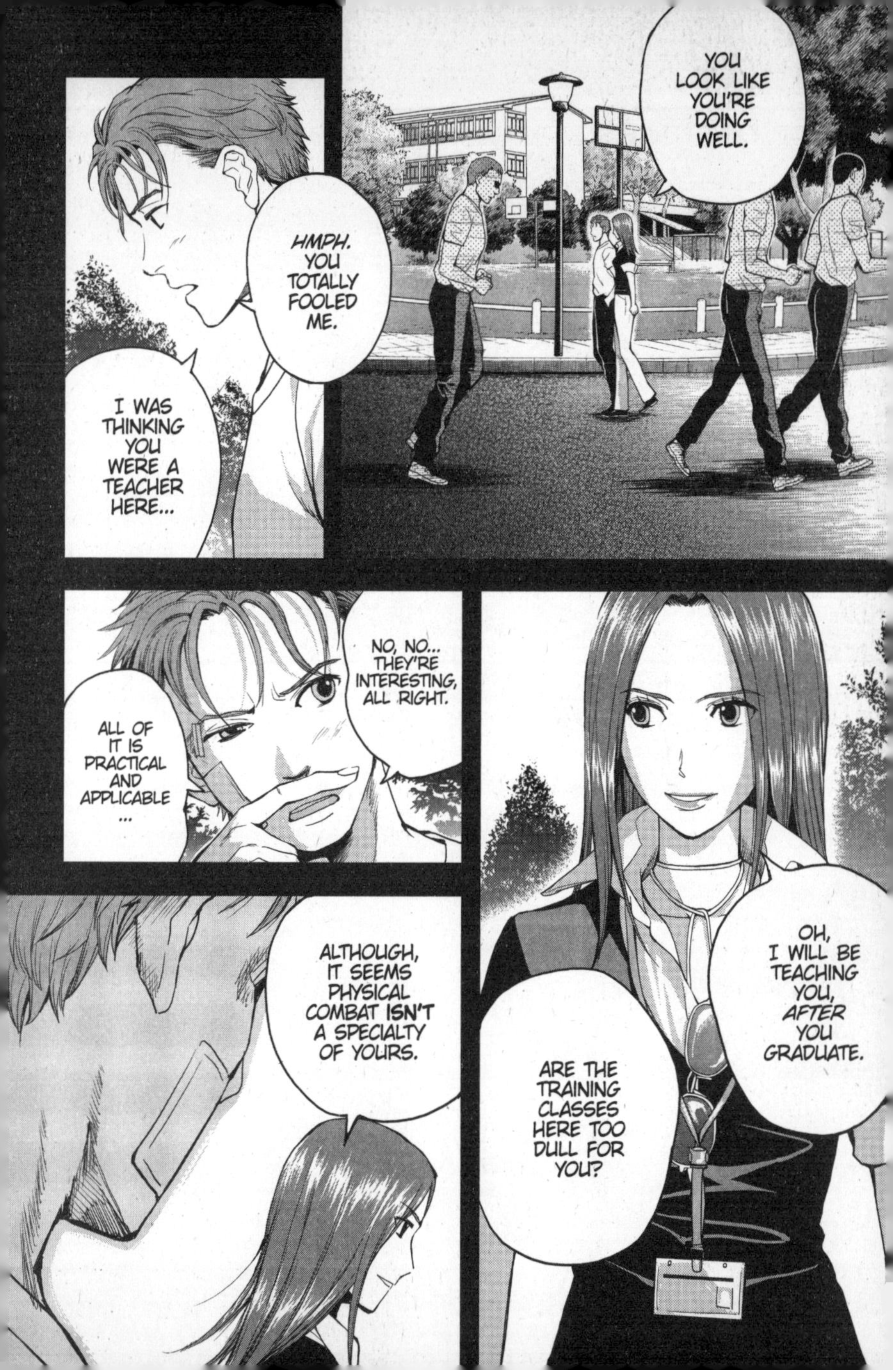
YOU LOOK LIKE YOU'RE DOING WELL.
HMPH. YOU TOTALLY FOOLED ME.
I WAS THINKING YOU WERE A TEACHER HERE...
OH, I WILL BE TEACHING YOU, *AFTER* YOU GRADUATE.
ARE THE TRAINING CLASSES HERE TOO DULL FOR YOU?
NO, NO... THEY'RE INTERESTING, ALL RIGHT.
ALL OF IT IS PRACTICAL AND APPLICABLE ...
ALTHOUGH, IT SEEMS PHYSICAL COMBAT **ISN'T** A SPECIALTY OF YOURS.

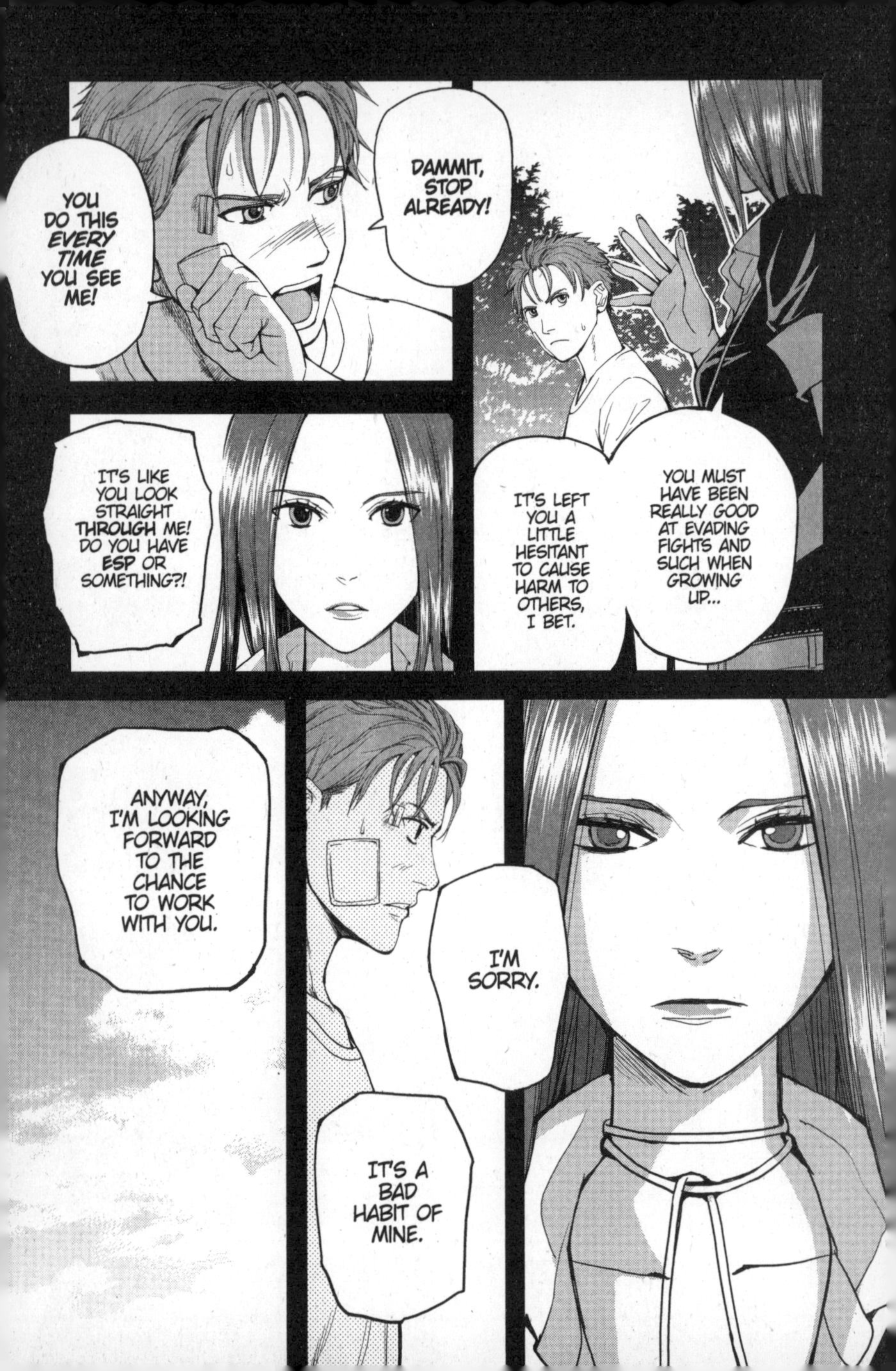
YOU MUST HAVE BEEN REALLY GOOD AT EVADING FIGHTS AND SUCH WHEN GROWING UP...
IT'S LEFT YOU A LITTLE HESITANT TO CAUSE HARM TO OTHERS, I BET.
DAMMIT, STOP ALREADY!
YOU DO THIS *EVERY TIME* YOU SEE ME!
IT'S LIKE YOU LOOK STRAIGHT THROUGH ME! DO YOU HAVE ESP OR SOMETHING?!
I'M SORRY.
IT'S A BAD HABIT OF MINE.
ANYWAY, I'M LOOKING FORWARD TO THE CHANCE TO WORK WITH YOU.

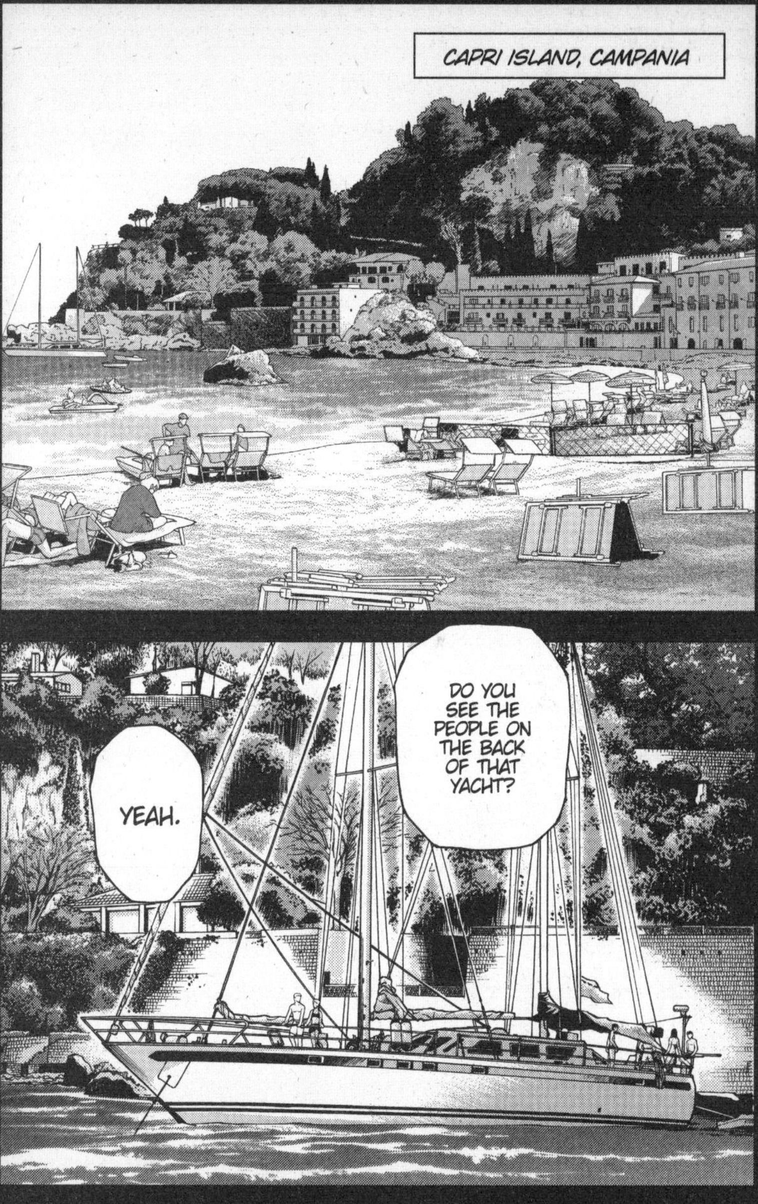
CAPRI ISLAND, CAMPANIA
DO YOU SEE THE PEOPLE ON THE BACK OF THAT YACHT?
YEAH.

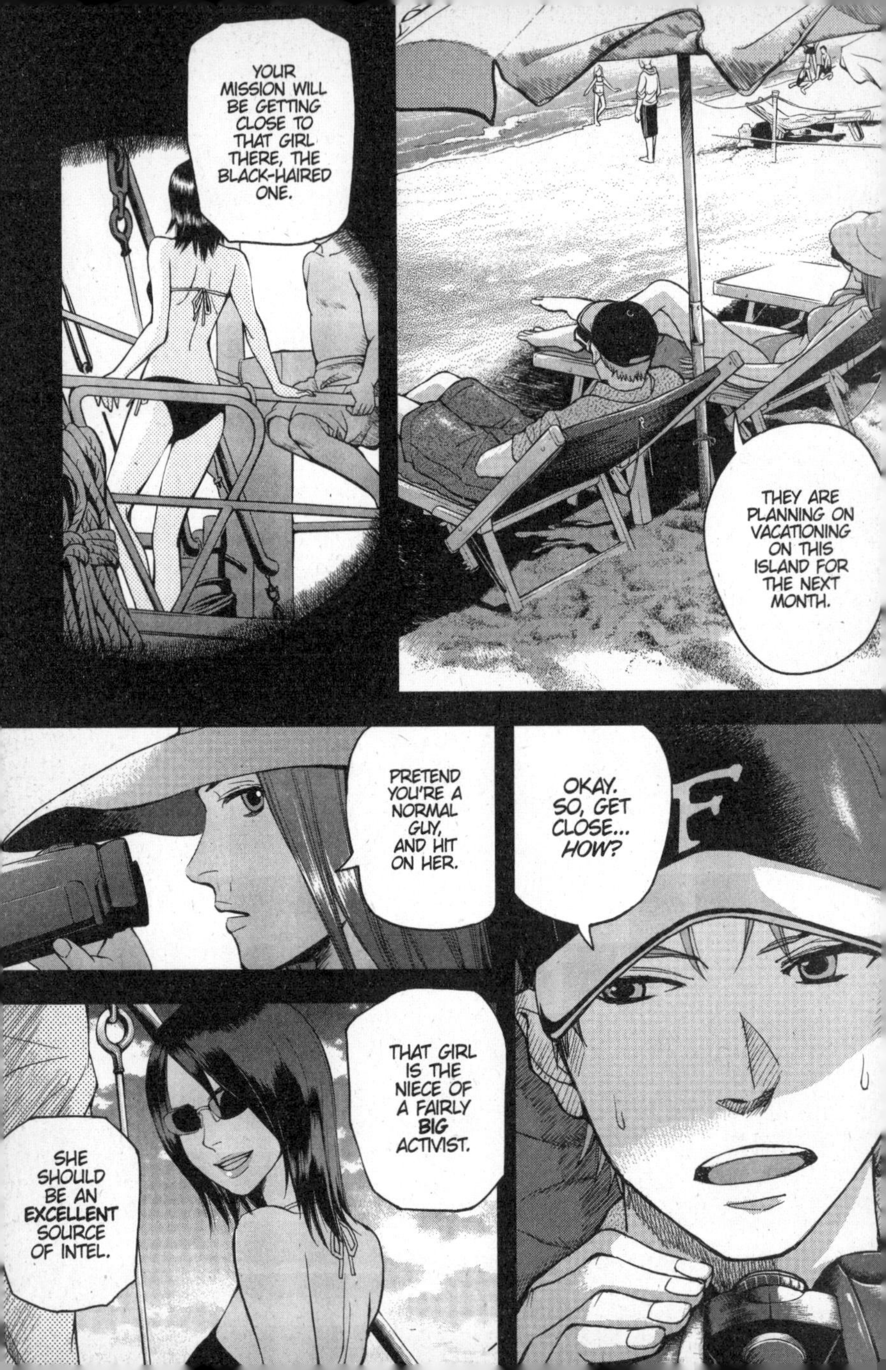
THEY ARE PLANNING ON VACATIONING ON THIS ISLAND FOR THE NEXT MONTH.
YOUR MISSION WILL BE GETTING CLOSE TO THAT GIRL THERE, THE BLACK-HAIRED ONE.
OKAY. SO, GET CLOSE... *HOW?*
PRETEND YOU'RE A NORMAL GUY, AND HIT ON HER.
THAT GIRL IS THE NIECE OF A FAIRLY **BIG** ACTIVIST.
SHE SHOULD BE AN **EXCELLENT** SOURCE OF INTEL.

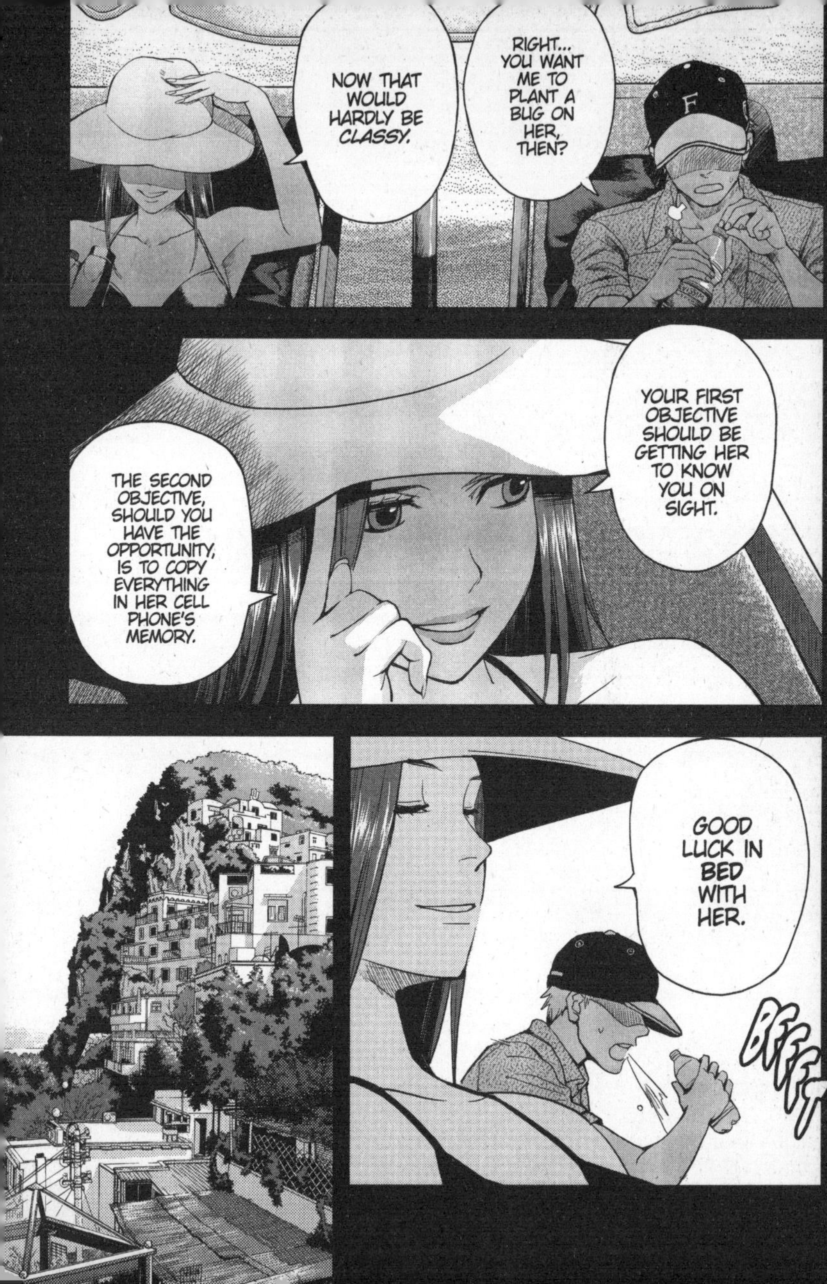
RIGHT... YOU WANT ME TO PLANT A BUG ON HER, THEN?
NOW THAT WOULD HARDLY BE *CLASSY.*
YOUR FIRST OBJECTIVE SHOULD BE GETTING HER TO KNOW YOU ON SIGHT.
THE SECOND OBJECTIVE, SHOULD YOU HAVE THE OPPORTUNITY, IS TO COPY EVERYTHING IN HER CELL PHONE'S MEMORY.
GOOD LUCK IN BED WITH HER.
BFFFT

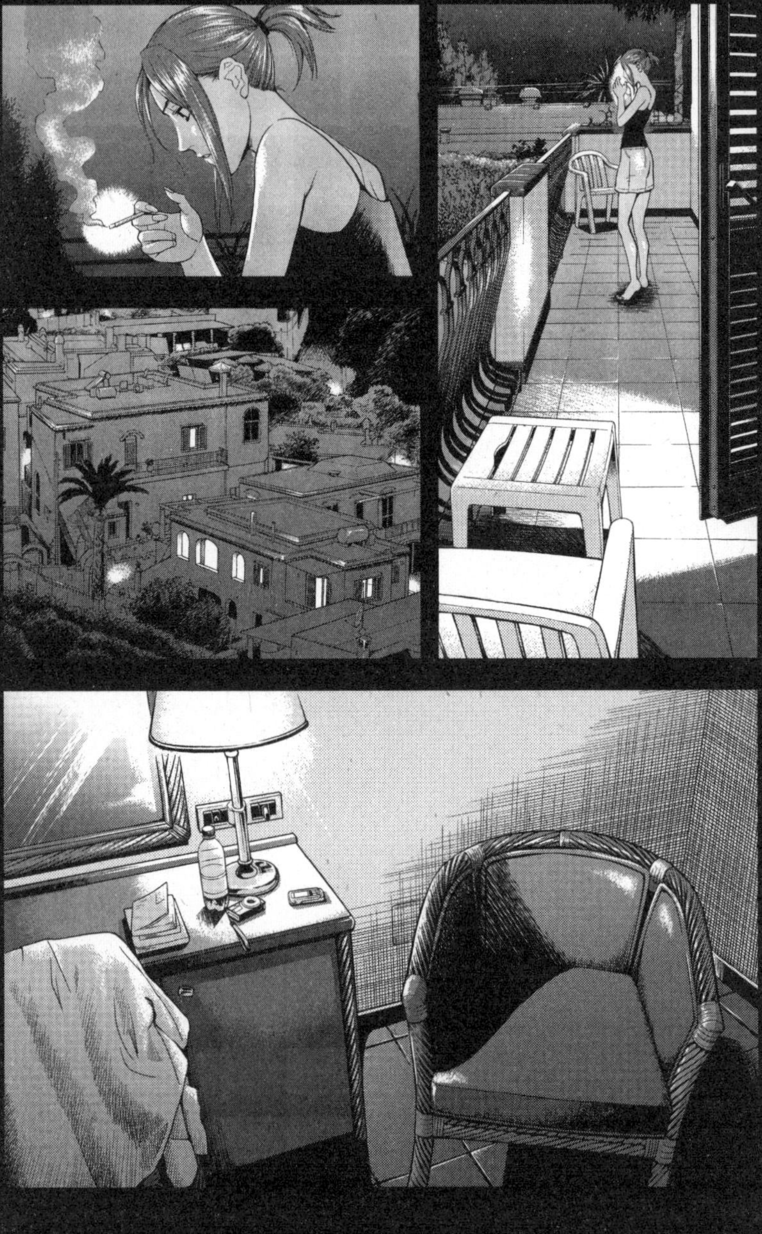

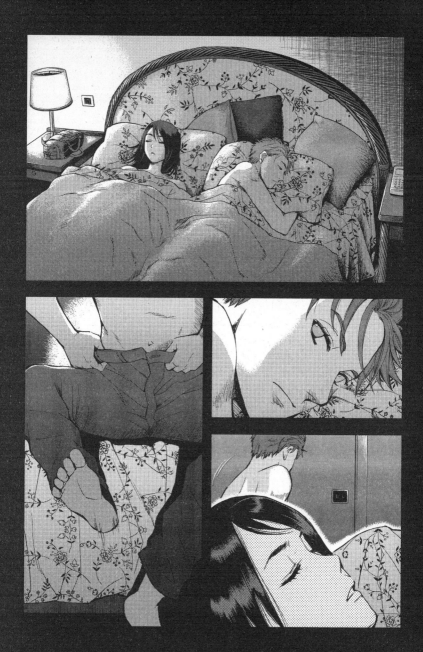

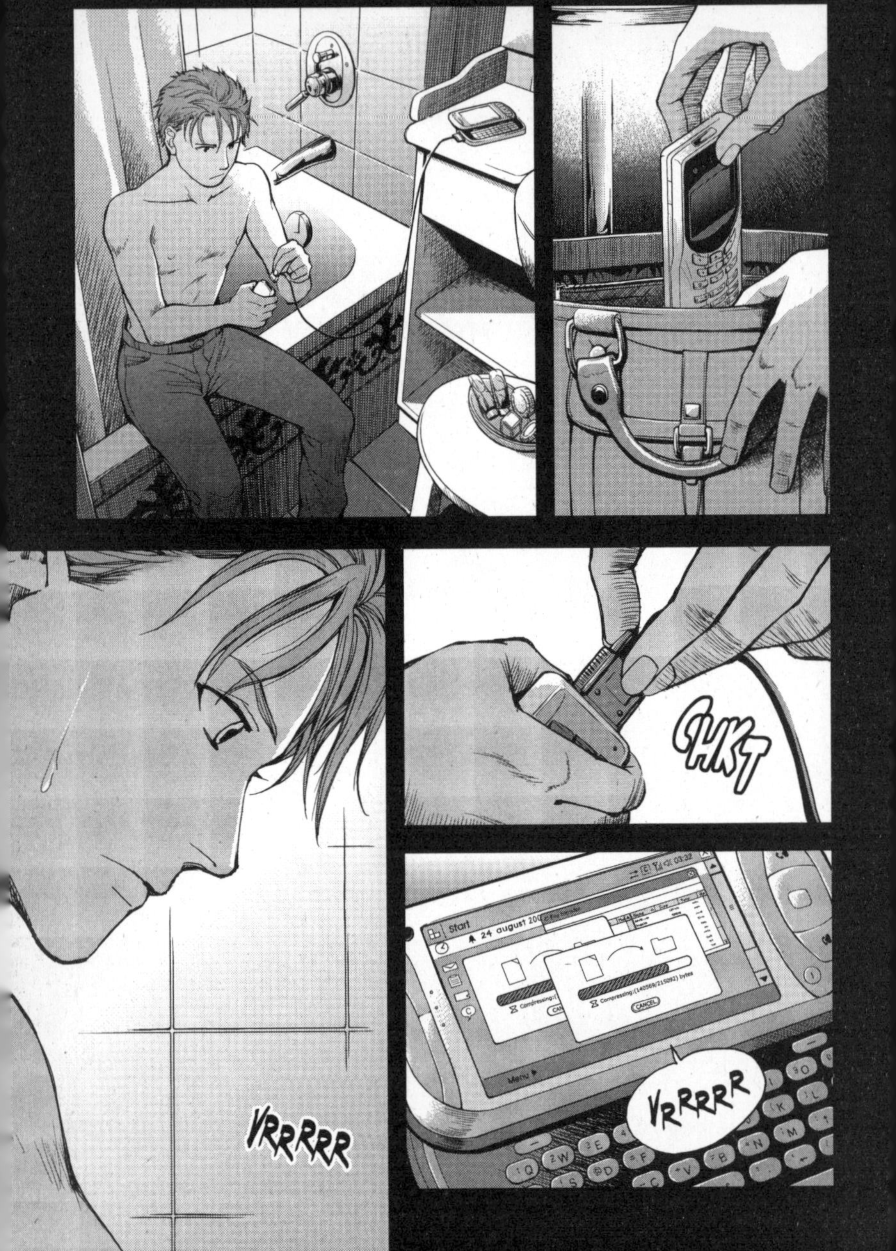
CHKT
Start
24 august 200
Compressing:(140569/215092) bytes
CANCEL
Menu
VRRRRR
VRRRRR

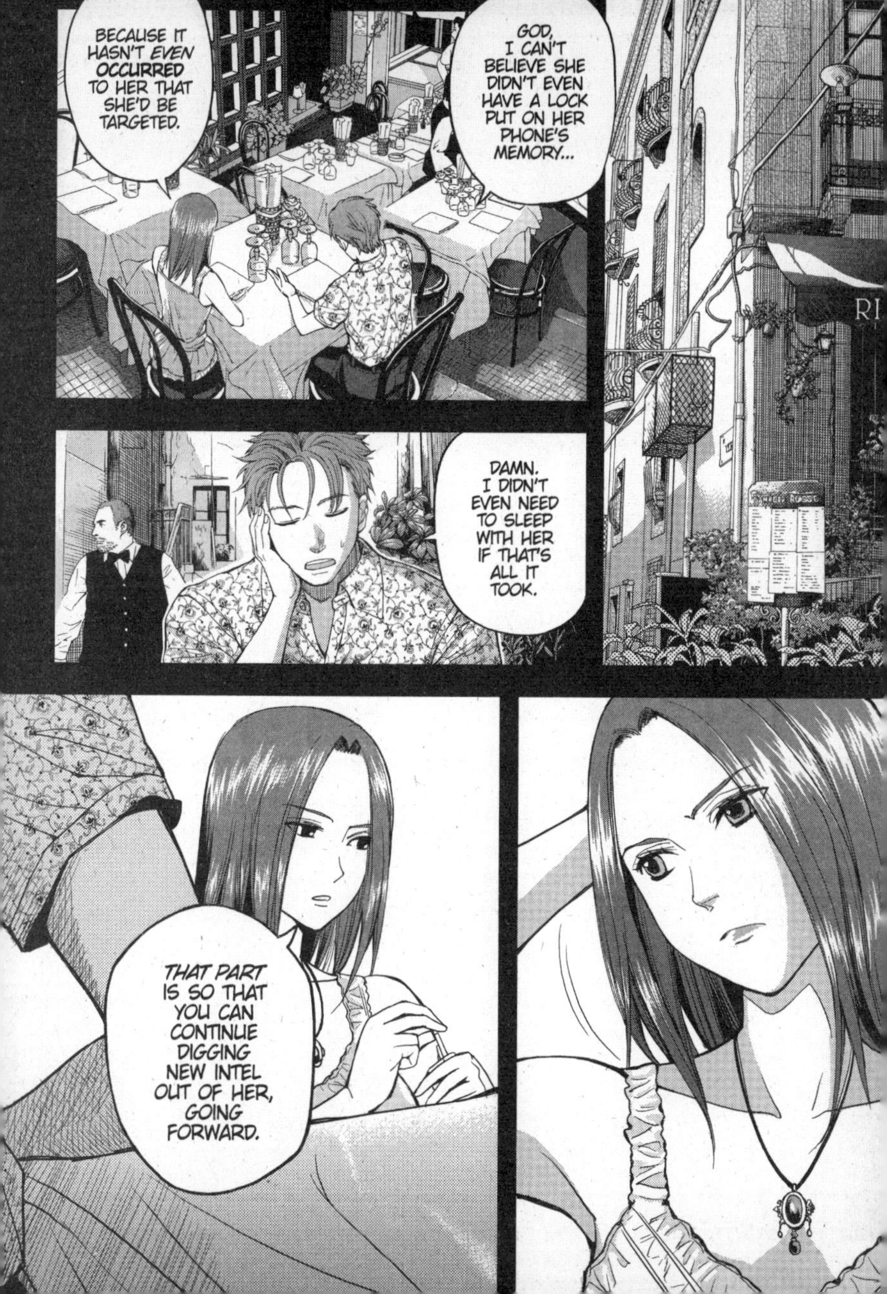
GOD, I CAN'T BELIEVE SHE DIDN'T EVEN HAVE A LOCK PUT ON HER PHONE'S MEMORY...
BECAUSE IT HASN'T *EVEN* **OCCURRED** TO HER THAT SHE'D BE TARGETED.
DAMN. I DIDN'T EVEN NEED TO SLEEP WITH HER IF THAT'S ALL IT TOOK.
THAT PART IS SO THAT YOU CAN CONTINUE DIGGING NEW INTEL OUT OF HER, GOING FORWARD.

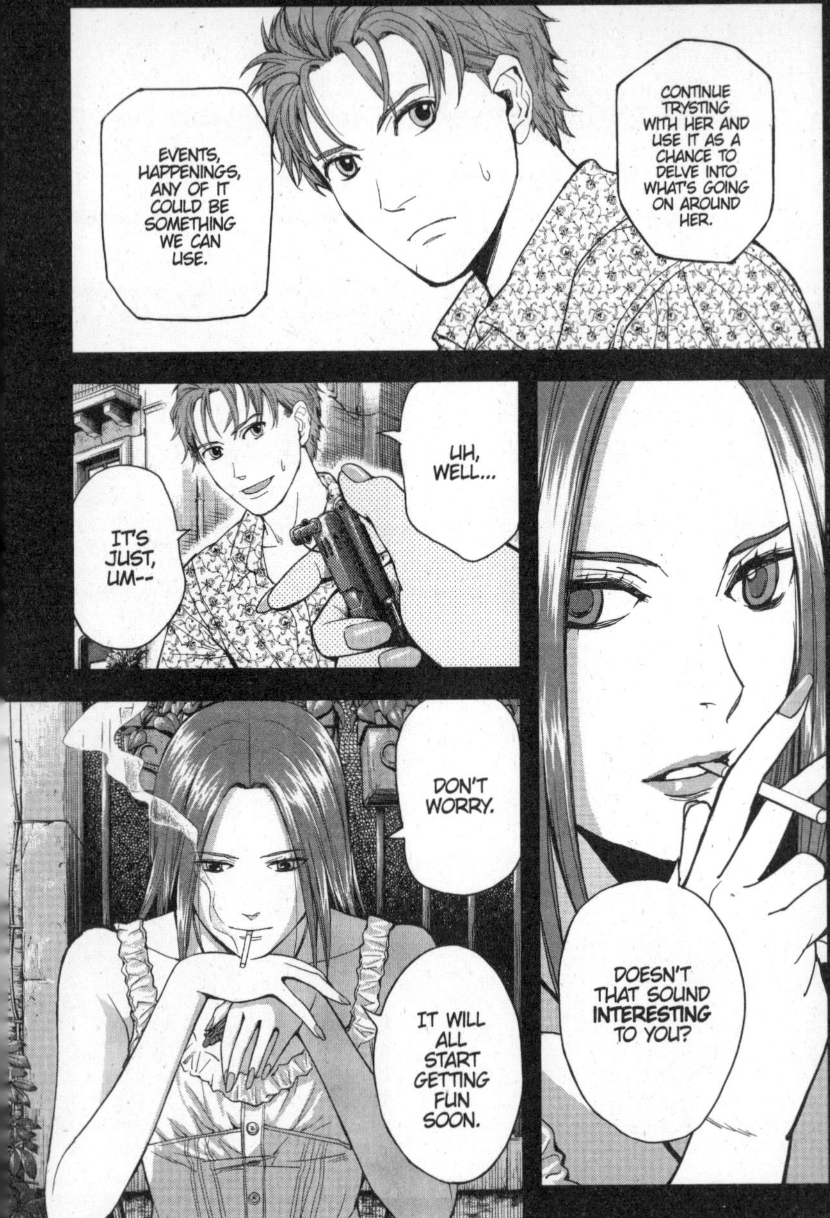
CONTINUE TRYSTING WITH HER AND USE IT AS A CHANCE TO DELVE INTO WHAT'S GOING ON AROUND HER.
EVENTS, HAPPENINGS, ANY OF IT COULD BE SOMETHING WE CAN USE.
DOESN'T THAT SOUND **INTERESTING** TO YOU?
UH, WELL...
IT'S JUST, UM--
DON'T WORRY.
IT WILL ALL START GETTING FUN SOON.

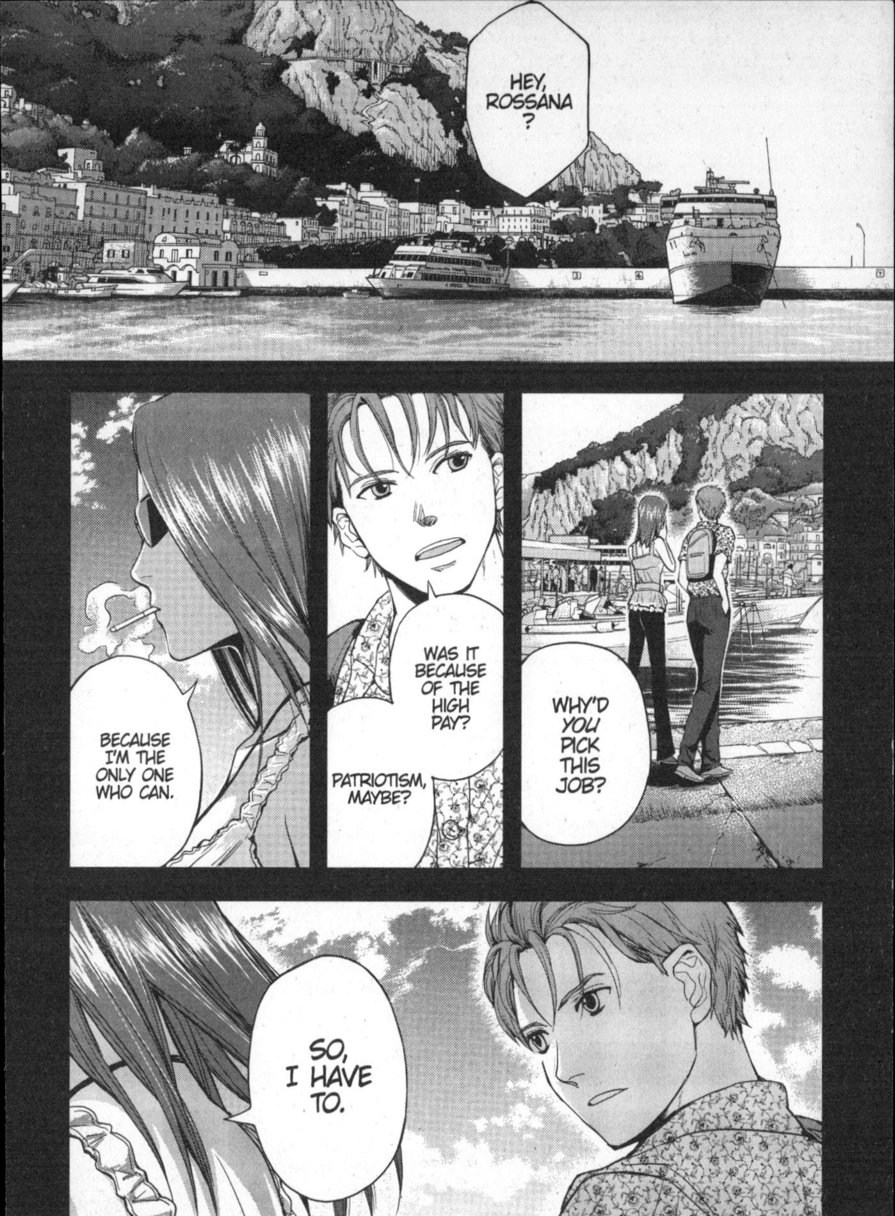
HEY, ROSSÁNA?
WHY'D YOU PICK THIS JOB?
WAS IT BECAUSE OF THE HIGH PAY?
PATRIOTISM, MAYBE?
BECAUSE I'M THE ONLY ONE WHO CAN.
SO, I HAVE TO.

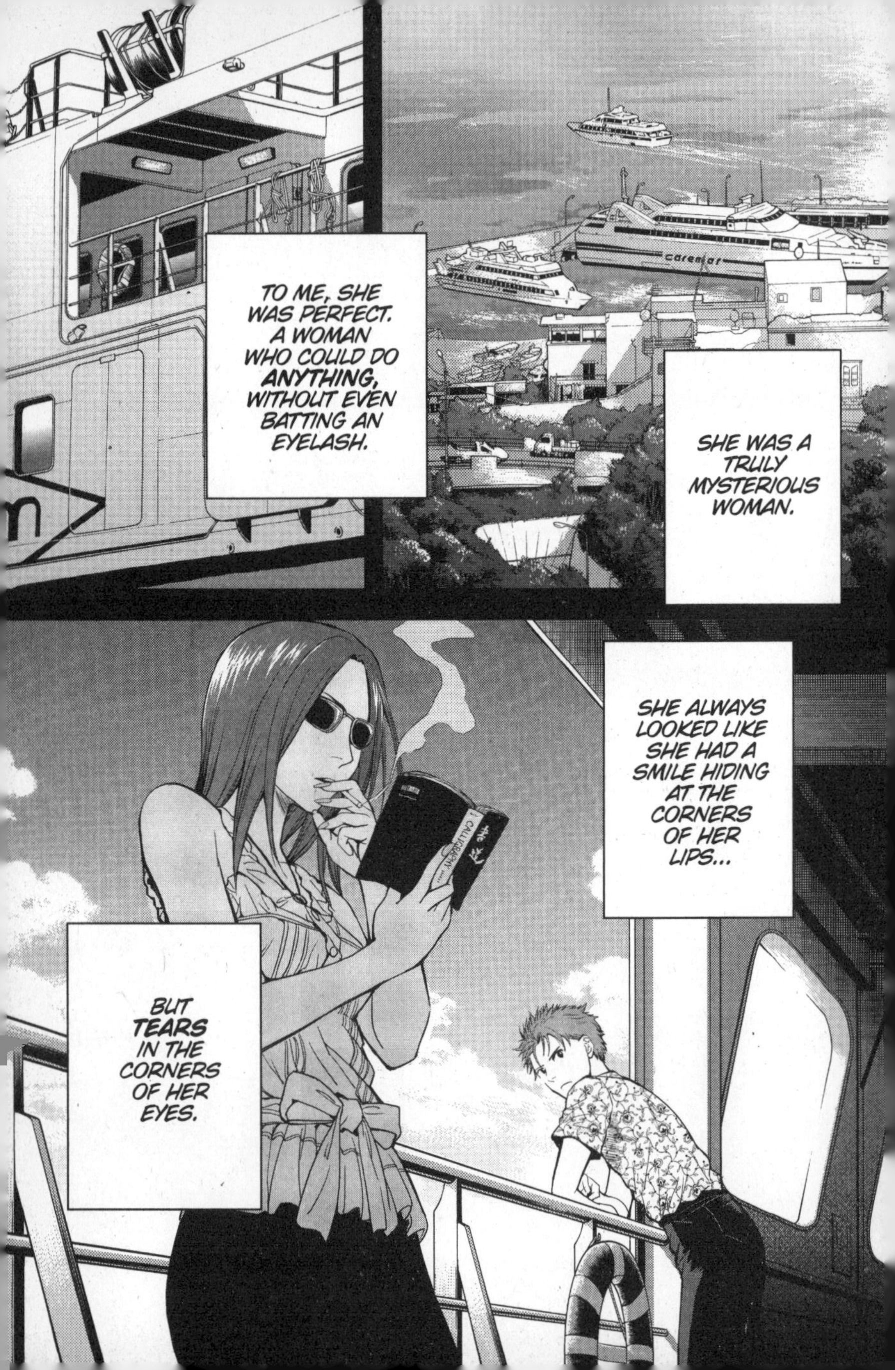
SHE WAS A TRULY MYSTERIOUS WOMAN.
TO ME, SHE WAS PERFECT. A WOMAN WHO COULD DO **ANYTHING**, WITHOUT EVEN BATTING AN EYELASH.
SHE ALWAYS LOOKED LIKE SHE HAD A SMILE HIDING AT THE CORNERS OF HER LIPS...
BUT **TEARS** IN THE CORNERS OF HER EYES.

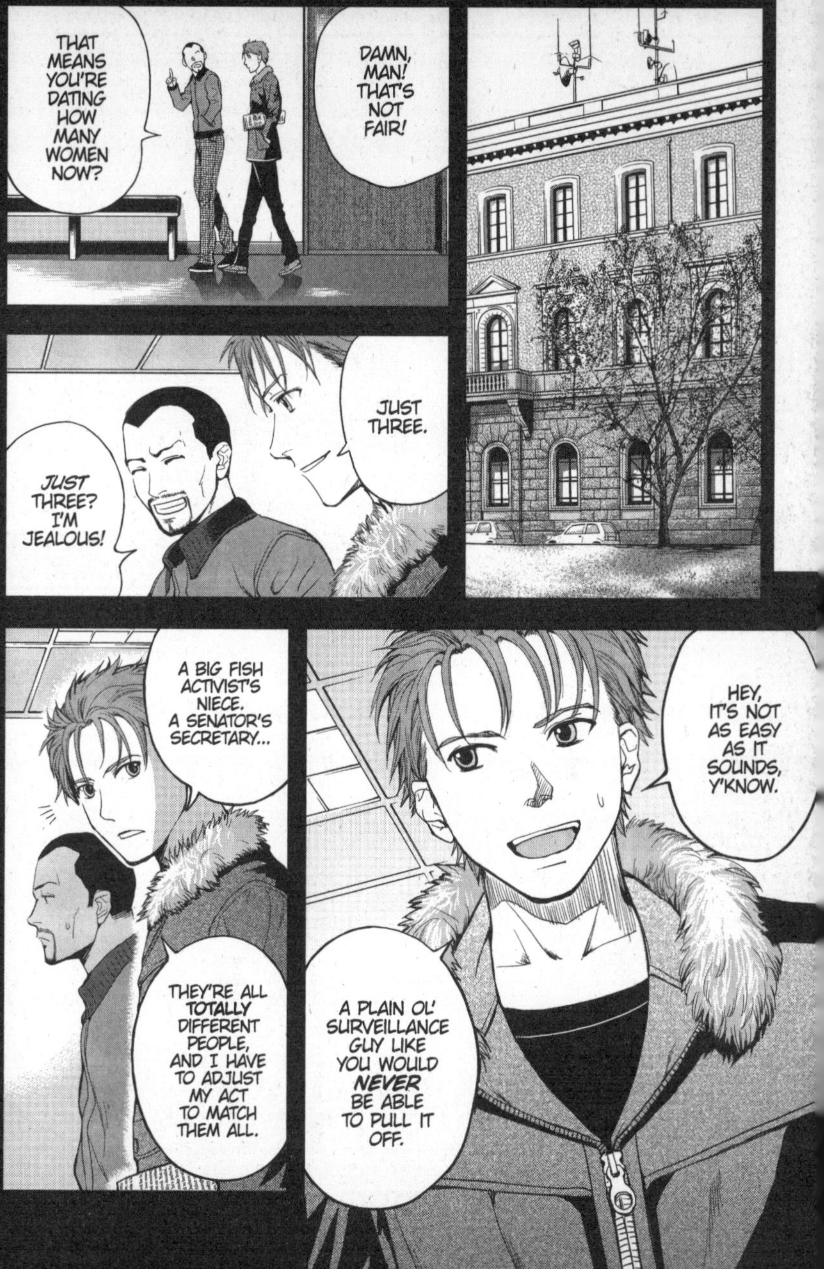
DAMN, MAN! THAT'S NOT FAIR!
THAT MEANS YOU'RE DATING HOW MANY WOMEN NOW?
JUST THREE.
JUST THREE? I'M JEALOUS!
HEY, IT'S NOT AS EASY AS IT SOUNDS, Y'KNOW.
A PLAIN OL' SURVEILLANCE GUY LIKE YOU WOULD NEVER BE ABLE TO PULL IT OFF.
A BIG FISH ACTIVIST'S NIECE. A SENATOR'S SECRETARY...
THEY'RE ALL TOTALLY DIFFERENT PEOPLE, AND I HAVE TO ADJUST MY ACT TO MATCH THEM ALL.

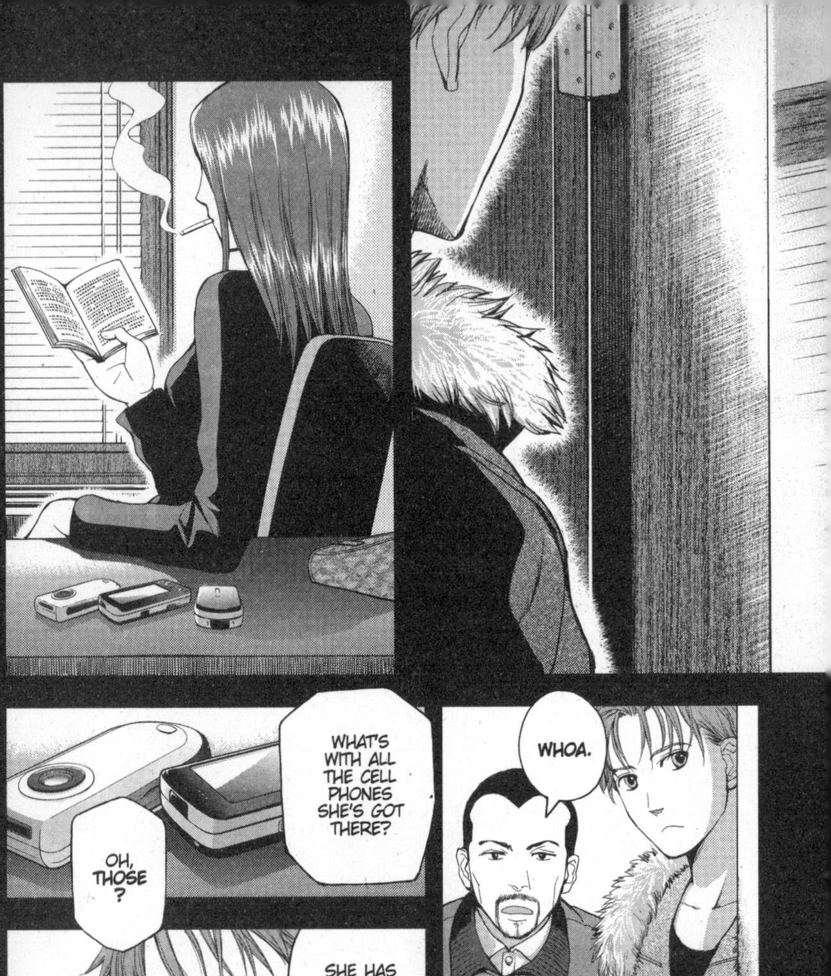
WHOA.
NOW HERE'S SOMETHING YOU DON'T SEE EVERY DAY. ROSSANA'S *ACTUALLY* IN HER OFFICE.
WHAT'S WITH ALL THE CELL PHONES SHE'S GOT THERE?
OH, THOSE?
SHE HAS A DIFFERENT ONE FOR EACH OF HER IDENTITIES.
IT'S PRETTY TOUGH FOR HER, JUST KEEPING UP WITH ALL THE EMAILS AND TEXTS SHE GETS.

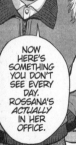

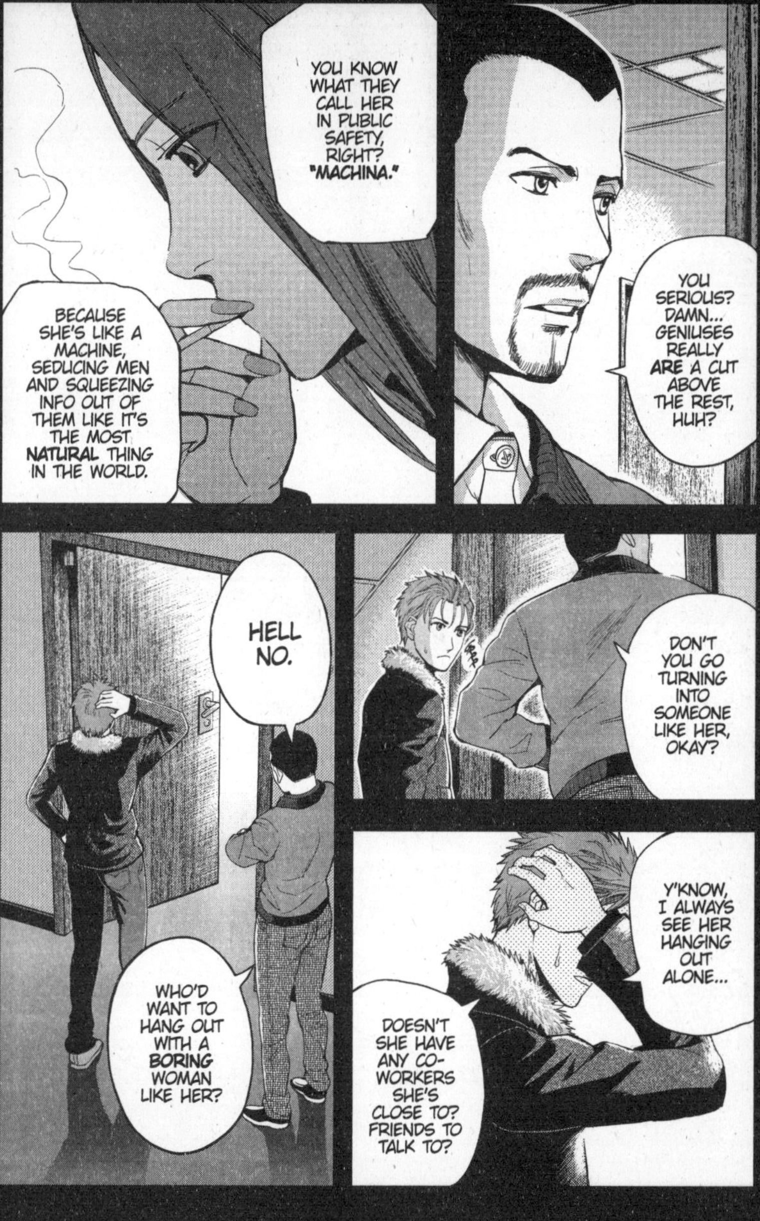
YOU SERIOUS? DAMN... GENIUSES REALLY ARE A CUT ABOVE THE REST, HUH?
YOU KNOW WHAT THEY CALL HER IN PUBLIC SAFETY, RIGHT? "MACHINA."
BECAUSE SHE'S LIKE A MACHINE, SEDUCING MEN AND SQUEEZING INFO OUT OF THEM LIKE IT'S THE MOST NATURAL THING IN THE WORLD.
DON'T YOU GO TURNING INTO SOMEONE LIKE HER, OKAY?
Y'KNOW, I ALWAYS SEE HER HANGING OUT ALONE...
DOESN'T SHE HAVE ANY CO-WORKERS SHE'S CLOSE TO? FRIENDS TO TALK TO?
HELL NO.
WHO'D WANT TO HANG OUT WITH A BORING WOMAN LIKE HER?

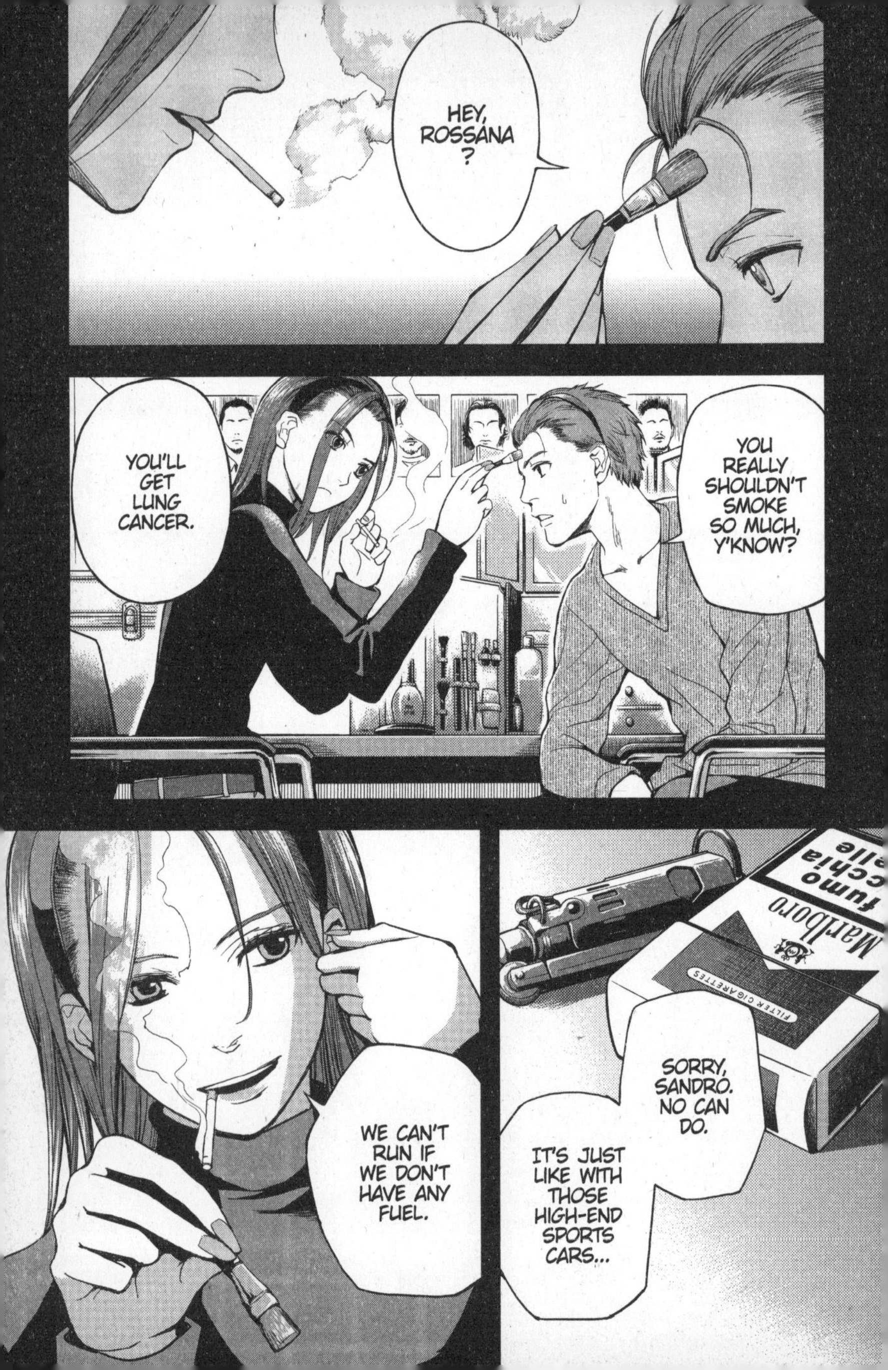
HEY, ROSSANA?
YOU REALLY SHOULDN'T SMOKE SO MUCH, Y'KNOW?
YOU'LL GET LUNG CANCER.
Marlboro
FILTER CIGARETTES
SORRY, SANDRO. NO CAN DO.
IT'S JUST LIKE WITH THOSE HIGH-END SPORTS CARS...
WE CAN'T RUN IF WE DON'T HAVE ANY FUEL.

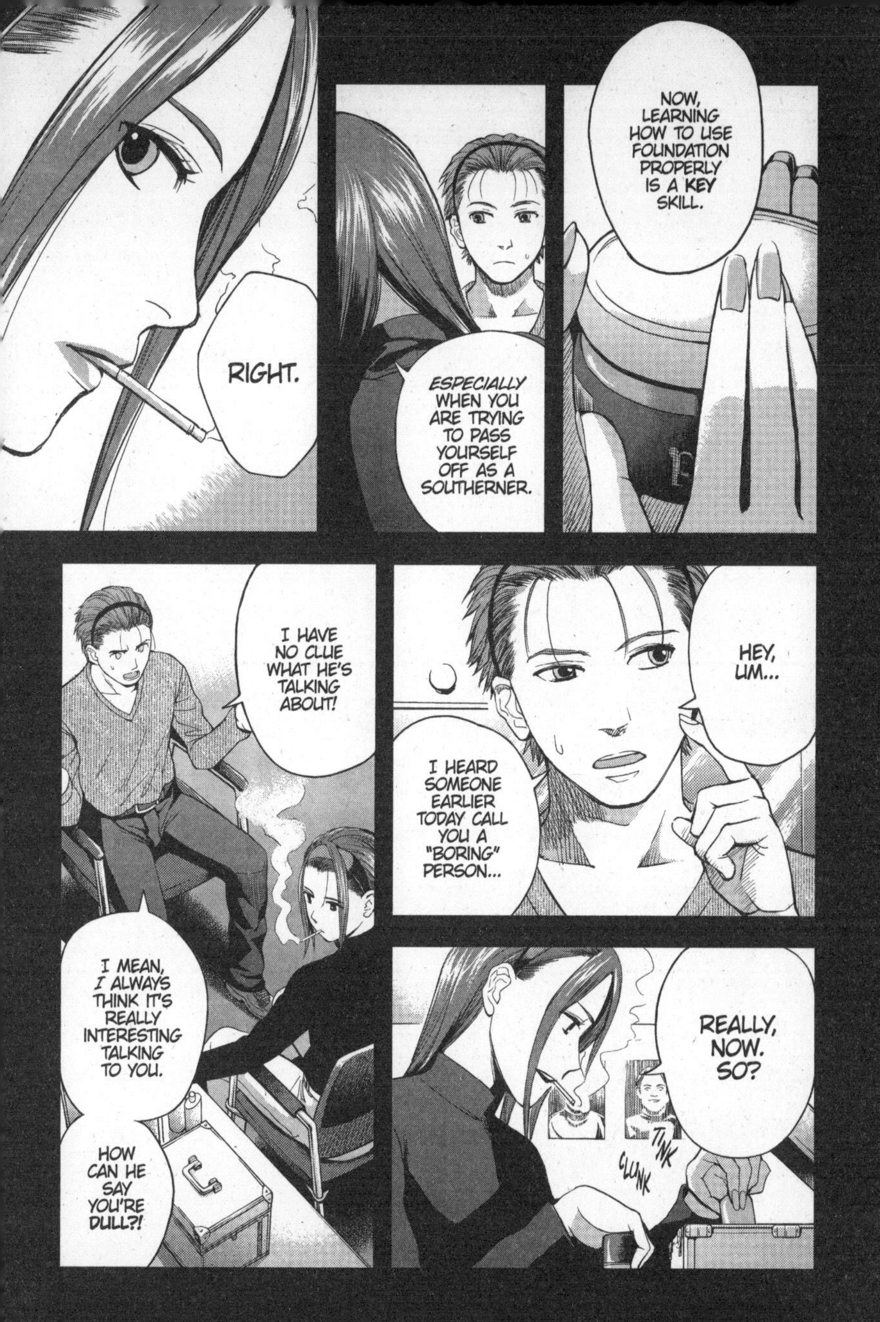
NOW, LEARNING HOW TO USE FOUNDATION PROPERLY IS A KEY SKILL.
ESPECIALLY WHEN YOU ARE TRYING TO PASS YOURSELF OFF AS A SOUTHERNER.
RIGHT.
HEY, UM...
I HEARD SOMEONE EARLIER TODAY CALL YOU A "BORING" PERSON...
REALLY, NOW. SO?
TINK
CLUNK
I HAVE NO CLUE WHAT HE'S TALKING ABOUT!
I MEAN, *I* ALWAYS THINK IT'S REALLY INTERESTING TALKING TO YOU.
HOW CAN HE SAY YOU'RE DULL?!

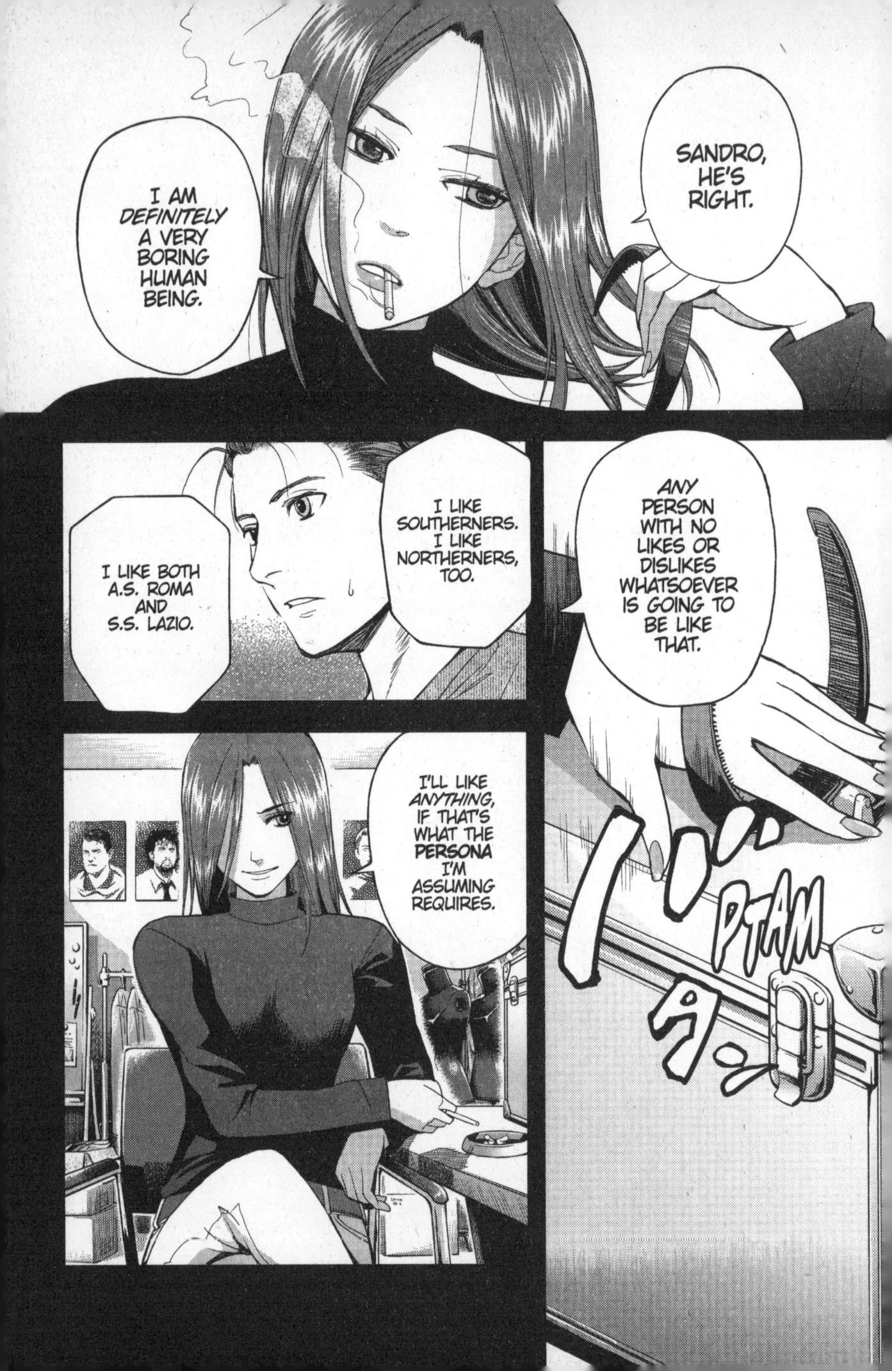
SANDRO, HE'S RIGHT.
I AM *DEFINITELY* A VERY BORING HUMAN BEING.
ANY PERSON WITH NO LIKES OR DISLIKES WHATSOEVER IS GOING TO BE LIKE THAT.
PTAM
I LIKE SOUTHERNERS. I LIKE NORTHERNERS, TOO.
I LIKE BOTH A.S. ROMA AND S.S. LAZIO.
I'LL LIKE *ANYTHING*, IF THAT'S WHAT THE **PERSONA** I'M ASSUMING REQUIRES.

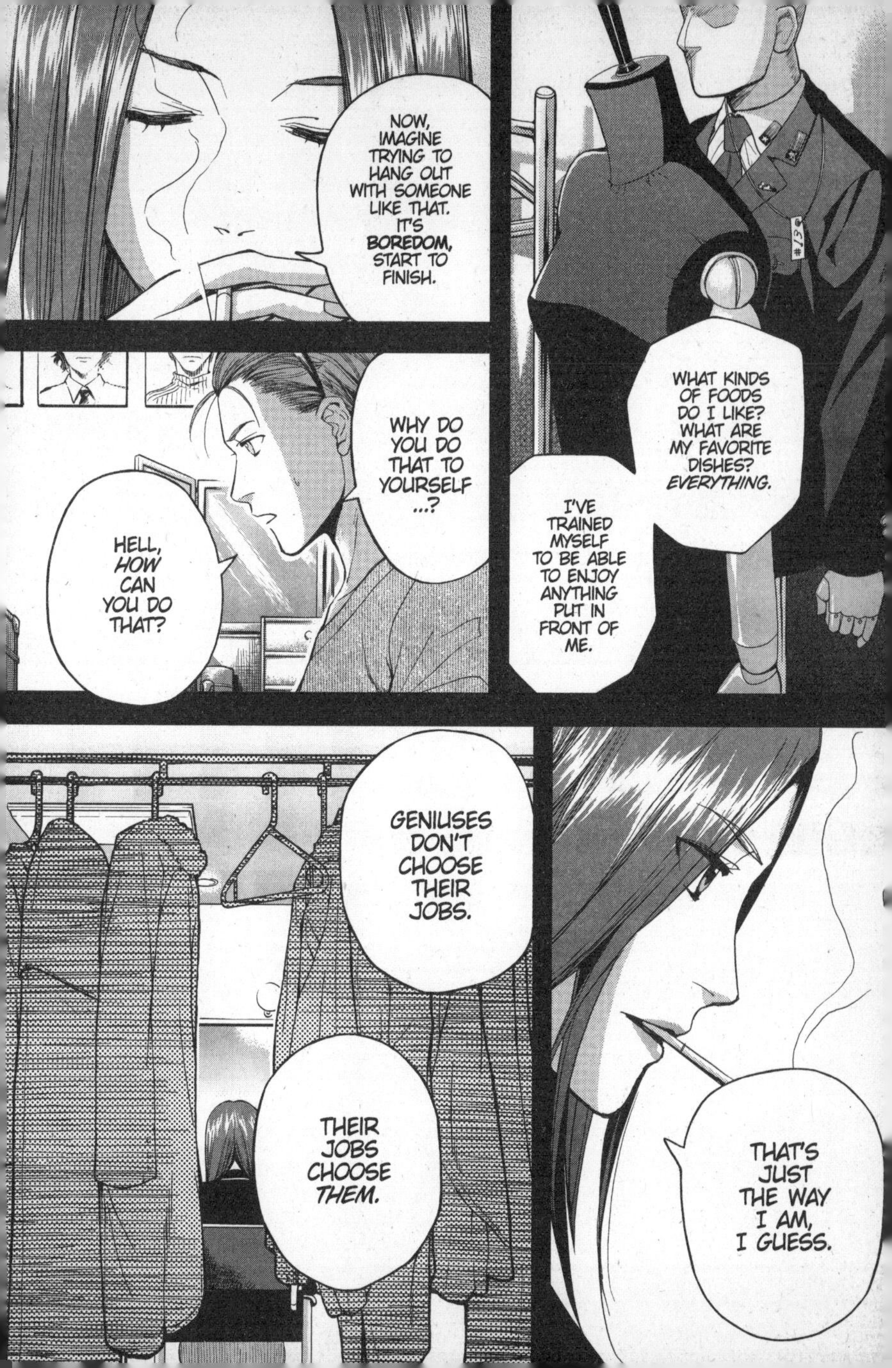
WHAT KINDS OF FOODS DO I LIKE? WHAT ARE MY FAVORITE DISHES? *EVERYTHING*.
I'VE TRAINED MYSELF TO BE ABLE TO ENJOY ANYTHING PUT IN FRONT OF ME.
NOW, IMAGINE TRYING TO HANG OUT WITH SOMEONE LIKE THAT. IT'S **BOREDOM**, START TO FINISH.
WHY DO YOU DO THAT TO YOURSELF ...?
HELL, *HOW* CAN YOU DO THAT?
THAT'S JUST THE WAY I AM, I GUESS.
GENIUSES DON'T CHOOSE THEIR JOBS.
THEIR JOBS CHOOSE *THEM*.

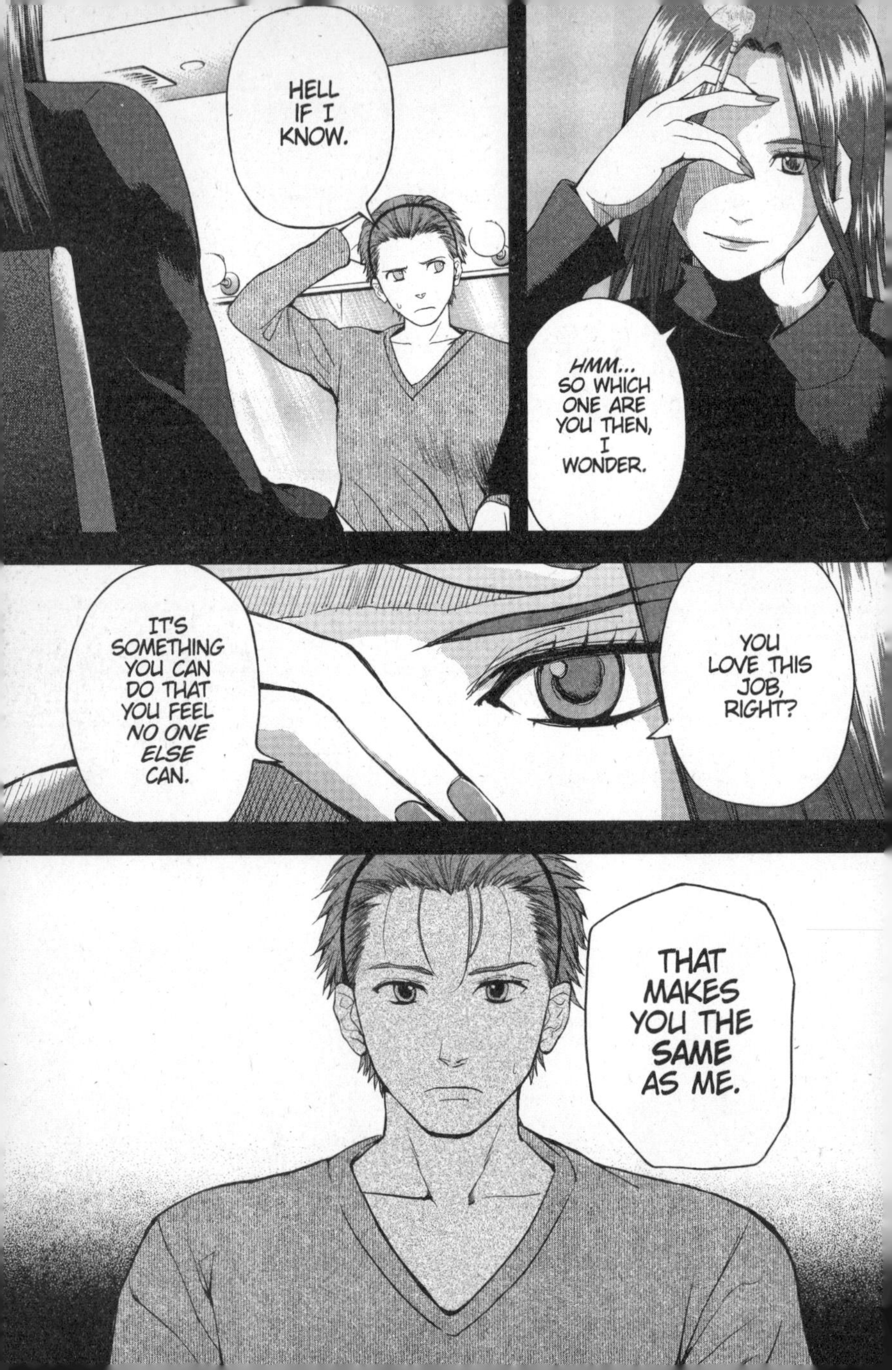
HMM... SO WHICH ONE ARE YOU THEN, I WONDER.
HELL IF I KNOW.
YOU LOVE THIS JOB, RIGHT?
IT'S SOMETHING YOU CAN DO THAT YOU FEEL NO ONE ELSE CAN.
THAT MAKES YOU THE SAME AS ME.

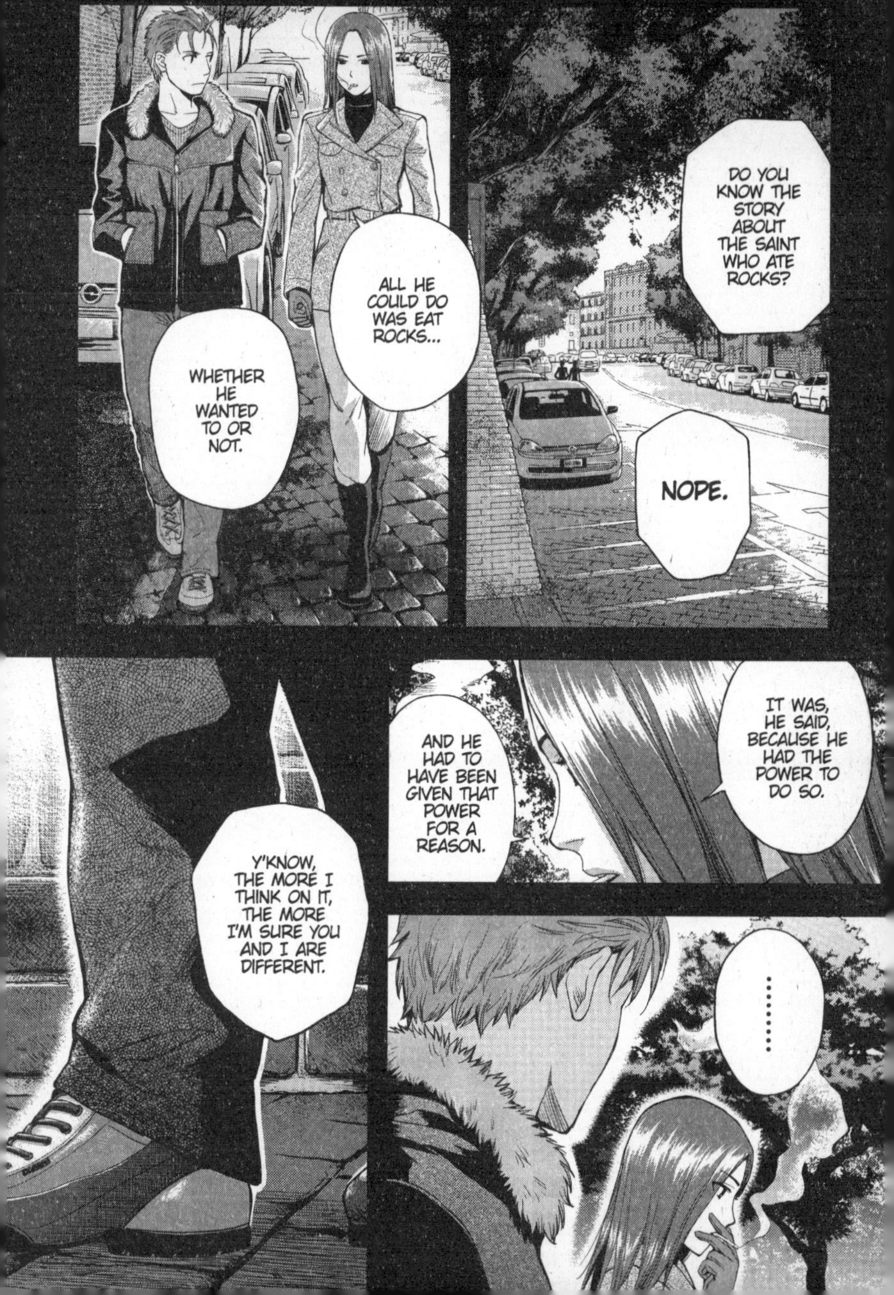
DO YOU KNOW THE STORY ABOUT THE SAINT WHO ATE ROCKS?
NOPE.
ALL HE COULD DO WAS EAT ROCKS...
WHETHER HE WANTED TO OR NOT.
IT WAS, HE SAID, BECAUSE HE HAD THE POWER TO DO SO.
AND HE HAD TO HAVE BEEN GIVEN THAT POWER FOR A REASON.
......
Y'KNOW, THE MORE I THINK ON IT, THE MORE I'M SURE YOU AND I ARE DIFFERENT.

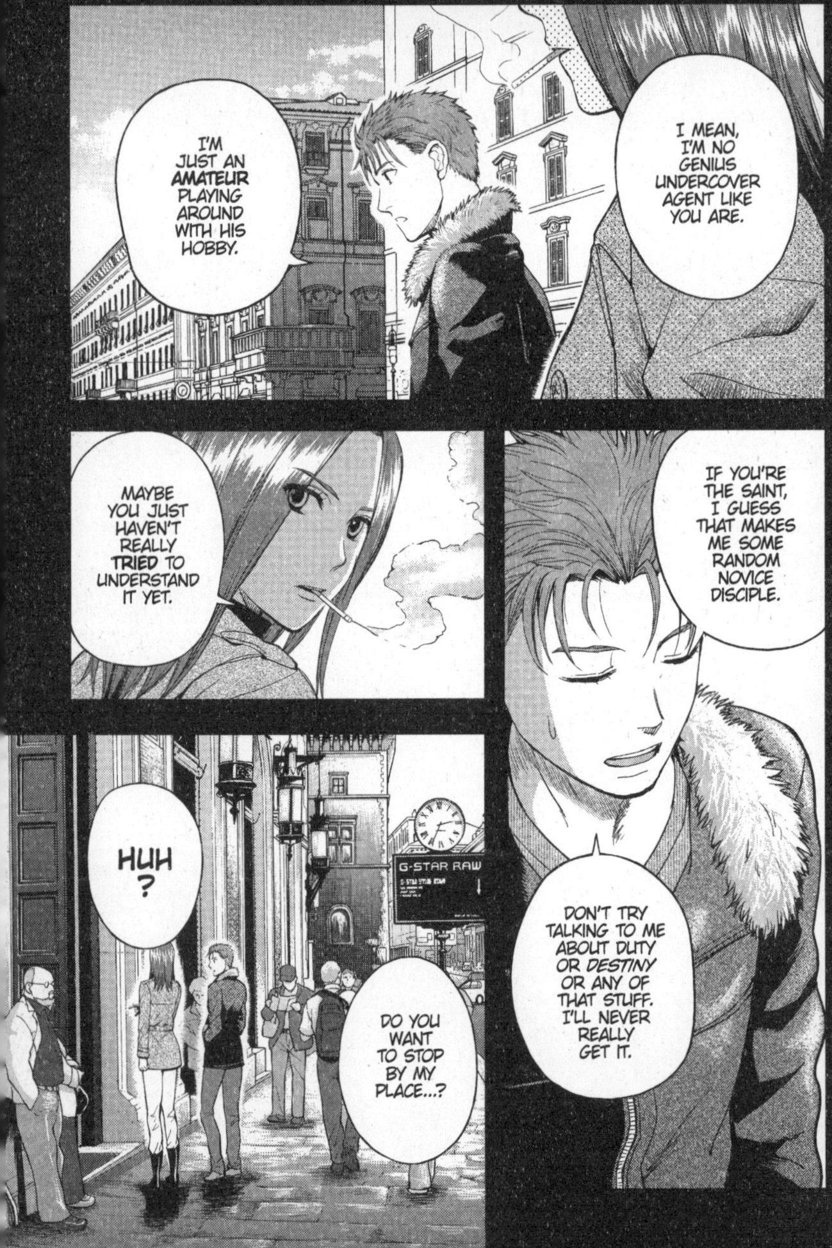
I MEAN, I'M NO GENIUS UNDERCOVER AGENT LIKE YOU ARE.
I'M JUST AN **AMATEUR** PLAYING AROUND WITH HIS HOBBY.
IF YOU'RE THE SAINT, I GUESS THAT MAKES ME SOME RANDOM NOVICE DISCIPLE.
DON'T TRY TALKING TO ME ABOUT DUTY OR *DESTINY* OR ANY OF THAT STUFF. I'LL NEVER REALLY GET IT.
MAYBE YOU JUST HAVEN'T REALLY **TRIED** TO UNDERSTAND IT YET.
G-STAR RAW
DO YOU WANT TO STOP BY MY PLACE...?
HUH ?

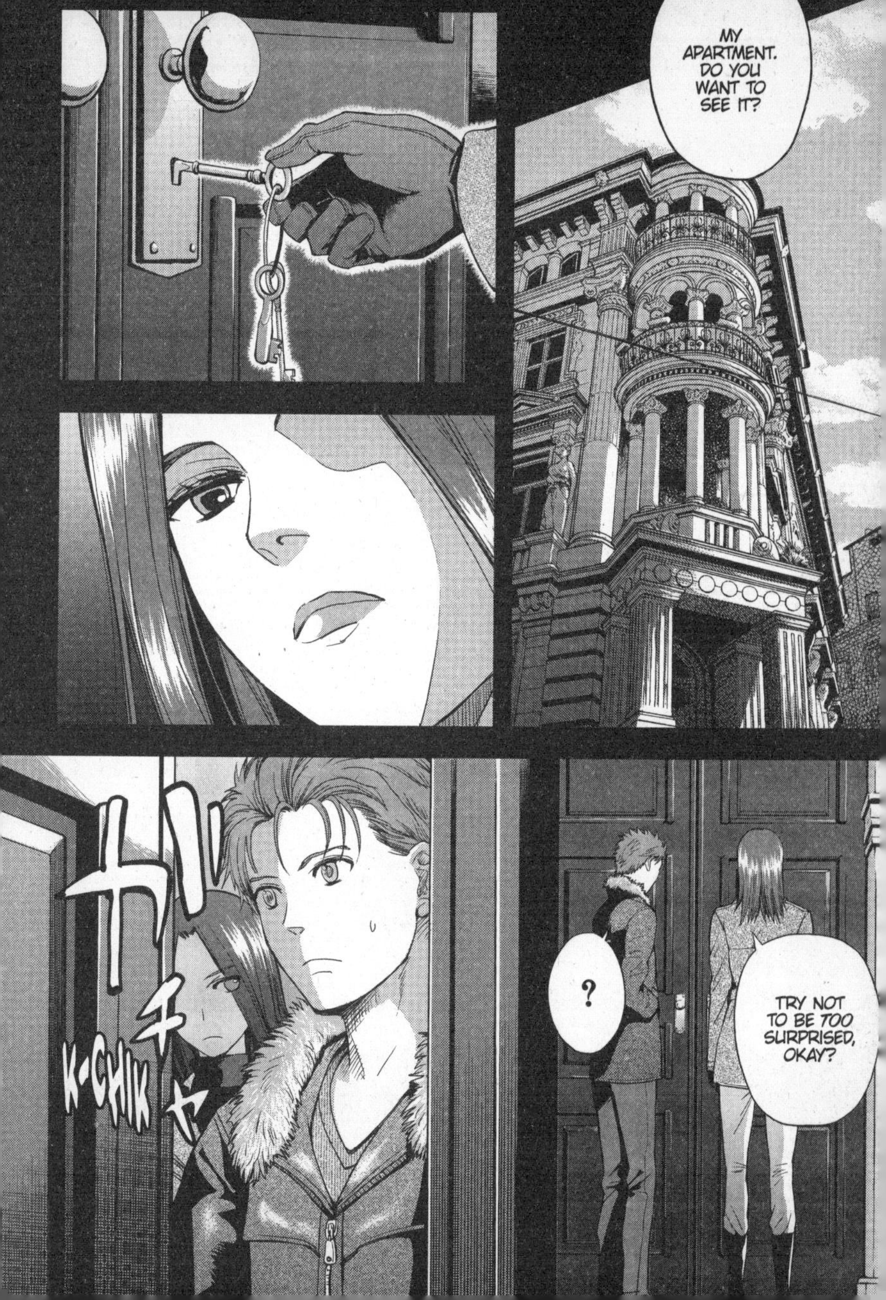
MY APARTMENT. DO YOU WANT TO SEE IT?
TRY NOT TO BE *TOO* SURPRISED, OKAY?
?
K-CHIK

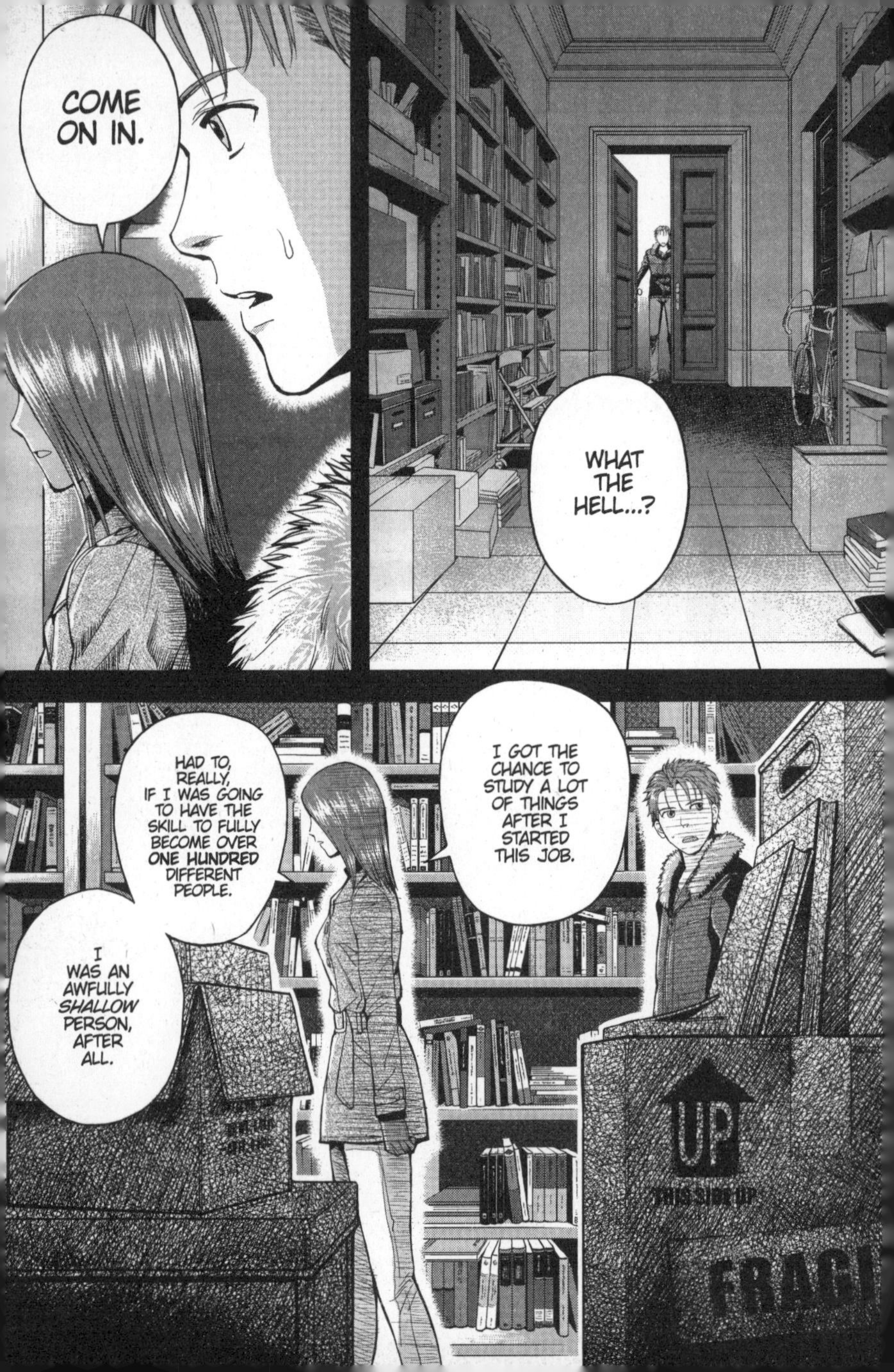
WHAT THE HELL...?
COME ON IN.
I GOT THE CHANCE TO STUDY A LOT OF THINGS AFTER I STARTED THIS JOB.
HAD TO, REALLY, IF I WAS GOING TO HAVE THE SKILL TO FULLY BECOME OVER **ONE HUNDRED** DIFFERENT PEOPLE.
I WAS AN AWFULLY *SHALLOW* PERSON, AFTER ALL.
UP
THIS SIDE UP

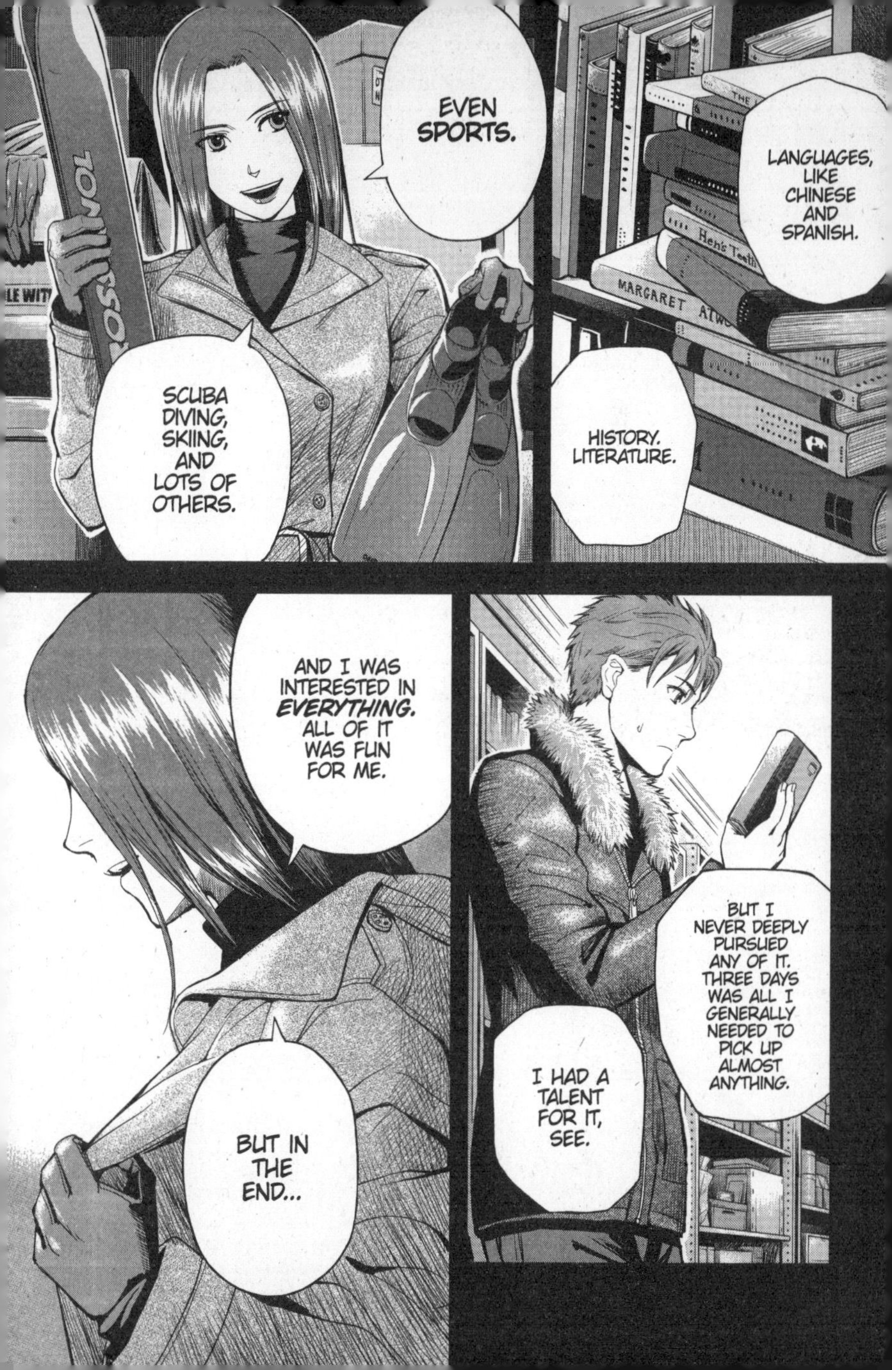

LANGUAGES, LIKE CHINESE AND SPANISH.
HISTORY. LITERATURE.
EVEN SPORTS.
SCUBA DIVING, SKIING, AND LOTS OF OTHERS.
BUT I NEVER DEEPLY PURSUED ANY OF IT. THREE DAYS WAS ALL I GENERALLY NEEDED TO PICK UP ALMOST ANYTHING.
I HAD A TALENT FOR IT, SEE.
AND I WAS INTERESTED IN *EVERYTHING.* ALL OF IT WAS FUN FOR ME.
BUT IN THE END...

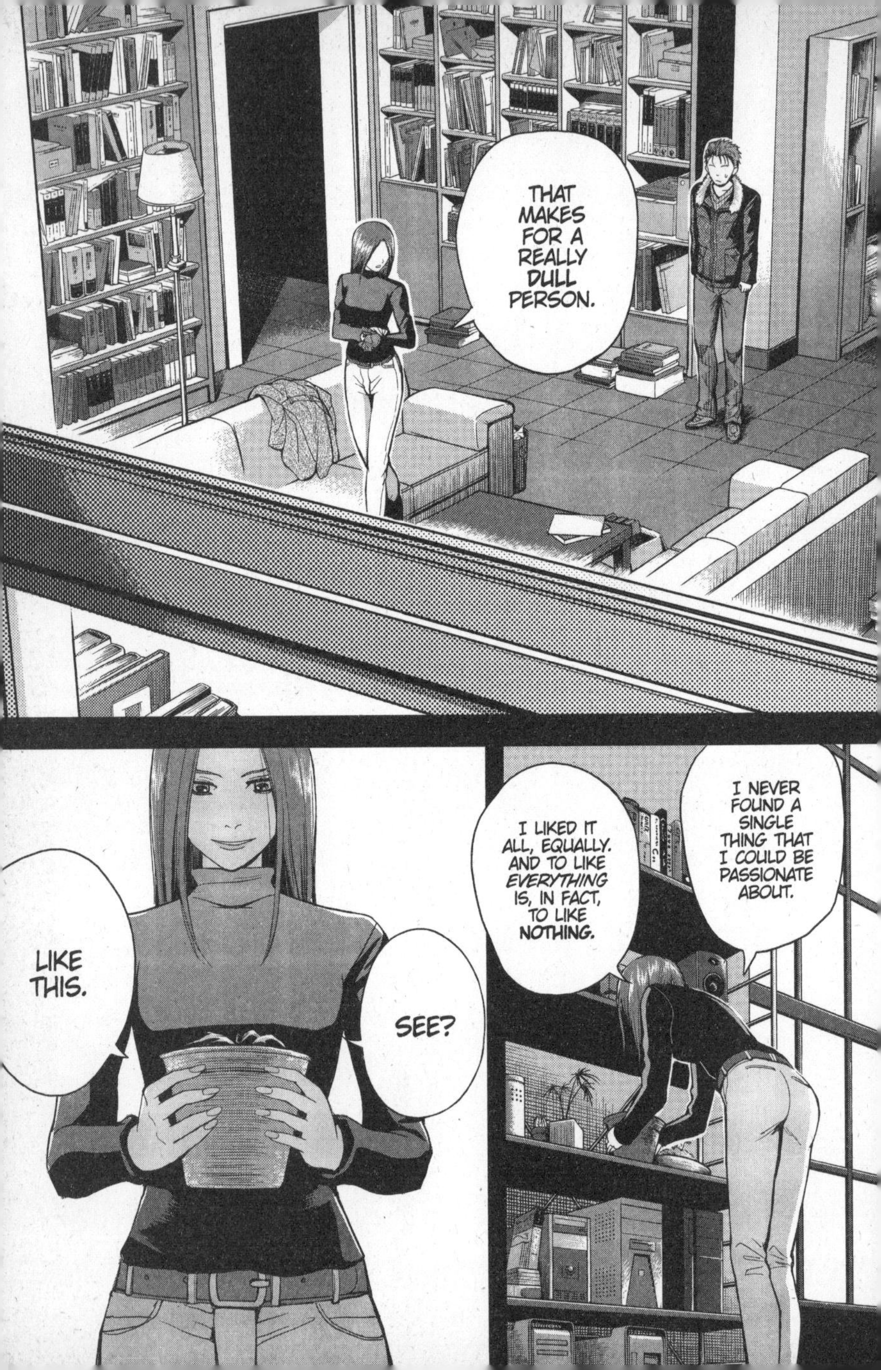
THAT MAKES FOR A REALLY DULL PERSON.
I NEVER FOUND A SINGLE THING THAT I COULD BE PASSIONATE ABOUT.
I LIKED IT ALL, EQUALLY. AND TO LIKE *EVERYTHING* IS, IN FACT, TO LIKE **NOTHING**.
SEE?
LIKE THIS.

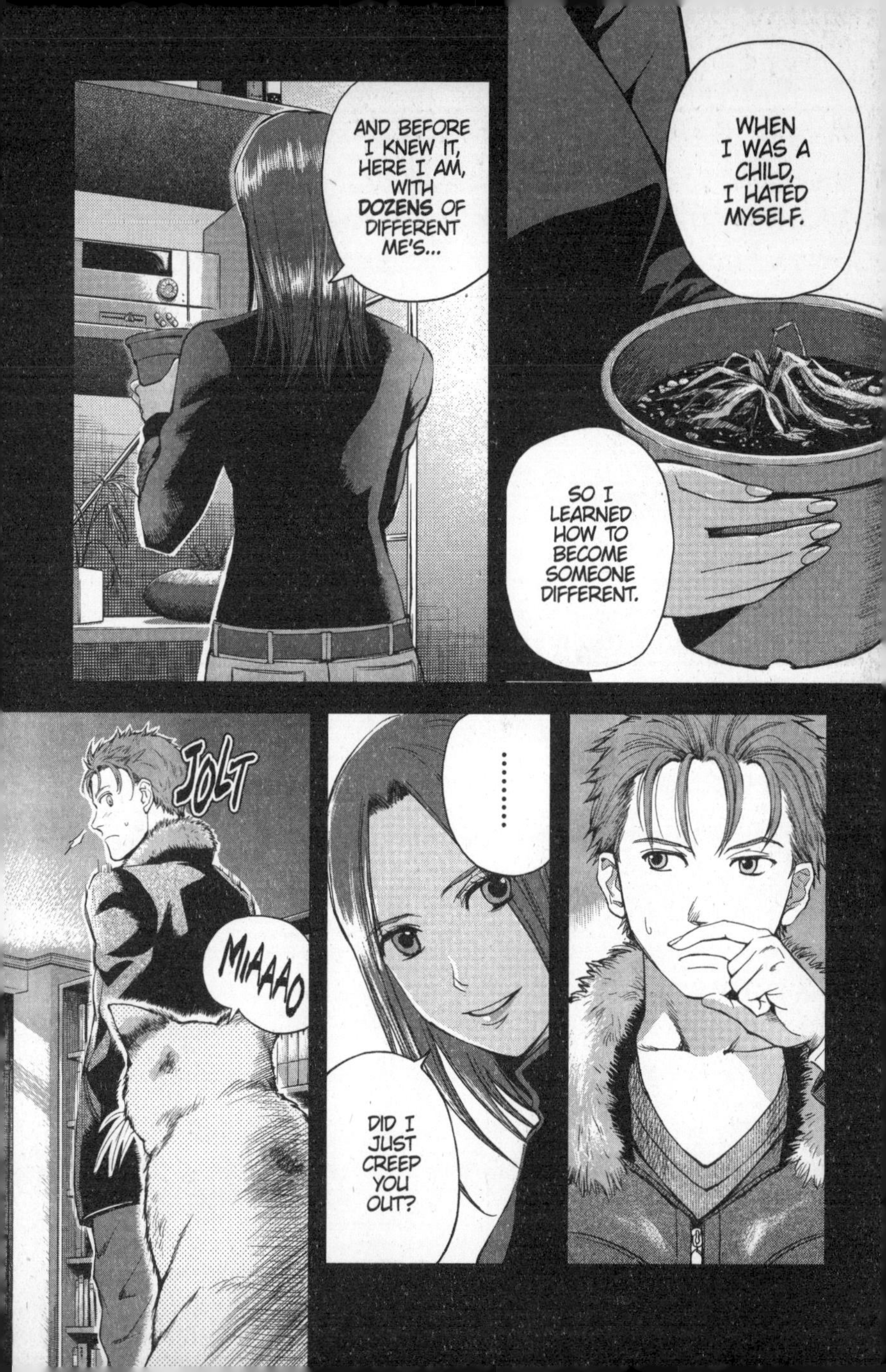

WHEN I WAS A CHILD, I HATED MYSELF.
SO I LEARNED HOW TO BECOME SOMEONE DIFFERENT.
AND BEFORE I KNEW IT, HERE I AM, WITH DOZENS OF DIFFERENT ME'S...
......
DID I JUST CREEP YOU OUT?
JOLT
MIAAAO

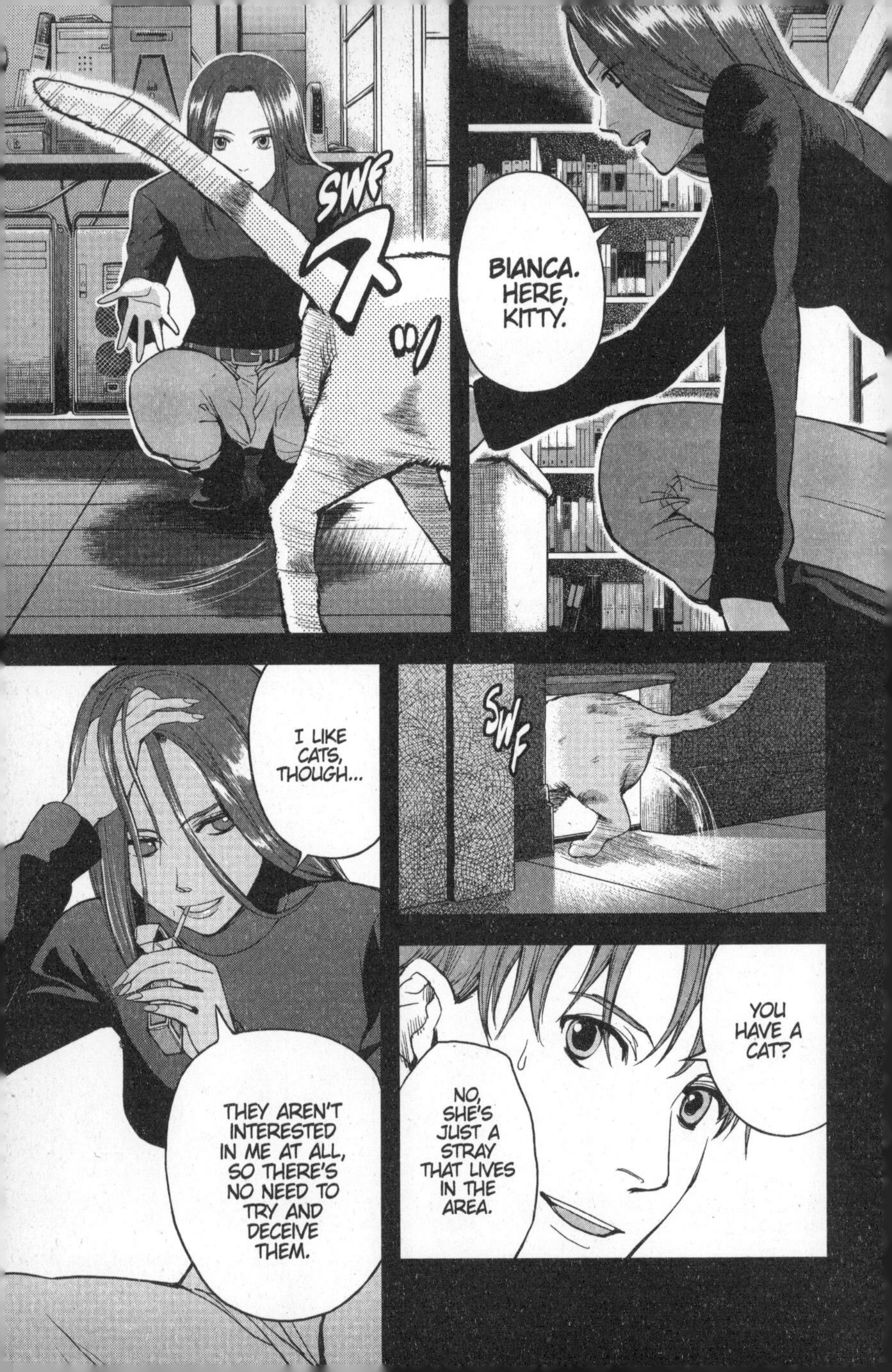
BIANCA. HERE, KITTY.
SWF
SWF
YOU HAVE A CAT?
NO, SHE'S JUST A STRAY THAT LIVES IN THE AREA.
I LIKE CATS, THOUGH...
THEY AREN'T INTERESTED IN ME AT ALL, SO THERE'S NO NEED TO TRY AND DECEIVE THEM.

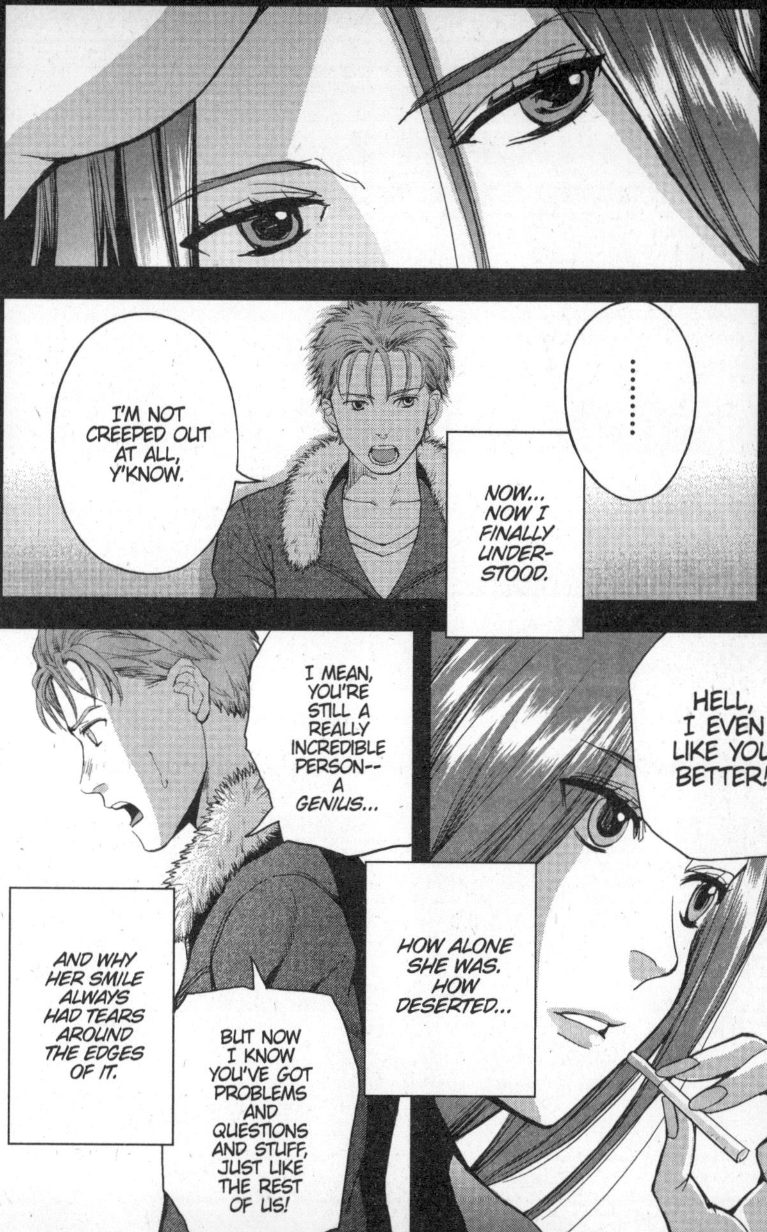
......
I'M NOT CREEPED OUT AT ALL, Y'KNOW.
NOW... NOW I FINALLY UNDERSTOOD.
HELL, I EVEN LIKE YOU BETTER!
HOW ALONE SHE WAS. HOW DESERTED...
I MEAN, YOU'RE STILL A REALLY INCREDIBLE PERSON-- A GENIUS...
BUT NOW I KNOW YOU'VE GOT PROBLEMS AND QUESTIONS AND STUFF, JUST LIKE THE REST OF US!
AND WHY HER SMILE ALWAYS HAD TEARS AROUND THE EDGES OF IT.

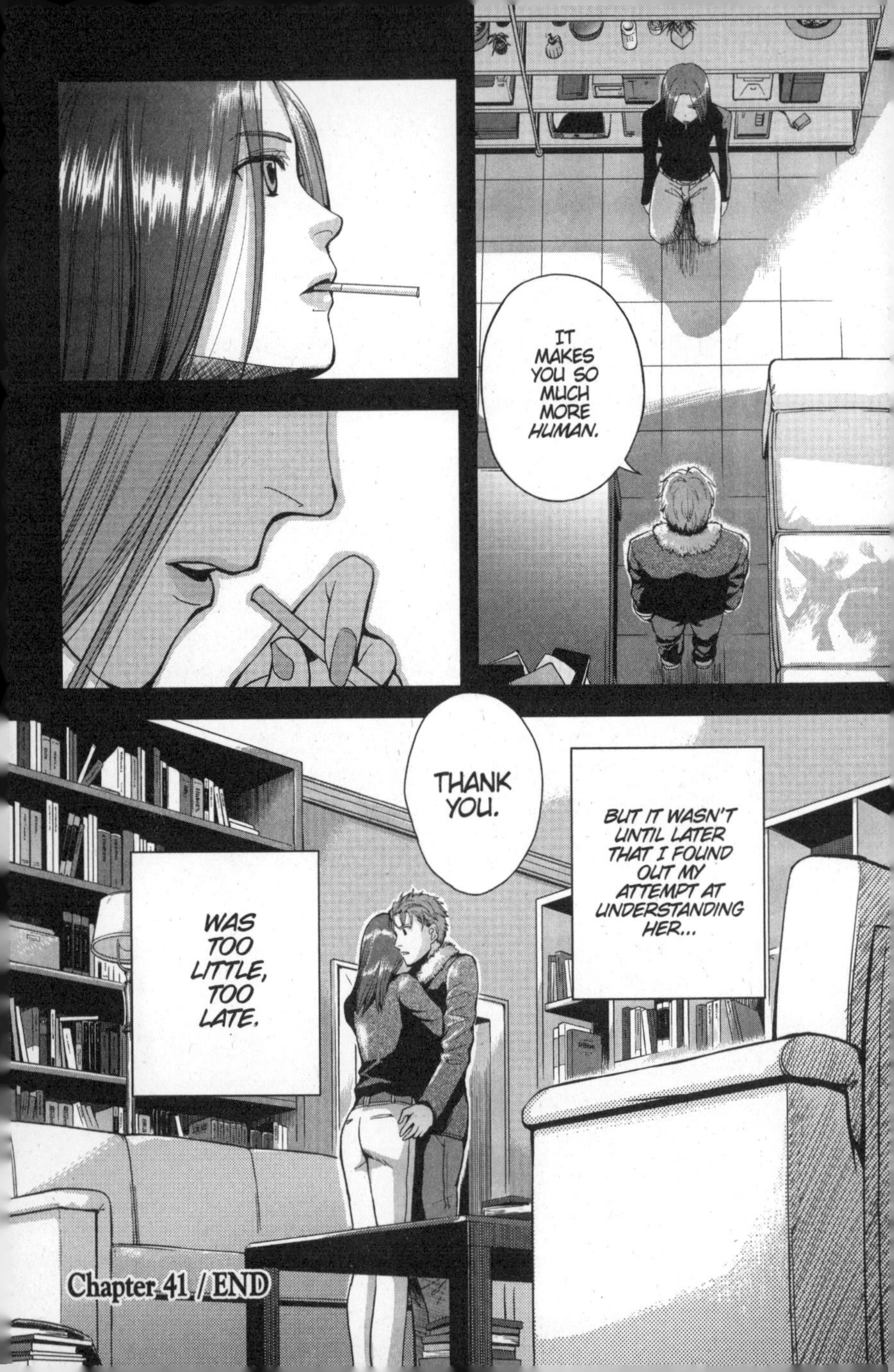
IT MAKES YOU SO MUCH MORE HUMAN.
THANK YOU.
BUT IT WASN'T UNTIL LATER THAT I FOUND OUT MY ATTEMPT AT UNDERSTANDING HER...
WAS TOO LITTLE, TOO LATE.
Chapter 41 / END

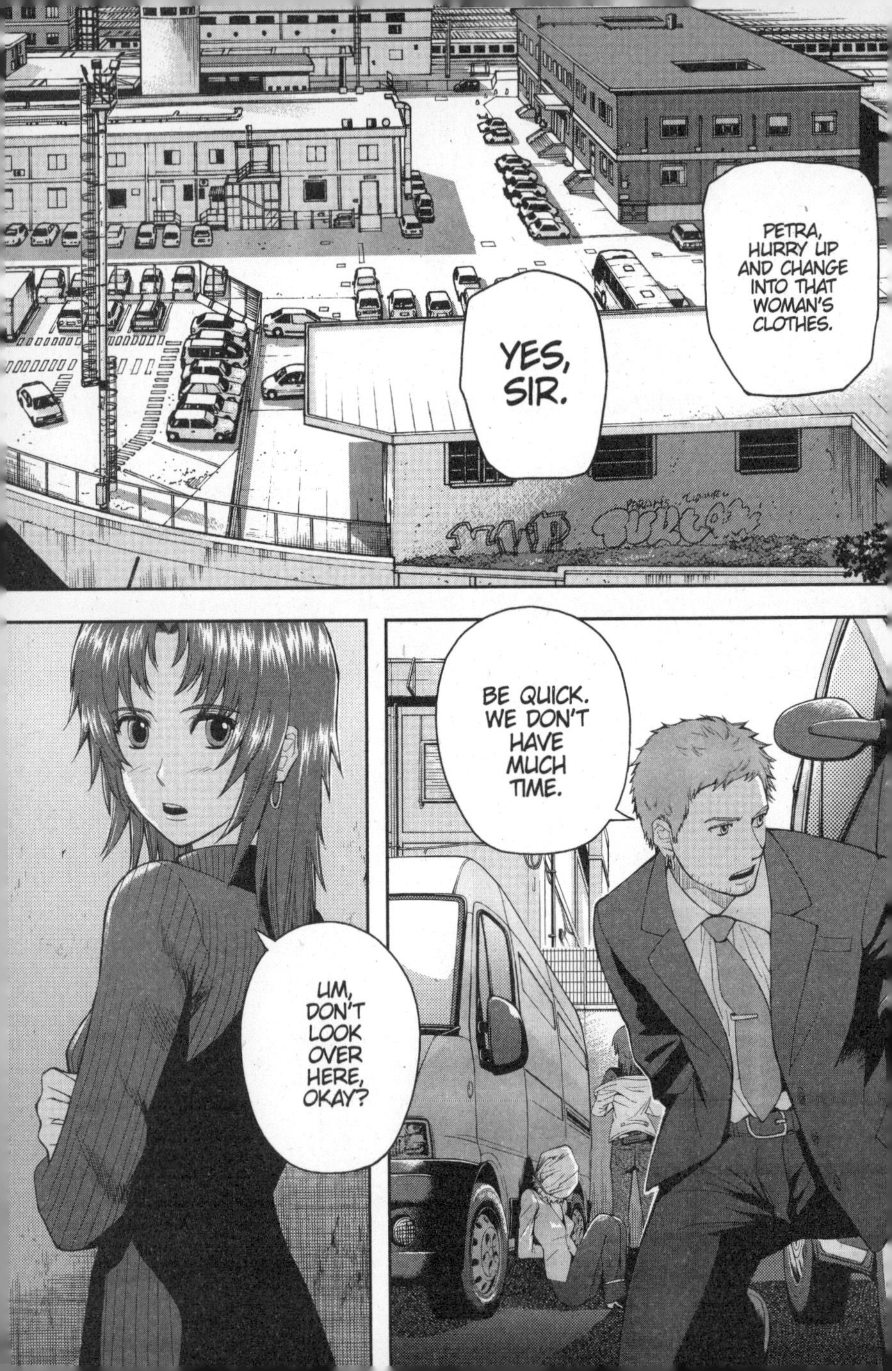
PETRA, HURRY UP AND CHANGE INTO THAT WOMAN'S CLOTHES.
YES, SIR.
BE QUICK. WE DON'T HAVE MUCH TIME.
UM, DON'T LOOK OVER HERE, OKAY?

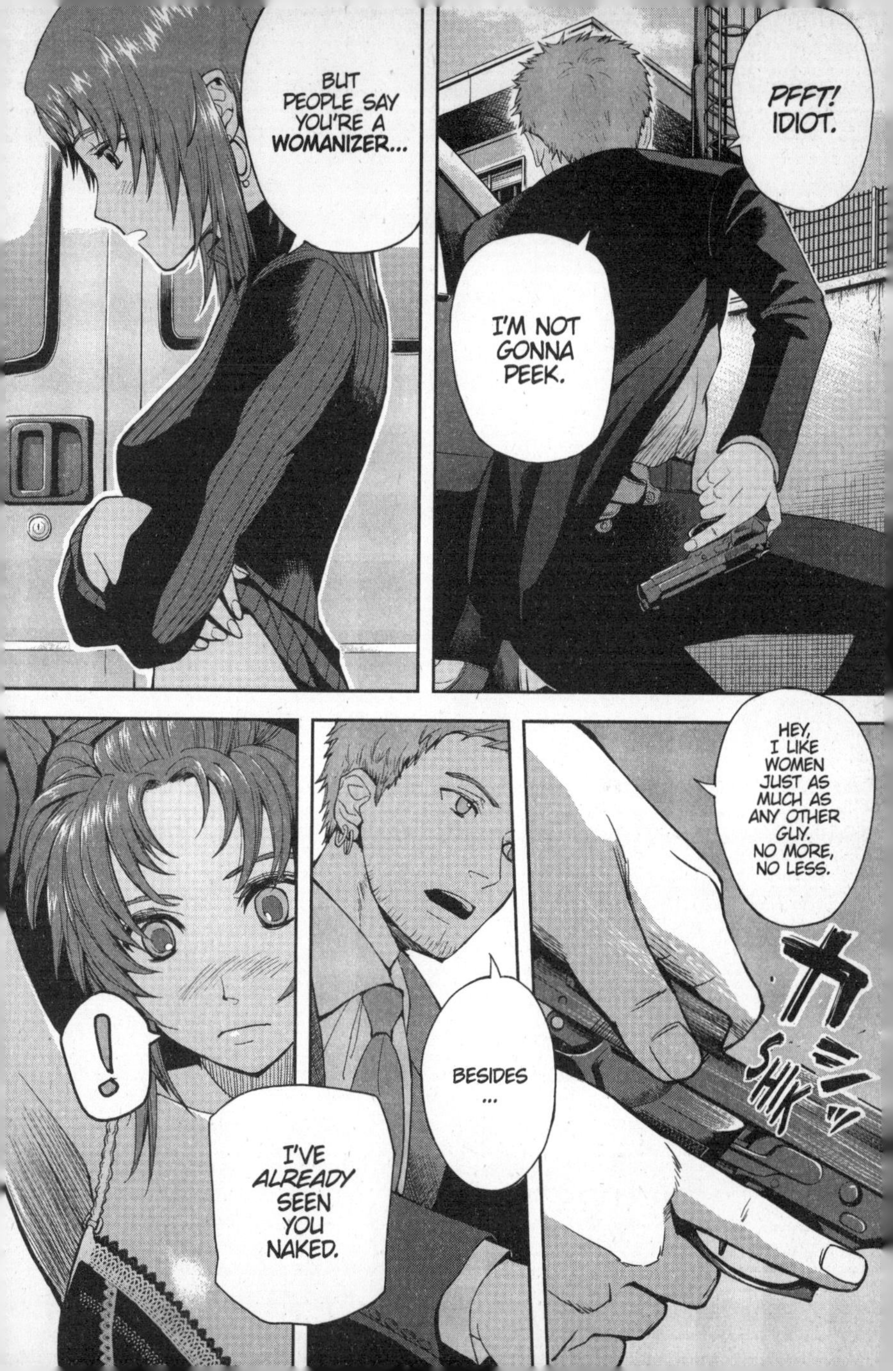
PFFT! IDIOT.
I'M NOT GONNA PEEK.
BUT PEOPLE SAY YOU'RE A WOMANIZER...
HEY, I LIKE WOMEN JUST AS MUCH AS ANY OTHER GUY. NO MORE, NO LESS.
SHIK
BESIDES ...
!
I'VE ALREADY SEEN YOU NAKED.

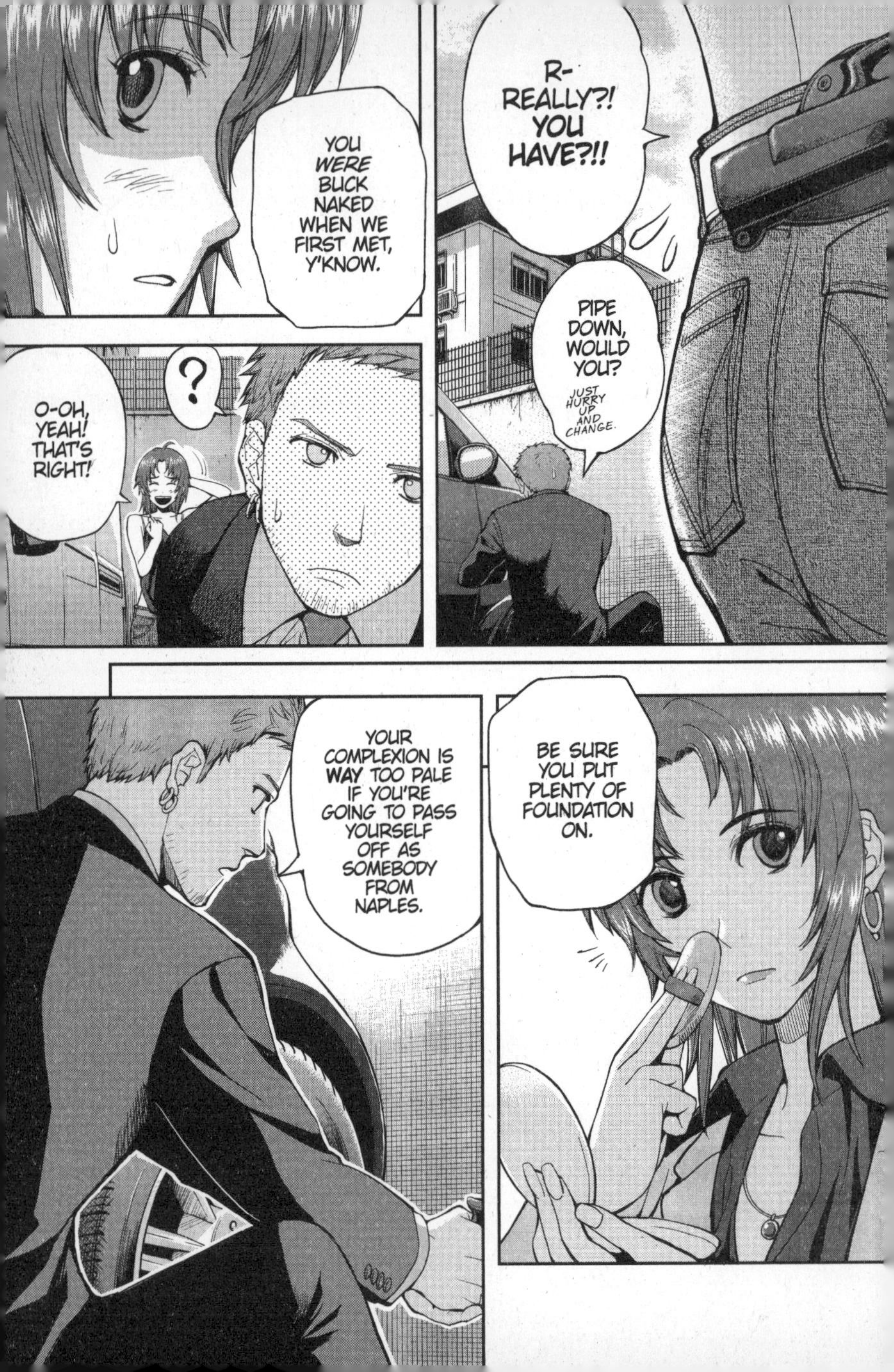
R-REALLY?! YOU HAVE?!!
PIPE DOWN, WOULD YOU?
JUST HURRY UP AND CHANGE.
YOU WERE BUCK NAKED WHEN WE FIRST MET, Y'KNOW.
?
O-OH, YEAH! THAT'S RIGHT!
BE SURE YOU PUT PLENTY OF FOUNDATION ON.
YOUR COMPLEXION IS WAY TOO PALE IF YOU'RE GOING TO PASS YOURSELF OFF AS SOMEBODY FROM NAPLES.

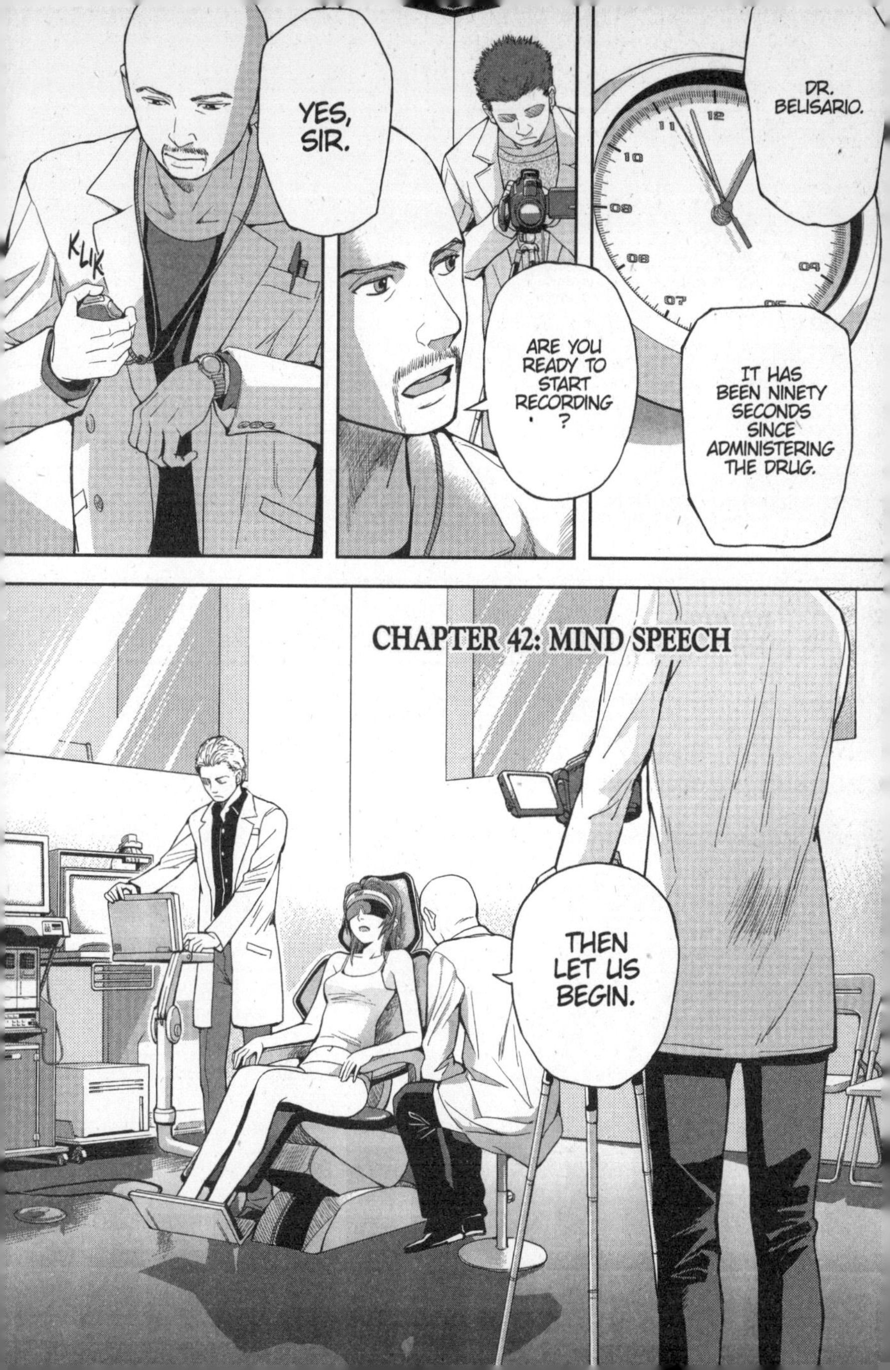
DR. BELISARIO.
IT HAS BEEN NINETY SECONDS SINCE ADMINISTERING THE DRUG.
ARE YOU READY TO START RECORDING?
YES, SIR.
KLIK
CHAPTER 42: MIND SPEECH
THEN LET US BEGIN.

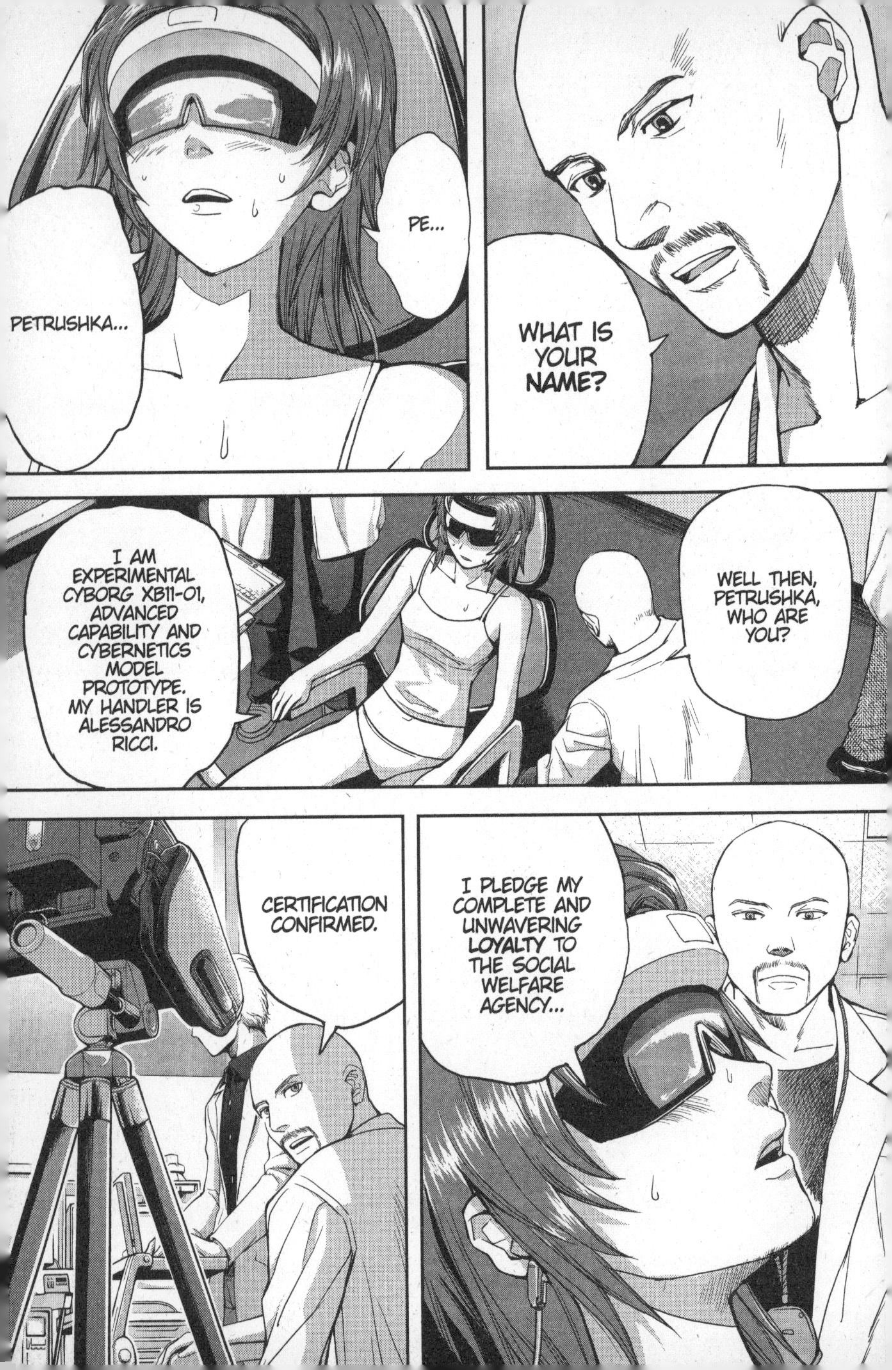
WHAT IS YOUR NAME?
PE...
PETRUSHKA...
WELL THEN, PETRUSHKA, WHO ARE YOU?
I AM EXPERIMENTAL CYBORG XB11-01, ADVANCED CAPABILITY AND CYBERNETICS MODEL PROTOTYPE. MY HANDLER IS ALESSANDRO RICCI.
I PLEDGE MY COMPLETE AND UNWAVERING LOYALTY TO THE SOCIAL WELFARE AGENCY...
CERTIFICATION CONFIRMED.

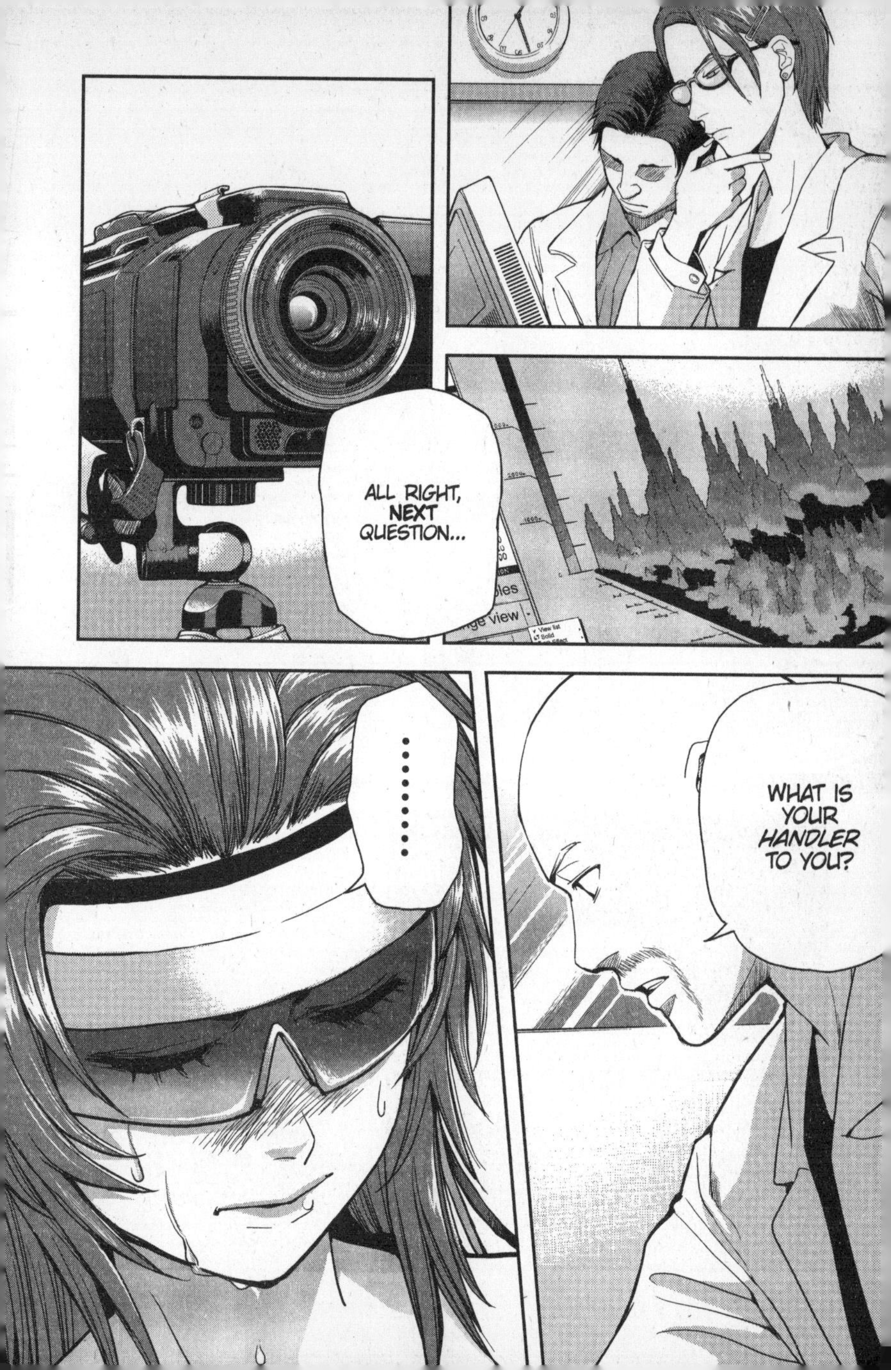
ALL RIGHT, NEXT QUESTION...
WHAT IS YOUR *HANDLER* TO YOU?
....

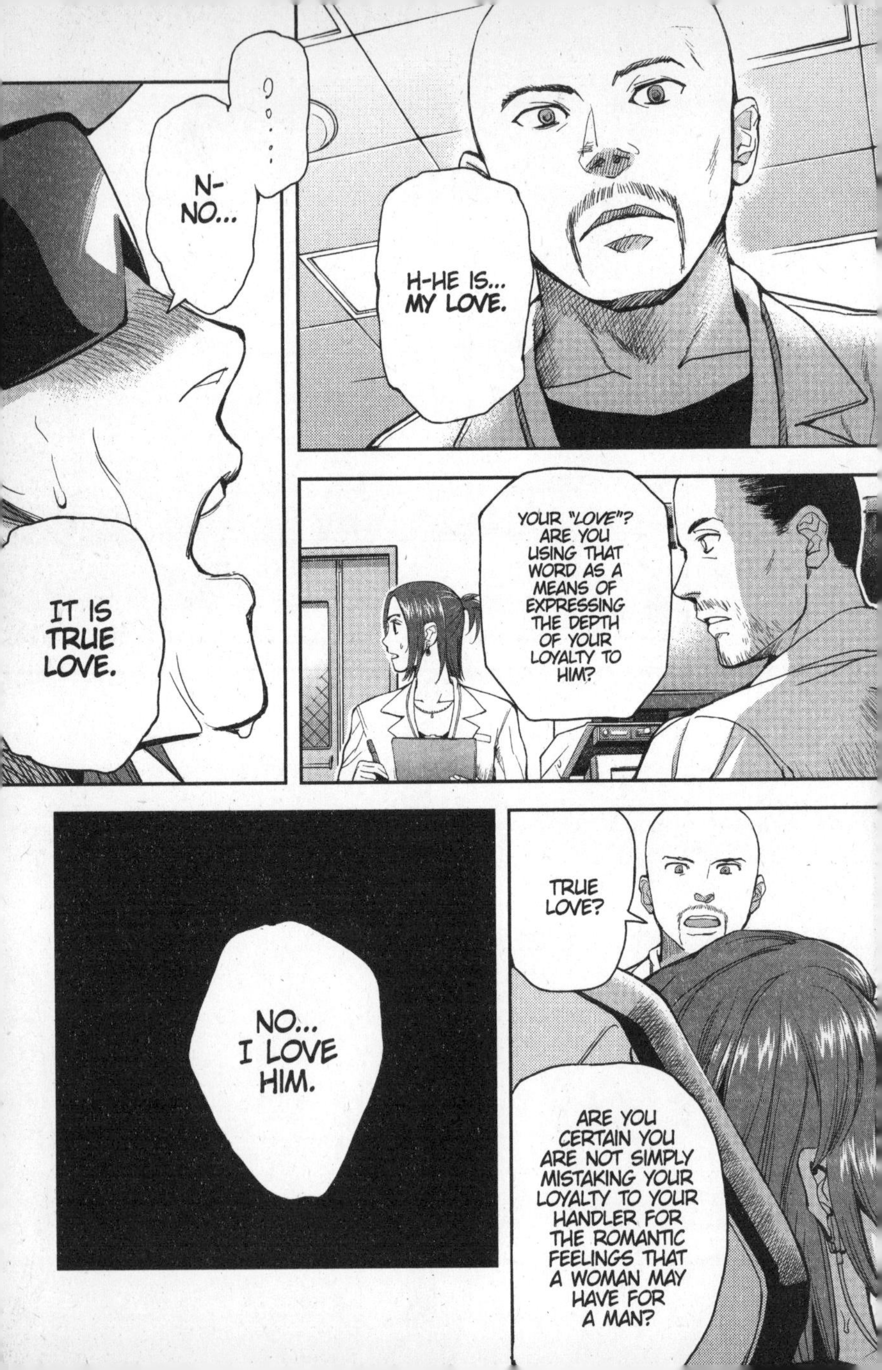
H-HE IS... MY LOVE.
YOUR "LOVE"? ARE YOU USING THAT WORD AS A MEANS OF EXPRESSING THE DEPTH OF YOUR LOYALTY TO HIM?
N- NO...
IT IS TRUE LOVE.
TRUE LOVE?
ARE YOU CERTAIN YOU ARE NOT SIMPLY MISTAKING YOUR LOYALTY TO YOUR HANDLER FOR THE ROMANTIC FEELINGS THAT A WOMAN MAY HAVE FOR A MAN?
NO... I LOVE HIM.

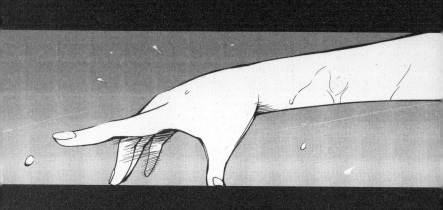

DANCING...

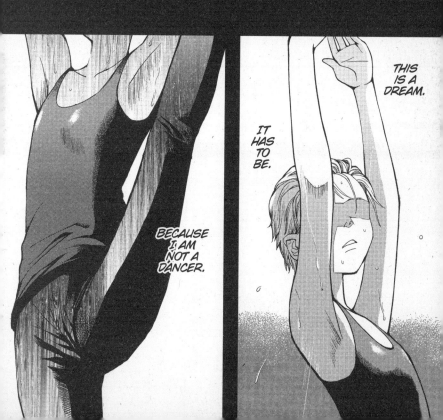

THIS IS A DREAM.

IT HAS TO BE.

BECAUSE I AM NOT A DANCER.

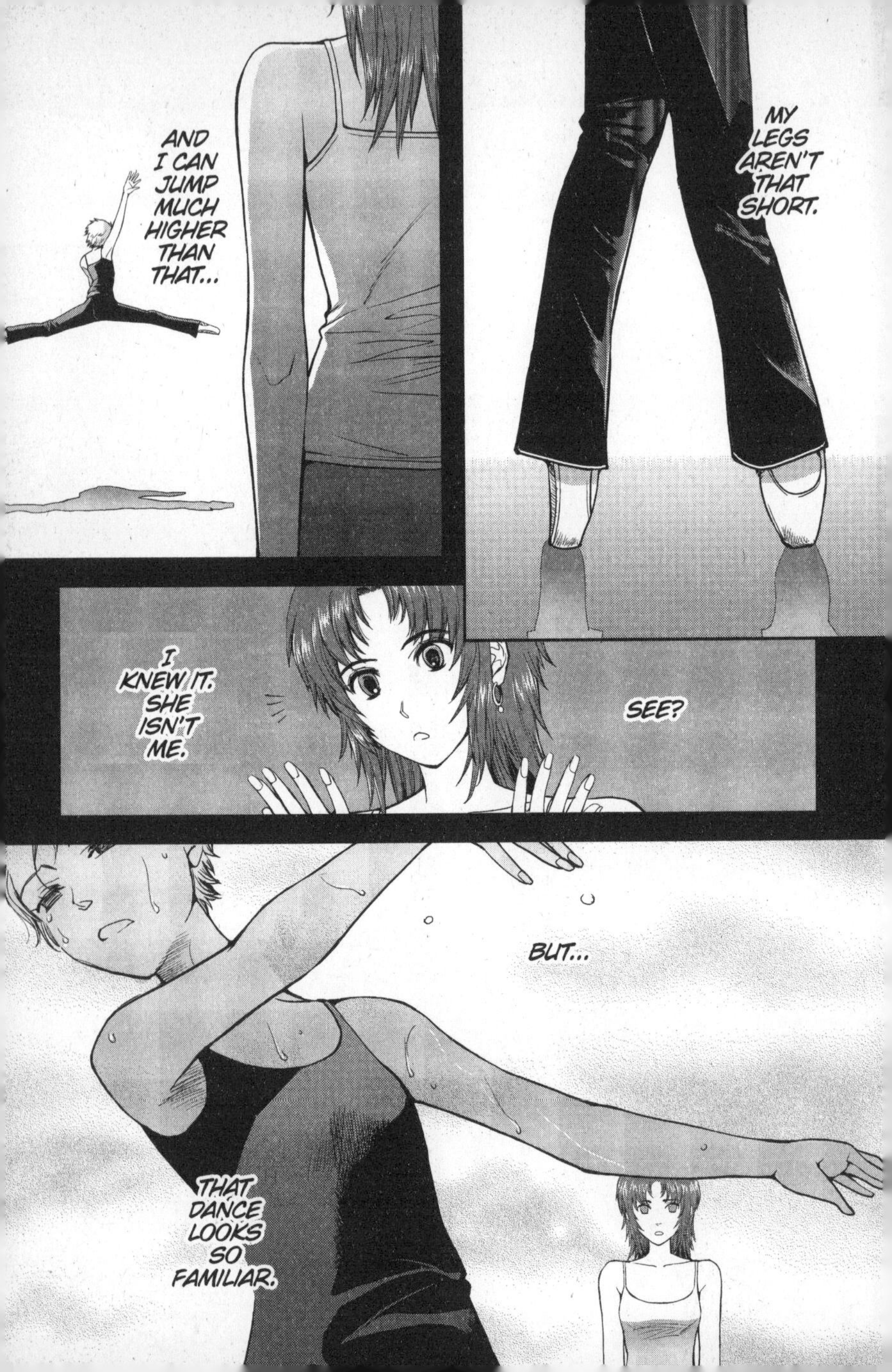
MY LEGS AREN'T THAT SHORT.
AND I CAN JUMP MUCH HIGHER THAN THAT...
SEE?
I KNEW IT. SHE ISN'T ME.
BUT...
THAT DANCE LOOKS SO FAMILIAR.

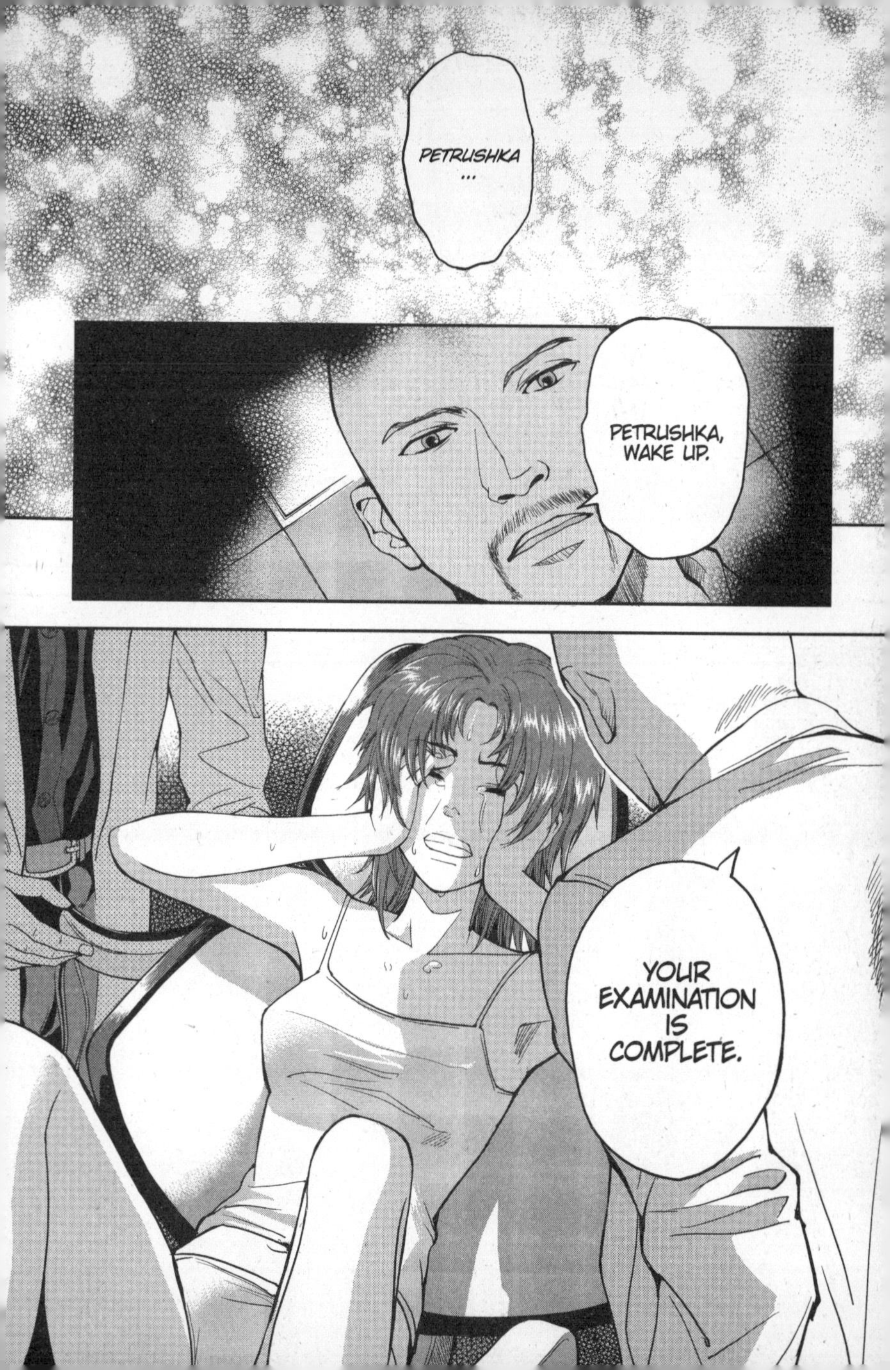
PETRUSHKA ...
PETRUSHKA, WAKE UP.
YOUR EXAMINATION IS COMPLETE.

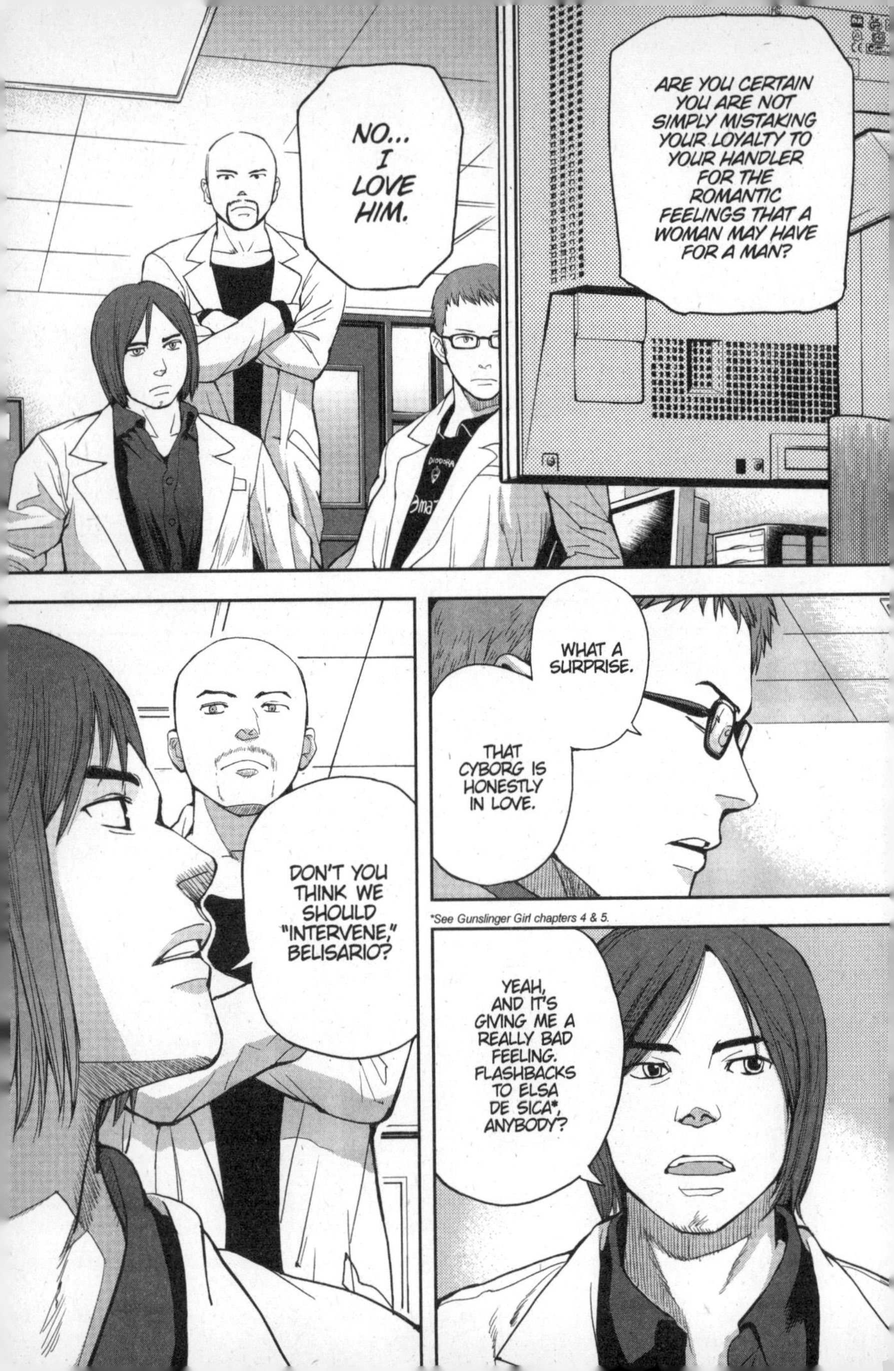
ARE YOU CERTAIN YOU ARE NOT SIMPLY MISTAKING YOUR LOYALTY TO YOUR HANDLER FOR THE ROMANTIC FEELINGS THAT A WOMAN MAY HAVE FOR A MAN?
NO... I LOVE HIM.
WHAT A SURPRISE.
THAT CYBORG IS HONESTLY IN LOVE.
YEAH, AND IT'S GIVING ME A REALLY BAD FEELING. FLASHBACKS TO ELSA DE SICA*, ANYBODY?
DON'T YOU THINK WE SHOULD "INTERVENE," BELISARIO?
*See Gunslinger Girl chapters 4 & 5.

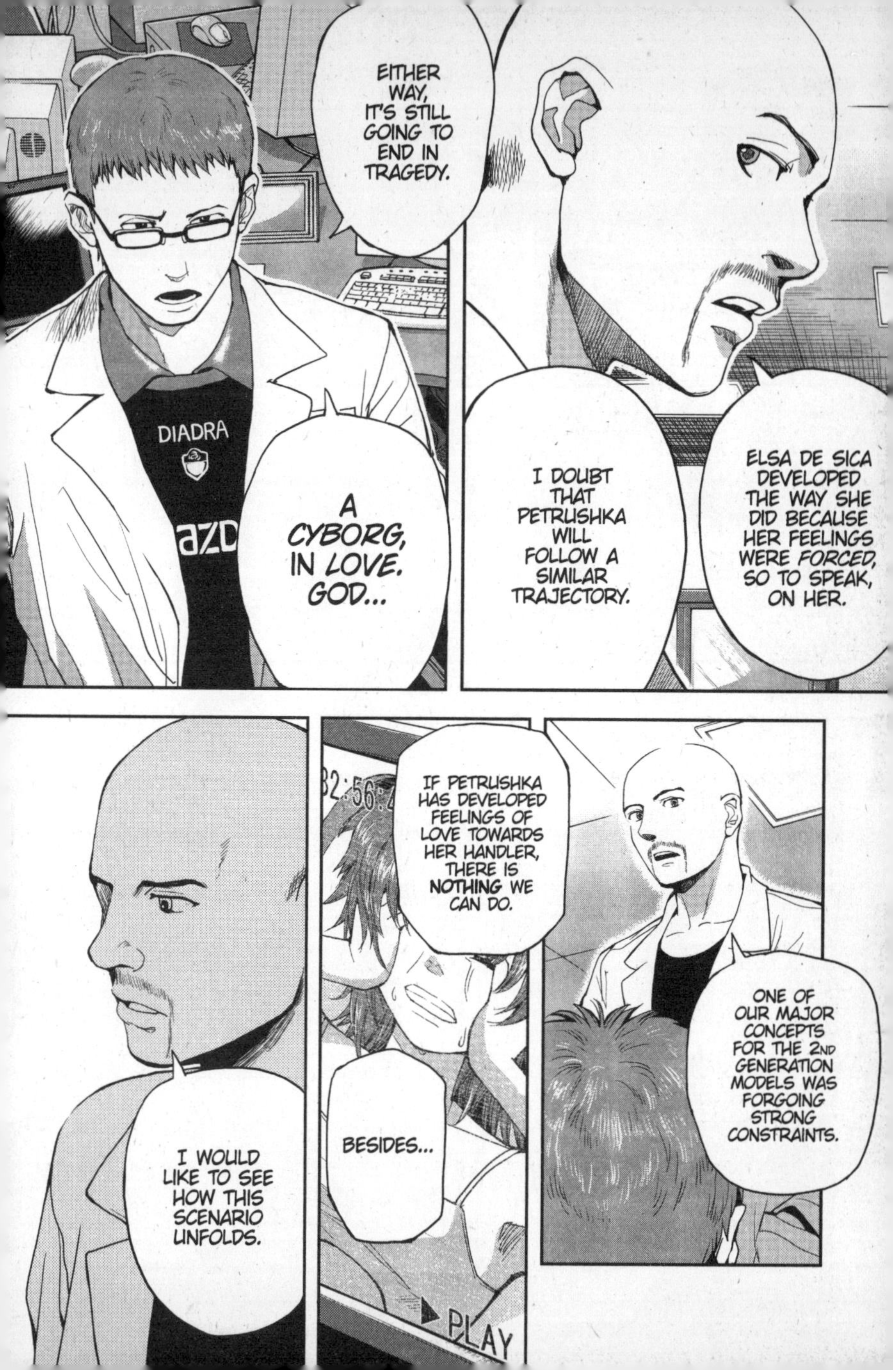
ELSA DE SICA DEVELOPED THE WAY SHE DID BECAUSE HER FEELINGS WERE *FORCED*, SO TO SPEAK, ON HER.
I DOUBT THAT PETRUSHKA WILL FOLLOW A SIMILAR TRAJECTORY.
EITHER WAY, IT'S STILL GOING TO END IN TRAGEDY.
DIADRA
A *CYBORG*, IN *LOVE*. *GOD*...
ONE OF OUR MAJOR CONCEPTS FOR THE 2ND GENERATION MODELS WAS FORGOING STRONG CONSTRAINTS.
IF PETRUSHKA HAS DEVELOPED FEELINGS OF LOVE TOWARDS HER HANDLER, THERE IS **NOTHING** WE CAN DO.
BESIDES...
▶PLAY
I WOULD LIKE TO SEE HOW THIS SCENARIO UNFOLDS.

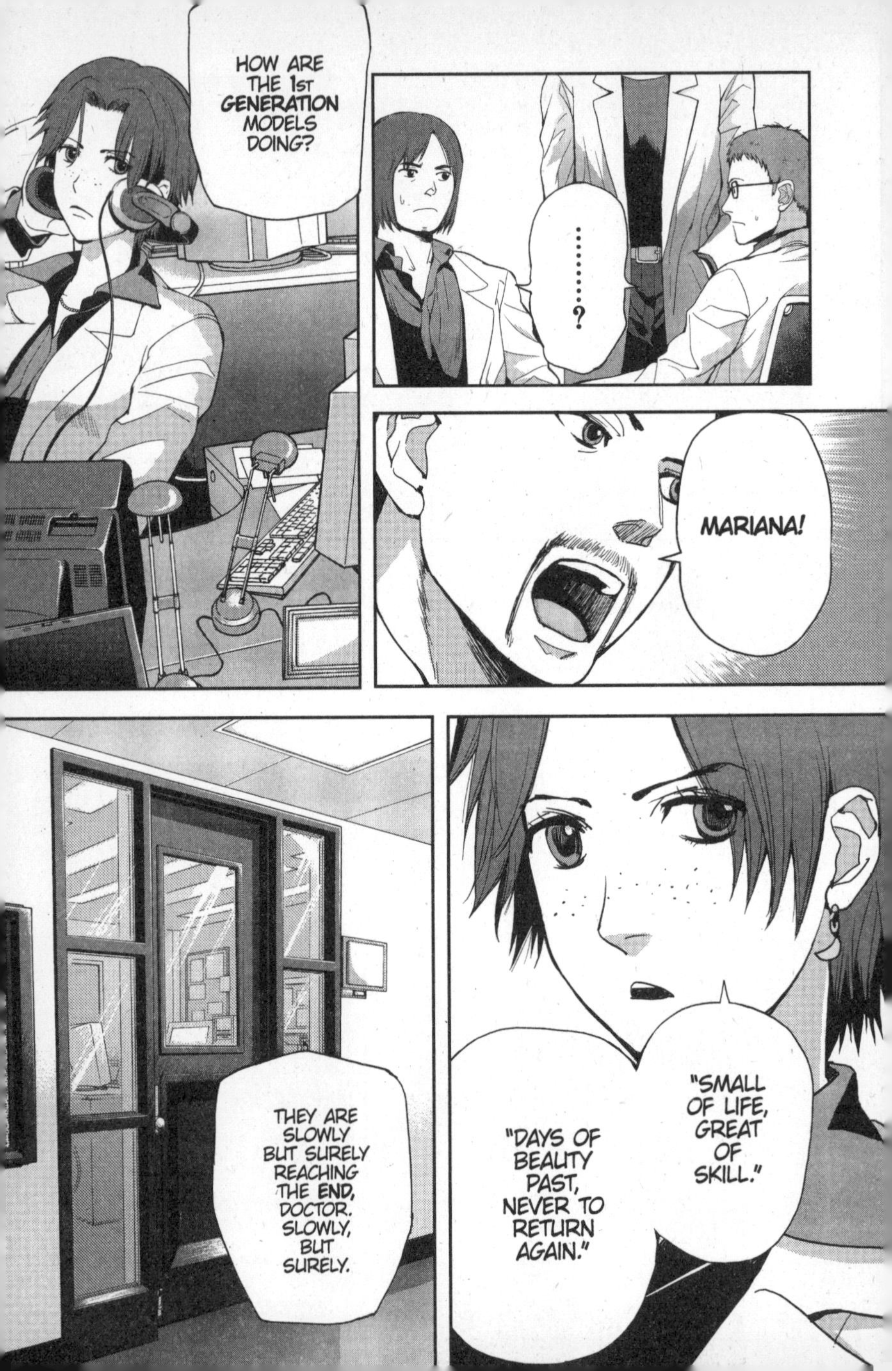
……?
MARIANA!
HOW ARE THE 1st GENERATION MODELS DOING?
"SMALL OF LIFE, GREAT OF SKILL."
"DAYS OF BEAUTY PAST, NEVER TO RETURN AGAIN."
THEY ARE SLOWLY BUT SURELY REACHING THE END, DOCTOR. SLOWLY, BUT SURELY.

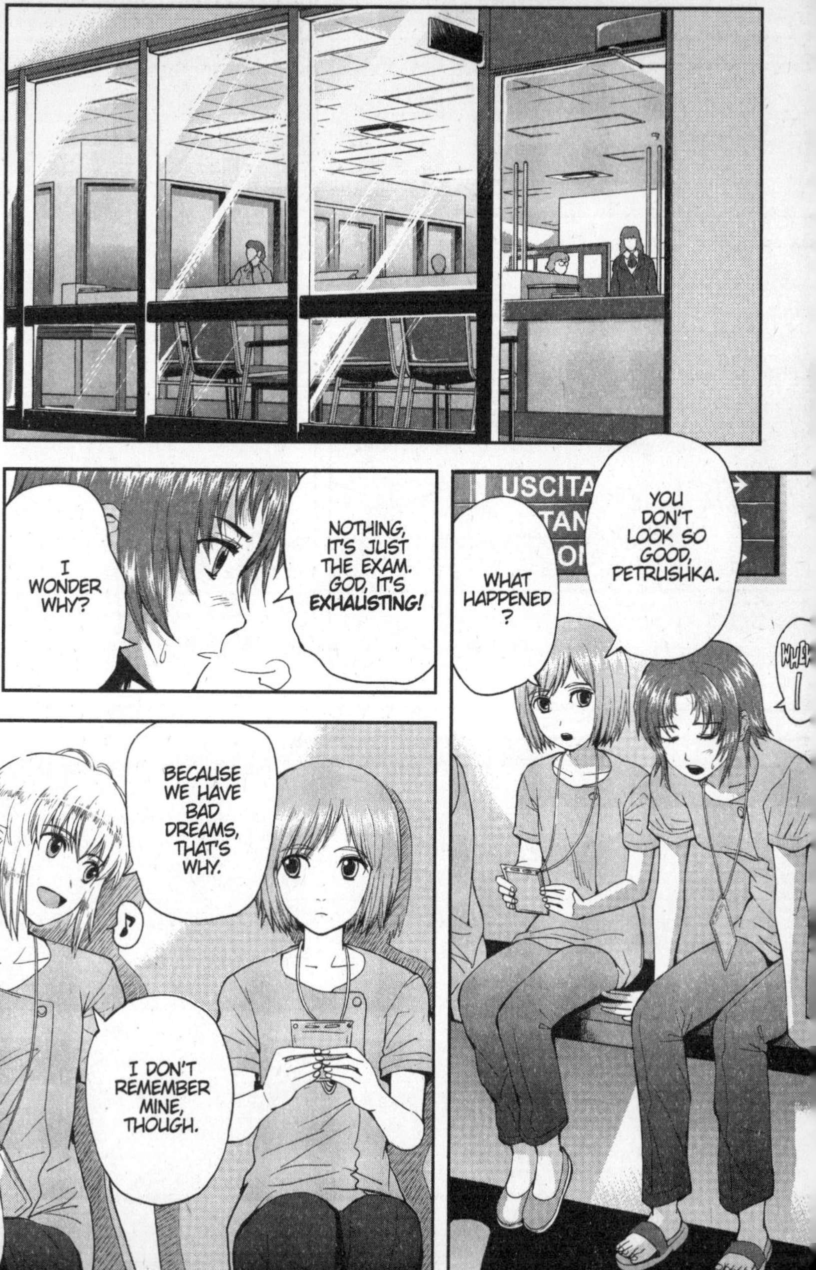
USCITA
YOU DON'T LOOK SO GOOD, PETRUSHKA.
WHAT HAPPENED?
NOTHING, IT'S JUST THE EXAM. GOD, IT'S EXHAUSTING!
I WONDER WHY?
BECAUSE WE HAVE BAD DREAMS, THAT'S WHY.
I DON'T REMEMBER MINE, THOUGH.

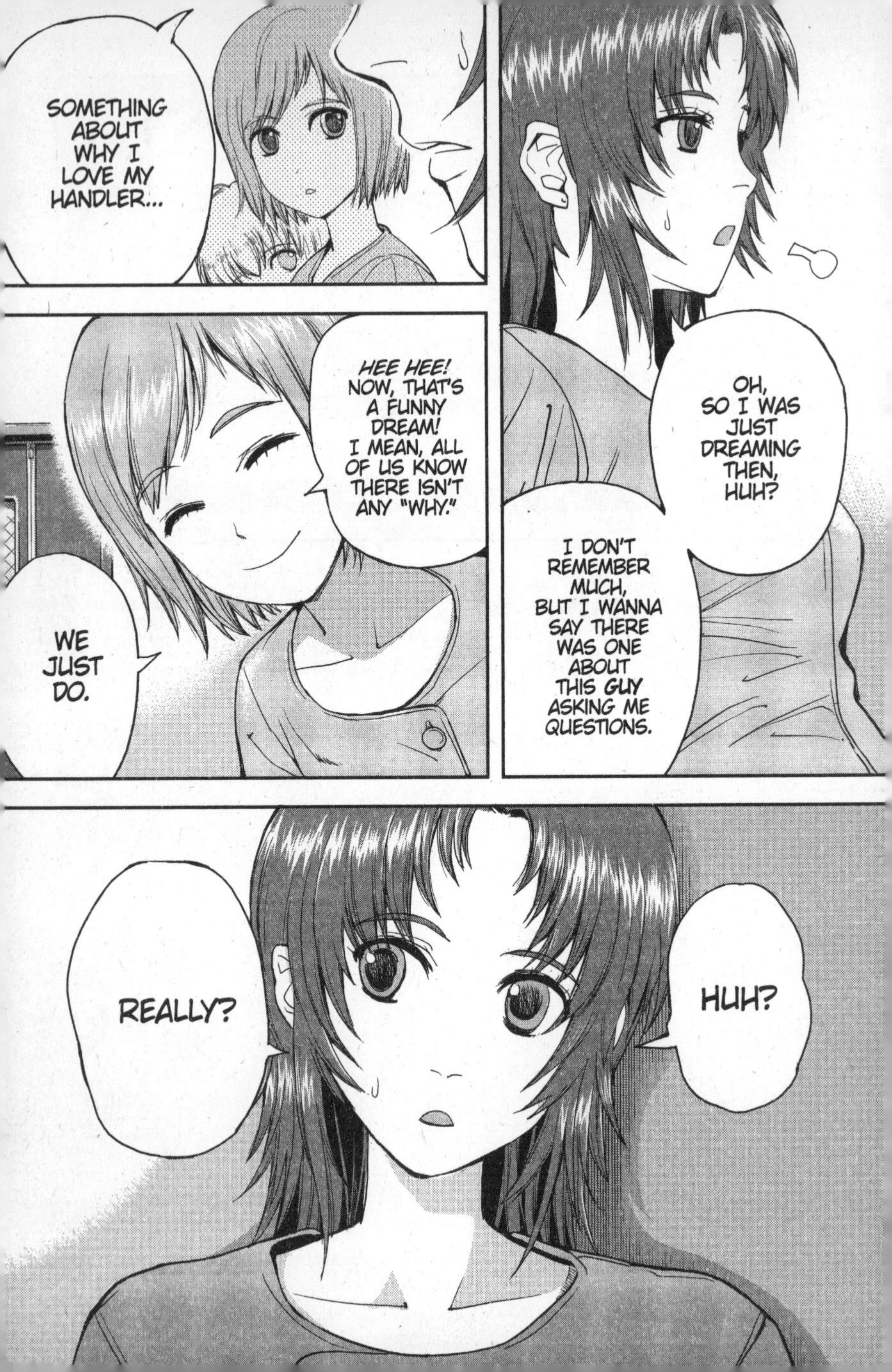
OH, SO I WAS JUST DREAMING THEN, HUH?
I DON'T REMEMBER MUCH, BUT I WANNA SAY THERE WAS ONE ABOUT THIS GUY ASKING ME QUESTIONS.
SOMETHING ABOUT WHY I LOVE MY HANDLER...
HEE HEE! NOW, THAT'S A FUNNY DREAM! I MEAN, ALL OF US KNOW THERE ISN'T ANY "WHY."
WE JUST DO.
HUH?
REALLY?

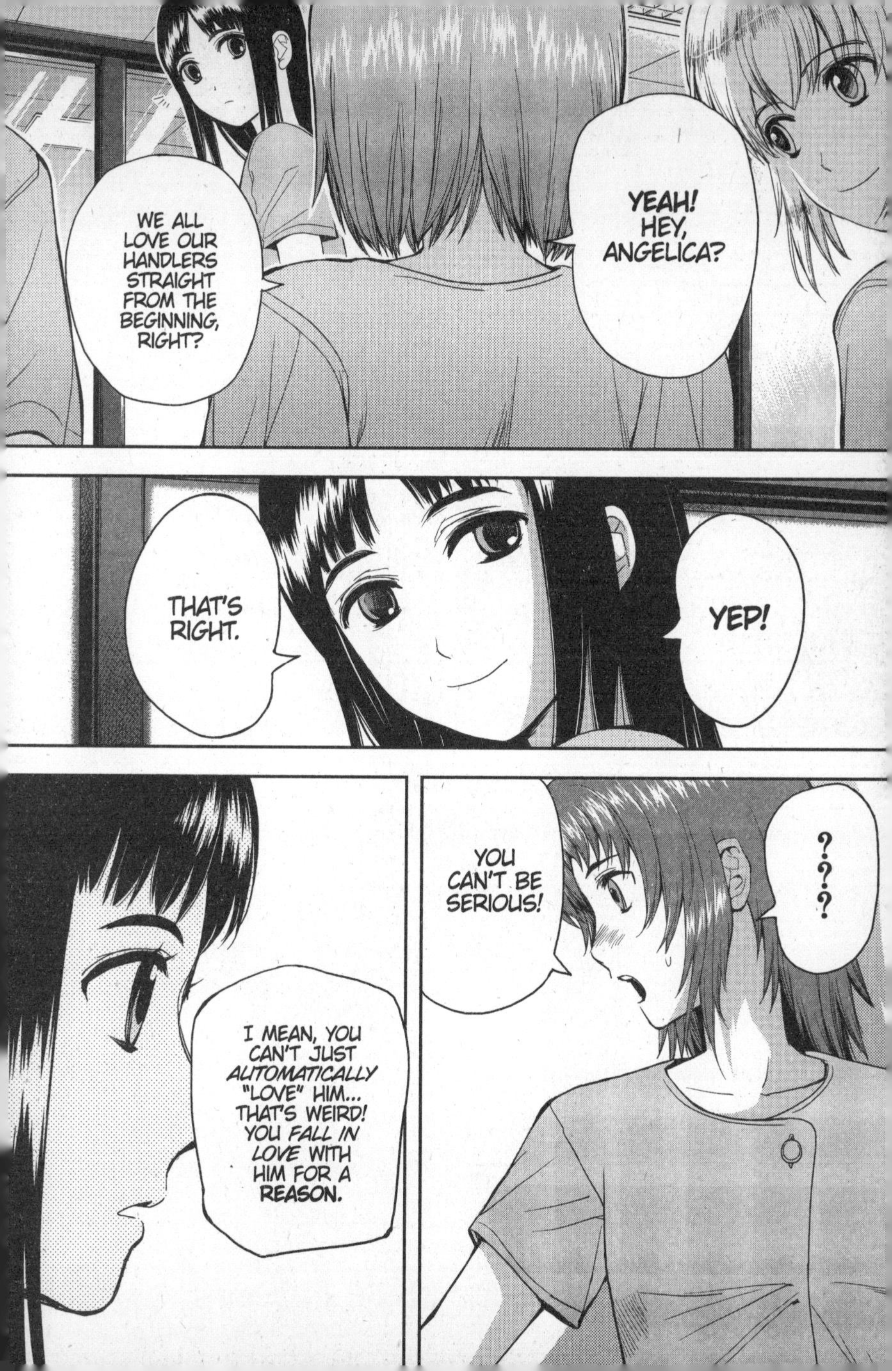
YEAH! HEY, ANGELICA?
WE ALL LOVE OUR HANDLERS STRAIGHT FROM THE BEGINNING, RIGHT?
YEP!
THAT'S RIGHT.
???
YOU CAN'T BE SERIOUS!
I MEAN, YOU CAN'T JUST *AUTOMATICALLY* "LOVE" HIM... THAT'S WEIRD! YOU *FALL IN LOVE* WITH HIM FOR A REASON.

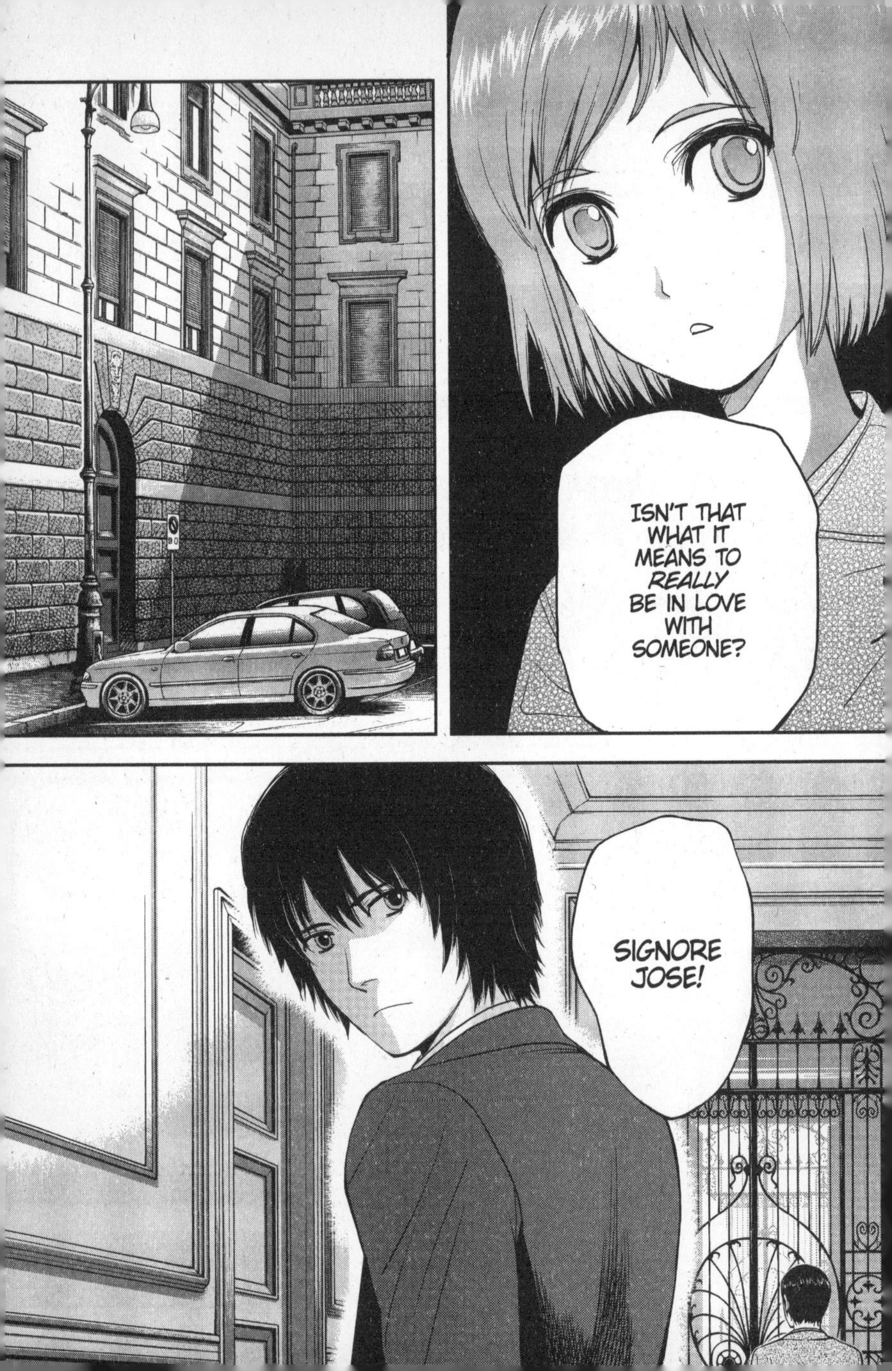
ISN'T THAT WHAT IT MEANS TO *REALLY* BE IN LOVE WITH SOMEONE?
SIGNORE JOSE!

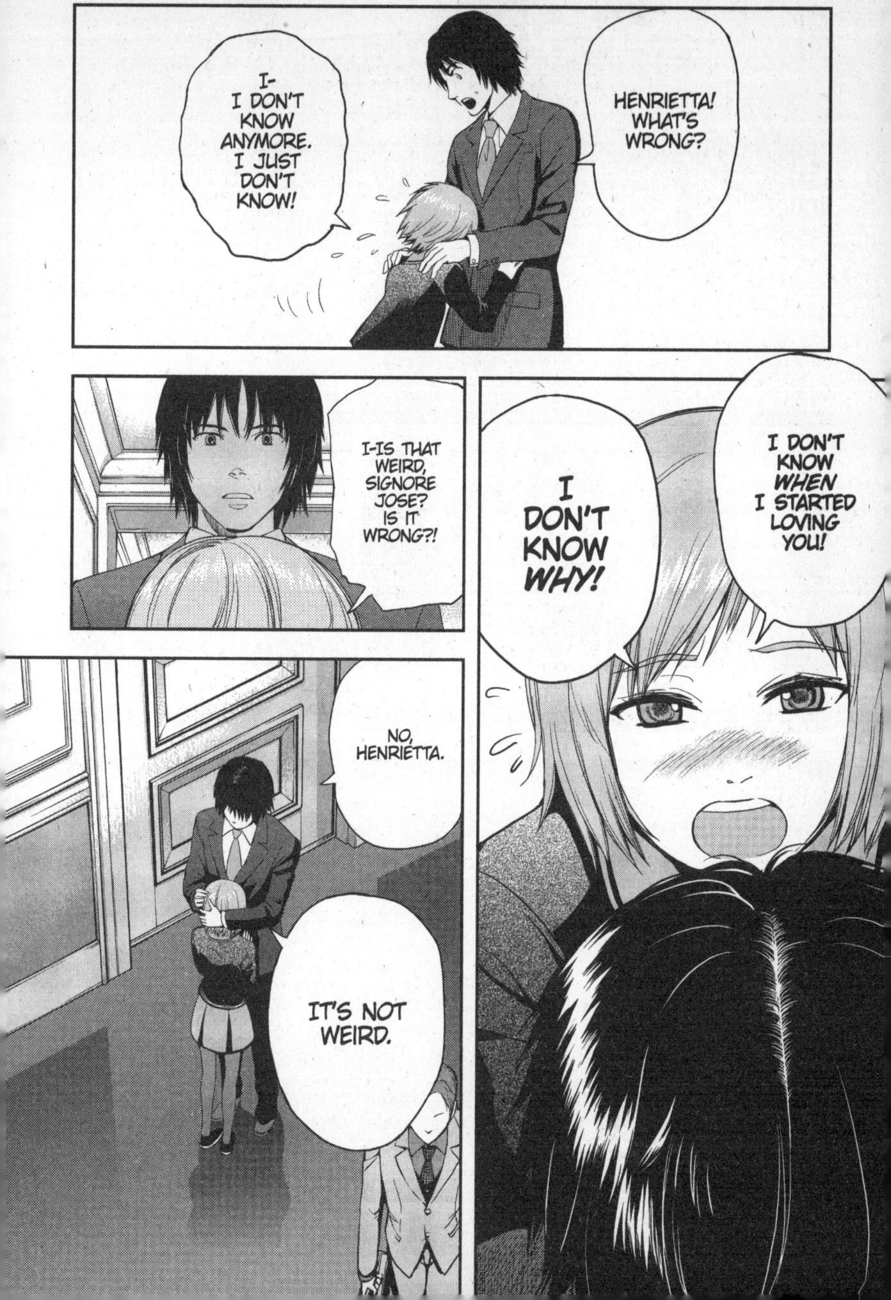
HENRIETTA! WHAT'S WRONG?
I- I DON'T KNOW ANYMORE. I JUST DON'T KNOW!
I DON'T KNOW *WHEN* I STARTED LOVING YOU!
I DON'T KNOW *WHY!*
I-IS THAT WEIRD, SIGNORE JOSE? IS IT WRONG?!
NO, HENRIETTA.
IT'S NOT WEIRD.

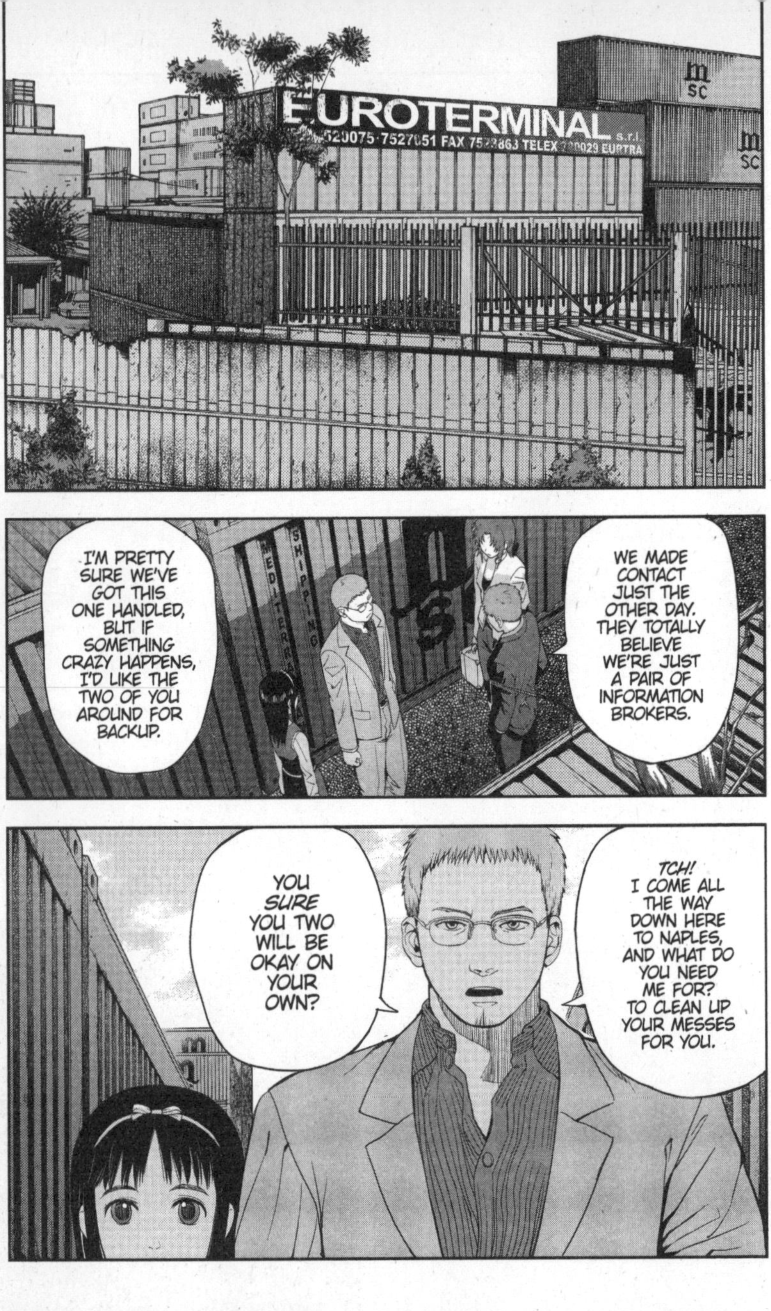
EUROTERMINAL s.r.l.
WE MADE CONTACT JUST THE OTHER DAY. THEY TOTALLY BELIEVE WE'RE JUST A PAIR OF INFORMATION BROKERS.
I'M PRETTY SURE WE'VE GOT THIS ONE HANDLED, BUT IF SOMETHING CRAZY HAPPENS, I'D LIKE THE TWO OF YOU AROUND FOR BACKUP.
TCH! I COME ALL THE WAY DOWN HERE TO NAPLES, AND WHAT DO YOU NEED ME FOR? TO CLEAN UP YOUR MESSES FOR YOU.
YOU *SURE* YOU TWO WILL BE OKAY ON YOUR OWN?

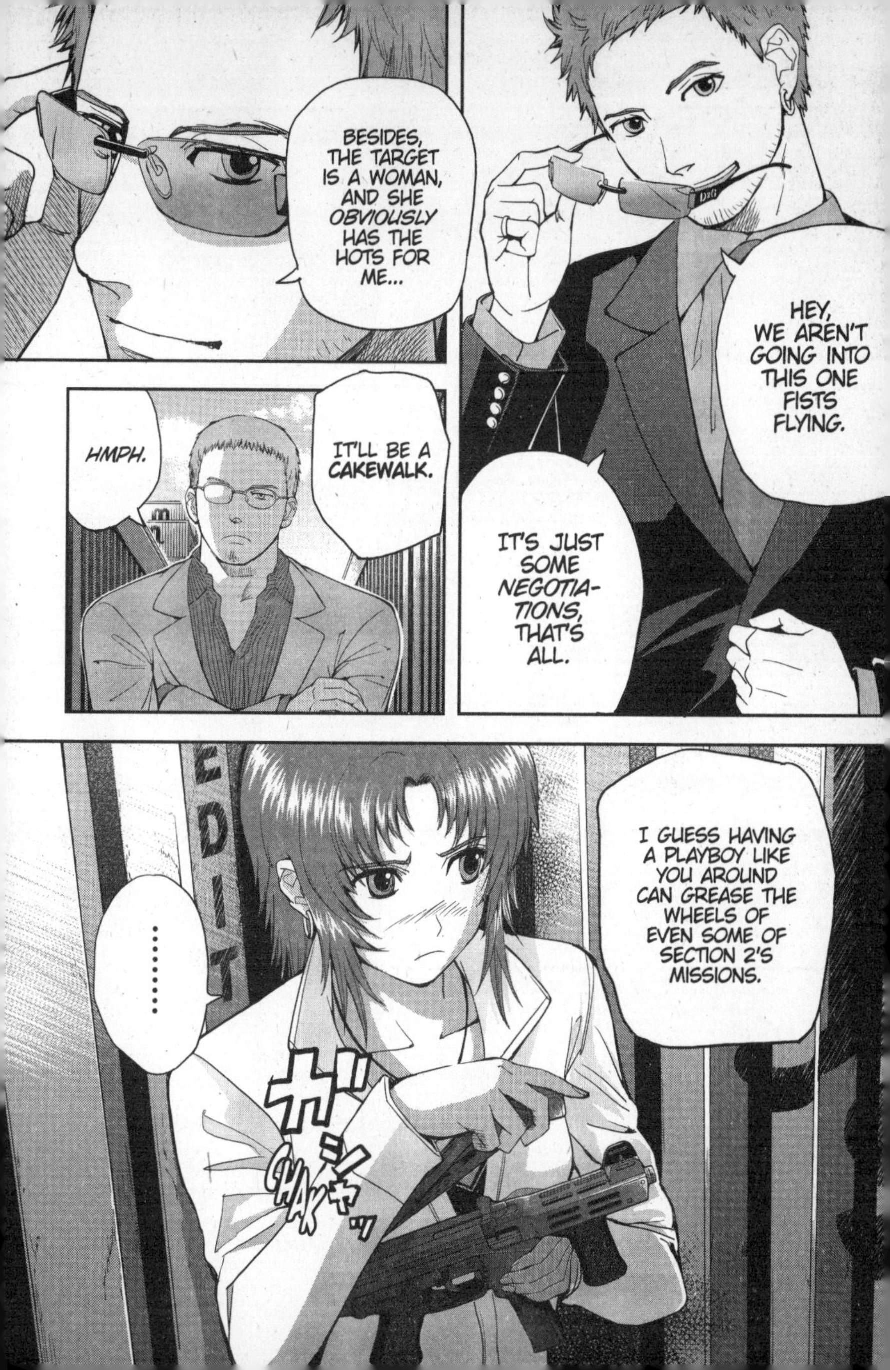
HEY, WE AREN'T GOING INTO THIS ONE FISTS FLYING.
IT'S JUST SOME NEGOTIATIONS, THAT'S ALL.
BESIDES, THE TARGET IS A WOMAN, AND SHE OBVIOUSLY HAS THE HOTS FOR ME...
IT'LL BE A CAKEWALK.
HMPH.
I GUESS HAVING A PLAYBOY LIKE YOU AROUND CAN GREASE THE WHEELS OF EVEN SOME OF SECTION 2'S MISSIONS.
....
CHAK

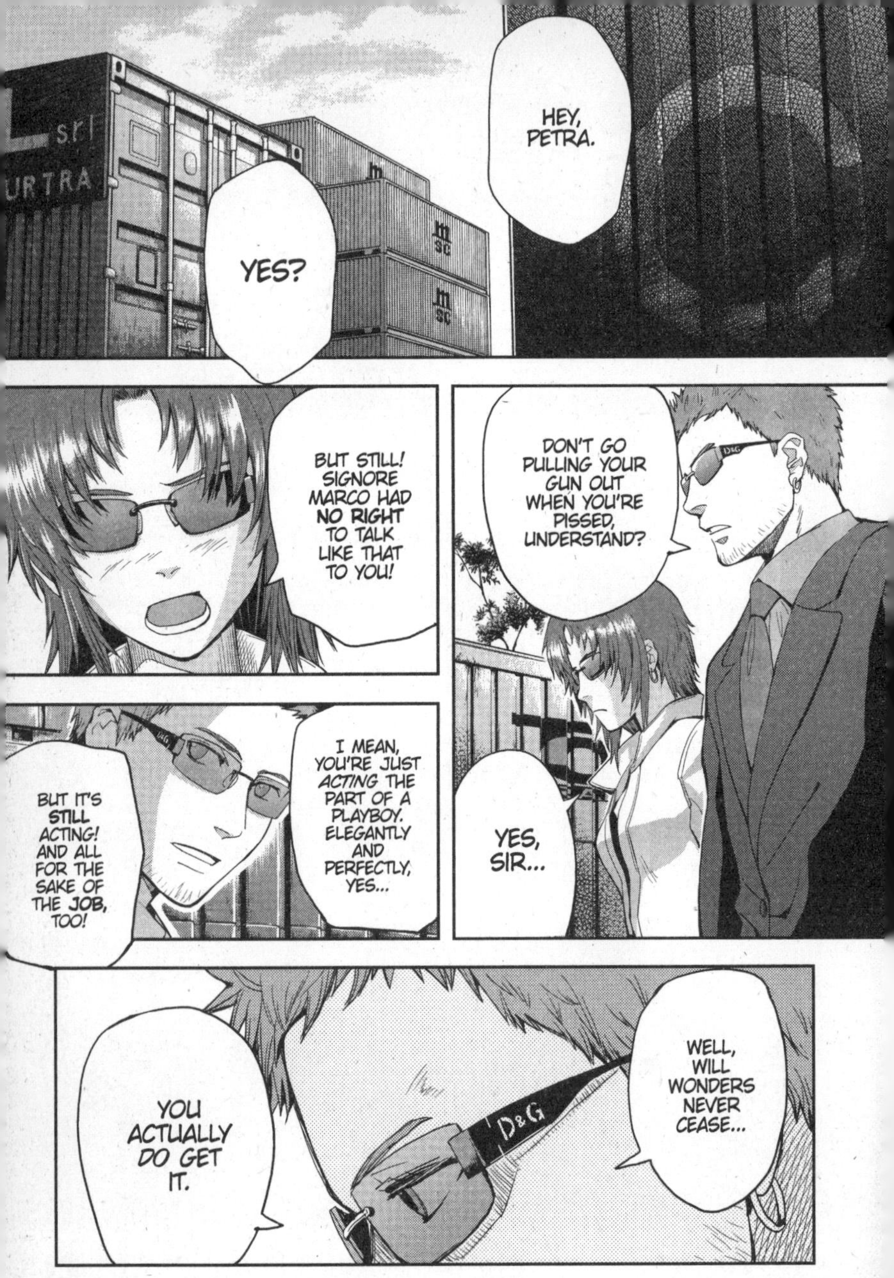
HEY, PETRA.
YES?
DON'T GO PULLING YOUR GUN OUT WHEN YOU'RE PISSED, UNDERSTAND?
YES, SIR...
BUT STILL! SIGNORE MARCO HAD **NO RIGHT** TO TALK LIKE THAT TO YOU!
I MEAN, YOU'RE JUST *ACTING* THE PART OF A PLAYBOY. ELEGANTLY AND PERFECTLY, YES...
BUT IT'S **STILL** ACTING! AND ALL FOR THE SAKE OF THE **JOB**, TOO!
WELL, WILL WONDERS NEVER CEASE...
YOU ACTUALLY DO GET IT.

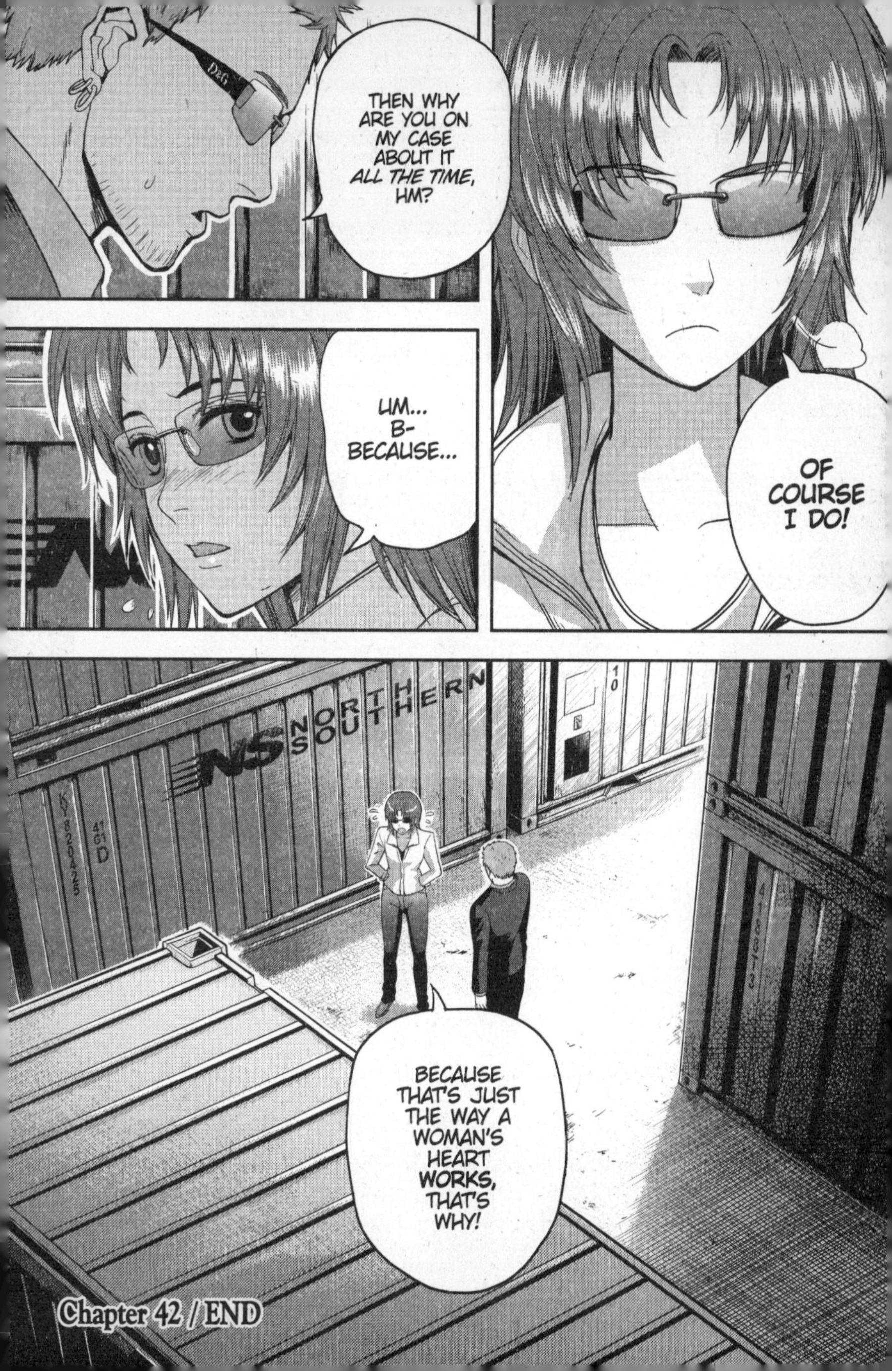
OF COURSE I DO!
THEN WHY ARE YOU ON MY CASE ABOUT IT *ALL THE TIME*, HM?
UM... B-BECAUSE...
NS NORTH SOUTHERN
BECAUSE THAT'S JUST THE WAY A WOMAN'S HEART **WORKS**, THAT'S WHY!

Chapter 42 / END

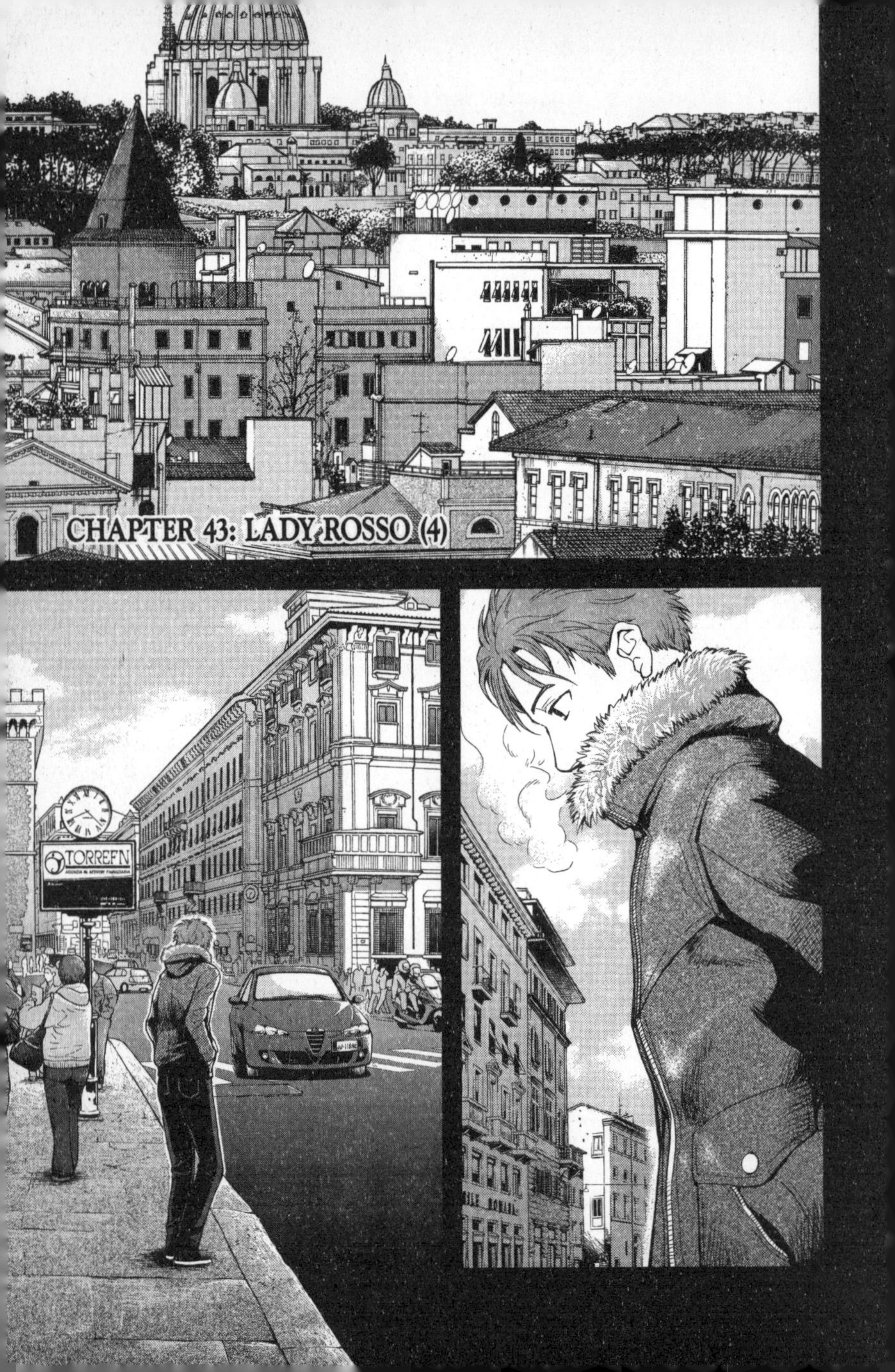
CHAPTER 43: LADY ROSSO (4)
TORREFN

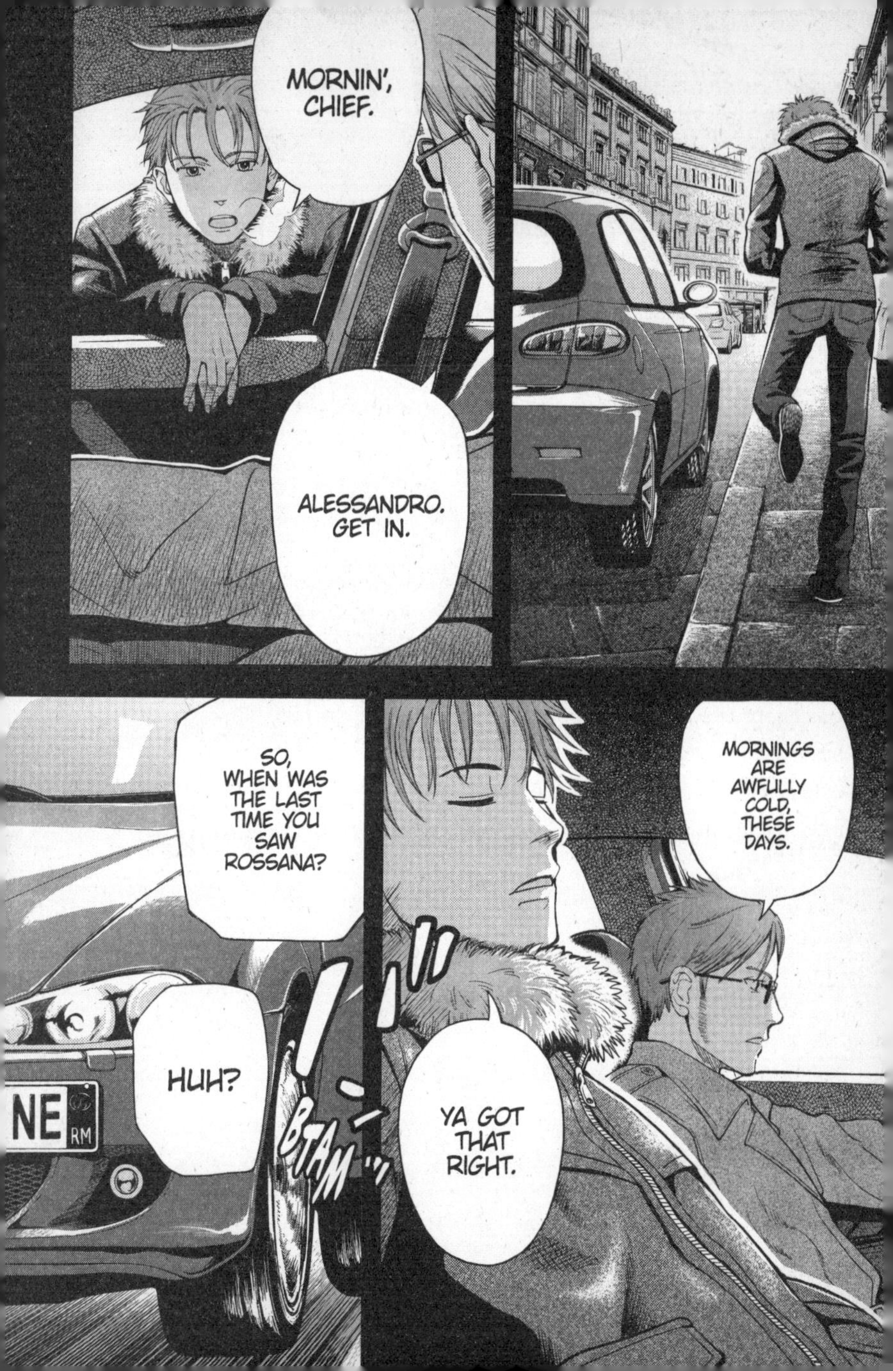
MORNIN', CHIEF.
ALESSANDRO. GET IN.
MORNINGS ARE AWFULLY COLD, THESE DAYS.
YA GOT THAT RIGHT.
BTAM
SO, WHEN WAS THE LAST TIME YOU SAW ROSSANA?
HUH?

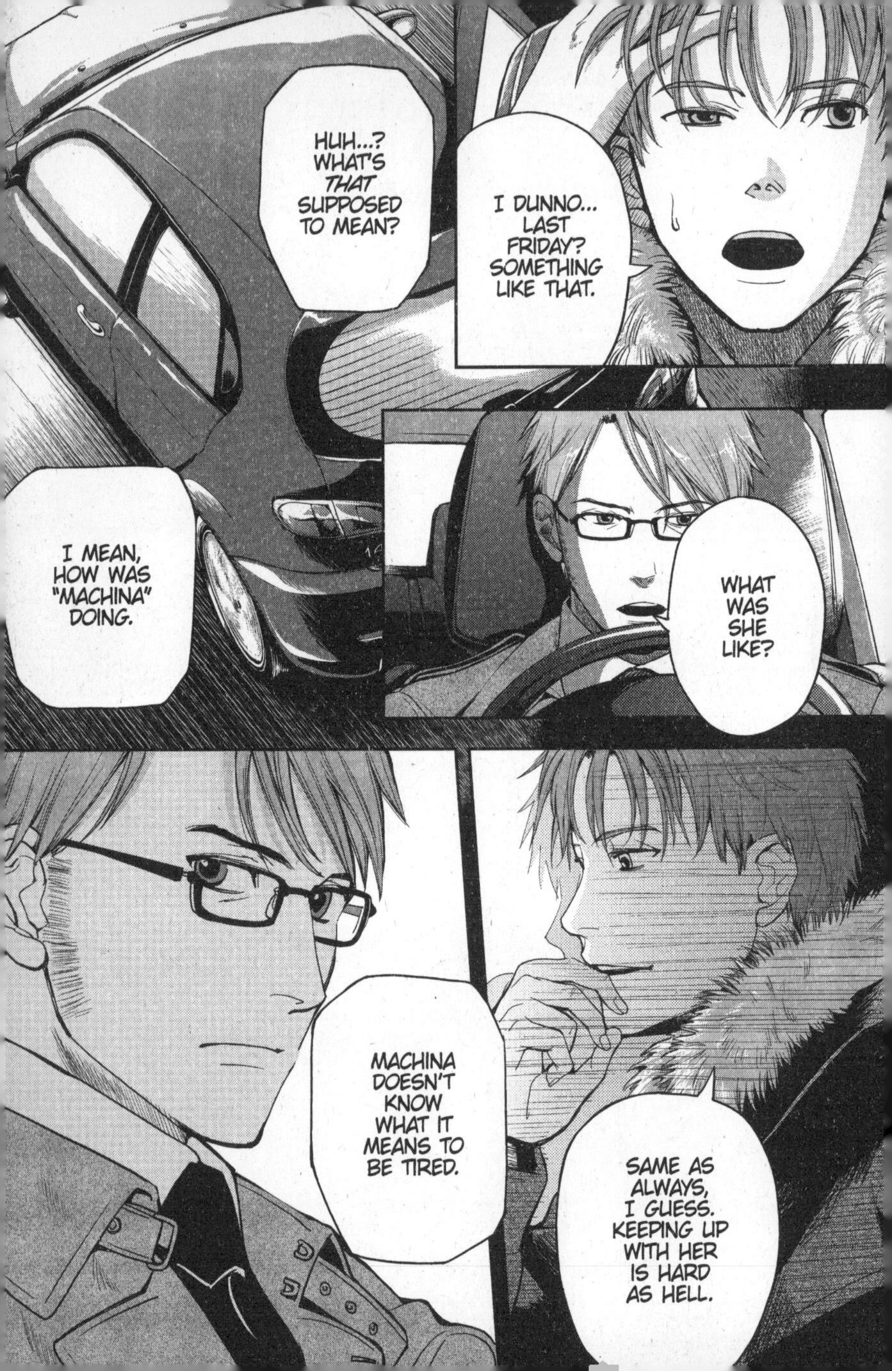
I DUNNO... LAST FRIDAY? SOMETHING LIKE THAT.
HUH...? WHAT'S *THAT* SUPPOSED TO MEAN?
I MEAN, HOW WAS "MACHINA" DOING.
WHAT WAS SHE LIKE?
SAME AS ALWAYS, I GUESS. KEEPING UP WITH HER IS HARD AS HELL.
MACHINA DOESN'T KNOW WHAT IT MEANS TO BE TIRED.

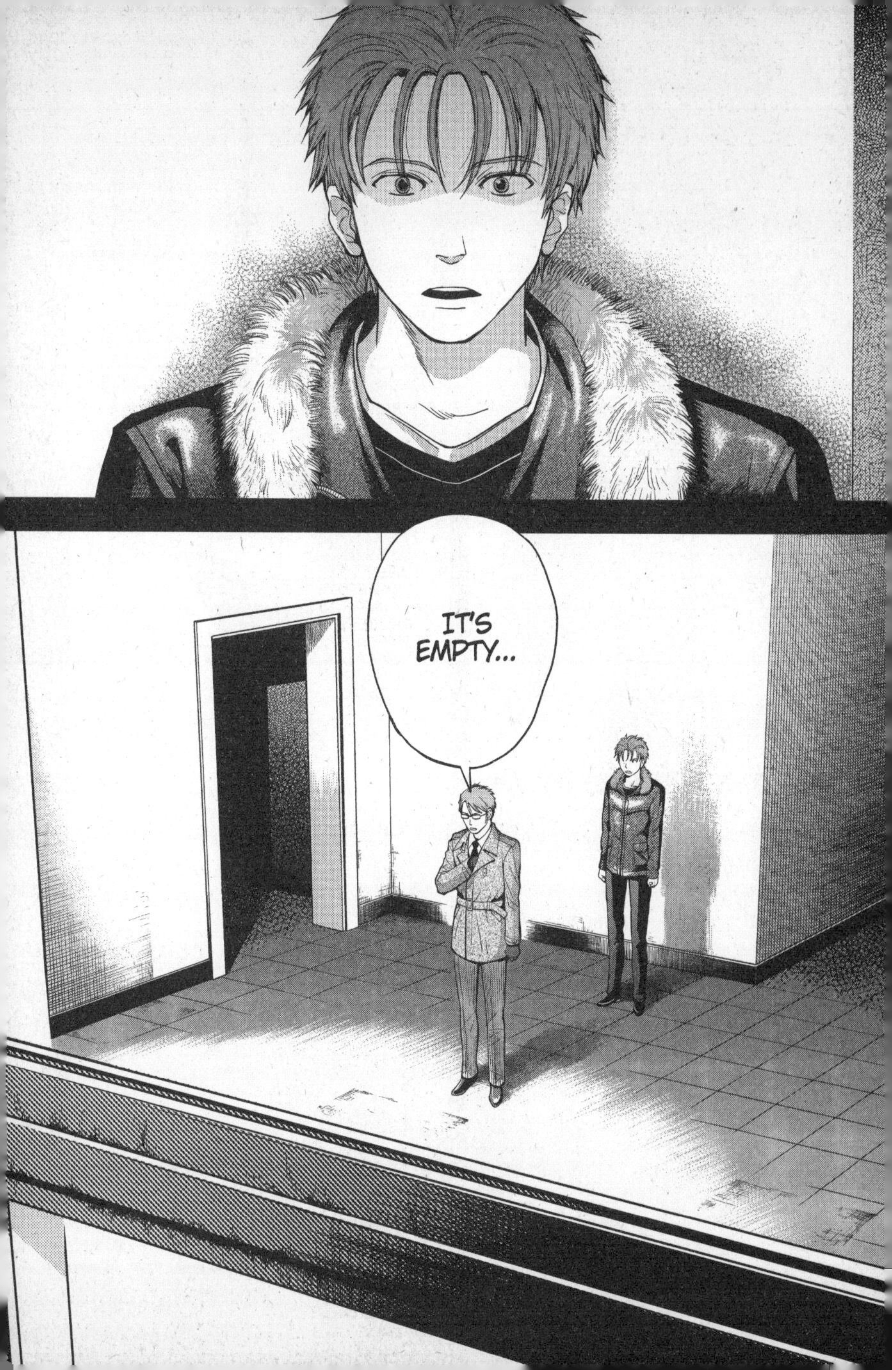
IT'S EMPTY...

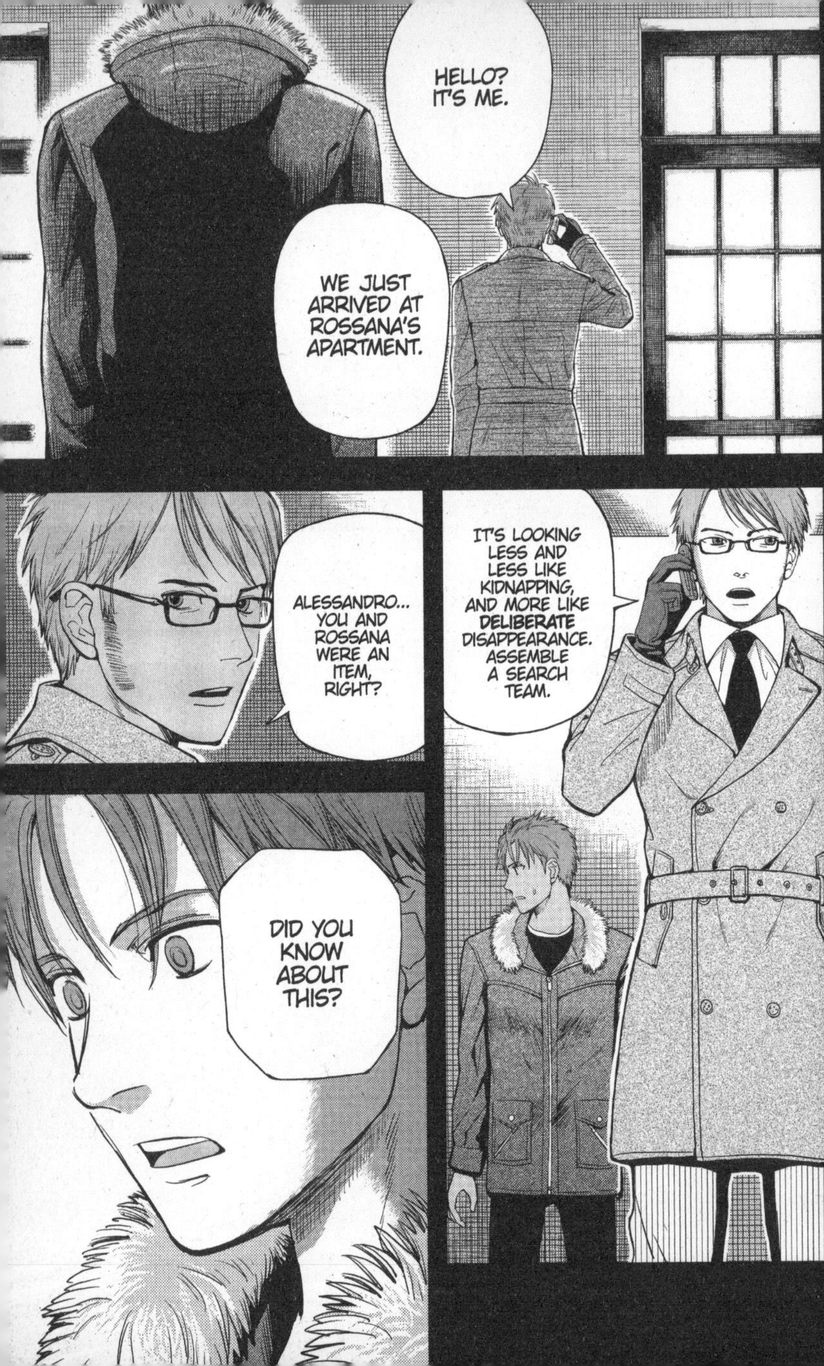
HELLO? IT'S ME.
WE JUST ARRIVED AT ROSSANA'S APARTMENT.
IT'S LOOKING LESS AND LESS LIKE KIDNAPPING, AND MORE LIKE **DELIBERATE** DISAPPEARANCE. ASSEMBLE A SEARCH TEAM.
ALESSANDRO... YOU AND ROSSANA WERE AN ITEM, RIGHT?
DID YOU KNOW ABOUT THIS?

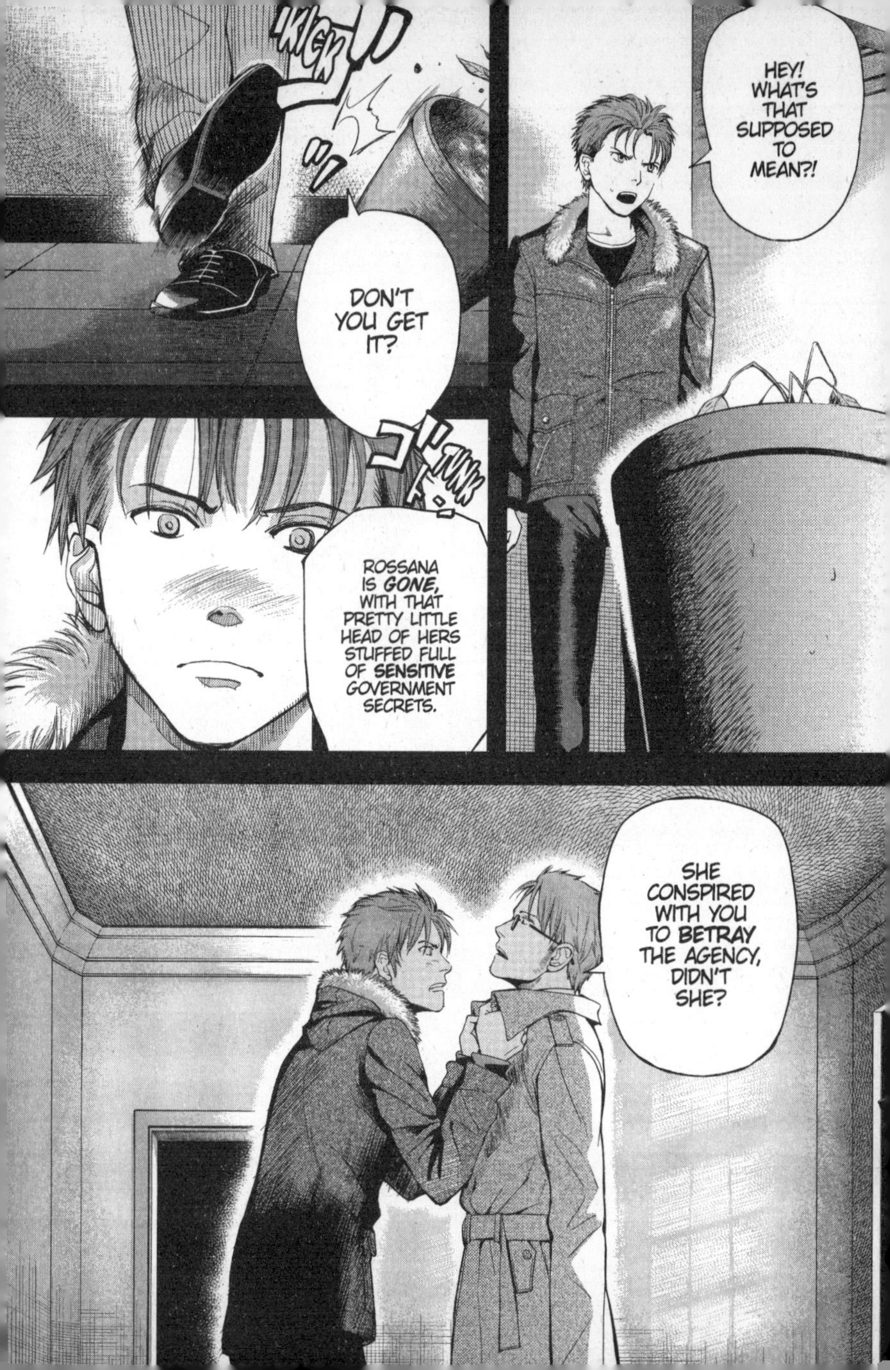
HEY! WHAT'S THAT SUPPOSED TO MEAN?!
KICK
DON'T YOU GET IT?
THUNK
ROSSANA IS **GONE**, WITH THAT PRETTY LITTLE HEAD OF HERS STUFFED FULL OF **SENSITIVE** GOVERNMENT SECRETS.
SHE CONSPIRED WITH YOU TO **BETRAY** THE AGENCY, DIDN'T SHE?

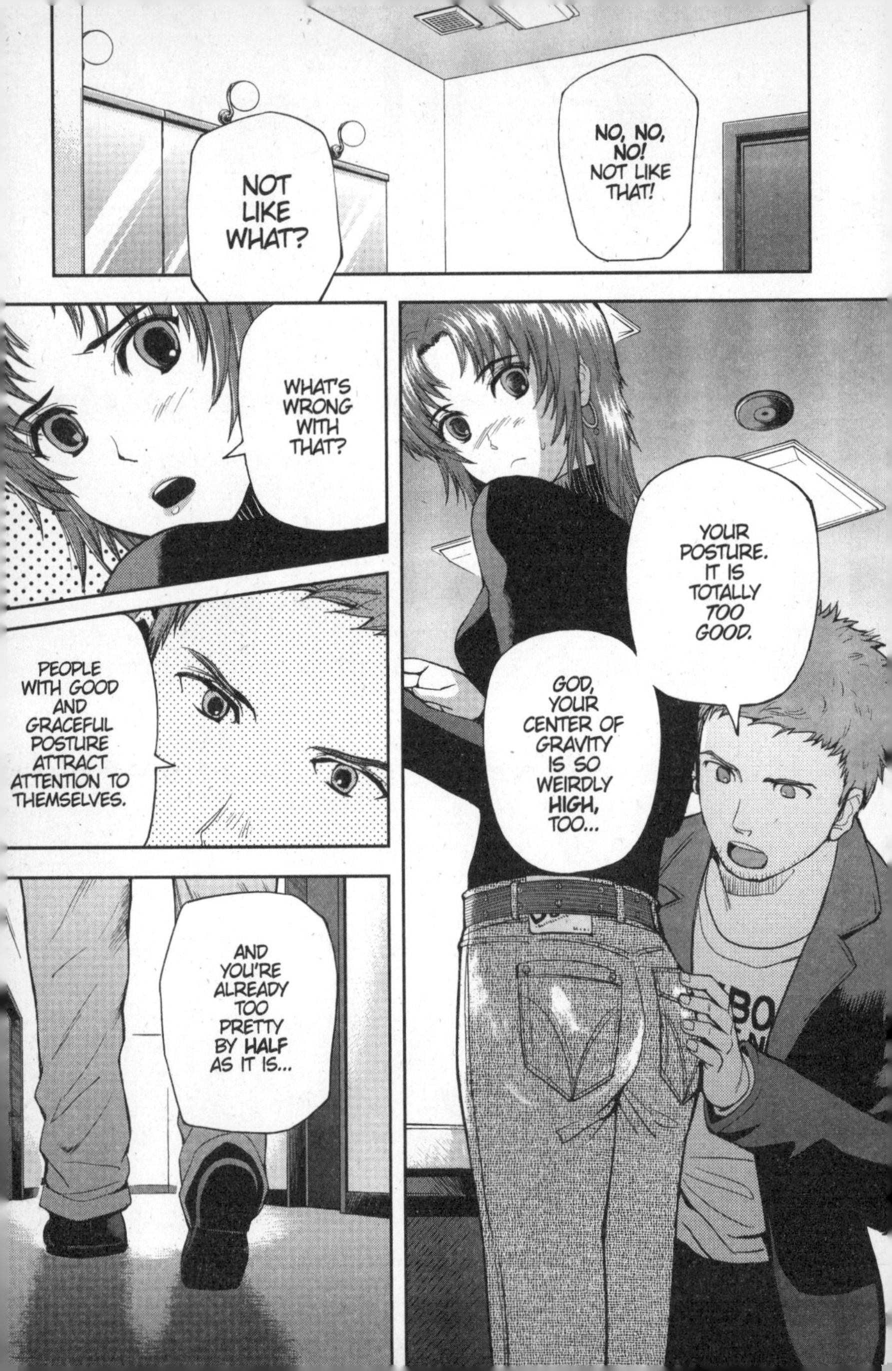
NO, NO, NO! NOT LIKE THAT!
NOT LIKE WHAT?
YOUR POSTURE. IT IS TOTALLY *TOO* GOOD.
GOD, YOUR CENTER OF GRAVITY IS SO WEIRDLY **HIGH**, TOO...
WHAT'S WRONG WITH THAT?
PEOPLE WITH GOOD AND GRACEFUL POSTURE ATTRACT ATTENTION TO THEMSELVES.
AND YOU'RE ALREADY TOO PRETTY BY **HALF** AS IT IS...

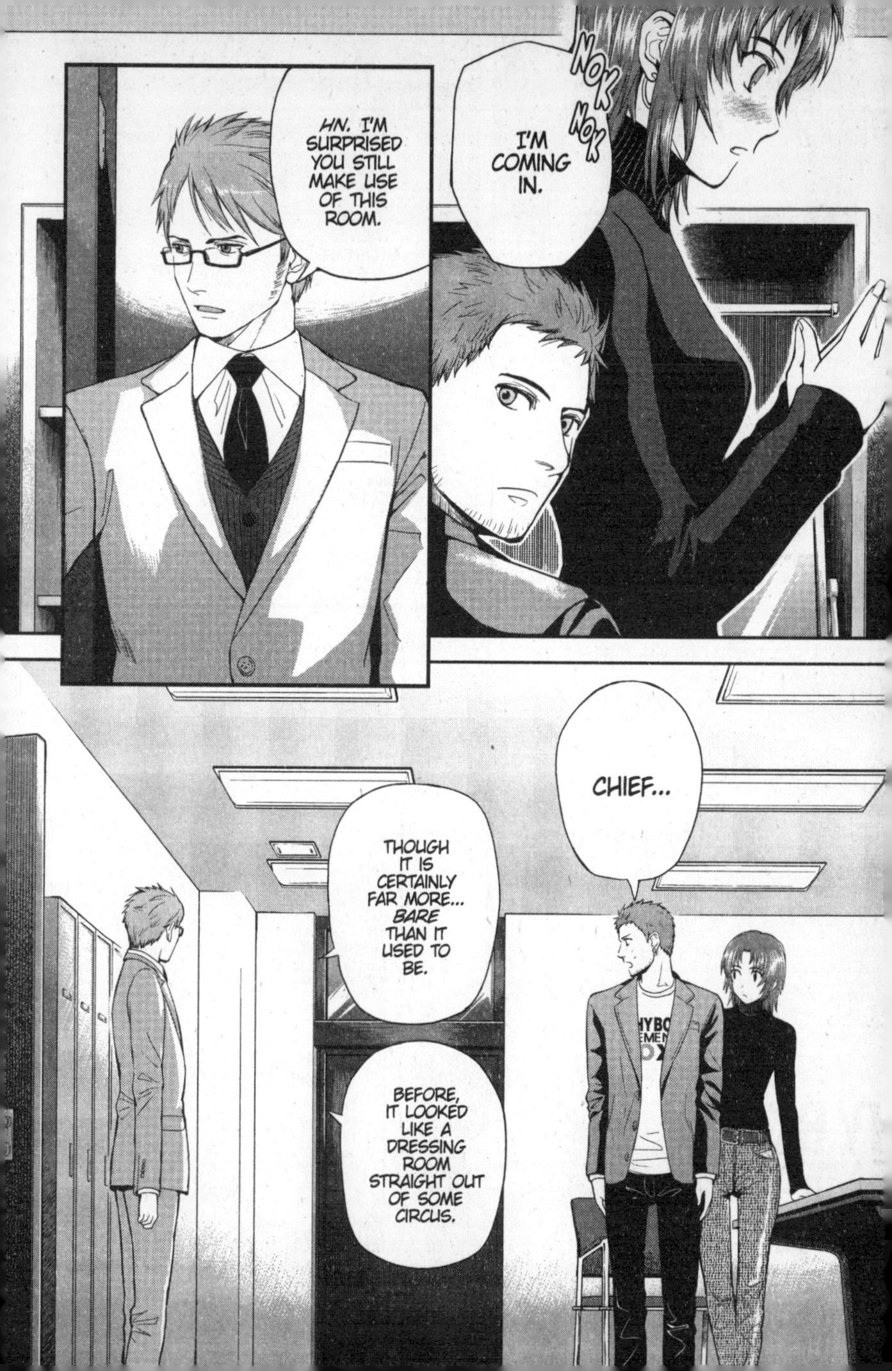
NOK NOK
I'M COMING IN.
HN. I'M SURPRISED YOU STILL MAKE USE OF THIS ROOM.
CHIEF...
THOUGH IT IS CERTAINLY FAR MORE... *BARE* THAN IT USED TO BE.
BEFORE, IT LOOKED LIKE A DRESSING ROOM STRAIGHT OUT OF SOME CIRCUS.

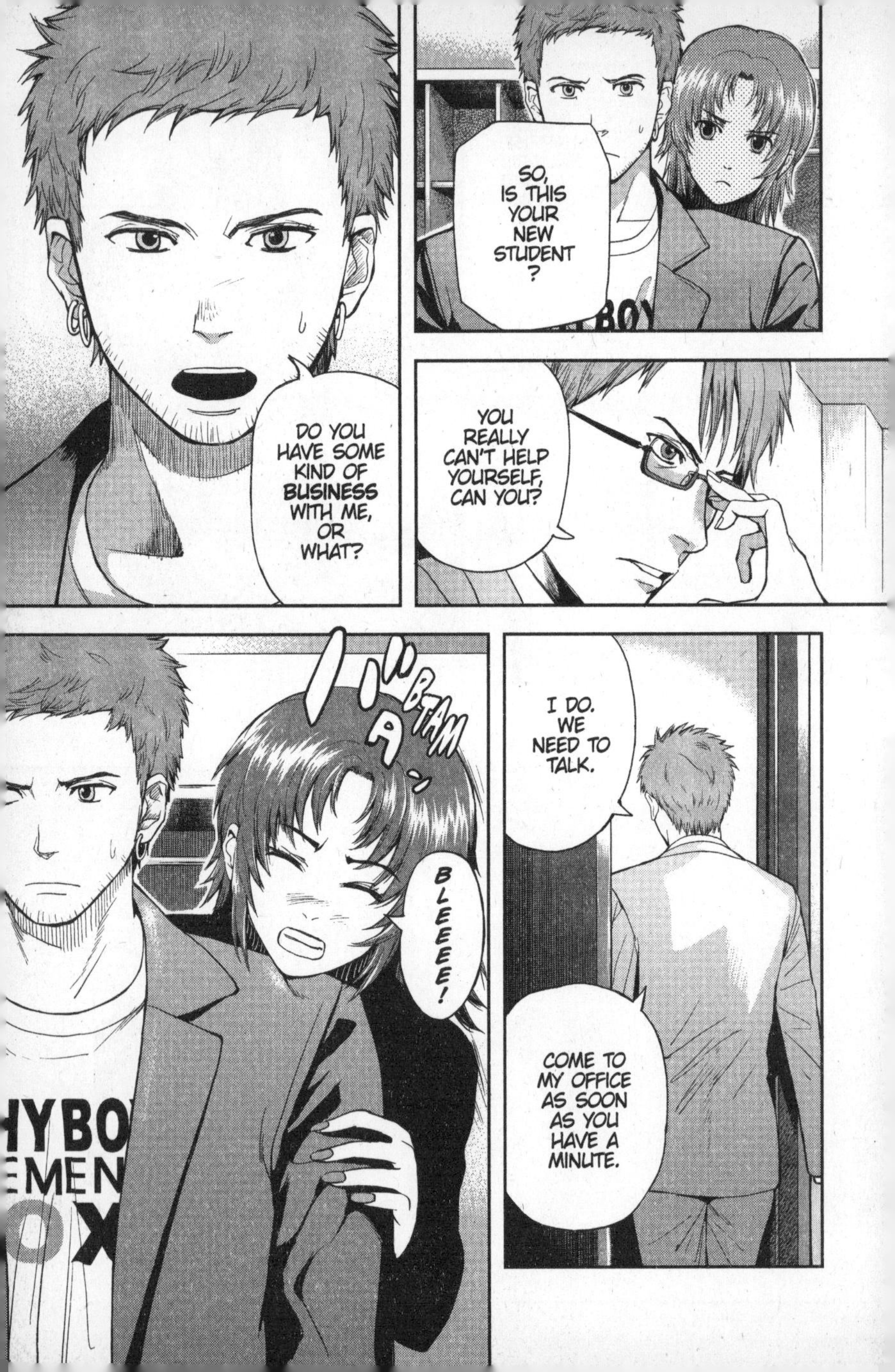
SO, IS THIS YOUR NEW STUDENT?
YOU REALLY CAN'T HELP YOURSELF, CAN YOU?
DO YOU HAVE SOME KIND OF BUSINESS WITH ME, OR WHAT?
I DO. WE NEED TO TALK.
COME TO MY OFFICE AS SOON AS YOU HAVE A MINUTE.
BLEEEEE!

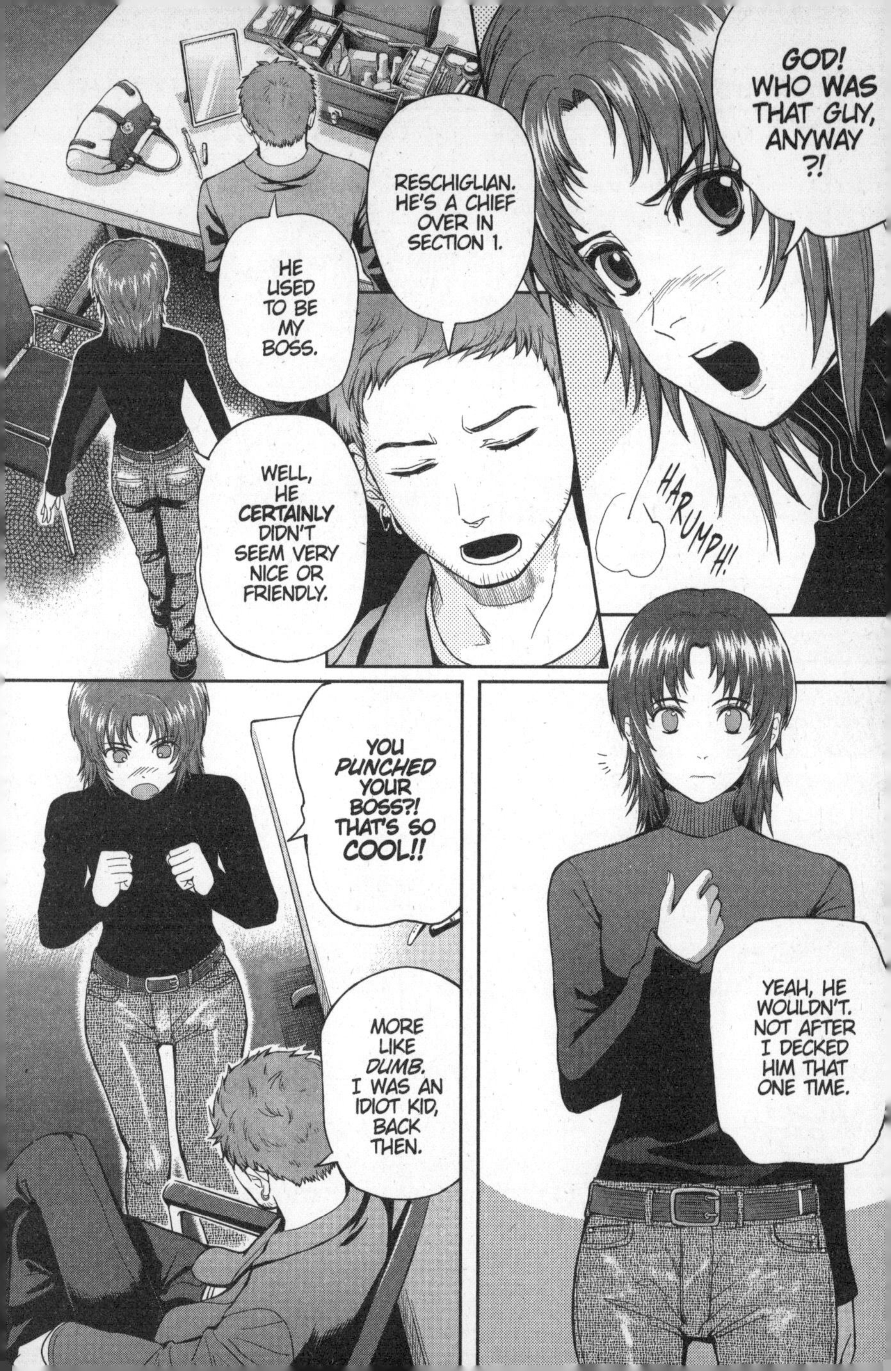
GOD! WHO WAS THAT GUY, ANYWAY?!
HARUMPH!
RESCHIGLIAN. HE'S A CHIEF OVER IN SECTION 1.
HE USED TO BE MY BOSS.
WELL, HE CERTAINLY DIDN'T SEEM VERY NICE OR FRIENDLY.
YEAH, HE WOULDN'T. NOT AFTER I DECKED HIM THAT ONE TIME.
YOU PUNCHED YOUR BOSS?! THAT'S SO COOL!!
MORE LIKE DUMB. I WAS AN IDIOT KID, BACK THEN.

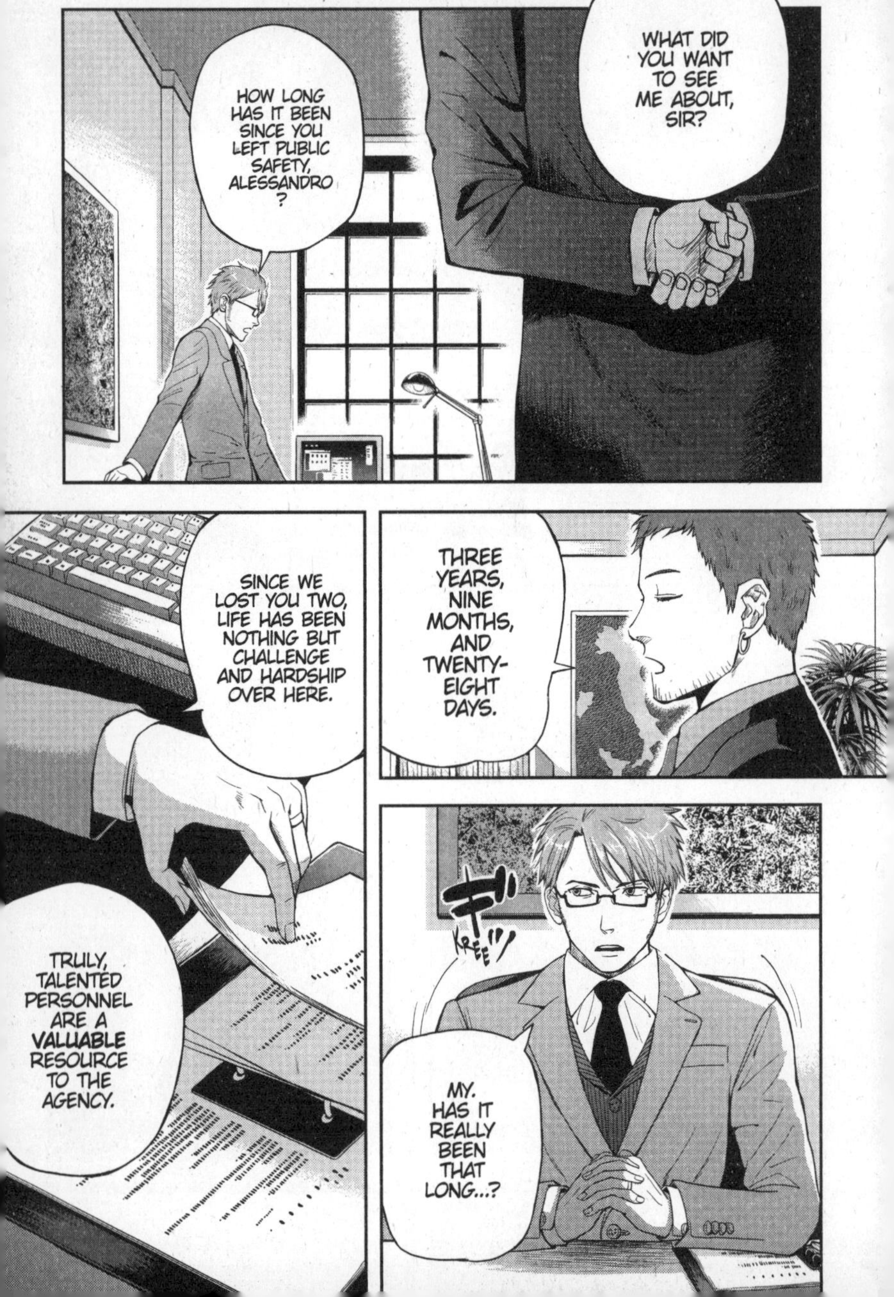
WHAT DID YOU WANT TO SEE ME ABOUT, SIR?
HOW LONG HAS IT BEEN SINCE YOU LEFT PUBLIC SAFETY, ALESSANDRO?
THREE YEARS, NINE MONTHS, AND TWENTY-EIGHT DAYS.
KREE
MY. HAS IT REALLY BEEN THAT LONG...?
SINCE WE LOST YOU TWO, LIFE HAS BEEN NOTHING BUT CHALLENGE AND HARDSHIP OVER HERE.
TRULY, TALENTED PERSONNEL ARE A VALUABLE RESOURCE TO THE AGENCY.

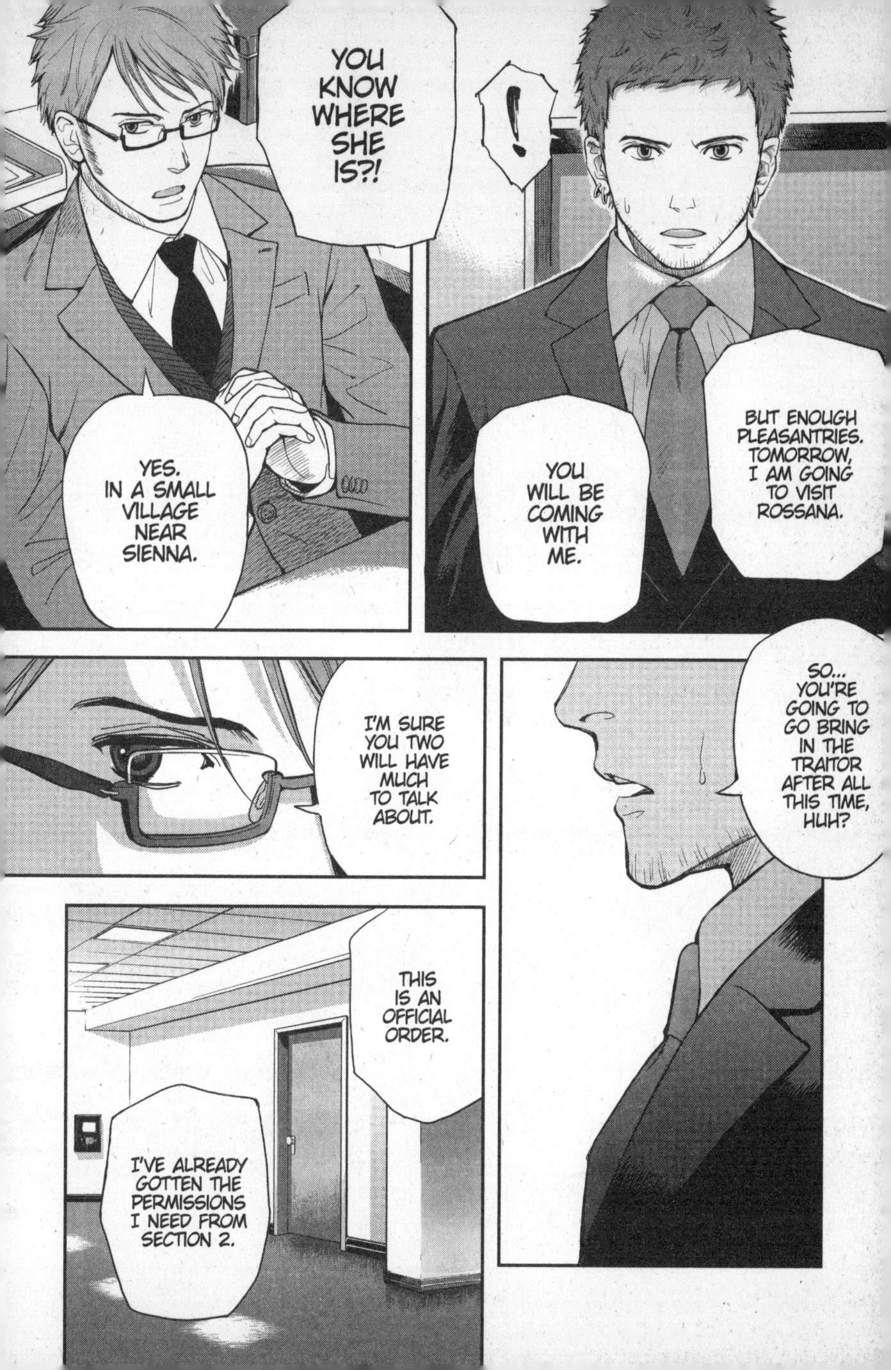
!
BUT ENOUGH PLEASANTRIES. TOMORROW, I AM GOING TO VISIT ROSSANA.
YOU WILL BE COMING WITH ME.
YOU KNOW WHERE SHE IS?!
YES. IN A SMALL VILLAGE NEAR SIENNA.
SO... YOU'RE GOING TO GO BRING IN THE TRAITOR AFTER ALL THIS TIME, HUH?
I'M SURE YOU TWO WILL HAVE MUCH TO TALK ABOUT.
THIS IS AN OFFICIAL ORDER.
I'VE ALREADY GOTTEN THE PERMISSIONS I NEED FROM SECTION 2.

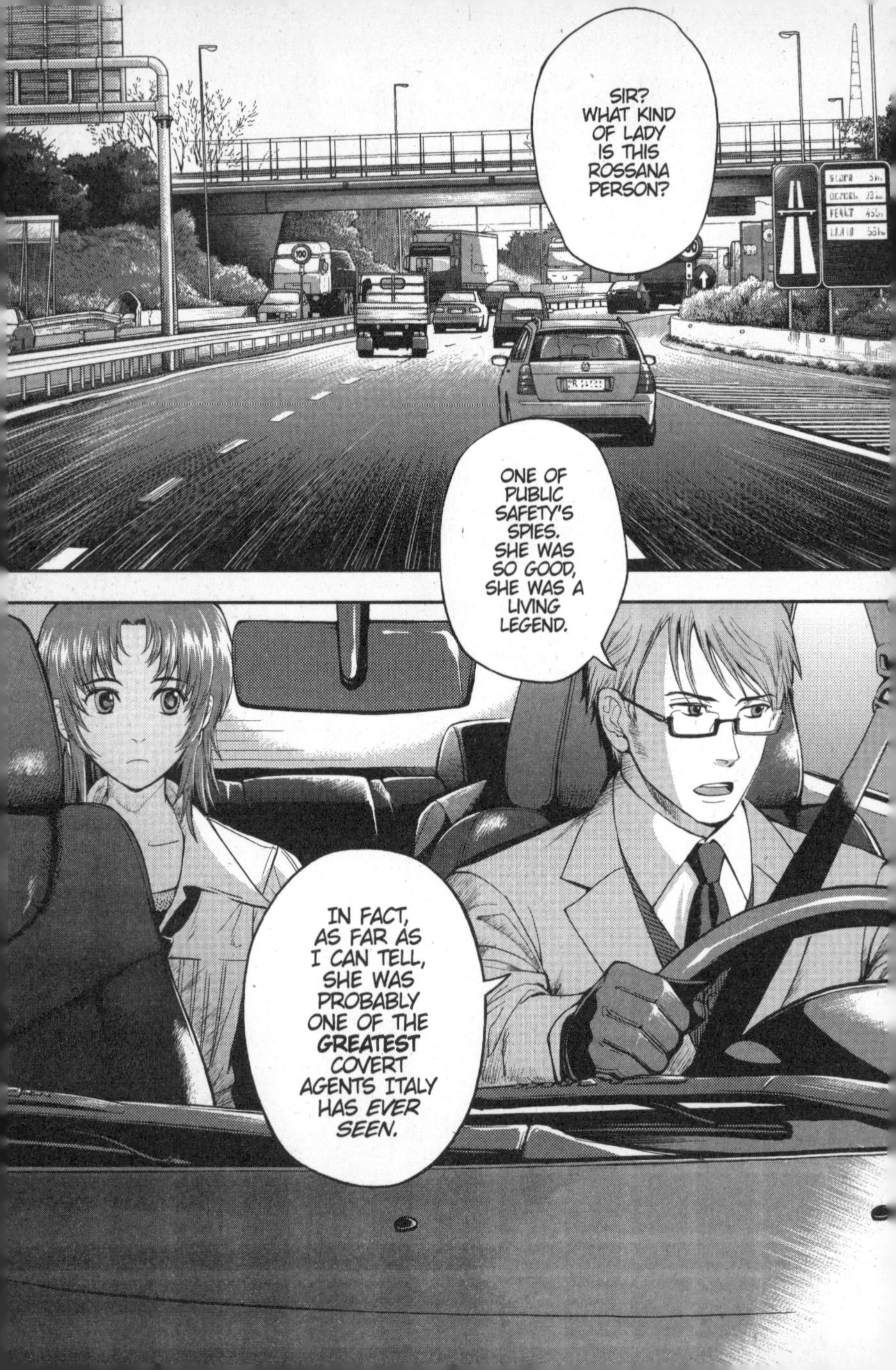
SIR? WHAT KIND OF LADY IS THIS ROSSANA PERSON?
ONE OF PUBLIC SAFETY'S SPIES. SHE WAS SO GOOD, SHE WAS A LIVING LEGEND.
IN FACT, AS FAR AS I CAN TELL, SHE WAS PROBABLY ONE OF THE **GREATEST** COVERT AGENTS ITALY HAS *EVER* SEEN.

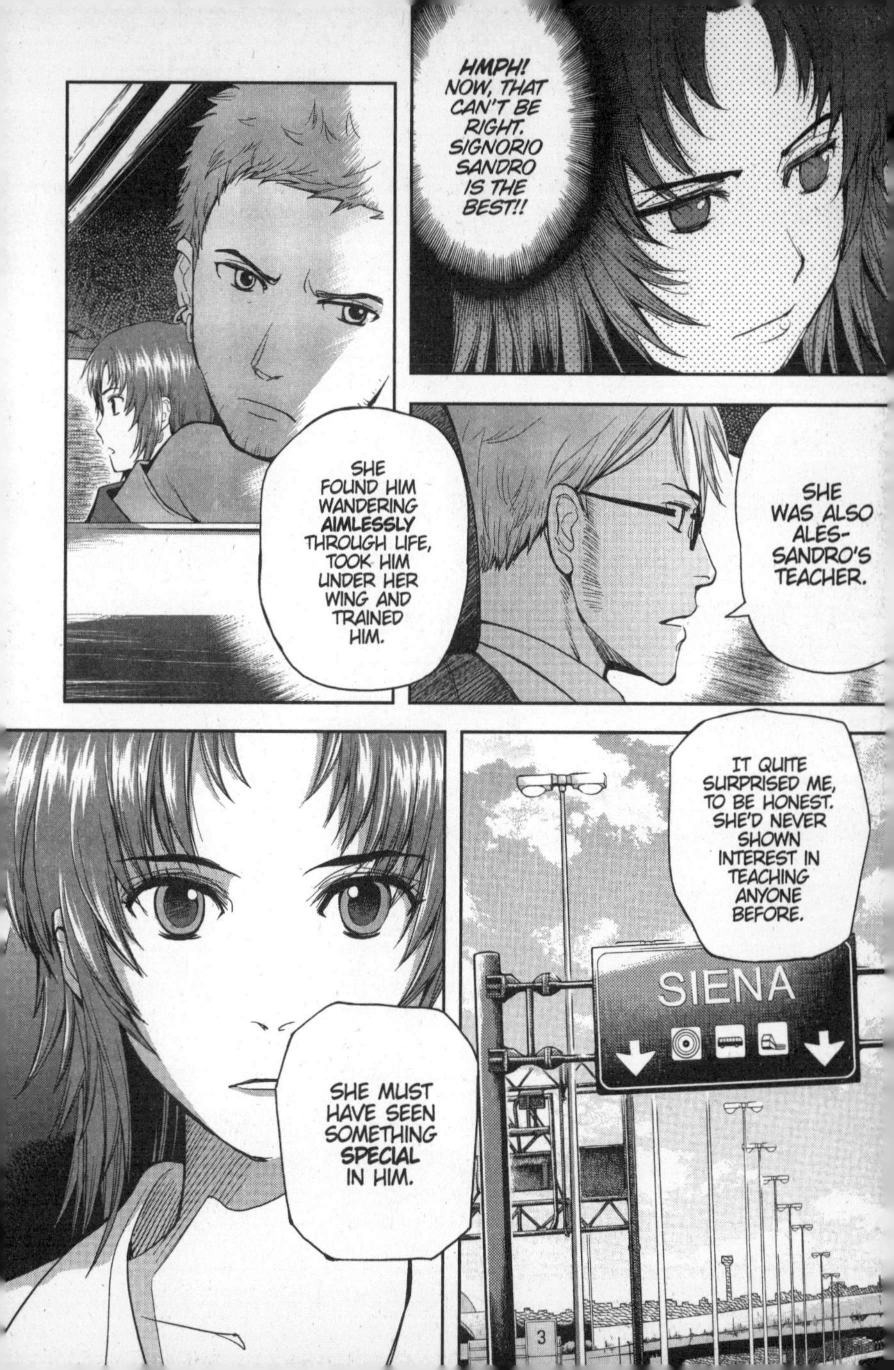
HMPH! NOW, THAT CAN'T BE RIGHT. SIGNORIO SANDRO IS THE BEST!!
SHE WAS ALSO ALES-SANDRO'S TEACHER.
SHE FOUND HIM WANDERING **AIMLESSLY** THROUGH LIFE, TOOK HIM UNDER HER WING AND TRAINED HIM.
IT QUITE SURPRISED ME, TO BE HONEST. SHE'D NEVER SHOWN INTEREST IN TEACHING ANYONE BEFORE.
SIENA
SHE MUST HAVE SEEN SOMETHING **SPECIAL** IN HIM.

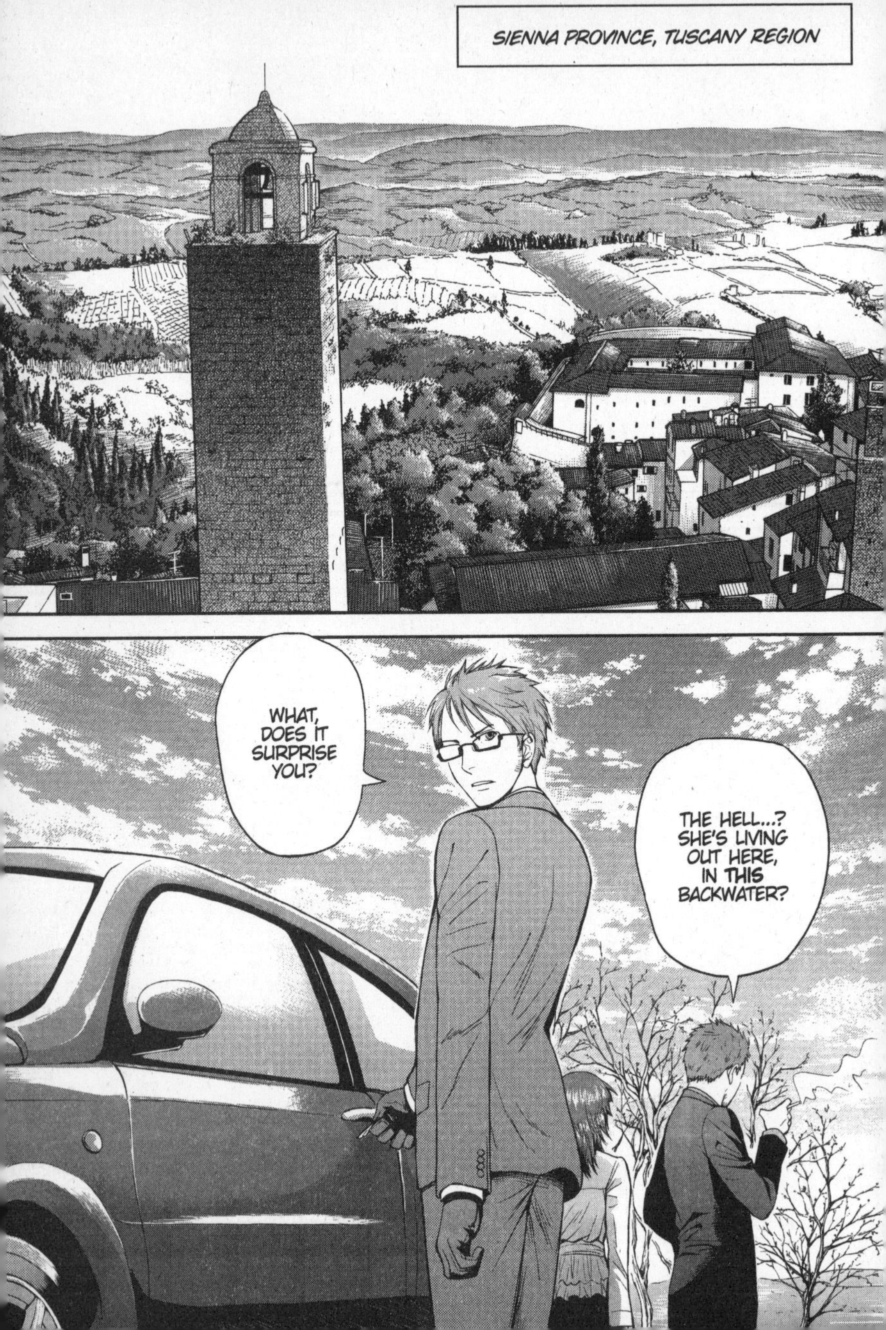
SIENNA PROVINCE, TUSCANY REGION
THE HELL...? SHE'S LIVING OUT HERE, IN THIS BACKWATER?
WHAT, DOES IT SURPRISE YOU?

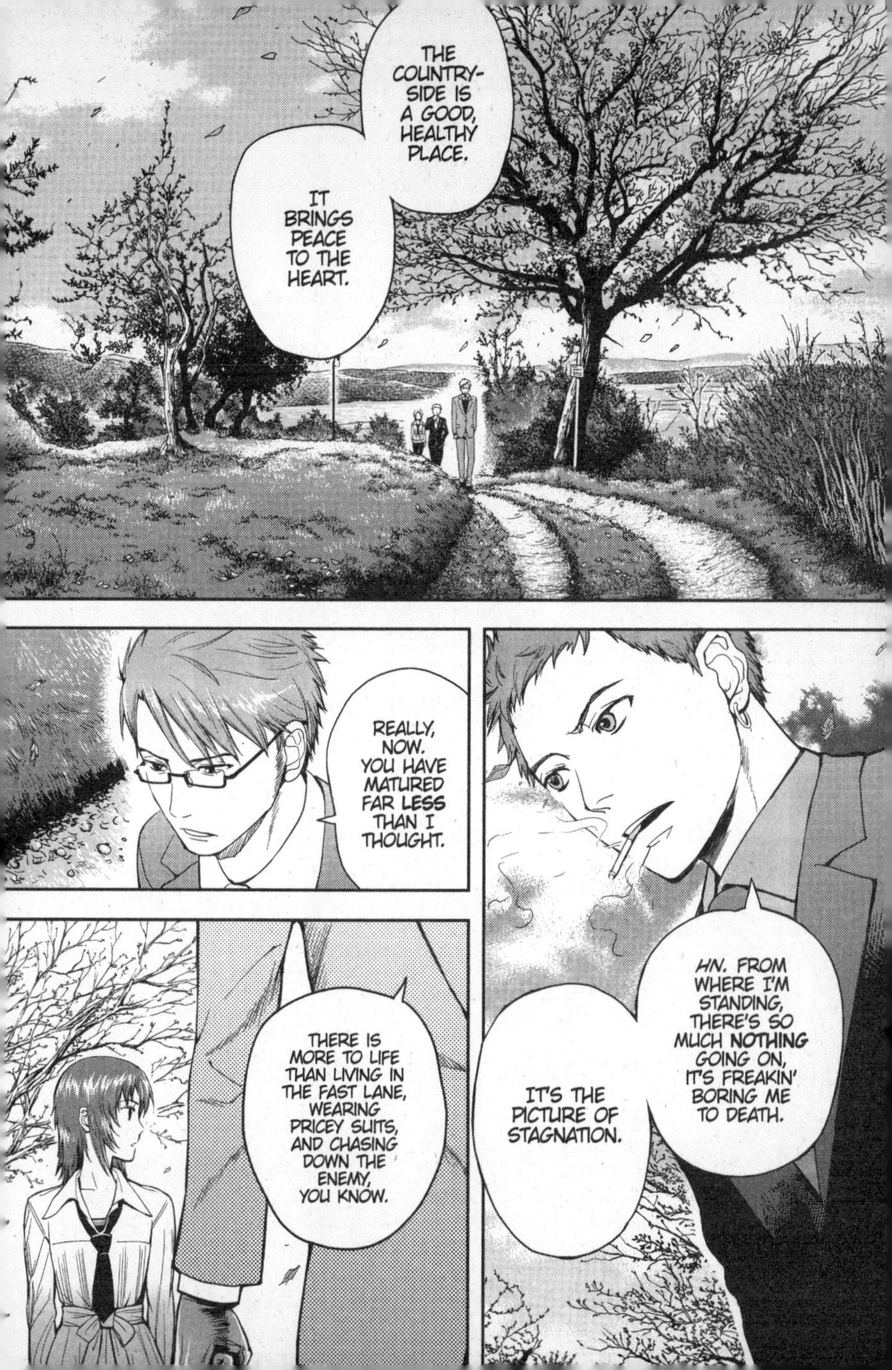
THE COUNTRY-SIDE IS A GOOD, HEALTHY PLACE.
IT BRINGS PEACE TO THE HEART.
HN. FROM WHERE I'M STANDING, THERE'S SO MUCH **NOTHING** GOING ON, IT'S FREAKIN' BORING ME TO DEATH.
IT'S THE PICTURE OF STAGNATION.
REALLY, NOW. YOU HAVE MATURED FAR **LESS** THAN I THOUGHT.
THERE IS MORE TO LIFE THAN LIVING IN THE FAST LANE, WEARING PRICEY SUITS, AND CHASING DOWN THE ENEMY, YOU KNOW.

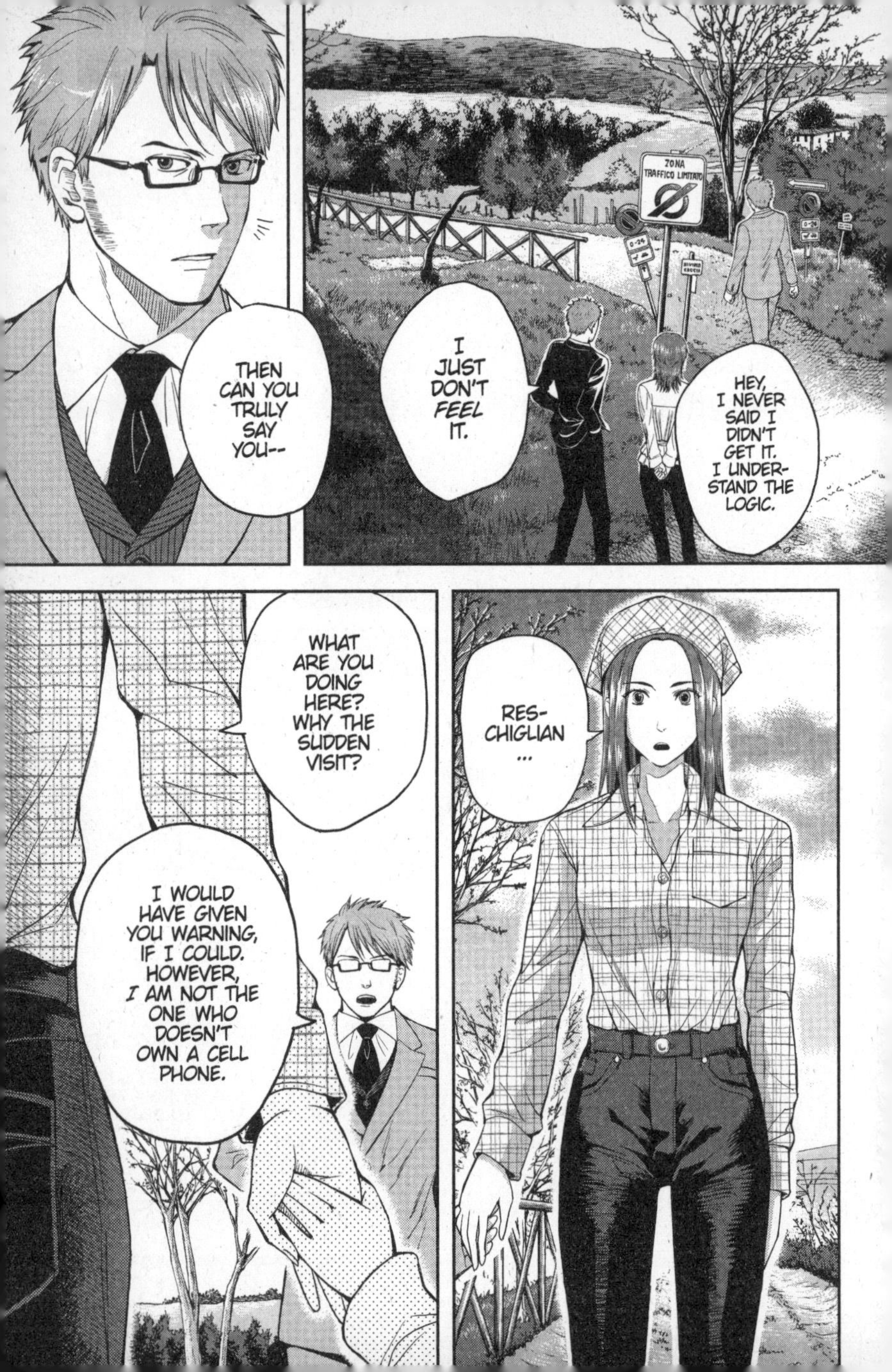
ZONA TRAFFICO LIMITATO
HEY, I NEVER SAID I DIDN'T GET IT. I UNDERSTAND THE LOGIC.
I JUST DON'T *FEEL* IT.
THEN CAN YOU TRULY SAY YOU--
RES-CHIGLIAN ...
WHAT ARE YOU DOING HERE? WHY THE SUDDEN VISIT?
I WOULD HAVE GIVEN YOU WARNING, IF I COULD. HOWEVER, *I* AM NOT THE ONE WHO DOESN'T OWN A CELL PHONE.

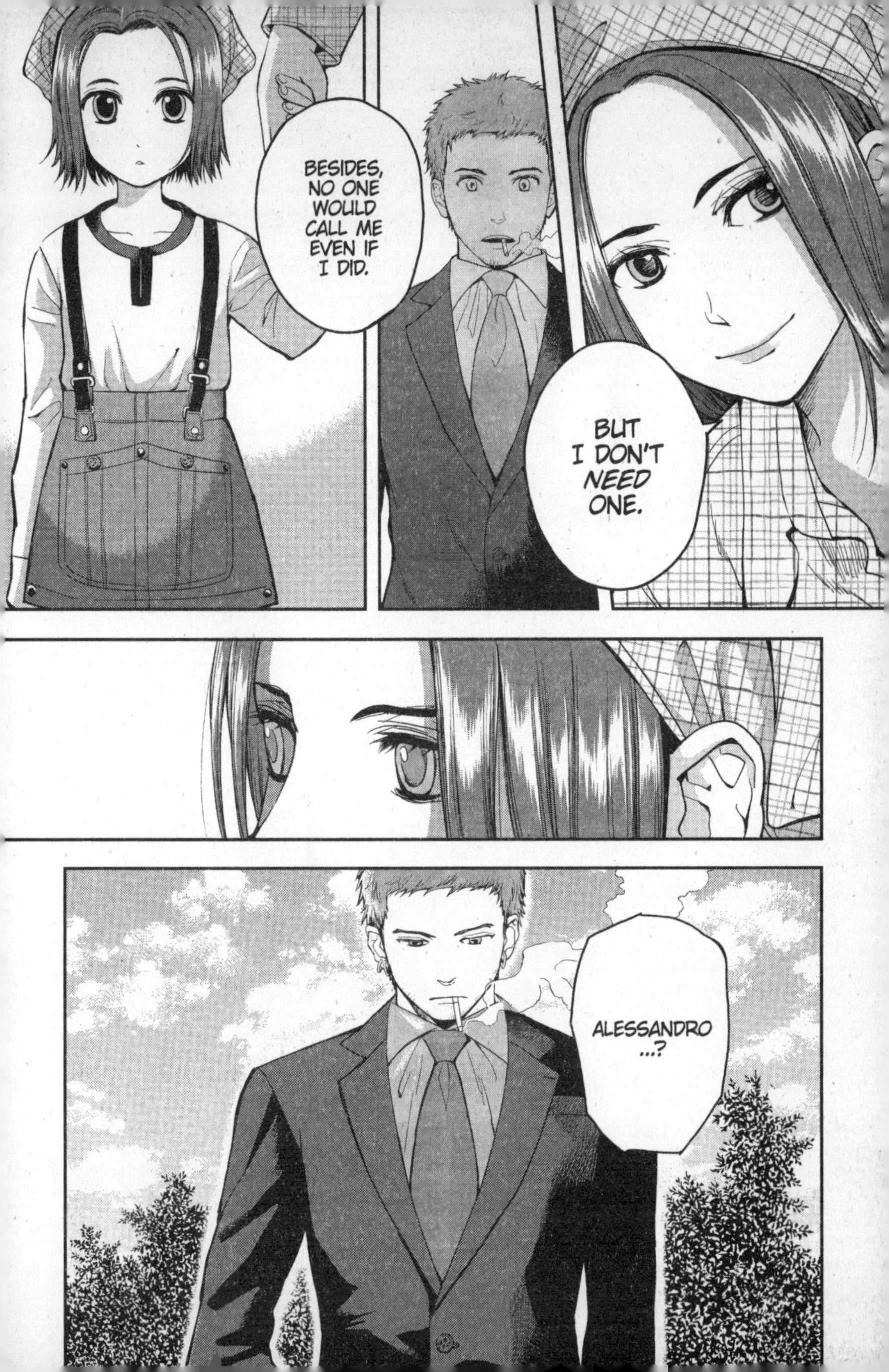
BUT I DON'T NEED ONE.
BESIDES, NO ONE WOULD CALL ME EVEN IF I DID.
ALESSANDRO ...?

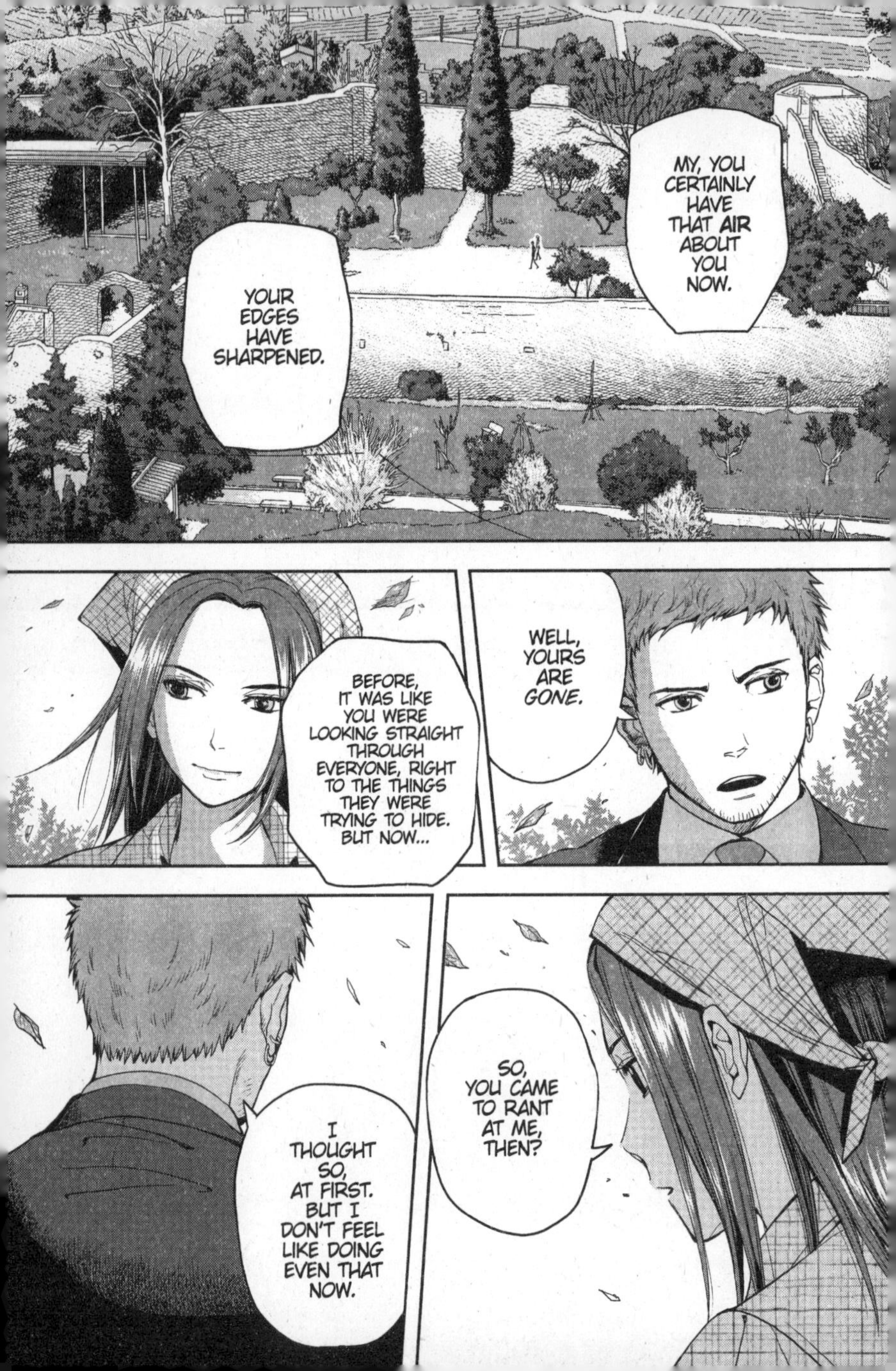
MY, YOU CERTAINLY HAVE THAT AIR ABOUT YOU NOW.
YOUR EDGES HAVE SHARPENED.
WELL, YOURS ARE GONE.
BEFORE, IT WAS LIKE YOU WERE LOOKING STRAIGHT THROUGH EVERYONE, RIGHT TO THE THINGS THEY WERE TRYING TO HIDE. BUT NOW...
SO, YOU CAME TO RANT AT ME, THEN?
I THOUGHT SO, AT FIRST. BUT I DON'T FEEL LIKE DOING EVEN THAT NOW.

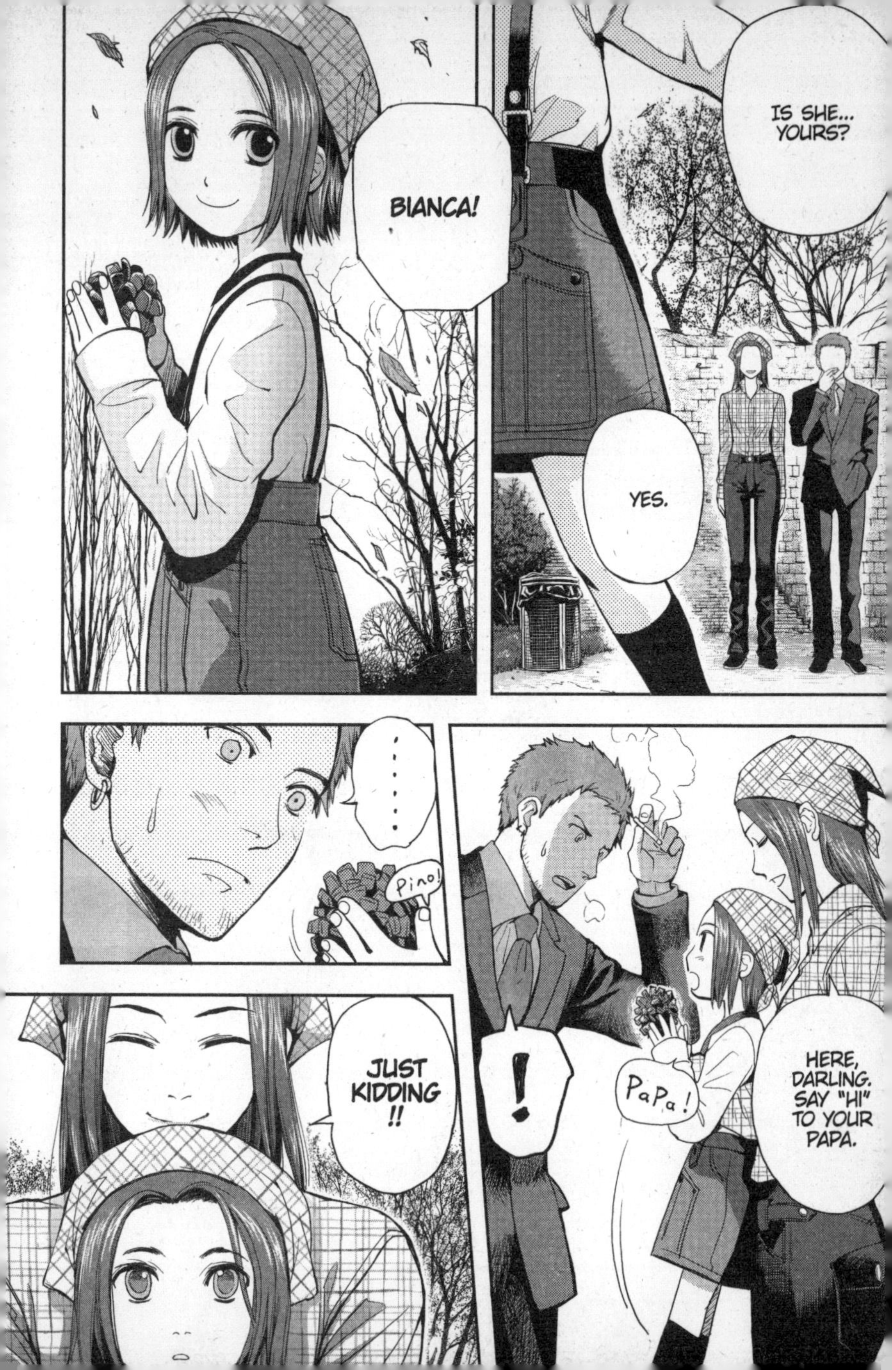
IS SHE... YOURS?
YES.
BIANCA!
HERE, DARLING. SAY "HI" TO YOUR PAPA.
PaPa!
!
......
Pino!
JUST KIDDING!!

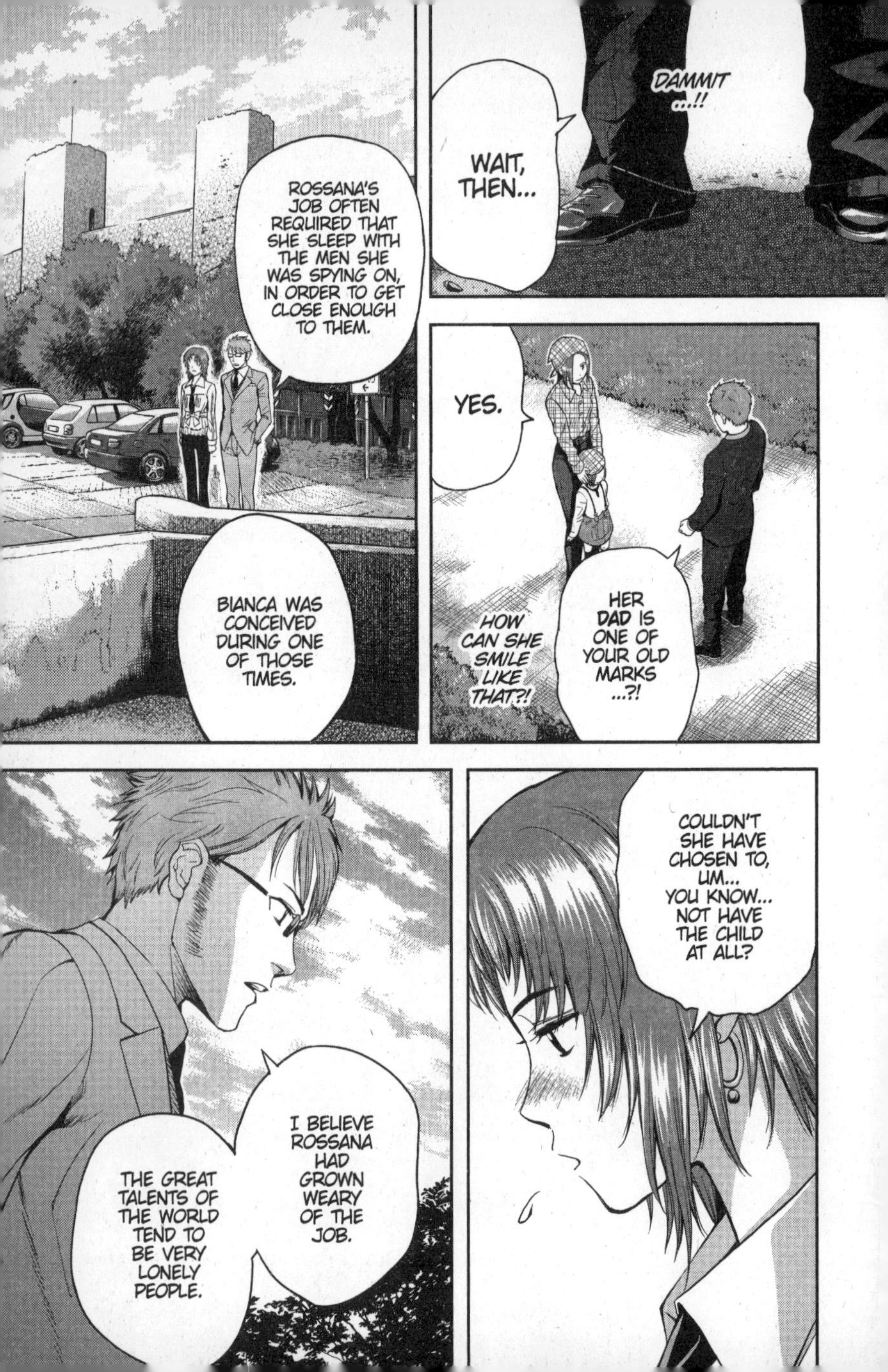
DAMMIT ...!!
WAIT, THEN...
YES.
HER DAD IS ONE OF YOUR OLD MARKS ...?!
HOW CAN SHE SMILE LIKE THAT?!
ROSSANA'S JOB OFTEN REQUIRED THAT SHE SLEEP WITH THE MEN SHE WAS SPYING ON, IN ORDER TO GET CLOSE ENOUGH TO THEM.
BIANCA WAS CONCEIVED DURING ONE OF THOSE TIMES.
COULDN'T SHE HAVE CHOSEN TO, UM... YOU KNOW... NOT HAVE THE CHILD AT ALL?
I BELIEVE ROSSANA HAD GROWN WEARY OF THE JOB.
THE GREAT TALENTS OF THE WORLD TEND TO BE VERY LONELY PEOPLE.

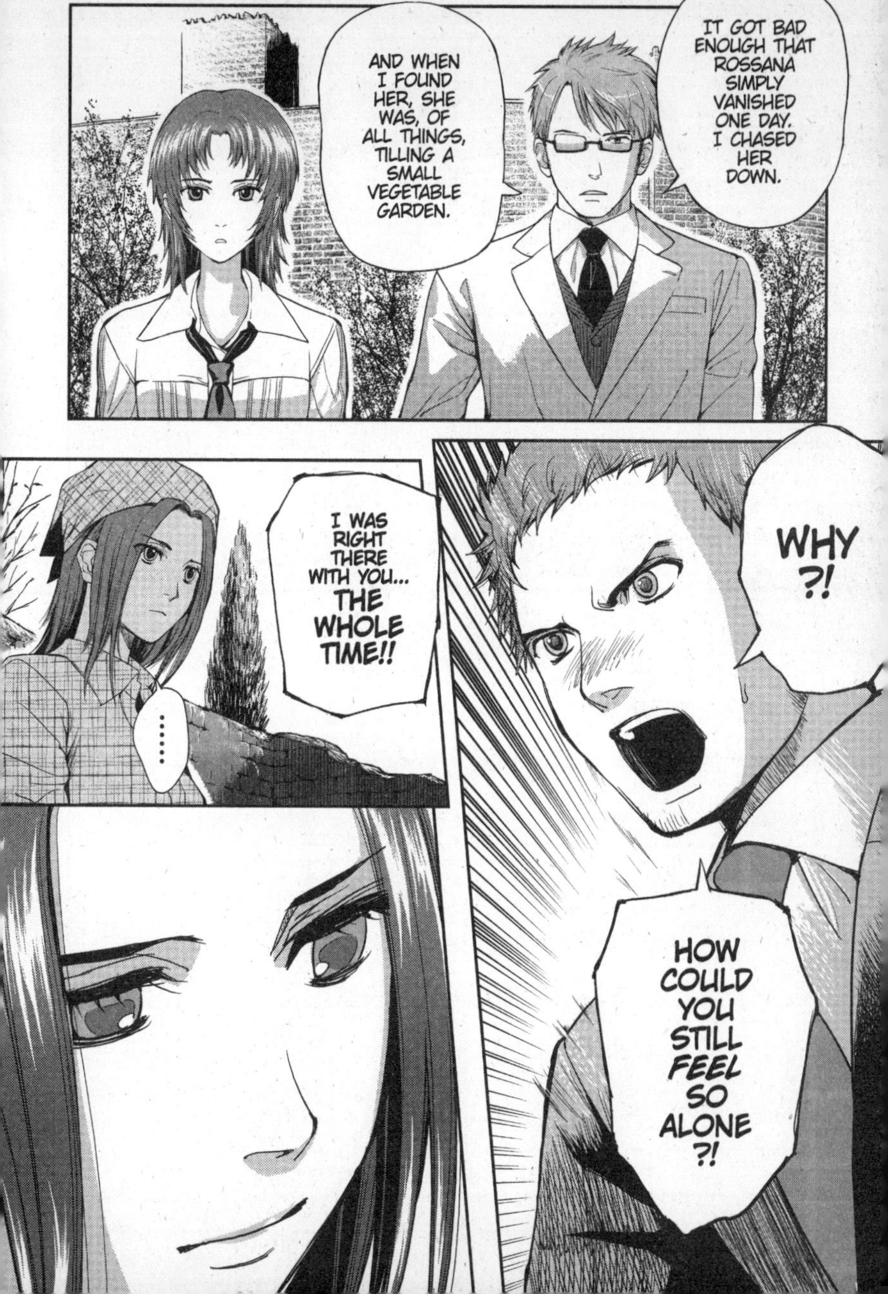
IT GOT BAD ENOUGH THAT ROSSANA SIMPLY VANISHED ONE DAY. I CHASED HER DOWN.
AND WHEN I FOUND HER, SHE WAS, OF ALL THINGS, TILLING A SMALL VEGETABLE GARDEN.
WHY ?!
HOW COULD YOU STILL *FEEL* SO ALONE ?!
I WAS RIGHT THERE WITH YOU... **THE WHOLE TIME!!**
......

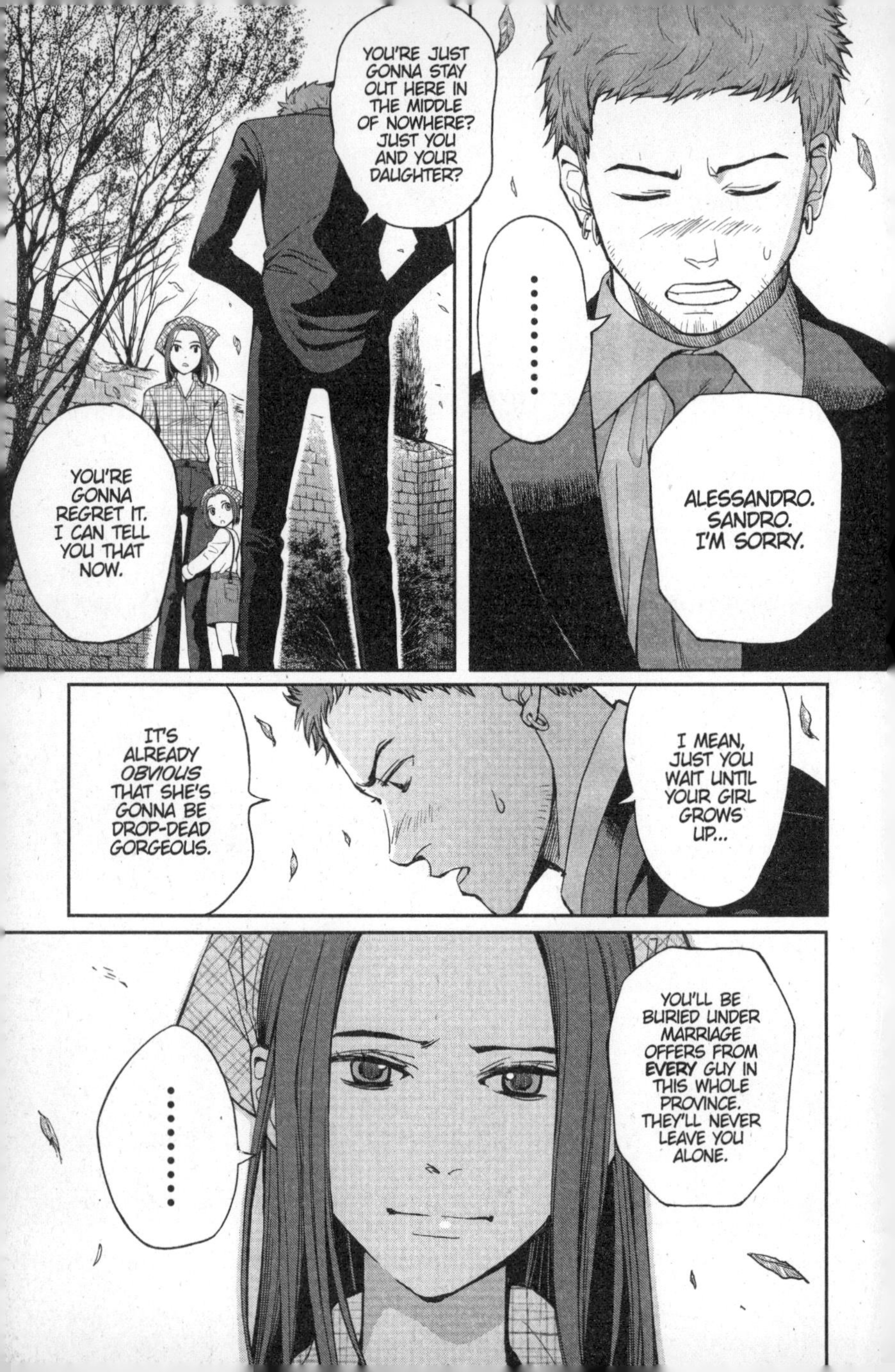
......
ALESSANDRO. SANDRO. I'M SORRY.
YOU'RE JUST GONNA STAY OUT HERE IN THE MIDDLE OF NOWHERE? JUST YOU AND YOUR DAUGHTER?
YOU'RE GONNA REGRET IT. I CAN TELL YOU THAT NOW.
I MEAN, JUST YOU WAIT UNTIL YOUR GIRL GROWS UP...
IT'S ALREADY *OBVIOUS* THAT SHE'S GONNA BE DROP-DEAD GORGEOUS.
YOU'LL BE BURIED UNDER MARRIAGE OFFERS FROM **EVERY** GUY IN THIS WHOLE PROVINCE. THEY'LL NEVER LEAVE YOU ALONE.
......

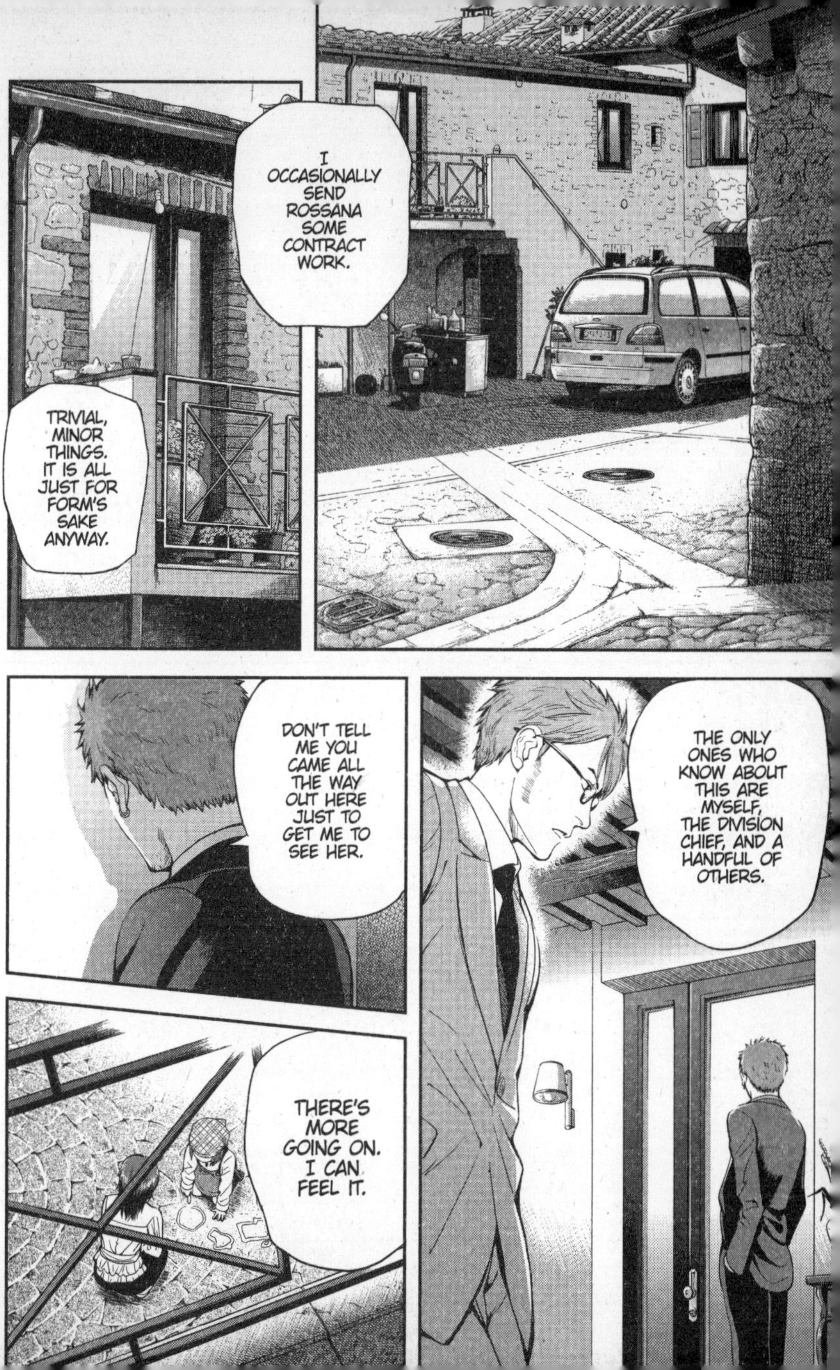
I OCCASIONALLY SEND ROSSANA SOME CONTRACT WORK.
TRIVIAL, MINOR THINGS. IT IS ALL JUST FOR FORM'S SAKE ANYWAY.
THE ONLY ONES WHO KNOW ABOUT THIS ARE MYSELF, THE DIVISION CHIEF, AND A HANDFUL OF OTHERS.
DON'T TELL ME YOU CAME ALL THE WAY OUT HERE JUST TO GET ME TO SEE HER.
THERE'S MORE GOING ON. I CAN FEEL IT.

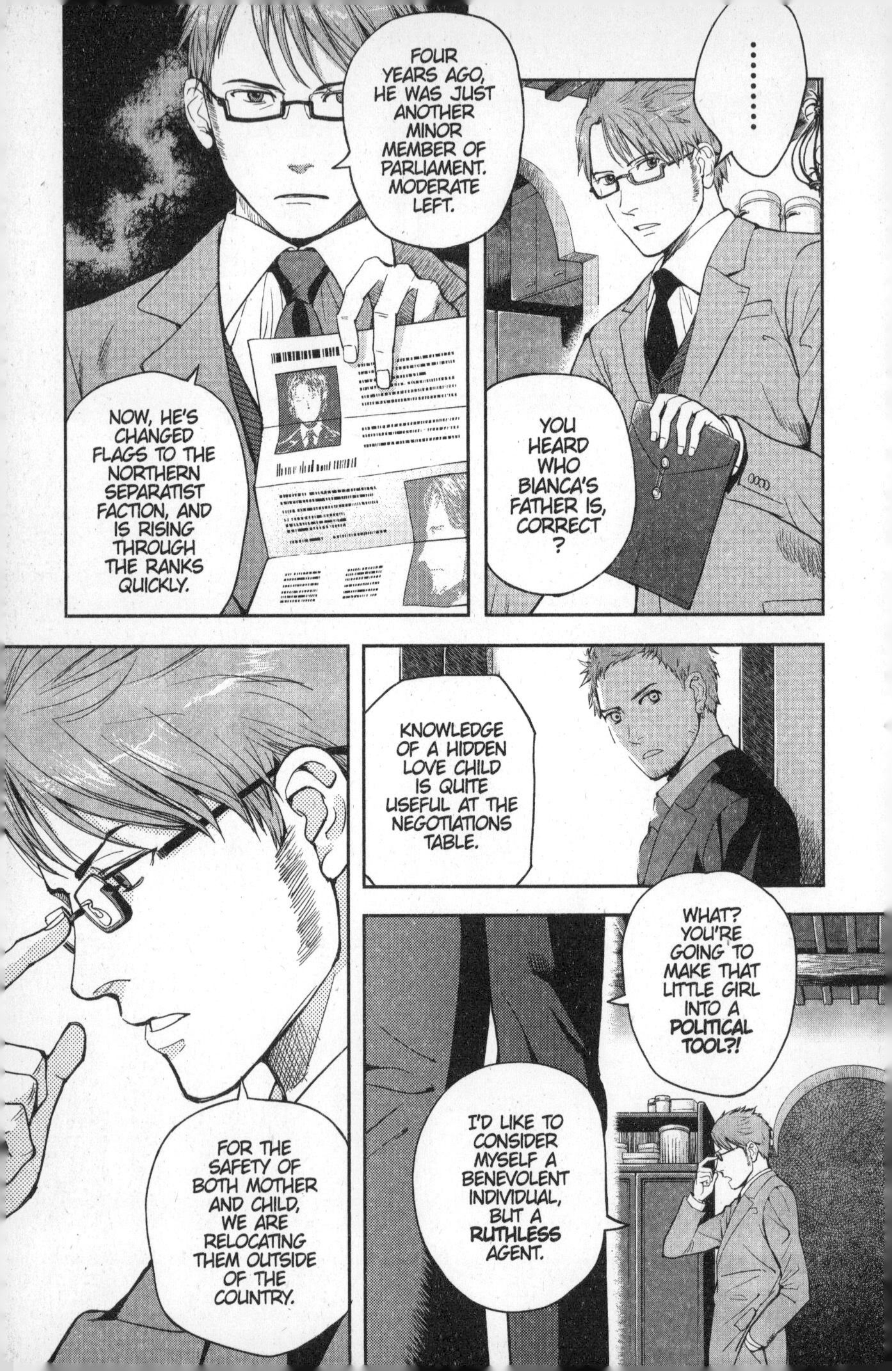
……
YOU HEARD WHO BIANCA'S FATHER IS, CORRECT?
FOUR YEARS AGO, HE WAS JUST ANOTHER MINOR MEMBER OF PARLIAMENT. MODERATE LEFT.
NOW, HE'S CHANGED FLAGS TO THE NORTHERN SEPARATIST FACTION, AND IS RISING THROUGH THE RANKS QUICKLY.
KNOWLEDGE OF A HIDDEN LOVE CHILD IS QUITE USEFUL AT THE NEGOTIATIONS TABLE.
WHAT? YOU'RE GOING TO MAKE THAT LITTLE GIRL INTO A POLITICAL TOOL?!
I'D LIKE TO CONSIDER MYSELF A BENEVOLENT INDIVIDUAL, BUT A RUTHLESS AGENT.
FOR THE SAFETY OF BOTH MOTHER AND CHILD, WE ARE RELOCATING THEM OUTSIDE OF THE COUNTRY.

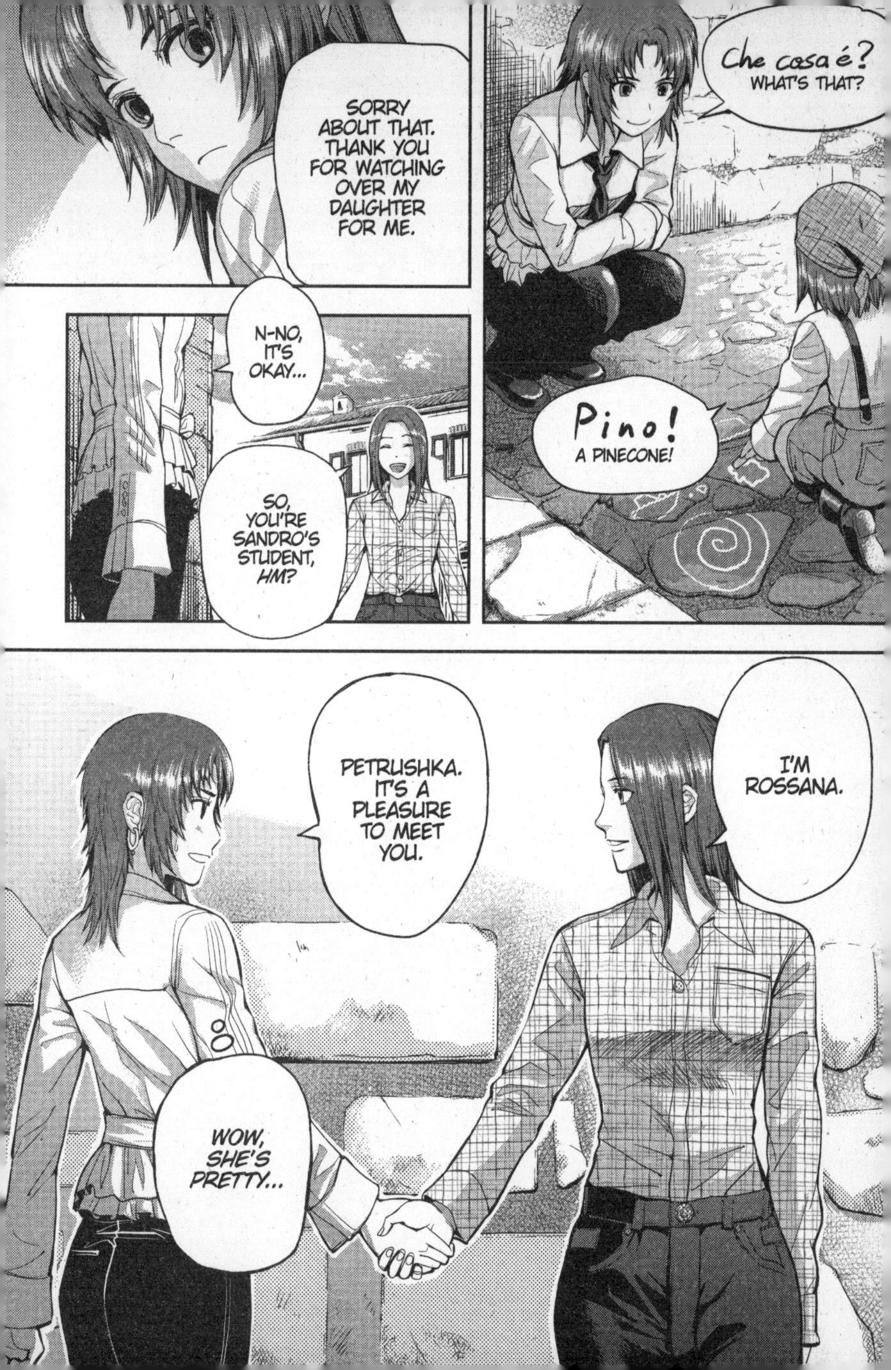
Che cosa é? WHAT'S THAT?
Pino! A PINECONE!
SORRY ABOUT THAT. THANK YOU FOR WATCHING OVER MY DAUGHTER FOR ME.
N-NO, IT'S OKAY...
SO, YOU'RE SANDRO'S STUDENT, HM?
I'M ROSSANA.
PETRUSHKA. IT'S A PLEASURE TO MEET YOU.
WOW, SHE'S PRETTY...

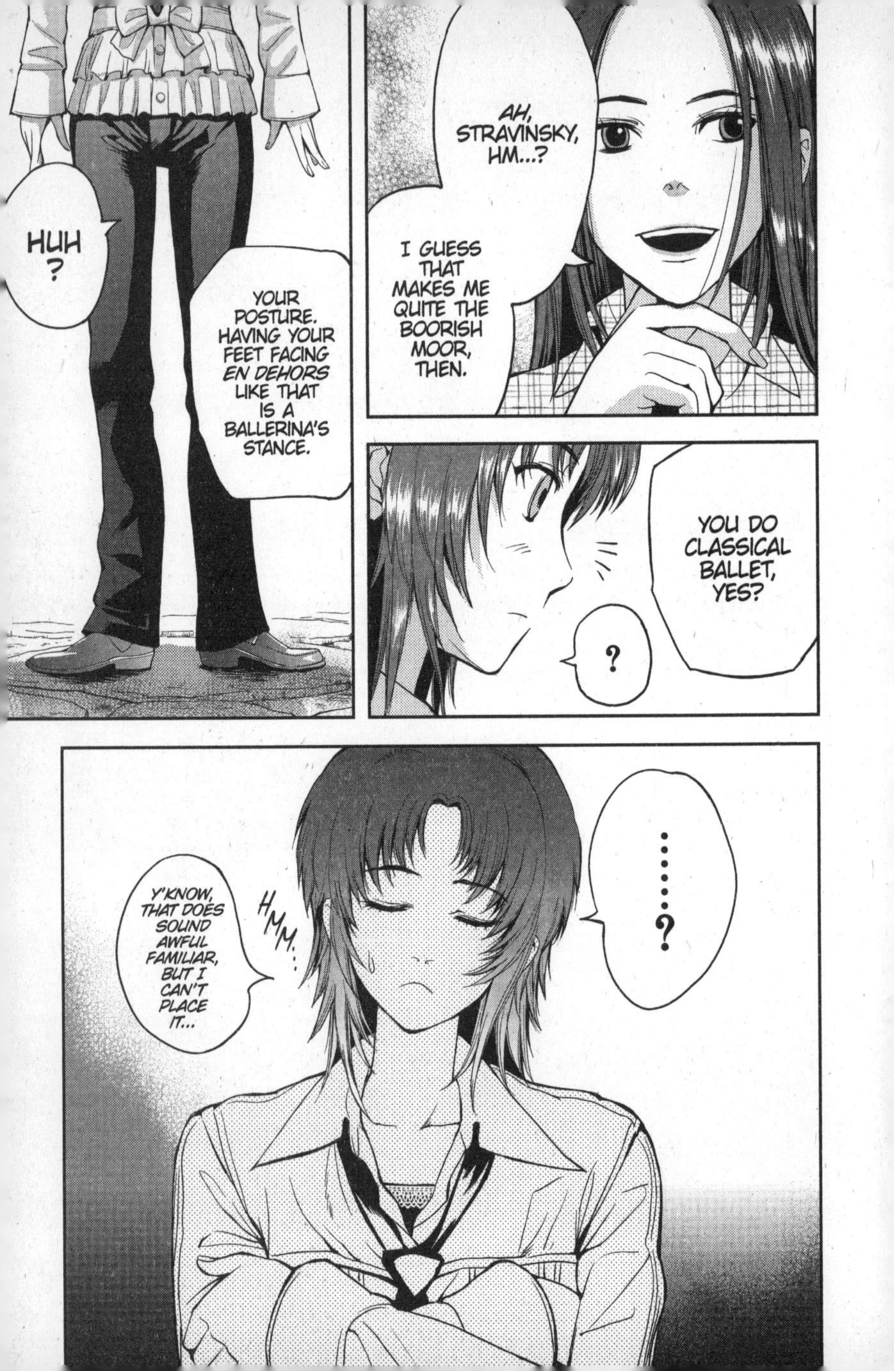
AH, STRAVINSKY, HM...?
I GUESS THAT MAKES ME QUITE THE BOORISH MOOR, THEN.
YOU DO CLASSICAL BALLET, YES?
?
HUH ?
YOUR POSTURE. HAVING YOUR FEET FACING EN DEHORS LIKE THAT IS A BALLERINA'S STANCE.
......?
HMM...
Y'KNOW, THAT DOES SOUND AWFUL FAMILIAR, BUT I CAN'T PLACE IT...

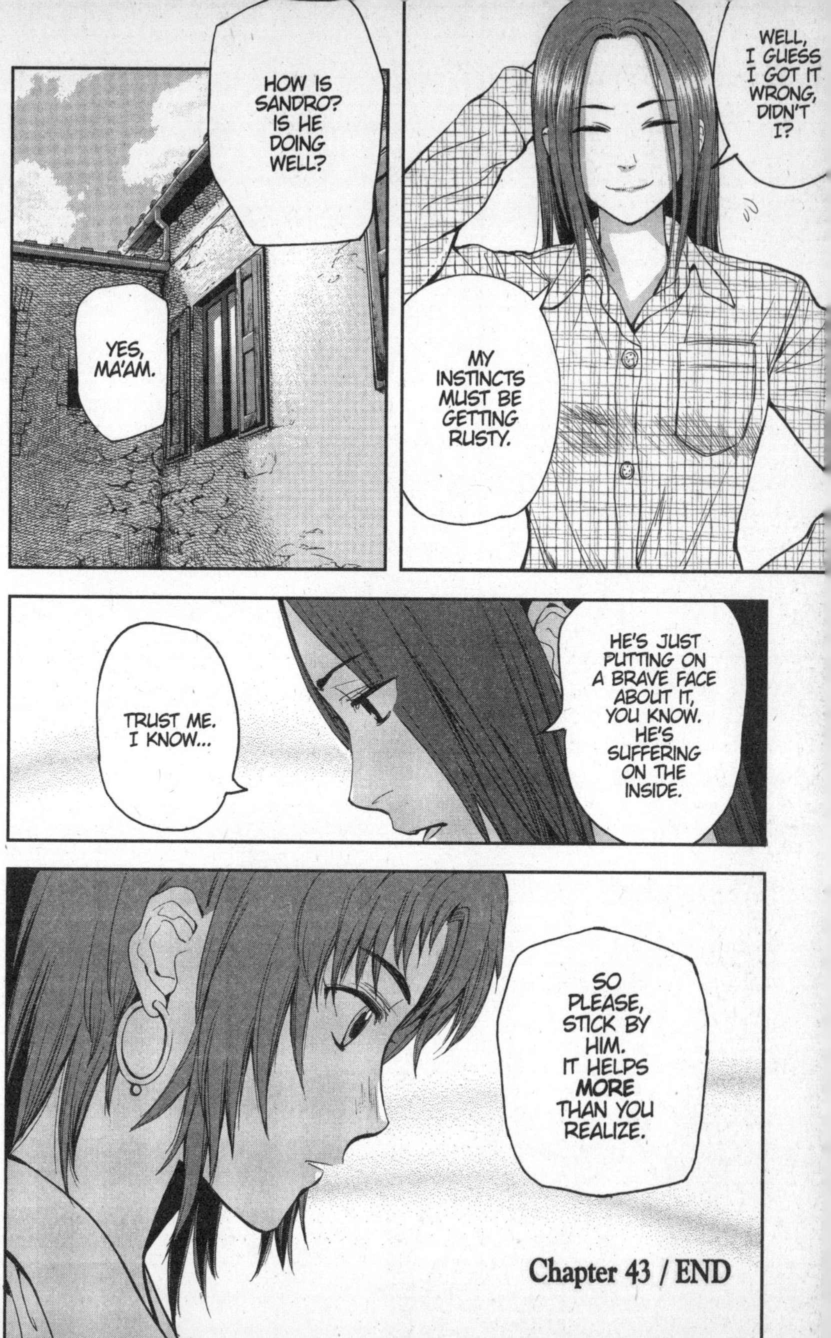
WELL, I GUESS I GOT IT WRONG, DIDN'T I?
MY INSTINCTS MUST BE GETTING RUSTY.
HOW IS SANDRO? IS HE DOING WELL?
YES, MA'AM.
HE'S JUST PUTTING ON A BRAVE FACE ABOUT IT, YOU KNOW. HE'S SUFFERING ON THE INSIDE.
TRUST ME. I KNOW...
SO PLEASE, STICK BY HIM. IT HELPS **MORE** THAN YOU REALIZE.

Chapter 43 / END

CHAPTER 44: LADY ROSSO (5)

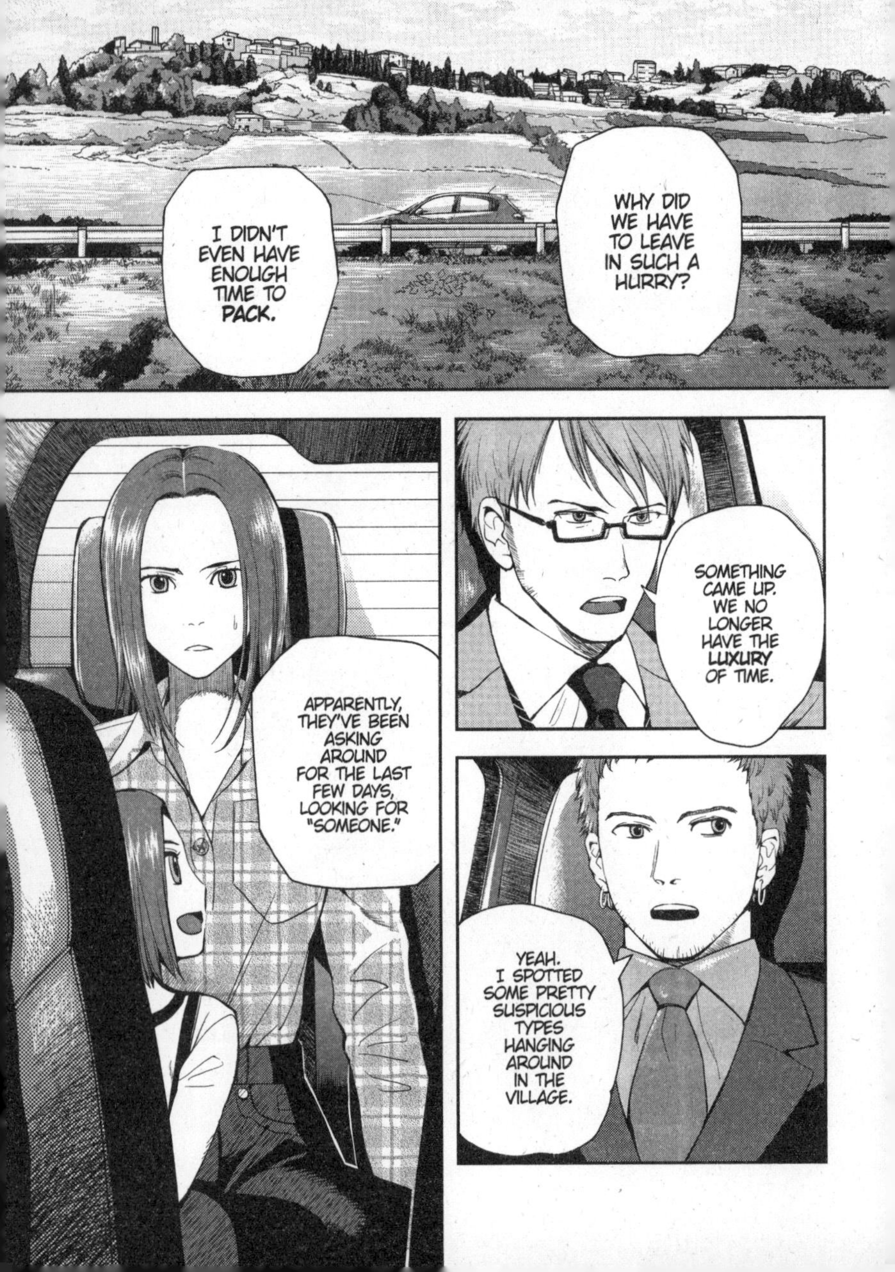
WHY DID WE HAVE TO LEAVE IN SUCH A HURRY?
I DIDN'T EVEN HAVE ENOUGH TIME TO PACK.
SOMETHING CAME UP. WE NO LONGER HAVE THE LUXURY OF TIME.
YEAH. I SPOTTED SOME PRETTY SUSPICIOUS TYPES HANGING AROUND IN THE VILLAGE.
APPARENTLY, THEY'VE BEEN ASKING AROUND FOR THE LAST FEW DAYS, LOOKING FOR "SOMEONE."

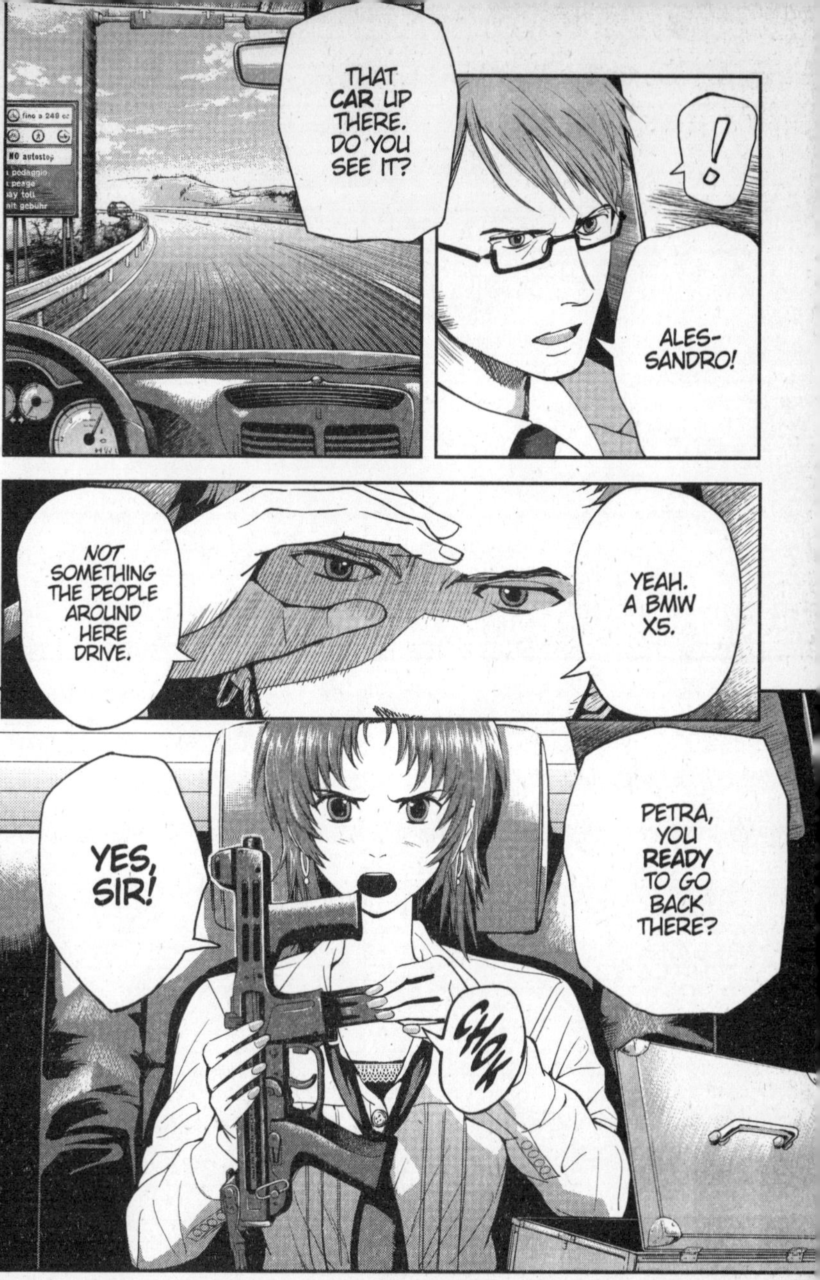
!
ALES-SANDRO!
fino a 249 cc
NO autostop
THAT CAR UP THERE. DO YOU SEE IT?
YEAH. A BMW X5.
NOT SOMETHING THE PEOPLE AROUND HERE DRIVE.
PETRA, YOU READY TO GO BACK THERE?
CHOK
YES, SIR!

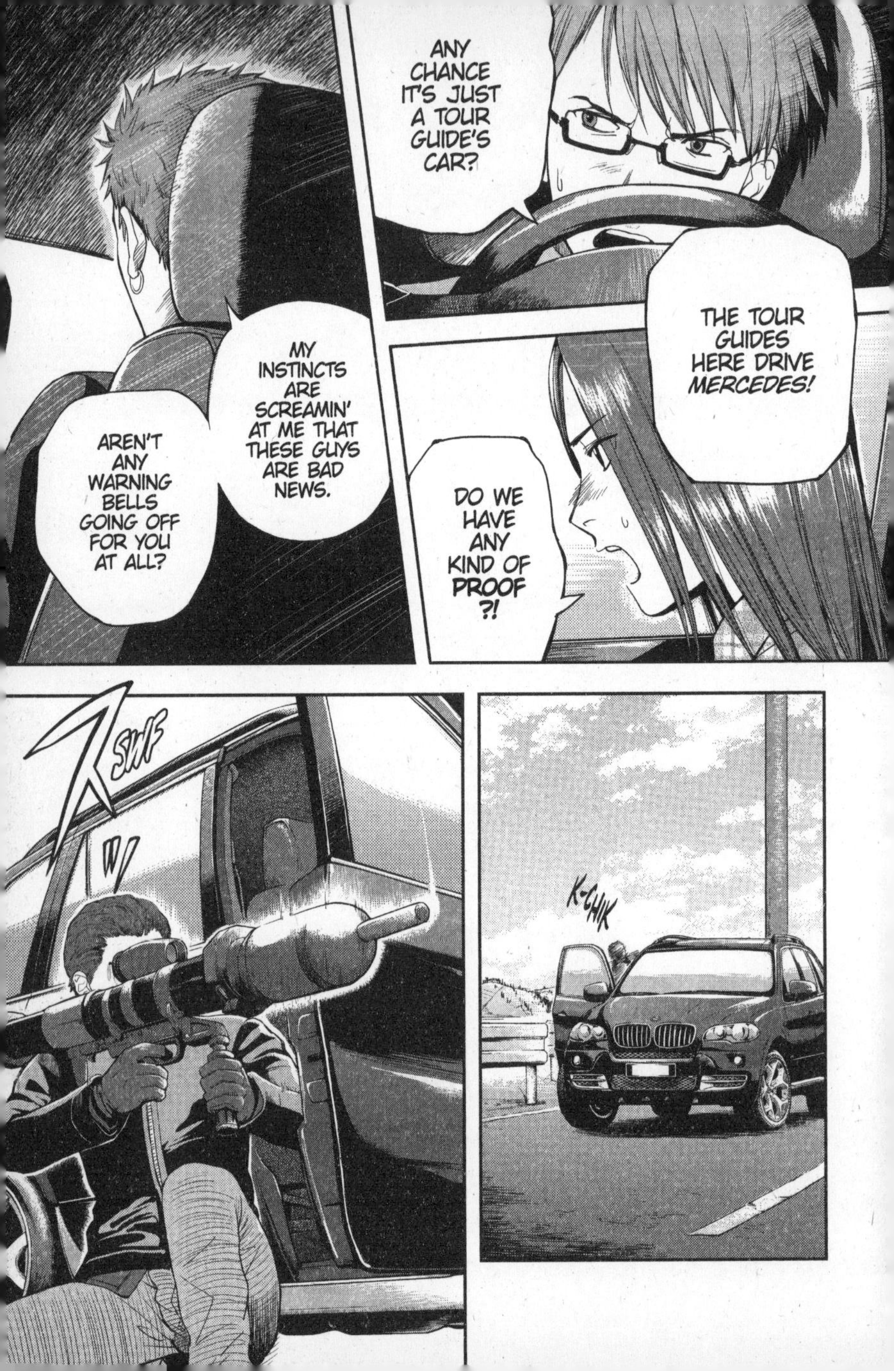
ANY CHANCE IT'S JUST A TOUR GUIDE'S CAR?
THE TOUR GUIDES HERE DRIVE MERCEDES!
DO WE HAVE ANY KIND OF PROOF ?!
MY INSTINCTS ARE SCREAMIN' AT ME THAT THESE GUYS ARE BAD NEWS.
AREN'T ANY WARNING BELLS GOING OFF FOR YOU AT ALL?
K-CHIK
SWF

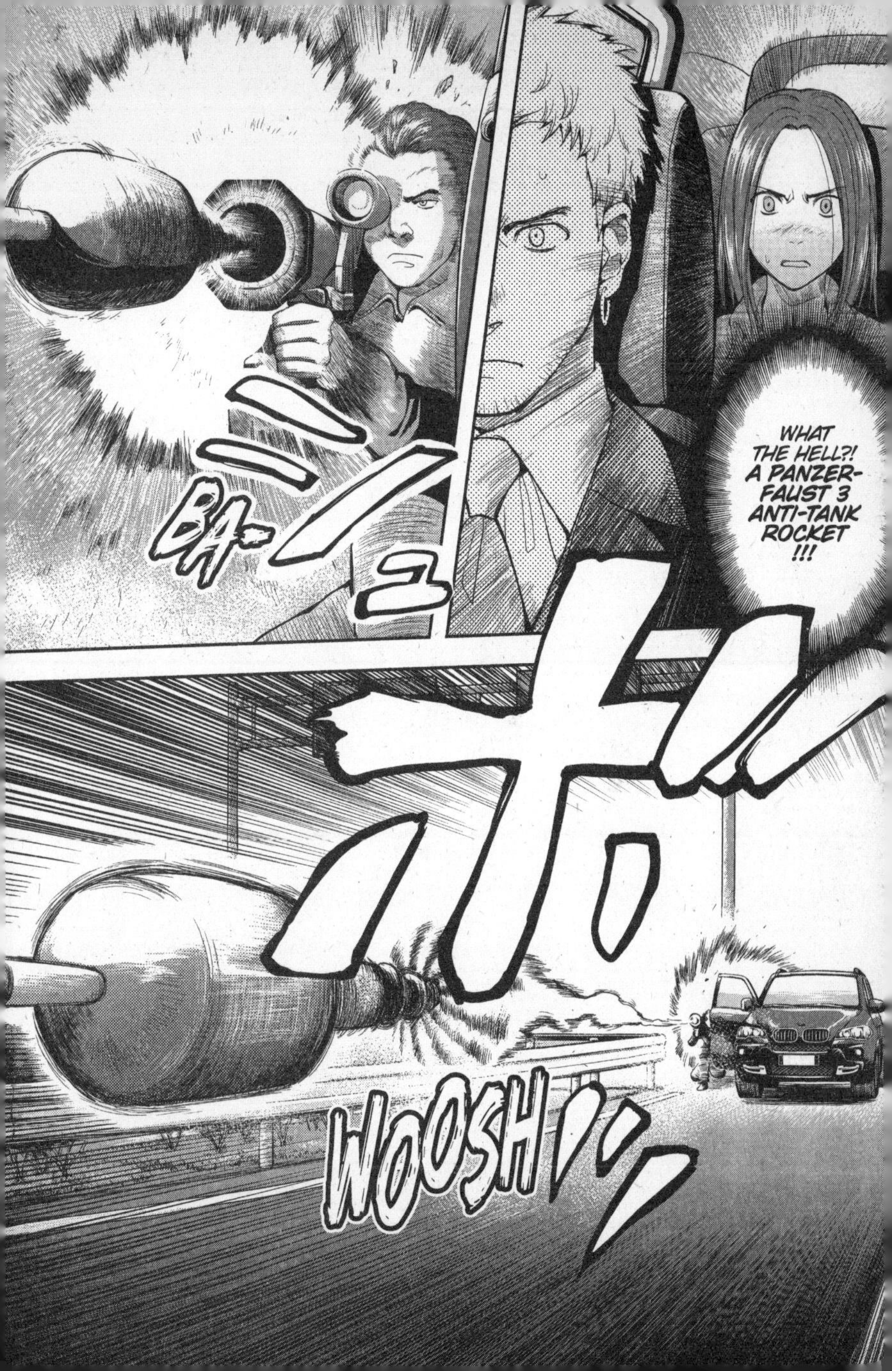
WHAT THE HELL?! A PANZER-FAUST 3 ANTI-TANK ROCKET !!!
BA-
WOOSH

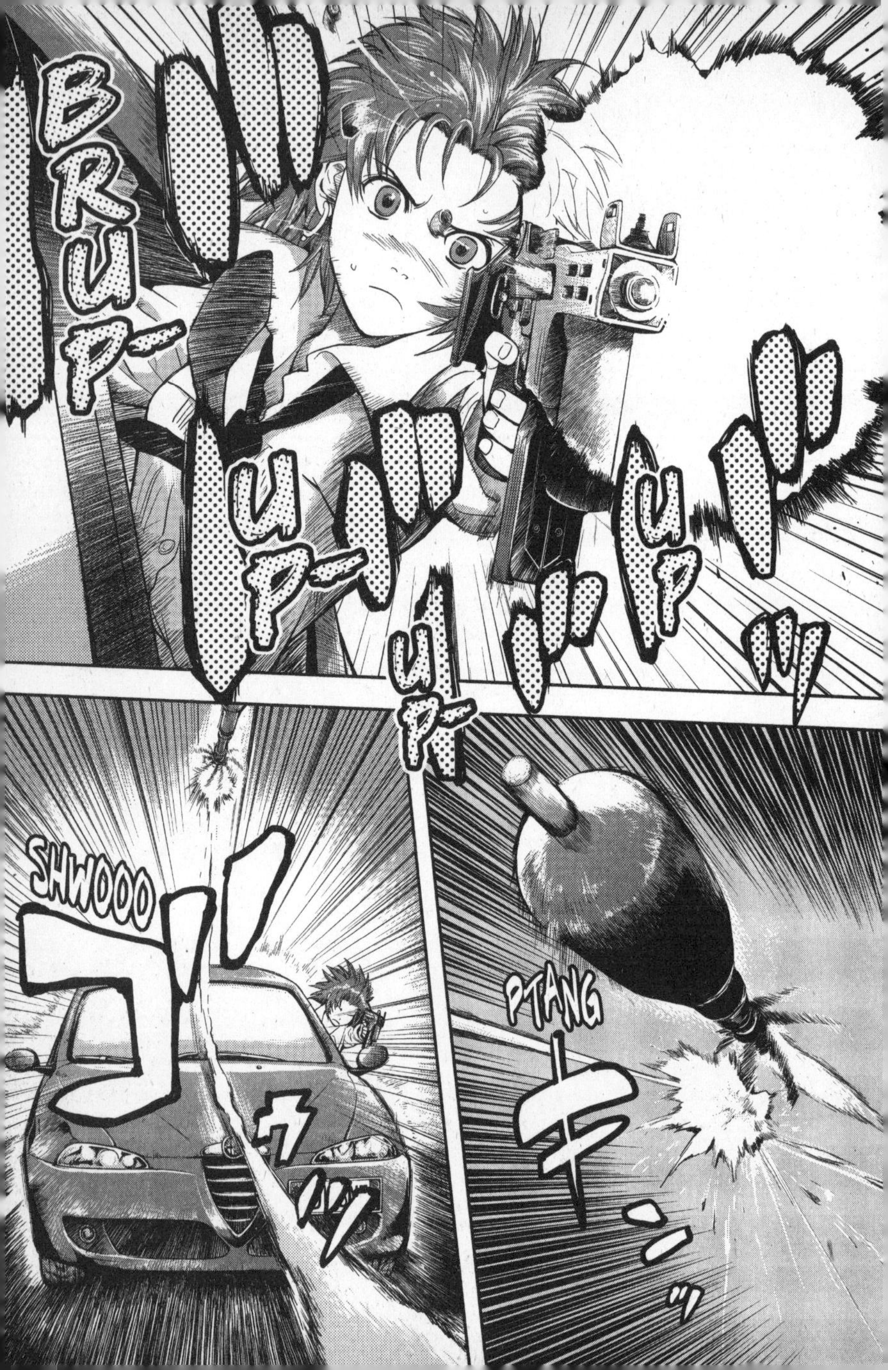
BRUP-
UP-
UP
UP-
PTANG
SHWOOO

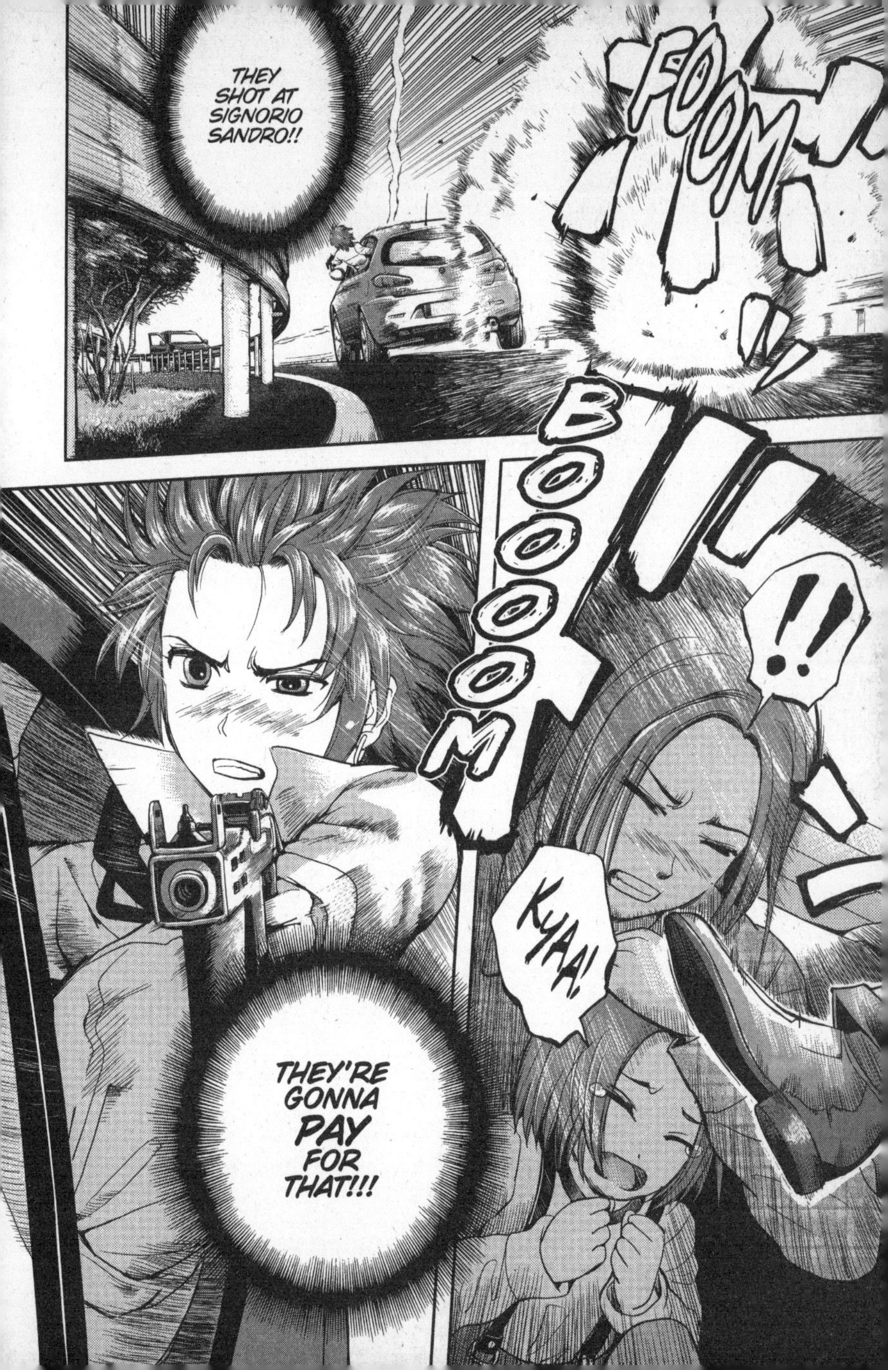
FOOM
THEY SHOT AT SIGNORIO SANDRO!!
BOOOOOOM
!!
KYAA!
THEY'RE GONNA PAY FOR THAT!!!

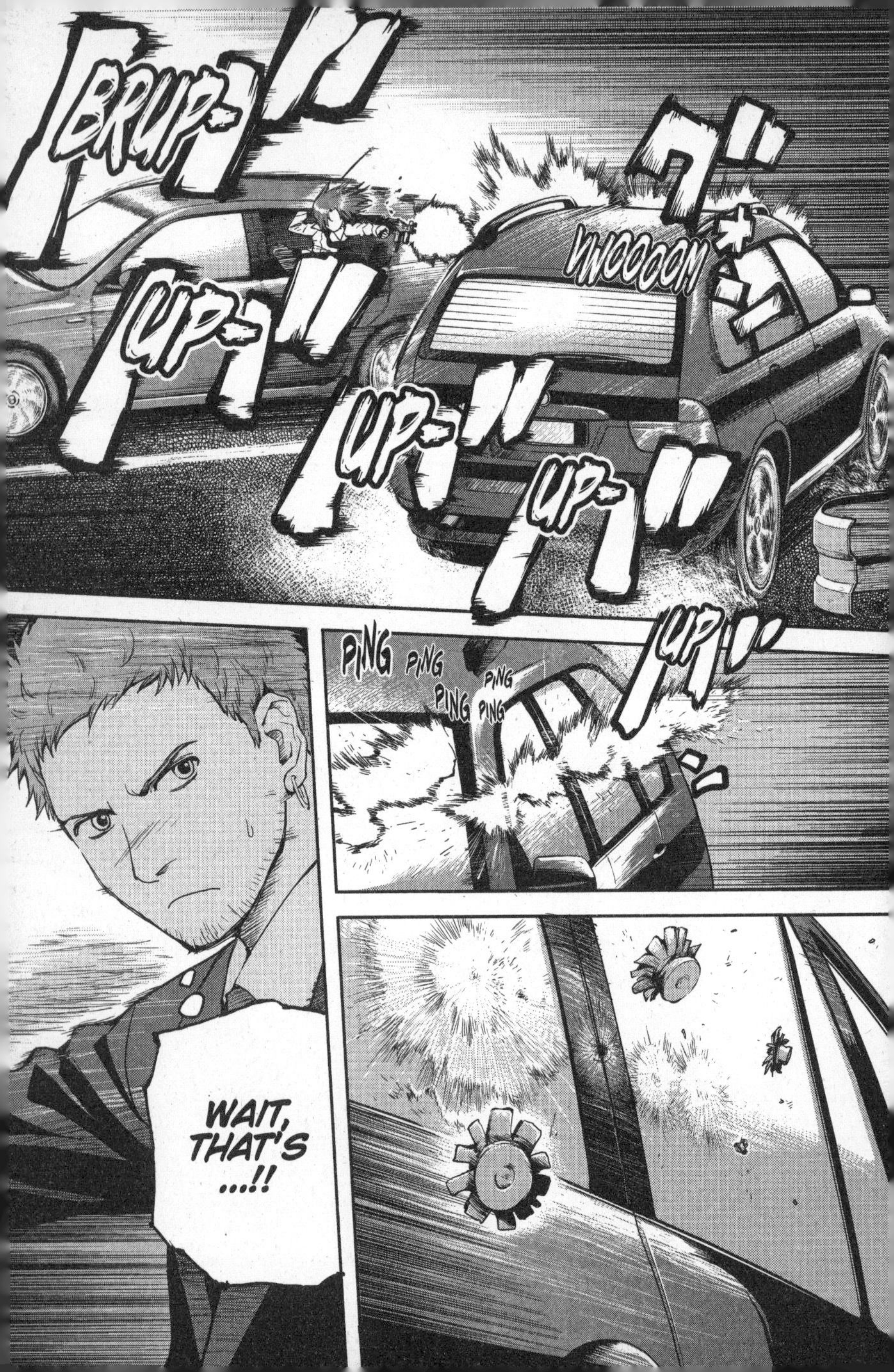

VWOOOOM
BRUP-!!
UP-!!
UP-!!
UP-!!
UP!!
PING PING PING PING PING
WAIT, THAT'S ...!!

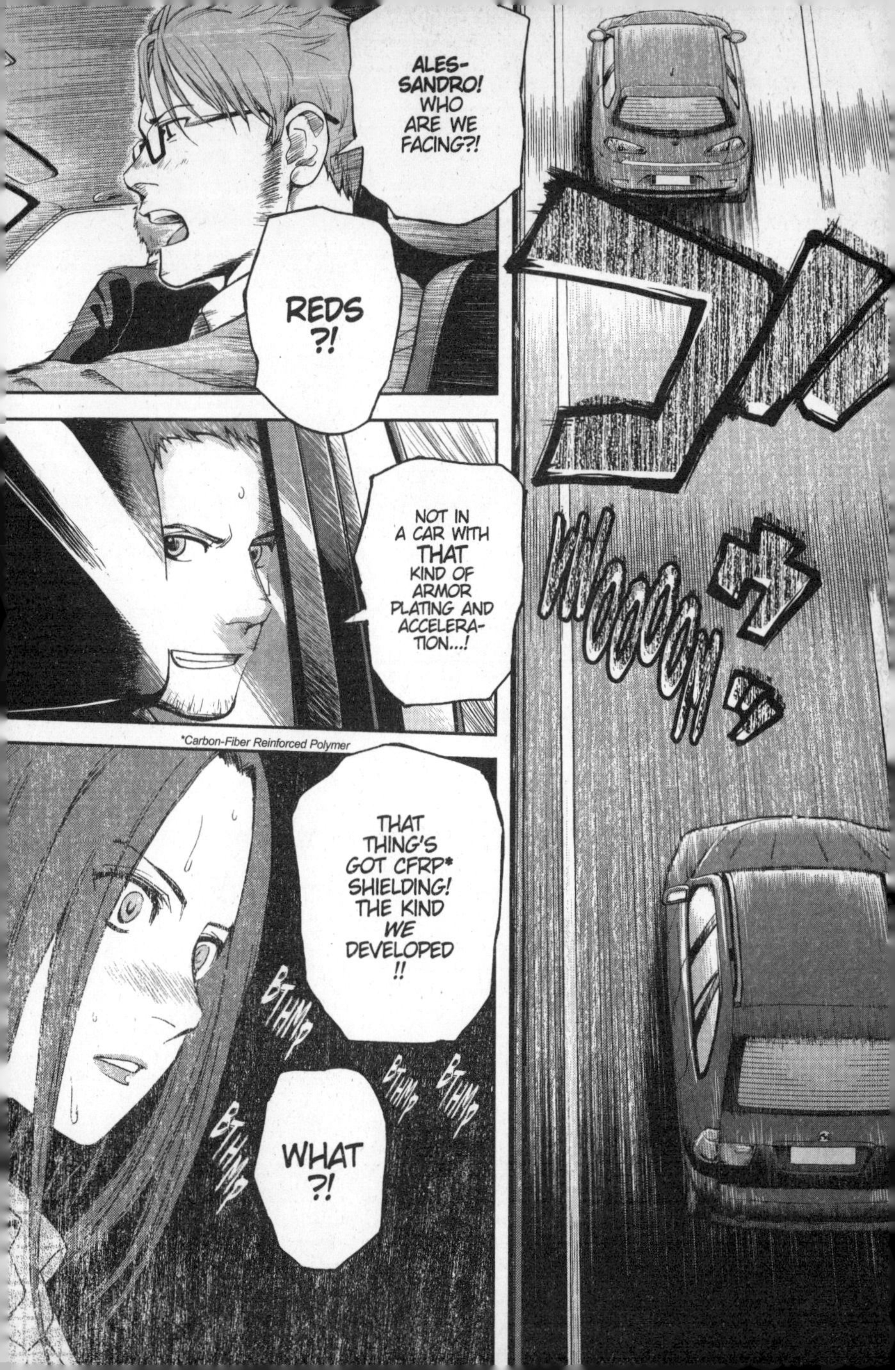
ALES-SANDRO! WHO ARE WE FACING?!
REDS ?!
NOT IN A CAR WITH THAT KIND OF ARMOR PLATING AND ACCELERA-TION...!
*Carbon-Fiber Reinforced Polymer
THAT THING'S GOT CFRP* SHIELDING! THE KIND WE DEVELOPED !!
BTHMP
BTHMP
BTHMP
BTHMP
WHAT ?!

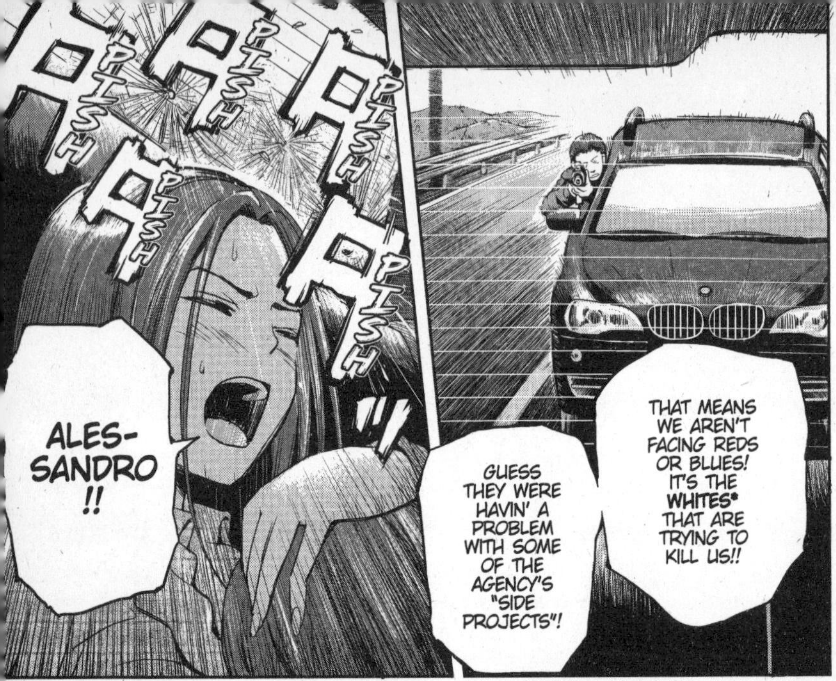
THAT MEANS WE AREN'T FACING REDS OR BLUES! IT'S THE **WHITES*** THAT ARE TRYING TO KILL US!!
GUESS THEY WERE HAVIN' A PROBLEM WITH SOME OF THE AGENCY'S "SIDE PROJECTS"!
PISH
PISH
PISH
PISH
PISH
ALES-SANDRO!!

Reds = radical left; Blues = radical right; Whites = the government.

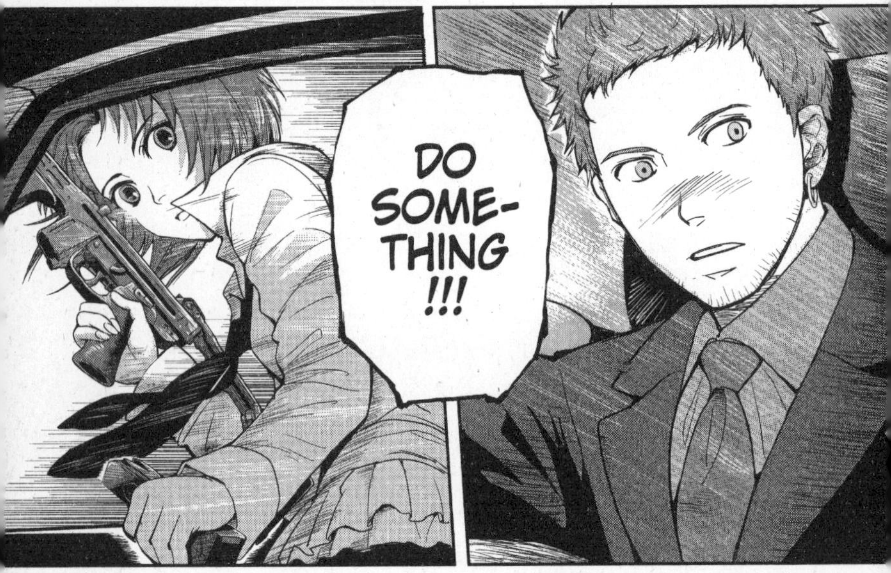
DO SOME-THING!!!

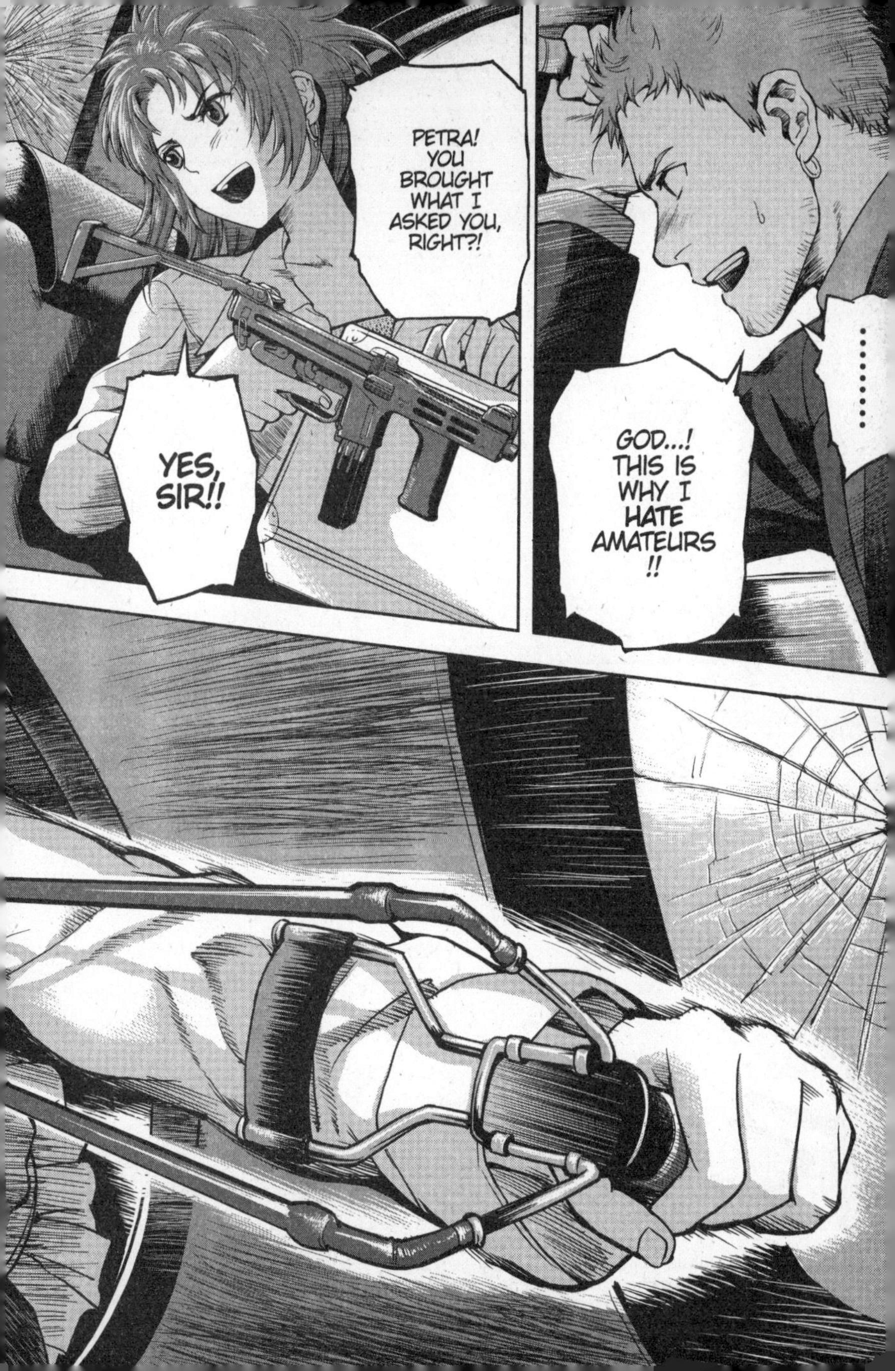
......
GOD...! THIS IS WHY I HATE AMATEURS !!
PETRA! YOU BROUGHT WHAT I ASKED YOU, RIGHT?!
YES, SIR!!

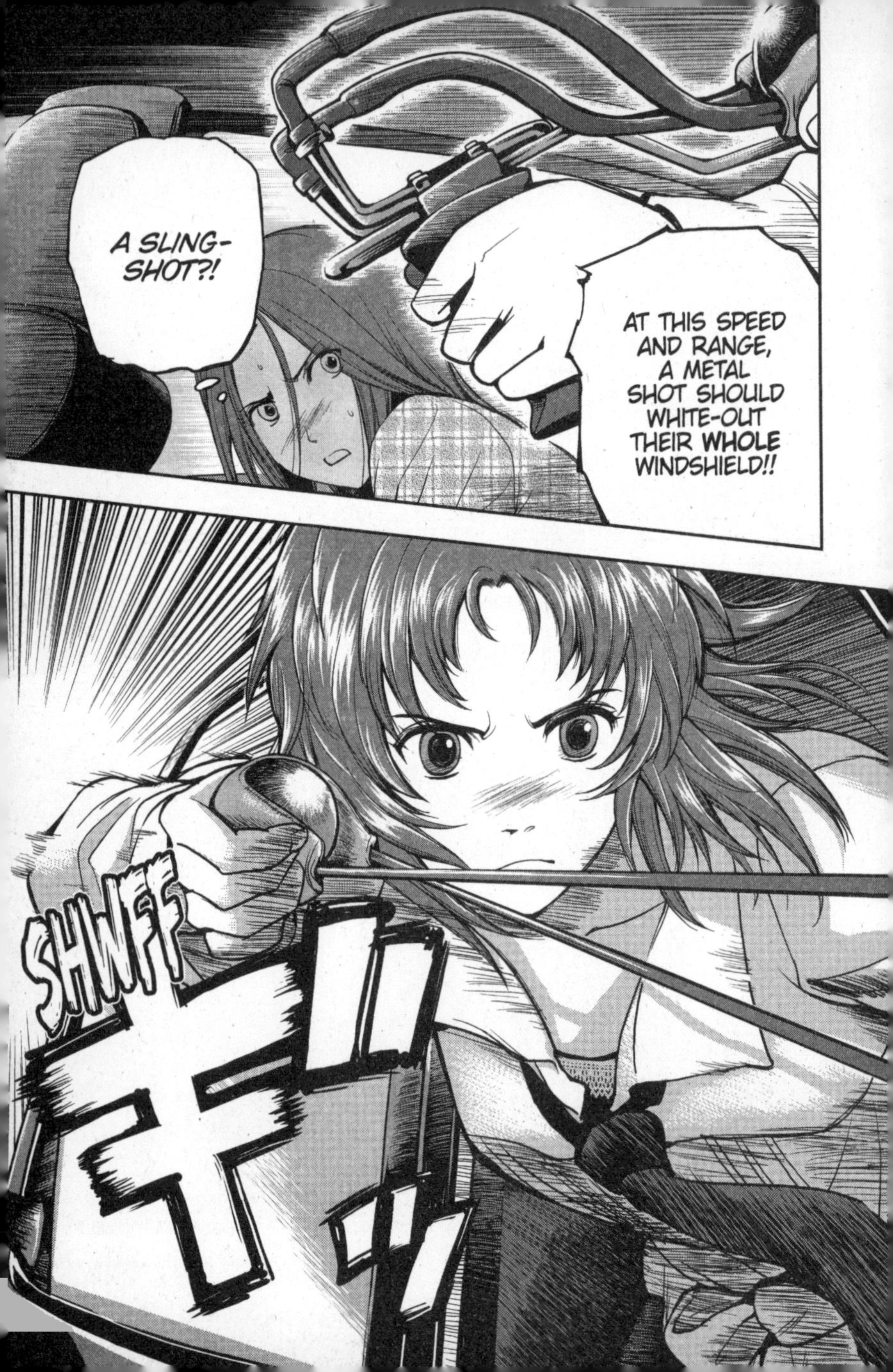
AT THIS SPEED AND RANGE, A METAL SHOT SHOULD WHITE-OUT THEIR WHOLE WINDSHIELD!!
A SLING-SHOT?!
SHWFF

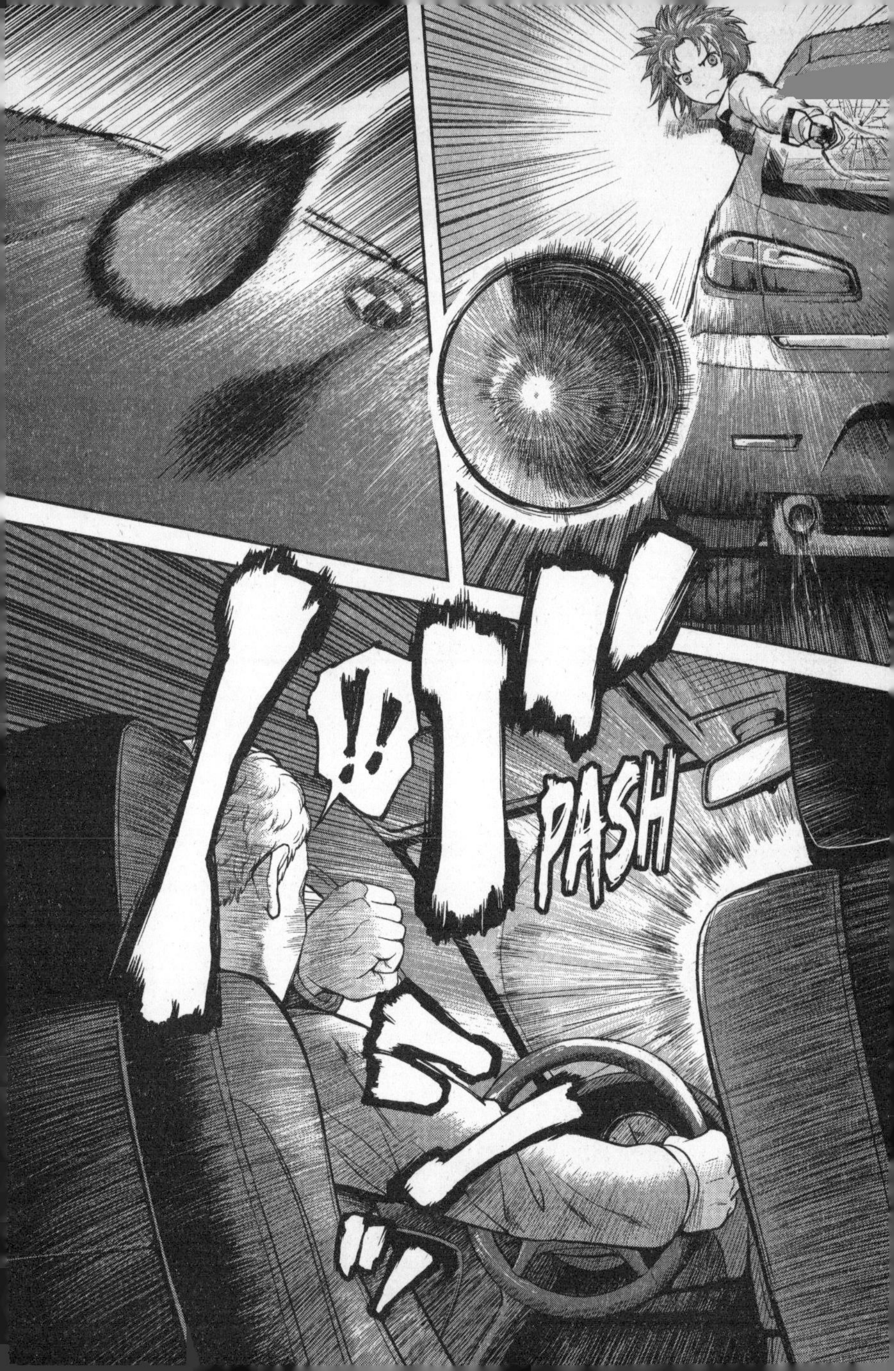
PASH
!!

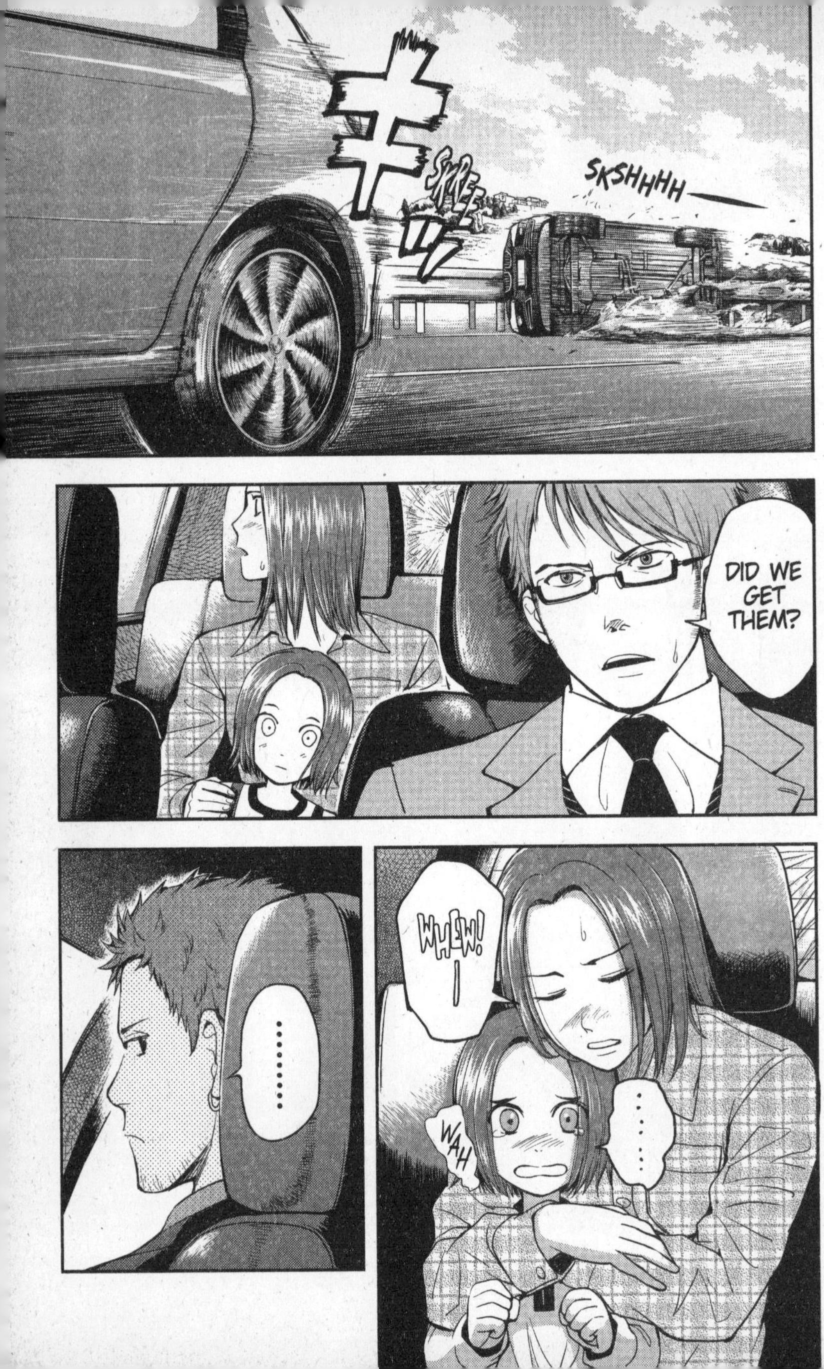
SKSHHHH—
SKREE
DID WE GET THEM?
WHEW! I—
......
WAH
....

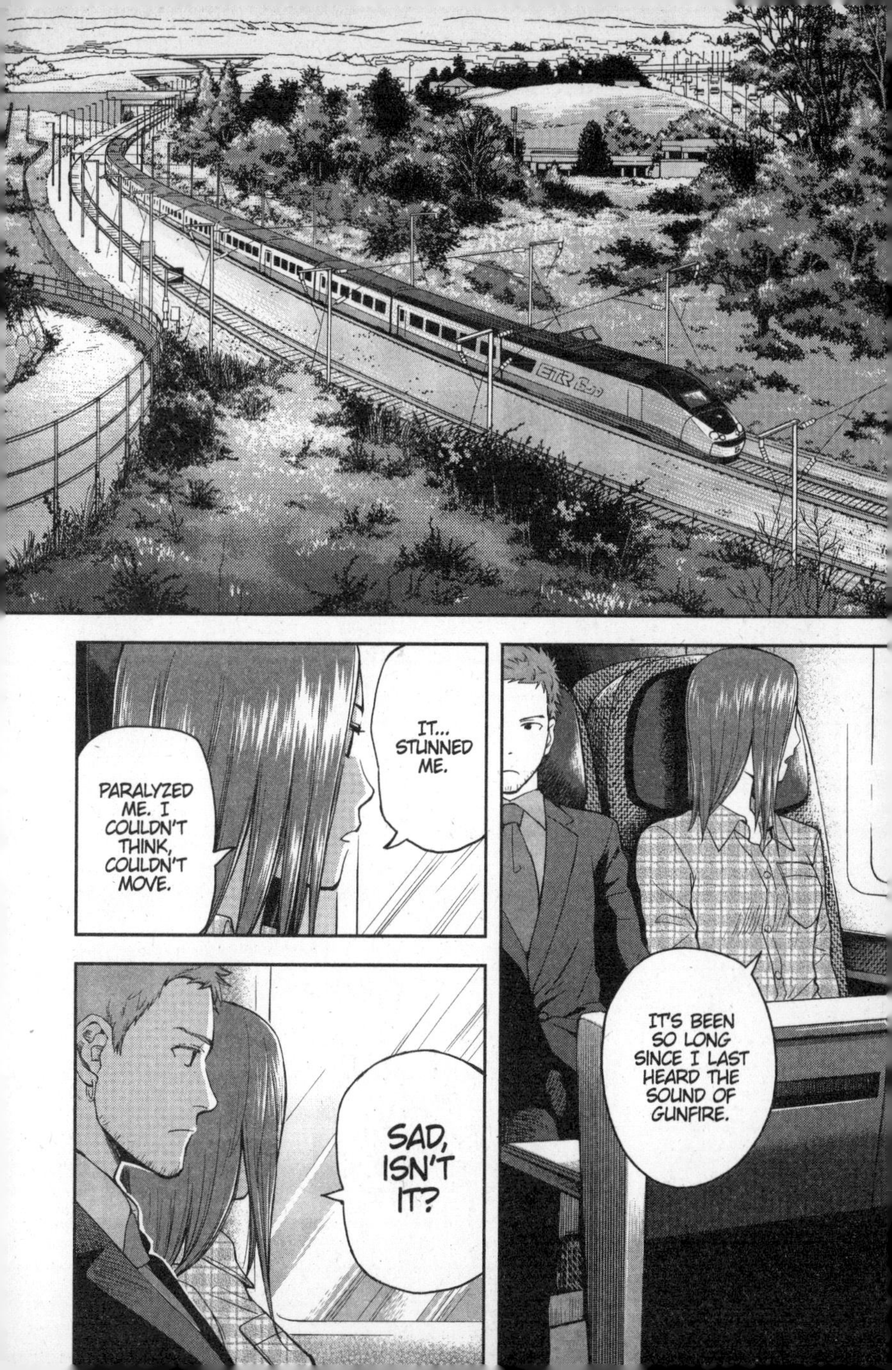
IT'S BEEN SO LONG SINCE I LAST HEARD THE SOUND OF GUNFIRE.
IT... STUNNED ME.
PARALYZED ME. I COULDN'T THINK, COULDN'T MOVE.
SAD, ISN'T IT?

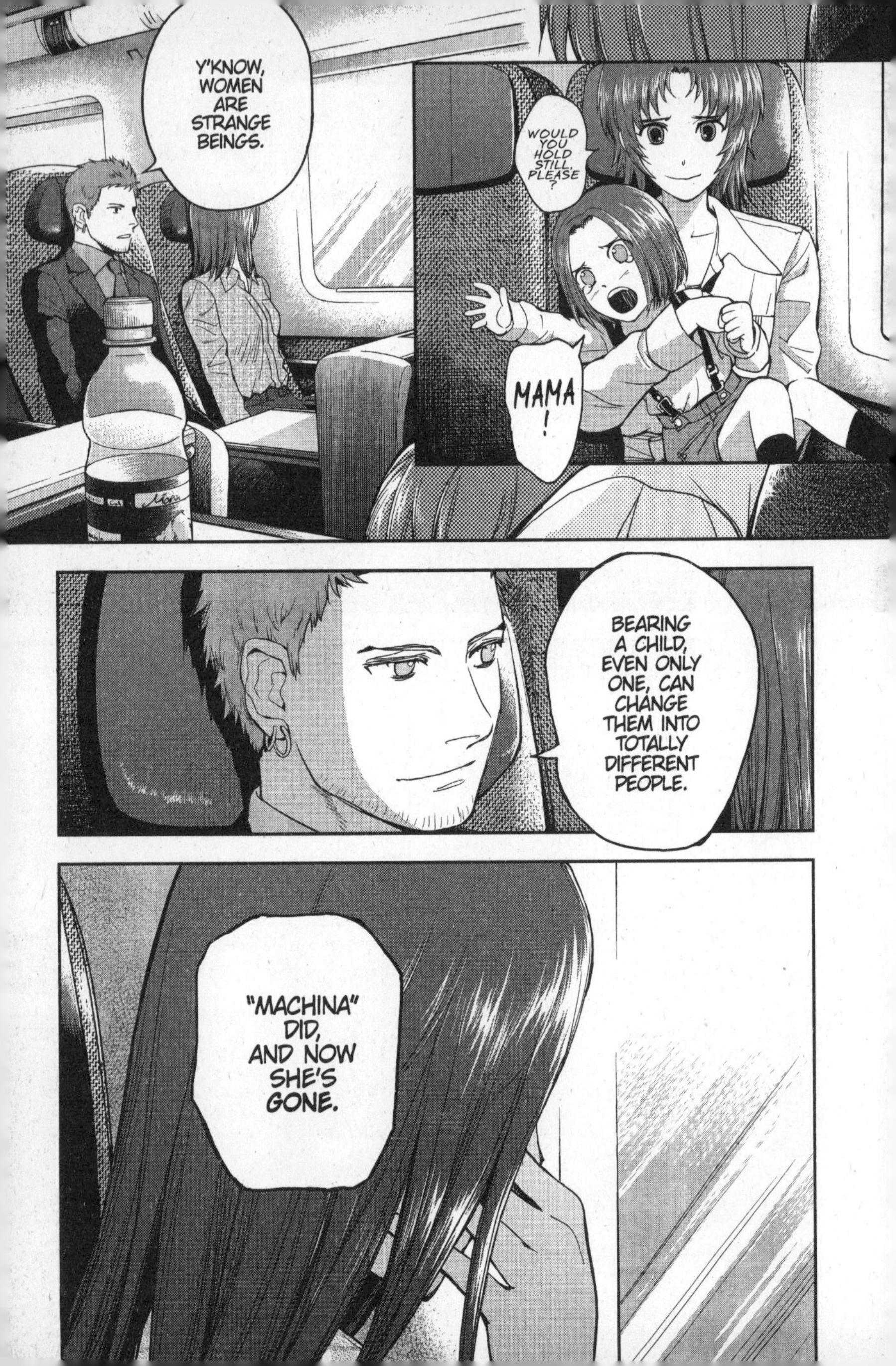
WOULD YOU HOLD STILL, PLEASE?
MAMA!
Y'KNOW, WOMEN ARE STRANGE BEINGS.
BEARING A CHILD, EVEN ONLY ONE, CAN CHANGE THEM INTO TOTALLY DIFFERENT PEOPLE.
"MACHINA" DID, AND NOW SHE'S GONE.

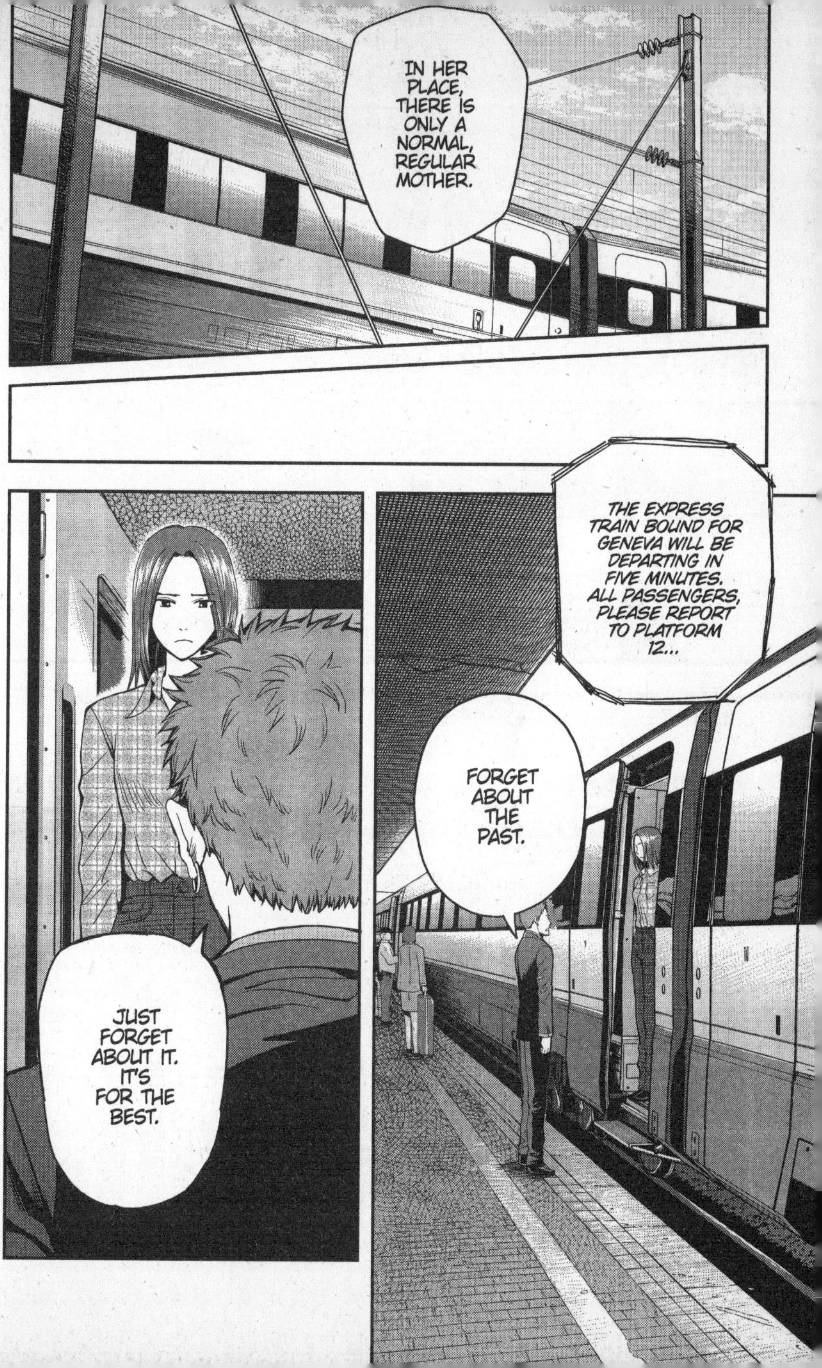
IN HER PLACE, THERE IS ONLY A NORMAL, REGULAR MOTHER.
THE EXPRESS TRAIN BOUND FOR GENEVA WILL BE DEPARTING IN FIVE MINUTES. ALL PASSENGERS, PLEASE REPORT TO PLATFORM 12...
FORGET ABOUT THE PAST.
JUST FORGET ABOUT IT. IT'S FOR THE BEST.

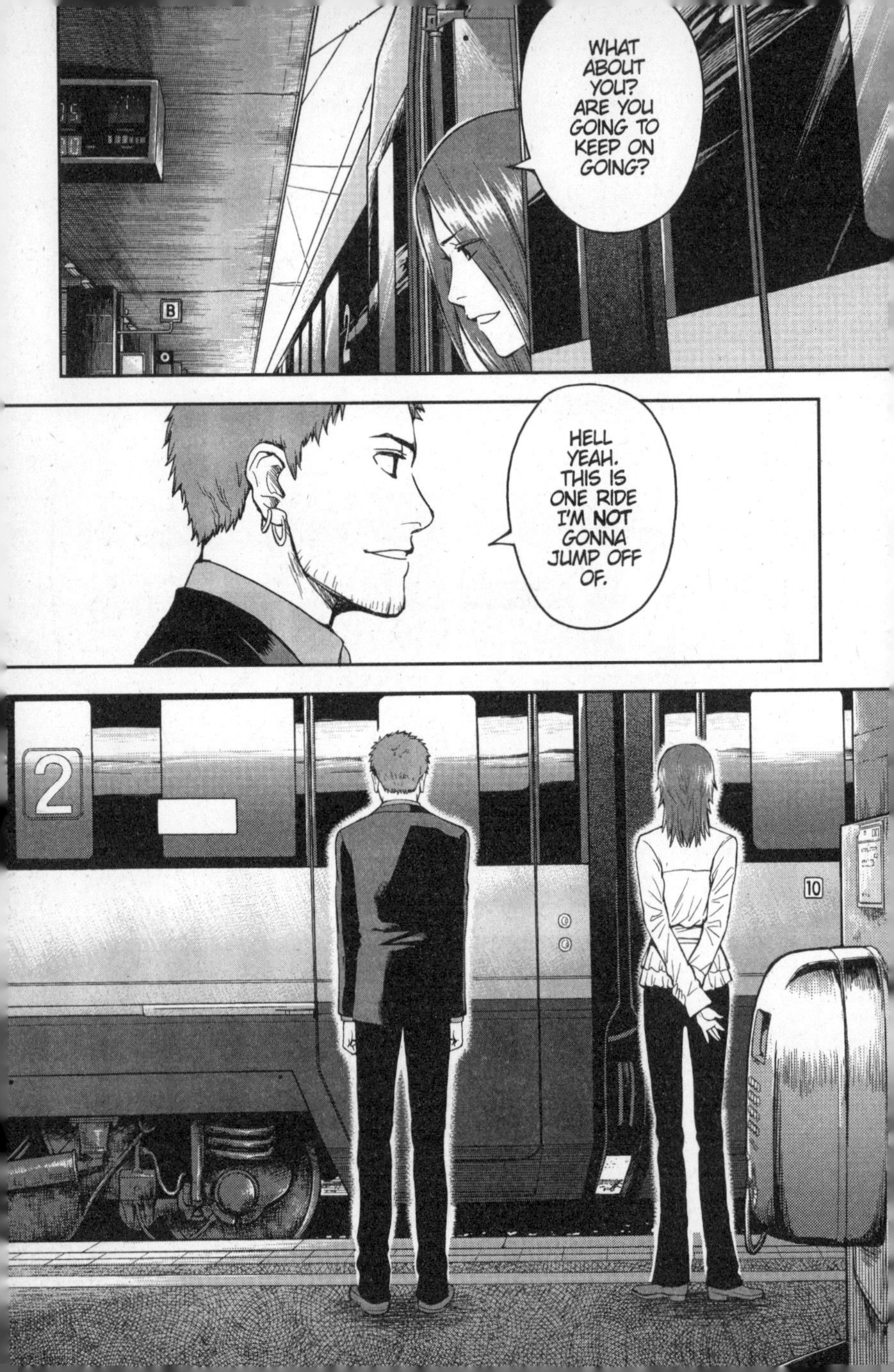
WHAT ABOUT YOU? ARE YOU GOING TO KEEP ON GOING?
HELL YEAH. THIS IS ONE RIDE I'M NOT GONNA JUMP OFF OF.

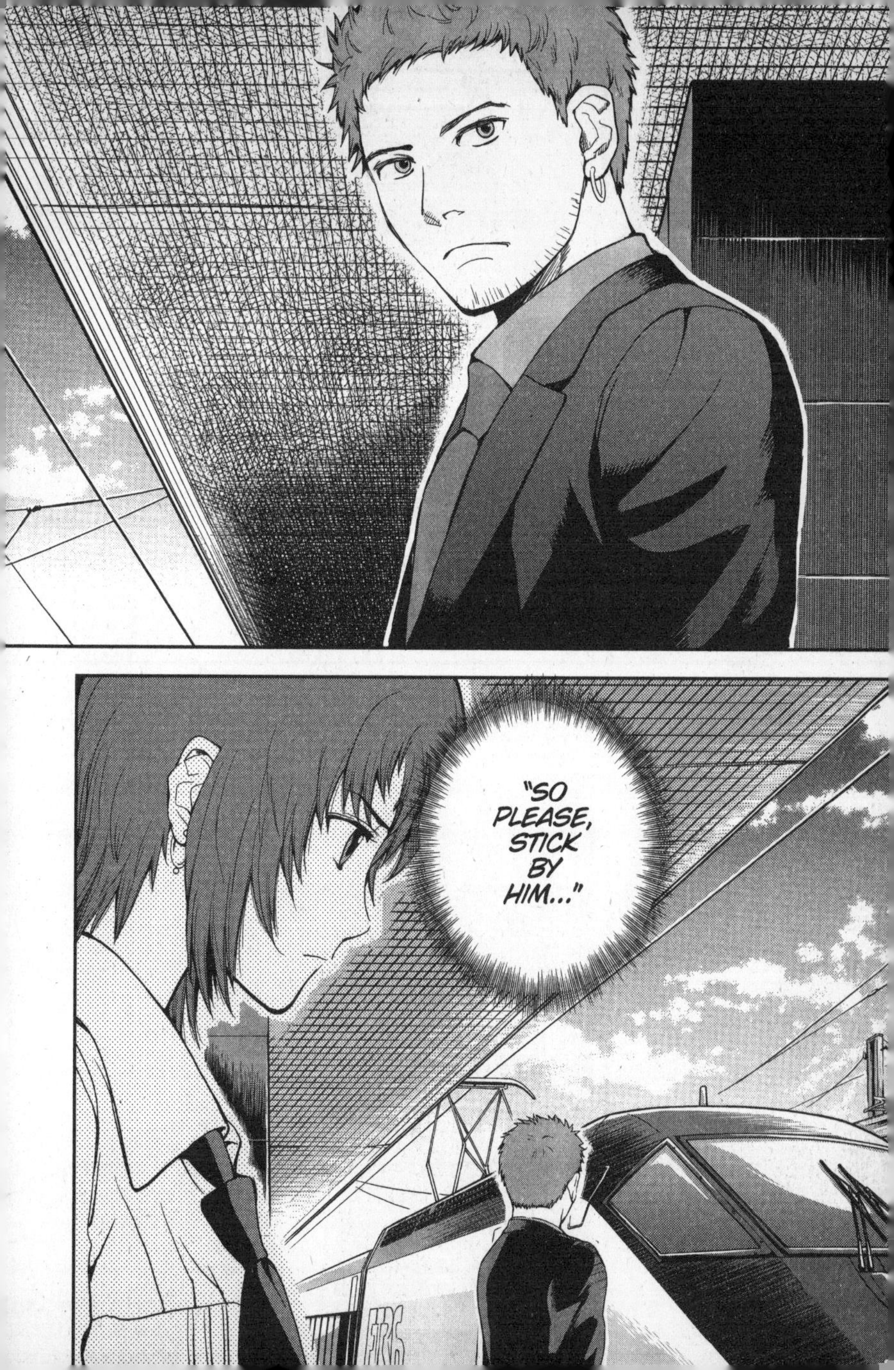
"SO PLEASE, STICK BY HIM..."

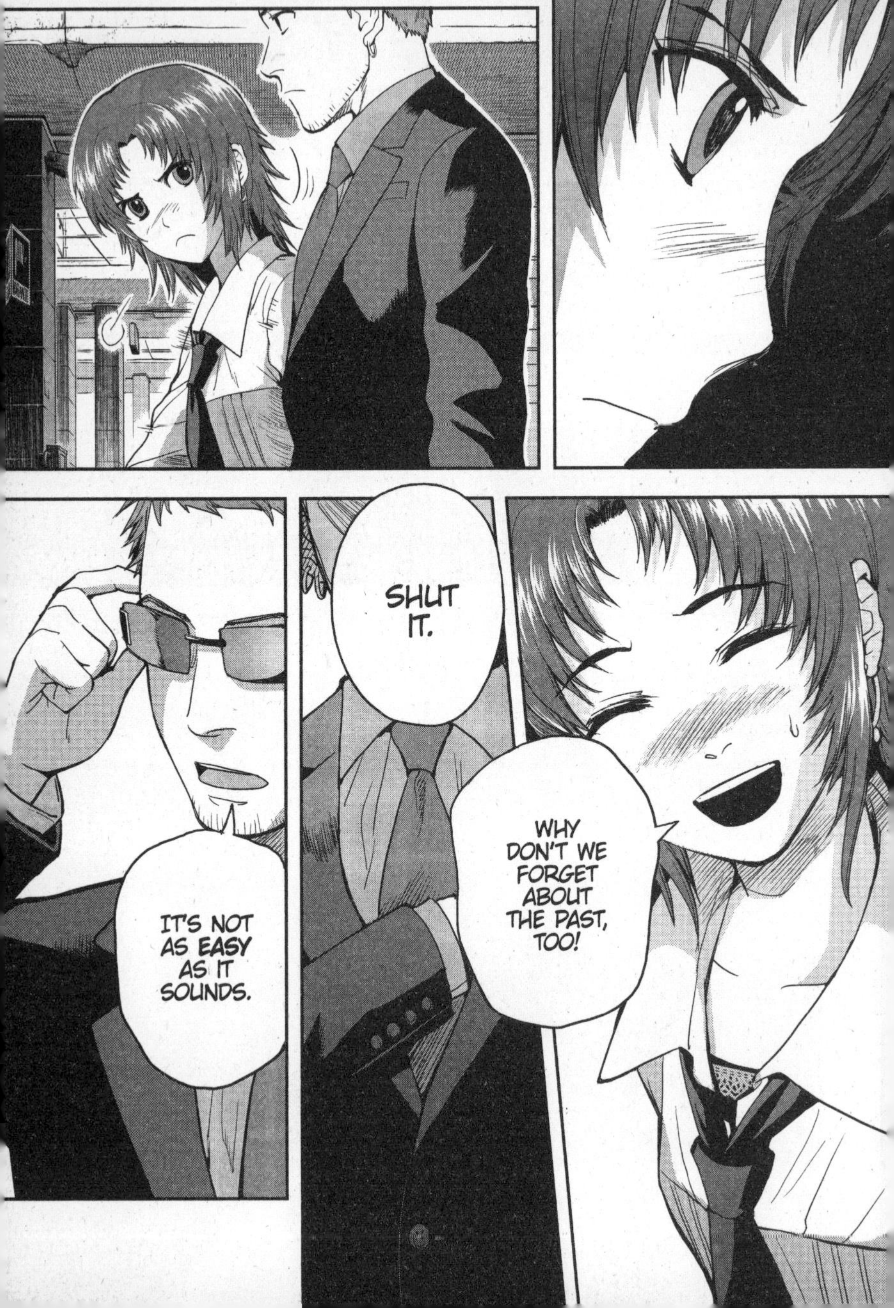
WHY DON'T WE FORGET ABOUT THE PAST, TOO!
SHUT IT.
IT'S NOT AS EASY AS IT SOUNDS.

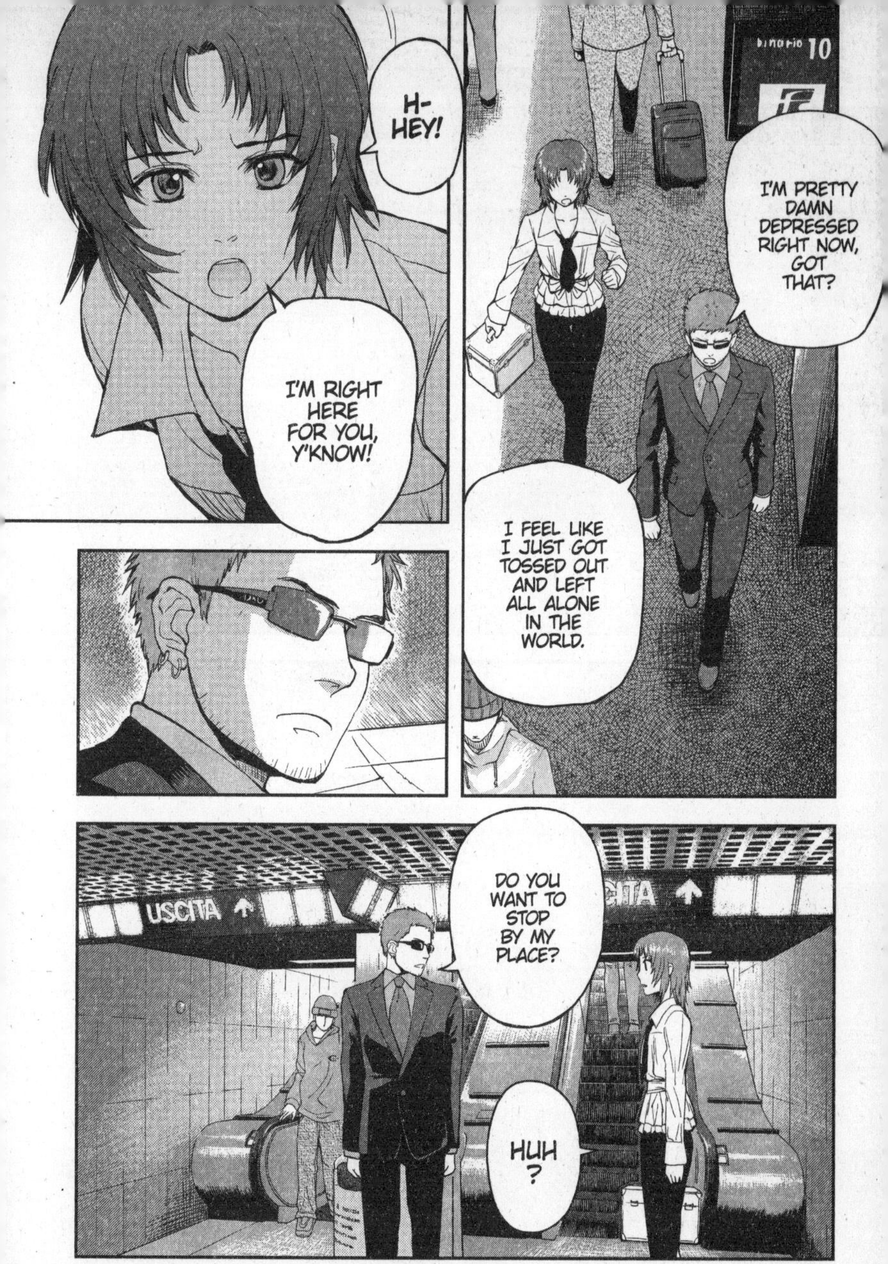
binario 10
I'M PRETTY DAMN DEPRESSED RIGHT NOW, GOT THAT?
I FEEL LIKE I JUST GOT TOSSED OUT AND LEFT ALL ALONE IN THE WORLD.
H-HEY!
I'M RIGHT HERE FOR YOU, Y'KNOW!
USCITA
DO YOU WANT TO STOP BY MY PLACE?
HUH?

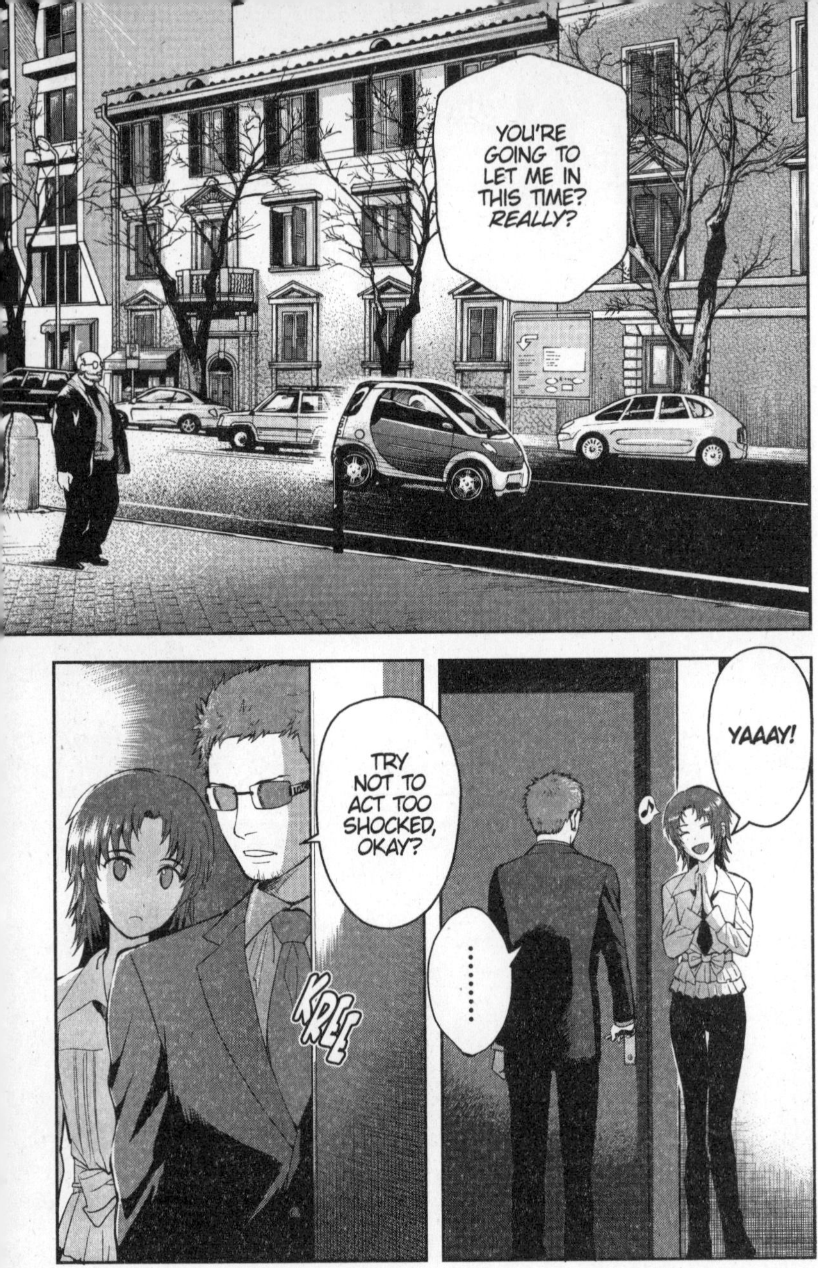
YOU'RE GOING TO LET ME IN THIS TIME? *REALLY?*
YAAAY!
♪
......
TRY NOT TO ACT TOO SHOCKED, OKAY?
KREE

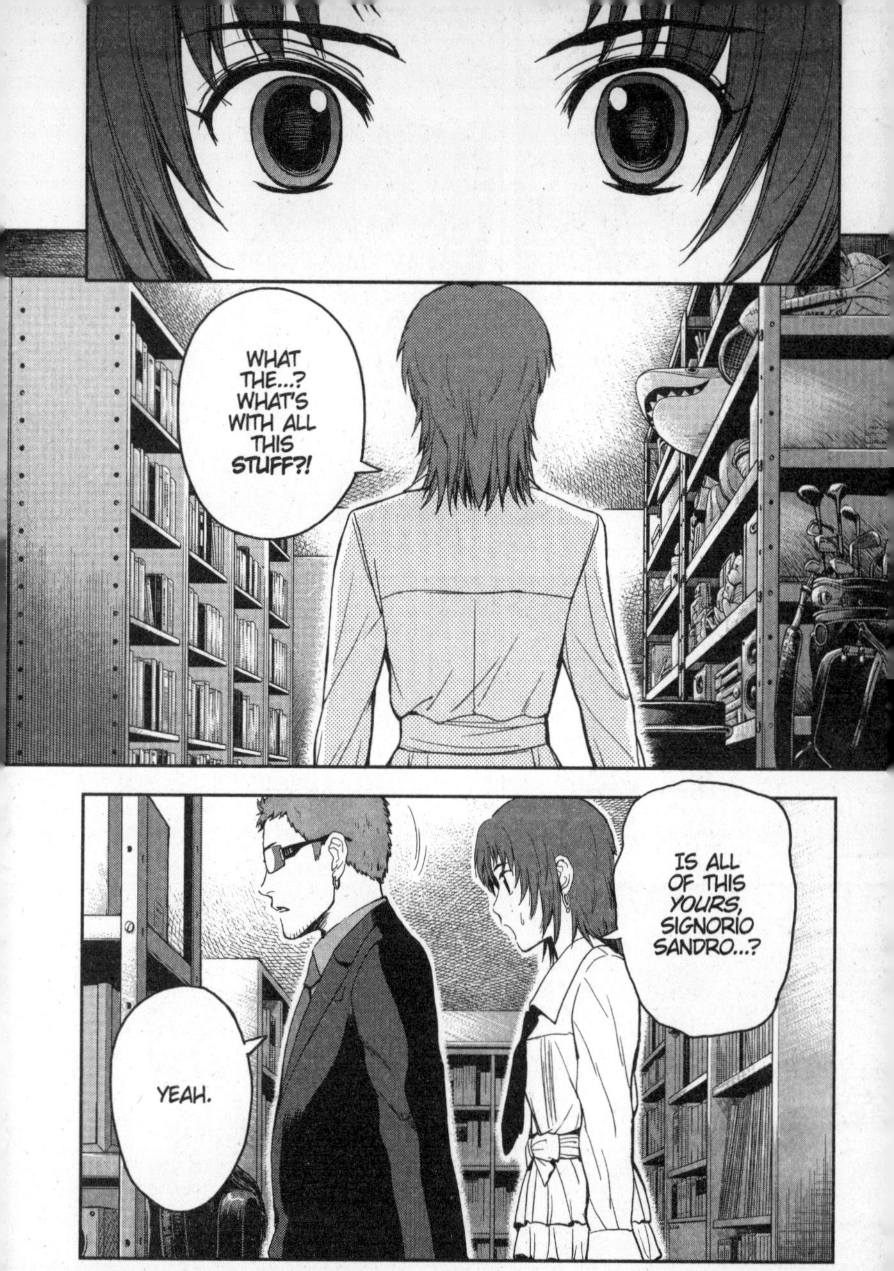
WHAT THE...? WHAT'S WITH ALL THIS STUFF?!
IS ALL OF THIS *YOURS,* SIGNORIO SANDRO...?
YEAH.

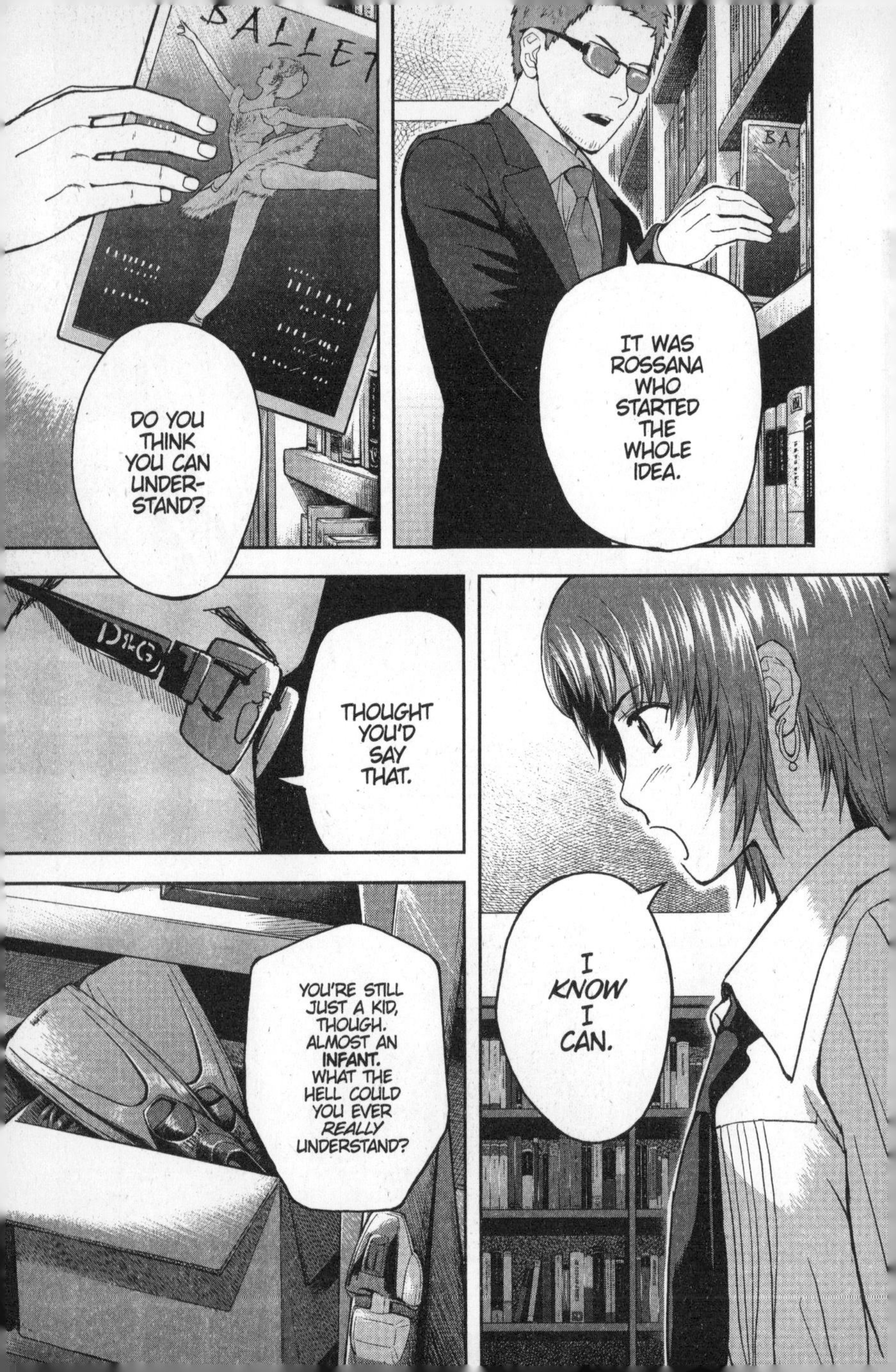
BALLET
IT WAS ROSSANA WHO STARTED THE WHOLE IDEA.
DO YOU THINK YOU CAN UNDERSTAND?
I *KNOW* I CAN.
THOUGHT YOU'D SAY THAT.
D&G
YOU'RE STILL JUST A KID, THOUGH. ALMOST AN **INFANT**. WHAT THE HELL COULD YOU EVER *REALLY* UNDERSTAND?

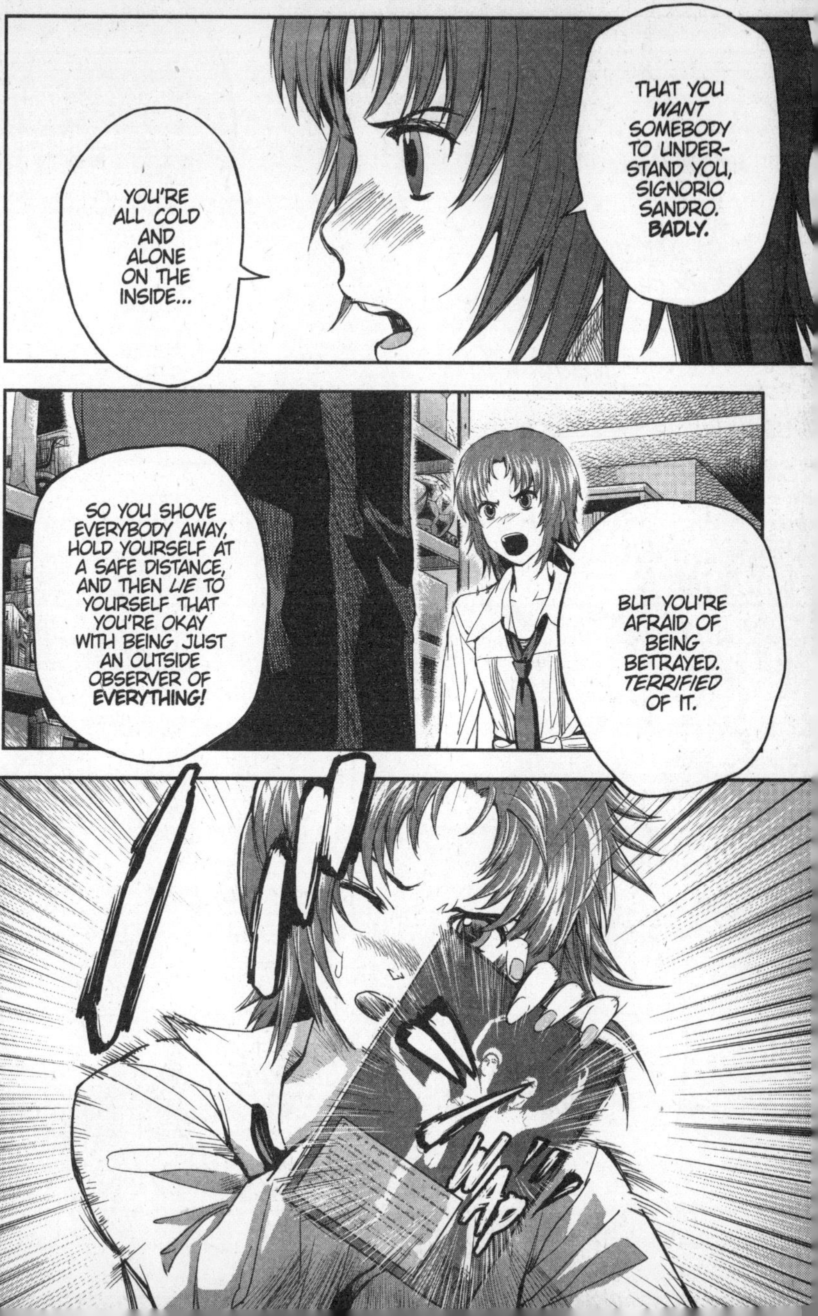
THAT YOU *WANT* SOMEBODY TO UNDER-STAND YOU, SIGNORIO SANDRO. BADLY.
YOU'RE ALL COLD AND ALONE ON THE INSIDE...
BUT YOU'RE AFRAID OF BEING BETRAYED. *TERRIFIED* OF IT.
SO YOU SHOVE EVERYBODY AWAY, HOLD YOURSELF AT A SAFE DISTANCE, AND THEN *LIE* TO YOURSELF THAT YOU'RE OKAY WITH BEING JUST AN OUTSIDE OBSERVER OF **EVERYTHING!**
WAP

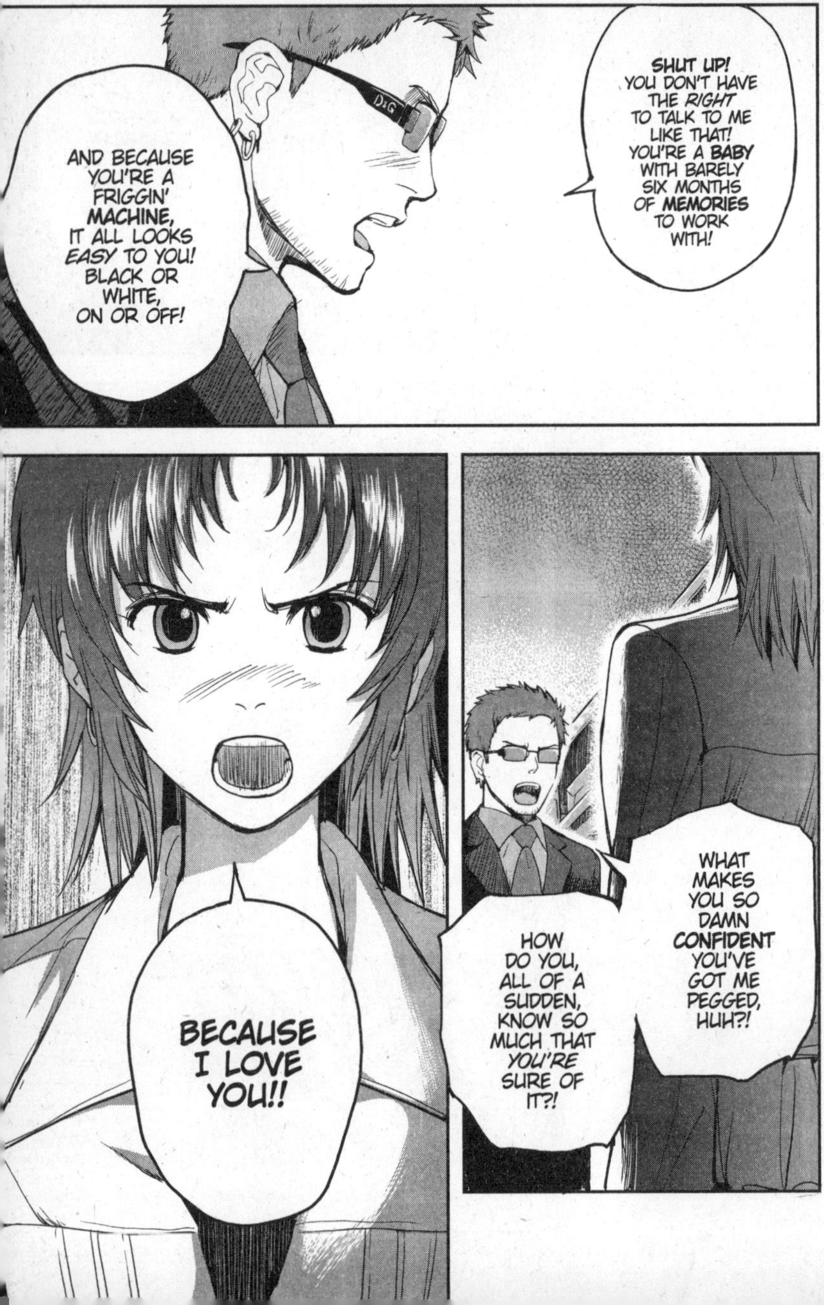
SHUT UP! YOU DON'T HAVE THE RIGHT TO TALK TO ME LIKE THAT! YOU'RE A BABY WITH BARELY SIX MONTHS OF MEMORIES TO WORK WITH!
AND BECAUSE YOU'RE A FRIGGIN' MACHINE, IT ALL LOOKS EASY TO YOU! BLACK OR WHITE, ON OR OFF!
WHAT MAKES YOU SO DAMN CONFIDENT YOU'VE GOT ME PEGGED, HUH?!
HOW DO YOU, ALL OF A SUDDEN, KNOW SO MUCH THAT YOU'RE SURE OF IT?!
BECAUSE I LOVE YOU!!

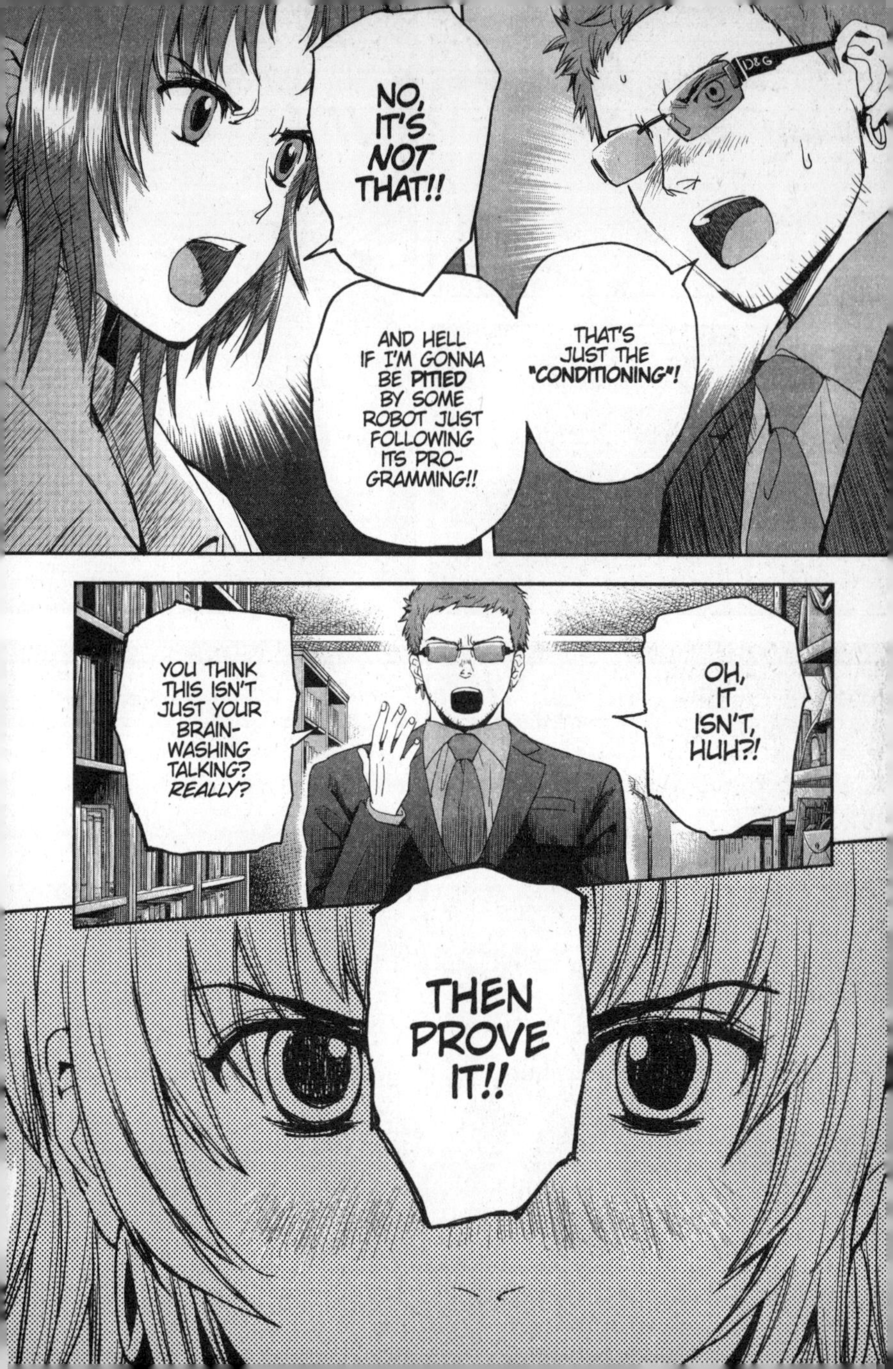
NO, IT'S NOT THAT!!
THAT'S JUST THE "CONDITIONING"!
AND HELL IF I'M GONNA BE PITIED BY SOME ROBOT JUST FOLLOWING ITS PRO-GRAMMING!!
OH, IT ISN'T, HUH?!
YOU THINK THIS ISN'T JUST YOUR BRAIN-WASHING TALKING? REALLY?
THEN PROVE IT!!

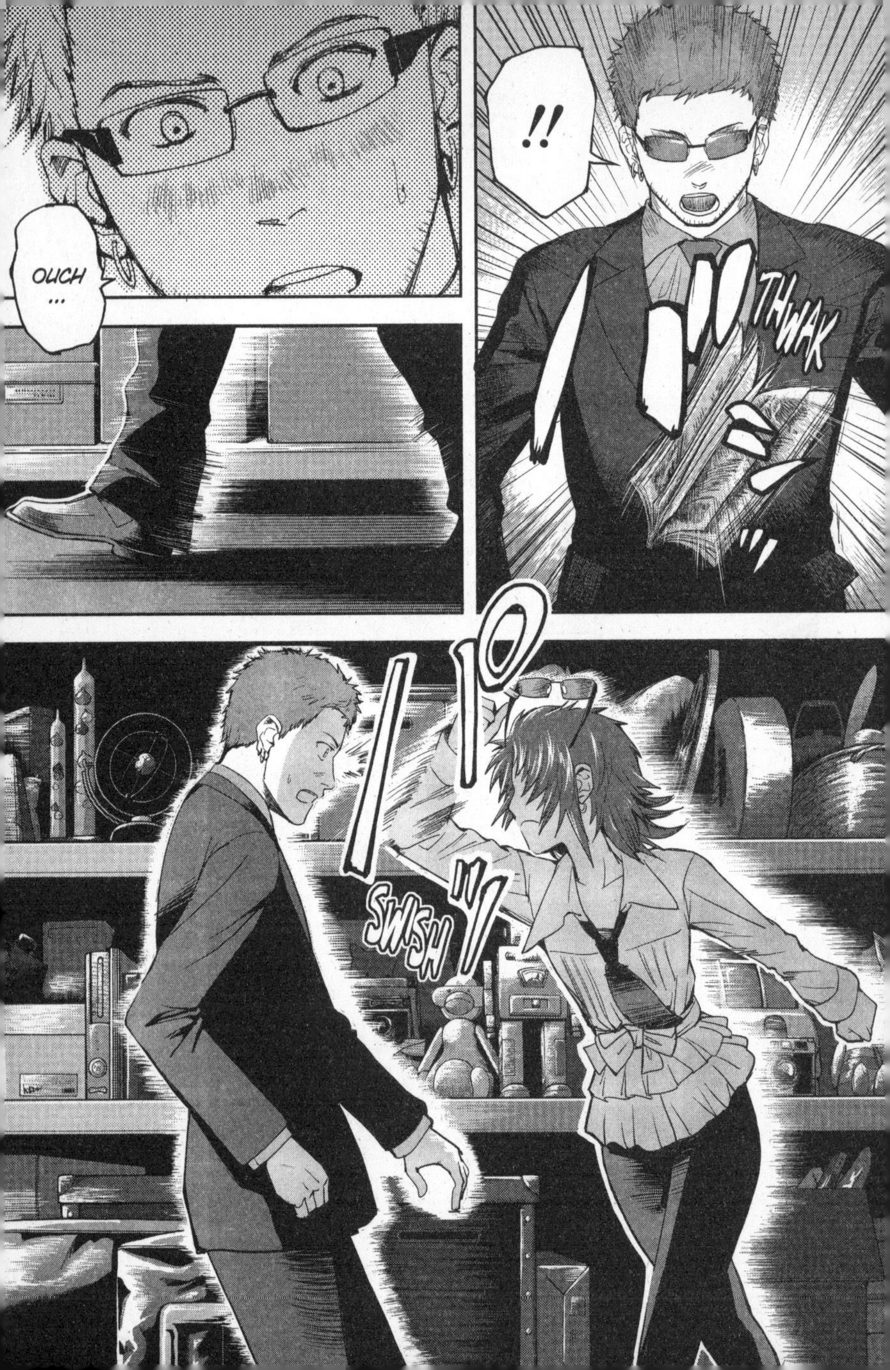

!!
THWAK
OUCH ...
SWISH

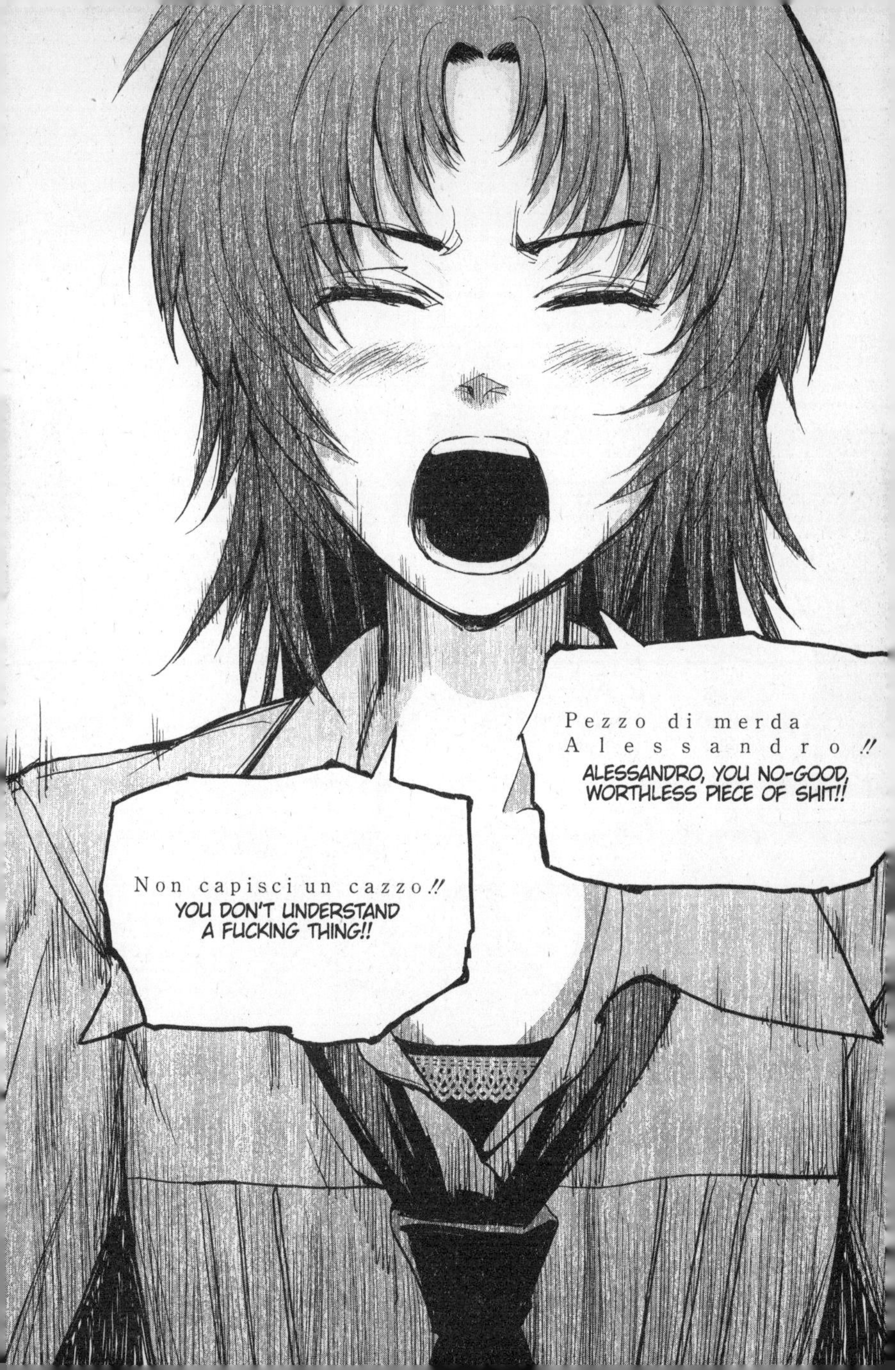
Pezzo di merda Alessandro!!
ALESSANDRO, YOU NO-GOOD, WORTHLESS PIECE OF SHIT!!
Non capisci un cazzo!!
YOU DON'T UNDERSTAND A FUCKING THING!!

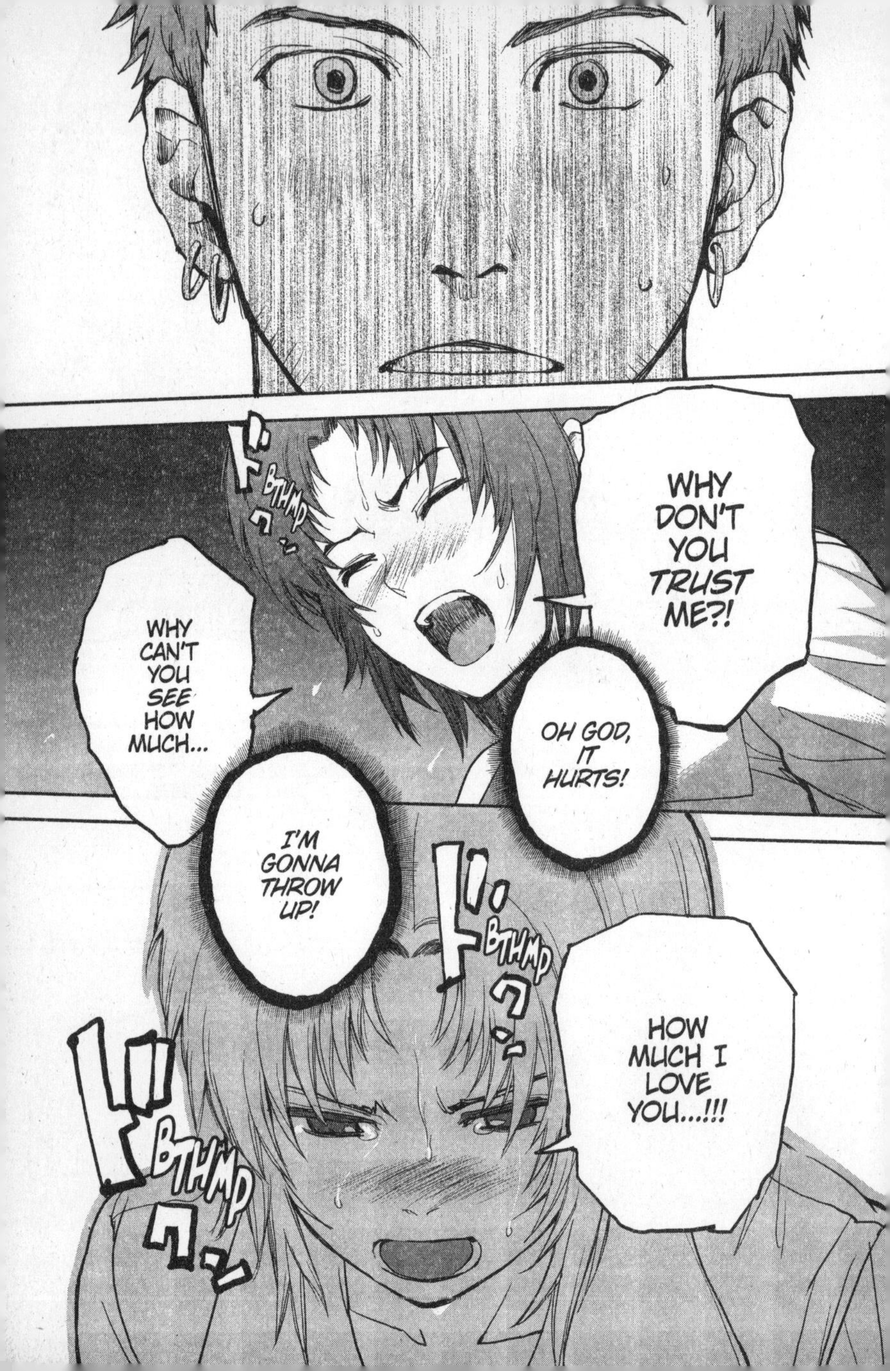
BTHMP
WHY DON'T YOU TRUST ME?!
OH GOD, IT HURTS!
WHY CAN'T YOU SEE HOW MUCH...
I'M GONNA THROW UP!
BTHMP
HOW MUCH I LOVE YOU...!!!
BTHMP

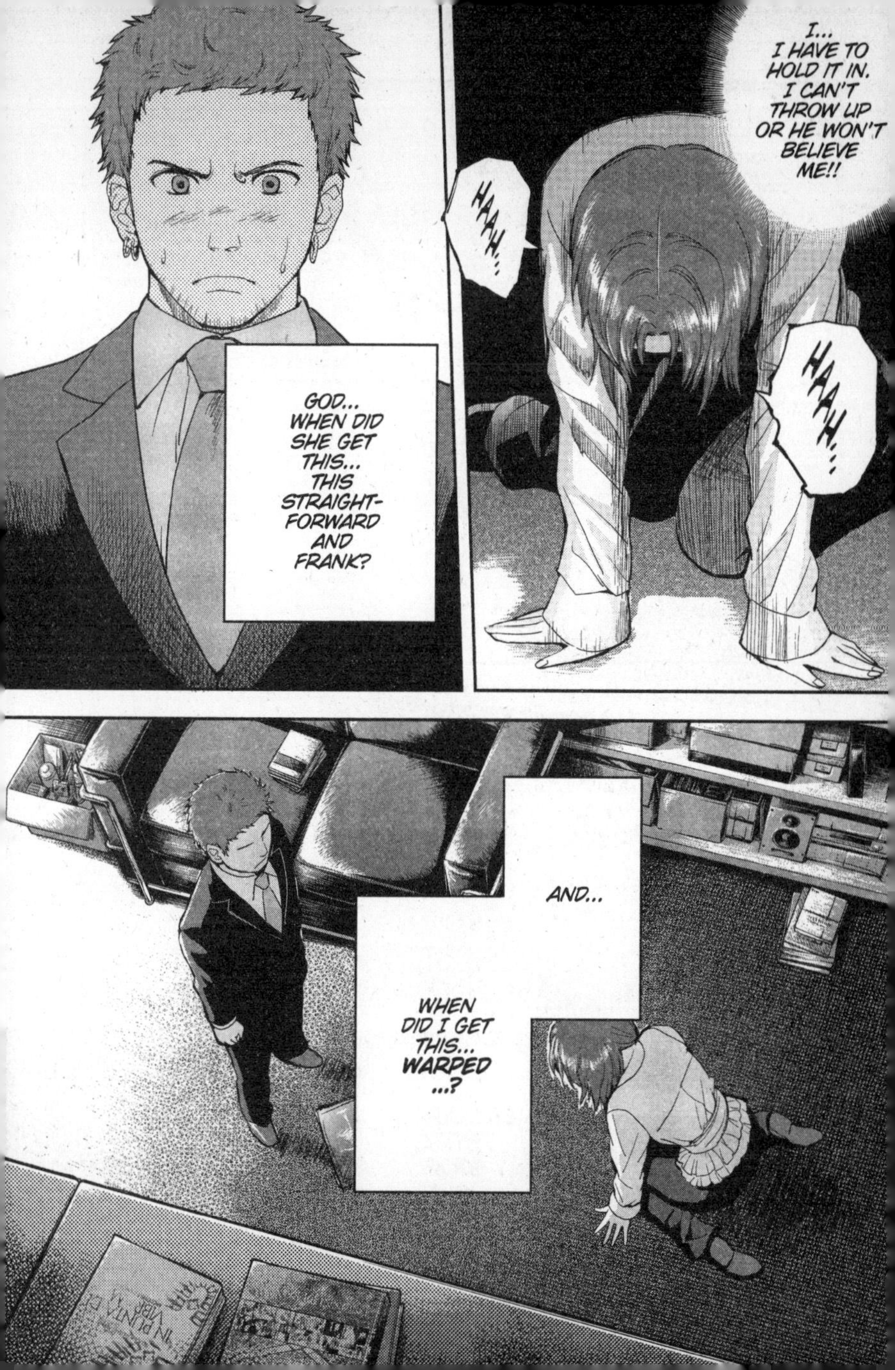
I... I HAVE TO HOLD IT IN. I CAN'T THROW UP OR HE WON'T BELIEVE ME!!
HAAAH...
HAAAH...
GOD... WHEN DID SHE GET THIS... THIS STRAIGHT-FORWARD AND FRANK?
AND...
WHEN DID I GET THIS... **WARPED**...?

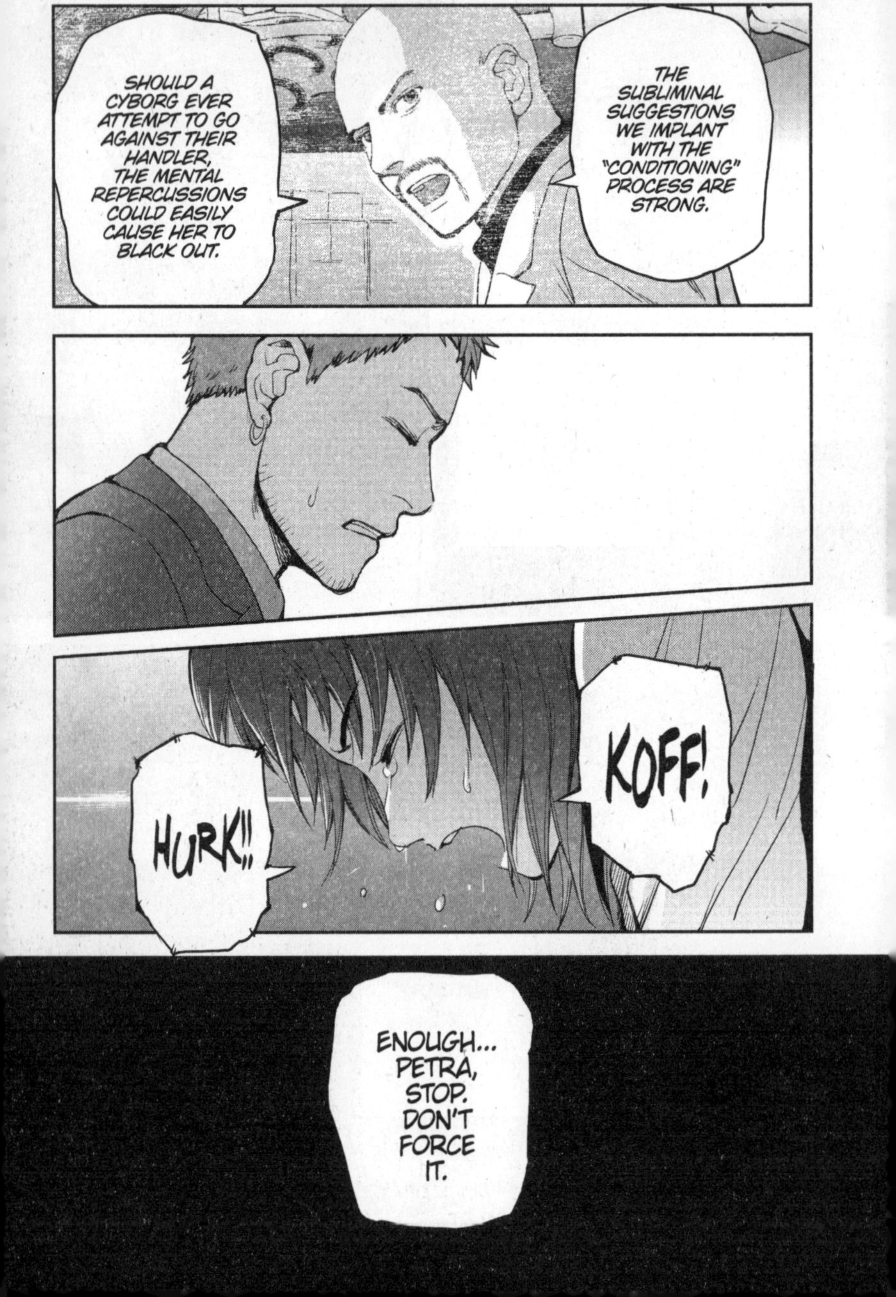
THE SUBLIMINAL SUGGESTIONS WE IMPLANT WITH THE "CONDITIONING" PROCESS ARE STRONG.
SHOULD A CYBORG EVER ATTEMPT TO GO AGAINST THEIR HANDLER, THE MENTAL REPERCUSSIONS COULD EASILY CAUSE HER TO BLACK OUT.
KOFF!
HURK!!
ENOUGH... PETRA, STOP. DON'T FORCE IT.

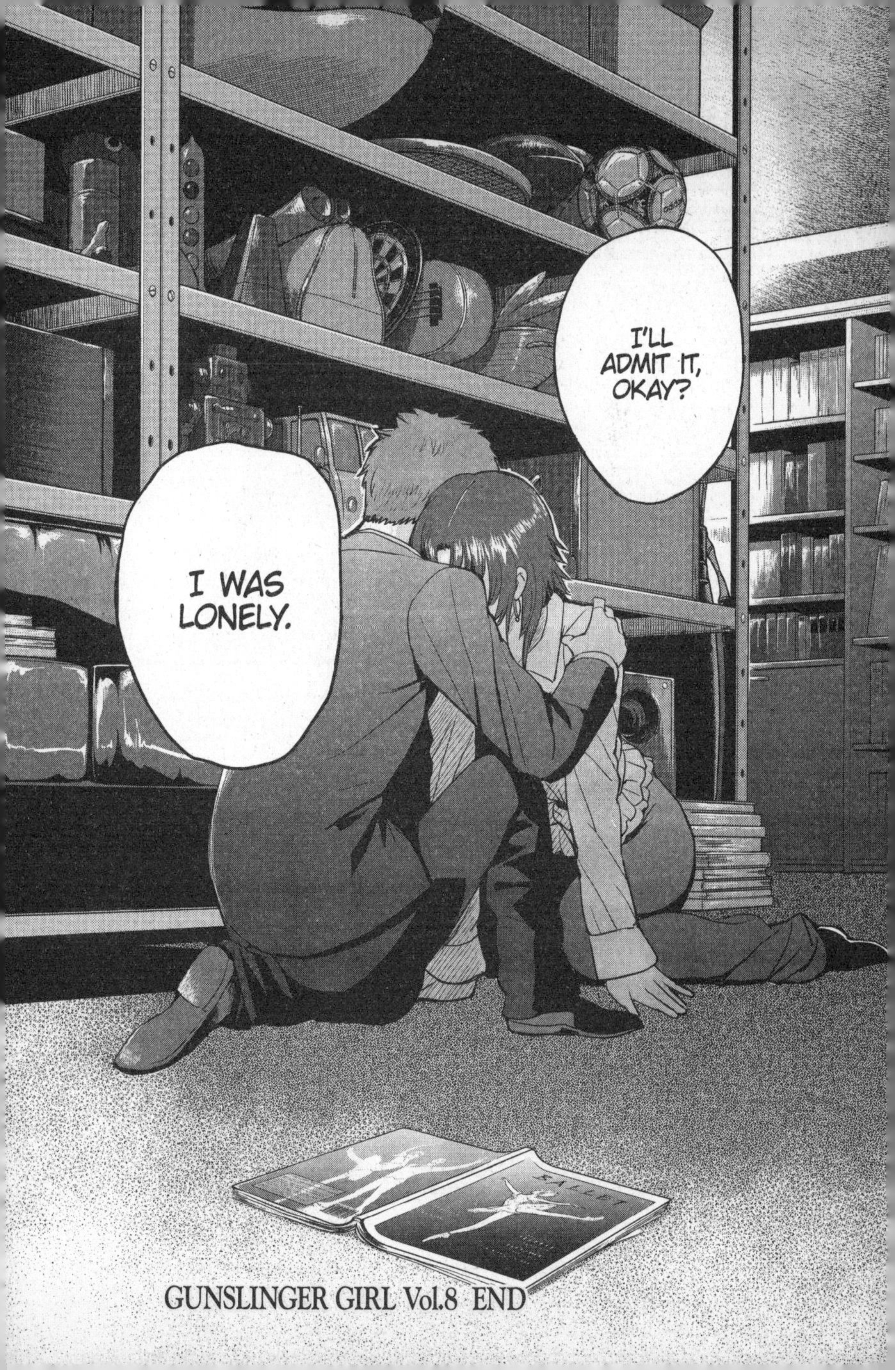
I'LL ADMIT IT, OKAY?
I WAS LONELY.
GUNSLINGER GIRL Vol.8 END

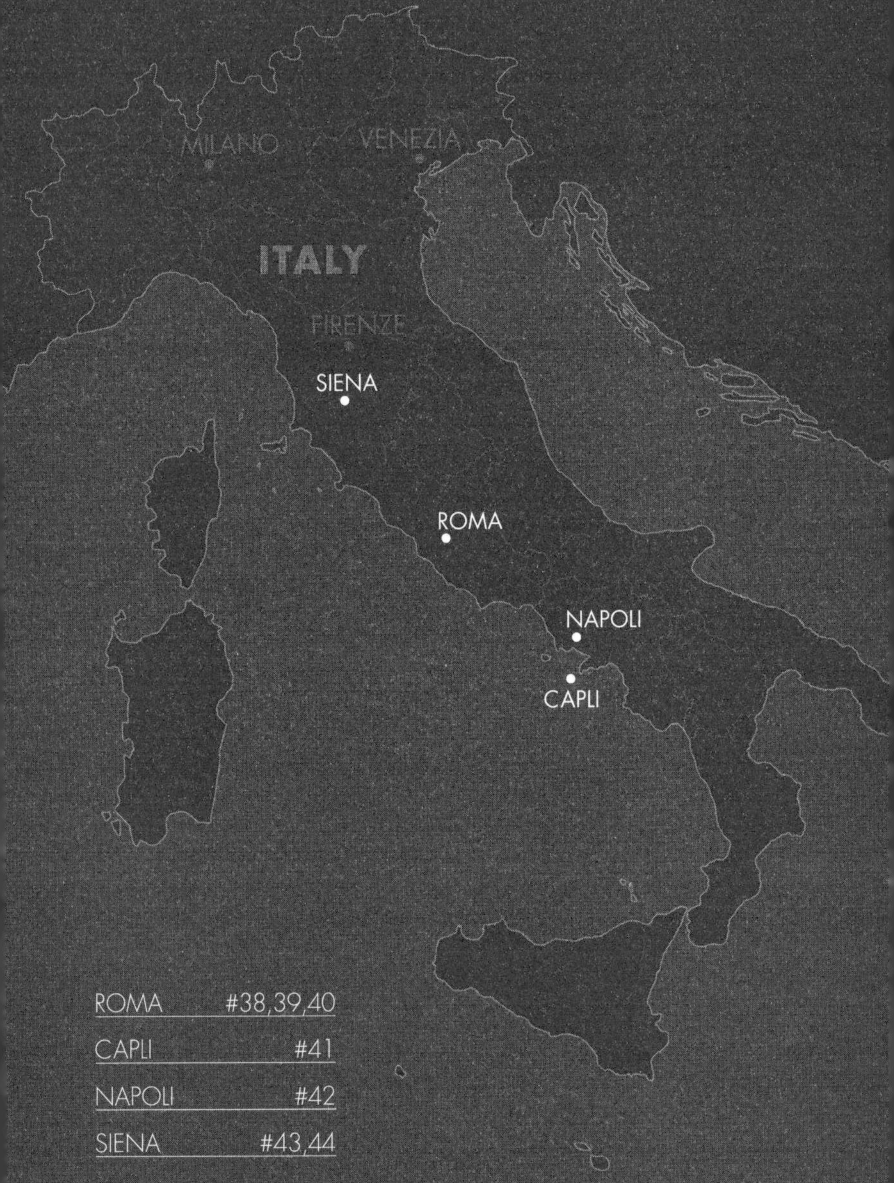
MILANO
VENEZIA
ITALY
FIRENZE
SIENA
ROMA
NAPOLI
CAPLI

"HOW DID YOU KNOW THAT?"

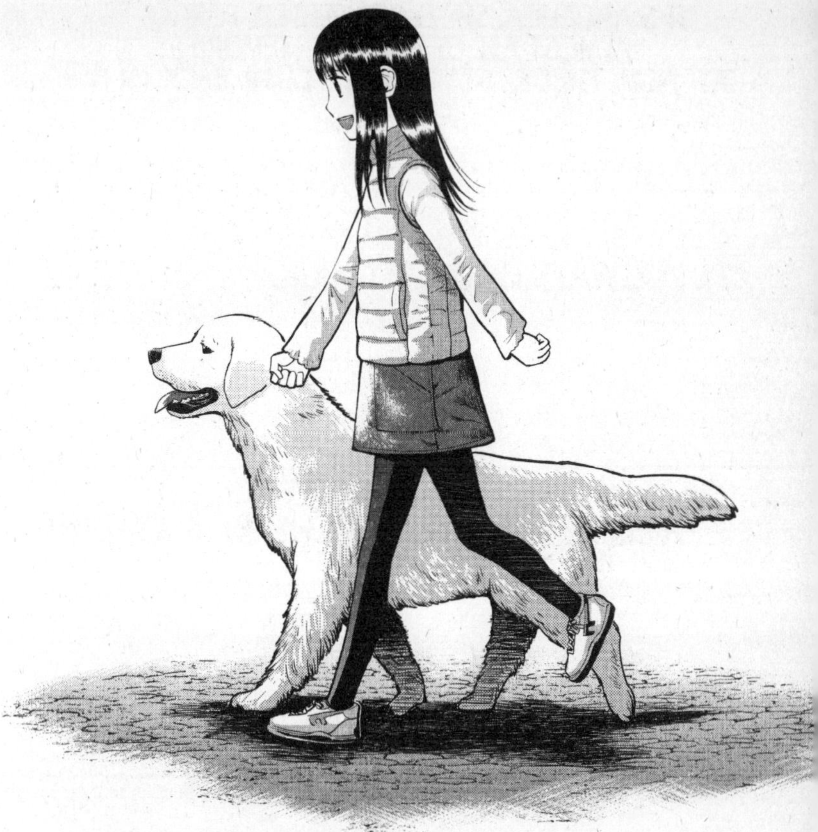

"RIGHT NOW, I'M NOT NEARLY TALL ENOUGH TO BE A GOOD SHIELD FOR HIM."

GUNSLINGER GIRL OMNIBUS COLLECTION 4

"IT'S ANGELICA. SHE'D COMPLETELY FORGOTTEN
ALMOST ALL OF HER OLD MEMORIES...
BUT NOW THEY'RE STARTING TO COME BACK TO HER."

"I'VE ALWAYS HAD BAD LUCK..."

"Y'KNOW,
ANGIE'S BEEN REALLY CHEERFUL OF LATE."

"I CAN'T HELP BUT FEEL THEY'RE A REALLY BAD SIGN..."

COMING SOON...

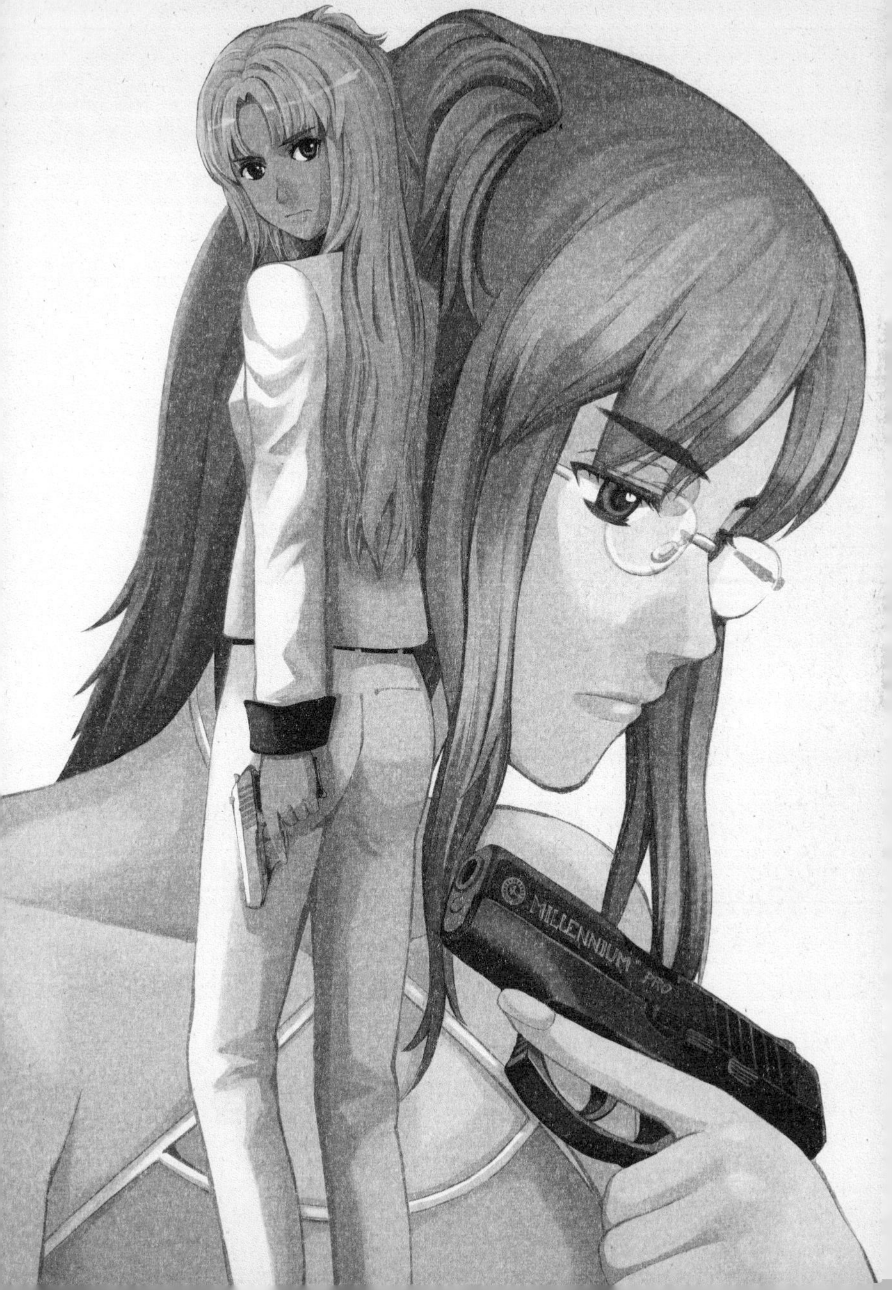
MILLENNIUM PRO

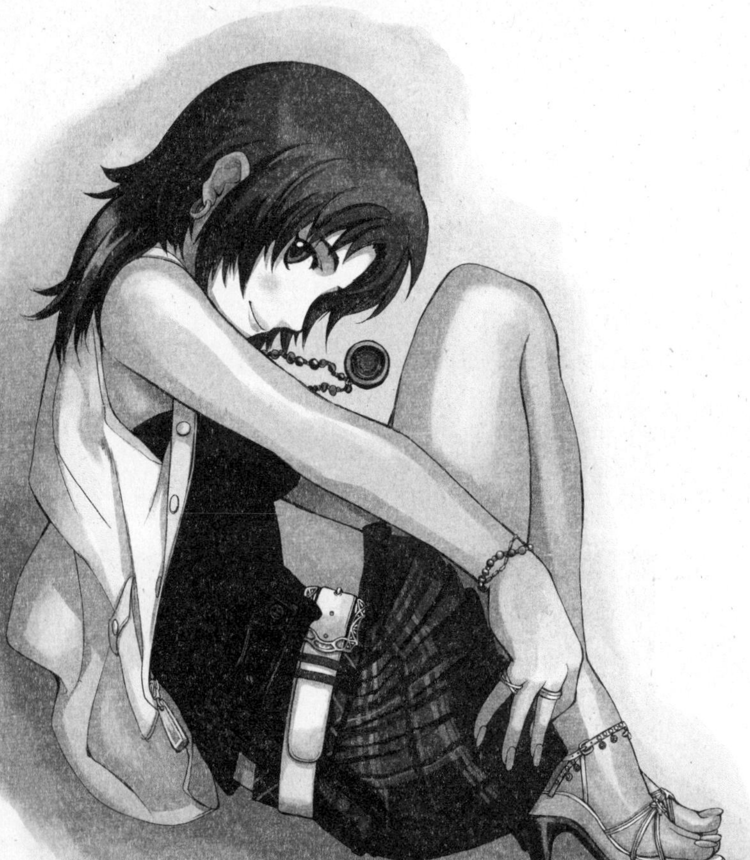

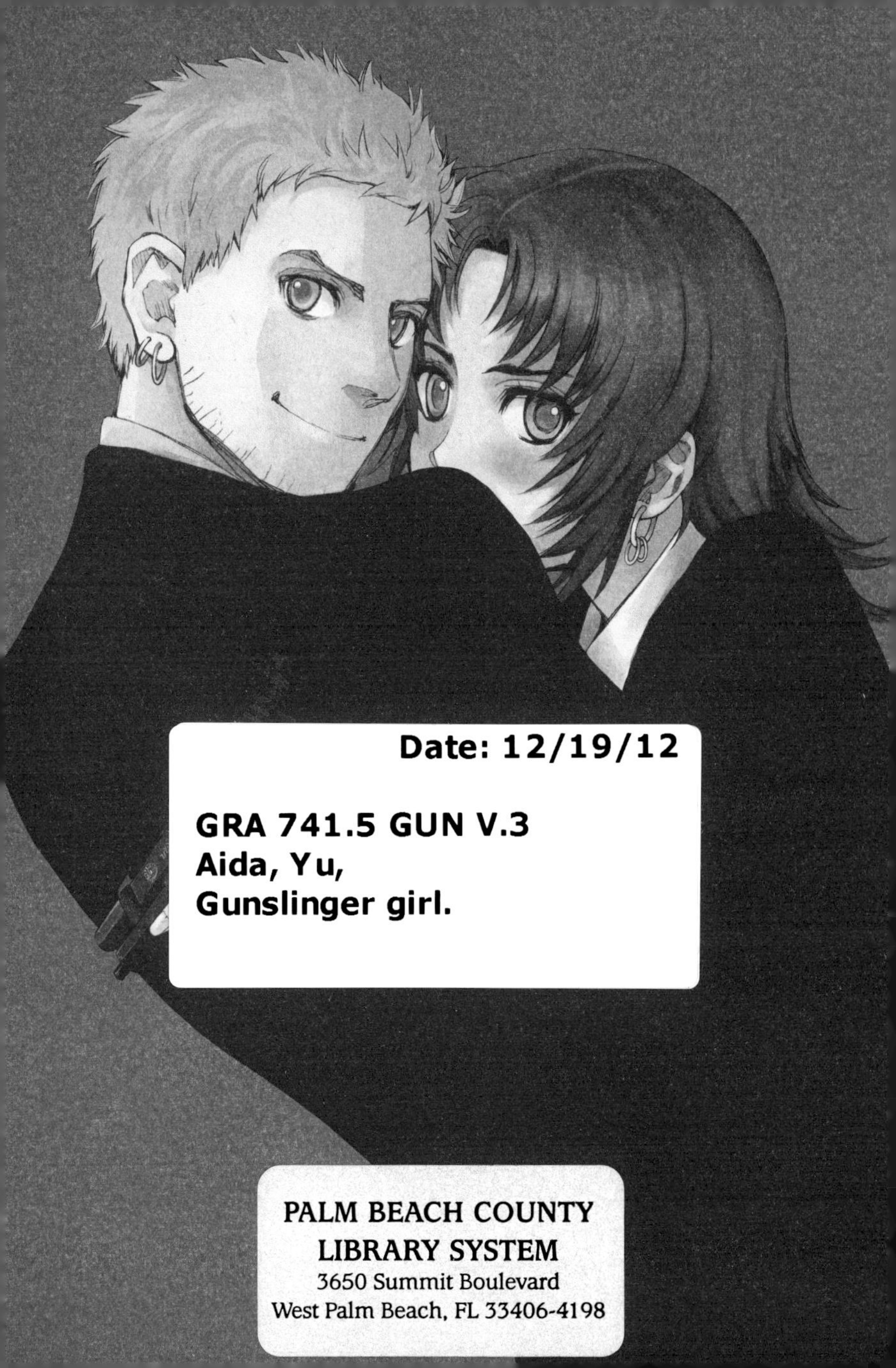

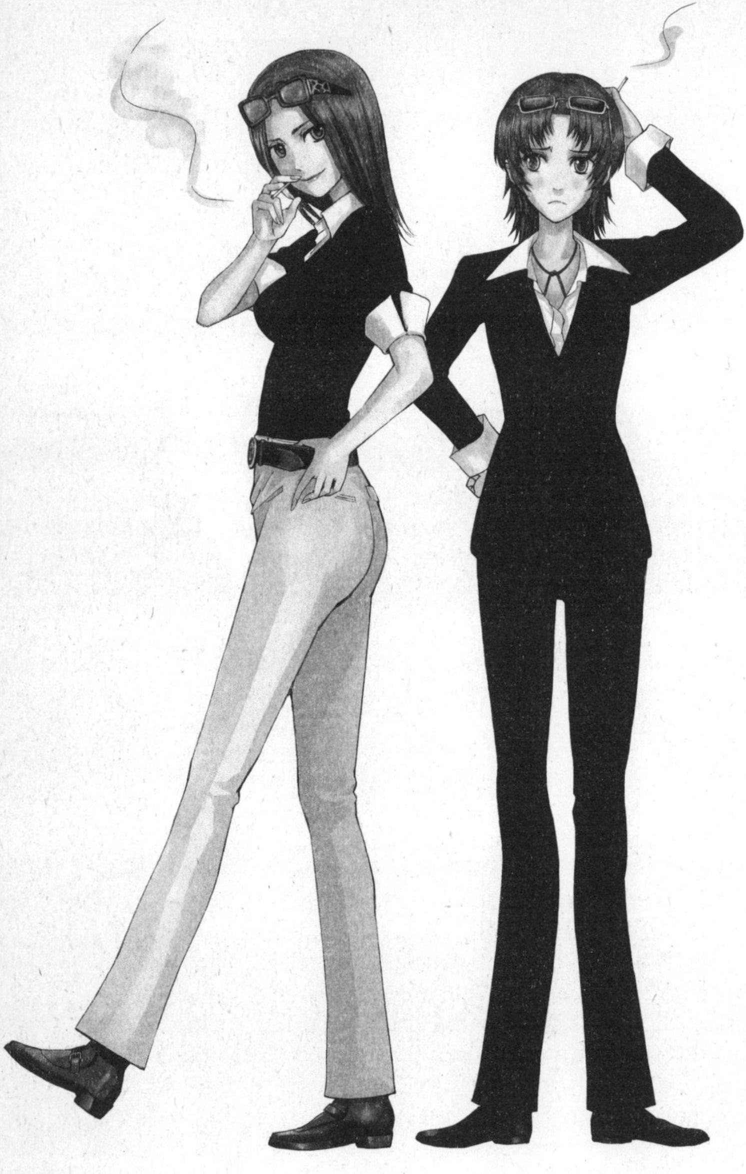

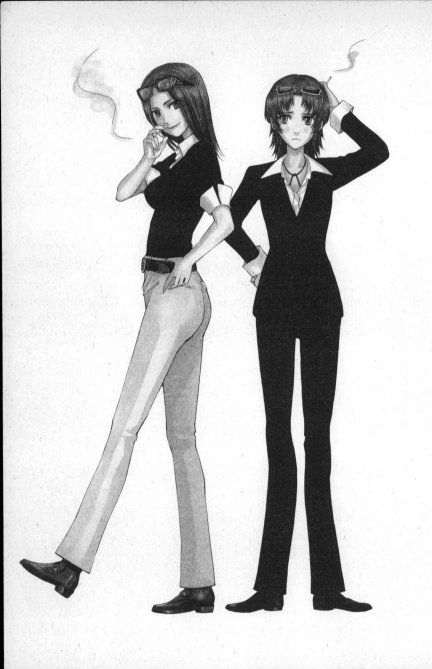

TRANSLATION NOTES

CHAPTER 38

In the ballet "Swan Lake," Odile is the black swan, the temptress character who seeks to trick Prince Siegfried into breaking his vow to Odette, the white swan princess.

CHAPTER 41

A.S. Roma **(Associazione Sportiva Roma)** and S.S. Lazio **(Società Sportiva Lazio)** are rival football clubs both based out of Rome.

Rossana's cat meows in Italian: "miao"

CHAPTER 43

"Petruska" is a ballet by Russian composer Igor Stravinsky, composed in 1910-11. The story is about a traditional Russian puppet made of straw and sawdust who comes to life and develops emotions. Another of the central characters in the ballet is the Moor, another puppet who is handsome and lives a life of luxury. The Moor attempts to seduce the Ballerina (another puppet character), but is interrupted by Petruska. The Moor chases down Petruska, and eventually kills him. The puppets' master, the Charlatan reminds everyone at the end of the ballet that Petruska was just a puppet, not even a real person.
ring World War II, it gets its name because when triggered, it first bounces up approximately 3 feet before exploding.